Processes of Change in Brain and Cognitive Development

Attention and Performance

Processes of Change in Brain and Cognitive Development
Attention and Performance XXI

Edited by

Yuko Munakata
Department of Psychology
University of Colorado at Boulder
Boulder, USA
and

Mark H. Johnson
Centre for Brain and Cognitive Development
School of Psychology
Birkbeck, University of London
London, UK

This book is based on the papers presented at the **Twenty-First International Symposium on Attention and Performance** held at Winter Park, Colorado, July 26–Aug 1, 2004.

OXFORD
UNIVERSITY PRESS

OXFORD
UNIVERSITY PRESS

Great Clarendon Street, Oxford OX2 6DP

Oxford University Press is a department of the University of Oxford.
It furthers the University's objective of excellence in research, scholarship,
and education by publishing worldwide in

Oxford New York

Auckland Cape Town Dar es Salaam Hong Kong Karachi
Kuala Lumpur Madrid Melbourne Mexico City Nairobi
New Delhi Shanghai Taipei Toronto

With offices in

Argentina Austria Brazil Chile Czech Republic France Greece
Guatemala Hungary Italy Japan Poland Portugal Singapore
South Korea Switzerland Thailand Turkey Ukraine Vietnam

Oxford is a registered trade mark of Oxford University Press
in the UK and in certain other countries

Published in the United States
by Oxford University Press Inc., New York

A catalogue record for this title is available from the British Library

Library of Congress Cataloging in Publication Data
(Data available)
ISSN   1047–0387

Typeset by SPI Publisher Services, Pondicherry, India
Printed in Great Britain
on acid-free paper by
Biddles Ltd, King's Lynn

ISBN 0–19–856874–6 (Hbk)   978–0–19–856874–2 (Hbk)

10 9 8 7 6 5 4 3 2 1

Preface

The twenty-first meeting of the International Association for the Study of Attention and Performance took place July 27–31, 2004 in the secluded alpine setting of the Iron Horse Resort, Winter Park, Colorado. The meeting brought together scientists addressing cognitive and brain development at multiple levels, including phylogeny, genetics, neurophysiology, brain imaging, behavior, and computational modeling, across both typically and atypically developing populations. Over 5 days, we discussed some of the most promising advances and approaches in understanding developmental change. This book is the result.

The plan for a symposium on cognitive and brain development began with a meeting of the Association's Executive Committee in July, 2002. At that time, there was increasing agreement among contemporary researchers that developmental psychology needed to move away from static descriptions of the cognitive system at different ages, and strengthen its focus on the underlying mechanisms that generate change. Two important advances in this endeavor are research on learning mechanisms that drive developmental change, and research on the types of representational change that occur in development. A third advance comes in the form of methods of investigation, arising from the recent convergence between developmental psychology and cognitive neuroscience – 'developmental cognitive neuroscience'. However, as yet there had been no systematic investigation of progress and problems associated with these three advances. Moreover, developmental investigations had too often been separated from related work on cognitive change in adults. We planned to address these issues at Attention and Performance XXI.

By all accounts, the 2004 meeting was successful in meeting these goals. In paper after paper, employing a variety of methods, we heard about *how* developmental changes might be occurring, rather than merely *what* developmental changes were occurring. These papers stimulated intense and productive discussions, across a diverse group of researchers. For example a spirited debate on the nature of constraints on learning engaged scientists investigating these issues in newborns and scientists working with adult learners. Another debate fleshed out the relations between different types of approaches to modeling development (e.g. neural network vs. Bayesian). All of these discussions showed great promise for moving the field forward, away from static descriptions and toward mechanisms that generate developmental change.

The book has five major sections, corresponding to the 5 days of the meeting. These sections fall under the broad topics of learning (Parts 1 and 2), representational change (Parts 3 and 4), and an assessment of cognitive neuroscience methods in the study of developmental change (Part 5). The first section covers various types of learning mechanisms that drive developmental change (e.g. self-organizing, constructivist, and dynamically guided learning). These are not necessarily mutually exclusive learning mechanisms, but they have been studied separately to some degree. Each chapter in this section aims to explore the potential of certain learning mechanisms for understanding specific examples of developmental change. Given that there are a number of powerful learning mechanisms that could be involved in development, it becomes relevant to investigate how these mechanisms are constrained such that children learn about stimuli or events that are of adaptive relevance. Learning is not infinitely flexible or general during development; instead, constraints appear to govern what can be learned and when. For example, early in development, learning can be highly stimulus-specific, such that children exhibit learning only when the testing context very closely matches that of the learning context. In addition, learning in some domains appears to be guided by constraints relevant to stimuli in those domains. The chapters in Part 2 discuss these constraints on learning across a variety of domains: object processing, face processing, social cognition, memory, and word learning. The third section focuses on the nature of transformations in mental representations during development. Although there is much controversy about the appropriate definition of 'representation', we use the term in its most general sense to refer to patterns of activation within the brain that correspond to aspects of the external environment. The chapters in this section consider what we have learned about changes in representations from the perspective of cognitive analyses, computational modeling, and neuroimaging work, with both typical and special populations. The fourth section explores two, apparently opposing, proposals about the transformation of information during development. One view is that perceptual and cognitive development involves a process of the increasing integration of streams of information, while the other view is that development involves increasing segregation or dissociation of processing streams. The chapters in this section present compelling evidence that both of these processes occur during development, and examine the potential benefits of developing and integrating pathways with different computational trade-offs. Cognitive neuroscience approaches to development are discussed across all of these sections. However, the fifth and final section contains chapters that specifically focus on evaluating what we have learned about cognitive developmental change from the different methodologies and approaches offered by cognitive neuroscience. In each case, the authors were also asked to take a prospective look at what potentially could be learned about cognitive change from applying their methodology or through the study of a particular participant group. This section culminates, and the book closes, with a discussant chapter that looks back over the meeting (and book) and raises issues for the future. A brief summary of the themes of the meeting can also be read in Johnson and Munakata (2005) Processes of change in brain and cognitive development, *Trends in Cognitive Science*, March 2005.

The book also includes an opening chapter from Tim Shallice, based on his Association Lecture at the meeting. This chapter assesses evidence relating to the influential Supervisory System model of prefrontal cortex function, and concludes that different functional components of the system have different anatomical bases within the frontal lobes.

A number of people and organizations were instrumental in making this meeting and book possible. Jennifer Brace and Erin Phinney provided superb assistance with the meeting logistics. Molly Turk and Linda Williams of the Iron Horse Resort attended to all of our needs – lodging, dining, meeting, and recreating. Agnes Volein provided invaluable support managing all of the book details, and Leslie Tucker helped with a multitude of tasks associated with the meeting. The organization's Executive Committee and Advisory Council offered helpful guidance throughout the process of organizing this meeting. Finally, we are extremely grateful for the generous financial support provided by the following organizations: Birkbeck (University of London) School of Psychology, The British Academy, Coleman Institute, University of Colorado Boulder Psychology Department, Office of Naval Research, James S. McDonnell Foundation, Sackler Institute for Developmental Psychobiology, Trends in Cognitive Sciences, and University of Colorado Boulder Institute of Cognitive Science.

YM
MHJ
2006

Contents

The Attention and Performance Symposia

Since the first was held in The Netherlands in 1966, the Attention and Performance Symposia have become an established and highly successful institution. They are now held every 2 years, in a different country. The original purpose remains: to promote communication among researchers in experimental cognitive psychology and cognate areas working at the frontiers of research on 'attention, performance and information processing'. The format is an invited workshop-style meeting, with plenty of time for papers and discussion, leading to the publication of an edited volume of the proceedings.

The International Association for the Study of Attention and Performance exists solely to run the meetings and publish the volume. Its Executive Committee selects the organizers of the next meeting, and develops the program in collaboration with them, with advice on potential participants from an Advisory Council of up to 100 members. Participation is by invitation only, and the Association's Constitution requires participation from a wide range of countries, a high proportion of young researchers, and a substantial injection of new participants from meeting to meeting.

Held usually in a relatively isolated location, each meeting has four and a half days of papers presented by a maximum of 26 speakers, plus an invited Association Lecture from a leading figure in the field. There is a maximum of 65 participants (including the current members of the executive committee and the organizers). There are no parallel sessions, and all participants commit themselves to attending all the sessions. There is thus time for substantial papers followed by extended discussion, both organized and informal, and opportunities for issues and ideas introduced at one point in the meeting to be returned to and developed later. Speakers are encouraged to be provocative and speculative, and participants who do not present formal papers are encouraged to contribute actively to discussion in various ways, for example as formal discussants, by presenting a poster, or as contributors to scheduled discussion sessions. This intensive workshop atmosphere has been one of the major strengths and attractions of these meetings. Manuscript versions of the papers are refereed anonymously by other participants and external referees and published in a high-quality volume edited by the organizers, with a publication lag similar to many journals. Unlike many edited volumes, the Attention and Performance series reaches a wide audience and has considerable prestige. Although not a journal, it is listed in journal citation indices with the top dozen journals in experimental psychology. According to the Constitution, 'Papers presented at meetings are expected to describe work not previously published, and to represent a substantial contribution...' Over the years, contributors have been willing to publish original experimental and theoretical research of high quality in the volume, and this tradition continues. A and P review papers have also been much cited. The series has attracted widespread praise in terms such as 'unfailingly presented the best work in the field' (S. Kosslyn, Harvard), 'most distinguished series in the field of cognitive psychology' (C. Bundesen, Copenhagen), 'held in high esteem throughout the field because of its attention to rigor, quality and scope... indispensable to anyone who is serious about understanding the current state of the science' (M. Jordan, MIT), 'the books are an up to the minute tutorial on topics fundamental to understanding mental processes' (M. Posner, Oregon).

In the early days of the Symposium, when the scientific analysis of attention and performance was in its infancy, thematic coherence could be generated merely by gathering together the most active researchers in the field. More recently, experimental psychology has ramified, 'cognitive science' has been born, and converging approaches to the issues we study have developed in neuroscience. Participation has therefore become interdisciplinary, with neuroscientists, neuropsychologists, and computational modelers joining the experimental psychologists. Each meeting now focuses on a restricted theme under the general heading of 'attention and performance'. Recent themes include: Synergies in Experimental Psychology: Artificial Intelligence and Cognitive Neuroscience (USA, 1990); Conscious and Unconscious Processes (Italy, 1992); Integration of Information (Japan, 1994); Cognitive Regulation of Performance: Interaction of Theory and Application (Israel, 1996); and Control of Cognitive Processes (UK, 1998); Common Processes in Perception and Actions (Germany, 2000); and Functional Brain Imaging of Visual Cognition (Italy, 2002).

Authors and Participants

Karen Adolph
Department of Psychology
New York University
6 Washington Place
New York, NY 10003
USA
karen.adolph@nyu.edu

Dima Amso
Sackler Institute for Developmental
Psychobiology
Weill Medical College of Cornell
University 1300 York Avenue, Box 140
New York, NY 10021
USA
da547@nyu.edu

Richard N. Aslin
Department of Brain and Cognitive
Sciences
Meliora Hall, River Campus
University of Rochester
Rochester, NY 14627
USA
aslin@cvs.rochester.edu

Renée Baillargeon
Department of Psychology
University of Illinois
603 E. Daniel
Champaign, IL 61820
USA
rbaillar@s.psych.uiuc.edu

Marie T. Banich
Department of Psychology
University of Co at Boulder
E-213-E Muenzinger Hall, Box 345
Boulder, CO 80309
USA
mbanich@psych.colorado.edu

April Ann Benasich
CMBN, Rutgers University
197 University Ave.
Newark, NJ 07102
USA
benasich@axon.rutgers.edu

Jennifer Brace
Department of Psychology
Carnegie Mellon University
Pittsburgh, PA 15213
USA
jbrace@andrew.cmu.edu

Andrew J. Bremner
Cognitive Science Research Unit
Université Libre de Bruxelles
Av F. -D. Roosevelt, 50
1050 Ixelles
Belgium
abremner@ulb.ac.be

John T. Bruer
James S. McDonnell Foundation
1034 South Brentwood Blvd., Suite 1850
Saint Louis, MO 63117
USA

Claus Bundesen
Center for Visual Cognition
Department of Psychology
University of Copenhagen
Njalsgade 90, DK-2300
Copenhagen S
Denmark
bundesen@psy.ku.dk

Susan Carey
Department of Psychology
Harvard University
33 Kirkland St.
Cambridge, MA 02138
USA
scarey@wjh.harvard.edu

B. J. Casey
Sackler Institute for Developmental
Psychobiology
Weill Medical College of Cornell
University
1300 York Avenue, Box 140
New York, NY 10021
USA
bjc2002@med.cornell.edu

Susan Chipman
Office of Naval Research, BCT1
800 North Quincy Street
Arlington, VA 22217–5660
USA
chipmas@onr.navy.mil

Desmond Tak-Ming Cheung
Department of Psychology
B63 Uris Hall
Cornell University
Ithaca, NY 14853–7601
USA
dtc22@cornell.edu

Eliana Colunga
Department of Psychology
University of Colorado at Boulder
345 UCB
Boulder, CO 80309–0345
USA
colunga@psych.colorado.edu

Gergely Csibra
Centre for Brain and Cognitive
Development
School of Psychology
Birkbeck
University of London
Malet Street
London WC1E 7HX
UK
g.csibra@bbk.ac.uk

Richard B. Darlington
Department of Psychology
228 Uris Hall
Cornell University
Ithaca, NY 14853–7601
USA
rbd1@cornell.edu

Matthew C. Davidson
Department of Psychology
Room 416
University of Massachusetts
Amherst, MA 01002
USA
davidson@psych.umass.edu

Judy S. DeLoache
Department of Psychology
University of Virginia
P. O. Box 400400,
Charlottesville, VA 22904–4400
USA
jdeloache@virginia.edu

Frederic Dick
Centre for Brain and Cognitive
Development
School of Psychology
Birkbeck
University of London
32 Torrington Square
London WC1E 7JL
UK
f.dick@bbk.ac.uk

Karen R. Dobkins
Department of Psychology, 0109
University of California, San Diego
La Jolla, CA 92093
USA
kdobkins@ucsd.edu

John Duncan
MRC Cognition and Brain Sciences Unit
15 Chaucer Road
Cambridge, CB2 2EF
UK
john.duncan@mrc-cbu.cam.ac.uk

Teresa Farroni
Centre for Brain and Cognitive
Development
School of Psychology
Birkbeck
University of London
32 Torrington Square
London WC1E 7JL
UK
Dipartimento di Psicologia dello
Sviluppo e della Socializzazione
Via Venezia 8
35131 Padova
Italy
t.farroni@psychology.bbk.ac.uk

Barbara L. Finlay
Department of Psychology
248 Uris Hall
Cornell University
Ithaca, NY 14853–7601
USA
blf2@cornell.edu

Isabel Gauthier
Department of Psychology
Vanderbilt University
301 Wilson Hall
Nashville, TN 37203
USA
isabel.gauthier@vanderbilt.edu

György Gergely
Institute for Psychological Research
Hungarian Academy of Sciences
1132 Budapest
Victor Hugo u. 18–22
Hungary
gergelyg@mtapi.hu

Rick O. Gilmore
Department of Psychology
Pennsylvania State University
622 Moore Building
University Park, PA 16802
USA
rogilmore@psu.edu

Clark Glymour
Department of Philosophy
Carnegie-Mellon University
Baker Hall 135L
Pittsburgh, PA 15213
USA
cg09@andrew.cmu.edu

Rebecca L. Gómez
Department of Psychology
University of Arizona
Tucson, AZ 85721–0068
USA
rgomez@u.arizona.edu

Daniel Gopher
William Davidson Faculty of
Industrial Engineering and Management
Technion – Israel Institute of Technology
Technion City
Haifa 32000
Israel
dgopher@ie.technion.ac.il

Alison Gopnik
Department of Psychology
University of California
3317 Tolman Hall, #1690
Berkeley, CA 94720–1650
USA
gopnik@socrates.berkeley.edu

William Greenough
Beckman Institute
University of Illinois
405 N. Mathews Avenue
Urbana, IL 61801
USA
wgreenou@cyrus.psyc.uiuc.edu

Marshall M. Haith
University of Denver
Department of Psychology
Frontier Hall, 2155 S. Race St.
Denver, CO 80208
USA
mhaith@du.edu

Harlene Hayne
Psychology Department
University of Otago
PO Box 56,
Dunedin
New Zealand
hayne@psy.otago.ac.nz

John R. Hesselink
Department of Radiology
UCSD Medical Center
200 West Arbor Drive
San Diego, CA 92103–8756
USA
jhesselink@ucsd.edu

Kazuo Hiraki
Department of Systems Science
University of Tokyo
Komaba 3–8–1, Meguro-ku
Tokyo 15–8902
Japan
khiraki@idea.c.u-tokyo.ac.jp

Almut Hupbach
Department of Psychology
University of Arizona
Tucson, AZ 85721
USA
almut.hupbach@mail.mcgill.ca

Mark H. Johnson
Centre for Brain and Cognitive
Development
School of Psychology
Birkbeck
University of London
32 Torrington Square
London WC1E 7JL
UK
mark.johnson@psyc.bbk.ac.uk

Nancy Kanwisher
McGovern Institute
Bldg NE20–454, MIT
Cambridge, MA 02139
USA
ngk@mit.edu

Annette Karmiloff-Smith
Neurocognitive Development Unit
Institute of Child Health
30 Guilford Street
London, WC1N IEH
UK
a.karmiloff-smith@ich.ucl.ac.uk

Mitsuo Kawato
National Institute for
Physiological Sciences
38 Nishigonaka Myodaiji
Okazaki, Aichi, 444–8585
Japan 8

Roberta L. Klatzky
Carnegie Mellon University
Department of Psychology
Baker Hall 342c
Pittsburgh, PA 15213
USA
klatzky@cmu.edu

Arthur F. Kramer
2247 Beckman Institute
University of Illinois
405 N. Mathews Ave.
Urbana, IL 61801
USA
a-kramer@uiuc.edu

Irene Leo
Dipartimento di Psicologia
dello Sviluppo e della Socializzazione
Università di Padova
Via Venezia, 8
35131 Padova
Italy
irene.leo@unipd.it

Jie Li
Department of Psychology
University of Illinois
603 E. Daniel
Champaign, IL 61820
USA
jieli@uiuc.edu

Yuyan Luo
Stanford University
Department of Psychology
450 Serra Mall
Stanford, CA 94305
USA
yluo@psych.stanford.edu

Denis Mareschal
School of Psychology
Birkbeck
University of London
Malet St
London WC1E 7HX
UK
d.mareschal@bbk.ac.uk

Lori Markson
Department of Psychology, Newoscience
and Behauiou
University of California
3210 Tolman Hall MC1650
Berkeley, CA 94720
USA
markson@berkeley.edu

Daphne Maurer
Department of Psychology, Neuroscience
and Behaviour
McMaster University
Hamilton, Ontario L8S 4K1
Canada
maurer@mcmaster.ca

Bruce McCandliss
Sackler Institute for Developmental
Psychobiology
Weill Medical College of Cornell
University
1300 York Avenue, Box 140
New York, NY 10021
USA
bdm2001@med.cornell.edu

James L. McClelland
Center for the Neural Basis of Cognition
and Department of Psychology
Carnegie Mellon University
115 Mellon Institute
4400 Fifth Avenue
Pittsburgh, PA 15213
USA
jlm@cnbc.cmu.edu

Elinor McKone
School of Psychology (Building 39)
Australian National University
Canberra ACT 0200
Australia
elinor.mckone@anu.edu.au

Catherine J. Mondloch
Department of Psychology
Brock University
500 Glenridge Avenue
St Catharines, Ontario L2S 3A1
Canada
cmondloch@brocku.ca

J. Bruce Morton
Department of Psychology
University of Western Ontario
1151 Richmond Street, Suite 2
London, Ontario N6A 5B8
Canada
b.morton@uwa.ca

Yuko Munakata
Department of Psychology
345 UCB
University of Colorado at Boulder
Boulder, CO 80309–0345
USA
munakata@psych.colorado.edu

Lynn Nadel
Department of Psychology
University of Arizona
Tucson, AZ 85721
USA
nadel@u.arizona.edu

Helen J. Neville
Psychology Department
1227 University of Oregon
Eugene, Oregon 97403–1227
USA
neville@uoregon.edu

Richard K. Olson
Department of Psychology
University of Colorado
Boulder, CO 80309–0345
USA
rolson@psych.Colorado.edu

Takashi Omori
Faculty and Graduate School of
Engineering
Hokkaido University, Kita 8 Nishi 5
Sapporo 060–8628
Japan
omori@complex.eng.hokudai.ac.jp

Randall C. O'Reilly
Department of Psychology
University of Colorado Boulder
345 UCB
Boulder, CO 80309–0345
USA
oreilly@psych.colorado.edu

Brianna Paul
SDSU/UCSD Joint Doctoral Program in
Clinical Psychology
University of California, San Diego
9500 Gilman Drive, 0515
La Jolla, CA 92093–0515
USA
bpaul@crl.ucsd.edu

Bruce F. Pennington
University of Denver
Department of Psychology
Frontier Hall, 2155 S. Race St.
Denver, CO 80208
USA
bpenning@nova.psy.du.edu

Mary A. Peterson
Department of Psychology
University of Arizona
Tucson, AZ 85721
USA
MAPeters@u.arizona.edu

Erin Phinney
University of Denver
Department of Psychology
Frontier Hall, 2155 S. Race St.
Denver, CO 80208
USA
ephinney@du.edu

Kim Plunkett
Department of Experimental Psychology
Oxford University
South Parks Road
Oxford OX1 3UD
UK
kim.plunkett@psy.ox.ac.uk

Wolfgang Prinz
Max-Planck-Institut für
Kognitions- und Neurowissenschaften
Arbeitsbereich Psychologie/Kognition
und Handlung
Amalienstr. 33
D-80799 München
Germany
prinz@cbs.mpg.de

Shbana Rahman
Trends in Cognitive Sciences
Elsevier
84 Theobald's Road
London WC1X 8RR
UK
s.rahman@elsevier.com

Maartje Raijmakers
Department of Psychology
University of Amsterdam
Roetersstraat 15
1018 WB Amsterdam
The Netherlands
m.e.j.raijmakers@uva.nl

Fiona M. Richardson
School of Psychology
Birkbeck
University of London
Malet Street
London WC1E 7HX
UK
f.richardson@bbk.ac.uk

David Rosenbaum
Department of Psychology
Penn State University
642 Moore Building
University Park, PA 16802–3106
USA

Yves Rosetti
Espace et Action
Inserm U 534
16, avenue du Doyen Lépine
69500 Bron
France
rossetti@lyon.inserm.fr

Barbara W. Sarnecka
Department of Cognitive Sciences
University of California-Irvine
3151 Social Science Plaza
Irvine, CA 92697–5100
USA
sarnecka@uci.edu

Gaia Scerif
University of Nottingham
School of Psychology
University Park
Nottingham NG7 2RD
UK
gs@psychology.nottingham.ac.uk

Mark S. Seidenberg
Department of Psychology
University of Wisconsin-Madison
1202 W. Johnson St
Madison WI 53706
USA
seidenberg@wisc.edu

Atsushi Senju
Department of Cognitive and Behavioral
Science
Graduate School of Arts and Sciences
University of Tokyo, Komaba
3–8–1 Komaba, Meguro-ku
Tokyo, 153–8902
Japan
atsushi@darwin.c.u-tokyo.ac.jp

Tim Shallice
University College London
Institute of Cognitive Neuroscience
Alexandra House
17 Queen Square
London WC13AR
UK

Shinsuke Shimojo
California Institute of Technology
Simojo Psychophysics Laboratory
837 San Rafael Terrace
Pasadena, CA 91105
USA
sshimojo@its.caltech.edu

Thomas R. Shultz
Department of Psychology
McGill University
1205 Penfield Avenue
Montreal, Quebec H3A 1B1
Canada
thomas.shultz@mcgill.ca

Francesca Simion
Dipartimento di Psicologia dello
Sviluppo e della Socializzazione
Università degli Studi di Padova
Via Venezia, 8
35131 Padova
Italy
francesca.simion@unipd.it

Linda Smith
Indiana University
Department of Psychology
1101 E. Tenth St
Bloomington, IN 47405
USA
smith4@indiana.edu

Kelly A. Snyder
University of Denver
Department of Psychology
Frontier Hall, 2155 S. Race St
Denver, CO 80208
USA
ksnyder@nova.psy.du.edu

Joan Stiles
Department of Cognitive Science
University of California, San Diego
9500 Gilman Drive, 0515
La Jolla, CA 92093–0515
USA
stiles@ucsd.edu

Michael S. C. Thomas
School of Psychology
Birkbeck
University of London
Malet Street
London WC1E 7HX
UK
m.thomas@bbk.ac.uk

Chiara Turati
Dipartimento di Psicologia
dello Sviluppo e della Socializzazione
Università degli Studi di Padova
Via Venezia, 8
35131 Padova
Italy
chiara.turati@unipd.it

Eloisa Valenza
Dipartimento di Psicologia
dello Sviluppo e della Socializzazione
Università degli Studi di Padova
Via Venezia, 8
35131 Padova
Italy
eloisa.valenza@unipd.it

Su-hua Wang
Department of Psychology
University of California
273 Social Sciences 2
Santa Cruz, CA 95064
USA
suhua@ucsc.edu

Jason D. Zevin
Sackler Institute for Developmental
Psychobiology
Weill Medical College of Cornell
University
1300 York Ave., Box 140
New York, NY 1002
USA
jdz2001@med.cornell.edu

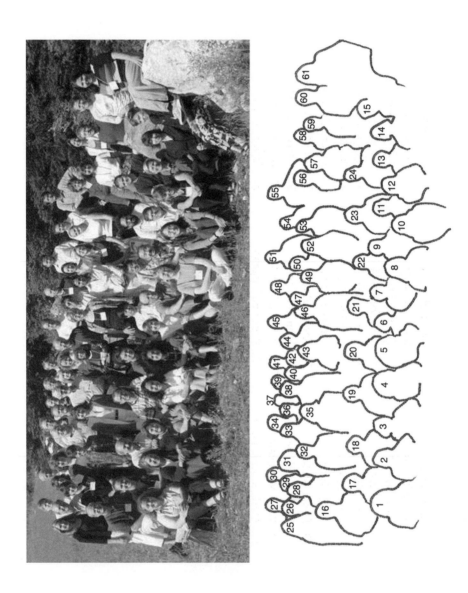

1. Kelly Snyder
2. Marie T. Banich
3. Judy S. DeLoache
4. Gaia Scerif
5. Teresa Farroni
6. Lori Markson
7. Lynn Nadel
8. Elinor McKone
9. Shinsuke Shimojo
10. Yuko Munakata
11. Mark S. Seidenberg
12. Nancy Kanwisher
13. Joan Stiles
14. Alison Gopnik
15. Linda Smith
16. Richard N. Aslin
17. Jennifer Brace
18. David Rosenbaum
19. Rick O. Gilmore
20. Atsushi Senju
21. Takashi Omori
22. Kazuo Hiraki
23. Jason D. Zevin
24. Frederic Dick
25. Mary Peterson
26. Tim Shallice
27. Kim Plunkett
28. Harlene Hayne
29. Karen Adolph
30. John Duncan
31. Barbara L. Finlay
32. Renée Baillargeon
33. James McClelland
34. Mark H. Johnson
35. Annette Karmiloff-Smith
36. Tom Shultz
37. Randall C. O'Reilly
38. Bruce F. Pennington
39. Wolfgang Prinz
40. April Ann Benasich
41. Claus Bundesen
42. Helen J. Neville
43. Francesca Simion
44. Richard K. Olson
45. J. Bruce Morton
46. Susan Carey
47. Mitsuo Kawato
48. Daniel Gopher
49. Shbana Rahman
50. Rebecca L. Gómez
51. Gergely Csibra
52. Isabel Gauthier
53. Erin Phinney
54. Michael Thomas
55. Denis Mareschal
56. Maartje Raijmakers
57. Daphne Maurer
58. B.J. Casey
59. Bruce McCandliss
60. Roberta L. Klatzky
61. Eliana Colunga

Association lecture

Chapter 1

Contrasting domains in the control of action: The routine and the non-routine

Tim Shallice

Abstract

The Supervisory System model, in which there are two cognitive levels in the control action, is assessed. It is argued that there is a modulatory relation between the levels. It is further argued that standard connectionist variables, such as age of acquisition, familiarity, and frequency, are particularly useful for characterizing behavior produced by contention scheduling, the lower-level system, when Supervisory System function is impaired. By contrast, an analogy with symbolic AI models is used to theoretically motivate a fractionation of Supervisory System processing as created by a set of functionally selective and anatomically partially separable subsystems. It is argued that the systems for the Supervisory System's top–down selection of schemas in contention scheduling has a different lateralization of dorsolateral prefrontal cortex from the systems concerned with non-evident error detection and checking. The former are held to be the more left lateralized in comparison with the latter.

1.1 Introduction

The idea that there is a hierarchical organization of the processes that control action, with the higher levels modulating the operation of the lower ones, is very old, going back at least to Hughlings Jackson. Moreover, in the more neurobiological versions it is commonplace to view the prefrontal cortex as the summit of the hierarchy (e.g. Luria 1966; Fuster 1989; Dehaene and Changeux 1997; Miller and Cohen 2001).

A second very common idea in experimental psychology is that there are two domains of the control of action – automatic and non-automatic (controlled) (e.g. Shiffrin and Schneider 1977) – and there are related models in developmental psychology (e.g. Karmiloff-Smith 1986). The model of Norman and myself (1980, 1986) (see also Shallice 1982) essentially combines these two ideas in proposing two domains of processing – that of the Supervisory System and of contention scheduling – with the former only realizing its effects through modulation of the latter and with the Supervisory System localized in prefrontal cortex (Fig. 1.1).

In these respects, the Norman–Shallice model may be thought of as merely one variant of the combination of two, now standard although not universally accepted, perspectives in cognitive neuroscience. It has, though, an additional rather different conceptual dimension. It was developed not only from a conflation of the experimental psychology and the neurobiology of levels of action control; it also represented in two respects an interface between two different modeling traditions – the connectionist, at that time represented by interactive activation modeling (e.g. McClelland and Rumelhart 1981) and of symbolic AI.

Thus as far as the selection of which schemas control the processing and effector systems they require, contention scheduling, the system the Supervisory System

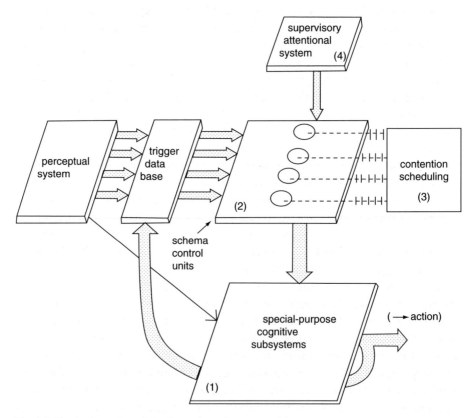

Fig. 1.1 The basic version of the Supervisory System model.

modulates, is viewed as operating in an interactive activation fashion with units corresponding to overlearned single motor or cognitive skills – action and thought schemas. In routine mode, schemas receive activating input from both higher-level (source) schemas and from object-trigger systems. In non-routine mode, additional activation to schemas is provided by the Supervisory System. However, in addition, it is also useful to conceive of the overall system within a more symbolic framework as operating in an analogous fashion to production systems. The symbolic aspect is used principally in the processes that follow selection and in particular how the 'arguments' of schemas are set on selection – where, with what, and on what the thought or action skill operates – which depend upon the simultaneous state of object representation systems. Moreover, the initial verbal account has been realized more recently computationally in interactive activation simulations of Cooper and Shallice (2000) based on the everyday task of coffee preparation.

The intellectual origins of the Supervisory System concept were different. In earlier discussions of the automatic/controlled distinction (e.g. Shiffrin and Schneider 1977) what processes lead to controlled processing was only vaguely specified. In the Norman–Shallice model it was held to be a materially and conceptually separable system. The idea that different systems could be involved in routine and non-routine operations came from classical artificial intelligence. There the idea was quite standard that in addition to the processes used for the effecting of routine selection of routine operations, there are special processes that come into play in situations where routine responding does not lead to the attaining of goals (e.g. Sussman 1975; Newell 1990). The main thrust of the model developed by Norman and myself (1986) was to argue for a prefrontally located Supervisory System, coming into play in non-routine situations to modulate the operation of a system which effects routine action – contention scheduling. Thus the distinction between the situations in which the two types of system come into play was derived from symbolic AI.

One may view the contrast in the computational principles on which the two systems operate from a related but not identical perspective. Perner (2003) has argued that the lower-level system representations involved in contention scheduling are implicit, as they are procedural representations. By contrast he argues that the higher (Supervisory) level 'is defined by the necessity to entertain *predication* and *fact-explicit* representation and to exercise *content control* over the lower level' (p. 225). He illustrates this with the example of a child given the instructions 'Put the green cards into the left box', where the child cannot represent their meaning in a 'predication-implicit' way, as no card is actually being presented. He continues 'That also means that not only predication to instances but also that they are not real but only hypothetically considered instances needs to be made explicit … The same explicitness is, of course, also required for planning, reasoning and entertaining hypotheses before one can come to a conclusion which action sequence is best to employ.' (p. 225).

It is possible to consider the computations carried out by the cognitive subsystems on two dimensions. One concerns the number of input variables that need to be taken into account and the complexity of their interactions. As these increase computational procedures which optimize constraint satisfaction, ones using gradient descent principles are likely to be optimal, that is systems operating on broadly connectionist principles, of which interactive activation models are a simple version. The second dimension is the degree to which the values of intermediate products, of input variables themselves, and indeed which are the critical input variables, may be subject to revision. As these characteristics increase in importance for a computation so the value of having explicit how and why intermediate products are arrived at becomes increasingly valuable. One basic theme of this paper is that high values on the first dimension are more critical in the computations of contention scheduling and high values on the second for those of many aspects of the Supervisory System.

More recently the model has been developed by Stuss *et al.* (1995) and Shallice and Burgess (1996) to confront a major conceptual inadequacy in the original model. How the Supervisory System enabled the organism to confront non-routine situations was completely unspecified. Thus the concept is derided by Dennett (1998) as 'an ominously wise overseer – homunculus who handles the hard cases in the workshop of consciousness' (p. 288). Since the logic of the original paper was partially derived from the idea that the postulating of homunculi of reduced power could be progressive, itself derived from Dennett (1978), the source of this criticism was rather odd. However, the sentiment was common (e.g. Baddeley 1996). One major strand of development of the model has been to confront this objection. However, this has principally been done by analogy with the deeply unfashionable conceptual framework which was critical in the initial development of the model, namely symbolic artificial intelligence. The essence of the Mark II model of Shallice and Burgess (1996) was the assumption that in confronting non-routine situations a number of qualitatively very different types of computational operations are required, which were held to be the province of anatomically separable higher-level subsystems (Fig. 1.2). It further used the assumption of functional specialization, which can be broadly but unrigorously specified, as that if the phenotype of homo sapiens includes cognitive tasks sufficiently different in their computational requirements from all others in its repertoire then they would be implemented at least in part in separable regions of cortex[1].

Four interlinked issues are addressed through this paper. One major issue is whether the distinction between higher and lower-level control of action is well captured by the idea of their being the provinces of different systems with 'modulation' being an appropriate characterization of their relation. The second major issue is whether 'routine-ness' is an appropriate concept to use to contrast the different properties of the two levels of systems. The third concerns the relevant saliency of the constraint satisfaction and explicitness dimensions respectively. Thus I will argue that a broadly

---

[1] For simplicity I will adopt the terminology of the Shallice–Burgess paper.

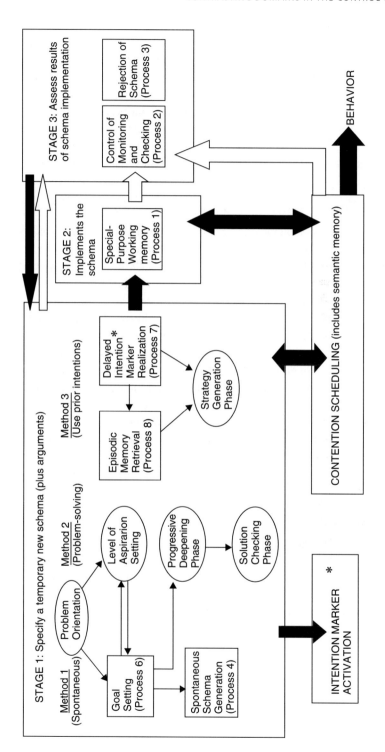

Fig. 1.2 The Mark II Supervisory System model of Shallice and Burgess (1996).

connectionist framework is particularly useful in characterizing the lower-level contention scheduling system, as discussed above. This is considered in the next section. Then I will address whether symbolic AI ideas are of value when considering the Supervisory System; in particular I will consider the perspective derived from symbolic AI that the 'ominously wise overseer-homonculus' can be tamed by its being fractionated into different subsystems. This is addressed in the following two sections. The final issue, considered in the last section, is whether the division relates to the phenomenological one between willed and automatic action.

1.2 Basic findings: associationism and contention scheduling

The finding from functional imaging, that the activation of prefrontal cortex declines as tasks become less novel, has been shown in a variety of paradigms (e.g. Raichle *et al.* 1994; Jueptner *et al.* 1997). Moreover, lesions to prefrontal cortex affect the ability to confront non-routine situations appropriately (e.g. Shallice and Evans 1978; Knight 1984). This fits with a prefrontally localized system being critical for non-routine tasks. However, while the absence of such evidence would undermine the current approach, it could be explained in a variety of ways; for instance non-routine situations may make greater demands on working memory.

Stronger evidence is provided by the findings that lesions to prefrontal cortex lead to behavior characterizable as that controlled by contention scheduling alone. Through the last 100 years of its history, psychology has been concerned to model routine operations – initially through S–R psychology, then somewhat separately, in more computational form, through production systems, and in a more neurobiological one through connectionism. A key aspect of the model is the role that stimulus–response (action schema) associations play in the genesis of action. For such frameworks, factors such as frequency, familiarity, age-of-acquisition, priming, interference, and so on become important dependent variables. Predictions made from accounts of contention scheduling inherit this tradition. A key aspect of the model is the role that stimulus–response (or better trigger-stimulus representation to action-schema) associations play in the genesis of action. So prefrontally impaired behavior should be especially sensitive to: (i) familiarity, (ii) age-of-acquisition, and (iii) (implicitly) frequency-of-application of a rule.

In a variety of prefrontal syndromes the patient's actions are behaviors triggered by stimuli with which they are strongly associated even when they have been instructed not to respond in this way and gain nothing by so doing. These include the grasp reflex (De Renzi and Barbieri 1992), utilization behavior (Lhermitte 1983; Shallice *et al.* 1989), failures in the anti-saccade type of tasks (Paus *et al.* 1991), and forms of the anarchic hand syndrome (Della Sala *et al.* 1991; Humphreys and Riddoch 2003). In such syndromes, action selection can be at the level of effector selection (Riddoch *et al.* 1998) or of so-called 'source' schema (Shallice *et al.* 1989).

The analogue of these behaviors in problem-solving is the especial vulnerability of frontal patients in situations in which the elicitation of 'capture errors' (Reason 1979; Norman 1981) is potentiated by stimulus displays (Della Malva *et al.* 1993). In other words, prefrontal patients have difficulty in suppressing inappropriate responses triggered by familiar S–R bonds in contention scheduling; they cannot overcome potentiated but incorrect responses. A second relevant problem-solving phenomenon is the strikingly good performance of prefrontal patients in situations where rule abstraction is required if the rule is one which corresponds to the inbuilt tendencies of the contention scheduling system. Thus Verin *et al.* (1993) found that an alternation rule was attained more rapidly by prefrontal patients than normal adults when the subject must make one choice once every 15 s; the prefrontal patients made virtually no errors. Moreover, 5- and 6-year-old children, but not those of 7+, also found the task very easy (Houde *et al.* 2001), supporting the assumption that the contention scheduling system obeys age-of-acquisition principles.

Where frequency is concerned, perhaps the most direct support is provided by the use of the random generation task. In the random generation task the subject must produce a sequence of numbers which approximate randomness as closely as possible; that is the responses must not satisfy any given rule inappropriately frequently. Baddeley (1986) analyzed the task. He argued that as there were no external stimuli, any schema controlling the obeying of a rule which is operating to elicit any one response must be inhibited prior to the next response and an alternative schema activated. On the model both these steps would require the Supervisory System. Jahanshahi *et al.* (1998) using transcranial magnetic stimulation showed that by comparison with a sham TMS control a single TMS pulse to the left dorsolateral prefrontal cortex led to a rough doubling in the rate of responses which involved counting up or down in ones. In other words, a response which followed the most frequently applied rule occurred much more often following rTMS to left prefrontal cortex, even when it was clearly inappropriate. Moreover, using fMRI Jahanshahi *et al.* (2000) found that as the speed of generation was increased so the degree of randomness plunged dramatically as rates increased from 1 per 3 s to 1 per 0.5 s. The curve was mirrored in the activation of one area of cortex, again the left dorsolateral prefrontal cortex (Fig. 1.3). Thus with the proviso, to be discussed later, that the effects were essentially restricted to one part of the prefrontal cortex – the left dorsolateral region – the predictions were well corroborated using this paradigm.

These neuropsychological effects of activating selection of action schema only from representations of trigger stimuli – an S–R type of operation – fit well with a phenomenon described from the normal literature on task switching. Allport and Wylie (2000) investigated how switching was affected by the specific stimuli used on a previous run of the other task. Subjects alternated between short runs of two tasks – color naming and (color) word reading – so creating a Stroop-type situation. However, only some of the colors presented for naming had occurred in the preceding (color) word reading task. Allport and Wylie found that on 'switch' trials, but not on

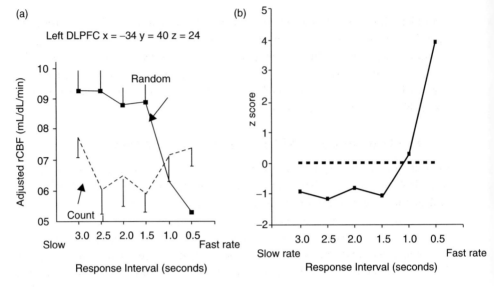

Fig. 1.3 (a) Activation levels of a left dorsolateral prefrontal voxel in Jahanshahi *et al.*'s (2000) fMRI study of random generation showing the effect of generation rate in the experimental task and in a control counting task. (b) The degree of measured randomness related to rate of generation in the experimental task (up is less random; the broken line indicates perfect performance on the measure; 'supra-perfect' performance arises from the avoidance of repeats). (DLPFC=dorsolateral prefrontal cortex)

non-switch trials, subjects were slower to give the first color naming response if the name had been previously primed than if it was in the 'unprimed' set. It is on switch trials that the schema unit controlling the effecting of one task set has to be inhibited and a second unit activated which controls the other task set. The pattern of results is well simulated on an interactive activation model which is essentially isomorphic with contention scheduling in the relevant respect (Gilbert and Shallice 2002).

The Allport and Wylie result is only one of a range of results from the classical Attention–Performance areas reviewed by Hommel (2000) that show that S–R effects *can* occur independently of the conscious intentions of the subject and be in conflict with them. Moreover, in line with standard associationism, such effects of irrelevant S–R associations increase with practice (McLeod and Dunbar 1988). At the same time, Hommel also showed that 'automatic' S–R translation effects do not generally occur independently of the conscious intentions of the subject, in that the degree to which they are manifested depends typically upon the conscious intention of the subjects concerning the task that they are attempting to carry out. As will be discussed in the last section, on the current approach, conscious volitional responses require the Supervisory System. The first type of effect Hommel described then corresponds on the model to a situation where a schema is selected which had activation derived only from triggering by external stimuli in contention scheduling and producing responses in conflict with those of other schemas elicited by top–down modulation from the Supervisory System. However, typically the two types of environmentally driven and top–down influences would combine to lead to schema selection, so giving rise to his second type of phenomenon. Moreover, the 'determining tendency' conceptual framework of Ach (1905), to which Hommel appeals, is, as we will see, entirely compatible with the current model.

1.3 The fractionation of the Supervisory System

How does the cognitive system enable subjects to cope with non-routine situations? In symbolic AI, architectures based on classical planning systems were found to be slow, cumbersome, and fragile in their operation (see Russell and Norvig 1995, for review). This led to their replacement by decentralized reactive-planning systems such as those of Brooks (1991). However, more recently a number of defects of reactive-planners have become apparent and researchers have developed three-layer architectures (e.g. Gat 1991; Elsaesser and Slack 1994) (see Glasspool 2004). In a three-level planner, such as that of Gat (1998), the bottom layer is a Brooks-style reactive controller. The highest level is a 'deliberative' system capable of reasoning and goal-directed behavior. It can be viewed as performing the overall function of the Supervisory System. The middle layer assembles sequences of single behaviors and enables higher-level goals to be achieved by different lower-level behaviors depending on the overall situation. Glasspool has argued that the middle layer of the Gat-type architecture is analogous to contention scheduling on the current approach. So current planning frameworks used in symbolic AI have a set of systems on different levels which resemble those in the Norman–Shallice model.

A system for coping with non-routine situations does not have to be internally unitary. Indeed, in a recent model of the deliberative level used in medical expert decision-making – the Domino model – Fox and Das (2000) argue that six different computational domains are required in order to carry out the key processes necessary from the detection of the existence of a potential symptom to the execution of the care procedure. The processes may however be called recursively. Fox and Das argue that these six different domains each need to be underpinned by a different logic, that is that the logical constraints which the implementation aims to satisfy involve six different sets of axioms.

There are a number of approaches to conceptualizing executive functions which have an origin in symbolic AI; one example is EPIC (Kieras *et al.* 2000). In this paper I will follow the Supervisory System mark II model (Shallice and Burgess 1996) (Fig. 1.2) where this conceptual approach is combined with the use of dissociation logic to isolate subsystems neuropsychologically. However, the model fits well with the stages outlined by Fox and Das, namely:

1. The first computational domain is that required in the articulation of a goal. This involves abstracting from the current situation aspects that are important to improve.

2. The second is that involved in the production of one or more procedures for attaining the goal.
3. The third is selection between them and the consequent decision to act.
4. The fourth is the articulation of the selected procedure into a sequence of implementable steps.
5. The fifth is the realization of the steps as actions.
6. The final one is the checking that these actions are indeed ameliorating the situation, that is they assist in realizing the goal or goals. If not, the cycle begins again with a new goal of patching the procedure or aborting it.

Such a division of the whole process into a series of stages of this type is far from original to the Domino model (e.g. Ben-Yishay and Diller 1983). However, what is original is that each of the stages is held to correspond to different domains which are each sufficiently computationally distinct to require a separate underlying logic.

The current approach, which is based on the Supervisory System mark II model, presupposes that processes requiring the Supervisory System are involved in each of these stages. However, only the processes involved in the second, fifth, and sixth of the above stages will be considered in this paper. The approach aims to show that in carrying out these stages, processes involving the Supervisory System are used which are partially anatomically distinct from each other. This partial anatomical separability corresponds to the different underlying logics on the Fox and Das model. Whether other stages also involve separable processes in prefrontal cortex remains to be investigated.

Consider the second stage – the articulation of a possible procedure for attaining the goal specified in the first stage, when this is not directly elicited through the use of learned contingencies by the combination of situation and goal. On the model the procedure corresponds to a series of outputs from the Supervisory System which lead to the activation of a set of schemas in contention scheduling. For reasons to be given in the final section, outputs from a Supervisory System to contention scheduling correspond to conscious states of the organism. Articulated procedures then are 'strategies'. Strategies which normal subjects typically develop and apply in confronting a novel situation are much less used by frontal patients (e.g. Owen *et al.* 1990; Burgess and Shallice 1996a). For instance, in the Owen *et al.* (1990) study, subjects were presented with a set of randomly arranged outline boxes on a monitor. The subject can select any box to open. For any one search-cycle only one such target is available and the subject must search through the boxes until it is found. Then a target will become available in another box and so on until there has been a target in each of the boxes. Normal subjects generally learn the strategy of searching in a fixed spatial pattern, for each configuration of boxes. Frontal patients use this strategy much less. It should be noted that using a fixed spatial search procedure requires subjects to abstract that they will have a memory problem if they search randomly. So production of an appropriate strategy has a critical prior stage of abstracting over the situation, behavior, and thought processes. That the prefrontal cortex should be involved in the determination of the procedure by which the Supervisory System actively modulates the activation level of schemas in contention scheduling fits well the now standard idea that dorsolateral prefrontal cortex produces top–down modulatory control over lower level structures (e.g. Dehaene and Changeux 1997; Frith 2000; Miller and Cohen 2001).

One can differentiate at least three different ways by which humans achieve a strategy in a non-routine situation: by spontaneous strategy production, by explicit problem solving, and by having previously determined on a procedure to use if the situation arises – intention realization. I will return later to the second and third (which can be considered part of stage five on the Domino model). I will assume that the first of the three is the evolutionarily primary, and restrict consideration to it for the present.

I will contrast strategy production with a second supervisory subprocess, which is a key part of stage six of the Domino model. This is the process of detecting a discrepancy between the situation resulting from the implementation of the strategy and the requirements of satisfying a goal. If such a discrepancy is detected then this leads to a new goal being set up to 'patch' the 'bug' or abandon the goal. Very frequently the environment forces us to detect an error that we have made. However, spontaneous detection of non-evident errors also frequently occurs in everyday life situations (e.g. Rizzo *et al.* 1995). These authors argue for a four-stage process of coping with errors: production of the evidence for detecting a mismatch, explicit detection of the mismatch as arising from the subject's own behavior, error identification, and error recovery. As mismatches, in particular, can be complex, specific mechanisms for non-evident error detection would seem likely to be required. Thus a mismatch can be based on rather abstract properties such as the length of time an operation is taking, it can involve a comparison with the intuitive value a result should have, and can even involve inferences (Rizzo *et al.* 1995; Burgess and Shallice 1996b).

As with the processes responsible for strategy production, this subprocess comes in an explicit and in a non-explicit form. The evolutionarily primary form is spontaneous non-evident error detection. In its explicit form it is checking. Checking is sometimes viewed as merely the repeating of cognitive operations that have already been carried out. However there is critical difference. On the second pass the non-evident error detection system is potentiated. Moreover, in many cases even deliberate checking is more than mere recapitulation. It can, for instance, involve the attempt to obtain further information compatible or not with a putative solution (e.g. Burgess and Shallice 1996b).

The essence of the computation in non-evident error detection is a matching operation very different from the active construction process required in strategy production. The two processes collectively correspond to the 'manipulation and monitoring' of Petrides's (1994) characterization of dorsolateral prefrontal function. However, within the Supervisory System model they are complimentary. The former is concerned with positively modulating the contention scheduling system from above in order to achieve goals. The latter is concerned with negatively interrupting the operation of the contention scheduling system because it is failing to achieve task goals. Therefore, on the argument for functional specialization given earlier, it would seem likely that the two types of process – strategy production and non-evident error detection – are partially anatomically separable. In the next section I consider evidence that while both involve dorsolateral prefrontal cortex, the former is relatively more lateralized to the left and the latter relatively more to the right. The contrasting lateralizations are not assumed to be all-or-none. Moreover, in any particular case one would also expect an additional influence orthogonal to this one of the well-known material specific lateral biases in the operation of prefrontal cortex (see Wagner 1998).

1.4 The relative differential lateralization of strategy production and non-evident error detection processes

The neuropsychological investigations of prefrontal function referred to in Section 1.2 were mainly conducted before the early 1990s when most patients did not have MRI scans. Where comparisons were carried out of possible contrasting effects of prefrontal lesions, the contrast was typically whether the lesion affected the left or right prefrontal cortex. This conflated the very differing effects of lateral, medial, and orbital prefrontal lesions. It was not until the mid-1990s, when Stuss and Alexander introduced the method of contrasting Left Lateral, Right Lateral, Superior Medial, and Inferior Medial prefrontal lesions (e.g. Stuss *et al.* 1998), that contrasting effects of right and left lesions began to be reliably obtained (with respect to lateral prefrontal lesions).

Thus of the studies discussed in Section 1.2 only one showed differing effects of left and right prefrontal lesions. This was the study of random number generation of Jahanshahi *et al.* (1998), where the effect of rTMS to induce a routine procedure (counting) was much greater if applied to the left lateral prefrontal cortex than to the right. Moreover, as far as the avoidance of counting in ones is concerned, the functional imaging study of Jahanshahi *et al.* (2000) gave a similar left lateralized result.

However there is a simple alternative explanation for such effects. Representations of number to which alternative rules or procedures can be applied are verbal and so may involve specifically left hemisphere regions for this reason. To avoid simple stimulus-based explanations of this sort it is important to contrast two theoretically important processes when both use the same material.

Our first contrasting set of findings with respect to lateralization when the same material is used occurred in a surprising area – memory for categorized word lists (Fletcher *et al.* 1998a; Fletcher *et al.* 1998b). In free recall of word lists where the words are selected from a small number of categories, it is well known that the optimal strategy is to organize the encoded words into categories (Mandler 1967). It was also known from neuropsychological studies that the prefrontal cortex is critical for use of this strategy, if words are presented randomly so that the appropriate categories have to be abstracted (Incisa and Milner 1993; Gershberg and Shimamura 1995). In our study (Fletcher *et al.* 1998a), when this process was disrupted by a demanding secondary task there was a specific loss of activation in left dorsolateral prefrontal cortex.

However, might one not just argue that this condition involved verbal material and so the lateralization of the effect would be explained in terms of the material used? Such an explanation would not account for a contrasting lateralization which was unexpectedly obtained in a complementary retrieval experiment (Fletcher *et al.* 1998b). In this experiment encoding had taken place outside the scanner. In the experimental condition subjects had to retrieve the whole word list by free recall at a one per 4 s rate with the next word to be recalled cued only by the instruction 'Next'. This was compared with a condition in which subjects had to retrieve 16 words in paired associate fashion, each being elicited by its previously presented individual subcategory label, for example *poet → Browning*. Here when the activations involved in carrying out the different tasks were compared the effects obtained were in the right frontal lobe. In particular, retrieval of the organized list activated right dorsolateral cortex significantly more than did retrieval of an equal number of words through individual paired associate recall.

Why might this have occurred? In a neuropsychological investigation of a closely related experimental procedure of free recall of 16-word categorized lists, Stuss *et al.* (1994) had found that patients with right frontal lesions, but not left, produce over twice as many words in their output protocols which are repeats as did normal subjects. As their memory performance was in other respects quite good and considerably better than that of patients with left frontal lesions, it appeared that it was not that the right frontal patients had forgotten but instead that they had an editing or checking impairment and did not remove from their output, prior to producing them, words which they had already recalled. Thus the two complimentary PET experiments on encoding and retrieval of categorical lists fit with the idea that there are relative differences in lateralization between strategy generation and non-evident error detection.

I will assume from the results just considered and the findings of Jahanshahi *et al.* that, at least for verbal material, spontaneous strategy production depends critically on left dorsolateral prefrontal cortex. I will therefore concentrate on the complementary non-evident error detection and checking processes which are less easy to investigate experimentally. As far as these processes are concerned it will be assumed that they will: (i) occur under conditions of uncertainty; (ii) occur when a plausible alternative needs to be rejected; and (iii) occur in time after the solution has been initially achieved. In addition, damage to such processes will be assumed to: (iv) lead to failures in criterion setting with subjects being more prone to false positive errors; and (v) make subjects particularly liable to capture errors. Moreover it will be assumed that: (vi) the control of non-evident error detection and checking cannot simply be reduced to the deployment of cognitive effort.

The studies of Fletcher *et al.* (1998a, b) involved encoding and retrieval in episodic memory. Memory experiments might not seem the most natural vehicle to use to analyze control processes. However, they have a great advantage when compared to, say, problem-solving, in allowing repeated trials which involve complex control processes in a domain where the other processes required vary little across trials (see e.g. Koriat and Goldsmith, 1996). Although episodic memory experiments can be used to analyze the nature of control processes, they also involve many other processes which are not well understood. I will therefore consider memory experiments only from the perspective of the properties discussed earlier in this section that non-evident error detection and checking processes should have.

I will consider four experiments which relate to the relative uncertainty of the subject in the memory retrieval situation – two of which used the remember/know paradigm (Henson *et al.* 1999a; Eldridge *et al.* 2000), one which used confidence judgments (Henson *et al.* 2000), and a fourth which examined incorrect versus correct source judgments given following prior correct item judgments (Cansino *et al.* 2002). If one contrasts the less confident (or accurate) compared with the more confident (or accurate) responses, that is the condition which should give rise to the greater checking activity, there was greater dorsolateral activation in all cases, in two cases being bilateral and in two cases specifically right (Henson *et al.* 1999a; Eldridge *et al.* 2000). By contrast, the more confident condition produced greater activation in mid-dorsolateral or anterior prefrontal sites on the left. This latter result is not predicted by the current model, but nor is it in conflict with it, while the former fits it.

The second type of situation in which error detection and checking is to be expected is when a highly plausible alternative must be rejected; a capture error is to be avoided. In the memory context, proactive interference provides a retrieval environment where the potential for capture errors is considerable. In Henson *et al.* (2002), the one cortical region which showed significantly greater activation in trials where proactive interference was present compared to control trials was the right dorsolateral prefrontal cortex.

A third criterion concerns the time at which an error detection or checking process should occur. fMRI lacks the temporal discriminatory power to give adequate timing of the activation of dorsolateral prefrontal cortex in memory retrieval studies. However, a variety of electrophysiological studies have reported a wave beginning more than 1 s after stimulus presentation occurring at electrodes over right dorsolateral prefrontal cortex (e.g. Wilding and Rugg 1996). To my knowledge no study using source analysis with this paradigm has been run. However, if the identification of where the source is by using the localization of the surface electrodes proves correct then this provides support that the right dorsolateral prefrontal response fits with criterion (iii) for checking. In general, across studies this wave occurs bilaterally but is greater over the right than left prefrontal cortex.

Criterion (iv) holds that an impairment in checking will lead to an inadequate setting of criteria. Evidence for this comes from a striking study of the effects of the creation of temporary lesions by rTMS on encoding or retrieval. Rossi *et al.* (2001) presented subjects with 96 magazine pictures for 2 s each at a roughly one per 20 s rate. An hour later they were presented with 48 of these together with 48 distractors at the same rate. rTMS or sham TMS was given over a left or right prefrontal site lasting for 500 ms, to coincide with the onset of the encoding of the recognition stimulus. rTMS over right prefrontal cortex at encoding or over left prefrontal at retrieval led to performance which was no different from the effects of sham TMS. However rTMS over left prefrontal cortex at encoding or over right prefrontal cortex at retrieval led to impaired performance with d' values between 0.5 and 0.8 by comparison with d' of about 1.4 for the two intact conditions. As critically, the criterion C was significantly reduced for only one condition from the value of 0.97 found in the baseline condition. When right prefrontal rTMS was given at retrieval, C was only 0.28 and there was a false alarm rate of 41 per cent, roughly double that in the sham and baseline conditions.

A second study of Sandrini *et al.* (2003) used word pairs. It too showed a strong effect of the laterality of rTMS at retrieval (with an effect for right but not for left prefrontal cortex), but unlike the earlier study rTMS had an effect at encoding, when administered at either left or right frontal sites. This study was a 2-alternative forced choice study and so criterion changes could not be directly assessed.

In all these studies, when comparing a putative non-evident error detection or checking process with an encoding process, the former was relatively speaking more strongly lateralized to the right. Moreover, the temporal and criterion evidence also supported a predominantly right prefrontal checking process.

It should be noted that in some of the memory experiments the contrast obtained for error detection or checking is with encoding rather than strategy generation or production. This can be justified on either of two assumptions. One is that effective episodic encoding depends on the formation of the structure which organizes what has to be remembered, as in the generation of a mediator (Mandler 1967). The other is that the key evolutionary function of episodic memory in humans is to provide a database for case-based reasoning when confronting novel situations; so it is intimately linked functionally to strategy selection (Burgess and Shallice 1996b).

Two other, more classical, neuropsychological studies outside the memory domain provide more direct evidence. The first – that of Reverberi *et al.* (2004) – was based on an fMRI source memory study of Henson *et al.* (1999b), which obtained a putative right prefrontal checking effect. In one condition of the Henson *et al.* study subjects were shown words in one of two positions on a card. At retrieval they had to indicate in one condition (inclusion) whether the word had been presented at all in the learning phase. In the other condition (exclusion) they had to say both whether it had been presented and, if so, whether it was in the same spatial position on the card; if it was not they had to give the same negative response as for new stimuli. Thus they frequently had to reject stimuli that were familiar because they had not occurred in precisely the same form as at encoding. The latter was held to involve greater checking, and led to a much larger right than left dorsolateral effect.

The Reverberi *et al.* study transposed key elements of the design into the problem-solving domain. It used a visuospatial analogue of the Wisconsin Card-Sorting – the Brixton Spatial Rule Attainment task – which had been shown by Burgess and Shallice (1996c) to be sensitive to frontal lesions. In the Brixton task the subject sees a series of cards one at a time on each of which there are 10 circles in a fixed 2 × 5 array. On each card one only of the circles is colored blue. The subject must attempt to abstract the rule which governs the movement of the blue circle across a sequence of cards, such as alternating between two specific positions, and so guess where the circle will be on the next card. Every five to nine cards the rule changes without warning.

In the Reverberi *et al.* study the first part of the experiment took exactly the same form as in the earlier work. In the second half, however, towards the end of the series of cards forming a rule the cards contained a red circle but not a blue one. The subjects, though, merely had to touch each red circle. For four cards the movement of the red circles followed a second interfering rule. Subjects were told that the rule followed by the red cards was irrelevant and when, as they did, the cards reverted to containing a blue circle, that the rule operative immediately before the red cards were presented became relevant again and they must apply it. This situation was therefore analogous to the Henson *et al.* exclusion condition. The subject has two putative rules activated and must select the less strongly primed one.

The study used the Stuss/Alexander subdivision of prefrontal lesion patients into four anatomically based groups. Patients with Left Lateral frontal lesions were impaired in abstracting the relevant rule for the blue cards, both if they were also impaired at a corresponding working memory task and if they were not. Patients with Right Lateral prefrontal lesions, however, were completely normal in their perform-ance on abstracting the rule from the blue cards. However, if one examined how the patients behaved in recovery of the rule after the intervening 'red' cards, the groups behaved in a quite different fashion. The Left Lateral prefrontal patients performed poorly even for rules that they had previously acquired. However, they showed no tendency to be captured by the irrelevant red-card rules. By contrast the Right Lateral patients produced three times the rate of capture errors as normal controls. One has a striking confirmation of the original findings of Stuss and colleagues (1994) in a quite different cognitive domain.

Can these effects I have been attributing to non-evident error detection or checking just be attributed to a lack of cognitive effort, one hypothesis that has been put forward in the memory domain for right prefrontal effects (Schacter *et al.* 1996)? In patient studies a double dissociation has been observed between a loss of behavior associated with cognitive effort and processes involved in monitoring or checking. Stuss *et al.* (2005) again used the Stuss/Alexander procedure for subdividing patients with frontal lesions into four anatomically based subgroups. They then compared the performance of the groups on two different types of reaction time foreperiod task. Both types of task have an interval between a warning signal and the stimulus. In one case, though, this foreperiod was fixed over a block of trials and different blocks with the effects of different foreperiods compared using a simple reaction time paradigm. In the other case, foreperiods varying within a block were compared in both simple and choice RT paradigms. In the fixed foreperiod conditions patients with lesions in the Superior Medial prefrontal area, which includes the anterior cingulate, were much slower than the other three frontal groups. Moreover, although control subjects were slower if the fixed foreperiod was 3 s rather than if it was 1 s (Fig. 1.4), this slowing was significantly greater in the Superior Medial group than in the other three groups. On Hockey's (1993) theory of effort, the effects can be explained by their having reduced cognitive effort to employ, or by reduced concentration capacities on the Stuss *et al.* (1995) subdivision of anterior attentional functions.

The varying foreperiod paradigms gave a very different pattern of effects from the fixed one, although again the Superior Medial group were overall the slowest. For the varying foreperiod paradigm, the foreperiod (which was actually the time between one stimulus and the next) could vary from 3 s to 7 s on each trial. In the simple RT experiment, normal controls and the patients in three of the frontal lobe subgroups were an average 30–35 ms faster for long interstimulus intervals (ISIs) (6 and 7 s) than for short ones (3 and 4 s). One group, however, was roughly 10 ms slower at the longer ISIs; it did not show that standard effect (Fig. 1.5). This was the Right Frontal group not the Superior Medial one. The pattern was similar in the choice RT paradigm. Normal controls and three of the frontal subgroups were 10–30 ms faster for long foreperiods than shorter ones. The Right Lateral subgroup were however 30 ms slower at the longer ISIs. In both cases the interaction was highly significant.

Two interpretations seem possible. One fits with classic 'expectancy' accounts of the variable foreperiod effect such as that of Drazin (1961), which holds that in the longer foreperiods subjects detect that no stimulus has yet arrived and as the conditional probability of a signal for any fixed period of time is now higher they deliberately increase their degree of cognitive effort. A second possibility which relates to the 'repreparation' theoretical perspective of Karlin (1959) is that the time course of cognitive effort over a trial autonomously tends to peak at the same time as the effective warning interval on the preceding trial – a Helson (1947) adaptation level type of effect. If the stimulus precedes the 'natural' peak of the cognitive effort distribution then RTs are longer. However if the subject detects that a stimulus has

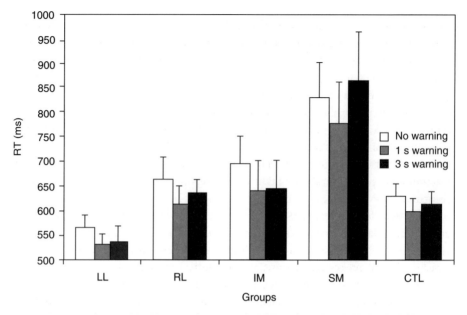

Fig. 1.4 The effect on reaction time of a fixed foreperiod of 1 s or 3 s on different subgroups of patients with prefrontal lesions (from Stuss *et al.*, in press). (LL = Left Lateral; RL = Right Lateral; IM = Inferior Medial; SM = Superior Medial; CTL = Controls.)

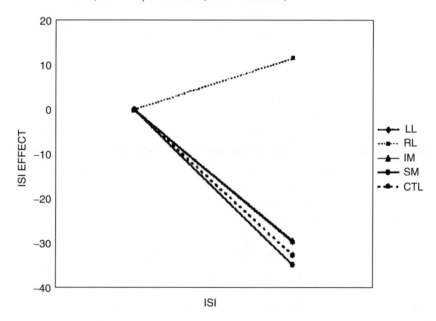

Fig. 1.5 The comparison between reaction time to a short foreperiod (3–4 s) and to a long one (6–7 s) in the critical variable foreperiod condition of Stuss *et al.* (2005). (ISI = interstimulus interval length of foreperiod; LL = Left Lateral; RL = Right Lateral; IM = Inferior Medial; SM = Superior Medial; CTL = Controls.)

not occurred, they can maintain the higher cognitive effort level autonomously achieved. However, this is a qualitatively different type of process which comes into play only when the absence of the anticipated stimulus has been detected. Both explanations then have in common that the subject must detect that no stimulus has yet occurred and then either in one case increase cognitive effort or in the other deliberately maintain the autonomously achieved maximum. Both these depend on realizing that a stimulus has not occurred, which again involves deliberate checking. Thus measures which depend upon checking are affected in a separate group of patients from those that depend on increasing more basic cognitive effort. Moreover, it is again the Right Lateral group who are impaired on the measure dependent upon checking.

In this section a variety of studies have been reviewed which involve aspects of non-evident error detection or checking functions. Overall, the control of such processes appears to be *relatively* lateralized to the right dorsolateral regions by comparison with other prefrontal processes. In some of the studies reviewed, these other prefrontal processes consist of the theoretically most critical ones of strategy generation which necessarily involves top–down schema selection and abstraction; in others there are contrasts with memory-encoding processes which can only be speculatively linked to strategy generation. However, there are still relatively few studies which contrast top–down schema selection and/or abstraction at input *per se* with non-evident error detection or checking at output using the same material and related paradigms. Thus the initial contrast made is supported but not completely unequivocally.

1.5 Other supervisory subsystems

I have concentrated on checking processes for one main reason. It is possible to accept the separation of a system for routine schema selection on the one hand from other control systems, without accepting that the latter themselves form a system. Humphreys and Riddoch (2003), for instance, suggest this type of possibility. Indeed, one can accept the division between certain systems involved in routine selection and others involved in non-routine selection, and just see this as a fairly arbitrary distinction within an overall multiple-module perspective on human cognitive functions. The argument for a system which controls non-evident error detection or checking derives, however, from a perspective that intelligent agents facing non-routine situations require both procedures for producing putatively relevant schemas or sets of schemas for tackling tasks *and* a procedure for checking their operation. They form a combined system such that when a schema selected by the former system is in operation the latter system would also be active. They do not represent individual take-it-or-leave-it independent accretions to the organism's cognitive armory.

However, on the Supervisory System perspective they are not the only such systems (see Shallice and Burgess (1996) and Glasspool (in press) for more extended discussion).

In particular, it was argued earlier that top–down schema selection could be in three modes. One is spontaneous schema selection, discussed earlier. A second is more explicit problem solving, which would require the processes involved in induction (closely related to abstraction) and deduction which Goel and Dolan (2004) have argued on the basis of verbal experiments to be left prefrontally localized. It seems likely that these processes are closely linked computationally to those of spontaneous strategy generation discussed earlier.

A third type of supervisory subprocess are those involved in the production, holding, and realization of intentions; this occurs when a particular putative procedure has been developed at an earlier time and can only be carried out later. On Fox and Das's approach this is part of their fifth stage: the realization over time of a previously selected procedure. That this process – intention generation and realization – might have a separate prefrontal localization was suggested by an analysis of three neurological patients investigated by Shallice and Burgess (1991). These patients performed well on a wide variety of clinical tests sensitive to dorsolateral and medial prefrontal impairment. However on one type of test – multitasking – they were grossly impaired. This is where they were presented with a group of open-ended tests of different types with a general instruction to complete all the tests but no specific signal as to when to move from one test to another. Two specific experiments were run. In one, subjects had to carry out six pencil and paper and dictation tasks in a testing room. In the other, they had to carry out eight simple everyday life tasks (e.g. sending a postcard with certain information) in a shopping centre environment. However, the pattern of performance was similar. They carried out far fewer tasks in a given time period than did normal subjects. They failed to start new tasks appropriately. This was not simply a motivational matter as when having to carry out a *single* demanding task for at least 30 minutes they performed well.

The patient with the best defined lesion had a bilateral frontopolar lesion affecting Brodmann areas 10 and 11 (Fig. 1.6). Moreover, in a later group study of a related test with three subtasks (Burgess *et al.* 2000) patients with anterior medial prefrontal lesions including frontopolar regions performed well on learning the rules of the task, forming a plan, and remembering how they carried it out. However, their overall 'score' – based on subtasks carried out, priorities applied within those subtasks, and rule-breaks – was impaired. Our hypothesis was that BA 10 was involved in the setting up, holding or realizing of intentions, so that, unlike a normal subject, a patient in this group fails to switch to attending to subtasks other than the one they are carrying out. In classical psychological terms, BA10 would control the operation of Ach's 'determining tendency.' Moreover, in functional imaging studies both Koechlin *et al.* (1999) and Burgess *et al.* (2001, 2003) have shown that lateral BA10 is activated if, in addition to performing a continuous on-line task, subjects have a second task they need to carry out, given that a certain type of stimulus occurs while they are carrying out the first task. Moreover, in one of the conditions of the Burgess *et al.* (2001) study, the

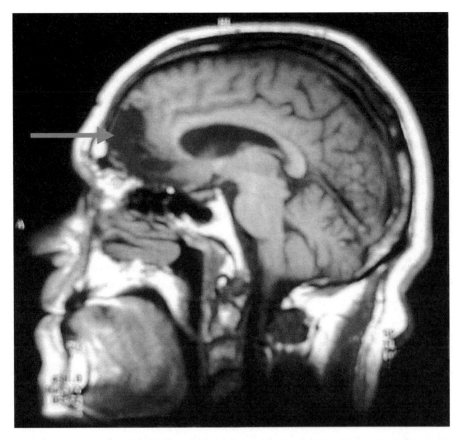

Fig. 1.6 MRI scan 6 years post-injury of the patient with the most focal lesion in the study of Shallice and Burgess, 1991. The lesion principally involves Brodmann areas 10 and 11. (From Shallice, 2004).

activation of BA10 occurs when this second task is potentially relevant throughout the scan period, but in fact the critical stimuli do *not* occur during the scan, so the second task is never executed. Again these studies fit with the idea that BA10 is involved in the deferred execution of a strategy, that is in later switching control of voluntary action from one task-schema to another if the second task becomes relevant but *when the need to switch is not explicitly signaled by well-learned aspects of the eliciting stimuli.*

1.6 The relation to volition, awareness, and explicitness

Norman and Shallice when developing the model used William James's (1890) phenomenological distinction between 'ideo-motor' and 'willed' acts. For James 'wherever movement follows unhesitatingly and immediately the notion of it in the mind, we have ideo-motor action'. This he contrasted with acts which require will, which involve an additional conscious element in the shape of a fiat, mandate, or expressed consent. Norman and Shallice argued that only the latter involve the Supervisory System, and that willed action involves prefiguring its consequences.

Closely related to this view are two other positions. Jack and Shallice (2001) argued that the basic idea can be generalized to any conscious state. They argued that to be conscious of anything depends on the occurrence of what they call a C-process (for conscious-process). A C-process is the key supervisory subprocess that leads to the selection of the dominant schema and the setting of its arguments in contention scheduling. The perspective that conscious experience is critically linked to the operation of the Supervisory System that by top–down modulation lead to schema selection in contention scheduling (Jack and Shallice 2001) fits with cognitive neuro-science evidence that when one becomes conscious of a percept prefrontal systems become activated (Lumer and Rees 1999).

Perner (2003), too, develops his arguments about the need for the use of explicit representations in the operations of a Supervisory System. He argues that as conscious awareness implies that we know what we know, that this entails that his so-called 'predication-explicitness' is a prerequisite for conscious awareness, and that the same applies for 'fact-explicitness'. He continues, 'Fact-explicit representations minimally constitute some meta-awareness of what one knows, which satisfies the basic intuition behind the higher-order thought theory (of consciousness) that being consciously aware of a state of affairs entails knowing (or thinking) that one knows' (p. 230). In other words, the properties required of a Supervisory System to carry out the types of operation that are prototypic of it, mean that the representations used by it to activate schema in contention scheduling have properties that conscious representations need to have and plausibly ones which would require that they be conscious.

The phenomenological distinction between willed/ conscious/ explicit and ideo-motor (in the sense of James (1889)/ automatic/ implicit thus provides parallels to the processing contrast of the two different ways in which schema selection can occur in contention scheduling, that is with or without Supervisory System modulation. The argument of the paper is that there are two very different types and levels of processing domain in the cognitive control of action depending on the routineness and/or implicitness of the type of operation. Thus variables typical of connectionist systems characterize the operation of contention scheduling in the absence of the Supervisory System. Turning to the Supervisory System, subprocesses, such as the retention of working memory information or the specific processes which initiate and allow strategy induction, are currently valuably addressed by connectionist modeling too (e.g. Rougier and O'Reilly 2002). However, properties like being *predication-explicit* are currently far more likely to be implemented in symbolic AI systems than in non-symbolic ones. Moreover, that the higher-level control system – the Supervisory System – is itself internally specialized both functionally and anatomically into separable subsystems with complementary subfunctions is more easily derivable from symbolic AI principles.

Acknowledgements

I would like to thank John Duncan and Wolfgang Prinz for most helpful comments on an earlier version of this paper. Research relevant to this paper was assisted by grants from the Wellcome Foundation.

References

Ach N (1905). *Über den Willenstatigheit und das Denken*. Gottingen.

Allport DA and Wylie G (2000). 'Task-switching' stimulus-response bindings and negative priming. In: S Monsell and J Driver, eds. *Control of cognition processes: attention and performance*, vol. XVIII, pp. 35–70. Cambridge, Massachusetts, USA: MIT Press.

Baddeley AD (1986). *Working memory*. Oxford: Oxford University Press.

Baddeley AD (1996). Exploring the central executive. *Quarterly Journal of Experimental Psychology*, 49, 5–28.

Ben-Yishay Y and Diller L (1983). Cognitive remediation. In: M Rosenthal, ER Griffiths, MR Bond and JR Miller, eds. *Rehabilitation of the brain-damaged adult*, pp. 367–380. Philadelphia: F.A. Pais.

Brooks RA (1991). Intelligence without representation. *Artificial Intelligence*, 47, 139–160.

Burgess PW and Shallice T (1996a). Response suppression, initiation and strategy following frontal lobe lesions. *Neuropsychologia*, 34, 263–273.

Burgess PW and Shallice T (1996b). Confabulation and the control of recollection. *Memory*, 4, 359–412.

Burgess PW and Shallice T (1996c). Bizarre responses, rule detection and frontal lobe lesions. *Cortex*, 32, 241–260.

Burgess PW, Quayle A and Frith CD (2001). Brain regions involved in prospective memory as determined by positron emission tomography. *Neuropsychologia*, 39, 545–555.

Burgess PW, Scott SK and Frith CD (2003). The role of rostral frontal cortex (area 10) in prospective memory: a lateral versus medial dissociation. *Neuropsychologia*, 41, 906–916.

Burgess PW, Veitch E, Costello A and Shallice T (2000). The cognitive and neuroanatomical correlates of multitasking. *Neuropsychologia*, 38, 848–863.

Cansino S, Maquet P, Dolan RJ and Rugg MD (2002). Brain activity underlying encoding and retrieval of source memory. *Cerebral Cortex*, 12, 1048–1056.

Cooper R and Shallice T (2000). Contention scheduling and the control of routine activities. *Cognitive Neuropsychology*, 17, 297–338.

Dehaene S and Changeux JP (1997). A hierarchical neuronal network for planning behaviour. *Proceedings of the National Academy of Science, USA*, 94, 13293–13298.

Della Malva CL, Stuss DT, D'Alton J and Willmer J (1993). Capture errors and sequencing after frontal brain lesions. *Neuropsychologia*, 31, 363–372.

Della Sala S, Marchetti C and Spinnler H (1991). The anarchic hand: a fronto-medial sign. In: F Boller and J Grafman, eds. *Handbook of neuropsychology*, vol. 9. Amsterdam: Elsevier.

Dennett DC (1978). *Brainstorms: philosophical reflections on mind and psychology*. Hassocks, Sussex: Harvester Press.

Dennett DC (1998). Reflections on language and mind. In: P Carruthers and J Boucher, eds. *Language and thought – interdisciplinary themes.* Cambridge: Cambridge University Press.

De Renzi E and Barbieri C (1992). The incidence of the grasp reflex following hemisphere lesion and it relation to frontal damage. *Brain,* 115, 293–313.

Dobbins IG, Foley H, Schacter DL and Wagner AD (2002). Executive control during episodic retrieval: multiple prefrontal processes subserve source memory. *Neuron,* 35, 989–996.

Drazin DH (1961). Effects of foreperiod, foreperiod variability and probability of stimulus occurrence in simple reaction time. *Journal of Experimental Psychology,* 62, 43–50.

Eldridge LL., Knowlton BJ, Furmanski CS, Bookheimer SJ and Engel SA (2000). Remembering episodes: a selective role for the hippocampus during retrieval. *Nature Neuroscience,* 3, 1149–1152.

Elsaesser C and Slack MG (1994). Integrating deliberative planning in a robot architecture. In: *Proceedings of the AIAA/NASA conference on intelligent robots in field, factory, service and space (CIRFFSS '94),* pp. 782–787. Houston.

Fletcher PC, Shallice T and Dolan RJ (1998a). The functional roles of prefrontal cortex in episodic memory. I Encoding. *Brain,* 121, 1239–1248.

Fletcher PC, Shallice T, Frith CD, Frackowiak RSJ and Dolan RJ (1998b). The functional roles of prefrontal cortex in episodic memory. II Retrieval. *Brain,* 121, 1249–1256.

Fox J and Das SK (2000). *Safe and sound: artificial intelligence in hazardous applications.* Menlo Park, California: AAAI Press.

Frith CD (2000). The role of dorsolateral prefrontal cortex in the selection of action as revealed by functional imaging. In: S Monsell and J Driver, eds. *Control of cognitive processes: attention and performance,* Vol. XVIII, pp. 549–565. Cambridge, Massachusetts: MIT Press.

Fuster JM (1989). *The prefrontal cortex.* New York: Raven.

Gat J (1991). *Reliable, goal-directed reactive control of autonomous mobile robots.* PhD Dissertation. Virginia Polytechnic Institute.

Gat J (1998). On tree level architectures. In: D Kortenkamp, RP Bonnasso and R Murphy, eds. *Artificial intelligence and mobile robots.* Menlo Park, California: AAAI Press.

Gershberg FB and Shimamura AP (1995). Impaired use of organizational strategies in free recall following frontal lobe damage. *Neuropsychologia,* 33, 1305–1333.

Gilbert SJ and Shallice T (2002). Task switching: a PDP model. *Cognitive Psychology,* 44, 297–337.

Glasspool, DW (in press). The integration and control of behaviour: Insights from neuroscience and AI. In D.N. Davis (Ed.) Hershey PA, Idea group Inc.

Goel V and Dolan RJ (2004). Differential involvement of left prefrontal cortex in inductive and deductive reasoning *Cognition,* 93, B109–B121.

Helson H (1947). Adaptation level as frame of reference for prediction of psychophysical data. *American Journal of Psychology,* 60, 1–29.

Henson RNA, Rugg MD, Shallice T, Josephs O and Dolan RJ (1999a). Recollection and familiarity in recognition memory: an event-related fMRI study. *Journal of Neuroscience,* 19, 3962–3972.

Henson RNA, Rugg MD, Shallice T and Dolan RJ (2000). Confidence in word recognition: dissociating right prefrontal roles in episodic retrieval. *Journal of Cognitive Neuroscience,* 12, 913–923.

Henson RNA, Shallice T and Dolan RJ (1999b). The role of right prefrontal cortex in episodic retrieval: am fMRI test of the monitoring hypothesis. *Brain,* 122, 1367–1381.

Henson RNA, Shallice T, Josephs O, Dolan RJ (2002). Functional magnetic resonance imaging of proactive interference during spoken recall. *NeuroImage,* 17, 543–558.

Hockey GRJ (1993). Cognitive-emotional control mechanisms in the management of work demands and psychological health. In: AD Baddeley and L Weiskrantz, eds. *Attention: selection, awareness and control*, pp. 328–345. Oxford: Clarendon.

Hommel B (2000). The prepared reflex: automaticity and control in stimulus-response translation. In: S Monsell and J Driver, eds. *Control of cognitive processes: attention and performance*, vol. XVIII, pp. 247–273. Cambridge, Massachusetts, USA: MIT Press.

Houde AO, Agard N, Pillon B and Dubois B (2001). A new window on child prefrontal functions: inhibition of a non-strategic alternation-pointing scheme. *Current Psychology Letters*, 5.

Humphreys GW and Riddoch MJ (2003). Fractionating the intentional control of behaviour: A neuropsychological analysis. In: J Roessler and N Eilan, eds. *Agency and self awareness: issues in philosophy and psychology*, pp. 201–217. Oxford: Clarendon.

Incisa della Rocchetta A and Milner B (1993). Strategic search and retrieval inhibition: the role of the frontal lobes. *Neuropsychologia*, 31, 503–524.

Jack A and Shallice T (2001). Introspective physicalism as an approach to the science of consciousness. *Cognition*, 79, 161–196.

Jahanshahi M, Dirnberger G, Fuller R and Frith CD (2000). The role of the dorsolateral prefrontal cortex in random number generation: A study with positron emission tomography. *NeuroImage*, 12, 713–725.

Jahanshahi M, Profice P, Brown RG, Ridding MC, Dirnberger G and Rothwell JC (1998). The effects of transcranial magnetic stimulation over the dorsolateral prefrontal cortex on suppression of habitual counting during random number generation. *Brain*, 121, 1533–1544.

James W (1890). *The principles of psychology*. New York: Holt.

Jueptner M, Stephan KM, Frith CD, Brooks DJ, Frackowiak RSJ and Passingham RE (1997). Anatomy of motor learning. I. Frontal cortex and attention to action. *Journal of Neurophysiology*, 77, 1313–1324.

Karlin L (1959). Reaction time as a function of foreperiod duration and variability. *Journal of Experimental Psychology*, 58, 185–191.

Karmiloff-Smith A (1986). From metaprocesses to conscious access: Evidence from children's metalinguistic and repair data. *Cognition*, 23, 95–147.

Kieras DE, Meyer DE, Ballas JA and Lauber EJ (2000). Modern computational perspectives on executive processes and cognitive control: Where to from here? In: S Monsell and J Driver, eds. *Control of cognition processes: attention and performance*, vol. XVIII, pp. 681–712. Cambridge, Massachusetts, USA: MIT Press.

Knight RT (1984). Decreased response to novel stimuli after prefrontal lesions in man. *Electroencephalography and Clinical Neurophysiology*, 59, 9–20.

Koechlin E, Basso G, Pietrini P, Panzer S and Grafman J (1999). The role of prefrontal cortex in cognition. *Nature*, 399, 148–151.

Koriat A and Goldsmith M (1996). Monitoring and control processes in the strategic regulation of memory accuracy. *Psychological Review*, 103, 490–517.

Lhermitte F (1983). 'Utilization behaviour' and its relation to lesions of the frontal lobes. *Brain*, 106, 237–255.

Lumer ED and Rees G (1999). Covariation of activity in visual and prefrontal cortex associated with subjective visual perception. *Proceedings National Academy of Science, USA*, 96, 1669–1673.

Luria AR (1966). *Higher cortical functions in man*. London: Tavistock.

MacLeod CM and Dunbar K (1988). Training and Stroop-like interference: Evidence for a continuum of automaticity. *Journal of Experimental Psychology, Learning, Memory and Cognition*, 14, 126–135.

Mandler G (1967). Organizational Memory. In: K Spence and JT Spence, eds. *The psychology of learning and motivation*, pp. 327–372. New York: Academic Press.

McClelland JL and Rumelhart DE (1981). An interactive model of context effects in letter perception. Part I. An account of basic findings. *Psychological Review*, 88, 375–407.

Miller EK and Cohen JD (2001). An integrative theory of prefrontal function. *Annual Review of Neuroscience*, 24, 167–202.

Newell A (1990). *Unified theories of cognition*. Cambridge, Massachusetts: Harvard University Press.

Norman DA (1981). Categorisation of action slips. *Psychological Review*, 88, 1–15.

Norman DA and Shallice T (1986). Attention to action: willed and automatic control of behaviour. In: RJ Davidson, GE Schwartz and D Shapiro, eds. *Consciousness and self regulation: advances in research*, vol. IV, pp. 1–18. New York: Plenum.

Owen AM, Downes JD, Sahakian BJ, Polkey CE and Robbins TW (1990). Planning and spatial working memory following frontal lobe lesions in man. *Neuropsychologia*, 28, 1021–1034.

Paus T, Kalina M, Patockova L, Angerova Y, Gerny R, Mecir P, *et al.* (1991). Medial vs lateral frontal lobe lesions and differential impairment of central-gaze fixation maintenance in man. *Brain*, 114, 2051–2067.

Perner J (2003). Dual control and the causal theory of action: the case of non-intentional action. In: J Roessler and N Eilan, eds. *Agency and self-awareness: issues in philosophy and psychology*. Oxford: Clarendon.

Petrides M (1994). Frontal lobes and working memory: evidence from investigations of the effects of cortical excisions in nonhuman primates. In: F Boller and J Grafman, eds. *Handbook of neuropsychology*, pp. 59–84. Amsterdam: Elsevier.

Raichle ME, Fiez JA, Videen TO, MacLeod A.-MK, Pardo JV, Fox PT *et al.* (1994). Practice related changes in human brain functional anatomy during nonmotor learning. *Cerebral Cortex*, 4, 8–26.

Reason JT (1979). Actions not as planned. In: G Underwood and R Stevens, eds. *Aspects of consciousness*, vol. 1. London: Academic Press.

Reverberi C, Lavaroni A, Gigli GL, Skrap M and Shallice T (2005). Specific impairments of rule induction in different frontal lobe subgroups. *Neuropsychologia* 43, 460–472.

Riddoch MJ, Edwards MG, Humphreys GW, West R and Heafield T (1998). Visual affordances direct actions: neuropsychological evidence from manual interference. *Cognitive Neuropsychology*, 15, 645–684.

Rizzo A, Ferrante D and Bagnara S (1995). Handling human error. In: J-M Huc, PC Cacciabue and E Hollnegel, eds. *Expertise and technology*, pp. 195–212. Hillside, N.J. Erlbaum.

Rossi S, Cappa SF, Babiloni C, Pasualetti P, Miniussi C, Carducci F, *et al.* (2001). Prefrontal cortex in long-term memory: an 'interference' approach using magnetic stimulation. *Nature Neuroscience*, 9, 948–952.

Rougier NP and O'Reilly RC (2002) Learning representations in a gated prefrontal cortex model of dynamic task switching. *Cognitive Science*, 26, 503–520.

Russell SJ and Norvig P (1995). *Artificial intelligence: a modern approach*. Prentice Hall, Upper Saddle River N.J.

Sandrini M, Cappa SF, Rossi C, Rossini PM and Miniussi C (2003). The role of the prefrontal cortex is verbal episodic memory. *Journal of Cognitive Neuroscience*, 15, 855–861.

Schacter DL, Reiman E, Curran T, Yun LS, Bandy D and McDermott KB (1996). Neuroanatomical correlates of veridical and illusory recognition memory: evidence from positron emission tomography. *Neuron*, **17**, 267–274.

Shallice T (1982). Specific impairments of planning. *Philosophical Transactions of the Royal Society, London B*, **298**, 199–209.

Shallice T (2004). The fractionation of supervisory control. In M. S. Gazzaniga (Ed.). *The Cognitive Neurosciences III*, pp 943–956. Cambridge, Mass: MIT Press.

Shallice T and Burgess P (1991). Deficits in strategy application following frontal lobe damage in man. *Brain*, **114**, 727–741.

Shallice T and Burgess PW (1996). Domains of supervisory control and the temporal organisation of behaviour. *Philosophical Transactions of the Royal Society of London B*, **351**, 1405–1412.

Shallice T and Evans ME (1978). The involvement of the frontal lobes in cognitive estimation. *Cortex*, **14**, 294–303.

Shallice T, Burgess PW, Schon F and Baxter DW (1989). The origins of utilisation behaviour. *Brain*, **11**, 1587–1598.

Shallice T, Fletcher PC, Frith CD, Grasby P, Frackowiak RSJ and Dolan RJ (1994). Brain regions associated with the acquisition and retrieval of verbal episodic memory. *Nature*, **386**, 633–635.

Shiffrin RM and Schneider W (1977). Controlled and automatic human information processing: II. Perceptual learning, automatic attending and a general theory. *Psychological Review*, **84**, 127–190.

Stuss D, Alexander MP, Palumbo C, Buckle L, Sayer L and Pogue J (1994). Organisational strategies of patients with unilateral or bilateral frontal lobe injury in word list learning tasks. *Neuropsychology*, **8**, 355–373.

Stuss DT, Shallice T, Alexander MP and Picton TW (1995). A multidisciplinary approach to anterior attentional functions. *Annals of the New York Academy of Sciences*, **769**, 191–211.

Stuss DT, Alexander MP, Hamer L, Palumbo C, Dempster R, Binns M, *et al.* (1998). The effects of focal anterior and posterior brain lesions on verbal fluency. *Journal of the International Neuropsychological Society*, **4**, 265–278.

Stuss DT, Alexander MP, Shallice T, Picton TW, Binns MA, Macdonald R, *et al.* (2005). Multiple frontal systems controlling response speed. *Neuropsychologia* **43**, 396–417.

Sussman GJ (1975). *A computational model of skill acquisition*. American Elsevier, New York.

Verin M, Partiot A, Pillon, Malapani C, Agid Y and Dubois B (1993). Delayed response tasks and prefrontal lesions in man – Evidence for self-generated patterns of behaviour with poor environmental modulation. *Neuropsychologia*, **31**, 1379–1396.

Wagner AD, Poldrack, RA, Eldridge LL, Desmond JE., Glover, GH,. Gabrieli, JD (1998). Material-specific lateralization of prefrontal activation during episodic encoding and retrieval. *Neuroreport*. **9**, 3711–3717.

Wilding EL and Rugg MD (1996). An event-related potential study of recognition memory with and without retrieval of source. *Brain*, **119**, 889–906.

Part 1

Learning mechanisms

Chapter 2

How far can you go with Hebbian learning, and when does it lead you astray?

James L. McClelland

Abstract

This paper considers the use of Hebbian learning rules to model aspects of development and learning, including the emergence of structure in the visual system in early life. There is considerable physiological evidence that a Hebb-like learning rule applies to the strengthening of synaptic efficacy seen in neurophysiological investigations of synaptic plasticity, and similar learning rules are often used to show how various properties of visual neurons and their organization into ocular dominance stripes and orientation columns could arise without being otherwise preprogrammed. Some of the plusses and minuses of Hebbian learning are considered. Hebbian learning can strengthen the neural response that is elicited by an input; this can be useful if the response made is appropriate to the situation, but it can also be counterproductive if a different response would be more appropriate. Examples in which this outcome-independent Hebbian type of strengthening might account, at least in part, for cases in which humans fail to learn are considered, and computational models embodying the Hebbian approach are described that can account for the findings. At a systems level, Hebbian learning cannot be the whole story. From a computational point of view, Hebbian learning can certainly lead one in the wrong direction, and some form of control over this is necessary. Also, experimental findings clearly show that human learning can be affected by accuracy or outcome feedback. Several ways in which sensitivity to feedback might be incorporated to guide learning within a fundamentally Hebbian framework for learning are considered.

2.1 **Introduction**

Connectionist models that learn using error-correcting learning rules have long played a role in the exploration of issues in cognitive and linguistic development. In my own work in the late 1980s and early 1990s, I explored the idea that predictive error-driven learning provided the engine that drives cognitive development (McClelland, 1994). The central idea was that the developing child is continually making implicit predictions about the future state of the world based on current inputs, using an internal model embodied in a connectionist network. Any mismatch between the child's expectations and observed events provides an error signal, indicating that the child's internal model must be updated. Learning then occurs by adjusting the parameters of the mind—the connection weights in the network—to reduce the discrepancy between predicted and observed events. The necessary changes are determined by the use of the back-propagation algorithm (Rumelhart *et al.* 1986).

I applied this predictive error-driven learning approach in a series of models (McClelland, 1989; McClelland and Jenkins, 1991; McClelland, 1995) addressing aspects of cognitive development as revealed by the work of Siegler (1976) on the Inhelder and Piaget (1958) balance scale task. Other models that use back propagation to adjust connection weights to reduce the difference between predicted and observed events include Elman's (1990) model of the acquisition of syntax through learning to predict the next word from previous words, and St. John and McClelland's (1990) model of learning to comprehend sentences through learning to predict the characteristics of the events described by sentences. The approach has also been applied to the development of conceptual and physical knowledge during infancy (Munakata *et al.*, 1997) and to many aspects of conceptual development during childhood (Rogers and McClelland, 2004). Several papers in this volume present ongoing investigations that can be thought of as exemplifying this approach.

In spite of my own continuing reliance on error-driven learning (especially in the work with Rogers, cited above) I have recently begun exploring learning that can occur in the absence of an error signal (McClelland, 2001). Specifically, I have been exploring the possibility that Hebb's famous proposal for learning in neural systems may provide some guidance in addressing aspects of human learning—particularly some of its failures as well as its successes—that may not be fully addressed within the error-driven approach. In the course of this work I have also had occasion to begin to think more generally about the fact that we learn from our own reactions and behaviors, as well as from the sequences of events that we see in the world. The key questions addressed in this chapter are:

- How well do networks based on Hebbian learning work as computational systems, and when do they fail?
- How do the successes and failures of Hebbian systems compare to the successes and failures of human learning?

In the first part of this chapter, I will review Hebb's proposal for learning and describe briefly some of the neuroscience evidence that has supported the basic proposal and led to a family of Hebb-like learning rules used widely in biologically-oriented models of neural network learning. The second part of the chapter will explore some puzzling findings concerning successes and failures of learning that can be addressed with models in which learning occurs on the basis of these biologically-oriented learning rules. In the course of this we will encounter some evidence that makes it clear why the Hebbian approach is not fully sufficient without some elaboration to encompass sensitivity to outcome information. This will lead to a brief discussion of how such information may be accommodated within a fundamentally Hebbian framework. I will conclude by returning to the broader question of how we learn from our own behavior. I will suggest that even here Hebbian learning has its limits, and consider ways it may be regulated by internally-generated signals that can be used to help guide our learning in the right directions.

2.1.1 Hebb's proposal and the biology of Hebbian learning

In a famous passage in his 1949 book, Hebb proposed a neural mechanism for learning:

When an axon of cell A is near enough to excite a cell B and repeatedly or persistently takes part in firing it, some growth process or metabolic change takes place in one or both cells such that A's efficiency, as one of the cells firing B, is increased.

This passage captures the fundamental idea rather well, but is somewhat cumbersome to process. A simpler, catchier wording captures the key idea quite succinctly:

Cells that fire together wire together.

The source of this latter version is unknown, but it is oft-repeated in discussions of Hebbian learning in neuroscience.

Hebb's proposal has been the inspiration of a wide range of biological research on long-term potentiation, usually conducted in slices taken from the hippocampus of the rat. Long-term potentiation is explored by providing a train of impulses to a bundle of fibers projecting to a target neuron (or group of neurons) whose state of activation is being monitored (and potentially directly controlled). When the train of impulses is strong, so that the postsynaptic neurons fire, the efficacy of smaller test pulses arriving on the bundle of fibers is increased, or potentiated. Typically there is a short-lasting component that decays over minutes, to leave a longer-lasting increment that can persist for the lifetime of the preparation; it is this longer-lasting increment that we refer to with the phrase *long-term potentiation* (LTP). It is well-established that a weak input, itself insufficient to produce LTP, could result in potentiation if paired with a stronger input arriving on other fibers (Barrionuevo and Brown, 1983; McNaughton *et al.* 1978).

Research on LTP and related phenomena is ongoing, and several important additional facts have been established. One of these, the phenomenon of spike-time-dependent-plasticity (STDP), further supports Hebb's proposal. What STDP refers to is the finding that the exact timing of neural firing in pre- and postsynaptic neurons can influence LTP. Indeed, under some conditions, LTP is maximal if the sending neuron fires just before the receiving neuron fires, which it must if it is to participate in firing the receiving neuron; and LTP is reversed if the sending neuron fires after the receiving neuron fires. This phenomenon of STDP arises when individual pre- and postsynaptic events are considered at a fine time grain. The role of spike-time-dependence in the living, behaving organism is debated, since the timing of spikes tends to be quite variable; but STDP can help neurons become more selective for temporal coincidences (Abbott and Nelson, 2000; Song *et al.* 2000), and is likely to receive considerable further exploration as a mechanism for learning fine-grained temporal information.

In any case, most existing models aimed at system-level and behavioral phenomena, including all those to be considered here, do not address neuronal activity at this fine level of granularity. Instead such models use continuous activation values, thought to reference the mean firing rate of a population of neurons (generally it is assumed that a population is required to provide a sufficient signal to have an impact on receiving neurons). At this level, LTP is generally found to be well-captured as depending on the product of separate functions of pre- and postsynaptic activity:

$$\Delta w_{rs} = \varepsilon f_r(a_r) f_s(a_s) \tag{1}$$

Learning rules obeying relations of this form will be considered Hebbian; in the simple case where the functions are identify functions ($f_r(a_r) = a_r, f_s(a_s) = a_s$) and where a_r and a_s take on activation values of 1 or 0, this learning rule captures the simple 'cells that wire together fire together' idea in a straightforward and simple form. However, in this form the rule is not quite adequate, either to capture findings from LTP studies or to address issues in development and learning.

Two findings from LTP research have contributed to the specification of the functions f_r and f_s:

1. Early research by Levy and Steward (1979) established that LTP is accompanied by a corresponding depression of the efficacy of inputs that are not activated when the receiving neuron is activated. This phenomenon, known as 'heterosynaptic long-term depression' can be captured in models by assuming that the presynaptic function f_s in the equation above is given by the difference between the sending unit's activation and the existing value of the connection weight:

$$f_s(a_s) = (a_s - w_{rs}) \tag{2}$$

2. Under conditions where strong trains of input stimulation produce LTP, repeated weak trains tend to produce a long-term depression or reduction of synaptic

efficacy (Dudek and Bear, 1993). This phenomenon was predicted from a model of developmental stabilization in which the Hebbian update equation is assumed to be non-monotonic (Bienenstock *et al.* 1982). With very low levels of activity in the receiving neuron, a_r, the value of the postsynaptic term is 0; as activity increases it first becomes negative, then as activity increases further still it becomes positive. This non-monotonic function, called φ, was proposed because it tends to encourage the stabilization of neuronal responses and to promote sharp tuning of the receiving neuron's receptive field. This occurs because inputs that only weakly activate the neuron are weakened still further. Although the use of the φ function would likely improve most models, the slightly simpler form below, in which $φ(a_r)$ is approximated simply by a_r, is used in many computational models (Grossberg, 1976; Rumelhart and Zipser, 1985).

$$\Delta w_{rs} = \varepsilon a_r (a_s - w_{rs}) \tag{3}$$

A variety of different names have been given to this learning rule. Although the name is a bit cumbersome, I will refer to this rule as the Hebbian redistribution rule or the *Hebb_r* rule for short, since it redistributes the incoming weights to a unit so that they are aligned with the input pattern activating the unit.

2.2 Applications of Hebbian learning in biological and psychological development

Learning rules of the general form of Equation 1 have been used in many models addressing aspects of biological and psychological development. On the biological side, Linsker (1986a, 1986b, 1986c) has used a variant of Equation 1 to model the emergence of center–surround receptive fields, oriented edge detectors, and ocular dominance columns during prenatal development. Considering first center–surround receptive fields, what Linsker observed is that the postsynaptic or receiving neuron tends to strengthen the subset of its inputs that are most highly correlated with each other. To see why this should be, suppose there are three inputs to a receiving neuron, and suppose that the first two occur together but the third occurs when the other two do not (this very simple case represents the extreme of positive vs. negative correlation; the same principle applies to less extreme cases). As illustrated in Table 2.1, the postsynaptic term in the Hebbian learning rule will be larger, on average, when either the first or the second input is active than it is when the third is active, so Equation 1 will cause the weights to the receiver from the first and second units to increase more than the weight to the receiver from the third unit. This tendency, when opposed by an overall tendency for connection weights to decay, can result in a situation where the inputs that have relatively strong correlations with other inputs to the receiving unit end up with connection weights to the receiver that grow stronger over time, and those that are less correlated with the other inputs to the receiver end up with weights that grow increasingly more negative.

Table 2.1 Effect of input correlation on connection weights

event	a_1	a_2	a_3	a_4	$a_r a_1$	$a_r a_2$	$a_r a_s$
a	1	1	0	.20	.20	.20	0
b	0	0	1	.10	0	0	.10
sum of coproducts					.20	.20	.10
decay					−.15	−.15	−.15
net change to weight					.05	.05	−.05

Effect of correlation of input activations on Hebbian learning. Two events are illustrated, one in which input units 1 and 2 are both active, and one in which input unit 3 is active alone. In the first case, the resulting activation of the receiving unit is greater than in the second case, so the Hebbian coproducts ($a_r a_s$) are larger in the first case than the second case. For this case we are assuming $a_r = \Sigma_s a_s w_{rs}$ and $w_{rs} = .1$ for all s before either event is presented. Note that the coproducts are all positive. The value chosen for weight decay determines how strong the sum of the coproducts must be for the change in weight to be positive. Note also that changes in the weights will influence the activation of the receiving unit if the inputs are presented again; this tends to amplify the effect of the correlation in the inputs still further. Based on Linsker (1996a).

Linsker (1986a,b) considered a network consisting of several two-dimensional arrays of cells (similar to the retina and subsequent layers in the visual pathway), with the density of connections reaching a given cell in one layer from the preceding layer obeying a decreasing (Gaussian) function of distance between the positions of the cells in the two layers. He then considered what would happen if the cells in the first layer fired spontaneously and independently. Because of the distance-dependence in the initial connections, neighboring cells in the second layer are likely to receive connections from some of the same cells in the first layer, so that the inputs—and therefore the resulting activations—of these neighboring cells will be slightly correlated; the degree of correlation falls off with distance between the neighbors. Now, the crucial observation concerns the inputs to cells at the third layer. Each third-layer cell receives relatively dense projections from the cells at the corresponding location in the preceding layer, with density falling off with distance. As a result, cells near the center of the projection to the third-layer cell tend to have a greater correlation with all the other cells projecting to the third-layer cell than those near the edges. The result is that the connections from cells near the center of the projection end up with positive connections and those near the edges end up with negative values, thereby producing center–surround receptive fields. If the outputs of center–surround cells at the third layer are propagated forward through several further layers, Linsker (1986b) found that edge detectors can emerge. The reasons for this are less intuitive but still follow from the principle that the neurons at higher levels are maximizing their responsiveness to maximally correlated clusters of cells in their inputs.

In order to organize the edge detectors that emerge at higher levels into orientation columns, Linsker (1986c) assumed a particular 'cortical interaction function' in which nearby neurons tend to excite each other and neurons at a greater distance tend to inhibit each other. The result of this is that neighboring neurons tend to encourage each other to have similar response properties, while neurons with slightly greater separations tend to discourage this tendency. Orientation columns thus arise as the biproduct of Hebbian learning coupled with the local excitatory and midrange inhibitory interactions. Similar principles (most importantly, the assumption that the neighboring neurons in the same eye are more correlated during spontaneous prenatal activity than neurons in two different eyes) result in the emergence of eye-selective neurons and ocular dominance columns where inputs from the two eyes converge (Miller *et al.*, 1989).

It should be noted that there is now evidence that some aspects of cortical neural organization are laid down during early phases of development, before the developing neurons become active (Crowley and Katz, 2000). This organization may depend on chemical gradients and other mechanisms that channel axonal growth, providing an initial coarse framework that encourages map-like spatial organization and alternating stripes of innervation from the two eyes. Thus, by no means is it assumed that all aspects of neural organization depend on Hebbian mechanisms. What is widely assumed is that a very basic framework provided prior to the onset of activation is further refined and maintained by Hebbian learning mechanisms.

A particular network architecture that has proven fairly popular in models both of psychological and biological development is shown in Fig. 2.1. The particular network shown, based loosely on the proposals of Kohonen (1982), provides two two-dimensional sheets of neurons, corresponding perhaps to a sensory surface (on the retina or the skin) called the input layer and a second layer of units called the representation layer that receives projections from the input surface. As above, initial weak connections are assumed to have a weak topographic bias, so that a neuron at a given location in the input layer will tend to have slightly stronger connections to corresponding locations in the representation layer.

Within each layer, short-range excitatory connections and longer-range inhibitory connections are assumed to enforce a scenario in which a localized blob of activity at the input layer gives rise to a corresponding localized blob of activity at the receiving layer. (In Kohonen's idealization of this, the receiving unit with the strongest weighted input is simply chosen as the winning unit. It and its neighbors are assigned activation values ranging from 1 to 0, following a Gaussian falloff with distance from the winning unit. Similar architectures have frequently been used to model refinement of map-like cortical representations (e.g. Goodhill, 1993).

In addition to modeling structural features of the underlying neural substrate, networks similar to the one in Fig. 2.1 have also been used extensively in models of development at a behavioral level. Two cases in point are the models of category formation introduced by Schyns (1991) and the model of infant's sensitivity to causal even sequences introduced by Cohen, Chaput, and Cashon (2002). In both models, the tendency of such map-like representations to group similar inputs together and to learn to respond to patterns of coherent covariation in these inputs plays an important role in the accounts offered for important aspects of cognitive development.

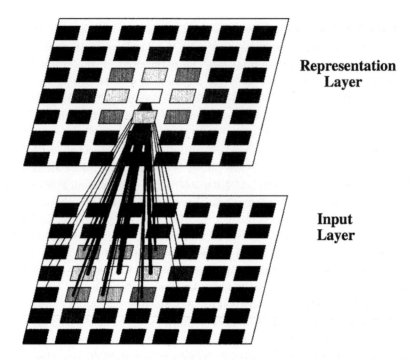

Fig. 2.1 A simple map-formation network similar to the architecture proposed by Kohonen (1982). Units are represented by tiles within each layer, and the activation of each unit is indicated by shading (white = 1.0; black = 0). The network is shown with a blob of activation centered just to the left of the middle of the input layer. This in turn has produced a blob of activation centered on the middle unit of the representation layer. Connections from the center unit on the representation layer to the units on the input layer are illustrated, with thicker lines indicating stronger connections. These connections were established through learning; before learning, the connections were largely random, with only a weak tendency for connections from a particular input unit to project more strongly to the corresponding unit in the representation layer. Reprinted from Figure 1 of McClelland *et al.* (1999).

2.3 Computational limitations of Hebbian learning

Hebbian learning is relatively weaker than error-correcting approaches, where there is an explicit measure of the network's error and an explicit procedure for adjusting weights so as to minimize the error. Such error-correcting learning algorithms have been very successful in allowing networks to solve hard problems, and in so doing to discover useful representations that aid in their solution. Networks trained using strictly Hebbian approaches are not really constrained in this way. Thus, the computational question, 'How well do networks based on Hebbian learning work as computational systems?' is answered by many modelers 'not very well at all'. However, it may be worth noting that it is possible to guide some types of networks that are trained with the Hebb$_r$ rule in Equation 3 to some extent. To see this, let us consider what happens in a simple competitive network of the kind used by Rumelhart and Zipser (1985). Competitive networks consist of two layers of units, as in the Kohonen model, but there is no lateral spread of activation: when an input is presented, one of the representation units is chosen as the winner and is allowed to adjust its connection weights according to Equation 3; the weights coming in to all other units are left unchanged. In such a network, each competitive unit tends to pick out its own cluster of similar inputs, a simple form of category formation. Each unit's weight vector ends up positioned at the centroid of its cluster, and the assignment of patterns to clusters tends to maximize within-cluster similarity. Thus the approach provides a simple, input driven category-formation algorithm.

However, sometimes the similarity structure in a set of inputs is not a sufficient guide to their correct categorization, as defined by environmental contingencies; at the very least, some aspects of similarity may be more important than others, for example. Figuring out how to weight different kinds of similarity is one of the strengths of error-correcting learning, and indeed, in such models, the similarity structure over inputs can sometimes be completely remapped at hidden layers using error-correcting learning. The point I would like to emphasize here, however, is that Hebbian learning mechanisms are not completely insensitive to guidance by such things as category labeling information (or any information reliably correlated with variable item properties). Specifically, within the Rumelhart and Zipser model, the clustering process can be influenced by providing additional input, such as a category label, along with each pattern. The label input is treated as just another part of the input pattern, and as such it tends to make the patterns that are assigned the same label more similar to each other, and those assigned different labels less similar, thereby altering the clustering of inputs. This method was used extensively to cause networks to group divergent inputs together in the simulations of Rumelhart and Zipser (1985) and a similar approach was used by Schyns in his Kohonen-network based model of perceptual category learning with and without labeling information.

My point here is not to suggest that Hebbian learning is sufficient to solve all hard learning problems. I would suggest, however, that the potential of this approach may be underestimated. Later in the paper I will turn to other ways in which an inherently Hebbian learning process may be guided. For now, however, I consider some characteristics of Hebbian learning which may help explain some successes and failures of learning in experiments with human subjects.

2.4 Some psychological plusses and minuses of Hebbian learning

A key observation about Hebbian learning is that it tends to strengthen the pattern of neural response that occurs to a particular input. When such responses are desirable, their strengthening can lead to increased accuracy, fluency, etc., of the perception, emotion, thought, or action associated with this neural response, and this may well underlie the increased fluency of performance that occurs with practice in many information-processing tasks.

However, when the response that is evoked by an input is not desirable, its strengthening may have deleterious consequences. One such deleterious consequence is the phenomenon of dystonia that can occur in musicians and writers. Dystonia appears to reflect a tendency for the various digits of a person's hand to lose their independence and often to enter into a state of chronic activation experienced as a cramp. Although the details are not fully clear about how these disorders develop, they do occur in individuals who persistently activate a set of muscles together, for example by gripping the neck of a violin or a writing implement with several digits simultaneously. This continual coactivation of muscles (and the neurons that drive them) could lead to Hebbian strengthening of synaptic connections among the neurons that control the muscles, such that the intent to move any one muscle would then lead to coactivation of all of them. Once set up, the dystonia may be very difficult to correct, especially in musicians who must continue to perform. A second kind of deleterious consequence could occur in phobias and in racism. If you react in fear upon seeing a snake or a person from a particular racial group, Hebbian synaptic strengthening may increase the tendency to respond in this way, even if nothing bad actually happens. A third kind of case may arise in persons—including scientists—who have long practiced a particular way of thinking, and are then confronted with an entirely new and incommensurate pattern of thought. The idea that such entrenched 'habits of mind' may provide barriers to the discovery and acceptance of new scientific ideas is discussed at length in two books by Howard Margolis (1987, 1993), a philosopher and historian of science. For example Margolis discusses nightmares Darwin had for years in which he was plagued by a vision of the complex structure of the human eye. The entrenched habit of thinking of the eye as too complex to arise without divine design was difficult, apparently, even for Darwin himself to shake.

In the remainder of the present article, I will provide an update on investigations of two other cases in which Hebbian learning may provide at least part of the explanation for failures of human learning, and where experimental evidence now suggests that procedures developed with the strengths and weaknesses of Hebbian learning in mind can allow us to arrange conditions so that learning will be more successful. Both puzzles arose within the context of the complementary learning systems model of McClelland, McNaughton and O'Reilly (1995). According to this model, there is a gradual or slow learning system, in the neocortex, which subserves the acquisition of language, conceptual knowledge, cognitive skills, and many other sorts of cognitive abilities that are acquired gradually in the course of development. This system is complemented by another, fast learning system, in the hippocampus and related structures in the medial temporal lobes, that allows for the rapid formation of arbitrary associative conjunctions such as the conjunction of a name with a face or the particular arbitrary combination of elements that together form an experienced episode. This theory continues to provide a guiding framework for my own thinking about learning and memory in the brain, but a few years ago two things began to puzzle me.

2.4.1 Paradox of new learning in amnesia

One of these puzzles arose in thinking about new learning in amnesia. The amnesic syndrome, as seen in patient HM (Scoville and Milner, 1957), results from removal or severe damage to the hippocampus and related structures, and leaves the cortical learning system intact, which, according to the theory, is capable of gradual learning. And indeed, there is evidence of some slow learning in patients like HM. For example Milner *et al.* (1968) had shown that HM was able to acquire some new declarative information. He was able to identify John F. Kennedy from his profile on a coin, and he could report that Kennedy had been the president and that he had been assassinated. Kennedy's election and assassination both occurred after HM became amnesic, so HM must have learned this while amnesic. Furthermore Gabrieli, Cohen, and Corkin (1988) report evidence that HM learned new words that entered the language after he became amnesic. Though his acquisition was certainly not normal, it was nevertheless clear that he had acquired the meanings of some new words. However, in a laboratory experiment, Gabrieli *et al.* made absolutely no progress in teaching HM the meanings of eight infrequent words. Several approaches were used to try to get HM to learn the words. The main one involved showing a definition and giving HM a chance to choose which of the eight words went with it. A response was required on every trial, and HM had to keep trying until he chose the correct answer. The answer was then eliminated as a possibility, and the definition of another word was then given. HM then had to choose from seven alternatives. This process iterated until a single choice remained. HM practiced this task extensively over a several week period, but never made any progress. At the end of the experiment he could define correctly only one of the words, a word he happened to know before the beginning of the experiment. Other studies with HM, reviewed in Milner *et al,* (1968) indicated that he was unable to learn even very short lists of arbitrary paired associates. I was puzzled by these failures, because I expected HM to be able to learn new things, albeit gradually, via his largely intact neocortical learning system, and because of the evidence that he had indeed learned some new things during the time he was amnesic.

While one could envisage a host of reasons for the apparent discrepancy indicated here, one possibility that occurred to me was as follows. Perhaps the discrepancy reflects a special disadvantage that would accrue in learning new material if a patient who is only able to learn slowly were forced to make a response on every learning trial. According to the complementary learning systems model, residual cortical learning is expected to be very gradual, depending on the cumulation of very slight connection adjustments on each learning opportunity. But many experiments (including paired-associate learning tasks and the version of the word-learning task used by Gabrieli *et al.*) combine a test of memory with every learning trial. Since the amnesic patient will have learned very little from the first exposure to the correct answer, the test of memory that occurs on the second exposure is very likely to result in an incorrect response. If this incorrect response is strengthened (as it would be under the Hebbian approach), this would tend to work against correct elicitation of the desired association. On subsequent trials this same process would continue. Depending on details (e.g. the likelihood of the same interfering response being repeatedly elicited by the test, etc.), this could result in a complete failure to show improvement, even though connection strengths are being adjusted on each learning trial. Possibly, connection weights promoting both the correct and the incorrect response would be strengthened on every learning trial. While strengthening the weights promoting the correct response would tend to lead to improvement, strengthening the weights promoting an error would tend to increase interference that would counteract the improvement.

2.4.2 Prediction and Experiment

An obvious prediction follows from this account: a procedure in which the patient is given repeated exposure to a set of cue-target pairs without requiring any reponse during exposure should be more likely to result in correct responding than a procedure that attempts to elicit a response from each cue alone, prior to exposure to the correct response. For future reference in this article, we call the former procedure a *study-only* procedure, while we call the second procedure a *generate-study* procedure. The standard procedure used in paired associate learning, often called the *method of anticipation* is, of course, an example of a generate-study procedure, and the multiple-choice procedure of Cohen *et al.* is similar to such a procedure in that it tends to result in the elicitation of many errors before exposure to the correct word–definition association.

Once this prediction became apparent, I quickly discovered several studies that have reported advantages for amnesic patients with the study-only procedure (Baddeley and Wilson, 1994; Hamman and Squire, 1995; Hayman *et al.*, 1993). The Hayman *et al.* study is perhaps the most dramatic. The investigators tested patient KC (an individual who became profoundly amnesic due to a closed-head injury arising from a motor-cycle accident) with what might be called amusing word definitions, similar to some crossword puzzle cues. KC was given repeated exposure to these materials to see if he would learn the experimenter's target response for each clue. Two examples were 'a talkative featherbrain' (parakeet) or 'Marlon Brando's wife' (godmother). Materials were divided into those for which KC had a pre-existing (incorrect) association and those for which he drew a blank, and half of each type were presented repeatedly using the study-only procedure, while the other half were presented using the generate-study procedure. Items were further subdivided into those studied once per session and those studied twice per session. When tested after several study sessions with all of the materials, KC showed a clear study-only advantage, and the results were most dramatic for the case in which KC had a pre-existing response. Among items presented only once per session, KC showed no progress in the generate-study condition, and he persisted in giving the same response he had generated himself in most cases. In contrast, he learned to produce the experimenter's response on 67 per cent of the cases in the corresponding study-only condition (items for which he had a pre-existing response, presented once per session). This finding is highly consistent with the idea that elicitation of incorrect responses results in their strengthening, thereby either blocking learning of the correct cue-target association or perhaps simply masking evidence of learning of the experimenter-defined cue-target association by maintaining the pre-existing response at sufficient strength to compete with the experimental target item.

The findings in the Hayman et al. experiment are supportive of an important role for Hebbian strengthening of incorrect responses. However, other studies have produced much smaller study-only advantages compared to a generate-study condition. For example Hamman and Squire (1995) used cue-target materials that form meaningful (but improbable) sentence-like units, such as 'Medicine cures HICCUPS'. Here 'Medicine cures' is the cue and 'HICCUPS' is the to-be-learned target response. Note that the response words were chosen to be unlikely but meaningful, and were pretested to ensure that they would be generated very infrequently to the cue prior to first exposure (<5 per cent). While Hamman and Squire did find a study-only advantage in this experiment, the effect was not large. Furthermore, the size of the effect was correlated with the degree to which the patient exhibited signs of a frontal deficit, and thus it was suggested that the study-only advantage might not be relevant to understanding failures of learning in relatively pure cases of amnesia.

In this context I was lucky to have the opportunity to revisit the issue in a collaborative study (Bird, et al. 2004) of patient VC, a severely amnesic patient that has been previously characterized by Cipolotti et al. (2001) as having severe retrograde as well as anterograde amnesia as a result of a hypoxic incident. VC's damage appears to be restricted to the medial temporal lobes, and he shows no signs of frontal deficits. As in the Hamman and Squire study, we used improbable but meaningful sentence-like materials. The study phase was not presented to VC as a memory experiment; rather he was told for the study-only (SO) items to listen to each item as it was read by the experimenter, repeat it, and then rate it for meaningfulness. For the generate-study (GS) items he was first given the cue, asked to produce his own completion (which could, for example, have been 'INFECTION' for the 'medicine cures ...' example) and then to listen to the experimenter's version, repeat it, and provide a meaningfulness rating. Thus our procedure ensured that a response was elicited on every generate-study trial, something that was not done in the Hamman and Squire experiment. The 20 GS and 20 SO items were presented eight times each in interleaved sequence (GS items alternated with SO items), and an additional 20 unstudied control items were included only at test. It may be worth noting that there is a contrast in the framing of the task for subjects between the Hamman and Squire experiment on the one hand and the present study (along with Hayman *et al.*) on the other. In Hamman and Squire, the subjects appear to have been instructed to try to learn the experiment's target word, as in the standard method of anticipation used in paired-associate learning experiments. This presumably engenders an effort to try to retrieve an episodic memory of the previously presented cue-target pair. In contrast, our study and Hayman *et al.* investigated incidental learning based on repeated encounters with the cues, self-generated responses, and target materials.

Combining the findings from two runs of the experiment produced very clear-cut results: when tested two minutes after the end of the study phase, VC produced the correct response for 45 per cent of the study-only items and only 15 per cent of the generate-study items. The difference was highly reliable, and the advantage for the generate-study condition compared to the control condition (5 per cent correct responses) was not significant. This finding thus confirms that elicitation of incorrect responses leads to strengthening of the elicited responses that can prevent or mask learning in a generate-study condition, and it is clearly consistent with the basic Hebbian notion that we strengthen whatever response we make to a given input.

It should be noted that a study-only advantage is rarely found in normal subjects (but see Baddeley and Wilson, 1994). Indeed, Hamman and Squire (1995) found an advantage for generate-study in several normal control conditions, including one that equated control performance with amnesic performance using a long delay between study and test. This may reflect the fact that in their study, normal subjects approached the generate phase of each study trial (excluding the very first study trial, of course) as an opportunity to recall the correct response. With the aid of their intact hippocampal system, the controls would then have been able to reinstate the correct experimenter-defined response in many cases, thereby reducing the likelihood of incorrect response generation, and providing the correct answer to the cortex so that this response, rather than some other incorrect one, is strengthened by Hebbian learning. A computational model based on these ideas has been used to simulate the results of several of the experiments discussed in this section (Kwok, 2003).

2.4.3 Why can't Japanese adults learn to distinguish /r/ and /l/?

A second puzzle that I contemplated in the context of the complementary learning system model concerns the apparent loss of plasticity for some aspects of language learning in adulthood. The question here was put to me by Helen Neville (personal communication): if the slow learning system in the cortex is as generally applicable to all forms of learning as I assume it to be, and if this system remains capable of new learning in adulthood, then why is it that acquisition of the phonology and syntax of a non-native language appears to be so hard for adults to learn? In fact it should be noted at the outset that the facts remain somewhat unclear on several relevant points. While some have emphasized differences in degree of mastery of subtle syntactic and semantic aspects of a language as a function of age of arrival in the new language context (Johnson and Newport, 1989), others have emphasized that there is in fact gradual acquisition even of some of the most difficult aspects of second languages, and have pointed out that age of arrival may be negatively correlated with degree of emersion in the new language culture; on this view, one account of the difficulty of later arrivals is that they simply have less exposure. The exact extent of reduced plasticity for language acquisition remains unclear, and accounts other than the one below are possible (see Seidenberg and Zevin, Chapter 25, this volume). Nevertheless, it occurred to me that the deleterious consequences of Hebbian learning might be a contributing factor, strengthening undesirable responses that interfere with new learning, just as with the failure of learning under generate-study conditions in amnesia.

Consider the case of Japanese adults confronted with the need to perceive the distinction between the English speech sounds /r/ and /l/. In their native language, Japanese speakers do not distinguish these sounds. They do have a sound often called 'the Japanese tap' that sounds to the English ear sometimes like an /r/ or an /l/, though it also bears some similarity to the reduced form of /d/ and /t/ that occurs intravocalically in 'cider'. Suppose that Japanese speakers hear both English /r/s and /l/s as examples of their native tap sound, and that this perception is, like that of other speech sounds, categorical, in that they have the very same percept for sounds they treat as belonging to the same category. Then if Hebbian learning is occurring, it may unhelpfully strengthen the tendency of /r/ and /l/ sounds to elicit this categorical percept. Note that under this account, the mechanisms of plasticity would be completely intact, but they would be unhelpfully working against the acquisition of a discrimination between /r/ and /l/.

My collaborators and I have developed two computational models illustrating how this process may work, using a Hebb-like learning rule like the one in Equation 3. The first of these (McClelland *et al.*, 1999) uses a Kohonen network architecture like the one shown in Fig. 2.1, while the second (Vallabha and McClelland, 2004) uses a three-layer recurrent neural network with attractor dynamics. The second model has several advantages over the first, but basically illustrates the same process in action. The second model has also been used to provide a simulation of many aspects of the data we obtained from an experiment designed to explore the implications of this Hebbian account for methods that might help us teach Japanese adults to hear the difference between the English /r/ and /l/ sounds. The studies partially supported the Hebbian account but also indicated that it is incomplete in its simplest form, so I consider the experiments before returning to further discussions of the modeling work.

2.4.4 Implications for teaching /r/-/l/ discrimination

Our experiments (McCandliss *et al.*, 2002) revolved around the following simple idea: if the Hebbian explanation is correct, it should be possible to help Japanese adults learn to distinguish /r/ and /l/ using versions of /r/ and /l/ stimuli that exaggerate the distinctions between them to the point that they will elicit distinct percepts for Japanese listeners. Hebbian learning would then operate to strengthen the tendency of each input to elicit a distinct percept. We might then be able to gradually reduce the difference between the stimuli, as long as we continue to ensure that they generally elicit distinct percepts, so that gradually, the listeners would come to perceive natural, unexaggerated tokens of /r/ and /l/ as different. Note that, from a Hebbian perspective, no outcome information should be necessary to allow listeners to learn to hear the /r/ and /l/ stimuli differently. Thus no information was given about response accuracy in our first experiment.

To construct the stimuli for our studies, we took two minimal pairs—'road–load' and 'rock–lock'—and used them to construct 60-step stimulus continua ranging from an exaggerated /r/ to an exaggerated /l/ (Fig. 2.2). A male native English speaker produced each word carefully several times, and examples of each pair were chosen such that the articulations could be aligned to each other over time. For each continuum, the shared word body ('_oad' or '_ock') was the same for all members of the continuum. The onset of each item was constructed from the set of coefficients obtained by linear predictive coding of the the natural /l/ and /r/ stimuli. Both continua were pretested with native English speakers to ensure that exaggerated stimuli were still identifiable as /l/ and /r/ and to determine the position of the boundary between the /l/ and /r/ percepts and also to identify the edges of the gray zone between the /r/ and /l/ categories for English speakers.

For our first experiment, we contrasted an adaptive training procedure that started with initially exaggerated /l/ and /r/ stimuli with a fixed training procedure using the stimuli just at the edge of the gray zone between the /l/ and /r/ percepts for native English speakers (Fig. 2.2). In the adaptive condition, training began with exaggerated stimuli falling outside the native English range and spaced an equal number of steps on either side of the native catgory boundary. Eight Japanese adults received training in each condition. Only subjects performing below 70 per cent correct in a pretest of their ability to correctly identify the fixed training stimuli were included in the experiment. Half of subjects in each group received training with 'rock–lock'; the other half received training with 'road–load'.

The training procedure was very simple. On each trial, the /r/ or the /l/ stimulus from the training continuum was presented. Subjects responded by pressing a key to choose /r/ or /l/. No accuracy feedback was given. In the adaptive condition only, stimuli were adjusted between trials based on the subject's performance. After each error, one of the two stimuli was replaced by the next easier (more exaggerated) token,

Native Speaker Identification Functions

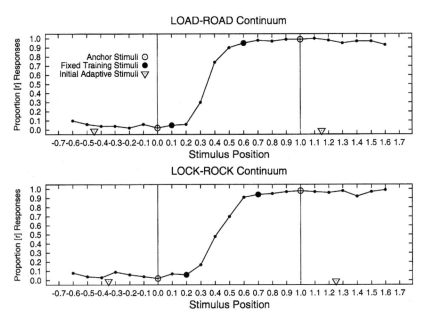

Fig. 2.2 Mean categorization functions of 12 native English speakers for synthesized speech stimuli from each of the two continua used in the experiments. The X axis represents the position on the stimulus in relation to the anchor stimuli, which are resynthesized versions of naturally spoken stimuli without exaggeration or interpolation. Percentages of trials eliciting R responses are plotted on the Y axis for each stimulus. Large empty circles represent the anchor stimuli resynthesized from the recorded base stimuli. Data points between the anchor stimuli are responses to stimuli interpolated between these anchors, and data points in the peripheral regions represent responses to extrapolated speech stimuli. Stimuli used for the fixed training condition are indicated with large filled circles. Triangles point to the positions of the initial stimuli used in the adaptive training condition. Reprinted from Figure 1, p. 92 in BD McCandliss, JA Fiez, A Protopapas, M Conway, and JL McClelland, Success and failure in teaching the /r/-/l/ contrast to Japanese adults: Test of a Hebbian model of plasticity and stabilization in spoken language perception. *Cognitive Affective, and Behavioral Neuroscience*, 2002, **2**, 89–108.

alternating which item was adjusted to maintain symmetry around the native boundary. After eight successive correct responses, one of the two stimuli was replaced by the next harder token, again alternating to maintain symmetry. Training took place over three 20-minute sessions, each involving 480 training trials and 50 probe trials (with the fixed training stimuli, so that performance of the two groups could be directly compared). Half of subjects in each group continued for three additional sessions.

The results of the experiment were very clear-cut, and consistent with the Hebbian analysis (Fig. 2.3, top panels). All eight subjects in the adaptive condition showed an

Effects of Training Without Feedback

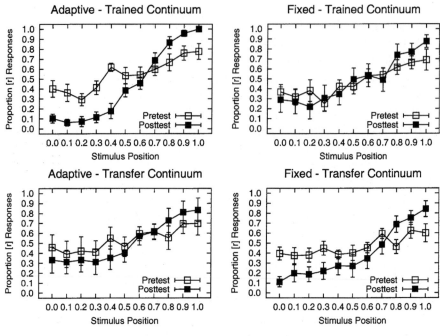

Effects of Training With Feedback

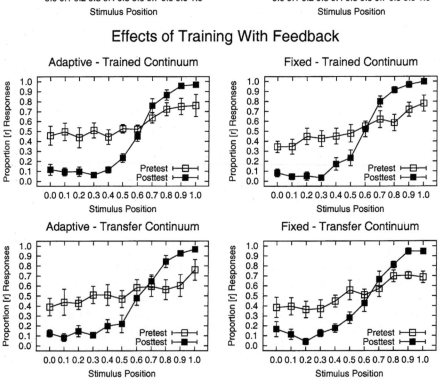

improvement in their identification of the stimuli on the trained continuum after three sessions of training (top left panel). There was only a slight improvement for the fixed training group overall (top right), and the amount of improvement was no larger than that seen in a control group (not shown in the figure) of eight additional subjects who received the same pre- and posttesting separated by the same number of days as the adaptive and fixed training groups, but had no training between tests.

The findings of our first study suggest that there is considerable residual plasticity in the phonological systems of Japanese adults. Their failure to learn under normal conditions may reflect not so much a loss of plasticity as a tendency for the mechanisms of learning to maintain strongly established perceptual tendencies, as expected under the Hebbian analysis.

Results of our experiment are also consistent with the predictions of a Hebbian account of perceptual learning: successful learning can occur without outcome information. If stimuli are exaggerated so that distinct percepts are produced, learning occurs. Learning is far less successful using the fixed training stimuli. However, it should be noted that several of the subjects in the fixed training condition did eventually begin to learn the /r/–/l/ distinction. It should also be noted that there were very large individual differences in the learning progress of subjects in the adaptive training condition. One thought about this, based on an analysis of learning in the recent model of Vallabha and McClelland (2004), revolves around the idea that the subjects should be viewed as falling on a continuum in terms of their initial tendency to hear the /r/ and /l/ stimuli as the same or different. This tendency occurs in the model because the perceptual representations formed in the model are patterns of activity that exhibit attractor-like properties that are essentially continuous or graded in nature. The representation of two different sounds tends to overlap, with the degree of overlap dependent on where the inputs lie within the attractor structure encoded in the weights in the network. When the overlap is initially very high, adaptive training proceeds slowly and fixed training does not progress at all. For those subjects for whom the overlap is initially lower, adaptive training proceeds very quickly and there is also progress in the fixed training condition.

Fig. 2.3 Mean categorization functions (with standard error bars) for four groups of Japanese subjects (n=8) before and after three 20-minute training sessions in the four training conditions of the experiment. Pre- and post-test results are shown on the continuum used in training and on the other continuum used to assess transfer. Adapted from Figure 2, p. 95, and Figure 6, p. 99, in BD McCandliss, JA Fiez, A Protopapas, M Conway and JL McClelland, Success and failure in teaching the /r/-/l/ contrast to Japanese adults: Test of a Hebbian model of plasticity and stabilization in spoken language perception. *Cognitive Affective, and Behavioral Neuroscience*, 2002, **2**, 89–108.

2.4.5 Incorporating a role for outcome information into Hebbian models of learning

While the results thus far suggest that we can go some distance in understanding the conditions under which human subjects succeed and fail to learn, relying only on the principle of Hebbian learning, it is also crucial to consider how other factors might shape the learning process. There are many studies in the literature indicating that mere exposure to stimuli that might elicit distinct percepts is not always enough to induce plasticity. An example from the extensive body of relevant work of Michael Merzenich and his associates will help illustrate this point. In one study (Recanzone *et al.*, 1992a, b) monkeys received vibratory stimulation when the surface of the middle finger of one hand was stimulated with a vibrating stylus. Monkeys who were required to discriminate different frequencies of vibration to obtain rewards showed improvement in their discrimination ability over training as well as dramatic reorganization of the sensory map representation for the stimulated hand, while monkeys who received yoked presentations of stimuli, but who were required to pay attention instead to other inputs, showed no reorganization.

With such results in mind, my collaborators and I wondered whether accuracy feedback might influence our Japanese listener's ability to learn the /r/–/l/ discrimination. To address this issue, we repeated our first experiment using fixed and adaptive training, but with the addition of visual feedback presented immediately after each response. Subjects received a row of three green checks if correct, or a row of three red x's if incorrect. The results of the experiment indeed confirmed that accuracy information can play a powerful role in enhancing learning: subjects in both the fixed and the adaptive group showed clear signs of learning (Fig. 2.3, bottom panels), and both groups now showed clear signs of transfer of what they had learned to the untrained continuum. To our surprise, we found that with feedback, learning was fastest in the fixed, and not the adaptive, training condition (Fig. 2.4). Subjects in the fixed-with-feedback condition showed marked performance improvements at the outset of training, although there was some decline in performance between sessions, and showed very sharp identification functions after 3 days of training. These subjects also showed strong generalization to the untrained continuum and a sharp peak at the boundary between the /r/ and /l/ categories, consistent with the establishment of distinct categories or perceptual magnets for the /r/ and /l/ categories. Subjects in the adaptive-with-feedback condition did nearly as well, and overall slightly better than their counterparts in the adaptive-without-feedback conditions.

2.5 Integrating outcome information into Hebbian learning mechanisms

Our findings on the role of accuracy feedback provide one of many indications that there is something more to learning than the simple strengthening of synaptic

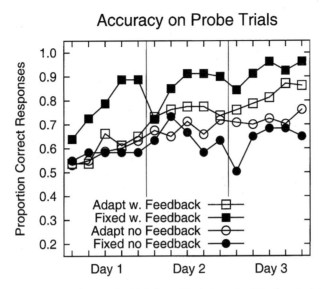

Fig. 2.4 Mean per cent correct on probe trials for subjects in each of the four training conditions over the course of training. Each data point is based on 10 probe trials per subject and encompasses 100 training trials. Data from two subjects in the fixed/no feedback condition have been excluded due to a data recording error on day 3. Their data were typical of the group on days 1 and 2. Reprinted from Figure 9, p. 102, in BD McCandliss, JA Fiez, A Protopapas, M Conway and JL McClelland, Success and failure in teaching the /r/-/l/ contrast to Japanese adults: Test of a Hebbian model of plasticity and stabilization in spoken language perception. *Cognitive Affective, and Behavioral Neuroscience*, 2002, **2**, 89–108.

connections among neurons that fire together. Yet our first experiment clearly indicates that outcome information is not always necessary for learning. This finding, together with the extensive support for Hebb-like learning mechanisms from LTP research, and the success of models using Hebbian mechanisms of learning in map-like neural structures to account for aspects of neural and cognitive development, suggests an important role for Hebbian learning mechanisms, or at least, some learning process that can operate to strengthen neural and behavioral responses in the absence of outcome information. Thus, my own inclination has been to consider ways in which a learning mechanism that operates according to Hebbian principles might be augmented by additional sources of information. Here I will briefly consider a few different possibilities. Note that this section is quite speculative in nature, but relates our work to that of others and raises points of general relevance to the possibility that a basically Hebbian mechanism is at work at the neural basis of learning and thus seems worth presenting in the present context.

One very simple proposal that can have dramatic effects within map-like representations is to modulate Hebbian learning as a function of attention. In fact, simply allowing attention to regulate neural activity *per se* provides one possible account for findings such as those of Recanzone *et al.* above, in which there is massive reorganization of representations of attended, task-relevant stimuli. If the extent of neural activity itself is attention-dependent, and if (as many indications suggest) strong neural activity is needed to gate Hebbian plasticity, then the effects of task-related attention can be accommodated without any special regulation of learning based on outcome information *per se.*

While the above seems very likely to play some role in regulating the degree of learning, two specific points should be born clearly in mind. First, there are clearly signs of learning in experiments in which subjects are simply exposed to interesting stimuli, even when these are just presented in the background without any task (Saffran, *et al.* 1996; Gomez, chapter 4, this volume). Of course it is not always clear in such studies whether subjects allocate covert attention to the stimuli, but the findings do suggest we need not assume that explicit task relevance and strong motivation to attend are always necessary for learning to occur. Second, it is not clear that a strictly attentional account provides a full basis for understanding the role of accuracy feedback within experiments where task demands are at least nominally held constant, as they are in the McCandliss *et al.* experiments. All subjects in these experiments were attempting to learn to discriminate the /l/ and /r/ sounds we used. Accuracy feedback may well help to keep subjects motivated and thereby keep their attention focused, so we cannot rule out some role for a simple attentional effect, but it seems likely that some additional role for specific feedback is operative, over and above any such global effect.

There are several ways to use accuracy feedback to augment Hebbian learning. One possibility, based on O'Reilly's LEABRA learning rule (O'Reilly, 1996; O'Reilly, Chapter 16, this volume), is simply to combine error correcting and Hebbian learning. In LEABRA, the signal that drives the connection weight combines the $Hebb_r$ learning rule of Equation 3 with an error-correcting term. If we were to apply this suggestion to capture the role of accuracy feedback in our /l/–/r/ learning experiment, we would need to imagine that the listener is able to translate the feedback signal into an indication of which response is correct, and then use this as the source of the correct target information required in standard error-correcting learning, which then augments the Hebbian part of the learning when accuracy feedback is available.

The LEABRA approach is certainly worth exploring, but does introduce some processing complexity that has led me to consider other alternatives. To compute the error-correction component of the weight update, LEABRA uses a second pass through the activation settling process with the teaching input provided, after the first pass of activation in the absence of the teaching input. O'Reilly and I are currently at work on a successor to the LEABRA algorithm that attempts to eliminate the separate second pass. In the meantime, the two proposals considered below are perhaps mechanistically simpler than the existing version of LEABRA, and have thus been the focus of the modeling effort by Vallabha and McClelland (2004).

The first of the two ideas is to use the feedback signal to produce a reward signal I will call $R(F)$, and then use this to modulate Hebbian learning:

$$\Delta w_{rs} = \varepsilon R(F) f_r(a_r) f_s(a_s) \qquad (4)$$

To apply this idea to the results of the experiments reviewed above, in which we see evidence of learning without any feedback, we would require that $R(F)$ have some positive value in the absence of any accuracy feedback. Feedback indicating that the response is correct could then increase the value of the $R(F)$ above its baseline value, and feedback indicating that the response is incorrect could reduce it below baseline, or potentially (as in many applications of reward-driven or *reinforcement* learning, c.f. Barto, 1992) reverse its sign. The second idea is to use the accuracy feedback signal to derive the identity of the correct response, and use this to adjust the activation of the output unit before applying the Hebb$_r$ rule of Equation 3. This approach treats the accuracy feedback as simply providing a source of activation to units representing the response alternatives.

In simulations, we have found that both of these approaches work fairly well to allow us to model the effects of accuracy feedback in the McCandliss *et al.* (2002) experiments, and at present we have little basis for choosing among them. There are a few advantages to the reward-modulated learning approach, however, that may be worth mentioning. First, the mechanism requires only a global modulation of the extent of synaptic change, which from a neuromechanistic point of view is consistent with the fact that the reward signal comes with a slight delay after the convergent pre- and postsynaptic activity. Second, it is consistent with recent findings from a brain imaging study by Tricomi, Delgado, McCandliss, McClelland, and Fiez (2005) indicating that Japanese adults may treat accuracy feedback on their identification responses to /r/ and /l/ stimuli the same way subjects treat monetary reward (positive and negative monetary outcomes): similar brain areas are activated with similar timecourses for /r/–/l/ responses receiving positive feedback and for positive monetary reward provided for correct guesses in a random guessing task, and similar areas and timecourses are also observed for incorrect /r/–/l/ responses and negative extrinsic reward in the random guessing task. The findings suggest that the subjects find accuracy feedback rewarding, and are consistent with the possibility that positive feedback gates the release of a global reward signal (e.g. dopamine) that could modulate synaptic plasticity (for a discussion of the role of dopamine as a reward signal, see Tricomi *et al.*, 2004).

2.6 Summary and conclusion

I have considered the idea of approaching human (and neural network) learning from an essentially Hebbian perspective. I have reviewed evidence from LTP studies and considered a range of computational models that incorporate Hebbian learning, and I have described experimental studies consistent with the idea, which seems to follow from a Hebbian approach, that there are processes at work strengthening the response a person makes to an input, either when this is incorrect, as in the apparent undesirable strengthening of incorrect associative responses in amnesia, or when there is no feedback, as in the adaptive-no-feedback condition of our experiment teaching Japanese adults to differentiate between /l/ and /r/. Hebbian learning can provide a basis for thinking about how we may learn from our own responses to things, in the absence of external teaching information, and such a process may also explain many cases of failures of learning, if circumstances conspire such that incorrect or unhelpful responses are elicited instead of correct or helpful ones. Based on these points, it seems likely that it will be worthwhile to consider the possible role of a Hebbian learning mechanism in other cases of successes and failures of learning and development besides those considered in the present article.

Clearly, though, Hebb's proposal by itself is insufficient to address all aspects of human learning and memory. If such a process operates at all, it must be subject to extensive regulation and/or supplementation with other processes. Furthermore, the process operates within an organized network of interacting brain structures that play important roles in guiding processing toward correct outcomes. More work is necessary to understand these regulatory and/or supplemental processes, and to fully understand how interactions among brain regions, particularly medial temporal structures and neocortical learning systems, work together to achieve a system that functions successfully as an integrated whole.

Acknowledgement

Preparation of this article was supported by MH 64445 from the National Institute of Mental Health (USA).

References

Abbott LF and Nelson SB (2000). Synaptic plasticity: Taming the beast. *Nature Neuroscience*, 3, 1178–1183.

Baddeley A and Wilson BA (1994). When implicit learning fails: Amnesia and the problem of error elimination. *Neuropsychologia*, 32, 53–68.

Barrionuevo G and Brown TH (1983). Associative long-term synaptic potentiation in hippocampal slices. *Proceedings of the National Academy of Sciences, USA*, 80, 7347–7351.

Barto AG (1992). Reinforcement learning and adaptive critic methods. In: DA White and DA Sofge, eds. *Handbook of intelligent control: Neural, fuzzy, and adaptive approaches*, pp. 469–491. New York: Van Nostrand Reinhold.

Bienenstock EL, Cooper LN and Munro PW (1982). Theory of the development of neuron selectivity: Orientation specificity and binocular interaction in visual cortex. *Journal of Neuroscience*, 2, 32–48.

Bird C, Cipolotti L, Kwok K and McClelland JL (2004). *Successes and failures of associative learning in amnesia*. Manuscript, Center for the Neural Basis of Cognition, Carnegie Mellon.

Cipolotti L, Shallice T, Chan D, Fox N, Scahill R, Harrison G, *et al.* (2001). Long-term retrograde amnesia...the crucial role of the hippocampus. *Neuropsychologia*, **39**, 151–172.

Cohen LB, Chaput HH and Cashon CH (2002). A constructivist model of infant cognition. *Cognitive Development*, **17**, 1323–1343.

Crowley JC and Katz LC (2000). Early development of ocular dominance columns. *Science*, **290**, 1321–1324.

Dudek SM and Bear MF (1993). Bidirectional long-term modification of synaptic effectiveness in the adult and immature hippocampus. *Journal of Neuroscience*, **12**, 2910–1918.

Elman JL (1990). Finding structure in time. *Cognitive Science*, **14**, 179–211.

Gabrieli JDE, Cohen NJ and Corkin S (1988). The impaired learning of semantic knowledge following bilateral medial temporal-lobe resection. *Brain and Cognition*, **7**, 157–177.

Goodhill GJ (1993). Topography and ocular dominance: A model exploring positive correlations. *Biological Cybernetics*, **69**, 109–118.

Grossberg S (1976). On the development of feature detectors in the visual cortex with applications to learning and reaction-diffusion systems. *Biological Cybernetics*, **21**, 145–159.

Hamman SB and Squire LR (1995). On the acquisition of new declarative knowledge in amnesia. *Behavioral Neuroscience*, **109**, 1027–1044.

Hayman CAG, MacDonald CA and Tulving E (1993). The role of repetition and associative interference in new semantic learning in amnesia: A case experiment. *Journal of Cognitive Neuroscience*, **5**, 375–389.

Hebb DO (1949). *The organization of behavior*. New York: Wiley.

Inhelder B and Piaget J (1958). *The growth of logical thinking from childhood to adolescence*. New York: Basic Books.

Johnson J and Newport E (1989). Critical period effects in second-language learning: The influence of maturational state on the acquisition of English as a second language. *Cognitive Psychology*, **21**, 60–99.

Kohonen T (1982). Self-organized formation of topologically correct feature maps. *Biological Cybernetics*, **43**, 59–69.

Kwok K (2003). *A computational investigation into the successes and failures of semantic learning in normal humans and amnesics.* Unpublished doctoral dissertation, Carnegie Mellon University, Department of Psychology.

Levy WB and Steward O (1979). Synapses as associative memory elements in the hippocampal formation. *Brain Research*, **175**, 233–245.

Linsker R (1986a). From basic network principles to neural architecture, III: Emergence of orientation columns. *Proceedings of the National Academy of Sciences, USA*, **83**, 8779–8783.

Linsker R (1986b). From basic network principles to neural architecture, II: Emergence of orientation-selective cells. *Proceedings of the National Academy of Sciences, USA*, **83**, 8390–8394.

Linsker R (1986c). From basic network principles to neural architecture, I: Emergence of spatial-opponent cells. *Proceedings of the National Academy of Sciences, USA*, **83**, 7508–7512.

Margolis H (1987). *Patterns, thinking, and cognition*. Chicago, IL: University of Chicago Press.

Margolis H (1993). *Paradigms and barriers*. Chicago, IL: University of Chicago Press.

McCandliss BD, Fiez JA, Protopapas A, Conway M and McClelland JL (2002). Success and failure in teaching the [r]-[l] contrast to Japanese adults: Tests of a Hebbian model of plasticity and stabilization in spoken language perception. *Cognitive, Affective and Behavioral Neuroscience*, **2**, 89–108.

McClelland JL (1989). Parallel distributed processing: Implications for cognition and development. In: RGM Morris, ed. *Parallel distributed processing: Implications for psychology and neurobiology*, pp. 8–45). New York: Oxford University Press.

McClelland JL (1994). The interaction of nature and nurture in development: A parallel distributed processing perspective. In: P Bertelson, P Eelen and G D'Ydewalle, eds. *International perspectives on psychological science, Volume 1: Leading themes*, pp. 57–88. Hillsdale, NJ: Erlbaum.

McClelland JL (1995). A connectionist perspective on knowledge and development. In: TJ Simon and GS Halford, Eds. *Developing cognitive competence: New approaches to process modeling*, pp. 157–204. Hillsdale, NJ: Erlbaum.

McClelland JL (2001). Failures to learn and their remediation: A Hebbian approach. In: JL McClelland and RS Siegler, Eds. *Mechanisms of cognitive development: Behavioral and neural perspectives*, pp. 97–121. Mahwah, NJ: Erlbaum.

McClelland JL and Jenkins E (1991). Nature, nurture, and connections: Implications of connectionist models for cognitive development. In: KV Lehn, Ed. *Architectures for intelligence*, pp. 41–73. Hillsdale, NJ: Erlbaum.

McClelland JL, McNaughton BL and O'Reilly RC (1995). Why there are complementary learning systems in the hippocampus and neocortex: Insights from the successes and failures of connectionist models of learning and memory. *Psychological Review*, 102, 419–457.

McClelland JL, Thomas A, McCandliss BD and Fiez JA (1999). Understanding failures of learning: Hebbian learning, competition for representational space, and some preliminary experimental data. In: JA Reggia E Ruppin and D Glanzman, Eds. *Progress in brain research*, Vol. 121, pp. 75–80. Amsterdam: Elsevier Science.

McNaughton BL, Douglas RM and Goddard GV (1978). Synaptic enhancement in facia dentata: Cooperativity among coactive afferents. *Brain Research*, 157, 277–293.

Miller KD, Keller JB and Stryker MP (1989). Ocular dominance column development: Analysis and simulation. *Science*, 245, 605–615.

Milner B, Corkin, S and Teuber H.-L (1968). Further analysis of the hippocampal amnesia syndrome: 14-year follow-up study of H.M. *Neuropsychologia*, 6, 215–234.

Munakata Y, McClelland JL, Johnson MH and Siegler R (1997). Rethinking infant knowledge: Toward an adaptive process account of successes and failures in object permanence tasks. *Psychological Review*, 104, 686–713.

O'Reilly R (1996). *The LEABRA model of neural interactions and learning in the neocortex*. Unpublished doctoral dissertation, Department of Psychology, Carnegie Mellon University, Pittsburgh, PA.

Recanzone GH, Merzenich MM, Jenkins WM, Grajski KA and Dinse HR (1992a). Topographic reorganization of the hand representation in cortical area 3b of owl monkeys trained in a frequency-discrimination task. *Journal of Neurophysiology*, 67, 1031–1056.

Recanzone GH, Merzenich MM and Schreiner CE (1992b). Changes in the distributed temporal response properties of SI cortical neurons reflect improvements in performance on a temporally-based tactile discrimination task. *Journal of Neurophysiology*, 67, 1071–1091.

Rogers TT and McClelland JL (2004). *Semantic cognition: A parallel distributed processing approach*. Cambridge, MA: MIT Press.

Rumelhart DE, Hinton GE and Williams RJ (1986). Learning representations by back-propagating errors. *Nature*, 323, 533–536.

Rumelhart DE and Zipser D (1985). Feature discovery by competitive learning. *Cognitive Science*, 9, 75–112.

Saffran JR, Aslin RN and Newport EL (1996). Statistical learning by 8-month-olds. *Science*, 274, 1926–1928.

Schyns PG (1991). A modular neural network model of concept acquisition. *Cognitive Science*, 15, 461–508.

Scoville WB and Milner B (1957). Loss of recent memory after bilateral hippocampal lesions. *Journal of Neurology, Neurosurgery, and Psychiatry*, 20, 11–21.

Siegler RS (1976). Three aspects of cognitive development. *Cognitive Psychology*, 8, 481–520.

Song S, Miller KD and Abbott LF (2000). Competitive Hebbian learning through spike-timing-dependent synaptic plasticity. *Nature Neuroscience*, 3, 919–926.

St. John MF and McClelland JL (1990). Learning and applying contextual constraints in sentence comprehension. *Artificial Intelligence*, 46, 217–257.

Tricomi EM, Delgado MR and Fiez JA (2004). Modulation of caudate activity by action contingency. *Neuron*, 41, 281–292.

Tricomi EM, Delgado, MR, McCandliss BD, McClelland, JL and Fiez, JA (2005). Performance feedback drives caudate activation in a phonological learning task. Manuscript, Center for the Neural Basis of Cognition, University of Pittsburgh and Carnegie Mellon.

Vallabha GK and McClelland JL (2004). *A hebbian model of speech perceptual learning*. Manuscript, Center for the Neural Basis of Cognition, Carnegie Mellon.

Chapter 3

Constructive learning in the modeling of psychological development

Thomas R. Shultz

Abstract

Although many computational models of psychological development involve only learning, this paper examines the advantages of allowing artificial neural networks to grow as well as learn in such simulations. Comparisons of static and constructive network simulations of the same developmental phenomena bring this issue into clear focus. Constructive algorithms are found to be better at learning and at covering developmental stages and stage sequences. The relatively new sibling–descendant cascade-correlation algorithm (SDCC) decides whether to install each newly recruited hidden unit on the current highest layer or on a new layer. SDCC is applied to the problem of conservation acquisition in children. Results show no differences in comparison to previous conservation simulations done with standard cascade-correlation except for fewer network layers and connections with SDCC.

3.1 Introduction

It is clear from publication counts that artificial neural networks have become the model of choice in developmental psychology, just as they have in several other psychological domains (Shultz 2003). The most popular type of neural network in psychological modeling, including developmental work, is the static feed-forward network. Such networks learn by adjusting their connection weights, but their initial topologies do not change across the developmental periods that they model. It is development by learning, with a dose of nativism thrown in because the topological structure of each network is fully specified at the start.

A principal alternative is constructive learning, which, like psychological constructivism, allows for qualitative growth as well as quantitative adjustments. In some theoretical approaches, development proceeds in a succession of stages. Constructive learning fits well with those stage theories emphasizing that cognitive systems themselves undergo significant changes during development (e.g. Piaget 1965). Constructive learning is also consistent with contemporary neuroscience findings of synaptogenesis and neurogenesis occurring under pressures to learn, not only in infancy but also in mature brains (cf. reviews by Gould *et al.* 1999; Kempermann and Gage 1999; Purves *et al.* 1996; Quartz 2003; Quartz and Sejnowski 1997; Shultz *et al.* 2006). This line of neuroscience research is developing rapidly and some of it, including the claim of learning-directed neurogenesis in primate cortex, is controversial. Synaptogenesis is much less controversial, and it is worth noting that the constructive algorithms discussed here are neutral with respect to whether their growth processes emulate synapto- or neurogenesis. The issue hinges on whether candidate recruits are already somewhere else in the system or are constructed afresh.

There are several computational arguments showing the advantages of constructive learning over static learning. First, constructive-network algorithms learn in polynomial time any problem that can be learned in polynomial time (i.e. a realistic amount of time) by any algorithm whatsoever (Baum 1988). In contrast, static-network algorithms may take considerably longer to master such problems (e.g. exponential time), or maybe never solve them, because there is no guarantee that a given network topology has been designed with the appropriate degree of computational power. A designer of a static network must find a network topology with the approximately correct degree of power. Static networks that are too weak fail to learn and those that are too strong fail to generalize. Constructive algorithms automatically try to find the right degree of network complexity for the problem being learned. At the same time they are searching in weight space, they are also searching in topology space.

Second, constructive learners may find optimal solutions to the bias/variance tradeoff that plagues static learners (Quartz 2003; Quartz and Sejnowski 1997). All learning algorithms face a potential tradeoff between bias and variance, both sources of error. Bias is the distance between the best hypothesis that a learning system can form and the correct hypothesis; variance is the distance of a learning system's current hypothesis from the correct hypothesis. An optimal learning system would manage to keep both bias and variance low, and thus finish close to the correct hypothesis. A small network restricts variance but is highly biased because it can express only a few hypotheses, all of which may be far from the correct hypothesis, thus contributing to error. In contrast, a large network reduces bias by expanding the hypothesis space, but also typically increases variance; because so many hypotheses are possible, the correct hypothesis may be difficult to find, keeping error high. Constructive algorithms may avoid this tradeoff by reducing bias (by adding hidden units to expand the network and the hypothesis space) while reducing variance (by adjusting connection weights to approach the correct hypothesis).

Third, constructive, but not static, learners can escape from Fodor's paradox that nothing genuinely novel can be learned (Mareschal and Shultz 1996; Quartz 1993). Fodor (1980) had argued, based on 1970s hypothesize-and-test learning algorithms, that a learning system can only learn what it can already represent. If a particular hypothesis cannot be represented then it cannot be tested, and if it cannot be tested then it cannot be learned. Constructive learners escape from this dilemma because their growth enables them to represent hypotheses that they could not represent previously with their limited computational power. In contrast, static learning systems are limited to those hypotheses permitted by their initial design. A static network with a particular number of units and a particular connection scheme may not be able to adjust its weights appropriately, no matter how favorable its training regime is; the network may be too weak to learn, too powerful to generalize, or may not have the right topology for the problem at hand.

In this paper, I explore the advantages that constructive learning algorithms have in modeling various phenomena in psychological development, a strategy that is distinct from, but supported by, the foregoing neurological and computational considerations.

3.2 Comparison of constructive and static networks

One way to highlight the unique benefits of constructive learning is to compare models whose networks are allowed to grow against models containing static networks. The neural algorithms most widely applied to simulating cognitive development are back-propagation (BP), a static learner, and cascade-correlation (CC), a constructive learner (Shultz 2003). Both of these algorithms employ feed-forward, multilayered networks that learn by adjustment of connection weights to reduce error. Unlike BP, CC grows its network structure by recruiting hidden units (Fahlman and Lebiere 1990). Neither BP nor CC is designed to model neural circuits in detail; they are instead functional algorithms inspired by neuroscience principles. Mathematical and computational details on these algorithms can be found in many other sources (e.g. Shultz 2003).

Both BP (Elman *et al.* 1996; Munakata and McClelland 2003; Shultz 2003) and CC (Shultz 2003) have been successfully applied to a wide range of developmental phenomena. Nonetheless, comparisons between BP and CC are difficult to make because these algorithms have most often been applied to distinct phenomena. A unique focus of the present paper is a series of direct *bakeoff* competitions in which CC and BP are applied to the same phenomena. Although common and valuable in machine learning research, simulation bakeoffs are still rare in developmental psychology.

There are three domains of cognitive development to which both of these algorithms have been applied: the balance scale, the integration of velocity, time, and distance cues for moving objects, and age changes in sensitivity to correlations vs. features in category learning by infants. These three competitions are reviewed before presenting a new bakeoff featuring static and constructive models of conservation acquisition.

3.2.1 Balance-scale

The balance-scale problem presents a child with rigid beam balanced on a fulcrum (Siegler 1976). The beam has several pegs spaced at regular intervals to the left and right of the fulcrum. The experimenter places some number of identical weights on a peg on the left side and some number of weights on a peg on the right side. While supporting blocks prevent the beam from moving, the child predicts which side of the beam will descend, or whether the scale will balance, when the supporting blocks are removed.

The rules children use to make such predictions can be diagnosed by presenting children with six different types of problems. Three of these problems are simple because one cue (weight or distance from the fulcrum) perfectly predicts the outcome while the other cue is constant on both sides of the scale. The other three problems are more complex because these two cues conflict with each other, weight predicting one outcome and distance predicting another outcome. The pattern of predictions across these six problem types can be used to diagnose the rule the child uses to guide predictions. In a connectionist network, such rules are not symbolic propositions, but are instead emerging epiphenomena of network structure and function.

The major psychological regularity in the balance-scale literature is progression through four different stages (Siegler 1976). In stage 1, children use weight information to predict that the side with greater weight will descend or that the scale will balance when the two sides have equal weights. In stage 2, children also begin to use distance information when the weights are equal on each side, predicting that in such cases the side with greater distance will descend. In stage 3, weight and distance information are emphasized equally, but the child guesses when weight and distance information conflict on the complex problems. In stage 4, children respond correctly on all types of problems, whether simple or complex.

In perhaps the first connectionist simulation of cognitive development, McClelland and Jenkins (1991) found that a static BP network with two groups of hidden units segregated for either weight or distance information developed through the first three of these stages and into the fourth stage. However, their networks did not settle in stage 4, instead continuing to cycle between stages 3 and 4. Subsequent simulations showed that BP networks could settle into stage 4, but only at the cost of skipping stages 1 and 2 (Shultz 2003). In contrast, the first CC model of cognitive development naturally captured all four balance-scale stages, without requiring segregation of hidden units (Shultz *et al.* 1994).

The ability of neural networks to capture stages 1 and 2 on the balance scale is due to a bias towards equal-distance problems in the training set. These are problems with the weights placed equally distant from the fulcrum on each side. A preponderance of equal-distance problems forces the network to emphasize weight information first because weight information is more relevant to reducing network error. Once weight-induced error is reduced, then the network can turn its attention to distance information. In effect, the learning algorithm must find the particular region of connection-weight space that allows it to emphasize the numbers of weights on the scale before moving to another region of weight space that allows multiplication of equally important weight and distance information. A powerful learning algorithm is required to make this move in connection-weight space. Apparently a static network, once committed to using weight information in stage 1, cannot easily find its way to a stage-4 region merely by continuing to reduce error. In contrast, a constructive algorithm has an easier time with this move because each newly recruited hidden unit changes the shape of connection-weight space by adding a new dimension to this space. A new dimension provides a path on which to move towards a stage-4 region. The fact that several other algorithms fail to reach stage 4 on the balance scale means that the CC model is somewhat unique in predicting the occurrence of stage 4, a stage consistently found in psychological research.

Our CC networks also predicted the other major psychological regularity in the balance-scale literature, the so-called *torque-difference* effect, which is that problems with large torque differences from one side of the scale to the other are easier for children to solve at every stage than problems with small torque differences. We subsequently discovered that this somewhat ignored phenomenon had already been noted with children and could also be obtained from the BP model (Shultz 2003).

3.2.2 Integration of velocity, time, and distance cues

In classical physics, the velocity of a moving object equals the ratio of distance traveled to the time of the journey: velocity = distance / time. Algebraic manipulations show that distance = velocity × time, and time = distance / velocity. Some of the clearest evidence on children's acquisition of these ideas was provided by Wilkening (1981), who asked children to predict one dimension from knowledge of the other two. For example three levels of velocity information were represented by motion of a turtle, a guinea pig, and a cat. These three animals were said to be fleeing from a barking dog, and children were asked to imagine these animals moving while the dog barked. The child's task was to infer how far an animal would travel given the duration of the barking, an example of inferring distance from velocity and time.

We diagnosed rules in CC simulations based on correlations between network outputs and the various algebraic rules observed in children (Buckingham and Shultz 2000). To be diagnosed, an algebraic rule had to correlate positively with network responses, account for most of the variance in network responses, and account for more variance than any other rules did. For velocity and time inferences, CC networks first developed an equivalence rule (e.g. velocity = distance), followed by a difference rule (e.g. velocity = distance - time), followed in turn by the correct ratio rule (e.g. velocity = distance / time). Results were similar for distance inferences, except for the absence of an equivalence rule. For distance inferences, there is no reason for a network to favor either velocity or time information because both vary positively with distance. Six of these stages had been previously found with children, and two others were predictions of CC network models subsequently confirmed with children. The two predicted stages were the final stage of velocity inferences (velocity = distance / time) and the first stage of time inferences (time = distance). Stage progressions resulted from continued recruitment of hidden units.

In contrast to constructive networks, static networks were unable to capture these stage sequences (Buckingham and Shultz 1996). If a static BP network has too few hidden units, it fails to reach the correct multiplicative rules; if it has too many hidden units, it fails to capture the intermediate additive (difference) stages on velocity and time inferences. Extensive exploration of a variety of network topologies and variation in learning parameters suggests that there is no static network topology capable of capturing all three stages in this domain. Even the use of cross-connections that bypass hidden layers failed to improve the stage performance of BP networks. There is no apparent way to get static networks to cover all stages because the difference between underpowered and overpowered BP networks is a single hidden unit. Thus, the ability to grow in computational power seems essential in simulating stages in this domain.

3.2.3 Age changes in early category learning

A third comparison concerns age changes in sensitivity to correlations vs. features in category learning by infants. Using a familiarization paradigm to study categorization, Younger and Cohen (1983, 1986) found that 4-month-olds process information about independent features of visual stimuli, whereas 10-month-olds additionally abstract relations among those features. These results relate to a classic controversy about the extent to which perceptual development involves integration or differentiation of stimulus information. Developing ability to understand relations among features suggests that perceptual development involves integration, a view compatible with constructive learning.

Infants are conventionally assumed to construct representational categories for repeated stimuli, and afterwards to ignore novel stimuli that are consistent with a category, while concentrating on novel stimuli that are not members of an existing category. After repetitions of visual stimuli with correlated features, 4-month-olds recovered attention to stimuli with novel features more than to stimuli with either correlated or uncorrelated familiar features (Younger and Cohen 1983, 1986). In contrast, 10-month-olds recovered attention both to stimuli with novel features and to stimuli with familiar uncorrelated features more than to stimuli with familiar correlated features. This pattern of recovery indicates that young infants learned about individual stimulus features, but not about the relationships among features, whereas older infants also learned how these features correlate with one other.

These phenomena were recently simulated with CC encoder networks (Shultz and Cohen 2004). Encoder networks have the same number of inputs as outputs. Their task is to reproduce their input values on their output units. Encoder networks learn to do this by encoding an input representation onto a relatively small number of hidden units and then decoding that representation onto output units. Such networks develop a recognition memory for the stimuli they are exposed to. Network error, the discrepancy between inputs and outputs, can be used as a measure of stimulus novelty. Both static and constructive encoder networks were applied to these phenomena (Shultz and Cohen 2004). In CC networks, age was implemented by setting the score-threshold parameter higher for 4-month-olds than for 10-month-olds. Because learning stops only when all network outputs are within score-threshold of their target values for all training patterns, this parameter governs how much learning occurs. We assumed that older infants learn more from the same exposure time than younger infants do. On the further assumption that network error reflects stimulus novelty and interest, CC networks covered the infant data by showing more error to the uncorrelated test stimulus than to the correlated test stimulus only at the smaller score-threshold.

In contrast, a wide range of static BP networks failed to capture these effects. A BP simulator was modified to use a score-threshold parameter to decide on learning success like CC does. A wide variety of score-threshold values were explored in a systematic attempt to get BP networks to cover the infant data. Initially BP networks were given three hidden units, the modal number recruited by CC networks on this task. BP network topology was then varied to explore the roles of network depth and the presence of cross connections in simulation success. Both flat and deep BP networks were tried, both with and without cross-connection weights. Although BP networks did show some learning, they covered neither the 4-month-old nor 10-month-old data nor the transition between these ages. We ran nine BP networks in each of 80 simulations (2 familiarization sets × 10 score-threshold levels × 4 network topologies).

Only the CC networks generated a crossover prediction, with deep learning showing a correlation effect, and very superficial learning showing the opposite – a similarity effect, in the form of more error to (or interest in) the correlated test item than to the uncorrelated test item. This is termed a *similarity* effect because the uncorrelated test item was most similar to those in the familiarization set. The simulation predicted a correlation effect under optimal learning conditions and a similarity effect with less than optimal familiarization learning. Tests of this prediction found that 10-month-olds who tired of the training stimuli looked longer at the uncorrelated than the correlated test stimulus, but those who did not so tire did the opposite, looking longer at the correlated than the uncorrelated test stimulus (Cohen and Arthur 2004).

Although the static network simulations did not cover the infant data, they were useful in establishing why constructive networks were successful because these static networks employed topologies copied from the final constructive networks. Network growth seems critical to capturing detection of correlations between features and the developmental shift from earlier feature-value learning. An initially underpowered network focuses only on the stimulus features, allowing later network growth to use those features in detecting correlations.

3.3 Conservation phenomena

Conservation is one of the most well-studied phenomena in cognitive development with over 1000 publications. It most often involves a belief in the continued equivalence of two physical quantities over a transformation that appears to alter one of them. A prime example of conservation presents a child with two identical rows of evenly spaced objects. After the child agrees that the two rows have the same number of objects, the experimenter transforms one of the rows, for example by spreading its items out. The child is then asked whether the two rows still have the same amount or whether one of them now has more. Children below about 6 years of age respond that one of the two rows, usually the longer row, now has more than the other (Piaget 1965). This is in contrast to older children who respond that the two rows still have equal amounts. That is, older children conserve equivalence of the two amounts over the compressing transformation.

In the vast literature on conservation, there are four well-known empirical regularities:

1. A shift from non-conservation to conservation beliefs (acquisition effect).
2. A sudden spurt in performance during acquisition (spurt effect).
3. Emergence of correct conservation judgments for small quantities before larger quantities (problem-size effect).
4. Non-conservers' choice of the longer row as having more items than the shorter row (length-bias effect).

Regularities 1, 3, and 4 have been replicated many times with children (cf. Shultz 1998 for a more complete review).

3.3.1 Simulations of conservation with CC networks

Simulations with CC networks covered all of these phenomena without having to bias the training environment in any particular way (Shultz 1998). Inputs to the networks described conservation problems in which rows of objects were coded for their perceptual characteristics, namely their length and density. Transformations included those that alter number (addition and subtraction) and those that preserve number (elongation and compression). Addition and subtraction transformations each changed the quantity of a row by one item. Elongation and compression transformations altered the density of the row by one level. Target feedback supplied to the network concerned relative numerical equality judgments comparing the two rows. There were five levels of length and five levels of density, ranging from 2 to 6 in the initial rows, which could be either equal or unequal in number. Reflecting physical and mathematical reality, the number of items equals length $\times$ density of the row. Table 3.1 shows some example transformations of a 6-item row with initial length of 3 and initial density of 2. Typical psychology experiments, starting with only equal rows and using only equality-preserving transformations, can be seen as a special case of this more general scheme. This more general scheme, however, is necessary to capture what children eventually come to know about conservation problems.

Length and density values were coded as real numbers for each of the rows, both before and after the transformation. The identity of the transformed row was coded on a binary unit as 1 or -1. The four transformation types were coded in a binary, nth-unit fashion as 1 for the unit corresponding to the transformation type and -1 on the other three units. Two target output units with sigmoid activation functions were coded as $(0.5\ -0.5)$ if the first row had more items, $(-0.5\ 0.5)$ if the second row had more items, and $(-0.5\ -0.5)$ if the two rows had equal numbers of items after the transformation. Thus the networks had as inputs the same information that children in conservation experiments have regarding how the rows look, both before and after the transformation, as well as which transformation was applied and the row it was applied to. What the networks had to learn are functions relating these inputs to a decision about which row has more or whether the rows have the same number.

For each network, 420 of the 600 possible conservation problems were randomly selected as training patterns and 100 others were randomly selected as test patterns. Because networks started from randomly-selected connection weights and learned in a randomly-designed environment, they differed from each other in both heredity and environment, something like children do. Training was stopped at 1500 epochs, by which time most networks had learned all of the training patterns, a state called 'reaching victory'. A single epoch is a pass through all of the training patterns. Testing of a network was done on its 100 test patterns not used in training. All four of the principal conservation phenomena were captured by these CC networks.

3.3.2 Simulations of conservation acquisition with SDCC networks

The CC algorithm has occasionally been criticized for constructing overly deep networks that may not generalize as well as flatter networks do. The reason CC

Table 3.1 Example transformations holding density constant when number is altered

Transformation	Length	Density	Number
Pretransformation	3	2	6
Add	3.5	2	7
Subtract	2.5	2	5
Elongate	6	1	6
Compress	2	3	6

networks are so deep is that each new hidden unit is installed on its own layer with cascaded weights from any previous hidden units. A variant called flat CC puts all hidden units on the same layer and eliminates the cascaded weights between these hidden units, in the fashion of a three-layered BP network. In a research design that had flat and standard CC networks learning either flat or deep problems, we found that, on simpler problems (with less than 20 hidden units), there were no differences between flat and standard CC. On more complex problems (with more than 20 hidden units), there were several differences: 1) each algorithm performed better on its own problem type than on the opposite problem type, 2) standard CC learned more efficiently and accurately than flat CC, and 3) flat CC required fewer weights and generalized better than standard CC.

A relatively new variant called sibling–descendant CC (SDCC) dynamically decides whether to install a new hidden unit on the current highest layer (as a sibling) or on a separate, higher layer (as a descendant) (Baluja and Fahlman 1994). In SDCC, the candidate pool (conventionally eight candidate units) is divided in half, with an equal number of sibling and descendant candidates. The single candidate whose activations correlate most highly with network error is the one actually recruited, following conventional CC policy. To counter the natural tendency to always recruit a descendant unit, the descendant correlation values are multiplied by a penalty factor. Empirical exploration discovered that a penalty factor of 0.8 limited network depth without harming generalization (Baluja and Fahlman 1994).

Systematic comparisons show that SDCC's performance lies somewhere between flat and standard CC, but is closer to the latter (Dandurand 2004). There are generally no significant differences between SDCC and standard CC on most performance measures. The only exception is that SDCC generates networks with significantly fewer layers than does standard CC. Hence our interest in applying SDCC in simulations of psychological data with the aim of building networks with more realistic depths than in standard CC.

3.3.2.1 Acquisition of conservation

Twenty SDCC networks were trained and tested in the same fashion as CC networks were. In all SDCC simulations reported here, the penalty factor for descendant units was 0.8. A wide range of hidden-unit topologies were spontaneously constructed as

Table 3.2 Hidden-unit topologies of 20 SDCC networks

2–4–4	1–3–5	2–2–2–1	2–3–1–3	1–3–2–2–1–1
2–3–6	2–7	3–3–3	1–1–5–1	2–3–2
5–3	1–1–5–3	2–2–3–1	2–3	2–2
3–1–1–1	4–3–3	3–1–2–2	7–1	3–2–1

Table 3.3 Mean performance of 20 CC and 20 SDCC networks on conservation acquisition

Variable	CC	SDCC	$t(38)$	$p <$
Train % correct	99.13	99.24	−0.24	ns
Test % correct	93.35	94.20	−0.47	ns
Train error	0.008	0.009	−0.38	ns
Test error	0.041	0.039	0.23	ns
Epochs to victory	1257	1292	−0.40	ns
% reaching victory	50	65	−0.95	ns
Hidden units	7.95	8.10	−0.23	ns
Layers of hidden units	7.95	3.25	8.63	0.0001

shown in Table 3.2. For example a topology of 2–4–4 means two hidden units on the first layer, four on the second layer, and four on the third layer. All of these networks had 13 input units and two output units.

To compare overall performance of these SDCC networks with ordinary CC, a fresh experiment was run with 20 CC networks, a replication of the first experiment in Shultz (1998). Table 3.3 presents mean results on several variables of interest, along with independent-sample t-tests. The two algorithms do not differ on any measure except for the obvious one of the number of layers of hidden units. Because SDCC often installs sibling hidden units, it used fewer layers and saved a mean of 4.25 connection weights per network, the saved weights being cascaded weights eliminated for hidden units installed on the same layer. These results establish that SDCC performs just as effectively as CC on conservation acquisition, while saving on both network depth and number of connection weights. In the following sections, whether SDCC covers other conservation phenomena as well as CC does will be evaluated.

Proportion of correct training and test patterns is shown in Fig. 3.1 for network 14. This network reached victory in 802 epochs, recruiting two hidden units in a first layer and three more in a second layer, for a final 13–2–3–2 topology. The output epochs are grouped into 100 equal-size blocks for the plot. The plot shows excellent generalization to the test patterns and a substantial spurt in performance, both of which are representative of all other CC and SDCC networks. The epochs at which hidden units were recruited are shown by triangles for descendant units and squares for sibling units. One unusual feature of this network is the close proximity of the second and third recruits. The second recruit, a sibling unit, did not improve performance so

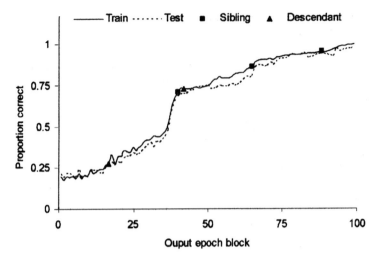

Fig. 3.1 Acquisition of conservation by SDCC network 14.

recruitment of another unit, a descendant unit, quickly followed. This and other hidden units continued to improve performance of the network to near perfect.

3.3.2.2 Problem size

The problem-size effect is that children develop conservation with small numbers before large numbers. For the simulations, a problem was considered to be small if the number of the smaller row had less than 12 items; large if the number of the smaller row had more than 24 items. These particular values split the patterns so that small and large problems were about equally frequent. Proportions of small and large problems correct for the 20 networks are plotted in Fig. 3.2 over ten equal-size blocks of output epochs. Proportions were transformed to arcsins to uncorrelate the relation between means and variances, and these arcsin values were subjected to ANOVA in which epoch block and problem size served as repeated measures. There were main effects of size, $F(1,19) = 15$, $p < 0.001$, and block, $F(9,171) = 172$, $p < 0.0001$, and an interaction between them, $F(9,171) = 8.7$, $p < 0.0001$. Problem-size means at each block were compared with dependent-sample t-tests. At every block, except 7 and 10, the difference was significant, $p < 0.05$, although the direction was reversed at block 1 where understanding of conservation was still very poor. The magnitude of the problem-size effects in networks (0.1) is about the same as reported in children, at least over blocks 2–6 (cf. Shultz 1998).

The fact that the networks performed better on small-number problems than on large-number problems is a manifestation of the Weber–Fechner law, wherein larger proportional differences are easier to discriminate than smaller proportional differences. Such effects naturally fall out of neural networks, although one could have captured this effect in other, more obvious ways suggested in the psychological

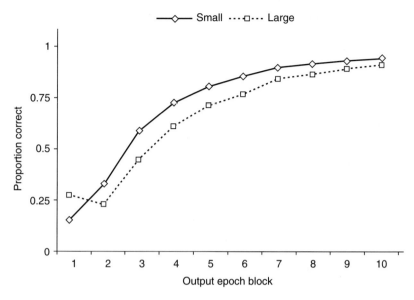

Fig. 3.2 Mean proportion correct on small- and large-number conservation test patterns over ten equal-size blocks of output epochs for 20 SDCC networks.

literature, namely, that children get relatively more practice with small numbers, or that children's estimation techniques are relatively more accurate with small numbers.

3.3.2.3 Length bias

Length bias, in the context of conservation of discrete quantities, refers to choosing a longer row as having more items than a shorter row. Analogous errors have been reported among non-conservers in a variety of other conservation tasks. The test for length bias conventionally uses only elongation and compression problems that have initially equal rows. Thirty of the 100 such equality-conserving problems were randomly selected as test problems. The remaining 70 equality-preserving problems entered the training set, conforming to a policy of training on 70 per cent of the relevant problems, along with 350 other randomly-selected training problems. The alternative of choosing the shorter, denser row as having more items in these equality-conserving problems is considered a density bias.

If the first output activation was more than 0 and the second output activation was less than 0, then a network was deemed to have chosen the first row as having more. Conversely, if the first output activation was less than 0 and the second output activation was greater than 0, then a network was considered to have chosen the second row as having more. Finally, if both output activations were less than 0, then a network was considered to have decided that the rows are numerically equal.

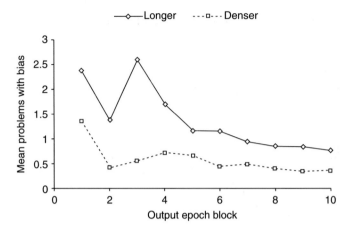

Fig. 3.3 Length and density bias over blocks of output epochs in 20 SDCC networks.

The numbers of test problems on which a network showed either a length or density bias each output epoch were collapsed into mean problems showing each bias at each of ten equal-size blocks of output epochs. These mean numbers of biased answers were subjected to ANOVA in which epoch block and type of bias served as repeated measures. There were main effects of bias, $F(1, 19) = 9.6$, $p < 0.01$, and block, $F(9, 171) = 12$, $p < 0.001$, and an interaction between them, $F(9, 171) = 4.9$, $p < 0.001$. Relevant means are shown in Fig. 3.3.

Bias-type means at each block were compared with dependent-sample t-tests. Only at blocks 1–4 and 6 was this difference significant, $p < 0.05$. Although this length bias was evident in the first two blocks, it increased in size in the third and fourth blocks before starting to diminish. This pattern suggests a bias that increases and then decreases with learning.

When expressed as a proportion of errors reflecting a length bias, such proportions ranged from 0.64 to 0.83 across the ten blocks. This approximates the values of 0.69 to 0.86 reported in various experimental conditions by Miller *et al.* (1973) with clay sausages, representing the proportion of length-bias errors in conservation of continuous quantities.

3.3.2.4 Explaining length bias

Length bias on conservation tasks has been conventionally attributed to either perceptual salience (length is more salient than number) or learning that longer rows often have more items than shorter rows. Although the source of length bias has not been settled by psychological research, it has been noted that very young children do not show a length bias (cf. review by Shultz 1998). This finding is consistent with the idea that time is required for children to learn that length is a somewhat reliable cue to number.

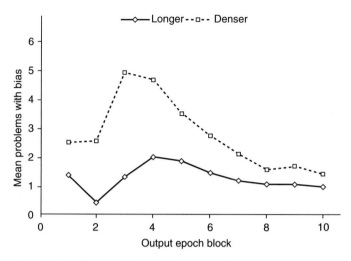

Fig. 3.4 Length and density bias over blocks of output epochs in 20 SDCC networks trained in an environment in which length was held constant during number-altering transformations.

The learning explanation is attractive in that addition and subtraction transformations could introduce a correlation between number and length, as long as density is held constant during such transformations. When density is constant, adding an item makes a row longer as well as more numerous; subtracting an item makes a row shorter as well as less numerous. The impact of this correlation between length and number on conservation acquisition was tested by creating an alternate environment in which length, rather than density, is held constant during number-altering transformations. In this alternative environment, when an item is added to a row, the row is compressed so that density increases and length does not change. Likewise, during subtraction, a row is elongated so that density decreases and length again remains constant. To maintain consistency with the previous simulation, length rather than density is changed by one unit in elongation and compression transformations. With this change, the previous simulation was repeated with 20 fresh networks.

Mean test problems showing length and density bias are plotted in Fig. 3.4 for this strange training environment. ANOVA yielded main effects of bias, $F(1, 19) = 10.5$, $p < 0.01$, and block, $F(9, 171) = 15$, $p < 0.001$, and an interaction between bias and block, $F(9, 171) = 5.5$, $p < 0.001$. Bias-type means at each block were again compared with dependent-sample t-tests, revealing significant density bias only in blocks 1–4, $p < 0.01$. As with length bias, density bias increases in strength and then disappears as the network continues to learn about conservation phenomena.

These results show that early non-conservation biases are strongly influenced in SDCC simulations by the correlation of either length or density with number during number-altering transformations. When density is held constant in these transformations, number correlates better with length than with density, and length then predicts number. But when length is held constant, number correlates with density, and thus density predicts number. Due to human laziness, the default condition is undoubtedly constant density because it takes more effort to adjust density when adding or subtracting an item.

These perceptual bias effects underscore the tension between perceptual and cognitive processes in conservation tasks. Piaget designed these tasks to create a particular conflict between perception and cognition. What the child knows (that a transformation does not alter a quantity) appears to conflict with what she sees (that one row is longer, and thus seems more numerous than the other row). It is well known that perceptual solutions dominate early in children's conservation acquisition, but eventually lose out to cognitive solutions involving reasoning about the effects of transformations (cf. review by Shultz 1998). Results in the last two simulations are consistent with this literature.

3.3.2.5 Knowledge-representation analysis

Although SDCC networks covered all four principal conservation phenomena (acquisition, spurt, problem size, and length bias), it would be premature to conclude that they provide an adequate model without analyzing the knowledge representations that they construct at various points in development. One of the most effective techniques for this is a Principal Components Analysis (PCA) of network contributions. Contributions are products of sending-unit activations and connection weights entering output units. As such, contributions summarize all of the relevant information influencing a network's outputs and typically produce sensible abstract descriptions that generalize well across cross-connected networks that otherwise appear to be idiosyncratic in topology and connection weights (Shultz *et al.* 1995).

Table 3.4 shows the developmental history of knowledge representations in network 8. This network ended up with a 13–4–3–2 topology, that is with 13 input units, four hidden units on one layer, three hidden units on the next layer, and two output units. Without any hidden units, the PCA of contributions yields two components explaining 92 per cent of the variance in contributions. The first component has loadings from the four density inputs, and the second component has loadings from the four length inputs. At this point, the network is performing well below chance, being correct on only 19 per cent of the training problems and 8 per cent of the test problems. Because this network, like most networks, began near the chance level of 33 per cent correct, it is now well into the phase of non-conservation errors, consistently selecting a longer row as being more numerous than a shorter row.

After recruiting a first hidden unit, network 8 substantially increases performance to 40 per cent correct on training problems and 44 per cent of test problems. A PCA of contributions at this point reveals the presence of three components – one continuing to deal with row density, and another with row length. The third, new component has

Table 3.4 Developmental history of knowledge representations in conservation network 8

Hidden units	Component						% Correct		% Variance explained
	1	2	3	4	5	6	Train	Test	
0	dnst	lngth	–	–	–	–	19	8	92
1	dnst	lngth	h1, id, add, elng	–	–	–	40	44	85
2	lngth, h2	h1, sub	id, sub, elng	–	–	–	66	58	82
3	lngth, h2	h3, cmpr, dnst	h1, sub, id	h2, elng, h3	–	–	73	76	86
4	lngth, h2	h3, cmpr, dnst, add	h1, sub, id	h2, elng, h3	–	–	74	73	91
5	lngth, h2	cmpr, h3	h4, h5, add	h1, id	elng, h3, sub	–	94	90	89
6	lngth, h2	cmpr, h6, h3	h4, h5	id, h1	add, sub, h6, h1	elng, h3, sub	99	97	93
7	lngth, h2	cmpr, h6, id	h1, id	h4, h5	elng, sub, h3	add, id, h7	100	99	93

dnst = density, lngth = length, h = hidden unit, id = identity of transformed row, add = addition, sub = subtraction, elng = elongation, cmpr = compression. The horizontal lines within the table demarcate the layers of hidden units.

loadings of decreasing size from the first hidden unit, and inputs concerning the identity of the transformed row, and the addition and elongation transformations. The non-linear power of the first hidden unit, plus consideration of these more conceptual inputs, accounts for the large increase in performance. Knowing the identity of the transformed row is essential to correctly interpreting any additional information on the applied transformation.

To perform even better, network 8 next recruits a second hidden unit, allowing it to reach correct percentages of 66 on training and 58 on test problems. A PCA of contributions still yields three components, but their organization is different than previously. The first component has loadings from the four length inputs and the new hidden unit. The second component has loadings from hidden unit 1 and subtraction input. And the third component has loadings from identity of the transformed row, and the subtraction and elongation transformations. Density inputs have temporarily disappeared from consideration.

After recruiting a third hidden unit, this network further increases its performance to 73 and 76 per cent correct on training and test problems, respectively. It now has four components to its contributions. The first still deals with length inputs and hidden unit 2. The second component has loadings from the new hidden unit, the compression transformation, and a smaller contribution from density inputs. Component 3 has loadings from hidden unit 1, the subtraction transformation, and the identity of the transformed row. The fourth component has loadings from the second and third hidden units and the elongation transformation. The fact that length input continues to be accompanied by a hidden unit means that mere length is not used to decide which row has more, as was the case in the first two stages, before the network had at least two hidden units. Instead, length information is now being combined with other inputs in a nonlinear fashion to make decisions on relative number. At this stage, the network is considering inputs on only two of the four types of transformation, subtraction and elongation. So this network still has some distance to go in fully understanding conservation. Namely, it lacks sufficient computational power to process and co-ordinate other information on addition and compression transformations.

Not much has changed with the recruitment of hidden unit 4. PCA still reveals four components with loadings on the same factors as before, apart from some new, minor consideration of the addition transformation. Somehow the new hidden unit is not important enough to load on any of these four components. This explains why performance does not increase beyond the previous level. Percent correct is now 74 on training problems and 73 on test problems. All of the first four hidden units reside on the same first hidden-unit layer – they have no cascaded connections. As if sensing that further non-linearity is required, the algorithm recruits its next hidden unit on a different level, with cascaded connection weights from all of the four existing hidden units.

This results in a PCA with five components and a big jump in performance to 94 and 90 per cent correct on training and test problems, respectively. The first component looks the same as before, length conditioned by hidden unit 2, but the rest of the components look substantially different. Component 2 deals with compression and hidden unit 3; component 3 with hidden units 4 and 5, and addition; component 4 with hidden unit 1 and the identity of the transformed row; and component 5 with elongation, subtraction, and hidden unit 3. Note that all existing hidden units are used, even the previously unused hidden unit 4. It is probably important that the new computational power afforded by hidden unit 5 enables an additional knowledge component allowing a greater spreading out of the various contributions. Spreading out these different functions is important to avoid the confusions caused by overloading of too much information on too few components.

Further representation spreading is enabled by recruitment of the sixth and seventh hidden units. The sixth hidden unit brings performance up to 99 and 97 per cent correct, respectively, on training and test problems. And the final, seventh hidden unit brings the network to nearly perfect performance on conservation problems. Notice the liberal use of information on the identity of the transformed row in three of the final six components. Identity is a key piece of information in many of the functions computed by the network in the final stage of learning. All of the important information on the conservation problem is well represented in these final solutions, although density information has been neglected since the second and last layer of hidden units began to form. As might be expected, in the strange environment where length is held constant in number-altering transformations, it is density inputs that are retained in network contributions and length inputs that are eventually ignored.

In effect, the network has progressed from responding based on how the rows look in terms of their length and density to reasoning about the effects of the transformation on the initial quantitative relation between the two rows. Such reasoning requires non-linear integration of information on the initial relation and the type and target of the transformation. For example adding an item has different results depending on both the row being added to and whether or not the two rows were initially equal in number.

In all of the conservation networks I have analyzed, whether constructed by the CC or SDCC algorithm, there is evidence of this progression from using the perceptual information of length and density to reasoning about the effects of particular transformations. This is the sort of shift that Piaget (1965) found with children. The knowledge-representation analyses presented here support Piaget's analysis, while specifying more fully, in computational terms, how such knowledge can be implemented and acquired within a plausible neural framework.

3.3.2.6   Summary of SDCC simulations

Like CC networks, SDCC networks covered all four principal conservation phenomena (acquisition, spurt, problem size, and length bias) and built knowledge representations mimicking the struggle between perceptual and cognitive solutions to the conservation task, a struggle eventually won in a comeback by cognitive strategies. At the same time, SDCC saved on numbers of network layers and connection weights. Past research, on a few non-psychological benchmark problems, found no reduction in connection weights with SDCC (Baluja and Fahlman 1994).

3.3.3   Conservation simulations with BP

Exactly the same training and testing scheme used with SDCC networks was tried with static BP networks. My original hypothesis was that, once finding a BP simulation that acquired conservation, knowledge-representation analysis might reveal that BP would not bother with perceptual solutions. Because these networks start with all the computational power they need, they might move directly to a more cognitive solution. As noted earlier, similar problems in capturing stages were reported for

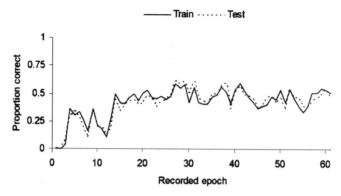

Fig. 3.5 Performance on conservation problems by a 13–10–10–2 BP network over 3000 epochs.

BP networks in the domain of integrating time, distance, and velocity cues for moving objects.

However, even when endowing BP networks with considerable computational power (one or two layers of 10 hidden units each), training them for extraordinary numbers of epochs (3000 to 12000 epochs), with systematic variation in key parameters of *epsilon* (learning rate, 0.1 to 0.5) and *mu* (momentum, 0.4 to 0.9), I have not been able to discover even a single case of successful acquisition of conservation. Best results were obtained with a large 13–10–10–2 topology, a low *epsilon* of 0.1, and a default *mu* of 0.9. Variation in training epochs did not matter much because there was no improvement after about 1000 epochs.

Figure 3.5 shows results from a representative network, designed with a 13–10–10–2 topology. *Epsilon* was lowered to 0.1; *mu* was the default 0.9. The learning-rate parameter scales the sizes of weight changes and needs to be set to a moderate value to allow reasonably fast learning, but not so fast that weight changes oscillate wildly over more optimal values. With the *split-epsilon* technique used here, *epsilon* is divided by unit fan-in, which is 13 for the first hidden layer, 10 for the second hidden layer, and 10 for the outputs, all of which brings the effective *epsilon* values down to the vicinity used in the CC and SDCC conservation simulations. The momentum parameter provides weights with a relative degree of inertia, so that they will change less when the last change was small and change more when the last change was large. The idea is to induce larger weight changes when the weight is far from the error minimum, and smaller weight changes when the weight is approaching the error minimum. This network was trained for 3000 epochs. The results in the figure were recorded at 60 equally-spaced epochs. Some learning does occur here in early epochs, but performance never goes much above 50 per cent correct. The BP algorithm was modified here to stop learning when all output activations are within score-threshold

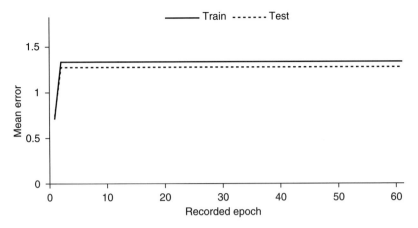

Fig. 3.6 Performance on conservation problems by a 13–10–10–2 BP network over 12 000 epochs.

of their targets for all of the training patterns, just as in CC and SDCC, so it did not stop until the 3000-epoch limit.

Figure 3.6 shows a different pattern that occurs often in these tests, also from a 13–10–10–2 BP network, but trained for 12 000 epochs. Again, *epsilon* was 0.1 and *mu* was 0.9, the optimal values. Per-pattern error values were recorded at 60 equally-spaced epochs. Because this network shows no change in error from the second recorded epoch, it must be stuck in a local error minimum.

With a very large number of possible designs for BP networks and a wide range of parameter settings to try, it is difficult to demonstrate that a particular learning algorithm cannot succeed, even on a difficult task like conservation acquisition. However, these results suggest that it will not be easy to get BP networks to acquire conservation as defined here.

3.4 Summary of comparison between static and constructive learning

In each of the four developmental domains where both static and constructive network algorithms have been applied, there is a clear superiority of constructive learning. Constructive algorithms, whether CC or SDCC, covered all of the basic psychological regularities in a natural and principled manner and generated sensible knowledge representations. In contrast, static BP networks suffer from any of three problems: they miss stages, fail to capture key psychological phenomena, or do not learn the training patterns.

BP networks missed important stages in the domain of integrating velocity, time, and distance cues for moving objects. They were either too underpowered to reach the terminal multiplicative stages, or else by virtue of starting with just one more unit they were too overpowered to capture intermediate additive stages. Network growth allowed constructive algorithms to capture all three levels of stages in this domain. Static BP networks also missed either stages 1 or 4 in the balance-scale domain. By changing biases in the training patterns, BP networks can be prodded to capture either stage 1 or stage 4, but they seem incapable of capturing both of these balance-scale stages. Moving from one region of connection-weight space to another can be difficult for a learning algorithm that cannot change its topology. The inability of BP networks to capture a full range of stages in these two domains points to a key reason for the success of CC networks in these domains. The gradual increase in computational power due to recruitment of hidden units allows CC networks to first perform at a more primitive level and then progress to more advanced stages, thus capturing the stages seen in children. Moving from a particular region of connection-weight space in stage 1 to a very different region in stage 4 of the balance scale is not a problem for CC networks because recruitment of hidden units effectively increases the dimensionality of that space, allowing greater flexibility in traversing the space.

In the domain of early category learning, BP networks did not capture any of the key phenomena. They could learn about the stimuli in the sense of reducing error, but they did not capture the results of either younger or older infants, showing neither a consistent similarity effect nor any correlation effect at all. Both of these effects, and the developmental transition between them, are captured by a network that is capable of growing while learning. Starting with little computational power requires CC networks to begin solving a relatively simple problem, discovery of stimulus features. Once the features have been noticed, then recruitment of additional computational power allows CC networks to track correlations among features.

Static BP networks have so far not mastered the conservation problem, despite designing networks that should have had sufficient computational power and time to learn and varying key learning parameters. The reasons for learning difficulty can be challenging to identify. But I would suggest that BP suffers from not being able to start from a simpler, under-powered perspective, a conjecture that is mindful of the benefits of starting small (Elman 1993). Both CC and SDCC start small in a topological and computational-power sense that does not require staging of the learning environment or limiting the window of processing, as Elman implemented with grammar learning. In constructive learning, starting with a small, underpowered network ensures that simple ideas are acquired first and progressively more complex ideas are built on top of simpler ones.

Another advantage of constructive learning is that networks can more easily move off from local error minima in their continuing search for more global error minima in a high-dimensional weight space. Recruiting a new hidden unit effectively adds another dimension to weight space enabling a network to find a path to lower error.

These and other simulations make it clear that the superiority of CC over BP in covering developmental phenomena is not merely a matter of CC discovering more advantageous network topologies than the human designers of static networks were able to achieve. First it is noteworthy that CC and especially SDCC networks automatically construct a wide variety of network topologies. It is unlikely that all of these topologies are somehow fortuitously and exclusively optimal for every algorithm. Recall also that our BP simulations of the infant category-learning experiments used a modal CC network topology, in some conditions complete with cross connections that bypass hidden layers as in CC networks (Shultz and Cohen 2004). In none of these simulations did a BP network cover the basic characteristics of either younger or older infants, nor the transition from younger to older, despite having a topology identical to that of the final stage of successful CC networks.

We have also studied this issue of network topology in a non-developmental context. CC networks were trained on exclusive–or, parity, encoding, symmetry, binary addition, and negation problems. After training, weights in the CC networks were reset to small random values and each resulting network was trained with the BP algorithm. These pairs of CC and BP networks were compared in terms of whether they could learn these tasks, how fast they learned, and how well they generalized to novel examples. Their knowledge representations were also assessed. In contrast to their BP yoked controls, CC networks always learned the task with the default learning parameters, usually learned faster, and learned with less computation. These are relatively easy tasks, designed to exercise the BP algorithm. It is well known that BP can solve them, but it is interesting that BP networks do not always solve them. Thus, discovery of magically optimal network topologies is not the key to explaining the differences between static and constructive learning. The key difference seems to be a simultaneous search of connection-weight space (to find the right weight values) and topology space (to find the right network structure). Because topology space is searched during the learning of connection weights and progresses from simple to complex, learning is facilitated and psychological stages of acquisition are simulated.

3.5 Conclusions

In addition to the neurological and computational advantages of constructive learning, the present modeling shows advantages for capturing psychological phenomena in several domains of cognitive development. By starting small and building new conceptualizations on top of old ones, the CC and SDCC algorithms cover data that elude static BP learning. In some cases, BP was unable to learn, making data coverage impossible. In other cases, even if BP could learn the problem, it was unable to cover stages and stage sequences.

Another potential advantage of CC and SDCC over static learners is their essential continuity with knowledge-based algorithms. Knowledge-based cascade-correlation

(KBCC) recruits previously learned subnetworks as well as single hidden units, providing the capacity for existing knowledge to either facilitate or interfere with new learning (Shultz and Rivest 2001). It is difficult to see how static BP networks could find and use existing knowledge in so natural a fashion.

All of this is not to suggest that the BP algorithm has no place in developmental simulations. BP has probably generated more successful simulations in psychology and development than any other algorithm has and this success speaks for itself (Elman *et al.* 1996). It is also noteworthy that simple recurrent networks trained on small, finite-state grammars with back-propagation of error encode progressively longer temporal contexts as learning continues (Servan-Schreiber *et al.* 1991). This shows that recurrently-connected static networks can sometimes learn simple functions before complex ones. The present bakeoff simulations show that constructive learning does a better job than static algorithms at covering certain developmental phenomena involving stage sequences and particularly difficult learning.

Comparison of SDCC to CC in the domain of conservation acquisition suggests equivalent performance in all aspects except that SDCC requires fewer, and more realistic, levels of hidden units and fewer connection weights. Such results point to the promising nature of SDCC while not invalidating interpretations of the many earlier simulations using CC. The results also suggest that the details of network topology may not be as important as the increasing computational power of the network. The fact that SDCC creates such a wide variety of network topologies expressing the same functionality supports this conjecture.

Acknowledgements

This work is supported by a grant from the Natural Sciences and Engineering Research Council of Canada. This paper benefited from comments by Yoshio Takane, J-P Thivierge, Frédéric Dandurand, several participants attending the Attention and Performance meeting, and an anonymous reviewer.

References

Baluja S and Fahlman SE (1994). Reducing network depth in the cascade-correlation learning architecture. *Technical Report CMU-CS-94-209*, School of Computer Science, Carnegie Mellon University.

Baum BE (1989). A proposal for more powerful learning algorithms. *Neural Computation,* 1, 201–207.

Buckingham D and Shultz TR (1996). Computational power and realistic cognitive development. In: *Proceedings of the Eighteenth Annual Conference of the Cognitive Science Society, pp.* 507–511. Mahwah, NJ: Erlbaum.

Buckingham D and Shultz TR (2000). The developmental course of distance, time, and velocity concepts: A generative connectionist model. *Journal of Cognition and Development,* 1, 305–345.

Cohen LB and Arthur AE (2004). *The role of habituation in 10-month-olds' categorization.* Unpublished paper, Department of Psychology, University of Texas.

Elman JL (1993). Learning and development in neural networks: The importance of starting small. *Cognition*, 48, 71–99.

Elman JL, Bates EA, Johnson MH, Karmiloff-Smith A, Parisi D and Plunkett K (1996). *Rethinking innateness: A connectionist perspective on development.* Cambridge, MA: MIT Press.

Fahlman SE and Lebiere C (1990). The cascade-correlation learning architecture. In: DS Touretzky, ed. *Advances in neural information processing systems 2*, pp. 524–532. Los Altos, CA: Morgan Kaufmann.

Fodor JA (1980). Fixation of belief and concept acquisition. In: M Piatelli-Palmarini, ed. *Language and learning: The debate between Chomsky and Piaget*, pp. 143–149. Cambridge, MA: Harvard Press.

Gould E, Tanapat P, Hastings NB and Shors TJ (1999). Neurogenesis in adulthood: A possible role in learning. *Trends in Cognitive Sciences*, 3, 186–192.

Kempermann G and Gage FH (1999). New nerve cells for the adult brain. *Scientific American*, 280, 48–53.

Mareschal D and Shultz TR (1996). Generative connectionist networks and constructivist cognitive development. *Cognitive Development*, 11, 571–603.

McClelland JL and Jenkins E (1991). Nature, nurture, and connections: Implications of connectionist models for cognitive development. In: K van Lehn, ed. *Architectures for intelligence: The twenty-second (1988) Carnegie symposium on cognition*, pp. 41–73. Hillsdale, NJ: Erlbaum.

Miller PH, Grabowski TL and Heldmeyer KH (1973). The role of stimulus dimensions in the conservation of substance. *Child Development*, 44, 646–650.

Munakata Y and McClelland JL (2003). Connectionist models of development. *Developmental Science*, 6, 413–429.

Piaget J (1965). *The child's conception of number.* New York: Norton.

Purves D, White LE and Riddle DR (1996). Is neural development Darwinian? *Trends in Neuroscience*, 19, 460–464.

Quartz SR (1993). Neural networks, nativism, and the plausibility of constructivism. *Cognition*, 48, 223–242.

Quartz SR (2003). Learning and brain development: A neural constructivist perspective. In: PT Quinlan, ed. *Connectionist models of development: Developmental processes in real and artificial neural networks*, pp. 279–309. New York: Psychology Press.

Quartz SR and Sejnowski TJ (1997). The neural basis of cognitive development: A constructivist manifesto. *Behavioural and Brain Sciences*, 20, 537–596.

Servan-Schreiber D, Cleeremans A and McClelland JL (1991). Graded state machines: The representation of temporal contingencies in simple recurrent networks. *Machine Learning*, 7, 161–193.

Shultz TR (1998). A computational analysis of conservation. *Developmental Science*, 1, 103–126.

Shultz TR (2003). *Computational developmental psychology.* Cambridge, MA: MIT Press.

Shultz TR and Cohen LB (2004). Modeling age differences in infant category learning. *Infancy*, 5, 153–171.

Shultz TR, Mareschal D and Schmidt WC (1994). Modeling cognitive development on balance scale phenomena. *Machine Learning*, 16, 57–86.

Shultz TR, Mysore SP and Quartz SR (2006, in press). Why let networks grow? In: D Mareschal, S Sirois, and G Westermann, eds. *Constructing cognition: Perspectives and prospects.* Oxford: Oxford University Press.

Shultz TR, Oshima-Takane Y and Takane Y (1995). Analysis of unstandardized contributions in cross connected networks. In: D Touretzky, G Tesauro and TK Leen, eds. *Advances in neural information processing systems 7*, pp. 601–608. Cambridge, MA: MIT Press.

Shultz TR and Rivest F (2001). Knowledge-based cascade-correlation: Using knowledge to speed learning. *Connection Science, 13,* 43–72.

Siegler RS (1976). Three aspects of cognitive development. *Cognitive Psychology, 8,* 481–520.

Wilkening F (1981). Integrating velocity, time, and distance information: A developmental study. *Cognitive Psychology, 13,* 231–247.

Younger BA and Cohen LB (1983). Infant perception of correlations among attributes. *Child Development, 54,* 858–867.

Younger BA and Cohen LB (1986). Developmental change in infants' perception of correlations among attributes. *Child Development, 57,* 803–815.

Chapter 4

Dynamically guided learning

Rebecca L. Gómez

Abstract

Recent research on human learning has revealed a pervasive ability to track statistical structure in adulthood and infancy. Because statistical information abounds in visual and linguistic structure, statistical learning has potential for playing an important role in the acquisition of complex skill. This chapter summarizes the literature on statistical learning and evaluates it in terms of its potential for circumventing problems that have been traditionally posed for learners, such as over generalization and how learners choose among multiple forms of structure. Empirical findings suggest that statistical learning is highly data driven. Additionally, learning appears to be constrained by preferred structure (structure that is particularly salient or easy to process), but also by the pressures exerted by the environment (learners tend to seek out invariant structure). Learning arises in the interaction of these two forms of constraint, resulting in a dynamically guided process.

4.1 Introduction

Statistical structure abounds in perceptual information. Whether auditory, visual, or tactile, stimulation is rich in frequent associations and patterns. Humans show a striking capacity for tracking such information. 'Statistical' learning, as this capacity has come to be known, is at the very root of development as evidenced by its emergence in early infancy (Gómez and Gerken 1999; Kirkham *et al.* 2002; Saffran *et al.* 1996). Research in this area complements the two plus decades of work on computational models of learning and has been a major contributor to a renaissance of learning in psychological research.

For many years, especially in the area of language acquisition, learning was assumed to have little influence on language development other than explaining how children acquire the variations between different languages (see Chomsky 1965). Rather, innate mechanisms were thought, almost solely, responsible for guiding acquisition. Such mechanisms were not only language specific, but were thought to operate at a fairly high level (for instance the knowledge that sentences in one's language either do or do not require overt subjects). However, recent findings raise key questions about the form of innate sensitivities and the interplay of these with learning. Although innate sensitivities are most certainly involved in development, characterizing them accurately may be dependent on a more thorough understanding of learning. Identifying the scope and limits of learning should bring us closer to specifying the initial state.

I have organized this paper with two goals in mind. One is to review key literature on statistical learning and to convey an up-to-date summary of this work. I will do this with an eye toward evaluating how this research addresses fundamental challenges to learning theories having to do with understanding how learning might be constrained, how learners might recover from faulty generalizations, and how they might choose among multiple kinds of structure. The second goal is to explore the extent to which current work on learning addresses these challenges. Much work on statistical learning has been conducted in the context of language acquisition, and thus this chapter will reflect that perspective, but the issues generalize to other developmental domains.

The organization of the paper is as follows. First I will outline two fundamental issues for learning theories—how learners recover from overgeneralizations and the question of how learners choose among multiple kinds of structure. Next I will summarize the literature on statistical learning. I will go on to explore a mechanism for understanding how learners might choose among multiple kinds of structure and, in doing so, will consider the extent to which learners are likely to overgeneralize. Finally, I will highlight recent work in the area of memory and its implications for theories of learning.

4.1.1 Fundamental learning issues

There are numerous puzzles and questions that can be raised about basic learning mechanisms. Are they domain general or domain specific? Are they fundamentally different for child and adult learners? How rapid is learning? How permanent is it? What is the connection between learning and memory? What types of learning mechanisms do humans share with other species? What is the relationship between innate abilities and learning? Where do innate sensitivities leave off and where does learning begin? Obtaining answers to these questions is challenging, but not impossible. There are problems of a logical nature, however, that seem insurmountable – in particular, the problem of how learners recover from erroneous generalizations.

Pinker (1995) outlines four ways in which children's hypothesizes may differ from the rules of the target language and thus how children might acquire erroneous information. First, children's hypotheses may be entirely non-overlapping with the target language. This would be the case if children had only ungrammatical sentences in their repertoire. The second is that some, but not all, of children's hypotheses overlap with the target language. In this case, they would use some grammatical sentences but would also use ungrammatical ones. The third scenario is that children's hypotheses form a subset of the target language such that all of their sentences are grammatical, but they have not yet mastered all of the grammatical structures of the target language. None of these scenarios pose major problems for children because they will presumably continue to generate hypotheses in the course of continued (or 'positive') exposure. However, the fourth scenario, in which children's hypothesized language is a superset of the target language, does pose a problem, because the only way children can recover from such errors is by exposure to negative evidence (Gold 1967). This is because positive evidence only continues to confirm the overly general hypotheses. Negative evidence could come in the form of parental feedback; however such feedback appears to occur only sporadically (Marcus 1993) and, when present, has minimal impact (Brown and Hanlon 1970). As noted in Pinker (1995), without negative evidence children 'must have some mechanism that either avoids generating too large a language – the child would be conservative – or that can recover from such overgeneration' (p. 153). Otherwise, children will not be able to converge on their target language.

This puzzle has figured prominently in the literature on language learnability (e.g. Gold 1967; Wexler and Culicover 1980) and, in turn, has greatly influenced fundamental assumptions in language acquisition theory. Yet work on this problem has primarily been conducted using formal mathematical approaches and thus has tended to ignore key aspects of human cognition. Taking human cognition into account might lead us to question these assumptions. For instance, we might ask whether humans are actually likely to overgeneralize. We might also inquire about the nature of human memory to determine the extent to which overgeneralizations are likely to survive in memory. Answers to such questions may shed a different light on the degree to which learning may be incapacitated by the generation of erroneous hypotheses.

A second related challenge is the question of how learners choose among multiple competing hypotheses. Traditional views of learning have assumed that learning mechanisms would be too rudimentary to separate relevant from irrelevant structure and instead would make all possible generalizations, leading to a combinatorial explosion of possibilities (Pinker 1984). As with the problem of overgeneralization, this problem has been framed in formal terms instead of taking human cognitive capabilities into account. However, it is important to ask whether the problem of combinatorial explosions in human learning is a realistic concern. To determine this, we must characterize human learning mechanisms more fully. I will explore these issues in detail in ensuing sections.

4.1.2 A few notes about methodology

First, I will convey some key methodological details. Infants learn a great deal about natural language in a few short months, so in order to assess their learning abilities, they must be exposed to novel stimuli. Additionally, natural language is rich in correlated cues, making it difficult to pinpoint the exact source of learning. Artificial language materials are used in statistical learning studies to control for prior learning and to have more precise control over the types of cues presented to learners. Because the materials are novel they can also be used to assess learning in adults.

Statistical learning procedures usually involve two phases, a familiarization phase followed by a test. Length of familiarization varies from 2 to 3 min in infant studies to 10 to 20 min (or more) in adult studies. Adult participants are often used to obtain detailed information that cannot easily be obtained from infants and to investigate age-independent learning. Most studies use a two-language design so that half of the learners are exposed to Language A and half to Language B. At test, learners are exposed to strings from both languages. Language A strings violate the constraints of Language B and *vice versa*. Thus, both groups receive the same test but what is grammatical for one group is ungrammatical for the other. This design ensures that the structure of the languages, as opposed to something idiosyncratic about one language or the other, is responsible for learning. Great care is taken in the design of the materials to ensure that the critical grammatical structure will drive learning.

Infants are tested using visual or auditory preference procedures (Kemler Nelson *et al.* 1995) that record the amount of time they attend to different stimulus types[1]. Adult learning is assessed by means of grammaticality judgments or two-alternative forced choice. In all cases, learners discriminate between strings that conform to their training language and strings that do not. Adult learning gains tend to be modest, hovering between 60 and 70 per cent.

4.2 Statistical learning

Statistical learning is the discovery of statistical structure in the environment. Statistical structure can take many forms, including the frequency of cues or events, the co-occurrence frequency of cues or events, or the conditional probability on one cue or event given another. As an example, co-occurrence frequency is defined as the probability of two events occurring together. Conditional probability is the probability of the occurrence of an event given that another event has previously occurred; the probability of Event B given Event A is the probability of Event A and Event B divided by the probability of Event A, $P(B|A) = P(A \text{ and } B)/P(A)$. There are other forms of statistical structure but common to all forms is the characteristic that cues or events occur with some regularity.

---

[1] Much has been made of the fact that in some studies infants listen longer to strings from their training language whereas in others they listen longer to the other language. Although there is some reason to think that direction of preference may be linked to the complexity of the stimulus (Hunter and Ames 1988), this issue is largely unresolved. Because it is impossible to predict the direction of preference with absolute certainty, orienting reliably longer to one stimulus type or the other is taken as an indication of discrimination, regardless of direction.

Sensitivity to statistical structure has been shown in infants as young as 2 months of age. Kirkham *et al.* (2002) habituated infants to a continuous stream of three randomly ordered shape pairs (e.g. pink diamond, green triangle; yellow circle, turquoise square; blue cross, red octagon). Shapes followed each other with 1.0 probability within pairs and with a 0.33 probability between pairs. Additionally, all shapes were equally frequent. Because the shapes were presented continuously, looking time differences to legal versus illegal combinations at test would indicate sensitivity to the statistical information. Infants looked longer on trials containing illegal shape sequences suggesting that they had tracked the statistical information. Because sequence pairs occurred more frequently than non-sequence pairs, it is difficult to know whether infants of this age are tracking conditional probabilities between adjacent events, the co-occurrence frequency of events, or both.

However, infants are definitely able to track conditional probabilities by 7 to 8 months of age (Aslin *et al.* 1998; Fiser and Aslin 2002a; Saffran *et al.* 1996a). Saffran *et al.* exposed 8-month-olds to continuous streams of randomly ordered three-syllable words (e.g. tupiro, golatu). Additionally, the frequency of individual syllables was held constant. The primary cue to word boundaries was the higher conditional probabilities occurring between syllables within words versus the lower conditional probabilities occurring for syllables spanning words. Infants were able to use this information to identify word boundaries in running speech. Although the co-occurrence frequency of syllables within words and syllables spanning word boundaries was not held constant in the initial study, Aslin *et al.* (1998) equated co-occurrence frequency during training and still showed learning. All studies reported by Saffran and colleagues since then have controlled for this variable. For instance, Thiessen and Saffran (2003) have reported learning of conditional probabilities by 7 months of age. Other studies have demonstrated similar learning with multielement scenes (Fiser and Aslin 2002a) and tone sequences (Saffran *et al.* 1999), and with non-human primates (Hauser *et al.* 2001), showing that this learning is not specific to language or to humans.

By 12 months, infants are able to track conditional probabilities of words in strings (Gómez and Gerken 1999; Saffran and Wilson 2003), and can generalize their knowledge of frequent patterns to strings in new vocabulary (Gómez and Gerken 1999; Marcus *et al.* 1999). Between 12 and 17 months of age infants have begun to abstract categories from words in sequence and can learn phrase structure relationships between them (Gómez and Lakusta 2004; Gerken *et al.* 2005). By 15 months, infants are able to track non-adjacent dependencies in sequential structure (Gómez 2002; Gómez and Maye 2005; Santelmann and Jusczyk 1998).

Infants also appear able to learn under especially challenging conditions. Saffran and Wilson (2003) investigated infants' ability to use one source of information as input to another. Twelve-month-olds were familiarized with strings of novel words in continuous speech. Word ordering within strings was constrained by a finite-state grammar such that only certain orders of words were legal. This stimulus design required infants to identify words before they could learn the relationships among them in sequence. Infants were able to discriminate legal from illegal strings at test, demonstrating that they had both segmented units at the word level and had learned how words could be combined to form sentences. In another study, Gómez and Lakusta (2004) asked whether infants would generalize even when inconsistent strings were present. They did this by manipulating the extent to which training strings were drawn from a predominant artificial language. Infants in an 84/16 condition heard strings from their predominant language 84 per cent of the time and strings from another counterbalanced language 16 per cent of the time (other infants were exposed to 100/0 or 68/32 ratios). Infants in the 84/16 condition performed as well as those in the 100/0 condition, showing that they were able to tolerate some inconsistency in their input. However, with a high percentage of intrusions (the 68/32 condition), infants failed to discriminate, demonstrating reasonable limits on this learning.

Finally, a number of reports show remarkable similarities in adult, infant, and child learning, suggesting that abilities are present early on and persist into adulthood. For instance, adults, children, and infants process conditional probabilities similarly such that they are able to detect words and tones in continuous speech (Saffran 2002; Saffran et al. 1996b; Saffran et al. 1997; Saffran et al. 1999). They are equally adept at detecting conditional probabilities in sequentially presented visual stimuli (Fiser and Aslin 2002a, b). Infants and adults also appear to generalize similarly, regardless of whether they are abstracting patterns of repeating elements (Gómez and Gerken 1999; Gómez et al. 2000; Marcus et al. 1999) or category structure (Braine 1987; Gerken et al. 2005; Gómez and Lakusta 2004). Finally, similar factors are at play in how infants and adults come to detect remote dependencies in sequential structure (Gómez 2002; Gómez and Maye in press)

This section paints a picture of significant learning capacities, with infants showing discrimination after brief exposure to fairly complex structure (e.g. Gerken et al. 2005; Gómez 2002; Gómez and Maye 2005; Gómez and Lakusta 2004; Saffran and Wilson 2003). But with such seemingly raw power, what might constrain learning? This issue is important because the very success of statistical approaches hinges on learners' ability to distinguish relevant from irrelevant information (Pinker 1995). With such precocious abilities, what is to keep learners from making erroneous generalizations? In addition to the principles and parameters approach in which Universal Grammar is thought to consist of the principles common to all languages and the parameters that vary among languages (Chomsky 1981), several possibilities have been proposed. One is that humans are constrained by their perceptual apparatus to consider only certain possibilities (Saffran 2002, 2003; Newport and Aslin 2004). Another is that learning is constrained by the presence of correlated cues such that learning is more likely to be successful when multiple cues are present (e.g. Morgan and Demuth 1996; Morgan *et al.* 1987). A final constraint is prior learning, the extent to which prior experience affects the type of structure learners seek out (Lany *et al.* 2004; Lany and Gómez 2004). We will go into these proposals in more detail in the next section.

4.3 Constraints on learning

The problem of how learning might be constrained is a particularly thorny one for statistical learning approaches. Criticisms are that learning is not sophisticated enough to cope with the complex structure found in language (Chomsky 1965), or that it is too powerful, resulting in attention to irrelevant information and unchecked generalization (Pinker 1984, 1995). In response, a number of constraints have been proposed to explain how learners converge on appropriate structure.

A widely held view is that innate tendencies (congruent with linguistic universals) constrain language (Chomsky 1981). Such universals take the form of principles true of all languages and parameters that differ among languages. Parameters that vary among a small number of options are thought set on initial exposure to a particular language. However, there is little evidence that parameters are set in this manner Gerken 2005. Rather, acquisition appears to occur over an extended period of time beginning early in infancy. Although the one-exposure criterion could be relaxed, this begins to move parameter setting into the realm of learning. Additionally, as outlined above, there is mounting evidence that statistical processes contribute to acquisition, suggesting that learning may be more central to language acquisition than previously thought. Saffran (2003) and Newport and Aslin (2004) have suggested that learning is constrained by human perceptual sensitivities maping onto the kinds of structure that occur across languages. Saffran (2003) refers to this as constrained statistical learning. Thus, instead of innate principles driving learning, human perceptual constraints guide what is learned such that some kinds of information are learned more readily than others, particularly in certain domains (e.g. Saffran 2002). Consistent with this proposal is the idea that languages are shaped by human information processing capabilities. Aspects of language that are particularly learnable are likely to be those that persist in the evolution of language. Thus, there is a symbiosis between language and human learning such that perceptual sensitivities are tuned to the structure of human language and in turn languages are constrained to be learnable by human perceptual systems (Bever 1970).

According to a multiple cue integration view, learning is constrained by multiple, overlapping cues that may be statistical, phonological, or prosodic in nature (Billman 1989; Christiansen and Dale 2001; Christiansen and Curtin 2004; Morgan and Demuth 1996; Morgan *et al.* 1987). Whereas no one cue may occur with enough predictability to support learning (Fernald and McRoberts 1996), multiple occurring cues are more reliable. In human language learning, multiple cue integration results in better generalization (Billman 1989; Braine 1987; Frigo and McDonald 1998; Gerken *et al.* 2005). In connectionist models, multiple cue integration leads to faster, more uniform acquisition of syntax (Christiansen and Dale 2001), and to superior segmentation (Christiansen and Curtin 2004).

With respect to human learning, a case in point comes from work on generalization in which grammatical classes are given arbitrary labels such as a, X, b, and Y (Braine 1987; Frigo and McDonald 1998; Smith 1969). Words from these classes are combined to form legal phrases. For instance, aX and bY might be legal whereas aY and bX are not (this is analogous to relationships in English between determiners and nouns or auxiliaries and verbs, where children have to learn that determiners precede nouns but not verbs). Learners are exposed to most, but not all, aX and bY phrases, then are tested to see if they will discriminate legal phrases they have not yet encountered from illegal ones. As in natural language, 'functor-like' a- and b-categories have fewer members than 'lexical-like' Xs and Ys. Although learners readily acquire the legal positions of words in terms of which occur first versus second (Smith 1969), categories and their relationships (that words belong to particular a, b, X, and Y classes and that a-words go with Xs and not Ys) are virtually impossible to acquire unless some subset of the X- and Y-category members are marked with multiple conceptual or perceptual cues (Braine 1987; Frigo and McDonald 1998; Gerken *et al.* 2005; Gómez and Lakusta 2004; Wilson 2002).

In the case of infants, Gerken *et al.* (2005) created a set of stimuli in which feminine lexical stems appeared with the case endings –oj and –u and masculine stems appeared with the case endings -ya and -em. Case endings in these experiments were equivalent to a- and b-elements. Additionally, cues distinguishing Xs and Ys were present for a subset of category members. For instance, some of the X-words contained the derivational suffix –k (e.g. 'polkoj,' 'polku') whereas some of the Y-words contained the suffix –tel (e.g. 'zhitelya,' 'zhitelyem'). Seventeen-month-olds were first familiarized and then were tested to see if they would attend differentially to novel aX and bY stimuli versus ungrammatical aY and bX ones. Infants were able to generalize to new grammatical test items in which the suffixes were absent, generalizing to words such as 'vannoj' and 'pisarem' after hearing 'vannu' and 'pisarya.' As with adults, learning is impossible for infants to attain without multiple cues to category structure. Gómez and Lakusta (2004) investigated a precursor to this learning in 12-month-old infants.

Another type of constraint is prior experience. The importance of this constraint stems from the fact that, while key structure occurs in many forms in language not all forms occur with equal frequency or are as richly cued as others. For instance, nouns and verbs in English are both cued by co-occurring function morphemes ('the,' 'a' and '-s' in the case of nouns and 'was', 'is,' and '-ing' in the case of verbs), but cues occur with greater statistical likelihood for nouns. Thus, children might be more attuned to the statistical information cueing noun categories than the information cueing verbs, and fail to learn the less well-cued form. However, learners can circumvent this problem if they can use knowledge of a well-cued form to detect one that is less well cued Lany et al. 2005. Consistent with this idea, Saffran and Theissen (2003) found that prior exposure to a particular phonological pattern influences which words infants are likely to identify in a segmentation task. Infants exposed to CVCV words in a prior training phase (C = consonant, V = vowel) listened longer to new CVCV words than to words of the form CVCCVC (the opposite held true for infants exposed to CVCCVC forms during training). In the realm of syntax acquisition, Lany *et al.* (2005; see also Lany and Gómez 2004) found that prior experience with syntactic categories can guide learners' subsequent generalizations. In particular, after exposure to a language involving a key syntactic relationship (the aX/bY language detailed above), learners were able to detect relationships between a-, X-, b-, and Y-elements in a more complex language involving acX and bcY structure. This language was particularly challenging because the intervening c-element required learners to keep track of non-adjacent dependencies, which are harder to acquire than adjacent ones (Newport and Aslin 2004). Additionally, the more complex language was instantiated in novel vocabulary, forcing learners to draw on their knowledge of the abstract structural relationships of the aX/bY language. In the absence of prior exposure to the more simple language, learners were unable to achieve the more complex generalization. This finding is important for showing how learners might build more complex structures by scaffolding on simpler ones.

Thus, constraints appear to play an important role in learning. In most of these studies researchers have asked whether learners can acquire some particular type of structure (frequency, co-occurrence, or conditional probabilities, etc.; see Gómez and Gerken 2000, 2001 for review), but in the real world children need to discriminate among multiple sources of structure. The next section addresses this topic.

4.4 Choosing among multiple kinds of structure

Learners faced with multiple types of structure have to determine which is relevant to the particular learning problem at hand. Various solutions to this problem weight the influence of innate sensitivities and sensitivity to statistical structure, and their degree of interaction, differentially. For instance, the emphasis in the principles and parameters view is predominantly on innate linguistic constraints. Structure in language plays only a minor role in triggering parameters. While the constrained statistical learning view emphasizes perceptual constraints on learning it does not specify the extent to which constraints interact with statistics when learners are faced with two or more kinds of information. Multiple cue integration emphasizes statistical information but does not specify how such information might interact with perceptual constraints. The prior experience view is agnostic on this issue. Thus, whereas constraints and statistics both play a role in learning theories, we know little about their interaction, especially when learners are faced with multiple sources of structure.

The possibilities range along a continuum. Learners at one end could be driven primarily by statistical structure, such that they simultaneously attend to multiple types of information and weight the importance of a particular type in terms of its statistical regularity. As such, learning should closely mirror statistical structure. Thus learners encountering two types of information should favor the more statistically probable one a greater proportion of the time. I will refer to this as the statistics-driven approach. A second possibility factors a hierarchy of constraints into the picture such that learners will attend more heavily to a favored structure even if the less favored one has greater statistical certainty. This solution assumes a more minimal role for statistical processing. I will refer to this possibility as the constraints-driven approach[2]. A possibility somewhere in the middle assumes some ordering of constraints, but further that learning will only adhere to a preferential structure to the extent that it occurs with some minimum degree of statistical certainty. Below that point learners will begin to track alternative sources of structure. Although certain kinds of information may have a more privileged status than others (because of perceptual salience, ease of processing, or prior learning), the ability to track statistical structure plays a key role in determining whether learners will focus on one type of structure or another. I will refer to this as the constraints + statistics approach.

In the next sections I will report a series of studies aimed at investigating the question of how learners choose among multiple types of structure. The first set of studies asks this question in the context of learning non-adjacent (or remote) dependencies in sequential structure.

4.4.1 Non-adjacent dependency learning

Remote dependencies in sequential structure feature in numerous high-level cognitive tasks including language (relationships between auxiliaries and inflectional morphemes as in '*is* runn*ing*' or '*has* eat*en*'), event knowledge (involving scripts that may have varying subevents), means-ends analysis in problem solving, and high-level planning. Such dependencies pose a considerable challenge in requiring learners to form relationships over irrelevant intervening material and are extremely difficult to acquire compared to adjacent dependencies (Newport and Aslin 2000, 2004). In contrast, adjacent dependencies appear to be privileged in terms of ease of learning or salience. As such, what might prompt learners to direct attention away from adjacent dependencies to some other form of structure?

---

[2] It is well understood in the machine learning literature that learning of any great complexity is impossible unless some constraints are part of the architecture (Geman *et al.* 1992). Overly constrained learning mechanisms will fail to register important variations in the environment and will have difficulty generalizing. In contrast, learning mechanisms driven only by statistics will show idiosyncratic variance as a function of the training set. Thus, a key objective in understanding learning is determining what constraints are necessary and the type and degree of interaction necessary between constraints and statistics.

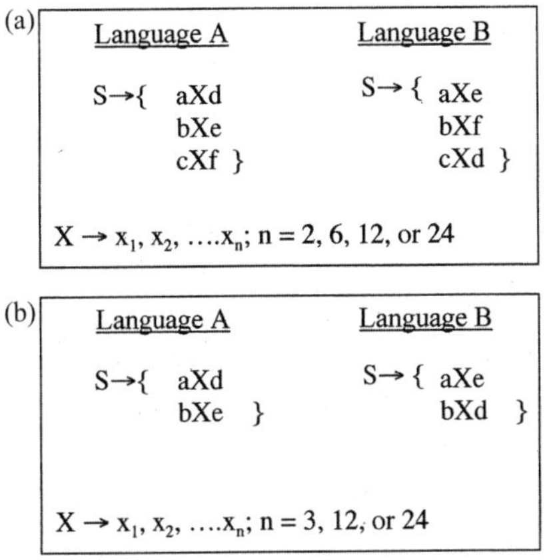

Fig. 4.1 (a) Languages used in with adult participants; (b) languages used with 18-month-old infants. From Gómez R (2002). Variability and detection of invariant structure. *Psychological Science*, **13**, 431–436. Reproduced with permission from Blackwell Publishing.

I first investigated this question by exposing adults to one of two artificial languages producing three-element strings (Gómez 2002). Strings were of the form aXb, cXd, and eXf in Language A (e.g. pel-kicey-jic) and aXd, bXf, and cXb in Language B (e.g. pel-kicey-rud) (Fig. 4.1). The elements a–f were pel, vot, dak, rud, jic, and tood. The 24 X-elements were wadim, kicey, puser, fengle, coomo, loga, gople, taspu, hiftam, deecha, vamey, skiger, benez, gensim, feenam, laeljeen, chila, roosa, plizet, balip, malsig, suleb, nilbo, and wiffle. Both languages contained the same adjacent dependencies, so these were not informative. Learners could only distinguish the languages by acquiring the non-adjacent dependencies. I systematically increased the size of the pool from which the middle element was drawn (set size = 2, 6, 12, 24) while holding the total number of strings heard during training constant to determine whether increasing variability (in the form of decreasing predictability between adjacent elements) would lead to better detection of non-adjacent dependencies (the set of 12 X-elements consisted of the first 12 words in the list, the set of six consisted of the first six, and so on). After an 18-min training phase, adult learners were tested on strings from the training language versus strings from the other language.

If learning were primarily driven by statistical structure, then learners should show a gradual increase in sensitivity to non-adjacent dependencies with an increase in set size. This is because conditional probabilities for adjacent dependencies go down as the variability of the middle element increases. However, if perceptual constraints are playing a role, learners might continue to track the privileged adjacent structure well beyond what is reasonable in terms of statistical regularity, then show an abrupt increase in sensitivity to non-adjacent structure when conditional probabilities are extremely low.

Consistent with the latter hypothesis, learners acquired non-adjacent dependencies only when the middle element was most variable, when adjacent dependencies were least predictable in set-size = 24. Accuracy across conditions in the adult study was 60 per cent (SEM = 8), 66 per cent (8.5), 65 per cent (8.5), and 90 per cent (5.5) for set sizes 2, 6, 12, and 24, respectively. In essence, performance was only slightly above chance for all but the condition with the highest variability. There was a similar pattern of results with 18-month-old infants as indicated by different listening times to strings from the training language versus the other language in a preferential listening procedure (Gómez 2002). Differences in the infant studies were that familiarization lasted for 3 min instead of 18 and infants were exposed to two non-adjacent dependencies instead of three. The infants discriminated the non-adjacent dependency when set size was 24 (mean looking time difference to grammatical versus ungrammatical strings = −2.07 s, SEM = 0.40), but not when it was 3 (mean difference = −0.04 s, SEM = 0.57) or 12 (mean difference = 0.35 s, SEM = 0.83).

One explanation for this finding is that learners focused on conditional probabilities between adjacent elements when these were relatively high (in the small set-size conditions), but when conditional probabilities between adjacent elements were sufficiently low (when set size was 24) the adjacent dependencies were no longer stable sources of structure. In this case learners focused instead on non-adjacent dependencies. Notably, learners did not show incremental increases in sensitivity to non-adjacent structure with incremental increases in variability of the middle element, a pattern we would expect if learners were responding primarily to the statistical structure. Rather they seemed to focus on adjacent dependencies long after these ceased providing reliable information. In set size 2 in the adult study, for example, the probability of the initial word being followed by a particular X-element was 0.33 (or 1 in 3). This probability decreased to 0.17, 0.08 and 0.04 with set sizes of 6, 12, and 24, respectively. In contrast, in all conditions the probability of the initial element being followed by a third element was 1. If responses to changes in conditional probabilities had been veridical, we might have expected to see learning of non-adjacent structure in the set size 6 condition (given the low conditional probability of 0.17). However, it was only after substantial variability was introduced in the middle that learners appeared to rely on the non-adjacent structure.

Subsequent research has shown that there is nothing special about a set size of 24. Gómez and Maye (2005) found that 17-month-olds can track non-adjacent structure with a set size of 18, but as in the original Gómez study, not with a set size of 12. Thus, what appears to be critical for getting learners to notice the non-adjacent dependencies is sufficient variability in the middle element where what constitutes 'sufficient' presumably varies as a function of the difficulty of the learning problem.

These results are important for increasing our understanding of how learners negotiate multiple kinds of structure and shed light on how constraints and statistical

Language A	Language B
S→{ aX	S→{ bX
Yb }	Ya }
a → a_1; b → b_1	
X → $x_1, x_2, \ldots x_n$; n=24	
Y → $y_1, y_2, \ldots x_n$; n=24	

Fig. 4.2 Languages used to contrast learning of co-occurrence and position with adult participants.

structure both contribute to this process. They provide insight into how structure in language input can steer learning in a dynamically guided process, one that arises in the interaction of preferences that guide learning initially but that change in response to environmental pressure. The structure motivating learning appears to change as learners encounter other more stable forms of structure.

One question we might ask is whether sensitivity to different kinds of structure implies different learning mechanisms. Work with simple recurrent networks suggests that the same mechanism may be engaged in both adjacent and non-adjacent forms of learning (Elman, personal communication; Onnis *et al.* 2004). However, other learning problems may require learners to choose among very different kinds of structure. Thus, as a next step we might ask whether learners will switch the focus of their learning for fundamentally different kinds of structure.

4.4.2 Learning to attend to position versus co-occurrence

My students and I (Gómez *et al.* 2005) selected a scenario that would potentially lead to learning of one kind of structure (co-occurrence) under one set of variability conditions and of an altogether different kind of structure (position) under another set of conditions, all the while keeping information about position the same. During training, adults were exposed to auditory strings of the form aX and Yb and on a later grammaticality test they had to distinguish these strings from strings of the form bX and Ya (Fig. 4.2). Additionally, X and Y elements were drawn from a set of 1 or 24 words. There was one a-element and one b, such that in the small set-size condition participants could either focus on specific bigrams (co-occurring elements) or on the position of particular words (or both). However, when set size was large, X and Y elements varied in relationship to the more stable as and bs, and so participants might pay more attention to a- and b-words as anchor points in strings (see Valian and Coulsen 1988). Importantly, participants could extract information about both co-occurrence and position in the small set-size condition because knowledge of the aX and Yb bigrams automatically yields knowledge of position. However, we were interested in determining whether learners would be more likely to notice one form of structure over another as a function of the variability of X- and Y-elements.

Introductory Psychology students at the University of Arizona were exposed to strings from one of two artificial languages during training. Language A produced sentences of the form aX and Yb. Language B produced sentences of the form bX and Ya. The a-word was pel and the b-word was vot. Learners in set size 1 were exposed to one X- and one Y-word, and thus heard two unique strings. Those in set size 24 were exposed to the 24 Xs and 24 Ys and thus heard 48 unique strings. The frequency of a- and b-words was held constant so that, for example, learners of Language A with set size 1 heard 24 instances of pel-coomo and 24 instances of wadim-vot and learners of set size 24 heard pel preceding each of 24 X-words and vot following 24 Y-words. The strings were presented in random order in a series of blocks with training lasting approximately 9 min.

We tested learners on strings with old versus new Xs and Ys. Participants should show different patterns of responding if the differences in variability of X- and Y-elements have led them to focus on different kinds of structure. Those who have focused on co-occurrence should accurately discriminate old grammatical strings from ungrammatical ones, but should perform poorly on strings with novel X- and Y-elements. Alternately, participants who have focused on the position of a- and b-elements should perform equally well regardless of whether test strings have old or new Xs and Ys.

After acquisition, participants were told they had been listening to an artificial language that followed a set of grammatical rules. Learning was tested in two ways, by a grammaticality test and by verbal report. The type of test was counterbalanced so that half of the participants received a grammaticality test followed by verbal report (the other half were tested in the opposite order). During the grammaticality test a string was played and learners were asked to judge whether it belonged to their training language by responding 'Yes' or 'No.' We obtained verbal reports by querying learners in increasing specificity, first asking whether they noticed any patterns or rules in the strings, next whether they could report specific strings, and finally we asked them to clarify and elaborate on their answers.

We measured grammaticality performance as the percentage of correct responses to items on the grammaticality test. The data resulted in a significant two-way inter-action of set size and old vs. new XYs such that learners in the set size 1 condition learned more about co-occurrence (M = 78 per cent accuracy, SEM = 1.5) than they did about position (M = 62 per cent, SEM = 2.2). Although there was some sensitivity to position (reflected in a comparison to chance [0.50]), learning was significantly greater for co-occurrence. In contrast, learners in the set size 24 conditions performed equally well when probed with strings containing old (M = 68 per cent, SEM = 1.7) versus new (M = 73 per cent, SEM = 2.3) X- and Y-elements. Furthermore, learning was significantly greater than chance.

The verbal reports were also revealing. We coded participants' responses in terms of their knowledge of rules and patterns characterizing strings. Co-occurrence knowledge was indicated by participants' ability to generate specific two-word phrases or by a general rule stating that there were four unique words combined as to form two two-word phrases. Participants received a verbal co-occurrence score of 1 for producing two grammatical strings or for stating the general rule, a score of 0.5 for producing one grammatical string, and a score of 0 for no verbal knowledge. Verbal knowledge of position was evidenced by stating that a particular word began strings, whereas, another ended them. Participants who stated this general rule and further specified the words used in a and b positions were given a score of 1. Those exhibiting verbal knowledge of only one a or b position were given a score of 0.5 and those exhibiting no verbal position knowledge were given a zero.

Consistent with the grammaticality judgments, verbal knowledge of co-occurrence was significantly higher for set size 1 (M = 0.73, SEM = 0.08) than for set size 24 learners (M = 0.17, SEM = 0.07). Thirty of 48 participants received the maximum score of 1 in set size 1. Six of 48 participants received the maximum score of 1 in set size 24.

Verbal knowledge of position was significantly lower for set size 1 (M = 0.02, SEM = 0.004) than for set size 24 learners (M = 0.54, SEM = 0.11). One participant (of 48) received a maximum score of 1 in set size 1, whereas 23 received the maximum score in set size 24.

In summary, verbal information generated by participants in set size 1 almost entirely reflected knowledge of co-occurrence. In contrast, verbal knowledge of position predominated in the set size 24 condition. Furthermore, seven participants in this condition spontaneously reported that the a- and b-words 'popped out,' whereas none of the participants in set size 1 reported such an effect. Although information about position was available to learners in the set size 1 condition, what was most relevant to them was the co-occurrence relationship between adjacent items. In set size 24, the relevant information was position of the a and b-elements.

The purpose of this pilot study was to determine whether variability of the X- and Y-elements would cause learners to focus on one type of structure in the stimulus over another, and to do so under conditions that would require very different forms of learning. If information about co-occurrence is privileged, then with a set size of 1 learners might focus on specific bigrams even though information about position was present. With a larger set size, however, learners might focus on anchor points in strings created by the relative stability of a- and b-elements in relationship to the changing Xs and Ys. Consistent with our hypothesis, learning appeared to be guided primarily by the most stable structure.

It could be protested that the extreme set sizes of 1 and 24 trivialized learning. After all, participants in set size 1 heard the same two strings repeatedly for a period of minutes and so it is not surprising to find learning of this information. However, the choice of extremes was deliberate given the desire to maximize learning, especially in the set size 1 condition where learners were more likely to acquire two kinds of structure. Nevertheless, only one participant (of 48) in set size 1 abstracted a rule involving anchor position, even though position should be easy to infer from memory of specific bigrams. It appears that what people learn is entirely different in the two conditions.

With that said, additional empirical work is in order. In particular, it will be important to test less extreme set size manipulations. We will also want to test increments of increasing variability between the extremes to explore how much variability in X- and Y-elements is necessary before learners become aware of position. How closely will sensitivity to position match the statistical decrease in conditional probabilities that accompanies an increase in set size? Will this reflect a different relationship between constraints and statistics than was suggested by Gómez (2002)? It will also be important to investigate these questions with younger learners. Such studies are currently underway.

The current study was useful for determining the conditions that might lead to attention to position versus co-occurrence; however, both forms of structure were concrete. Given that a critical milestone in learning is generalization, it is important to ask what might lead learners to focus on abstract versus concrete structure. We investigated this with 12-month-old infants in the context of form-based category abstraction.

4.4.3   The role of variability in category-based abstraction

Abstraction is the very root of complex learning. Indeed, the generative power of human language stems from our human ability to generalize from one instance to another. Once a novel word is categorized, language learners can automatically apply syntactic constraints associated with other words in its category. Given the centrality of categorization in language, it becomes necessary to ask how children achieve this kind of generalization.

A widely held view emphasizes the discovery of categories by first noting semantic or referential information (Grimshaw 1981; Pinker 1984); however, it is crucial to ask how children might begin to identify categories in the sound structure of language. Although semantic information most certainly plays a role, prelinguistic infants are limited in their knowledge of semantics. In contrast, they are acutely attuned to the sound properties of language (Juszcyk 1997). If infants can identify categories in the speech stream by means of phonological cues, they might then use this informa- tion to learn predictive relationships between categories. In English, for example, children must learn that function words such as 'the' and 'a' precede nouns and not verbs, whereas 'will' and 'can' precede verbs but not nouns. Infants who have identified categories in speech and the relationships between them will be at an advantage with respect to the later task of mapping between meaning and form, compared to children who only begin this process once semantic knowledge is more fully in place (Gómez and Gerken 2000).

In previous work (Gómez and Lakusta 2004), we have explored the foundations of this process by asking whether 12-month-olds would learn the relationship between functor-like a- and b-words and X- and Y-categories. During training infants were exposed to one of two training languages. One language consisted of aX and bY pairings, the other consisted of aY and bX pairs. Xs were instantiated as disyllabic words and Ys were monosyllabic. Syllable number was used as an abstract feature because information like this abounds in language. In English for instance, nouns tend to have more syllables than verbs and also tend to receive first syllable stress (Kelly 1992). Additionally, children are sensitive to these phonological cues (Cassidy and Kelly 1991). We tested infants on new phrases from their training language versus phrases from the other language. All X- and Y-words were novel at test. Infants were able to generalize to the novel sentences, suggesting that they had become sensitive to the relationships between the particular a- and b-elements and an abstract feature (syllable number). It is important to point out that although prosody is a factor (infants have to notice that X- and Y-words have either one or two syllables), this is not merely a prosodic effect. Infants had to learn to associate certain a- and b-words with particular syllable features.

I am currently using this paradigm to determine the conditions that might lead learners to focus on abstract versus concrete information by asking whether the same age infants will generalize with a smaller set size. If so, this would suggest that they are equally able to extract abstract features under conditions of low and high variability, implying that variability manipulations do not contribute to abstraction. However, if infants fail to discriminate, this suggests that abstraction is aided by exposure to a larger number of instances.

Twenty-four 12-month-old infants exposed to six Xs and six Ys (these data were originally reported in Gómez and Lakusta 2004, Experiment 1) were compared with another group exposed to a set size of 3 (Fig. 4.3). During training infants were exposed to strings from one of two training languages, A or B. Each language contained two a-elements (alt, ush) and two bs (ong and erd). In the Set-size 6 condition, there were 6 X-s (coomo, fengle, kicey, loga, paylig, wazil), and six Ys (deech, ghope, jic, skige, vabe, tam). A subset of these was used in the Set-size 3 condition so that there were three Xs and three Ys. X-elements were disyllabic and Ys were monosyllabic, thus infants could either attend to specific X- and Y-words or to the abstract feature of syllable number. The elements were combined to form grammatical phrases (e.g. alt coomo and erd deech in Language A). Strings were uttered in the same infant-directed speech with the same rising intonation structure. For each language in set-size 6 there were 24 phrases presented in random order. For Set-size 3, there were 12 phases. These were presented twice as often as in Set-size 6 to preserve the frequency of a- and b-words with the one- and two-syllable forms. Thus in both

Language A	Language B
$S \rightarrow \{$ aX	$S \rightarrow \{$ bX
bY $\}$	aY $\}$
$a \rightarrow a_1, a_2$; $b \rightarrow b_1, b_2$	
$X \rightarrow x_1, x_2, ... x_n$; $n = 3$ or 6	
$Y \rightarrow y_1, y_2, ... y_n$; $n = 3$ or 6	

Fig. 4.3 Languages used to contrast learning of co-occurrence versus abstract marker-feature relationships with 12-month-old infants.

set-size conditions the relationship between the a- and b-words and the abstract features were the same. The only difference was in the variability of the X- and Y-category members. The question was whether higher variability would aid abstraction of the category cue.

Each infant was tested using an auditory preference procedure. X- and Y-words were novel at test and thus differential listening times for legal versus illegal strings would indicate generalization of the abstract feature. Per the results of Gómez and Lakusta (2004), infants in the set size 6 condition listened longer to strings from their training language than to strings from the other language, M = 8.44 s (SEM = 0.72) versus M = 7.06 s (SEM = 0.6). Eighteen out of 24 infants showed this pattern, suggesting that they had acquired some sensitivity to the category-based structure of their training grammar. There were no differences in listening times in the set size 3 condition however, M = 8.25 s (SEM = 2.07) to strings from the training grammar and 9.66 s (SEM = 2.01) to the other grammar. Twelve out of 24 infants listened longer to strings from their training grammar. This is interesting in light of the fact that infants this age are extremely sensitive to prosodic structure induced by one-versus two-element words. Apparently prosody was not a strong enough cue to produce generalization to strings containing novel X- and Y-elements even though these strings maintained the prosody from training.

The ability to discriminate legal from illegal marker-feature pairings in the set size 6 condition, despite the fact that X and Y elements were novel at test, reflects sensitivity to the co-occurrence relations between markers and X and Y categories based on their abstract features. Such learning is complex – infants had to track four markers, associate them with abstract features, and generalize to pairings containing novel words. The fact that infants were able to generalize to novel X- and Y-elements suggests that learning was abstract (involving grouping of the X- and Y-elements according to syllable number). However abstraction appears to be dependent on the amount of variability in the X- and Y-elements. Infants in the set size 3 condition showed no generalization. One interpretation is that learners in the high variability condition learned a relationship between a- and b-words and abstract features whereas learners in the low variability condition were tracking specific co-occurrence relationships. I am currently collecting data to determine whether learners in the set size 3 condition will distinguish strings heard during training from ungrammatical ones. This is important for establishing whether infants in this condition were tracking specific aX and bY bigrams. If so, this would add to the argument that under conditions of low variability infants focus on the co-occurrence relation between specific aX or bY pairs, whereas with enough variability they abstract higher-order prosodic features. It would also add to the argument that learning is driven by an interaction between innate sensitivities and environmental structure. Under certain conditions learners show a tendency to track co-occurrence (possibly a default sensitivity), but with enough variability in their input, they will seek out other forms of reliably cued structure. Thus, it is in the interaction of particular sensitivities (or constraints) and environmental structure that learning unfolds dynamically.

4.5 **Summary**

The aim of this chapter has been to summarize the literature on statistical learning, especially with regard to addressing the problem of how learners might choose among multiple kinds of structure, whether the process might be guided primarily by constraints, primarily by statistics, or whether it might arise in the interaction of constraints and statistics. In all three of the cases highlighted (adjacent vs. non-adjacent dependencies, co-occurrence vs. position, and co-occurrence vs. abstraction) we see similar patterns. Learners easily track information about co-occurrence suggesting that this may be a preferred form of structure, but with enough variability in their input, they will focus on alternate structure, suggesting how learning might be guided in the interaction of constraints and the pressures exerted by the structure learners hear.

At first glance, it might seem paradoxical that variability can aid learning. Indeed, on most accounts high variability should result in increased noise and thus decreased learning. However, high variability acts to increase the salience of information, and in this way may facilitate learning. This is consistent with the idea that learning involves a tendency to seek out invariant structure, or structure remaining constant across varying contexts (EJ Gibson 1969; JJ Gibson 1966). More specifically, even though multiple types of structure were present, learners in these studies appeared to rely on one type of structure at a time. For example in the case of learning long-distance dependencies, even though the information about these was identical in all of the set-size conditions (the conditional probability of the non-adjacent dependencies was 1.0), adjacency appeared invariant when adjacent conditional probabilities were relatively high (in the small set-size conditions). It was only when adjacent conditional probabilities were sufficiently low (as when the middle element was drawn from a set of 24) that the non-adjacent dependencies stood out as invariant structure. Additionally, in the study comparing learning of co-occurrence and position, information about position of a-and b-elements was the same in the low (set size = 1) and high variability (set size = 24) conditions. Yet, learners showed little sensitivity to position when variability was low. Finally, variability appears to play a role in abstraction. Although 12-month-old infants generalized an abstract feature (syllable number) in a high variability condition (set size = 6) they did not do so with set size = 3. Although there is still much to do in this line of research, the initial findings are intriguing. They suggest that learning arises in the interaction of perceptual sensitivities and statistical structure and suggest how structure learners encounter might guide learning.

What of Pinker's contention that children need either to be constrained from erroneous hypothesizing or have a means for recovery when they do overgeneralize? If these studies are to be believed, there is little evidence of rampant overgeneralization in statistical learning. Instead learners appear to be conservative in their hypothesizing. In particular, in the case of non-adjacent dependencies learners seem to need a great deal of variability to reveal the invariance of the non-adjacent structure. Learners are also quite conservative about certain types of generalizations. The studies of Braine (1987), Frigo and McDonald (1998), and Gerken *et al.* (2005) demonstrate this fact. In particular, learners will not abstract categories in an aX/bY paradigm unless they have good reason to do so, namely when cues are present for distinguishing at least some of the category structure.

In the event that children do make erroneous generalizations, how might they recover? Recent work in memory reconsolidation is relevant to this issue. According to this literature, memory is much more dynamic than was previously thought (Nader 2003). Far from being permanent, when accessed, memories are put into a labile state. Once in this state memories can be reinforced, but just as easily changed or overridden. Especially relevant to the problem of how learners might recover from overgeneralizations, Walker *et al.* (2003) found that knowledge of a reactivated sequence (in a sequence learning task) could be overwritten by a new sequence if exposure to the new sequence was immediate. Learners showed robust memory for a sequence after both 1- and 2-day delays, but if another sequence was presented immediately after activating the first, then memory of the first sequence was hindered. In contrast, memory of the second sequence was intact.

A similar process could be instrumental in language acquisition. If we assume that hypotheses are activated by memory, then we must also assume that engaging them puts them into a fragile state. Once activated, erroneous hypotheses become subject to change. In particular, because of the data-driven nature of learning, overly general hypotheses are likely to be replaced by more specific ones. In short, given the dynamic nature of memory and its reconsolidation processes, as well as the data driven nature of learning, it seems unlikely that learners will hold fast to erroneous or overly general hypotheses without good evidence for doing so. We are currently conducting studies investigating this hypothesis.

With this said, there are many challenges for learning approaches. One has to do with better characterizing learning processes. A particular challenge goes out to computational modelers. Although a Simple Recurrent Network has been successful at modeling acquisition of adjacent and non-adjacent dependencies (Onnis *et al.* 2005), the model did not exhibit the abrupt increase in performance found in the Gómez (2002) data. Instead, it showed an incremental increase in sensitivity to non-adjacent structure. Although connectionist models are capable of exhibiting non-linear behavior, this particular model did not do so. It is also important to know more about the accuracy with which learners track statistical structure. Do learners keep track of fine gradations or do they track structure by means of broad categories or thresholds? Support for the latter would be consistent with a constraints + statistics approach. There is also a great deal more to learn about the initial state. We may be able to characterize constraint hierarchies of learning (how different forms of learning are ordered in terms of salience or learnability) in terms of how easily certain types of structure are learned compared to others. Memory studies may also be informative in this respect in terms of the extent to which different forms of learning can be reinforced or disrupted. Tenacity, in terms of the amount of variability necessary for switching learners to another state, may also reveal the ordering of sensitivities in a constraint hierarchy.

In all, the present literature on learning paints a very different picture from that portrayed in traditional characterizations (Chomsky 1965; Pinker 1995). Indeed, the conservative nature of learning, combined with a dynamic memory process, conspires against traditional assumptions. Statistical learning appears to be a process akin to perceptual tuning, partially guided by constraints, but also to a great extent by environmental structure, yielding in the interaction of these pressures a dynamic, adaptive, and flexible process.

Acknowledgements

Writing of this chapter was supported by NSF BCS-0238584 and NIH R01 HD42170–01. I would like to thank Y. Munakata, R. Schvaneveldt, and two anonymous reviewers for helpful comments and suggestions.

References

Aslin R, Saffran J and Newport E (1998). Computation of conditional probability statistics by 8-month-olds infants. *Psychological Science*, **9**, 321–324.

Bever T (1970). The cognitive basis for linguistic structures. In: J Hayes, ed. *Cognition and the development of language*, pp. 279–362. New York: Wiley.

Billman D (1989). Systems of correlations in rule and category learning: Use of structured input in learning syntactic categories. *Language and Cognitive Processes*, **4**, 127–155.

Braine M (1987). What is learned in acquiring words classes: A step toward acquisition theory. In: B MacWhinney, ed. *Mechanisms of language acquisition*, pp. 65–87. Hillsdale, New Jersey: Erlbaum.

Brown R and Hanlon C (1970). Derivational complexity and order of acquisition in child speech. In: JR Hayes, ed. *Cognition and the development of language.* pp. 11–53 New York: Wiley.

Cassidy K and Kelly M (1991). Phonological information for grammatical category assignments. *Journal of Memory and Language,* **14**, 333–352.

Chomsky N (1965). *Aspects of the theory of syntax.* Cambridge, Massachusetts: MIT Press.

Chomsky N (1981). *Lectures on government and binding.* Dordrecht, Netherlands: Foris.

Christiansen M and Curtin S (2004). Integrating multiple cues in language acquisition: a computational study of early infant speech segmentation. In: G Houghton, ed. *Connectionist models in cognitive psychology.* Hove, UK: Psychology Press.

Christiansen M and Dale R (2001). Integrating distributional, prosodic, and phonological information in a connectionist model of language acquisition. In: J Moore and K Stenning, eds. *Proceedings of the 23rd Annual Conference of the Cognitive Science Society,* pp. 220–225. Mahweh, New Jersey: Lawrence Erlbaum.

Fernald A, and McRoberts G (1996) Prosodic bootstrapping: a critical analyses of the argument and the evidence. In: J Morgan and K Demuth, eds. *Signal to syntax: Bootstrapping from speech to grammar in early acquisition,* pp. 365–88. Mahwah, NJ: Lawrence Erlbaum Associates

Fiser J and Aslin R (2002a). Statistical learning of new visual feature combinations by infants. *Proceedings of the National Academy of Sciences,* **99**, 15822–15826.

Fiser J and Aslin R (2002b). Statistical learning of higher-order temporal structure from visual shape sequences. *Journal of Experimental Psychology: Learning, Memory, and Cognition,* **28**, 458–467.

Frigo L and McDonald J (1998). Properties of phonological markers that affect the acquisition of gender-like subclasses. *Journal of Memory and Language,* **39**, 218–245.

Gemen S, Bienenstock E, and Doursat, R (1992). Neural Networks and the Bias/Variance Dilemma. *Neural Computation,* **4**, 1–58.

Gerken LA (2005). What develops in language development? In: R Kail, ed., Advances in Child Development and Behavior (Vol. 33, pp. 153–92). San Diego, CA: Elsevier.

Gerken LA, Wilson R and Lewis W (2005). Seventeen-month-olds can use distributional cues to form syntactic categories. *Journal of Child Language.*

Gibson EJ (1969). *Principles of perceptual learning and development.* New York: Meredith Corporation.

Gibson JJ (1966). *The senses considered as perceptual systems.* Boston: Houghton Mifflin.

Gold E (1967). Language identification in the limit. *Information and Control,* **16**, 447–474.

Gómez R (2002). Variability and detection of invariant structure. *Psychological Science,* **13**, 431–436.

Gómez R and Gerken LA (1999). Artificial grammar learning by one-year-olds leads to specific and abstract knowledge. *Cognition,* **70**, 109–135.

Gómez R and Gerken LA (2000). Infant artificial language learning and language acquisition. *Trends in Cognitive Sciences,* **4**, 178–186.

Gómez R and Gerken LA (2001). Artificial language learning as a means for investigating language acquisition. In: M Tomasello and E Bates, eds. *Essential readings in language development,* pp. 42–48. Oxford/New York: Basil Blackwell.

Gómez R, Gerken LA and Schvaneveldt R (2000). The basis of transfer in artificial grammar learning. *Memory and Cognition,* **28**, 253–263.

Gómez R and Lakusta L (2004). A first step in form-based category abstraction by 12-month-old infants. *Developmental Science,* **7**, 567–580.

Gómez R and Maye J (in press). The developmental trajectory of nonadjacent dependency learning. *Infancy*.

Gómez R, Welch K and Lany J (2005). Statistically guided learning. In preparation.

Grimshaw J (1981). Form, function, and the language acquisition device. In: C Baker and J McCarthy, eds. *The logical problem of language acquisition*. pp. 165–82 Cambridge, Massachusetts: MIT Press.

Hauser M, Newpor E, Asli R (2001). Segmentation of the speech stream in a non-human primate: statistical learning in cotton-top tamarins. *Cognition*, 78, B53–B64.

Hunter M and Ames E (1988). A multifactor model of infant preferences for novel and familiar stimuli. *Advances in Infancy Research*, 5, 69–95.

Jusczyk P (1997). *The discovery of spoken language*. Cambridge, MA: MIT Press.

Kelly M (1992). Using sound to solve syntactic problems: The role of phonology in grammatical category assignments. *Psychological Review*, 99, 349–364.

Kemler Nelson D, Jusczyk P, Mandel D, Myers J, Turk A and Gerken LA (1995). The head-turn preference procedure for testing auditory perception. *Infant Behavior and Development*, 18, 111–116.

Kirkham N, Slemmer J and Johnson S (2002). Visual statistical learning in infancy: evidence for a domain general learning mechanism. *Cognition*, 83, B35–B42.

Lany J and Gómez R (2004). The role of prior learning in biasing generalization in artificial language learning. *Proceedings of the 26th Annual Conference of the Cognitive Science Society, Chicago, IL*.

Lany J, Gómez R and Gerken LA (2005). The role of prior learning in the transfer of category structure. Submitted.

Marcus G (1993). Negative evidence in language acquisition. *Cognition*, 46, 53–85.

Marcus G, Vijayan S, Bandi Rao S and Vishton P (1999). Rule learning by seven-month-old infants. *Science*, 283, 77–80.

Morgan J and Demuth K, eds. (1996). *Signal to syntax*. Mahwah, New Jersey: Erlbaum.

Morgan J, Meier R and Newport E (1987). Structural packaging in the input to language learning: Contributions of prosodic and morphological marking of phrases to the acquisition of language. *Cognitive Psychology*, 19, 498–450.

Nader K (2003). Memory traces unbound. *Trends in Neurosciences*, 26, 65–72.

Newport E and Aslin R (2000). Innately constrained learning: Blending old and new approaches to language acquisition. In: S Howell, S Fish and T Keith-Lucas, eds. *Proceedings of the 24th Annual Boston University Conference on Language Development*, pp. 1–21. Somerville, MA: Cascadilla Press.

Newport E and Aslin R (2004). Learning at a distance: I. Statistical learning of non-adjacent dependencies. *Cognitive Psychology*, 48, 127–162.

Onnis L, Destrebecqz A, Christiansen M, Chater N and Cleeremans A (2005). Processing nonadjacent dependencies: A graded, associative account. Submitted.

Pinker S (1984). *Language learnability and language development*. Cambridge, MA: Harvard University Press.

Pinker S (1995). Language acquisition. In: L Gleitman and M Liberman, eds. *Language. An invitation to cognitive science*, 2nd edn, vol. 1. Cambridge, MA: MIT Press.

Saffran J (2002). Constraints on statistical language learning. *Journal of Memory and Language*, 47, 172–196.

Saffran J (2003). Statistical language learning: Mechanisms and constraints. *Current Directions in Psychological Science*, 12, 110–114.

Saffran J, Aslin R and Newport E (1996a) Statistical learning by eight-month-old infants. *Science,* 274, 1926–1928.

Saffran J, Johnson E, Asli R and Newport E (1999). Statistical learning of tonal structure by adults and infants. *Cognition,* 70, 27–52.

Saffran J, Newport E and Aslin R (1996b). Word segmentation: The role of distributional cues. *Journal of Memory and Language,* 35, 606–621.

Saffran J, Newport E, Aslin R, Tunick R and Barrueco S (1997). Incidental language learning: Listening (and learning) out of the corner of your ear. *Psychological Science,* 8, 101–105.

Saffran J and Thiessen E (2003). Pattern induction by infant language learners. *Developmental Psychology,* 39, 484–494.

Saffran J and Wilson D (2003). From syllables to syntax: Multi-level statistical learning by 12-month-old infants. *Infancy,* 4, 273–284.

Santelmann L and Jusczyk P (1998). Sensitivity to discontinuous dependencies in language learners: evidence for limitations in processing space. *Cognition,* 69, 105–134.

Smith K (1969). Learning co-occurrence restrictions: Rule learning or rote learning? *Journal of Verbal Behavior,* 8, 319–321.

Thiessen E and Saffran J (2003). When cues collide: Use of stress and statistical cues to word boundaries by 7- to 9-month-old infants. *Developmental Psychology,* 39, 706–716.

Valian V and Coulson S (1988). Anchor points in language learning: The role of marker frequency. *Journal of Memory and Language,* 27, 71–86.

Walker M, Brakefield T, Hobson J and Stickgold R (2003). Dissociable stages of human memory consolidation and reconsolidation. *Nature,* 425, 616–620.

Wexler K and Culicover P (1980). *Formal principles of language acquisition.* Cambridge, MA: MIT Press.

Wilson R (2002). *Category induction in second language learning: What artificial grammars can tell us.* Unpublished Ph.D. dissertation. University of Arizona.

Chapter 5

Core mechanisms of word learning

Lori Markson

Abstract

Children's striking ability to learn new words quickly and efficiently has spurred scholars to pinpoint the mechanism at its core. An ongoing controversy has concerned whether word learning results from a domain-specific mechanism or depends on more general abilities. One prevalent view is that children utilize multiple cues when acquiring new word meanings, suggesting a host of capacities may be influential in this process. Such capacities include more general cognitive abilities of attention and memory, lexical-specific constraints, and sensitivity to the intentions of others. What cognitive capacities are fundamental to word learning? Two approaches my colleagues and I have taken to address this question are comparing children's learning of words with the learning of non-linguistic information, and investigating the impact of children's understanding of communicative intent on the acquisition of words and facts. The findings of these studies, combined with those from diverse research programs, favor the view that word learning is not the result of a specialized language mechanism. Rather, some human capacities that are in place and used for other purposes are recruited for the task of learning words. Preliminary findings from recent studies with infants further explore the capacities that underlie early word learning.

5.1 Introduction

A fundamental question in the study of the mind is how children learn the meanings of words. To a naïve observer the act of learning a word might look fairly straightforward. A pancake is flipped onto a child's plate, she is handed a fork and told '...eat your pancake, Sophie', and a new word is learned over breakfast. But scholars intimate with the problem of word learning know that children must overcome a number of obstacles before the meaning of a word is acquired.

First, the child must isolate the word from the stream of speech in which it is spoken. Thus, in the example above, the novel form *pancake* must be segmented from the rest of the phrase. Second, the child must determine that the form *pancake* refers to the thing that recently fell onto her plate, and not the fork she was given to eat the pancake with, the syrup that was poured onto the pancake, just those parts of the pancake that are covered in syrup, the action of the pancake hitting the plate, and so on. Since all of these interpretations (and an infinite number of others) are equally plausible, how can the child know which entity the new word describes? In order to solve this problem of referential indeterminacy the child must somehow pick out which concept a new word maps onto from an infinite number of logical possibilities (Quine 1960). Third, once the proper translation of the new word has been inferred, the mapping between form and meaning must be established, and this mapping must be remembered over time. Each of these steps is an essential component of integrating a new word into a child's lexicon.

Despite these hurdles, children do manage to learn the words of their language, and they do so with a swiftness and ease that allows one to pardon the naïve observer for overlooking the complexities of this task in the first place. It is estimated that children know thousands of words before formal education even begins, suggesting that they must be learning many words a day throughout the preschool years (Anglin 1993; Miller 1991). Given these striking statistics, Carey (1978, p. 265) speculated that:

The only way to begin to account for the child's wizardry as a word learner, given the sheer weight of how much there is to be learned, is to grant that the child brings a great deal to the 'original word game'.

Such speculation about how children solve the problem of word learning has also been raised by philosophers. Word learning has been described as a classic problem of induction. Upon hearing a new word, a child is faced with an infinite number of logically possible meanings. This question was elegantly posed by Quine (1960) in his classic 'Gavagai' example. Imagine a situation in which a linguist, who knows nothing of the language being spoken in a foreign land, witnesses a native say the word 'Gavagai' as a rabbit runs past. Quine argued that there is no way for the linguist to know with certainty that 'Gavagai' refers to *rabbit*, and not rabbit-tail, brown rabbit running, rabbit-hood, or any one of an infinity of other logical possibilities. Children face a similar problem when confronted with a new word. As a result, determining the referent of an unfamiliar word poses a formidable task for the young child. Yet, children manage to learn words, thus a solution must be available to them. How children solve this problem of reference that is inherent in word learning has been the subject of much debate, raising deep questions about the nature of the mechanisms underlying word learning.

This chapter concerns the skills children require to learn the words of their language. I will first discuss a prevalent view that posits that children possess special constraints that aid them in learning the meanings of words. I then offer an alternative proposal, based on converging findings from a number of studies, demonstrating that many so-called constraints are actually not specific to word learning. I propose, instead, that children's remarkable word learning abilities are the result of more general cognitive abilities that together comprise the core mechanisms of word learning (Markson 1999; Bloom 2000). I will then present some preliminary findings from two lines of current research that investigate the nature of one such capacity – children's ability to rapidly learn and remember information about objects.

5.1.1 Domain-general versus domain-specific learning

By now, a wealth of research has revealed infants are sensitive to prosodic cues, distributional information, and structure available in the input and use this informa-tion to parse the stream of spoken words infants regularly hear (Gomez 2002; Jusczyk 1997; Saffran *et al.* 1996). In addition, by 8 months infants have been found to recognize the sound pattern of spoken words and remember them as long as 2 weeks later (Jusczyk and Aslin 1995; Jucszyk and Hohne 1997). Since a critical component of learning a new word is remembering the relationship between a phonological form and the entity to which it refers, these findings show that by the end of the first year of life, infants have successfully tackled the first major obstacle of word learning.

But how *do* children determine the meaning of a word, and learn and remember so many of them? Is there a special mechanism underlying children's capacity to learn words? One possible explanation is that word learning results from a dedicated language mechanism. The idea that a specific part of the brain is dedicated to solving a particular task is not new, especially in the study of language acquisition. Support for a biological specialization for language comes from studies that reveal a matur-ational time course as well as critical periods for the development of certain aspects of language, such as syntax and phonology (Curtiss 1989; Newport 1990; cf. Seidenberg and Zevin, Chapter 25 this volume). Probably the most compelling argument for a biological specialization for language is based on the impoverished input available to language learners. That children acquire grammatical knowledge through limited and impoverished experience and in the absence of negative evidence has led linguists to posit internal mechanisms (Chomsky 1986; Marcus 1993; see also Hauser *et al.* 2002). However, this does not necessarily hold for *meaning*, as parents frequently check on their child's intended meaning, and often offer reformulations of children's errors that can serve as negative evidence (Chouinard and Clark 2003).

It is possible that word learning and grammar may involve different mechanisms (Pinker 1991). Research with neurologically impaired populations offers some sup-port for a neural dissociation between the memory systems responsible for lexical information and grammatical rules (Ullman *et al.* 1996). Further evidence for a dissociation between syntactic and lexical processes stems from event-related brain potential (ERP) studies showing that lexical information is processed differently from grammatical information in both children and adults. Studies measuring ERPs of deaf and bilingual populations reveal different critical periods for lexical and grammatical knowledge (Neville *et al.* 1992; Weber-Fox and Neville 1996). Finally, twin studies have revealed a dissociation between vocabulary and grammar for heritability. The results of one study suggest that environmental input may not be as necessary for grammatical development as vocabulary acquisition, and conversely that heritability might not be as important for word learning as it is for the acquisition of grammar, suggesting that these two aspects of language might be acquired differently (Ganger 1998). Taken together, the findings suggest that children's ability to learn words may depend on a separate mechanism than that which is responsible for the development of syntactic knowledge.

In contrast, there is ample evidence supporting the opposite position, that a single domain-general mechanism underlies children's grammatical and lexical development (Bates *et al.* 1988; Bates and Goodman 1997). Studies examining language development in normal and atypical children have found that the emergence of grammar is correlated with vocabulary size. These findings suggest that lexical and grammatical development are governed by the same mechanism. Simulations of language learning in connectionist models provide additional support for this unified approach to mechanisms underlying language acquisition (Elman 1993; Elman *et al.* 1996).

Irrespective of the outcome of these broader arguments, more specific to word learning is the proposal that children are equipped with internal constraints that allow them to narrow down the hypothesis space that must be considered in determining the referent of a novel word (Markman 1989, 1990). It is important to note that proponents of theories positing lexical constraints vary with regard to whether the biases children have about word meanings are innate or learned, although they agree (at least implicitly) that these constraints apply specifically to the task of word learning (Golinkoff *et al.* 1992; Markman 1992; Waxman 1990). This view has not gone unchallenged and will be revisited in more detail in the section that follows (Bloom 2000; Nelson 1988; Regier 2003; Smith *et al.* 1996).

5.1.2 Specialized word learning biases and constraints

How do children learn words so quickly and effortlessly given the ambiguity of the context in which things are named? For years, the predominant view of how children solve this induction problem was the constraints approach (Golinkoff *et al.* 1994; Markman 1989, 1990). Constraint theories posit that children have internal lexical constraints that bias them to favor certain inferences or hypotheses over others when determining the meaning of a new word, thereby drastically reducing the number of possible meanings a child must consider.

According to various constraint theories, if a child is shown an object and told to 'Look at the *blicket*,' children are more likely to assume that *blicket* denotes the whole-object rather than a part or property of the object. Golinkoff and her colleagues interpret this response bias as an adherence to a principle of object scope, and by Markman as a whole object constraint. Similarly, in the above situation, children tend to assume that *blicket* is a name for other objects similar in kind to the original object, what Golinkoff refers to as a principle of categorical scope, and Markman as a taxonomic constraint. Third, children will assume that *blicket* refers to an object for which they do not know a name, rather than to an object for which they already know the name. This response is thought to result from the novel-name nameless-category (N3C) principle (Golinkoff *et al.* 1992) or the mutual exclusivity assumption (Markman and Wachtel 1988).

The word learning constraints described above have traditionally been shown to be present in preschool age children, leaving open the question of whether constraints are in place at the start of word learning, or some learning must be accomplished before they kick in. More recently, a number of researchers have started exploring the origin of these so-called constraints by examining them in infants. Markman and her colleagues (2003) tested whether the mutual exclusivity assumption is in place before 18 months, an age at which children's word learning accelerates rapidly. In their studies, 15- to 17- and 18- to 20-month-old infants, resisted learning second labels for familiar objects, and tended to search for the referent of a novel name, if one was not immediately visible. The findings were taken to suggest that lexical constraints – and specifically the mutual exclusivity assumption – are in place prior to the time children become rapid word learners (see also Halberda 2003 for a different perspective). Interestingly, a recent study found that a border collie could infer the referent of a new word based on something akin to a mutual exclusivity principle (Kaminski *et al.* 2004); however, this claim has been challenged by a number of convincing alternative explanations to account for the dog's apparent learning by exclusion (Markman and Abelev 2004).

Smith and her colleagues offer a quite different explanation for another prominent bias observed in children's extension of novel names – the shape bias – which proposes that children tend to determine the name of a novel object on the basis of shape (Landau *et al.* 1988). This claim is based on countless studies which have shown that when 3- and 4-year-old children are taught a new name for a novel object, they tend to extend the name to other objects that are similar in shape, rather than other perceptual features such as size and color, or conceptual information such as function (Jones *et al.* 1991; Landau *et al.* 1998). A more recent study explored the origin of the shape bias, by asking whether experience learning new object names – particularly for categories based strongly on shape – would facilitate infants' learning of new words (Smith *et al.* 2002). Seventeen-month-old infants who were trained on hearing names for categories organized primarily by shape, showed a marked increase in word learning over the course of 9 weeks. The findings were interpreted as evidence that the shape bias is acquired through experience learning words. Specifically, as they learn words, children learn to attend to the perceptual properties relevant for lexical extension, namely shape.

The two examples provided above investigating the emergence of word-learning constraints or biases in infants address two different biases (mutual exclusivity, shape bias) and the results are taken to support two strongly divergent views. The constraints approach proposed by Markman and her colleagues (1990) argues for a specialized word learning mechanism, whereas Smith and her colleagues (1996) posit that more general mechanisms of attention suffice, a seemingly more parsimonious explanation.

5.1.3 Intentional understanding contributes to word learning

Another means by which children can solve the problem of reference inherent in word learning is through their pragmatic knowledge or theory of mind capacities, most specifically an ability to understand the referential intent of others. Over a decade of research has provided the field with solid evidence that children are sensitive to social and pragmatic cues available in the naming context and that they use this information to learn the meanings of words and interpret speakers' utterances (Akhtar 2004; Baldwin 1991; Diesendruck and Markson 2001; Tomasello and Barton 1994).

One pragmatic cue children can use in word learning is direction of a speaker's eye gaze. Children know that the direction of a speaker's eye gaze is a reliable cue to the referent of a speaker's utterance (Baldwin 1991). In one study, 18- to 19-month-olds were handed an object to play with while a second object was placed inside an opaque bucket. While the child was distracted with the toy in her hand, the experimenter stared into the bucket and said, 'It's a toma.' Despite the discrepancy between the child and experimenter's focus of attention, the infants mapped the new name to the object in the bucket. This finding suggests that infants checked the experimenter's direction of gaze, and used this cue to infer that the label *toma* was intended to refer to the object in the bucket, and not the one in the child's hand.

Children use emotional expressions, such as frowning, as cues to the intent of a speaker (Tomasello and Barton 1994). In one study, an experimenter announced, 'Let's find the toma,' and then one toy after another was picked up and placed in a bucket while she frowned. When one of the objects was picked up, however, the experimenter smiled and said, 'Ah!'. Two-year-olds mapped the new name onto this last object, suggesting that they used the emotional cues provided by the experimenter to infer which object she was intending to refer to. Children in the same study were also shown to learn verbs in this way, on the basis of whether actions occurred intentionally or accidentally.

Young children also understand that speakers tend to name things that are new to the discourse context (Akhtar *et al.*1996). In this study, 2-year-olds played with three novel objects with a parent and the experimenter. While the parent was momentarily absent, a new object was added to the collection. The parent returned and exclaimed, 'There's a toma!' Children mapped the new label onto the most recently added object (new to the parent), suggesting that 2-year-olds understand that speakers tend to comment on things that are new to the discourse context.

These findings highlight children's understanding of the mental states of others and their use of this intentional knowledge in the service of word learning. Children's reliance on pragmatic cues to infer word meanings is generally thought to operate independently of, and thus render unnecessary, constraints. However, it is possible that the two could operate in unison as complementary mechanisms, or be instantiated at different points in development depending on the requisite skills present at various ages (Markman *et al.* 2003; Hollich *et al.* 2000). Regardless of the contribution of constraints (if any) in this process, it is likely that an ability to infer the intentions of others is essential for learning words (Bloom 2000).

5.1.4 Fast mapping, a special word learning ability

Every act of word learning involves the learning and retention of an arbitrary pairing – the link between a form and concept. Thus, once the referent of a word has been established, children still have to learn the mapping and permanently store the pairing in their lexicon. Anecdotal evidence suggested that children could learn words after minimal exposure to a word and its referent, but Carey and Bartlett (1978) were the first to empirically test whether children could indeed learn a new word after a brief, incidental exposure, and retain its meaning over time.

In their seminal study, 3-year-old children incidentally heard their preschool teacher use a new color word for a familiar object by contrasting it with a known color term by asking them to 'get the *chromium* one, not the *red* one'. Children were able to retrieve the correct object and showed some knowledge of the meaning of the new word even when tested up to 5 weeks later. Thus, children actively try to map at least some meaning onto each word they hear – a process dubbed 'fast mapping' (Carey 1978). It is important to note that the term *fast mapping* describes only the initial phase of learning in which children rapidly and efficiently incorporate a new word into the lexicon. After the initial *fast* mapping comes a slower learning process in which children work out the full meaning of a new word and come to appreciate subtle distinctions among individual words, particularly those within the same category (Carey 1978). The findings of this study and its successors demonstrate that children can acquire some understanding of the meaning of a new word after limited experience (Carey and Bartlett 1978; Dollaghan 1985; Goodman *et al.*1998; Heibeck and Markman 1987; Markson and Bloom 1997). Even infants as young as 13 months can fast map in ideal testing situations (Schafer and Plunkettt 1998; Werker *et al.*1998), demonstrating learning and retention of a new word meaning as long as 24 hours later (Woodward *et al.* 1994). Fast mapping, although not a constraint *per se*, has typically been thought of as an exceptional linguistic ability that children have at their disposal for the learning of words.

5.2 Constraints on word learning?

Several lines of work have been presented that highlight the special capacities available to children to solve the problem of word learning. It is common to emphasize how difficult a particular task is to accomplish, demonstrate how good people are at it, and then propose the existence of a module or neural mechanism specific to this task, for instance the human ability to perceive and recognize faces (e.g. Farah *et al.* 2000; Kanwisher *et al.* 1997; but see Haxby *et al.* 2001 for an alternative view that posits that the representations of faces are distributed). However, converging evidence from a number of studies suggests that the contrary might be true for the learning of words. A number of recent experiments have revealed that some aspects of word learning – historically assumed to apply specifically to word learning – actually apply more generally. Collectively, these findings suggest an alternative account of the mechanisms that lie at the core of word learning.

The first study to directly test whether a phenomenon traditionally assumed to be special to words might apply more generally was conducted in the domain of fast mapping. Markson and Bloom (1997) asked whether fast mapping is restricted to words, or applies more generally. To test this, 3- and 4-year-old children and adults interacted with a collection of ten objects, six of which were unfamiliar. In the guise of a measuring activity, one object was referred to by a novel name (e.g. 'the koba') and a different object was referred to by a novel fact (e.g. 'the one my uncle gave to me'). In a subsequent test session, learning was assessed by presenting the array of ten objects and asking children and adults for the referent of the new name or fact. Children and adults reliably chose the correct object in both the word and the fact conditions, regardless of whether they were tested immediately, or after a delay of 1 week or 1 month. A subsequent series of studies replicated this effect in 2-year-olds (Markson 1999). Based on this finding, Markson and Bloom (1997) concluded that fast mapping is not specific to words. This claim has not gone unchallenged, however, and has stimulated much debate concerning the domain specificity of fast mapping (Behrend *et al.* 2001; Bloom and Markson 2001; Childers and Tomasello 2003; Waxman and Booth 2000). In fact, recent evidence for fast mapping by a border collie has been taken as support for the notion that this ability is mediated by general learning and memory abilities that are not specific to humans (Kaminski *et al.* 2004). However, a number of critical issues must first be resolved before this data can be accepted as convincing evidence that dogs can learn words as human infants do (Bloom 2004).

Both the shape bias and mutual exclusivity constraint have also been shown to apply more generally. Recall that the shape bias entails children's tendency to extend names to objects that are similar in shape (Landau *et al.* 1988, 1998). But in a non-naming context, when children are simply asked to find another object of the same kind, they show the same tendency, in both cases generalizing on the basis of object kind, which is often determined on the basis of shape (Diesendruck and Bloom 2003). The shape bias is thus not specific to word learning, instead it derives from children's more general knowledge of object kinds.

The mutual exclusivity assumption asserts that children assume labels are exclusive, and thus each thing has only one name. When children are told the name of a novel object ('This is a *bem*') and asked for the referent of a different word ('Get the *jop*'), they apply the new word to the object not already associated with a name (e.g. Markman and Wachtel 1988). Interestingly, when children are told a fact about an object ('My uncle gave this to me'), and asked then asked for the referent of a different fact ('Get the one that cats like to play with'), they apply the new fact to the object that is not already associated with a fact (Diesendruck and Markson 2001). Like the shape bias, the mutual exclusivity assumption is not restricted to words but, rather, applies to communicative utterances more generally.

A number of children's theory of mind abilities now thought to be important for word learning also apply more generally. Infants will follow the direction of a speaker's gaze and map a new word to the object the speaker was looking at during naming, even if the child's attention was on another object at the time (Baldwin 1991, 1993). Interestingly, this finding also holds for the emotions domain (Baldwin and Moses 1994). When 12- and 18-month-olds observe a person looking at an object and display a negative ('Yecch!') or positive ('Wow!') emotional outburst, infants map the emotion to the appropriate referent, subsequently avoiding or approaching the object depending on the type of emotional display that was directed towards it (Moses *et al.* 2001). Thus, infants use a person's line of regard as a cue to referential intent not only for the learning of words, but more generally.

Together these examples suggest that the proposed constraints or biases aren't restricted to word learning contexts. None of them are uncontroversial, and it is unlikely that they will go unchallenged. In addition, merely showing that constraints or other capacities typically thought to be special to word learning apply more generally, is not sufficient to refute the existence of a domain-specific mechanism for word learning. A plausible alternative theory of what instead underlies children's remarkable word learning abilities is still needed.

My colleagues and I have proposed elsewhere that children's striking ability to learn words might not be due to capacities that are specific to word learning. Rather, the ability to learn words might stem form more general capacities that children possess. These capacities include sophisticated conceptual capacities that enable children to quickly learn and remember relevant information about objects, sophisticated theory of mind abilities that support children's reasoning about the intentions of others, and syntactic knowledge (Bloom 2000; Diesendruck and Markson 2001; Markson 1999; Markson and Bloom 1997). These abilities are the core capacities of word learning.

I have focused on two here – children's ability to rapidly learn about objects and their sensitivity to the intentions of others. We have previously proposed a pragmatic account for children's avoidance of lexical overlap (Diesendruck and Markson 2001). The remainder of this chapter speculates on the origins and development of these rapid learning abilities in even younger children. I present two studies that explore the kinds of information children might be more adept at learning, and discuss some preliminary findings.

5.3 The origins and scope of rapid learning

Earlier I described a series of fast mapping studies revealing that 2- to 4-year-old children can rapidly learn and remember both names and arbitrary facts about novel objects (Markson 1999; Markson and Bloom 1997). The ability to quickly learn and remember arbitrary mappings is central to word learning. However, in addition to words, children must learn about the myriad of artifacts that clutter their everyday environment. We have begun exploring this issue in two lines of research. The first line addresses the role of language in fast mapping. Specifically, we ask whether information must be conveyed through language in order for rapid learning to occur. In addition, we consider this question with regard to the language capacities of the learner by testing children who are closer to the start of word learning. The second line of research asks whether children are better at learning information that is relevant to the category membership of an object, by testing young children's sensitivity to the functional parts of novel objects.

5.3.1 Rapid learning of words and non-linguistic properties of objects

To date, most studies testing children's fast mapping abilities have conveyed the relevant information verbally and tested children's knowledge in the same way. It therefore remains an open question whether infants have a broader ability to rapidly learn information about objects that extends beyond the domain of words, or whether these capacities for rapid learning might initially be specific to language and only later generalize to other types of information.

To address these questions, we tested 13- and 18-month-old infants' capacity to rapidly learn object names and non-obvious object properties that are not conveyed through language. In a series of experiments, infants were introduced to two novel objects and encouraged to play freely with them for several minutes. Each infant participated in either a word or property condition. Children in the word condition, were casually told the name of one of the objects (the target) while they interacted with it (e.g. 'Let's play with the *jippi*.'). Children in the property condition learned that one of the objects (the target) possessed a hidden, arbitrary property (e.g. it made a noise when shaken), which infants could discover while interacting with it, whereas the other object (the distracter) did not have such a feature. In both conditions, comparable attention was paid to the distracter object during this initial training phase.

Testing for each infant occurred either 1 day or 1 week after the initial training session. Infants returned to the lab after 1 day or 1 week and were tested on their memory of the word or property, depending on experimental condition. Memory for both the word and property was assessed using a standard multiple-choice procedure typically used in studies of word learning with children of this age (Baldwin 1991). Infants in the word condition were presented with the two objects from training and asked to 'find the *jippi*' on two consecutive trials with the lateral sides of the two objects reversed across trials. Infants in the property condition first heard the *noise* from behind the experimenter's back, and were then presented with the two objects and asked to find the one that had made that sound. At training, both objects now made the identical sound to avoid the possibility of infants hearing, and being influenced by, the target sound coming from one object over the other. Infants in the property condition received only one multiple-choice test since their choice was confirmed once they selected an object. However, prior to this test, infants in the property condition were given a different property test in which memory for the property was assessed using a violation-of-expectation object manipulation procedure. In this test, infants were sequentially presented with a replica of the target object that lacked the original hidden property (e.g. it no longer made a noise) and the original distracter object – which never made a noise – and encouraged to freely explore each object (Baldwin *et al.* 1993).

Infants' actions on the two objects were videotaped for later coding. We observed the number of target actions (e.g. shaking the object) that infants performed on the target object compared to both the actions of the same child on a different object (the distracter), and to the actions of different children, who had not previously been exposed to the target object's hidden property, on the same object. Infants in both age groups performed significantly more target actions on the target object compared to the distracter, and were above chance at selecting the target object in a multiple-choice task in both the word and property conditions at 18-months of age, but not at 13-months of age. It is likely that our word learning task was too stringent to tap into 13-month-olds' knowledge, since previous studies have demonstrated evidence of learning words using similar procedures (Woodward *et al.* 1994). Because infants successfully showed memory for the property in the more stringent object manipulation task, we conclude that even for these younger infants, rapid learning about objects is not restricted to language contexts.

The present findings demonstrate that 13- and 18-month-old infants can learn and remember a non-obvious object property after minimal exposure. These results move us one step closer to understanding whether children's capacity for word learning depends on a mechanism dedicated specifically to language, or results from a broader mechanism for learning and retaining arbitrary information in multiple domains of knowledge. These results also suggest that young children are skilled at learning non-obvious properties of objects, motivating the question of the scope of this rapid learning ability. Are children better at learning some kinds of information about unfamiliar objects over other kinds of knowledge? One possibility is that because categories are so essential to how we view and understand the world, that children are attuned to information that might be relevant for categorization from an early age. Both object names and object functions have been found to be useful cues to the category membership of an object in 18-month-old infants (Booth and Waxman 2002). Children of this age are also able to make inferences about non-obvious properties of objects on the basis of shared labels or perceptual features such as shape (Welder and Graham 2001). In the next study, we asked whether 18-month-old infants are sensitive to one particular object property that is relevant for categorization, namely the property of an object that supports its function.

5.3.2 Rapid learning about functional properties of novel objects

Words and certain object properties (e.g. shape, function) can provide useful information about the category or kind to which an artifact belongs. Perhaps humans are particularly adept at learning information that picks out the kind of thing something is (e.g. dangerous animal, musical instrument), because of the utility of such information. Category-relevant information is powerful – if you know that something is called 'lion', or for 'grating cheese' you're privy to essential information. In contrast, information that is irrelevant with respect to categorization – such as the box an object came in when it was purchased – is basically useless, and therefore less important to remember. Might humans, including very young children, be particularly skilled at learning the properties of novel artifacts that are relevant for categorization?

Following on the previous study, we asked whether 18-month-old infants would be sensitive to the features of objects that are relevant for its function. To test this, infants were shown the function of a novel opaque object (the standard) in a training session, in which the property of the standard object that was crucial to the function was concealed. For example one of the objects functioned as a scooper that was used to retrieve small toys from a bin. Importantly, the shelf that supported the objects being scooped was obscured. The experimenter demonstrated the function (e.g. scooping toys) as the child watched. The standard scoop object is shown in Fig 5.1. Immediately following the training trial, infants were shown two new, nearly identical objects in a test trial: one object that possessed the critical property (target) and one that lacked the critical property (distracter). The test objects were identical in shape and color, and differed only in the presence (target) and absence (distracter) of the functional properties (Fig. 5.1). In contrast to the opaque, standard object in which the func-

(a) standard

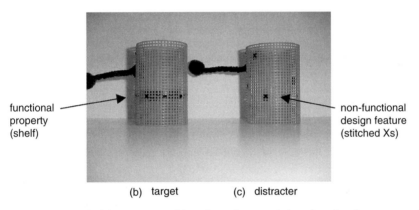

functional
property
(shelf)

non-functional
design feature
(stitched Xs)

(b) target   (c) distracter

Fig. 5.1 Example triad of the 'Scooper' objects from the non-obvious functional property study. (A) The 'standard' object. (B) The 'target' object with the non-obvious functional hidden property (shelf) indicated by an arrow. (C) The 'distracter' object lacking the target object's functional property, but similar in appearance with a non-functional design feature (black Xs stitched across the object in the same location as the shelf) indicated by the arrow.

tional property was obscured, the functional property (or lack of the property) was fully visible in the test objects. Infants were presented with the two test objects and were asked to choose the object appropriate to perform the action demonstrated in the preceding training trial. The two test objects were placed on opposite sides of the table, within the child's reach, and the child was allowed to choose one of the objects to explore and perform the function.

We observed infants' first reach for a test object (either target or distracter) and infants' performance of target actions (defined as an action resembling the demonstration of function by the experimenter during training) on both the target and distracter. Infants reached for the target significantly more than the distracter, and performed target actions on the target significantly more than on the distracter.

A control study was conducted to check that infants' preference for the target over the distracter was not due to the target's intrinsic salience. The control study was identical to the experimental study, except that there was no demonstration of the function of the standard object. Infants in the control condition chose between the target and distracter randomly, significantly less than in the experimental condition, suggesting that infants' successes in the experimental condition were due to functional knowledge.

These findings provide evidence that 18-month-old infants are sensitive to object functions and to the non-obvious properties that are responsible for these functions. Most importantly, infants are capable of understanding the correlation between function and structure. This provides direct evidence that infants can infer the possible function of an object from structure, consistent with the notion that children's learning and generalizing about objects is based in part on conceptual theories. It is also possible that infants in the present study were inferring structure from function (during the training trials), although it is not possible to draw this conclusion based on the present data.

A recent study found that when 2- to 4-year-old children were given the chance to ask questions about unfamiliar objects, children were satisfied when told the object's function alone, but persisted in asking questions about function when only an unknown name was provided (Kemler Nelson *et al.* 2004). This result was interpreted as suggesting that children's concepts of artifacts are intimately tied to the functions of objects because children were ultimately seeking information about the *kind* of thing the artifact was – what it *could do* or what it *was for*, rather than its name alone. Whereas names generally serve as useful indicators of an object's kind or category (and thus would explain based on this theory why they are learned so readily), a novel name alone may not necessarily prove sufficient for determining object kind. Our finding that 18-month-old infants are already attuned to the relevant features of artifacts suggests that even infants are motivated to discover the *kind* of thing an entity is, that is, the category to which a thing belongs. It remains an open question whether this type of learning is mediated by the same mechanism responsible for the learning of words.

5.4 Concluding remarks

I have argued that the ability to learn words might stem form more general cognitive capacities that humans possess. This view challenges a prevalent account of word learning that posits special constraints. However, the emerging evidence from a number of laboratories suggests that a number of capacities once thought to be specific to word learning, such as fast mapping and a bias to extend names on the basis of shape, in fact apply much more generally. In light of this evidence, it is reasonable to propose that the mechanism underlying word learning is not a single mechanism at all, but rather children recruit a host of more general cognitive capacities in the service of learning words, such as an ability to rapidly learn about objects and a sensitivity to the intentions of others (Bloom 2000). These are some of the capacities at the core of word learning, without them learning might look quite different.

One such capacity is the general learning and memory abilities that support the rapid learning and enduring memory of words. I have presented data showing that infants as young as 13 months readily learn about hidden, arbitrary properties of objects after minimal exposure, even in the absence of language, providing support for the notion that a broad mechanism for learning and retaining information about objects in multiple domains of knowledge subserves the learning of both names and properties. In addition, my colleagues and I have shown that 18-month-old infants learn about the functional properties of novel objects in a brief training session, suggesting an early sensitivity to object information that is relevant for categorization. By the second year of life, infants are actively engaged in developing not only a dictionary of words, but also an encyclopedia of knowledge. Whether a common mechanism is responsible for both kinds of learning poses a question for future research.

Acknowledgements

Thanks to Mark Johnson and two anonymous reviewers for very helpful comments and suggestions on a previous draft of this chapter. I am indebted to my collaborators Paul Bloom, Gil Diesendruck, Stella Christie, and Elizabeth Spelke for their invaluable ideas and discussion, and their assistance in carrying out this research.

References

Akhtar N (2004). Contexts of early word learning. In: DG Hall and SR Waxman, eds. *Weaving a lexicon*, pp. 485–508. Cambridge, MA: MIT Press.

Akhtar N, Carpenter M and Tomasello M (1996). The role of discourse novelty in early word learning. *Child Development*, **67**, 635–645.

Anglin J (1993). Vocabulary development: A morphological analysis. *Monographs of the Society for Research in Child Development*, **58**, (10, Serial No. 238), 1–166.

Baldwin DA (1991). Infants' contribution to the achievement of joint reference. *Child Development*, **62**, 875–890.

Baldwin DA (1993). Infants' ability to consult the speaker for clues to word reference. *Journal of Child Language*, **20**, 395–418.

Baldwin DA, Markman EM and Melartin RL (1993). Infants' ability to draw inferences about nonobvious object properties: Evidence from exploratory play. *Child Development*, **64**, 711–728.

Baldwin DA and Moses LJ (1994). Early understanding of referential intent and attentional focus: Evidence from language and emotion. In: C Lewis and P Mitchell, eds. *Children's early understanding of mind: Origins and development*. Hillsdale, NJ: Lawrence Erlbaum Associates.

Bates E, Bretherton I and Snyder L (1988). *From first words to grammar: Individual differences and dissociable mechanisms.* Cambridge: Cambridge University Press.

Bates E and Goodman JC (1997). On the inseparability of grammar and the lexicon. *Language and Cognitive Processes,* 12, 507–584.

Behrend DA, Scofield J and Kleinknecht EE (2001). Beyond fast mapping: Young children's extensions of novel words and novel facts. *Developmental Psychology,* 37, 698–705.

Bloom P (2000). *How children learn the meanings of words.* Cambridge, MA: MIT Press.

Bloom P (2004). Can a dog learn a word? *Science,* 304, 1605–1606.

Bloom P and Markson L (2001). Are there principles that apply only to the acquisition of words? A reply to Waxman and Booth. *Cognition,* 78, 89–90.

Booth AE and Waxman S (2002). Object names and object functions serve as cues to categories for infants. *Developmental Psychology,* 38, 948–957.

Carey S (1978). The child as word learner. In: M Halle, J Bresnan and GA Miller, eds. *Linguistic theory and psychological reality.* Cambridge, MA: MIT Press.

Carey S and Bartlett E (1978). Acquiring a single new word. *Papers and Reports on Child Language Development,* 15, 17–29.

Childers JB and Tomasello M (2003). Children extend both words and non-verbal actions to novel exemplars. *Developmental Science,* 6, 185–190.

Chomsky N (1986). *Knowledge of language.* New York: Praeger.

Chouinard MC and Clark EV (2003). Adult reformulations of child errors as negative evidence. *Journal of Child Language,* 30, 637–669.

Curtiss S (1989). The independence and task-specificity of language. In: M Bornstein and J Bruner, eds. *Interaction in Human Development,* pp.105–137. Hillsdale, NJ: Lawrence Earlbaum Associates.

Diesendruck G and Bloom P (2003). How specific is the shape bias? *Child Development,* 74, 168–178.

Diesendruck G and Markson L (2001). Children's avoidance of lexical overlap: A pragmatic account. *Developmental Psychology,* 37, 630–641.

Dollaghan CA (1985). Child meets word: Fast mapping in preschool children. *Journal of Speech and Hearing Disorders,* 28, 449–454.

Elman JL (1993). Learning and development in neural networks: The importance of starting small. *Cognition,* 48, 71–79.

Elman JL, Bates EA, Johnson MH, Karmiloff-Smith A, Parisi D and Plunkett K (1996). *Rethinking innateness.* Cambridge, MA: MIT Press.

Farah MJ, Rabinowitz C, Quinn GE and Liu GT (2000). Early commitment of neural substrates for face recognition. *Cognitive Neuropsychology,* 20, 117–123.

Ganger JB (1998). *Genes and environment in language acquisition: A twin study of vocabulary and syntactic development.* Unpublished doctoral dissertation, MIT.

Golinkoff RM, Hirsh-Pasek K, Bailey LM and Wenger NR (1992). Young children and adults use lexical principles to learn new nouns. *Developmental Psychology,* 28, 99–108.

Golinkoff RM, Mervis CB and Hirsh-Pasek K (1994). Early object labels: The case for a developmental lexical principles framework. *Journal of Child Language,* 21, 125–155.

Gomez R (2002). Variability and detection of invariant structure. *Psychological Science,* 13, 431–436.

Goodman JC, McDonough L and Brown NB (1998). The role of semantic context and memory in the acquisition of novel nouns. *Child Development,* 69, 1330–1344.

Halberda J (2003). The development of a word learning strategy. *Cognition,* 87, B23–B34.

Hauser MD, Chomsky N and Fitch Tecumseh W (2002). The faculty of language: What is it, who has it, and how did it evolve? *Science,* **298,** 1569–1579.

Haxby JV, Gobbini MI, Furey ML, Ishai A, Schouten JL and Pietrini P (2001). Distributed and overlapping representations of faces and objects in ventral temporal cortex. *Science,* **293,** 2425–2430.

Heibeck TH and Markman EM (1987). Word learning in children: An examination of fast mapping. *Child Development,* **58,** 1021–1034.

Hollich G, Hirsh-Pasek K and Golinkoff RM (2000). Breaking the language barrier: An emergentist coalition model for the origins of word learning. *Monographs of the Society for Research in Child Development,* **65,** (serial no. 262).

Jones SS, Smith LB and Landau B (1991). Object properties and knowledge in early lexical learning. *Child Development,* **62,** 499–512.

Jucszyk PW (1997). *The discovery of spoken language.* Cambridge, MA: MIT Press.

Jucszyk PW and Aslin RN (1995). Infants' detection of sound patterns of words in fluent speech. *Cognitive Psychology,* **29,** 1–23.

Jucszyk PW and Hohne EA (1997). Infants' memory for spoken words. *Science,* **277,** 1984–1986.

Kaminski J, Call J and Fischer J (2004). Word learning in a domestic dog: Evidence for 'fast mapping'. *Science,* **304,** 1682–1683.

Kanwisher N, McDermott J and Chun MM (1997). The fusiform face area: a module in human extrastriate cortex specialized for face perception. *Journal of Neuroscience,* **17,** 4302–4311.

Kemler Nelson DG, Egan LC and Holt MB (2004). When children ask, "What is it?" What do they want to know about artifacts? *Psychological Science,* **15,** 384–389.

Landau B, Smith LB and Jones SS (1988). The importance of shape in early lexical learning. *Cognitive Development,* **3,** 299–321.

Landau B, Smith LB and Jones SS (1998). Object shape, object function, and object name. *Journal of Memory and Language,* **38,** 1–27.

Marcus GF (1993). Negative evidence in language acquisition. *Cognition,* **46,** 53–85.

Markman EM (1989). *Categorization and naming in children: Problems of induction.* Cambridge, MA: MIT Press, Bradford Books.

Markman EM (1990). Constraints children place on word meanings. *Cognitive Science,* **14,** 57–78.

Markman EM (1992). Constraints on word learning: Speculations about their nature, origins and domain specficity. In: MR Gunnar and MP Maratsos, eds. *Modularity and constraints in language and cognition: The Minnesota Symposium on Child Psychology,* pp. 59–101. Hillsdale, NJ: Lawrence Erlbaum Associates.

Markman EM and Abelev M (2004). Word learning in dogs? *Trends in Cognitive Sciences,* **8,** 479–481.

Markman EM and Wachtel GF (1988). Children's use of mutual exclusivity to constrain the meaning of words. *Cognitive Psychology,* **20,** 121–157.

Markman EM, Wasow JL and Hansen MB (2003). Use of the mutual exclusivity assumption by young word learners. *Cognitive Psychology,* **47,** 241–275.

Markson L (1999). *Mechanisms of word learning: Insights from fast mapping.* Unpublished doctoral dissertation, University of Arizona.

Markson L and Bloom P (1997). Evidence against a dedicated system for word learning in children. *Nature,* **385,** 813–815.

Miller GA (1991). *The science of words.* New York: W.H. Freeman.

Moses LJ, Baldwin DA, Rosicky J and Tidball G (2001). Evidence for referential understanding of emotions at 12 and 18 months. *Child Development*, 3, 718–735.

Nelson K (1988). Constraints on word meaning? *Cognitive Development*, 3, 221–246.

Neville HJ, Mills DL and Lawson DS (1992). Fractionating language: different neural subsystems with different sensitive periods. *Cerebral Cortex*, 2, 244–258.

Newport EL (1990). Maturational constraints on language learning. *Cognitive Science*, 14, 11–28.

Pinker S (1991). Rules of language. *Science*, 253, 530–535.

Quine WVO (1960). *Word and object*. Cambridge, MA: MIT Press.

Regier T (2003). Emergent constraints on word learning: a computational perspective. *Trends in Cognitive Science*, 7, 263–268.

Saffran JR, Aslin RN and Newport EL (1996). Statistical learning by 8-month-old infants. *Science*, 274, 1926–1928.

Schafer G and Plunkett K (1998). Rapid word learning by fifteen-month-olds under tightly controlled conditions. *Child Development*, 69, 309–320.

Smith LB, Jones SS and Landau B (1996). Naming in young children: A dumb attentional mechanism? *Cognition*, 60, 143–171.

Smith LB, Jones SS, Landau B, Gershkoff-Stowe L and Samuelson L (2002). Object name learning provides on-the-job training for attention. *Psychological Science*, 13, 13–19.

Tomasello M and Barton M (1994). Learning words in non-ostensive contexts. *Developmental Psychology*, 30, 639–650.

Ullman MT, Corkin S, Coppola M, Hickok G, Growdon JH, Koroshetz WJ et al. (1996). A neural dissociation within language: Evidence that the mental dictionary is part of declarative memory, and grammatical rules are processed by the procedural system. *Journal of Cognitive Neuroscience*, 9, 266–276.

Waxman SR (1990). Linguistic biases and the establishment of conceptual hierarchies: Evidence from preschool children. *Cognitive Development*, 5, 123–150.

Waxman SR and Booth A (2000). Principles that are invoked in the acquisition of words, but not facts. *Cognition*, 77, B33–B43.

Weber-Fox CM and Neville HJ (1996). Maturational constraints on functional specializations for language processing: ERP and behavioral evidence in bilingual speakers. *Journal of Cognitive Neuroscience*, 8, 231–256.

Welder AN and Graham SA (2001). The influence of shape similarity and shared labels on infants' inductive inferences about nonobvious object properties. *Child Development*, 72, 1653–1673.

Werker JF, Cohen LB, Lloyd VL, Casasola M and Stager CL (1998). Acquisition of word-object associations by 14-month-old infants. *Developmental Psychology*, 34, 1289–1309.

Woodward AL, Markman EM and Fitzsimmons CM (1994). Rapid word learning in 13- and 18-month-olds. *Developmental Psychology*, 30, 553–566.

Part 2

Constraints on learning

Chapter 6

Developmental constraints on or developmental structure in brain evolution?

Barbara L. Finlay, Desmond Tak-Ming Cheung, and Richard B. Darlington

Abstract

The more we discover about the basic structure of vertebrate and invertebrate evolution, the more impressive the evidence of its conservative nature becomes. Evidence for commonalities versus special adaptations in brain evolution, with particular attention to rules for the proliferation of the cortex will be discussed. Conserved developmental rules that produce highly predictable brain organization seem best described as rules that produce generic, optimal organization rather than limiting constraints.

6.1 **Introduction**

How do we understand the structure of organisms, from body plan to brain to behavior? Ever since Darwin, the answer from evolutionary biology is simple: the characteristics of organisms are adaptations that have allowed their survival and reproductive success. We understand the nature of evolution to be competition between organisms on the basis of heritable variation in those adaptations that improve their reproductive success. This view, centered on the premise that adaptations are produced by accretion of small, adaptive changes, is best laid out in the various works of Richard Dawkins (Dawkins 1976, 1986). Excluding absurd 'just-so' stories, this view suggests that every feature of an organism should be subject to an adaptive account, usually in terms of the special niche of the organism. Remarkable cases of convergent evolution tend to reinforce the view that virtually every feature of an organism can be the target of special selection. For example the Tasmanian wolf (Fig. 6.1a), a marsupial, occupies the same niche as the North American timber wolf (Fig. 6.1b), and the similarity of the two, coming from such different stem species, is

(a)　　　　　　　　　　　　　　　　　(b)

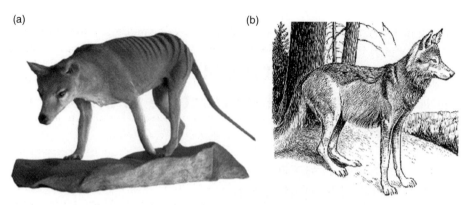

Fig. 6.1 (a) The thylacine (*Thylacinus cynocephalus*), also known as the Tasmanian wolf, was a large marsupial carnivore that lived in Australia and New Guinea. The last known captive animal died in 1936. (Image: http://collections.ucl.ac.uk/ zoology/highlights.asp). (b) Wolf (*Canis lupus*). (Image : www.nature.ca/notebooks/english/wolf/htm).

quite remarkable – the type of pelt (dark above, white below); the approximate size; the frontally placed eyes; the sharp canines; the behavioral adaptations for hunting. We can go further still in phylogenetic distance: consider the hawk moth, an invertebrate, compared to the hummingbird, both of which feed on trumpet-shaped blossoms, and both of which have made the elaborate adaptation of hovering flight and a long proboscis or beak, so much that they can be confused for each other where their habitats overlap. So, one aspect of understanding the structure of organisms is to take each feature as an adaptation to a functional role in a specific environment, from inference from species that have arisen from different origins but have converged on similar forms.

Another type of structure is common to all four of the organisms, the two mammals, the bird and the insect (and in fact is common to every complex invertebrate and vertebrate on earth), however, which defies this kind of account. This is the pattern of early regulatory gene expression, 'Hox genes', that controls the initial polarization, bilateral symmetry, and segmentation of both vertebrates and invertebrates. The pattern is complex, a series of nested and overlapping gradients of gene expression, and most important, very highly conserved across all of these creatures (Duboule and Dollé 1989; Graham *et al.* 1989; reviewed in Wilkins 2001). Further, this is only one of a number of highly conserved gene functions that control particular kinds of operations, or regulate the production of certain pieces of morphology. For example there is the Notch/Delta signaling complex, often employed as a generic 'symmetry breaker' which takes an initially uniform set of cells and sends them out on two separate developmental paths (Gerhart and Kirschner 1997). Or the famous Pax6, which controls the positioning of the eye, and is so conserved that if this gene is taken from the genome of the mouse and inserted into an atypical position and species, like the leg in a developing fruit fly, it will induce a fruit fly-appropriate compound eye in that location (Callaerts *et al.* 1997). Or, the Robo/Slit signaling complex, which directs the formation of axonal pathways that approach and then cross the body midline (Stein and Tessier-Lavigne 2001). Since it is highly unlikely that these rather complex, yet basic, organizational features represent convergent evolution, it is assumed they are conserved features, present in our ancestors and present in us. Are these universal developmental features 'developmental constraints'?

Stephen Jay Gould argued forcefully for understanding the role of history in the constraint of present form, and his arguments centered on how evolution, as a historical phenomenon, limits the possibilities of present form (Gould 1977, 2002). When selecting for better adaptations to particular niches, not all logical possibilities are presented for selection. In '*The Panda's Thumb*' he argued that the strongest evidence for developmental constraint are those cases when evolution produces out of a problematic substrate (the wrist bones of the proto-panda) an inefficient contrivance (the rather clumsy panda 'thumb'), an unhandy solution quite different from what engineers would choose to solve a problem were they given *carte blanche* on materials and manufacturing techniques (Gould 1980). The thumb itself is not the constraint, but rather the range of substrates and mechanisms evolution can use to address an adaptive problem. In developmental and cognitive psychology, constraint tends to be used in the same restrictive way, though prior form and history are not necessary parts of this kind of constraint argument. Out of the universe of multiple solutions to learning about or acting on real-world problems, the search space is constrained to particular facets of the information available, or particular tactics or heuristics used to take action on the information presented.

In this view, the instructions for the general invertebrate/vertebrate body and brain plan would appear be the most whopping 'constraint' possible on the paths of evolution, unchanged for some 600 million years. While the resultant types of species employing this plan on one hand seem almost unimaginably diverse, from lobsters to worms to elephants, there are significant aspects of conserved structure, including bilateral symmetry, retained topological relations of major organ systems, and most important, segmental organization.

Are we served by calling this kind of conservation 'constraint'? We will argue, along with various developmental biologists from whom the fundamental structure of these arguments are drawn (Gerhart and Kirschner 1997; Wilkins 2001; Ryan 2004), that these conserved pathways are not the crystallizations of an idiosyncratic, one-time choice of a single evolutionary path out of a universe of many possible paths, or even the best heuristic of many. Rather, they show us the nature of optimal, robust, and stable solutions to the survival problems of organisms operating in this world, as filtered by recurring catastrophe. We will go on to look at another highly conserved developmental pathway in mammalian evolution, this time the order of generation of neurons in the brain that produces the very reliable scaling of brain parts across animals as the brain enlarges, (Finlay and Darlington 1995; Finlay *et al.* 2001) and, finally, present new work on the conserved structure of the scaling of cortical areas and connectivity with brain size. In these last cases, we will attempt to evaluate whether robust developmental structure, developmental constraint, or specific adaptation is the best conceptual domain to capture the empirical results.

6.2 Adaptation, catastrophe, and evolvability

The scenario for evolution with which we started this chapter, of individuals struggling against members of their own species for reproductive success on the basis of their special adaptations in a stable world of available niches, only captures one aspect of the kind of challenges species face in evolutionary time, and only part of the nature of genetic change. The most salient single example for contrast is the meteor that hit the earth at the time of the Jurassic, suddenly and massively changing the environment – the light, the air quality, nutrients, every important feature of niche, costing the world the dinosaurs (Alvarez *et al.* 1980; Albritton 1989). The locus of the most massive source of variability in the Earth's collective genome in this kind of event is at the level of species or whole radiations of species, favoring those groups most able to survive and reproduce in the face of wholesale change. The range from global catastrophe, causing variation at the species level and higher, to the 'adaptive walk' where individuals compete and specialize in relatively stable settings, is a continuous range, not requiring wholesale catastrophe and extinction – there can be local catastrophes as well. The central issue is that a major source of genome variation across times of catastrophe, local or global, will reflect strategic variations that vary at the level of orders or classes, such as rapid development, homeothermy, circadian rhythmicity, behavioral plasticity, and that are executed by developmental and metabolic mechanisms that are stable and robust. Our genome contains the influence of both the recurring, general filter of great stress, and ongoing competition on the basis of subtly improved adaptations for reproductive success in stable environments.

'Evolvability' is a related idea that also carries import for how a genome will respond to challenge of any kind, and which genes will persist in a population. This idea has been used in two distinct ways in the allied fields of evolutionary biology, and in those areas of artificial intelligence and robotics that employ genetic algorithms. The first, and somewhat stricter, sense of this concept arose from the hypothesis and later the demonstration (in bacteria) that in times of extreme stress and crisis, 'deliberate' additional variation and mutation would arise as an adaptive mechanism, suppressed in favored environments (Radman *et al.* 1999). The second, more general, sense is the observation that some types of genomic or informational structures more readily produce usable adaptive changes and potential for evolution than others. This concept is now under intensive investigation in the growing field of evolutionary robotics and computation, thus coming around to integrate evolution with cognition from an unanticipated direction (Lipson and Pollack 2000; Nolfi and Floreano 2002; Baum 2004). Everything else equal, the 'evolvable' organism is more likely to be with us today. Central themes that have emerged, both in evolutionary biology and in evolutionary computation, are the importance of modules as high-level building blocks, standardized processes of linkage or integration between modules, and the ability to recursively construct higher-order modules that can be addressed evolutionarily (Baum 2004). In biological evolution, the concept of meaningful variation of a module springs directly from the segmented embryo that enjoyed such extreme evolutionary success. Even the derivation of the name 'Hox genes' comes from the observation of 'homeotic mutants', mutants which erroneously repeat a higher-order piece of structure in their body plans, like two adjacent regions both giving rise to wings, or to mouth parts (Gerhart and Kirschner 1997). Regulatory mutations are not the only mutations, of course – single amino acid to single protein mutations (such as might appear in species differences in photoreceptor or hemoglobin molecules) exist as well as this modular, Hox-level of alteration. We will give an example of the interaction of these two kinds of genetic change in the evolution of primate vision at the very end of this chapter.

In the next section, we will describe an initially surprising, conserved structure in the pattern of generation of the brain in mammals (and to a lesser degree, in vertebrates generally) that has direct consequences for the allometry of brain change in all mammalian radiations, and our own primate radiation. How can we discriminate whether we are looking at developmental constraint, a crystallized feature that limits the paths of brain change, or a developmental structure that gives some insight into the general nature of robust and adaptive solutions for making brains? Last we will turn this same approach to the particular case of the evolution of the cortex, and how the properties of the cortex reveal themselves in the various cases of imposed environmental, developmental, or genetic variability.

6.3 Scaling the whole brain

The Finlay laboratory has investigated, for some time, how spatially distributed systems in the brain and body evolve (Finlay *et al.* 1987, 1991, 1998, 2001; Finlay and Darlington 1995). The distributed systems we refer to are those with morphological specializations of the body and a number of associated brain parts coming from embryologically separate regions, such as the visual system which includes eyes, eye muscles, visual midbrain, visual cortex, and so forth, or sexual differentiation, which includes genitals, stereotypic motor pathways in the spinal cord, the cortical representation of social customs, and so on. We have approached this question in two complementary ways, introducing deviations into early development to look for system-wide reconfigurations, which is an aspect of 'evolvability', and also examining the patterns of observed evolutionary changes across species for the structure of the developmental mechanisms that underlie them. In the search for levels of 'grammar' in the variation in neuron number in the brains of different species, empirical work using the first strategy showed potential co-ordinating regressive processes, such as developmental neuron death and axon retraction, did not appear to have enough power to propagate changes in number and connectivity much past a connection or two in the brain (Finlay *et al.* 1987; Finlay and Pallas 1989). Therefore, wholesale changes in the size of a spatially distributed system could not be accounted for by developmental events occurring after cells were generated and differentiated.

The remaining logical possibility was neurogenesis, which we examined using the second strategy of looking for changes across species in development that could be plausibly related to adult differences. The structure of variation, both in the order and duration of neurogenesis and the structure of variation in the size of brain parts across species, could be directly compared. The intent was to quantify and understand the structure of variability in these directly related features (neurogenesis and the number of neurons in brain parts) at the level of individual structures; functional systems (like 'visual system', 'motor system'); brain geography ('midbrain', 'hindbrain'); and the whole brain. To our great surprise, both analyses of adult differences in brain volumes and neuron numbers, and early schedules of neurogenesis, returned an answer that the level of the variation of the whole brain, or the whole developmental schedule, grossly dominated the variation, the two sources of data congruent in detail. Not only that, brain parts varied both predictably and disproportionately as brains enlarged, and the disproportion was predicted by the conserved order in which structures were generated across species (Finlay and Darlington 1995).

6.4 The basic finding of conservation of the developmental timetable

Since the initial publication of our investigation into the linkage of neurogenesis and brain allometry (Finlay and Darlington 1995), we have published a number of further analyses and reviews to which we refer the reader for detail (Finlay *et al.*1998, 2001; Clancy *et al.* 1999, 2001; Kaskan and Finlay 2001; Kaskan *et al.* 2004). Here we will explore the specific issue of conservation of general brain scaling as a constraint.

Briefly, using the data collected for primates, insectivores, and bats by Stephan and collaborators (Stephan *et al.* 1981, 1988), a dataset that has been the subject of numerous analyses, we emphasized a finding that had been known before: that about 97 per cent of the variance in the sizes of brain parts was predicted by the size of the whole brain, and 99 per cent if a second 'limbic' or 'olfactory' factor was added. The human cortex (and all the large divisions as well) is just the size it should be for a primate brain our size (Hofman 1989) (Fig. 6.2). This was an unusual emphasis, because most investigators interested in mapping the differences in size of brain parts to differences in animal's behavior and niche disposed of the 99 per cent of shared variance, and examined the residual variance, using various statistical

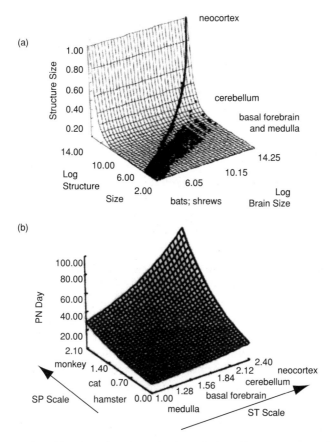

Fig. 6.2 (a) A combined log (y axis) and non-log (z axis) plot of brain structure volumes versus log brain volume (x azis) for the 131 primates, bats, and insectivores of the Stephan data set, redrawn from Finlay and Darlington (1995). This style of graphing is chosen to highlight both the predictable but disproportionate size of those structures scaling at the steepest slopes with respect to brain size, particularly the neocortex. (b) Model of the predictability of the birth date of a structure in a species given the ordinal position of each structure's birth date across animals (Structure Scale, ST) and the relative duration of neurogenesis in a species compared to others (Species Scale, SP). The seven species modeled in this analysis are hamsters, mouse, rat, spiny mouse, possum, cat, and monkey; 51 neural structures are modeled, from motor nuclei of the medulla to cortical layers. Those structures with high ST values are the latest generated ones, and are the same that become disproportionately large as brain volume enlarges.

approaches, even though the residual variance was so small. It is important to understand the actual physical characteristics of brain evolution to understand the nature of the shared and residual variance. In this dataset, brain weights vary from a fraction of a gram to over a kilogram, a factor of about 20 000. At any particular brain weight, the residual variance of individual structures is about 2.5 – that is, two species similar on the two factors (whole brain and limbic) might commonly have individual structures varying by over a factor of two, occasional pairs considerably larger, which would be very conspicuous to an investigator looking for individual or species differences in the sizes of brain components. It proves that the distribution of variance in volume across structures is quite uneven (Glendenning and Masterton 1998). This is an interesting aspect of species variation, and we do not discount it, but we have set our job to understand the significance of the factor of two in the context of the factor of 20 000, not the factor of two alone.

One potential answer to the question of the significance of brain size is that perhaps only ratios are important, and Harry Jerison, founder of much of the work in brain evolution and allometry, has shown that 'encephalization', essentially the ratio of brain size to body size, correlates much better with both our intuitions about and measures of behavioral complexity than does absolute brain size (Jerison 1973). Others have gone on to argue that there may be two different aspects of size, a scaling aspect and a species-difference aspect (Aboitiz 1996). This second argument, however, is perplexing when a second aspect of the regular structure of brain allometry is considered: disproportionality (Fig. 6.2). While the sizes of brain parts are predictable over brain scaling, a human brain does not look like a mouse brain enlarged a thousand times or so – each structure enlarges with brain size at its own characteristic rate, in particular, the cortex and cerebellum growing such as to completely dominate the volume of the brain in large-brained animals. If brain structures do not enlarge with increasing brain size at constant ratios, it is unclear how to understand what 'residual mass' is.

The proximate cause of the disproportionality in the enlargement of brain parts can be understood by looking at neurogenesis, how neurons are generated in early development across mammalian species (Fig. 6.2 b). The ordinal position of the peak day that neurogenesis ceases for each cell group and structure in the brain is very highly conserved (this end of neurogenesis is called the cell group or structure's 'birthday') although the total duration of neurogenesis varies from about 10 days in the mouse to over a hundred in monkeys. A two-factor equation can be written that captures 99 per cent of the variance in this species/structure matrix (Clancy *et al.* 1999, 2001). Curves of cell production in embryogenesis do not increase linearly, but exponentially, reflecting the doubling and redoubling nature of the 'symmetric' phase of cell division as the organism is first generated. The consequences of exponential growth for lengthening the period of neurogenesis by about a factor of 10, the ratio difference from mouse to monkey, are quite different for the end neuron number in structures with early birthdates (such as the medulla), middle birthdates (such as the midbrain), and late ones (such as the cortex). Our shorthand term for this relationship is 'late equals large' (Fig. 6.3). Thus, particular parts of the brain increase disproportionately *by a developmental rule.* This was quite a disturbing finding, in that most previous accounts of relative brain enlargement were cast as special adaptations due to the virtues of particular brain parts. Particularly, some special organization or advantage was often ascribed to the cortex – its efficient layering, the columnar structure. However, the

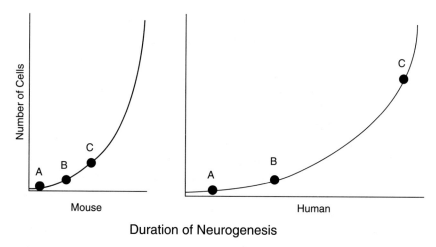

Fig. 6.3 'Late equals large.' A schematic of the consequences for eventual size of a structure generated early (A), intermediate (B), or late (C) in the order of neurogenesis for a species with a short period of neurogenesis and a small brain, like a mouse, versus one with a long period of neurogenesis and a large brain. In the long-development species, the precursor pool for late-generated structures has a longer time to multiply and becomes disproportionately large.

developmental rule that will produce a large cortex is already resident in those small stem mammals with their small cortices, who presumably had no particular plans of their own for generating a useful structure to house a 'language cortex' someday. Before we go on to discuss this perplexing observation as structure, constraint, or adaptation, we will go into a little more detail about just what the developmental rule is.

6.5 Forebrain segmental structure

Mammals are different from most other vertebrates by confining most of their neurogenesis to early development, rather than generating brain throughout life (there are exceptions to this generalization, of much current interest (Scharff 2000)). The conserved pattern of early neurogenesis we see, as well as where ongoing neurogenesis is found, can be explained by reference to a relatively new organizational scheme that finds a type of segmental structure in the forebrain. The patterns of expression of regulatory genes and transcription factors in early neurogenesis were used to establish this prosomere model (Rubenstein *et al.* 1994). The basic axes that define this structure are common to the entire brain, which begins as an extended plate, the 'neural plate', which subsequently rounds up and connects its lateral-most edges to become the 'neural tube'. The neural tube, whose original form is most obviously retained in the spinal cord, consists of repeating segments of similar fundamental structure with local variations. The part of the plate (and later tube) near the midline is called 'basal' for its position, and in the spinal cord this part gives rise to motor neurons. The lateral part is called 'alar', Latin for 'wing', and in the spinal

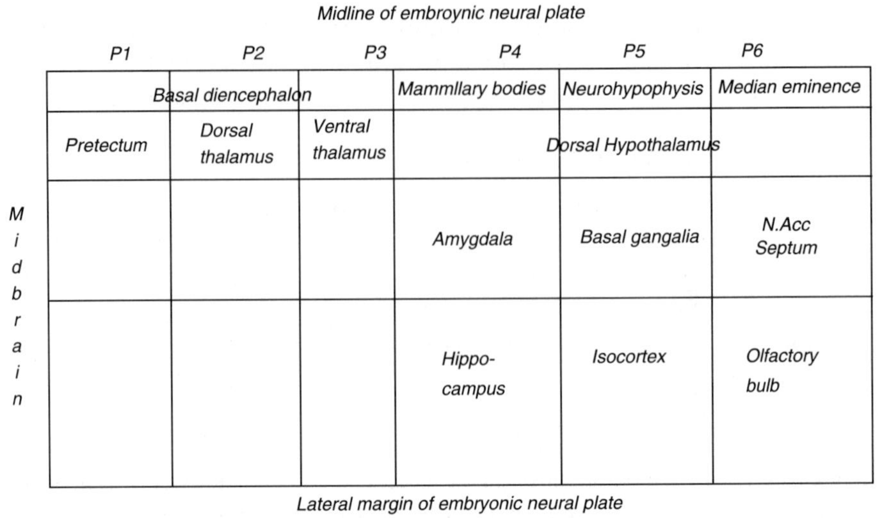

Midline of embroynic neural plate

	P1	P2	P3	P4	P5	P6
	Basal diencephalon			Mammllary bodies	Neurohypophysis	Median eminence
	Pretectum	Dorsal thalamus	Ventral thalamus	Dorsal Hypothalamus		
M i d b r a i n				Amygdala	Basal gangalia	N.Acc Septum
				Hippo-campus	Isocortex	Olfactory bulb

Lateral margin of embryonic neural plate

Fig. 6.4 Components of prosomeres, the embryonic segments of the telencephalon, described by Rubenstein *et al.* (1994). The lateral-most part of the early neural plate is the part that undergoes the most extended cell division and becomes disproportionately large in large brains. (N. ACC: Nucleus accumbens.)

cord contains sensory neurons. This embryonic basal–medial, alar–lateral plate-reconformed-into-a-tube structure can be tracked down in the adult with classical neuroanatomical methods up to about the level of the midbrain. The extended and eventually convoluted pattern of neurogenesis in the forebrain, however, makes it impossible to track cell groups from their origin. Examination of gene expression gradients was required in order to trace each cell group back to its position of origin on the two axes of the embryonic brain, anterior–posterior and basal–alar.

An assignment of the traditionally named brain parts to this axial system is given in Fig. 6.4 – for the most part (with some exceptions), as adult brain divisions reflect embryonic neural tube positions, these assignments can be made unambiguously. Hypothalamic and some basal forebrain structures are in the basal prosomeres, the large cellular masses of the forebrain, for example, the basal ganglia, are intermediate, and the cortical structures – olfactory bulb, hippocampus – most lateral or alar. If embryonic axial position is correlated with birth date (Finlay *et al.* 1998), both axes contribute to the solution, but the alar–basal axis predominates, with late birthdays for cell groups associated with alar positions, early birthdates with basal. Our short-hand for the relationship of timing of neurogenesis to brain part size 'late equals large' can now be extended to a spatial axis of gene expression 'lateral equals late equals large'. Note that for two of the most anterior structures in the most lateral-alar position, the olfactory bulb and hippocampus, there is in fact no terminal 'birthday' and neurogenesis continues throughout life, even in mammals (Bayer 1980, 1983).

Therefore, the conserved pattern of neurogenesis is not the crystallization of an arbitrary order that happened at some point in mammalian evolution, but is an expression of an axial pattern that, at least in part, is common to all vertebrates.

6.6 **The nature of constraints**

When this conserved pattern of neurogenesis producing disproportionate allometry is viewed in the language of special adaptation and constraint, the constraint is heavy. If it might be advantageous to select on the size of a brain part outside of the allowable factor of two, it appears that the only option to select on anything is to select on everything. For a hypothetical example, if a mouse could gather more food by increasing its auditory spatial resolution by increasing the size of the inferior colliculus more than a factor of two, all brain parts would have to be enlarged, with exceptional leverage on the size of the cortex and cerebellum, which would increase at a greater rate in size than the colliculus. This cost seems quite implausible, because brain tissue is metabolically expensive (with the possible exception of the largest cetaceans, where the fraction of metabolic energy allotted to the brain with respect to the body becomes negligible). An interesting example of the way minimal caloric requirements are defended can be found in the precise inverse relationship of brain size and intestine length (another expensive tissue) in primates – the more brain, the shorter the gut and the more limited the range of edible food becomes (Aiello and Wheeler 1995). So, if selection on the mouse increased auditory capacity happened in the way outlined, conserved neurogenesis would indeed be a constraint and the mouse would have to pay for its extra auditory capacity with the metabolic load incurred for useless neural tissue elsewhere.

If the premises of the hypothetical scenario for the improved mouse are taken apart, however, it has at least three interesting components for our argument:

1. Capacities like 'auditory acuity in foraging' can be appropriately localized to a brain part.

2. Increase in size of structures improves functionality.

3. Structure–function mappings in the brain are fixed.

We will discuss the first two concepts only briefly. For the first, it is interesting to note how rarely behaviors on which selection might act could be plausibly controlled by a single brain part, with the possible exception of features of sensory acuity. The coordination of increase in brain size over all brain parts should alert us to the fact that almost all functions are necessarily distributed, over sensory and motor neurons and almost everything in between. Recall, the problem of how to select for spatially distributed systems was the question that began this whole enterprise, and it may be that selecting on the whole brain is in fact the most economical way, the only way of increasing a distributed system. Interestingly, with the exception of the olfactory/limbic system, no other distributed functional system in the brain appears to show detectable covariation past directly connected structures (Barton and Harvey 2000; Finlay *et al.* 2001) or exhibits a genetic marker that identifies it in early development.

The second concept of the relationship of brain size to improved function is a major conundrum in brain evolution, and we cannot answer it here. Relative brain size is certainly linked to behavioral complexity, and has been directly linked to memory capacity in some cases (Nottebohm and Pandazis 1981; DeVoogd *et al.* 1993; Jacobs and Spencer 1994). Why absolute brain size does not necessarily have the same result is unclear.

The final statement 'structure–function mappings in the brain are fixed' deserves the closest attention, and we need to consider both the phylogenetic and epigenetic aspects of the question. There is no doubt that some functions are really fixed – the eyes just don't do well in somesthesis, and probably never will. The immediate connections of primary sensory and motor neurons are probably also somewhat limited in their potential functions. The multimodal, converging nature of the rest of the brain makes reassignment of functions to new structures, however, both plausible and likely, and can deliver us from the grip of a constraint that might appear crippling. Phylogenetically, it seems quite likely that new or modified functions might find their place in structures that become large easily by virtue of their embryonic position, rather than by modifying embryologically-disadvantaged locations. So, new functions find a place in the cortex because it becomes large, not the cortex becomes large because there are new functions in it. Many new observations in brain plasticity tell us that epigenetically, it is possible to map functions into structures where space is made available (one very interesting example and several reviews: Burton *et al.* 2002; Pallas 2001; Kingsbury and Finlay 2001; Finlay 2004). Especially, considering the requirement for robust, adaptive solutions in development, a general ability to map new functions into areas, as either new functions are required or new areas are available, seems a capacity to which we should now pay particular attention.

We will now go on to present some new data about the proliferation of areas in the cortex, as a particular example of the general argument we are making: does the proliferation of cortical areas represent special adaptation, as embodied in the special function of each cortical area, or the expression of developmental rules?

6.7 Proliferation of cortical areas

Since Brodmann (1909) first divided the isocortex into discrete areas on the basis of their cellular architecture, tremendous interest has been generated in mapping sensory, cognitive, and motor processes onto localized regions of cortex. A common core of areas responsible for the processing of visual, somatomotor, and auditory information have since been identified in the cortices of a variety of mammalian species (Krubitzer 1995). Claims for more specialized areas, from echolocation in bats (Schuller *et al.* 1991) to moral judgment in humans (Moll *et al.* 2002), have been made with increasingly refined electrophysiological and imaging techniques. The apparent modular organization of the cortex, that is the physical separation of modalities and modes of computation from initial analysis to upper-level functions, has been important in accounts of cortical evolution. For example the cortical area, as an anatomical and functional module, has been hypothesized to be a unit of selection in cortical evolution, with specialized cortical areas duplicating in response to selection pressure for particular sensory and cognitive abilities (Kaas 2000a).

Other functional and mechanistic accounts of cortical area proliferation exist, however, and many of these need not be mutually exclusive. At the functional level, the parcellation of cortex into areas might emerge from the computational require-ment to keep interactions local to maintain processing speed, or to 'save wire' in expanding, richly interconnected cortices (Ringo 1991; Cherniak 1992; Murre and Sturdy 1995). An experimentally produced alteration of early patterning molecules produces a kind of cortical proliferation: for example adding additional polarizing zones that control transcription factors that determine cortex polarity in an embryo can result in the duplication of cortical areas (Grove and Fukuchi-Shimogori 2003). The parcellation of the cortex into areas might emerge as an epiphenomenon of local organizational processes, such as activity-dependent stabilization of synapses, as the hexagonal structure of the honeybee comb arises from the construction of individual cells (Elman et al. 1996). A number of developmental models for the specification of cortical areas have been proposed (Rakic 1988, 1991, 1995; Kingsbury and Finlay 2001), but none have been linked explicitly with the pattern of areal proliferation in cortical evolution. In general, the number of cortical areas increases as overall brain size increases, but we do not know how predictable this increase is, nor what aspect of brain size best predicts it. Understanding scaling of cortical area proliferation is critical to understanding the developmental mechanisms that might produce an area.

We therefore examined the proliferation of the number of cortical areas with respect to brain size, in 24 mammals representing six orders, comparing visual, somatosen-sory, and total areal proliferation. Included in the dataset were eight insectivores, six marsupials, five primates, three rodents, one bat, and one carnivore (Table 6.1). For each species, we ascertained or measured overall brain weight and overall cortical surface area. These measurements were drawn primarily, but not exclusively, from the published mapping studies of Kaas, Krubitzer, and their colleagues (Kaas 1982, 1987, Krubitzer 1995; Krubitzer et al. 1986, 1993, 1994, 1997; Kaas et al. 1989; Krubitzer and Kaas 1990a, b, 1993; Felleman and Van Essen 1991; Northcutt and Kaas 1995; Beck et al. 1996; Gosh 1997; Beck and Kaas 1998, 1999; Lyon et al. 1998; Catania et al. 1999; Huffman et al. 1999; Rosa 1999; Kahn et al. 2000; Krubitzer and Huffman 2000; Lewis and Van Essen 2000a, b; Slutsky et al. 2000; Weller et al. 2000; Wu et al. 2000; Collins et al. 2001; Hui-Xin et al. 2002).

Table 6.1 Cortical areas for 24 mammalian species.

Common Name	Species Name	Bodyweight(g)	Brainweight(g)	Visual Areas	Somatomotor Areas	Total Areas	Cortical Area (mm²)
Owl Monkey	Aotus trivirgatus	935.00	18.20	23.00	13.00	36.00	5,485.85
Short-tailed Shrew	Blarina brevicauda	19.70	0.39	1.00	3.00	4.00	28.13
Marmoset	Callithrix jacchus	246.00	7.90	19.00	11.00	30.00	910.26
Least Shrew	Cryptotis parva	9.90	0.25	1.00	3.00	4.00	21.80
Striped Possum	Dactylopsila trivirgata	435.00		2.00	6.00	8.00	248.65
Northern Quoll	Dasyurus hallucatus	750.00		2.00	5.00	7.00	133.17
North American Opossum	Didelphis marsupialis	1,700.00	6.30	4.00	5.00	9.00	269.60
Tenrec	Echinops telfairi	87.55	0.62	2.00	3.00	5.00	24.24
Hedgehog	Erinaceus europaeus	874.16	3.29	2.00	6.00	8.00	106.69
Cat	Felis cattus	3,300.00	30.00	15.00	15.00	30.00	3,014.80
Galago	Galago sp.	201.00	4.80	13.00	11.00	24.00	382.83
Rhesus Macaque	Macaca sp.	7,950.00	95.00	32.00	22.00	54.00	10,598.20
Short-tailed Possum	Monodelphis domestica	150.00		3.50	3.00	6.50	44.94
Mouse	Mouse sp.	24.00	0.50	3.00	6.00	9.00	51.24
Flying Fox	Pteropus poliocephalus	695.00	7.23	6.50	8.00	14.50	219.63
Rat	Rattus sp.	217.00	1.79	4.00	7.00	11.00	90.69
Squirrel monkey	Saimiri sciureus	901.25	24.00	20.00	10.00	30.00	4,373.52
Fat-tailed Dunnart	Sminthopsis crassicaudata	20.00		2.00	3.00	5.00	11.37
Masked Shrew	Sorex cinereus	5.90	0.17	1.00	3.00	4.00	14.93
Southeastern Shrew	Sorex longirostris			1.00	3.00	4.00	9.48
Northern Water Shrew	Sorex palustris	14.60	0.28	1.00	3.00	4.00	25.55
Squirrel	Squirrel sp.	650.00	6.00	7.00	7.00	14.00	213.85
Brush-tailed Possum	Trichosurus vulpecula			2.00	5.00	7.00	208.35
Tree Shrew	Tupia belangeri	104.00	2.50	8.00			385.25

6.7.1 Cortical area enumeration and measurement

Topographic maps of cortical areas were gathered from the above-cited literature, choosing only those where an exhaustive map of the cortical representation of a designated modality had been attempted. Each unimodal area was counted as one area, and bimodal areas, such as the audiovisual area in *Monodelphis domestica*, were allotted half to each sensory division. The identified subdivisions of major areas, such as the division of M1 into rostral and caudal subdivisions, were each counted as a single area. In cases where the cortex of a single animal has been extensively mapped by a single laboratory, we deferred to their counting scheme. For instance, the macaque visual cortex has been most extensively mapped in Van Essen's laboratory, which counted 32 visual areas, a figure that is generally accepted by most researchers (Kaas 2000a). Finally, for the mouse and rat, we included in our count areas that have been mapped but not yet published (or named) in the literature (J. Kaas, personal communication). Most of the measurements of the area of the cortical surface, particularly for brains without extensive gyrification, come from flat-mounts of cortex (see Kaas (2000a) for details). For published maps of this type, we traced the perimeters of flattened cortices into NIMH Image v.4 using a WACOM data tablet and used their accompanying scale bars to obtain surface area estimates for each animal (Table 6.1).

Not all researchers agree on the definition or the number of cortical areas. Some make significantly fewer subdivisions (for example Zilles 1985) while others argue for the existence of a larger number of smaller areas even in small brains (for example Olavarria and Montero 1990). We chose to remain agnostic on the 'true' definition of a cortical area, and to rely instead on the pragmatic consideration of which explicit criteria allow us to examine the most species. The arguments of Kaas and Krubitzer on what constitutes an area are, however, compelling. Their criteria for identification of an area are multidimensional, and include the presence of a fully mapped visuotopic, somatotopic, or other computed dimension, internally consistent patterns of thalamic, intracortical, and callosal input and output, and in some cases identification of the features of cortical cytoarchitecture or neurotransmitter or modulator expression. The pragmatic concern that their work so dominates this data led us to preferentially employ their work and those who used similar criteria, in the interest of consistency and comparability. In cases of disagreement between investigators, such as the number of visual areas of the mouse and the rat, we deferred to the counting scheme of Kaas and Krubitzer.

6.7.2 Issues in analysis of phylogenetic data

Because species may share traits through common descent rather than through independent adaptation, we employed the method of the Comparison of Independent Contrasts (CAIC, Purvis and Rambaut, (1995)), in order to correct for the effects of phylogenetic relatedness. The resolved phylogenetic tree required for CAIC analysis was compiled from recent work by Murphy *et al.* (2001) and Kaskan *et al.* (2005). Branch lengths used for the computation of contrasts were set equivalent, assuming a punctuational model of change. This procedure yields contrasts upon which standard regression analyses can then be applied.

The number of cortical areas might be best predicted by one of several independent variables, including cortical surface area, or the weight of the whole brain, or 'encephalization', the ratio of brain to body weight. There was reason to suspect that in the case of two animals with equal brain sizes, the more encephalized one might have a greater number of cortical areas. Looking at the sole example in this dataset of three approximately similar brain weights where body weight varies substantially, between the Northern American opossum (brain weight 6.3 g, body weight 1700 g); the squirrel (brain weight 6 g, body weight 650 g); and the marmoset, (brain weight 7.3 g, body weight 248 g), the number of cortical areas was 9, 14, and 30, respectively. Unfortunately in this dataset overall, the biggest-bodied animals and most encephalized are all primates, and the smallest, and least encephalized are all insectivores. The two measures of cortical area and encephalization are highly correlated (r = 0.98. $R^2 = 0.96$, n = 19). In addition, brain weight also correlates highly with cortical surface area (r = 0.95, $R^2 = 0.91$, *n* = 19), rendering all three measures of brain size statistically indistinguishable for the set of animals we were able to examine. Since cortical area is the most proximate variable to the dependent variables we measured (number of cortical areas, ocular dominance column width, and axonal spread in the cortex) we have done our statistical analyses with respect to cortical area, but, in explanation of these data, the covariation of cortical area with other brain measures should not be forgotten.

6.7.3 Scaling of cortical area number

The number of cortical areas overall was well predicted by cortex surface area (log cortical areas = 0.000 + 0.250 log area, $R^2 = 0.78$ or 78 per cent of the variance captured, n = 22, p < 0.001) as were the number of somatomotor areas (log somatomotor areas = 0.000 + 0.240 log area, $R^2 = 0.79$, n = 22, p < 0.001). Though highly statistically significant, surface area captured less of the variance when predicting the number of visual areas (log visual areas = 0.000 + 0.250 log area, $R^2 = 0.48$, n = 23, p < 0.001). Figure 6.5a–c shows the simple regression of cortical area proliferation as predicted by cortical surface area for visual, somatomotor, and the total number of cortical areas.

The observation that the log of cortical area strongly predicts the log of the number of cortical areas suggests that the relationship is predictable, but this function is not directly instructive about the kind or number of developmental mechanisms underlying this pattern of proliferation. As most biological developmental mechanisms bear some relationship to cell size, they operate over finite physical distances and not their ratios. To better visualize the change in cortex size for comparison to developmental

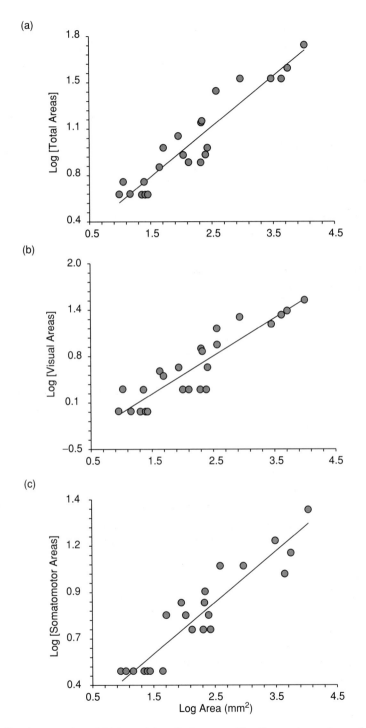

Fig. 6.5 Simple regression of (a) log total cortical area proliferation on log cortex surface area (**log total areas** = 0.172 + 0.379 log area, R^2 = 0.89, n = 23); (b) visual area proliferation (**log visual areas** = −0.529 + 0.509 log area, R^2 = 0.82, n = 24); and (c) somatomotor area proliferation (**log somatomotor areas** = 0.154 + 0.287 log area, R^2 = 0.87, n = 23).

mechanisms, the number of cortical areas was plotted against cortical surface area *without* logarithmic transformation in Fig. 6.6. The brains and grids adjoining the graph show the approximate number and surface area of visual and somatomotor areas for the smallest, medium-sized, and largest brains in comparable scales. For increases from the smallest cortices (from 10 to 400 mm^2), cortical area proliferation is rapid. Thereafter, however, only massive increases in cortical area produce new cortical areas.

6.8 Known developmental mechanisms which produce primary sensory areas

6.8.1 Setting initial positional information

Following Gould, the way cortical areas proliferate will depend not only on adaptation – selection on the basis of function – but also on what developmental mechanisms are available to modify cortical layout. At least two general classes of mechanism work in parallel to pattern the developing cortex, one through direct genetic specification of the cells of the cortex, and the second through instruction of the cortex by its major

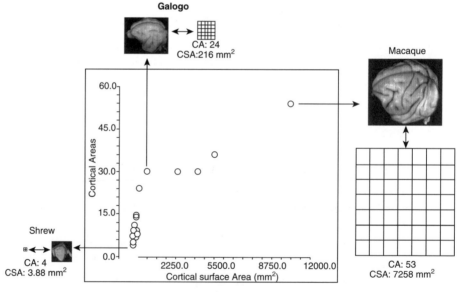

Fig. 6.6 The number of cortical areas plotted as a function of cortex surface area, without logarithmic transformation. To permit direct visual comparison, the approximate total cortical surface area of mapped visual and somatomotor areas (CSA) and number of cortical areas (CA) for the shrew, galago, and macaque are inset, as an example of small, medium, and large cortex area. Note that the entire cortex of the smaller brains would fit conveniently within any single cortical area of the rhesus monkey.

input, the thalamus. For the first class of mechanism, regions of the cortex are made distinct by the graded and overlapping expression of molecular markers, ranging from transcription factors such as Emx-2 and Pax 6 (Bishop *et al.* 2000; Grove and Fukuchi-Shimogori 2003) to the ephrin family of receptors and their ligands (Gao *et al.* 1996; Donoghue and Rakic 1999), to cell-adhesive molecules such as the cadherins (Redies and Takeichi 1996). While no single molecular gradient serves to define a particular cortical area *per se*, some cortical areas may be delineated by the combined or nested expression of multiple transcription factors. For instance, in the rat, the combined gradients of transcription factors Lhx-2, Emx-1, and SCIP appear to distinguish early auditory cortex from early visual cortex (Nakagawa *et al.* 1999). Experimental manipulation of the relative concentration of other molecules can shift cortical area boundaries rostrally or caudally, such as the transcription factors Pax6 and Emx2 appear to do (Bishop *et al.* 2000). Molecular gradients thus serve to set the basic polarity, position, and size of the primary areas (Grove and Fukuchi-Shimogori 2003). Some of the first-expressed molecules in these cortical areas designated by the transcription factors described above are axon-guidance molecules, such as the ephrins and their receptors, and contribute to the establishment of specific projections from the thalamus to the cortex, the next major developmental event.

6.8.2 Secondary thalamic instruction of the cortex

Once in place, thalamic projections represent the second major source of cortical patterning, driving multiple features of cortical organization. Thalamic projections can induce the expression of particular neurotransmitters, control cell number, and, in concert with molecular mechanisms, can induce topographic and organizational features such as barrel fields for whiskers or ocular dominance columns (Crowley and Katz 2002; review in Kingsbury and Finlay 2001).

6.8.3 Different control of primary and secondary regions?

However, as we now understand them, initial transcriptional control of cortical polarity and number account for the production of primary sensory and motor areas only. On the basis of similarities in cytoarchitecture, connectivity and response properties, Kaas, Krubitzer and their colleagues find evidence for three primary sensory areas, A1, V1, and S1 in a characteristic topographic relationship to each other in even the smallest brains, with secondary and tertiary representations elaborated in the zones between these areas as brains enlarge (Kingsbury and Finlay 2001). In addition, most, if not all, mammalian brains have at least one motor field, M1, which often overlaps with areas of the primary sensory cortex, S1, producing an M1/S1 area (Krubitzer 1998).

Many features distinguish primary somatomotor and visual areas from secondary and tertiary areas. The constant presence and topographic arrangement of the primary somatomotor, auditory and visual areas in all mammals but monotremes, and the conservation of their direct input from primary sensory thalamic nuclei has led to the hypothesis that these areas are a conserved, organizing 'core' of the cortex, as described above (Krubitzer 1998). Molecular gradients in early cortical development primarily demarcate primary somatomotor and visual areas (Ragsdale and Grove 2001). Relative to primary areas, secondary and tertiary sensory/motor areas are cytoarchitectonically indistinct with borders between areas lacking sharp transitions, and also, relative to V1, extrastriate areas tend to have more complex visuotopic maps with less defined visual topographies (with the notable exception of area MT (Rosa 2002)).

6.9 Axonal sorting as a candidate for segregation of secondary areas

The relationship of cortical surface area to cortical area number (Fig. 6.6) – rapid increase followed by slow change – could be consistent with a two-factor model of proliferation in which the effects of one factor become negligible at some size. Activity-dependent axonal sorting is a potential candidate for the first factor. What is the cortical area over which activity-dependent axonal sorting might operate? One rough quantitative assessment of this is the size of ocular dominance columns, which have been demonstrated by numerous manipulations in various species to depend on local activity and competition in the axonal populations (Tigges and Tigges 1979; Florence et al. 1986; Hess and Edwards 1987; Anderson et al. 1988; Law et al. 1988; Florence and Kaas 1992; Horton and Hocking 1996; Chappert-Piquemal et al. 2001; Cheng et al. 2001), though activity-independent factors also play a role in setting the size of these columns (Crowley and Katz 2002).

We thus obtained estimates of the spatial ranges over which various developmental processes are known to act, particularly activity-dependent sorting, in order to determine its plausibility as a developmental mechanism underlying areal proliferation. The absolute and relative dimensions of ocular dominance columns and axon arbor extents with respect to brain size were used to estimate the ranges over which axonal interactions might occur.

6.9.1 Ocular dominance columns

Ocular dominance columns have been described and their widths measured in a variety of species including galagos, macaques (Florence and Kaas 1992), spider monkeys (Florence et al. 1986), talapoin monkeys (Florence and Kaas 1992), capuchin monkeys (Hess and Edwards 1987), marmoset monkeys (Chappert-Piquemal et al. 2001), squirrel monkeys (Horton and Hocking 1996), ferrets (Law et al. 1988), cats (Anderson et al. 1988), humans (Cheng and Waggoner 2001; Goodyear 2001), and chimps (Tigges and Tigges 1979). To examine to what extent ocular dominance

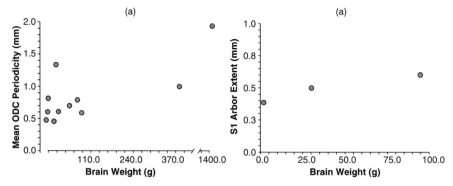

Fig. 6.7 (A) Mean ocular dominance column periodicity plotted against brain size, including humans, chimpanzees, six species of monkey the prosimian galago, the ferret, and domestic cat. Note that column periodicity varies only 4.5 times among brains that vary in size by a factor of 200. (B) Mean mediolateral extents of intracellularly-labeled thalamocortical axons terminating in primary somatosensory cortex for the rat, cat, and macaque monkey plotted against brain size. Note that axon extents vary only two times among brains that vary in size by a factor of 50.

columns scale with brain size, we plotted the average periodicity (average width of one light and one dark stripe) of ocular dominance columns against brain weight (Fig. 6.7A). Brain weights were obtained from various sources (Stephan 1981; Huffman *et al.* 1999; and varied from Kinser 2000).

The average width of ocular dominance columns remains in the range of 0.45 to 2 mm, varying very little, in species whose primary visual cortex area varies by a factor of approximately 38. Using the most permissive statistical technique, simple regression, this regression just reaches statistical significance, with a large component of this relationship clearly due to the human outlier data point (log ODC width $= -0.3097 + 0.1260$ log brain weight, $p = 0.0313, n = 11$).

6.9.2 Axon arbor extents in S1

For another estimation of the extent to which axon arbors vary in size in a comparable cortical context, we gathered measurements of the mediolateral extents of arbors in the primary somatosensory (S1) cortex of rats (Jensen 1987), cats (Landry and Deschenes 1981), and macaque monkeys (Garraghty and Sur 1990). Axons may have multiple arbors, widely spaced, but our intent in choosing this particular data source was to describe a single, spatially continuous arborization in a location specifiable across species. As Fig. 6.7B illustrates, the average mediolateral extents of arbors in the primary somatosensory cortices of rats, cats, and macaque monkeys vary only slightly (384–600 mm) among species whose brains vary in size by a factor of approximately 50.

Taking both examples together, both the widths of ocular dominance columns and the extents of thalamocortical axons in S1 vary very little over a wide range of brain sizes, both about two to five-fold, and both are the appropriate size to account for the fractionation of the cortex into areas at small-to-medium brain sizes. In addition, dendritic arbor size, which can also be affected by activity-dependent sorting mechanisms (Quartz and Sejnowski 1997), also does not vary appreciably with either brain size of cortical area size (Kaas 2000b). It is thus possible that co-ordinated size constraints apply to both localized axonal and dendritic arbors, and our explanation should include both factors.

The Southeastern shrew (*Sorex longirostris*) is has the smallest cortex in this set. The total surface area of somatomotor and visual cortex in this animal measures only $3.8 \, \text{mm}^2$, and the approximate dimensions of its average cortical area is $1.0 \times 1.0 \, \text{mm}$, a reasonable correspondence to the size range over which activity-dependent sorting has been shown to occur in the ocular dominance columns and somatosensory axon arbors of species with larger cortices (0.3–0.6 mm). Indeed V1 occupies only $0.5 \, \text{mm}^2$ in *Sorex longirostris* and typically occupies less than $1 \, \text{mm}^2$ in larger species of shrew (Catania *et al.* 1999). We hypothesize, as brains get bigger, more specific aspects of sensory stimuli may provide the correlational structure necessary to allow the segregation of new, functionally specific cortical areas once a minimum volume of tissue is made available. In fact the primary somatosensory areas, as they proliferate, segregate submodalities of sensory processing (Kaas 1997), and could be viewed as direct analogies to ocular dominance columns.

Axon-interaction forces may cease to be adequate to drive cortical area proliferation after topographically-mapped dimensions exceed 2–3 mm, and instead provide only substructure within cortical areas, the stripes, puffs, and blobs described in carnivore and primate cortex. At large brain sizes, other factors governing proliferation, such as molecular gradients released by patterning centers, may dominate, or the input to the cortex might reorganize. For example the targeted redirection of cell proliferation into the thalamus in great apes or humans may be a further evolutionary and developmental mechanism of further specification of the cortex through its thalamic input (Letinic and Rakic 2001).

6.10 A 'developmental constraint' account of cortical area proliferation

The degree to which the proliferation of cortical areas past the primary sensory areas is a straightforward function of cortex area suggests that either general functional constraints, or developmental mechanisms present in all brains, could account for their regular patterns of proliferation, as opposed to special selection on cortical areas specified for particular functions. The specializations and the relative size of the sensory and motor periphery may be the means of the functional differentiation of cortical areas in specialized species, transmitted to the cortex through 'generic' developmental mechanisms. Thus, new cortical areas may not necessarily emerge in response to selective pressure for novel or enhanced computational abilities, but may instead be inevitable consequences of size-constrained developmental processes scaling over a wide range of brain sizes. The fact that they emerge, however, does tell us something significant about the nature of cortical processing. Cortical areas are primarily defined as topographic maps, either of sensory surfaces or of a wide variety of computed dimensions, a representation that preserves local interactions in sensory and motor sheets. The principal role we hypothesize for Hebbian mechanisms in proliferation of new regions also emphasizes the importance of local interactions in the cortex. When this mechanism is placed in the context of intracortical feedforward and feedback, a potential for continual recombination and contextualization of new maps is created. Further discussion of how intracortical and thalamic connectivity have an interesting 'scalability' can be found in a recent review by Merker (2004).

6.11 Is predictable brain and cortex scaling a 'constraint' or a demonstration of robust structure comparable to the vertebrate body plan?

The observation that so much brain organization appeared to be the result of developmental rules first expressed in small brains and then extended with apparent grace into much larger ones was at first dismaying. Given that the usual account of brain structure was in terms of direct selection on brain parts, far too much precognition of future cortical needs was required of the first stem mammals for comfort. The growing realization of the conservation of fundamental developmental programs, and essential metabolic pathways, however, led to an analysis of their design features that permits both stability and adaptability. The conservation of body plan development suggests we should extend the same sort of analysis to the brain.

Our claim is not that all brains are the same, possessing no particular adaptations, but rather that our job is to understand just how the conserved structure we observe makes the brain permissive of adaptations. A premature mapping of species-specific adaptations onto brain parts, a sort of cross-species phrenology, is what we should avoid. The conservation of the Hox gene-generated body plan does not conserve antennae and exoskeletons, but rather, an 'evolvable' system of segmentation where different segments can diverge from a common organizational theme. The idea of 'computational tradeoffs' – that 'different brain areas are specialized to satisfy fundamental tradeoffs in the way that neural systems perform different kinds of learning and memory tasks' (O'Reilly, Chapter 16 this volume; Atallah *et al.* 2004) could be the key to understanding evolvable brain organization within conserved developmental structure. The cortex, particularly posterior cortex, appears specialized to acquire generalized statistical information about the environment, preserved over extended periods of time. Perhaps only those mammals which produced the necessary structure for this kind of computation in the alar prosomeres were able to make efficient use of the fact that neural structures generated in alar regions tended to increase disproportionately in size when body and brain size increased. Only those mammals were 'evolvable' and only those mammals are still here.

In the case of the cortex, we have an interesting window into evolution by looking at normal variations in development, and at pathology, because we can view many kinds of mutations or genetic change as a similar class of accidental event to which the cortex must equilibrate. We will consider one example each of normal variability, pathology, and genetic change to illustrate the properties of the cortex when encountering variation of different kinds.

The report of remarkable individual variability in the size of cortical areas, which would seem to be in direct contradiction with the very regular scaling across species described in all allometric studies and in this paper, is a perplexing observation. We will assume that published allometric studies have managed to determine representative mean structure sizes and address the more theoretical question of how we are to understand the importance of structure sizes if individual members may occasionally differ very substantially from one another in the relative sizes of brain parts (Adams *et al.* 2003; Purves and LaMantia 1993; Van Essen *et al.* 1984). What kinds of variations are reported at the individual level, within species? The best information comes from a number of studies of the primate visual system, particularly the rhesus macaque. Van Essen and colleagues (1984) have found individual animals whose primary visual cortex differed by a factor of two or more. Similarly, the variability of the human visual cortex exceeds substantially the variability of the entire cortex (Gilissen and Zilles 1995). There are no studies, to our knowledge, of the variability at the individual level of the number and arrangement of cortical areas. Few of these observations have as yet been tracked onto individual variation in visual capacity, and it would be interesting to do so, though at minimum a condition called 'reduced visual cortex syndrome' has not emerged! There is empirical reason to believe, however, that the basic processing of the visual system will be robust to wide variations in number of neurons in interconnecting populations, due to the equalizing effect of processes such as activity-dependent stabilization in early development (Pallas and Finlay 1989, 1991; Rezak *et al.* 2003) or compensatory perceptual processes in adulthood (for example Neitz *et al.* 2002).

Considering pathology, a variety of fascinating studies have now demonstrated that in both the early and late blind, the primary visual cortex may be redirected to participate in the process of Braille reading (Burton *et al.* 2002; Merabet *et al.* 2003). Thus, in both early development and adulthood, the occasion of underutilization of a cortical area for its typical function, even a primary sensory cortex, is either announced or can be detected, and it can subserve new functions.

Finally, an example in primate evolution illustrates a dramatic, species-specific niche adaptation arising apparently without genetic change in the cortex, though employing the new capacity requires the cortex. Several different radiations of primates have a mutation in one of their genes (just the difference of a DNA base pair or two) that make a photoreceptor protein (an opsin) change the frequency of light that best excites it, by substituting one or two amino acids that make up the opsin protein. Some of those primates couple the amino acid change with gene duplication, also a very common event in evolution (Jacobs 1998). Either of those changes is all that is required to produce primate trichromacy, three-receptor color vision, from the mammalian baseline dichromatic state. No other organizational changes of a genetic nature have been described in our visual systems – from the remaining retina to cortex, existing mechanisms for information extraction can take this small difference signal and produce a new perceptual world. The cortex is not disabled by the structural change in the photoreceptors that inform it but rather exploits the subtle new information offered.

We take these three examples as evidence that variability in cortical size can be assimilated gracefully into normal function both at the individual and the phylogenetic level; that the same piece of cortical tissue, in this case primary visual cortex, can subserve widely different functions; and that new, species-specific perceptual capacities need not require new cortical 'hardware' for their efficient use. In this functional context, it now seems likely that the predictability of disproportionate proliferation of the cortex with increasing brain size is not an unfortunate developmental constraint resulting in metabolic overload, but the precise placement of a tissue best serving adaptability across species.

Acknowledgements

We thank Jeremy Yost, Rick Dale and especially Jon H. Kaas for their invaluable comments in the preparation of this manuscript. This work was supported by NSF grant IBN 0138113 and NIH RO1 19245 grants to BLF.

References

Aboitiz F (1996). Does bigger mean better? Evolutionary determinants of brain size and structure. *Brain, Behavior and Evolution*, 47, 225–245.

Adams DL, Sincich LC and Horton JC (2003). Proportionate scaling of visual cortical areas revealed in complete flatmounts of macaque cerebral cortex. *Society for Neuroscience Abstracts*, 11, 818.

Aiello LC and Wheeler P (1995). The expensive-tissue hypothesis: the brain and digestive system in human and primate evolution. *Current Anthropology*, 36, 199–221

Albritton CC (1989). *Catastrophic episodes in earth history*. London and New York: Chapman and Hall.

Alvarez LW, Alvarez W, Asaro J and Michel HV (1980). Extraterrestrial cause for the Cretaceous-Tertiary extinction. *Science*, **208**, 1095–1108.

Anderson PA , Olavarria J and Van Sluyters RC (1988). The overall pattern of ocular dominance bands in cat visual cortex. *Journal of Neuroscience*, **6**, 2183–2200.

Atallah HE, Frank MJ and O'Reilly RC (2004). Hippocampus, cortex and basal ganglia: Insights from computational models of complementary learning systems. *Neurobiology of Learning and Memory*, in press.

Barton RA and Harvey PH (2000). Mosaic evolution of brain structure in mammals. *Nature*, **405**, 1055–1058.

Baum EB (2004). *What is thought?* Boston: MIT Press.

Bayer SA (1980). Development of the hippocampal region in the rat. I. Neurogenesis examined with 3H-thymidine autoradiography. *Journal of Comparative Neurology*, **190**, 87–114.

Bayer SA (1983). (3H) Thymidine-radiographic studies of neurogenesis in the rat olfactory bulb. *Experimental Brain Research*, **50**, 329–340.

Beck P and Kaas JH (1999). Cortical connections of the dorsomedial visual area in Old World macaque monkeys. *Journal of Comparative Neurology*, **406**, 487–502.

Beck PD and Kaas JH (1998). Cortical connections of the dorsomedial visual area in the new world owl monkeys (*Aotus trivirgatus*) and squirrel monkeys (*Saimiri scireus.*) *Journal of Comparative Neurology*, **400**, 18–34.

Beck PD, Pospichal MW and Kaas JH (1996). Topography architecture and connections of somatosensory cortex in opossums, evidence for five somatosensory areas. *Journal of Comparative Neurology*, **366**, 109–133.

Bishop KM, Gourdeau G and O'Leary DDM (2000). Regulation of area identity in the mammalian neocortex by Emx2 and Pax6. *Science*, **288**, 344–349.

Brodmann K (1909). *Vergliechende Lokalisationslehre der Grosshirnrinde in ihren Prinzipien dargestellt auf Grund der Zellenbaues.* Leipzig: Barth.

Burton H, Snyder AZ, Conturo TE , Akbudak E, Ollinger JM and Raichle ME (2002). Adaptive changes in early and late blind, An fMRI study of Braille reading. *Journal of Neurophysiology*, **87**, 589–607.

Callaerts P, Halder G and Gehring WJ (1997). Pax-6 in development and evolution. *Annual Review of Neuroscience*, **20**, 483–532.

Catania KC, Lyon DC, Mock OB and Kaas JH (1999). Cortical organization in shrews, evidence from five species. *Journal of Comparative Neurology*, **410**, 55–72.

Chappert-Piquemal C, Fonta C, Malecaze F and Imbert M (2001). Ocular dominance columns in the adult New World Monkey *Callithrix jacchus*. *Visual Neuroscience*, **18**, 407–412.

Cheng K and Waggoner RKT (2001). Human ocular dominance columns as revealed by high-field magnetic resonance imaging. *Neuron*, **32**, 359–374.

Cherniak C (1992). Local optimization of neuron arbors *Biological Cybernetics*, **66**, 503–510.

Clancy B, Darlington RB and Finlay BL (1999). The course of human events, predicting the timing of primate neural development. *Developmental Science*, **3**, 57–66.

Clancy B, Darlington RB and Finlay BL (2001). Translating developmental time across mammalian species. *Neuroscience*, **105**, 7–17.

Collins CE, Stepniewska I and Kaas JH (2001). Topographic patterns of V2 cortical connections in a prosimian primate *Galago garnetti*. *Journal of Comparative Neurology*, **431**, 155–167.

Crowley JC and Katz LC (2002). Ocular dominance development revisited. *Current Opinion in Neurobiology*, **12**, 104–109.

Dawkins R (1976). *The selfish gene.* Oxford: Oxford University Press.

Dawkins R (1986). *The blind watchmaker.* New York: W W Norton.

DeVoogd TJ, Krebs JR, Healy SD and Purvis A (1993). Relations between song repertoire size and the volume of brain nuclei related to song, comparative evolutionary analyses among oscine birds. *Proceedings of the Royal Society of London: B,* **254,** 75–78.

Donoghue MJ and Rakic P (1999). Molecular gradients and compartments in the embryonic primate cerebral cortex. *Cerebral Cortex,* **9,** 586–600.

Duboule D and Dollé P (1989). The structural and functional organisation of the mouse *Hox* gene family resembles that of *Drosophila* homeotic genes. *EMBO,* **8,** 1497–1505.

Elman J, Bates E, Johnson M, Karmiloff-Smith A, Parisi D and Plunkett K (1996). *Rethinking Innateness: A connectionist perspective on development.* Massachusetts: MIT Press.

Felleman DJ and Van Essen DC (1991). Distributed hierarchical processing in the primate cerebral cortex. *Cerebral Cortex,* **1,** 1–47.

Finlay BL (2004). Rethinking developmental neurobiology. In: M Tomasello and D Slobin, eds. *Beyond nature-nurture, essays in honor of Elizabeth Bates,* pp. 195–219. New York: Lawrence Earlbaum.

Finlay BL and Darlington RB (1995). Linked regularities in the development and evolution of mammalian brains. *Science,* **268,** 1578–1584.

Finlay BL and Pallas SL (1989). Control of cell number in the developing visual system. *Progress in Neurobiology,* **32,** 207–234.

Finlay BL, Darlington RB and Nicastro N (2001). Developmental structure in brain evolution. *Behavioral and Brain Sciences,* **24,** 263–307.

Finlay BL, Hersman MN and Darlington RB (1998). Patterns of vertebrate neurogenesis and the paths of vertebrate evolution. *Brain, Behavior and Evolution,* **52,** 232–242.

Finlay BL, Innocenti G and Scheich H (1991). *The neocortex, ontogeny and phylogeny.* New York: Plenum Press.

Finlay BL, Wikler KC and Sengelaub DR (1987). Regressive events in neurogenesis and scenarios for vertebrate brain evolution. *Brain, Behavior and Evolution,* **30,** 102–117.

Florence SL and Kaas JH (1992). Ocular dominance columns in area 17 of Old World macaque and talapoin monkeys. Complete reconstructions and quantitative analysis. *Visual Neuroscience,* **8,** 449–462.

Florence SL, Conley M and Casagrande VA (1986). Ocular dominance columns and retinal projections in New World spider monkeys (*Ateles ater*). *Journal of Comparative Neurology,* **234,** 234–248.

Gao PP, Zhang JH, Ceretti DP, Levitt P and Zhou R P (1996). Regulation of thalamic neurite outgrowth by the ephrin ligand ephrin A-5: implications for the development of thalamocortical projections. *Proceedings of the National Academy of Sciences, USA,* **95,** 5329–5334.

Garraghty PE and Sur M (1990). Morphology of single intracellularly stained axons terminating in area 3b of macaque monkeys. *Journal of Comparative Neurology,* **294,** 583–593.

Gerhart J and Kirschner M (1997). *Cell, Embryos and Evolution.* Malden, MA: Blackwell Science.

Gilissen E and Zilles K (1995). The relative volume of the primary visual cortex and its intersubject variability among humans, a new morphometric study. *Comptes Rendus Academie Sciences Paris,* **320,** 897–902.

Glendenning KK and Masterton RB (1998). Comparative morphometry of mammalian central auditory systems: Variation in nuclei and form of the ascending system. *Brain, Behavior and Evolution,* **51,** 59–89.

Goodyear BG (2001). Brief visual stimulation allows mapping of ocular dominance in visual cortex using fMRI. *Human Brain Mapping*, **14**, 210–217.

Gosh S (1997). Comparison of the cortical connections of areas 4g and 4d in the cat cerebral cortex. *Journal of Comparative Neurology*, **388**, 371–396.

Gould SJ (1977). *Ontogeny and phylogeny* Cambridge, MA: Harvard University Press.

Gould SJ (1980). *The panda's thumb*. New York: W W Norton.

Gould SJ (2002). *The structure of evolutionary theory*. Cambridge, MA: Belknap Press.

Graham A, Papalopulu N and Krumlauf R (1989). The murine and *drosophil* homeobox gene complex have common features of organisation and expression. *Cell*, **57**, 367–378.

Grove EA and Fukuchi-Shimogori T (2003). Generating the cerebral cortical area map. *Annual Review of Neuroscience*, **26**, 355–380.

Hess D and Edwards M (1987). Anatomical demonstration of ocular segregation in the retinogeniculate pathway of the New World capuchin monkey *(Cebus apella)*. *Journal of Comparative Neurology*, **264**, 409–420.

Hofman MA (1989). On the evolution and geometry of the brain in mammals. *Progress in Neurobiology*, **32**, 137–158.

Horton JC and Hocking DR (1996). Anatomical demonstration of ocular dominance columns in striate cortex of the squirrel monkey. *Journal of Comparative Neurology*, **16**, 5510–5522.

Huffman KJ, Nelson J, Clarey J and Krubitzer L (1999). Organization of somatosensory cortex in three species of marsupials *Dasyurus hallucatus Dactylopsila trivirgata* and *Monodelphis domestica*: Neural correlates or morphological specifications? *Journal of Comparative Neurology*, **403**, 5–32.

Hui-Xin Q, Lyon DC and Kaas JH (2002). Cortical and thalamic connections of the parietal and ventral somatosensory area in marmoset monkeys. (*Callithrix jacchus*). *Journal of Comparative Neurology*, **443**, 168–182.

Jacobs GH (1998). Photopigments and seeing – lessons from natural experiments – the Proctor Lecture. *Investigative Ophthalmology and Visual Science*, **39**, 2205–2216.

Jacobs LF and Spencer WD (1994). Natural space-use patterns and hippocampal size in kangaroo rats. *Brain, Behavior and Evolution*, **44**, 125–132.

Jensen K (1987). Terminal arbors of axons projecting to the somatosensory cortex of the adult rat: I The normal morphology of specific thalamocortical afferents. *Journal of Neuroscience*, 7, 3529–3543.

Jerison HJ (1973). *Evolution of the brain and intelligence*. New York: Academic Press.

Kaas JH (1982). Segregation of function in the nervous system: Why do sensory systems have so many subdivisions? In: W Neff, ed. *Contributions to sensory physiology*, pp. 201–240. New York: Academic Press.

Kaas JH (1987). The organization of the neocortex in mammals. *Annual Review of Psychology*, **38**, 129–151.

Kaas JH (1994). The organization of sensory and motor cortex in owl monkeys. In: JF Baer, RE Weller and I Kakoma eds, in *Aotus, the owl monkey*, pp 321–350. Orlando, Fl: Academic Press.

Kaas JH (1997). Topographic maps are fundamental to sensory processing. *Brain Research Bulletin*, **44**, 107–112.

Kaas JH (2000a). Why does the brain have so many visual areas? In: MS Gazzaniga, ed. *Cognitive neuroscience: a reader*, pp. 449–472. Malden, MA: Blackwell.

Kaas JH (2000b). Why is brain size so important: Design problems and solutions as neocortex get bigger or smaller. *Brain and Mind*, **1**, 1–25.

Kaas JH, Krubitzer L and Johanson KL (1989). Cortical connections of areas 17 (V-I) and 18 (V-2) of squirrels. *Journal of Comparative Neurology*, **281**, 426–446.

Kahn DM, Huffman KJ and Krubitzer L (2000). Organization and connections of V1 in *Monodelphis domestica*. *Journal of Comparative Neurology*, **428**, 337–354.

Kaskan PM and Finlay BL (2001). Encephalization and its developmental structure, how many ways can a brain get big? In: T Sanderson, ed. *Evolutionary anatomy of the primate cerebral cortex*, pp. 14–29. Cambridge: Cambridge University Press.

Kaskan P, Franco C, Yamada E, Silveira LCL, Darlington RB and Finlay BL (2005). Peripheral variability and central constancy in mammalian visual system evolution. *Proceedings of the Royal Society: Biological Sciences*, **272**, 91–100.

Kingsbury MA and Finlay BL (2001). The cortex in multidimensional space: Where do cortical areas come from? *Developmental Science*, **4**, 125–157.

Kinser, PA (2000). *http://serendip.brynmawr.edu/bb/kinser/size1.html*

Krubitzer L, Manger P, Pettigrew J and Calford M (1995). Organization of somatosensory cortex in monotremes: In search of the prototypical plan. *Journal of Comparative Neurology*, **351**, 261–306.

Krubitzer LA (1995). The organization of neocortex in mammals: Are species differences really so different? *Trends in Neurosciences*, **18**, 408–417.

Krubitzer LA (1998). What can monotremes tell us about brain evolution? *Philosopical Transactions of the Royal Society of London B*, **353**, 1127–1146.

Krubitzer LA and Huffman K J (2000). Arealization of the neocortex in mammals: genetic and epigenetic contributions to the phenotype. *Brain, Behavior and Evolution*, **55**, 323–333.

Krubitzer LA and Kaas JH (1990a). Cortical connections of MT in four species of primate, areal modular and retinotopic patterns. *Visual Neuroscience*, **5**, 165–204.

Krubitzer LA and Kaas JH (1990b). Organization and connections of somatosensory cortex in marmosets. *Journal of Neuroscience*, **10**, 952–974.

Krubitzer LA and Kaas JH (1993). The dorsalmedial visual area of owl monkeys, connections myleoarchitecture and homologies in other primates. *Journal of Comparative Neurology*, **334**, 497–527.

Krubitzer LA, Calford MB and Schmid LM (1993). Connections of somatosensory cortex in megachiropteran bats: The evolution of cortical fields in mammals. *Journal of Comparative Neurology*, **327**, 473–506.

Krubitzer LA , Kunzle H and Kaas JH (1997). Organization of somatosensory cortex in a Madagascan insectivore. *Journal of Comparative Neurology*, **379**, 399–414.

Krubitzer LA, Sesma MA and Kaas JH (1986). Microelectrode maps myeloarchitecture and cortical connections of three somatotopically organized representations of the body surface in parietal cortex of squirrels. *Journal of Comparative Neurology*, **253**, 415–434.

Landry P and Deschenes M (1981). Intracortical arborizations and receptive fields of identified ventrobasal thalamocortical afferents to the primary somatosensory cortex in the cat. *Journal of Comparative Neurology*, **199**, 345–371.

Law M, Zahs K and Stryker M (1988). Organization of primary visual cortex (area 17) in the ferret. *Journal of Comparative Neurology*, **178**, 157–180.

Letinic K and Rakic P (2001). Telencephalic origin of human thalamic GABAergic neurons. *Nature Neuroscience*, **4**, 931–936.

Lewis JW and Van Essen DC (2000a). Mapping of architectonic subdivisions in the macaque monkey with emphasis on parieto-occipital cortex. *Journal of Comparative Neurology*, **428**, 79–111.

Lewis J W and Van Essen DC (2000b). Corticocortical connections of visual sensorimotor and multimodal processing areas in the parietal lobe of the macaque monkey. *Journal of Comparative Neurology*, **428**, 112–137.

Lipson H and Pollack JB (2000). Automatic design and manufacture of artificial lifeforms. *Nature*, **406**, 974–978.

Lyon D, Jain N and Kaas JH (1998). Cortical connections of striate and extrastriate visual areas in tree shrews. *Journal of Comparative Neurology*, **401**, 109–128.

Merabet, LB, Theoret, H and Pascual-Leone, A (2003) Transcranial magnetic stimulation as an investigative tool in the study of visual function. *Optometry and Vison Science*, **80**, 356–368.

Merker B (2004). Cortex, countercurrent context and the logistics of personal history. *Cortex*, **40**, 550–583.

Moll J, De Oliveira-Souza R, Bramati I and Grafman J (2002). Functional networks in emotional moral and nonmoral social judgments. *Neuroimage*, **16**, 696–703.

Murphy WJ, Eizirik E, O'Brien S J, Madsen O, Scally M, Douady CJ, *et al.* (2001). Resolution of the early placental mammal radiation using Bayseian phylogenetics. *Science*, **294**, 2348–2351.

Murre J and Sturdy D (1995). The connectivity of the brain, multi-level quantitative analysis. *Biological Cybernetics*, **73**, 529–545.

Nakagawa Y, Johnson JE and O'Leary DDM (1999). Graded and areal expression patterns of regulatory genes and cadherins in embryonic neocortex independent of thalamocortical input. *Journal of Neuroscience*, **19**, 10877–10885.

Neitz J, Carroll J, Yamauchi Y, Neitz M and Williams DR (2002). Color perception is mediated by a plastic neural mechanism that is adjustable in adults. *Neuron*, **35**, 783–792.

Nolfi S and Floreano D (2002). Synthesis of autonomous robots through evolution. *Trends in Cognitive Science*, **6**, 31–37.

Northcutt R and Kaas JH (1995). The emergence and evolution of the mammalian cortex. *Trends in Neuroscience*, **18**, 373–378.

Nottebohm F and Pandazis CKS (1981). Brain space for a learned task. *Brain Research*, **213**, 99–109.

Olavarria J and Montero V (1990). Elaborate organization of visual cortex in hamster. *Neuroscience Research*, **8**, 40–47.

Pallas SL (2001). Intrinsic and extrinsic factors that shape neocortical specification. *Trends in Neuroscience*, **24**, 417–423.

Pallas S and Finlay BL (1991) Compensation for population size mismatches in the hamster retinotectal system: alterations in the organization of retinal projections. *Visual Neuroscience*, **6** 271–281.

Pallas SL and Finlay BL (1989). Conservation of receptive-field properties of superiorcolliculus cells after developmental rearrangements of retinal input. *Visual Neuroscience*, **2**, 121–135.

Purves D and LaMantia A (1993). Development of blobs in the visual cortex of macaques. *Journal of Comparative Neurology*, **334**, 169–175.

Purvis A and Rambaut A (1995). Comparative analysis by independent contrasts (CAIC), an Apple Macintosh application for analysing comparative data. *Computer Applications in Biosciences*, **11**, 247–251.

Quartz SR and Sejnowski TJ (1997). The neural basis of cognitive development, a constructivist manifesto. *Behavioral and Brain Sciences*, **20**, 537–556.

Radman M, Matic I and Taddei F (1999). Evolution of evolvability. *Annals of the New York Academy of Sciences*, **870**, 146–155.

Ragsdale CW and Grove EA (2001). Patterning the mammalian cerebral cortex. *Current Opinion in Neurobiology*, 11, 50–58.

Rakic P (1988). Specification of cerebral cortical areas. *Science*, 241, 170–176.

Rakic P (1991). Experimental manipulation of cerebral cortical areas in primates. *Philosophical Transactions of the Royal Society of London B*, 331, 291–294.

Rakic P (1995). A small step for the cell; a giant leap for mankind: a hypothesis of neocortical expansion during evolution. *Trends in Neurosciences*, 18, 383–388.

Redies C and Takeichi M (1996). Cadherins in the developing nervous system, an adhesive code for segmental and functional subdivisions. *Developmental Biology*, 180, 413–423.

Rezak KA, Huang L and Pallas SL (2003). NMDA receptor blockade in the superior colliculus increases receptive field size without altering velocity and size tuning. *Journal of Neurophysiology*, 90, 110–119.

Ringo J (1991). Neural interconnection as a function of brain size. *Brain, Behavior and Evolution*, 38, 1–6.

Rosa MG (2002). Visual maps in the adult primate cerebral cortex, some implications for brain development and evolution. *Brazilian Journal of Medical and Biological Research*, 35, 1485–1498.

Rosa MGP (1999). Topographic organization of extrastriate cortex in the flying fox: implications for the evolution of mammalian visual cortex. *Journal of Comparative Neurology*, 411, 503–523.

Rubenstein JLR, Martinez S, Shimamura K and Puelles L (1994). The embryonic vertebrate forebrain, the prosomeric model. *Science*, 266, 578–579.

Ryan M (2004). Ode to the code. *American Scientist*, 92, 494–498.

Scharff C (2000). Chasing fate and function of new neurons in adult brains. *Current Opinion in Neurobiology*, 10, 774–783.

Schuller G, Oapos-Neill W and Radtke-Schuller S (1991). Facilitation and delay sensitivity of auditory cortex neurons in CF – FM bats *Rhinolophus rouxi* and *Pteronotus p parnellii*. *European Journal of Neuroscience*, 3, 1165–1181.

Slutsky DA, Manger PR and Krubitzer LA (2000). Multiple somatosensory areas in the anterior parietal cortex of the California ground squirrel *(Spermophilus beechyi)*. *Journal of Comparative Neurology*, 416, 521–539.

Stein E and Tessier-Lavigne M (2001). Hierarchical organization of guidance receptors, silencing of netrin attraction by slit through a Robo/DCC receptor complex. *Science*, 291, 1928–1938.

Stephan H (1981). New and revised volumes of brain structures in insectivores and primates. *Folia Primatologica (Basel)*, 35, 1–29.

Stephan H, Baron G and Frahm H D (1988). Comparative size of brain and brain components *Comparative primate biology*, 4, 1–38.

Tigges J and Tigges M (1979). Ocular dominance columns in the striate cortex of chimpanzee *(Pan troglodytes)*. *Brain Research*, 166, 387–391.

Van Essen DC, Newsome WT and Maunsell JH (1984). The visual field representation in striate cortex of the macaque monkey, asymmetries anisotropies and individual variability. *Vision Research*, 24, 429–448.

Website (2001). *Brain and bodyweights of mammals*. University of New Mexico Department of Mathematics Website.

Weller RE , White DM and Walton MMG (2000). Intrinsic connections in the caudal subdivision of the dorsolateral visual area (DLc) in squirrel monkeys. *Journal of Comparative Neurology*, 420, 52–69.

Wilkins A S (2001). *The evolution of developmental pathways*. Sunderland, MA: Sinauer Associates.

Wu C, Bichot N and Kaas JH (2000). Converging evidence from microstimulation architecture and connections for multiple motor areas in the frontal and cingulate cortex of prosimian primates. *Journal of Comparative Neurology*, **423**, 140–177.

Zilles K (1985). *The cortex of the rat: A stereotaxic atlas*. Berlin: Springer-Verlag.

Chapter 7

Under what conditions do infants detect continuity violations?

Renée Baillargeon, Jie Li, Yuyan Luo, and Su-hua Wang

Abstract

According to Spelke (1994), infants interpret physical events in accord with a core principle of *continuity*, which states that objects exist and move continuously in time and space. Here we adopt a stronger definition of the principle, which states that objects not only exist and move continuously in time and space, but also retain their physical properties as they do so. We then present a new account of infants' physical reasoning that specifies under what conditions infants succeed and fail in detecting violations of the principle. Finally, we describe new lines of research that test specific predictions from the account.

7.1 Introduction

For the greater part of the 20th century, researchers generally assumed that young infants understand very little about the physical world. Two related factors contributed to this assumption. First, the leading theoretical accounts of the time tended to portray young infants as limited sensorimotor processors incapable of representation or thought (e.g. Bruner 1964, 1968; Piaget 1952, 1954). Second, a dearth of methodological tools forced investigators to rely primarily on infants' manual actions to assess their physical knowledge. For example, Piaget (1954) observed that young infants typically do not search for objects hidden behind or beneath other objects, and concluded that they do not yet realize that objects continue to exist when hidden.

The situation today is markedly different. New methods have brought to light new findings which indicate that even very young infants possess expectations about physical events (e.g. Baillargeon 1987; Goubet and Clifton 1998; Gredebäck and von Hofsten 2004; Hespos and Baillargeon in press; Hofstader and Reznick 1996; Hood and

Willatts 1986; Kaufman *et al.* in press; Lécuyer and Durand 1998; Leslie 1984; Newcombe *et al.* 1999; Spelke and Kestenbaum 1986; Wilcox *et al.* 1996). As a result of these empirical advances, there is now widespread (though by no means universal) agreement that physical reasoning constitutes one of the fundamental domains of human cognition, and that core principles within the domain facilitate infants' reasoning and learning about events (e.g. Baillargeon 2002; Carey and Spelke 1994; Gelman 1990; Gopnik and Wellman 1994; Keil 1991; Leslie 1995; Wellman and Gelman 1992).

This new theoretical perspective has given rise to many new research questions. In particular, what specific core principles are infants endowed with? And how do these principles operate? In this chapter, we focus on the principle of *continuity*. The original definition of the principle, as proposed by Spelke and her colleagues (e.g. Carey and Spelke 1994; Spelke 1994; Spelke *et al.* 1992, 1995), was that objects exist and move continuously in time and space. For reasons that will become clear, here we adopt a stronger definition of the principle, which states that objects not only exist and move continuously in time and space, but also retain their physical properties (e.g. their size, shape, pattern, and color) as they do so.

How does the principle of continuity operate? Under what conditions do infants succeed in detecting continuity violations, and under what conditions do they fail? Over the past few years, we have been developing an account of infants' physical reasoning that attempts to answer this question (e.g. Baillargeon 2002, 2004; Luo and Baillargeon 2005 c; Wang *et al.* 2005). This chapter is organized into three main sections: in the first, we review recent findings on the development of infants' physical knowledge; in the second, we present our account of infants' physical reasoning; finally, in the third, we introduce new lines of research which test specific predictions from the account.

7.2 How do infants acquire their physical knowledge?

Research over the past 15 years has shed considerable light on the development of infants' knowledge about physical events (for recent reviews, see Baillargeon 2002, 2004). Much of this research has used the violation-of-expectation (VOE) method. In a typical experiment, infants see two test events: an *expected* event, which is consistent with the expectation examined in the experiment, and an *unexpected* event, which violates this expectation. With appropriate controls, evidence that infants look reliably longer at the unexpected than at the expected event is taken to indicate that infants: (1) possess the expectation under investigation; (2) detect the violation in the unexpected event; and (3) are 'surprised' by this violation. The term 'surprised' is used here simply as a short-hand descriptor, to denote a state of heightened interest or attention induced by an expectation violation.[1]

---

[1] VOE reports that young infants possess rich cognitive abilities, such as the ability to represent hidden objects, have recently been criticized (e.g. Bogartz *et al.* 1997; Cashon and Cohen 2000; Haith and Benson 1998; Munakata *et al.* 1997; Rivera *et al.* 1999; Roder *et al.* 2000; Schilling 2000; Thelen and Smith 1994).

7.2.1 Event categories, vectors, and variables

Recent research suggests that infants 'sort' events into distinct categories. Many of these *event categories* capture relatively simple spatial relations between objects, such as 'object behind nearer object, or occluder' (occlusion events), 'object inside container' (containment events), and 'object under cover' (covering events) (e.g. Aguiar and Baillargeon 2003; Casasola *et al.* 2003; Hespos and Baillargeon 2001a; Luo and Baillargeon 2005b; McDonough *et al.* 2003; Munakata 1997; Wang *et al.* 2005; Wilcox and Chapa 2002; for a review, see Baillargeon and Wang 2002).

Each event category comprises one or more *vectors*, which correspond to separate problems that infants must solve in order to fully predict outcomes within the category. For example, in the case of occlusion events, infants must learn to predict whether an object will be hidden or visible when behind an occluder, and also how soon an object that moves behind an occluder will emerge from behind it; in the case of containment events, infants must learn to predict whether an object can be lowered inside a container, how much of an object inside a container will protrude above it, and whether the portion of an object that lies inside a container should be hidden or visible (e.g. Aguiar and Baillargeon 1998; Arterberry 1997; Gredebäck and von Hofsten 2004; Hespos and Baillargeon 2001b; Luo and Baillargeon 2005c; Sitskoorn and Smitsman 1995; Wang *et al.* 2004; Wilcox and Schweinle 2003).

For each vector in an event category, infants identify a sequence of *variables* that enables them to predict outcomes within the vector more and more accurately over time (e.g. Aguiar and Baillargeon 1999; Baillargeon and DeVos 1991; Hespos and Baillargeon 2001a; Luo and Baillargeon 2005a; Sitskoorn and Smitsman 1995; Wang *et al.* 2005; Wilcox 1999). Variables are akin to condition–outcome rules: for a set of contrastive outcomes, a variable specifies what condition produces each outcome. Each variable that is added along a vector revises and refines predictions from earlier variables. This process can be illustrated by a simple decision tree (for related ideas, see Mitchell 1997; Quinlan 1993; Siegler 1978). As an example, the decision tree in Fig. 7.1 depicts some of the variables infants identify as they learn when objects behind occluders should and should not be hidden.

At about 2.5 months of age, infants use only a simple *behind/not-behind* variable to predict when objects behind occluders should be hidden: they expect an object to be

---

Investigators have argued that VOE findings are often open to alternative, low-level interpretations, which cast doubt on claims that young infants possess rich cognitive abilities. However, converging evidence for VOE findings is steadily accumulating; at present, this evidence comes from action tasks (e.g. Goubet and Clifton 1998; Gredebäck and von Hofsten 2004; Hespos and Baillargeon in press; Hofstader and Reznick 1996; Hood and Willatts 1986), from habituation tasks (e.g. Casasola *et al.* 2003; McDonough *et al.* 2003), and from tasks tapping neural correlates (Kaufman *et al.* in press). In addition, experimental tests of specific alternative interpretations of VOE findings have not supported these interpretations (e.g. Luo and Baillargeon 2005c; Luo *et al.* 2003, 2005; Wang *et al.* 2004; for review and discussion, see Aslin 2000; Baillargeon 1999, 2000, 2004; Lécuyer 2001; Munakata 2000; Wang *et al.* 2004).

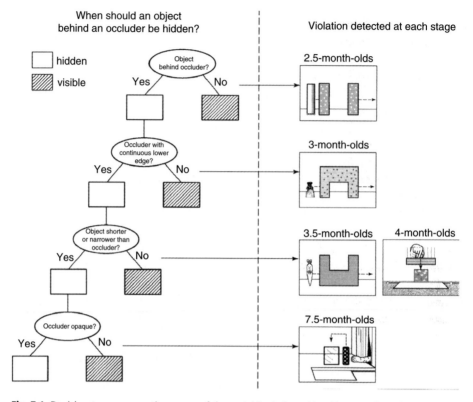

Fig. 7.1 Decision tree representing some of the variables infants identify to predict when objects behind occluders should be hidden or visible. The identification of each new variable enables infants to detect additional occlusion violations.

hidden when behind a closed occluder and to be visible when not (Aguiar and Baillargeon 1999; Lécuyer and Durand 1998; Luo and Baillargeon 2005c). Thus, when infants see an object move back and forth behind two screens placed a short distance apart, they expect the object to be hidden when behind each screen and to be visible when between them, because at that point the object does not lie behind any occluder. At about 3 months of age, infants identify a new occlusion variable, *lower-edge-discontinuity*: they now expect an object to be visible when behind a closed occluder whose lower edge is not continuous with the surface on which it rests, creating a gap between the occluder and surface (Aguiar and Baillargeon 2002; Luo and Baillargeon 2005c). Thus, infants expect an object to remain hidden when passing behind a screen shaped like a U, but not one shaped like an inverted-U. At about 3.5 to 4 months of age, infants identify *height* and *width* as occlusion variables: they now expect tall objects to remain partly visible when behind short occluders (Baillargeon and DeVos 1991), and wide objects to remain partly visible when behind narrow occluders (Wang *et al.* 2004; Wilcox 1999; Wilcox and Baillargeon 1998b).

Finally, at about 7.5 months of age, infants identify *transparency* as an occlusion variable: when an object is placed behind a transparent occluder, infants now expect the object to be visible through the front of the occluder, and are surprised if it is not (Luo and Baillargeon 2005a, 2005b).

7.2.2 Errors of omission and commission

We have just seen that, for each event category, infants identify variables – organized along vectors – which enable them to predict outcomes within the category more and more accurately over time. This description predicts that infants who have not yet identified a variable along a vector should err in two distinct ways in VOE tasks, when shown violation and non-violation events involving the variable. First, infants should respond to violation events consistent with their faulty knowledge as though they were expected. We refer to this first kind of error – viewing a violation event as expected – as an error of *omission*. Second, infants should respond to non-violation events inconsistent with their faulty knowledge as though they were unexpected. In other words, infants should respond to perfectly ordinary and commonplace events with increased attention, when these events happen to contradict their incomplete knowledge. We refer to this second kind of error – viewing a non-violation event as unexpected – as an error of *commission*.

To date, many investigations of infants' physical knowledge have revealed errors of omission: infants who have not yet identified a variable in a vector of an event category typically do not view violation events involving the variable as unexpected (e.g. Aguiar and Baillargeon 2002; Baillargeon and DeVos 1991; Hespos and Baillargeon 2001a; Luo and Baillargeon 2005c; Wang *et al.* 2005; Wilcox 1999). For example, 3-month-old infants, who have not yet identified height as an occlusion variable, view as expected a violation event in which a tall object remains fully hidden when passing behind a short occluder (Aguiar and Baillargeon 2002; Baillargeon and DeVos 1991; Luo and Baillargeon 2005c). At this age, infants have acquired only the variable lower-edge-discontinuity: as long as the lower edge of the occluder is continuous with the surface on which it rests, infants expect the object to remain hidden when behind the occluder, regardless of the heights of the object and occluder.

Recent experiments have also revealed errors of commission in infants' responses to occlusion events. In particular, there is now evidence that 2.5-month-olds, who have not yet identified the variable lower-edge-discontinuity, view as unexpected a non-violation event in which an object becomes visible when passing behind an inverted-U-shaped screen (Luo and Baillargeon 2005c). Similarly, 3-month-olds, who, as mentioned above, have not yet acquired the variable height, view as unexpected a non-violation event in which a tall object remains visible above a short occluder (Luo and Baillargeon 2005c). Finally, 7-month-olds, who have not yet identified transparency as an occlusion variable, view as unexpected a non-violation event in which an object placed behind a transparent occluder remains visible through the occluder (Luo and Baillargeon 2005a).

7.2.3 Event-specific acquisitions

We have seen that, for each event category, infants identify variables, ordered along vectors, which allow them to better predict outcomes within the category. Recent experiments suggest that this acquisition process is event-specific: infants learn separately about each event category. This specificity manifests itself in at least two ways, described below.

First, variables identified in one event category remain tied to that category – they are not generalized to other categories, even when equally relevant. For example we saw above that infants identify the variable height at about 3.5 months in occlusion events (Baillargeon and DeVos 1991): they are now surprised when a tall object becomes fully hidden behind a short occluder. However, infants this age are not surprised when a tall object becomes fully hidden inside a short container, under a short cover, or inside a short tube. The variable height is not identified until about 7.5 months in containment events (Hespos and Baillargeon 2001a), until about 12 months in covering events (Wang *et al.* 2005), and until about 14 months in tube events (Wang *et al.* 2005). Similarly, we saw above that the variable transparency is identified at about 7.5 months in occlusion events (Luo and Baillargeon 2005a): infants are now surprised when an object placed behind a transparent occluder is not visible through the occluder. However, it is not until infants are about 9.5 months of age that they identify the same variable in containment events, and expect an object placed inside a transparent container to be visible through the container (Luo and Baillargeon 2005b). We use the Piagetian term *décalages* to refer to the lags in infants' identification of the same variable in different event categories.

Second, the same variable may be associated (at least initially) with different vectors in different event categories. This conclusion is suggested by different error patterns in infants' responses to occlusion and containment events. In occlusion events, as we just saw, height is identified at about 3.5 months and transparency at about 7.5 months. Both variables belong to a single vector having to do with when objects behind occluders should be hidden (see Fig. 7.1). Thus, 7-month-old infants, who have identified height but not transparency: (1) are surprised when a tall object becomes fully hidden behind a short occluder (a correct response; Baillargeon and Graber 1987; Hespos and Baillargeon 2005); and (2) are also surprised when an object placed behind a transparent occluder is visible through the occluder (an error of commission; Luo and Baillargeon 2005b). At this age, infants expect an object to be hidden when behind an occluder that is taller than the object – even if this occluder is in fact transparent.

In containment events, as we saw in the last section, height is identified at about 7.5 months and transparency at about 9.5 months. If these variables belonged to a single vector specifying when objects inside containers should be hidden, then we should expect that at 8.5 months infants would produce responses similar to those described above for occlusion events. However, this is not the case. Although 8.5-month-old infants are surprised when a tall object becomes fully hidden inside a short container (a correct response; Hespos and Baillargeon 2001a, in press; Wang *et al.* 2005), they are not surprised when an object placed inside a transparent container is either visible or not visible through the container (an error of omission; Luo and Baillargeon 2005b). These results suggest that, in containment events, height and transparency belong to separate vectors: whereas height belongs to a vector specifying when an object inside a container should protrude above it, transparency belongs to a vector having to do with when an object inside a container should be hidden. Thus, when a short object is lowered inside a tall transparent container, 8.5-month-old infants bring to bear their knowledge of height to predict that no portion of the object will be visible above the container. However, they cannot make a prediction as to whether the portion of the object inside the container should be hidden or visible. Apparently, it is not until infants are about 9.5 months that they form a vector specifying when objects inside containers should be hidden.

This analysis leads to striking predictions concerning 7.5- and 8.5-month-old infants' responses to events involving transparent containers. When a tall object is lowered inside a short transparent container, infants should look reliably longer if the top of the object is not visible, as opposed to visible, above the container. However, as long as the top of the object protrudes above the container, infants should look about equally whether the bottom of the object is visible, or not visible, through the container. Experiments are planned to test these predictions.

7.2.4 Identifying variables

We have seen that, for each event category, infants identify variables which enable them to predict outcomes within the category more and more accurately over time. How do infants identify these variables? And why do they sometimes identify the same variable at different ages in different categories?

We have proposed that the process by which infants typically identify a new variable in an event category is one of explanation-based learning (EBL) and involves three main steps (Baillargeon 2002; Wang and Baillargeon 2005b; for a computational description of EBL in the machine learning literature, see DeJong 1993). First, infants must notice *contrastive outcomes* relevant to the variable (e.g. in the case of the variable height in covering events, infants must notice that when a cover is placed over an object, the object becomes sometimes fully and sometimes only partly hidden); because these contrastive outcomes are not predicted by infants' current physical knowledge, they serve to trigger learning. Second, infants must discover the *conditions* that map onto the outcomes (e.g. they must discover that an object becomes fully hidden when placed under a cover as tall as or taller than the object, and becomes partly hidden otherwise). Third, infants must build an *explanation* for these condition–outcome data using their prior knowledge, which includes their core knowledge (e.g. because of their continuity principle, infants would readily understand that a tall object can extend to its full height inside a tall but not a short cover). Thus, according to the EBL account, only condition–outcome observations for which infants can build causal explanations are identified as new variables. These explanations are undoubtedly shallow (e.g. Keil 1995; Wilson and Keil 2000), but they still serve to integrate new variables with infants' prior causal knowledge.

The EBL account suggests at least two reasons why infants may identify a variable in one event category several weeks or months before they identify it in another event category. One reason has to do with the first step in the EBL process: because exposure to appropriate contrastive outcomes is necessary to trigger learning, it follows that variables will be learned later when exposure is less frequent. Thus, infants may identify height as a containment variable several months before they identify it as a covering variable (Hespos and Baillargeon 2001a; Wang *et al.* 2005) simply because, in everyday life, infants have more opportunities to notice that objects placed inside containers sometimes extend above them and sometimes not, than to notice that objects placed under covers sometimes extend beneath them and sometimes not.

A second reason why infants may identify a variable sooner in one event category than in another has to do with the second step in the EBL process. After noticing the contrastive outcomes for a variable, infants must discover the conditions that map onto these outcomes; this discovery may be more difficult in some categories than in others. To illustrate, consider the finding that infants identify height as an occlusion variable several months before they identify it as a containment variable (Baillargeon and DeVos 1991; Hespos and Baillargeon 2001a). Prior research (e.g. Baillargeon 1994, 1995) indicates that when infants begin to reason about a continuous variable in an event category, they can reason about the variable qualitatively but not quantitatively: they are not able at first to encode and reason about absolute amounts. In order to encode the heights of objects and occluders or containers qualitatively, infants must compare them as they stand *side by side*. It may be that infants have more opportunities to perform such qualitative comparisons with occlusion than with containment events. In the case of occlusion events, infants will often see objects move behind the side edges of occluders, making it easy to compare their heights as they stand next to each other (e.g. when a cereal box is pushed in front of a bowl). In the case of containment events, however, there may be relatively few instances in which objects are placed first next to and then inside containers; caretakers will more often lower objects directly into containers, giving infants no opportunity to compare their heights (e.g. Hespos and Baillargeon 2001a; Wang *et al.* 2004).

The preceding analysis predicts that infants who are exposed in the laboratory to appropriate outcome and condition data for a variable should identify it earlier than they would otherwise. To test this prediction, we recently attempted to 'teach'

9-month-old infants the variable height in covering events (Wang and Baillargeon 2005b); recall that this variable is typically not identified until about 12 months of age (Wang *et al.* 2005). Our results were positive and as such support both the EBL process and the speculation above that the décalage in infants' identification of the variable height in containment and covering events stems from the fact that infants are typically exposed to appropriate observations for this variable at different ages in the two categories.

7.3 An account of infants' physical reasoning

Armed with the findings presented in the last section, we now return to the question raised in the Introduction: How does infants' principle of continuity operate? Over the past few years, we have been developing an account of infants' physical reasoning that attempts to answer this question (e.g. Baillargeon 2002, 2004; Luo and Baillargeon 2005c; Wang *et al.* 2005).

7.3.1 Four assumptions

Our reasoning account rests on four assumptions. First, when watching a physical event, infants build a specialized physical representation of the event which is used to predict and interpret its outcome. Second, all of the information, but only the information, in infants' physical representation of an event becomes subject to a few core principles, including that of continuity (e.g. Leslie 1994; Spelke 1994; Wang and Baillargeon 2005b).

Third, in the first weeks of life, infants' physical representation of an event typically includes only basic spatial and temporal information about the event (Fig. 7.2a; e.g. Kestenbaum *et al.* 1987; Leslie 1994; Needham 2000; Slater 1995; Spelke 1982; Yonas and Granrud 1984). This *basic information* specifies primarily: (1) how many distinct objects are involved in the event (e.g. are there two objects present?); (2) what is the geometry, or distribution of open/closed surfaces, of each object (e.g. is one object open at the top to form a container, open at the bottom to form a cover, or open at both ends to form a tube?); and (3) what is the spatial arrangement of the objects and how does it change over time as the objects move or are moved (e.g. is one object being placed behind, inside, or under the other object?). The basic information thus captures essential aspects of the event, but leaves out most of its details: for example it includes no information about the relative sizes of the objects (e.g. is one object taller or wider than the other object?), or about their surface appearance (e.g. are the objects transparent or opaque?).

Fourth, as they form event categories and identify variables for each category, infants include more and more of this detailed information, or *variable information*, in their physical representations (Fig. 7.2b). When watching an event, infants first represent the basic information about the event, and use this information to

(a)

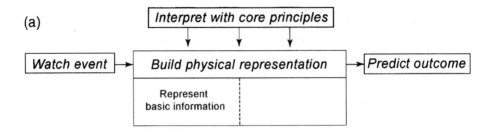

(b)

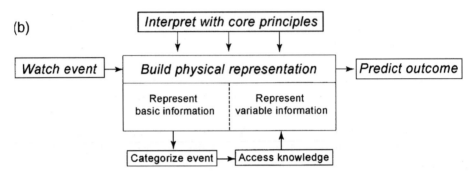

Fig. 7.2 Schematic presentation of the reasoning account for younger (a) and older (b) infants.

categorize it. Infants then access their knowledge of the event category selected. This knowledge specifies the variables that have been identified as relevant for predicting outcomes in the category, and hence that should be included in the physical representation of the event. Variables not yet identified are typically not included in the representation.

To illustrate our reasoning account, consider the finding that infants aged 7.5 months and older are surprised when a tall object is lowered inside a short container until it becomes hidden (Hespos and Baillargeon 2001a; Wang *et al.* 2005). The account suggests that, when watching this event, infants represent the basic information about the event and interpret this information in accord with their continuity principle ('object being lowered inside container'). Next, infants categorize the event as a containment event, and access their knowledge of this event category. Because at 7.5 months this knowledge includes the variable height, infants include information about the relative heights of the object and container in their physical representation of the event. This variable information then becomes subject to infants' continuity principle, making it possible for them to detect the continuity violation in the event: they recognize that the object is too tall to become hidden inside the short container. Infants younger than 7.5 months, who have not yet identified height as a containment variable, typically do not include height information in their physical representations of containment events. As a result, this information is not available and hence cannot be interpreted in accord with infants' continuity principle. Infants thus fail to detect continuity violations involving tall objects and short containers (Hespos and Baillargeon 2001a).

7.3.2 Basic continuity violations

According to our reasoning account, young infants should succeed in detecting any continuity violation that involves only the basic information they typically include in their physical representations of events. We refer to such violations as *basic continuity violations*.

There are now several reports indicating that 2.5- to 3-month-old infants (the youngest tested successfully to date with the VOE method) can detect basic continuity violations in occlusion, containment, and covering events (e.g. Aguiar and Baillargeon 1999; Hespos and Baillargeon 2001b; Luo and Baillargeon 2005c; Spelke *et al.* 1992; Wang *et al.* 2005; Wilcox *et al.* 1996). For example there is evidence that these young infants are surprised: (1) when an object disappears behind one occluder and reappears from behind another occluder without appearing in the gap between them (Aguiar and Baillargeon 1999; Luo and Baillargeon 2005c; Wilcox *et al.* 1996); (2) when an object is lowered inside a container through its closed top (Hespos and Baillargeon 2001b); (3) when an object is lowered inside an open container, which is then slid forward and to the side to reveal the object standing in the container's initial position (Hespos and Baillargeon 2001b); (4) when a cover is lowered over an object, slid to the side, and lifted to reveal no object (Wang *et al.* 2005); and (5) when a cover is lowered over an object, slid behind the left half of a screen taller than the object, lifted above the screen, moved to the right, lowered behind the right half of the screen, slid past the screen, and finally lifted to reveal the object (Wang *et al.* 2005).

To succeed in detecting the continuity violations in these events, infants need not represent any variable information, only basic information: in each event, they must specify how many objects are present, which of their surfaces are open/closed, how the objects are spatially arranged, and how this arrangement changes over time. This basic information, as it is represented, becomes subject to the continuity principle. When the event evolves in a manner inconsistent with the principle, it is tagged as a violation, causing infants to respond with increased attention.

To illustrate, consider the finding that infants are surprised when a cover is lowered over an object, slid to the side, and then lifted to reveal no object (Wang *et al.* 2005). We would argue that infants represent the following basic information: (1) an object open at the bottom, or cover, is held over a closed object; (2) the cover is lowered over the object [the continuity principle would specify at this point that the object continues to exist, in its same location, under the cover]; (3) the cover is slid to the side [the continuity principle would specify at this point that the object cannot pass through the sides of the cover and hence must be displaced with the cover to its new location]; and (4) the cover is lifted to reveal no object [the continuity principle would signal at this point that a violation has occurred: the object should have been revealed when the cover was lifted].

7.3.3 Variable continuity violations

According to our reasoning account, infants should fail to detect any continuity violation that involves a variable they have not yet identified as relevant to an event category, and hence do not yet include in their physical representations of events from the category. We refer to such violations as *variable continuity violations*.

When infants identify a variable earlier in one event category than in another, striking discrepancies can arise in their responses to perceptually similar events from the two categories: infants will detect a continuity violation involving the variable in one category, but not in the other. There are now several reports of such discrepancies (e.g. Hespos and Baillargeon 2001a; Luo and Baillargeon 2005b; Wang *et al.* 2005). For example, 4.5-month-old infants watched an experimenter lower a tall cylindrical object either behind (occlusion condition) or inside (containment condition) a container until only the knob at the top of the object remained visible (Hespos and Baillargeon 2001a). In one test event, the container was as tall as the cylindrical portion of the object (tall event); in the other test event, the container was only half as tall (short event), so that it should have been impossible for the cylindrical portion of the object to become fully hidden inside the container. The infants in the occlusion condition looked reliably longer at the short than at the tall event, but those in the containment condition tended to look equally at the two events. The infants thus detected the variable continuity violation in the occlusion but not the containment condition.

According to our reasoning account, the infants in the occlusion condition represented the basic information about each test event, categorized it as an occlusion event, and then accessed their knowledge of this event category. Because at 4.5 months this knowledge comprises the variable height (recall that this variable is identified at about 3.5 months; Baillargeon and DeVos 1991), the infants included information about the relative heights of the object and container in their physical representation of the event. This information became subject to the continuity principle, and the short event was marked as a violation event. The infants in the containment condition went through a similar reasoning process; however, because at 4.5 months infants' knowledge of containment events does not yet comprise the variable height (recall that this variable is not identified until about 7.5 months; Hespos and Baillargeon 2001a), the infants did not include information about the relative heights of the object and container in their physical representation of each test event. As a result, this (missing) information could not be interpreted in accord with the continuity principle, and the infants failed to detect the variable continuity violation in the short event.

In the experiments just described, the infants responded differently when an object was lowered behind or inside a container. These events were perceptually similar, but not identical. In a recent experiment, 9-month-old infants responded differently to perceptually *identical* events, when prior information led them to categorize the events as containment or as tube events (Wang *et al.* 2005). The infants watched two test events in which an experimenter lowered a tall object inside a container (containment condition) or a tube (tube condition) until it became fully hidden. In one event, the container or tube was slightly taller than the object (tall event); in the other event, the container or tube was only half as tall (short event), so that it should have been impossible for the object to become fully hidden. Prior to the test session, in an orientation procedure, the experimenter showed the infants each container (containment condition) or tube (tube condition) one at a time, calling attention to its top and bottom. When standing upright on the apparatus floor during the test events, the containers and tubes were indistinguishable. The infants in the containment and tube condition thus saw perceptually identical test events; only the information provided in the orientation procedure could lead them to believe that they were watching events involving containers or tubes.

The infants in the containment condition looked reliably longer at the short than at the tall event, but those in the tube condition tended to look equally at the two events. Thus, the infants detected the variable continuity violation in the containment but not the tube condition. According to our reasoning account, the infants in the containment condition categorized each test event as a containment event (based in part on information remembered from the orientation procedure), and then accessed their knowledge of this event category. Because at 9 months the variable height is known to be relevant for predicting outcomes in containment events (recall that this variable is identified at about 7.5 months; Hespos and Baillargeon 2001a), the infants included information about the relative heights of the object and container in their physical representation of each test event. This information became subject to the continuity principle, and the short event was tagged as violating the principle. The infants in the tube condition underwent a similar reasoning process; however, because height is not identified as a tube variable until about 14 months (Wang *et al.* 2005), the infants included no information about the relative heights of the object and tube in their physical representation of each test event. As a result, this (missing) information could not become subject to the continuity principle, and the infants failed to detect the violation in the short event.

The infants in this last experiment thus detected the variable continuity violation they were shown when they believed that they were facing containers, but not tubes. Such a finding provides strong evidence for our reasoning account and more specifically for the claim that: (1) infants detect a variable continuity violation in an event when they include information about the variable in their physical representation of the event; and (2) infants include this information when they have identified the variable as relevant for predicting outcomes in the event's category.

7.4 **Tests of our reasoning account**

The reasoning account presented in the last section suggests several interesting predictions. Two such predictions are examined here; both focus on infants' ability to detect variable continuity violations.

7.4.1 **Change blindness**

According to our reasoning account, infants who have not yet identified a variable as relevant to an event category typically do not include information about this variable in their physical representations of events from the category. If infants do not include information about a variable when representing an event, then they should be unable to detect surreptitious changes involving the variable: in other words, they should be *blind* to such changes (for related findings in the adult perception literature, see Rensink 2002; Rensink *et al.* 1997; Simons 1996, 2000).

7.4.1.1 Occlusion events

There have been many experiments over the past 30 years examining infants' ability to detect a change in an object that is briefly hidden (e.g. Bower 1974; Bower *et al.* 1971; Goldberg 1976; Gratch 1982; Meicler and Gratch 1980; Muller and Aslin 1978; Newcombe *et al.* 1999; Simon *et al.* 1995; Wilcox 1999; Wilcox and Baillargeon 1998a, 1998b). In the case of VOE tasks involving occlusion events, two factors appear to determine whether infants will respond with increased attention to an event in which one object disappears behind an occluder and a different object reappears (after an appropriate interval) from behind it. The first factor has to do with the width of the occluder relative to that of the objects. As we saw earlier, by 4 months of age, infants have identified width as an occlusion variable: they realize that a narrow occluder cannot hide a wide object, nor can it hide two narrow objects whose combined width is greater than that of the occluder (e.g. Wang *et al.* 2004; Wilcox 1999; Wilcox and Baillargeon 1998b). Infants who detect an object change in an occlusion event typically respond with increased attention only if the screen is too narrow to hide the two objects at the same time. If the screen is wide enough to hide both objects, infants do not respond with increased attention, because they can readily make sense of the event: they infer that two different objects are present behind the screen (e.g. Wilcox 1999; Wilcox and Baillargeon 1998a, 1998b).

The second factor has to do with the variable information infants include about the objects. In an extensive series of experiments using narrow-screen events, Wilcox (1999) found that infants detect differences in size and shape at about 4 months, differences in pattern at about 7.5 months, and differences in color at about 11.5 months. To restate this last result in terms of change blindness, infants younger than 11.5 months are blind to color changes in narrow-screen events. When a green ball disappears behind a narrow screen and a red ball reappears from behind it, infants do not realize that two different balls are present. Because they have not yet identified color as an occlusion variable, they do not include color information in their representation of the event. As a result, they assume that the event involves a single ball which becomes briefly occluded as it moves back and forth behind the screen.

7.4.1.2 Other events

We have recently begun to examine change blindness in event categories other than occlusion. Some experiments have focused on height changes in covering events (Wang and Baillargeon in press). Ongoing experiments (Li and Baillargeon 2005a) are focusing on height changes in containment and tube events. For example, in one experiment, 8-month-old infants first see a familiarization event in which an experimenter's gloved hand rotates a container (containment condition) or a tube (tube condition) forward and backward to show its top and bottom; the tube is identical to the container with its bottom removed. Next, all of the infants see the same change and no-change test event. At the start of the change event, the container/tube stands on the apparatus floor (because the container and tube are indistinguishable when standing upright, the infants can only assume that they are facing a container or tube based on the information provided in the familiarization event). Next to the container is a tall cylindrical object with a knob attached to its top; the container/tube is as tall as the cylindrical portion of the object. The experimenter's hand grasps the knob at the top of the object, lifts the object, and lowers it inside the container/tube until only the knob and very top of the object remain visible above the rim. The hand then gently twists the object back and forth for a few seconds. Finally, the hand lifts the object and returns it to its original position on the apparatus floor. When removed from the container/tube, the object is much shorter: its cylindrical portion is only half as tall as previously. The no-change event is identical to the change event, except that the short object is used throughout the event.

Because height is identified at about 7.5 months in containment events (Hespos and Baillargeon 2001a, 2005), we predict that the infants in the containment condition will include information about the relative heights of the object and container in their physical representation of each test event, and hence will detect the difference in the height of the object in the change event. As a result, the infants will look reliably longer at the change than at the no-change event. Conversely, because height is not identified until about 14 months in tube events (Wang et al. 2005), we predict that the infants in the tube condition will include no height information in their physical representations of the test events, will fail to detect the change in the height of the object, and hence will look about equally at the two test events.

Preliminary results support these predictions: although the infants in the two conditions view exactly the same test events, only the infants in the containment condition look reliably longer at the change than at the no-change event. Thus, at 8 months, infants appear to detect a change in the height of an object if this change takes place when the object is lowered inside a container – but not inside a tube.

7.4.1.3 A caveat

Before leaving this section, we offer an important caveat. When we say that infants do not include information about a variable in their physical representation of an event, we do not mean to claim that they do not represent this information *at all*. Whether they do or not is an empirical question we are currently investigating. Our working hypothesis is that when infants watch a physical event, different computational systems form different representations simultaneously, for distinct purposes. In particular, infants' *object-recognition* system represents detailed information about the objects in the event, for recognition and categorization purposes. At the same time, infants' *physical-reasoning* system forms a physical representation of the event, to predict and interpret its outcome. Thus, when infants determine that they must include information about a variable in their physical representation of an event, and this information is no longer perceptually available, they access their object-recognition system to retrieve the necessary information. On this view, the 8-month-old infants in the experiment just described (Li and Baillargeon 2005a) *all* encoded information about the relative heights of the object and container or tube in their object-recognition system. However, *only* the infants in the container condition retrieved this height information and included it in their physical representations of the test events.

These speculations suggest that even infants who fail to include variable information in their representation of an event could nevertheless have this information available in their object-recognition system. Tasks designed to tap this system directly should thus reveal this knowledge. This means, for example, that infants who have not yet identified the variable height in containment, covering, or tube events should nevertheless detect a change in the relative heights of an object and container, cover, or tube, when given a task that taps their object-recognition rather than their physical-reasoning system. Experiments are under way to test this prediction.

7.4.2 Inducing infants to detect variable continuity violations

We have argued that infants fail to detect a variable continuity violation in an event when: (1) they have not yet identified the variable as relevant to the event's category; (2) they do not include information about the variable in their physical representation of the event; and (3) the missing information cannot be interpreted in accord with the infants' continuity principle, so the event cannot be tagged as violating the principle. This analysis predicts that if infants could be *induced*, through various contextual manipulations, to include information about the variable in their physical representation of the event, then this information should become subject to the continuity principle, and infants should be able to detect the violation in the event. According to our reasoning account, the missing variable information, once represented, should be immediately interpretable by the continuity principle.

7.4.2.1 Priming effects

Recent evidence indicates that infants can be primed to include information about a variable they have not yet identified in their physical representations of events. Wilcox and Chapa (2004) built on the finding, described earlier, that infants younger than 11.5 months do not detect color changes in occlusion events: they are not surprised when a green ball and a red ball appear successively from behind a screen that is too narrow to hide them both (Wilcox 1999). Wilcox and Chapa set out to prime 7.5-month-old infants to attend to the color information in their narrow-screen event. Prior to the test trials, the infants received three pairs of priming trials. In each pair, the infants saw a pound event, in which a green cup was used to pound a peg, and a pour event, in which a red cup was used to pour salt. Green and red cups of different sizes and shapes were used in the three priming pairs. Next, the infants saw a test event in which a green and a red ball appeared successively from behind a narrow or a wide screen. The infants who saw the narrow-screen event looked reliably longer than those who saw the wide-screen event, suggesting that the priming trials had induced the infants to include color information in their physical representation of each test event. This priming effect was eliminated when the infants received only two priming pairs, or when the same cups were used across all three pairs.

Additional priming experiments built on the finding, reported earlier, that infants younger than 7.5 months do not detect pattern changes in occlusion events: they are not surprised when a dotted and a striped green ball appear successively from behind a screen that is too narrow to hide them both (Wilcox 1999). Using similar priming trials involving dotted and striped green cups, Wilcox and Chapa (2004) found that 5.5- and even 4.5-month-old infants could be primed to include pattern information in their physical representations of narrow- and wide-screen events.

These priming results provide strong support for the expanded definition of the continuity principle proposed in the Introduction – objects not only exist continuously in time and space, but also retain their physical properties as they do so. Young infants typically do not include color or pattern information in their representations of occlusion events. However, if primed to do so, infants immediately expect objects to retain these properties throughout the events. Thus, infants who are primed to represent an object as green and dotted expect it to remain green and dotted when passing behind an occluder. Note that this expectation is not a low-level response to a perceptual change: following priming, infants respond with increased attention when a green ball disappears behind an occluder and a red ball reappears from behind it *only* if the occluder is too narrow to hide the two balls at the same time. In other words, the priming experience does not merely heighten infants' sensitivity to color and pattern changes: rather, it leads them to include color and pattern information in their physical representations of events. This information, once included, becomes subject to infants' continuity principle, and events in which objects appear to spontaneously change color or pattern are tagged as violating the principle.

7.4.2.2 Carry-over effects

We have been developing a very different approach for inducing infants to detect variable continuity violations. The point of departure for this approach was the following question: What happens when infants see the same objects in two successive events from different event categories? Do they represent each event separately? Or do they carry over whatever variable information they included in their representation of the first event to their representation of the second event? The second alternative seemed to us more efficient and hence more plausible (e.g. Aguiar and Baillargeon 2003).

We reasoned that if infants carry over variable information from one event representation to the next, then infants who see an event in which a variable has been identified, followed by an event in which this same variable has not yet been identified, should show a *positive* carry-over effect: the variable information included in the first event representation should be carried over to the second event representation, allowing infants to detect continuity violations involving the variable earlier than they would otherwise. Exposure to a single initial event would thus be sufficient to induce infants to detect a variable continuity violation in a subsequent event: as long as infants spontaneously include the appropriate variable information in their representation of the first event, this information should be available to them when reasoning about the second event (e.g. Wang and Baillargeon 2005b).

At the same time, we realized that the converse should also be true: if variable information is carried over from one event representation to the next, then infants who see an event in which a variable has not yet been identified, followed by an event in which this same variable has been identified, should show a *negative* carry-over effect: the information about the variable should be absent from the second event representation, causing infants to fail to detect continuity violations they would otherwise have been able to detect.

Do infants show negative as well as positive carry-over effects when they see the same objects in two successive events from different categories? An ongoing experiment (Li and Baillargeon 2005b) addresses this question. This experiment examines 8.5-month-old infants' ability to detect a surreptitious change in the height of an object in an event sequence comprising an occlusion and a covering event.

The infants are assigned to an occlusion–covering or a covering–occlusion condition. The infants in the occlusion–covering condition receive a change or a no-change test trial. At the beginning of the change trial, a short cylindrical object stands next to a tall rectangular cover with a knob attached to its top; the object is half as tall as the rectangular portion of the cover. To start, an experimenter's gloved hand grasps the knob at the top of the cover, rotates the cover forward to show its hollow interior, and then replaces the cover next to the object (pretrial). Next, the hand slides the cover in front of the object, fully hiding it, and then returns it to its original position on the apparatus floor (occlusion event). Finally, the hand lowers the cover over the object, again fully hiding it, and then returns it to the apparatus floor (covering event). When the cover is removed from over the object in the covering event, the object is now as tall as the rectangular portion of the cover. In the no-change trial, the tall object is used throughout the trial. The infants in the covering-occlusion condition receive similar change and no-change trials, except that the occlusion and covering events are performed in the reverse order: the cover is placed first over and then in front of the object. The surreptitious change in the height of the object in the change trial thus takes place in the occlusion rather than in the covering event.

Because the variable height is identified at about 3.5 months in occlusion events (Baillargeon and DeVos 1991), but only at about 12 months in covering events (McCall 2001; Wang *et al.* 2005), we expect that the infants in the occlusion–covering condition will show a positive carry-over effect. When watching the occlusion event, the infants will categorize the event, access their knowledge of occlusion events, and include information about the relative heights of the cover and object in their physical representation of the event. When the infants next see the covering event, this height information will be carried over into this new representation; the information will then be interpreted in terms of the continuity principle, allowing the infants to detect the violation in the change event.

In contrast, the infants in the covering–occlusion condition should show a negative carryover effect. When watching the covering event, the infants will include no height information in their representation of the event. As a result, no height information will be carried over when the infants next represent the occlusion event. The infants will thus fail to detect the continuity violation in the change event.

Preliminary results support our predictions: in the occlusion–covering condition, the infants who see the change trial look reliably longer than those who see the no-change trial; in the covering–occlusion condition, the infants look about equally during the two trials.

These results are interesting for several reasons. First, they provide strong support for the notion that infants detect variable continuity violations when they include information about the relevant variables in their physical representations of the events. Second, they provide additional support for the expanded principle of continuity introduced in this chapter. Wilcox and Chapa (2004) found that young infants who were primed to encode the color or pattern of an object in an occlusion event were surprised when the object changed color or pattern behind the occluder. In a similar vein, the infants in the occlusion–covering condition who were induced to include height information in their representation of the covering event were surprised when the object changed height under the cover (see also Wang and Baillargeon 2005b). Together, these results make clear that infants who are led by contextual manipulations to represent the color, pattern, or height of an object in an event immediately expect these properties to remain stable – they do not need to learn that green balls cannot turn into red balls, dotted balls into striped balls, or short cylinders into tall ones (cf. Scholl and Leslie 1999).

Third, the present results suggest that when infants see objects involved in a sequence of two events from different event categories, they carry over whatever variable information they included in their physical representation of the first event to that of the second event. In some cases, this carry-over can *induce* infants to detect a variable continuity violation they would otherwise have failed to detect: the infants in the occlusion–covering condition detected at 8.5 months a violation that is typically not detected until about 12 months (Wang and Baillargeon 2005b; Wang *et al.* 2005). In other cases, the carry-over of variable information can *prevent* infants from detecting a variable continuity violation they would otherwise have been able to detect: the infants in the covering–occlusion condition failed to detect at 8.5 months a violation that is typically detected at 3.5 months (Baillargeon and DeVos 1991).

What mechanism might underlie these positive and negative carry-over effects between physical representations? One possibility is suggested by a recent model of object-based attention in infants (e.g. Kaldy and Leslie 2003; Leslie *et al.* 1998; Scholl and Leslie 1999; for related models of visual attention in adults, see Kahneman *et al.* 1992; Pylyshyn 1989, 1994). According to this model, when infants attend to an event involving a few objects, they assign an index to each object. These indexes serve as pointers that help keep track of the objects as the event unfolds (each index 'sticks to' its object as it moves). Typically, indexes are assigned based on spatiotemporal information and contain no featural information; however, such information can be added through a binding process. As the objects engage in first one and then another event, the same indexes continue to be used as long as the infants keep attending to the objects. Finally, in any event, the maximum number of indexes that can be assigned concurrently is three or four (four is the limit in adults).

This model suggests a simple explanation for the carry-over effects reported here. First, consider the infants in the occlusion–covering condition. When representing the occlusion event, the infants assigned an index to the cover and to the object, and bound height information to these indexes; when the infants next saw the covering event, which involved the same cover and object, they continued to use the same indexes, so that the height information bound to these indexes became, fortuitously, available to them. Next, consider the infants in the covering–occlusion condition. When representing the covering event, the infants again assigned an index to the cover and object – but bound no height information to these indexes. Because the occlusion event involved the same cover and object, the infants continued to use the same indexes and thus failed to detect the height continuity violation in the change event.

Blending together our reasoning account and Leslie's model of object-based attention (e.g. Kaldy and Leslie 2003; Leslie *et al.* 1998; Scholl and Leslie 1999) may thus provide useful insights into infants' representations of single as well as multiple events. In particular, such a hybrid account may help explain what variable information is bound to indexes in any one event representation, what variable information is carried over from one event representation to the next, and more generally what variable continuity violations infants succeed or fail to detect in the context of single and multiple events.

7.5 Concluding remarks

The research reviewed in this chapter indicates that infants detect continuity violations when they include in their physical representations the basic and variable information necessary to detect these violations. Violations that involve only basic information are typically detected at an early age, because even very young infants generally include adequate basic information in their physical representations (for exceptions, see Baillargeon 1987; Baillargeon and DeVos 1991). In contrast, violations that involve variable information are typically detected at later ages, because infants who have not yet identified a variable as relevant to an event category typically do not include information about this variable when representing events from the category. An infant who does not represent the heights of a tall object and short container cannot be surprised when the object becomes fully hidden inside the container.

Infants who have not yet identified a variable as relevant to an event category can nevertheless be induced to include information about this variable in their physical representations of events from the category, through appropriate contextual manipulations. For example infants can be induced to include information about the color or pattern of an object in an occlusion event (Wilcox and Chapa 2004), or about the height of an object in a covering event (Li and Baillargeon 2005b; Wang and Baillargeon 2005b). This variable information, once included in the physical representation, becomes subject to the continuity principle (objects exist and move continuously through time and space, retaining their physical properties as they do so), allowing infants to detect any surreptitious change or other continuity violation involving the variable. The world of infants is thus not a fairy-tale one: objects that are represented (either spontaneously or as a result of contextual manipulations) as small, green, and frog-like, are expected *not* to spontaneously turn into objects that are large, blond, and prince-like.

Acknowledgment

The preparation of this chapter was supported by a grant from the National Institute of Child Health and Human Development to the first author (HD-21104).

References

Aguiar A and Baillargeon R (1998). 8.5-month-old infants' reasoning about containment events. *Child Development*, **69**, 636–653.

Aguiar A and Baillargeon R (1999). 2.5-month-old infants' reasoning about when objects should and should not be occluded. *Cognitive Psychology*, **39**, 116–157.

Aguiar A and Baillargeon R (2002). Developments in young infants' reasoning about occluded objects. *Cognitive Psychology*, **45**, 267–336.

Aguiar A and Baillargeon R (2003). Perseverative responding in a violation-of-expectation task in 6.5-month-old infants. *Cognition*, **88**, 277–316.

Arterberry ME (1997). Perception of object properties over time. In: C Rovee-Collier and LP Lipsitt, eds. *Advances in infancy research*, Vol. 11, pp. 219–268. Greenwich, CT: Ablex.

Aslin RN (2000). Why take the cog out of infant cognition? *Infancy*, **1**, 463–470.

Baillargeon R (1987). Object permanence in 3.5- and 4.5-month-old infants. *Developmental Psychology*, **23**, 655–664.

Baillargeon R (1994). How do infants learn about the physical world? *Current Directions in Psychological Science*, **3**, 133–140.

Baillargeon R (1995). A model of physical reasoning in infancy. In: C Rovee-Collier and LP Lipsitt, eds. *Advances in infant research*, Vol. 9, pp. 305–371. Norwood, NJ: Ablex.

Baillargeon R (1999). Young infants' expectations about hidden objects: A reply to three challenges (article with peer commentaries and response). *Developmental Science*, **2**, 115–163.

Baillargeon R (2000). Reply to Bogartz, Shinskey, and Schilling; Schilling; and Cashon and Cohen. *Infancy*, **1**, 447–462.

Baillargeon R (2002). The acquisition of physical knowledge in infancy: A summary in eight lessons. In: U Goswami, ed. *Handbook of childhood cognitive development*, pp. 47–83. Oxford: Blackwell.

Baillargeon R (2004). Infants' reasoning about hidden objects: Evidence for event-general and event-specific expectations (article with peer commentaries and response). *Developmental Science*, **7**, 391–424.

Baillargeon R and DeVos J (1991). Object permanence in young infants: Further evidence. *Child Development*, **62**, 1227–1246.

Baillargeon R and Graber M (1987). Where's the rabbit? 5.5-month-old infants' representation of the height of a hidden object. *Cognitive Development*, **2**, 375–392.

Baillargeon R and Wang S (2002). Event categorization in infancy. *Trends in Cognitive Sciences*, **6**, 85–93.

Bogartz RS, Shinskey JL and Speaker CJ (1997). Interpreting infant looking: The event set x event set design. *Developmental Psychology*, **33**, 408–422.

Bower TGR (1974). *Development in infancy*. San Francisco: WH Freeman.

Bower TGR, Broughton JM and Moore MK (1971). Development of the object concept as manifested in the tracking behavior of infants between seven and twenty weeks of age. *Journal of Experimental Child Psychology*, **11**, 182–193.

Bruner JS (1964). The course of cognitive growth. *American Psychologist*, **19**, 1–15.

Bruner JS (1968). *Processes of cognitive growth: Infancy*. Worcester, MA: Clark University Press and Barre Press.

Carey S and Spelke ES (1994). Domain-specific knowledge and conceptual change. In: LA Hirschfeld and SA Gelman, eds. *Mapping the mind: Domain specificity in cognition and culture*, pp. 169–200. New York: Cambridge University Press.

Casasola M, Cohen L and Chiarello E (2003). Six-month-old infants' categorization of containment spatial relations. *Child Development*, **74**, 679–693.

Cashon CH and Cohen LB (2000). Eight-month-old infants' perceptions of possible and impossible events. *Infancy*, **1**, 429–446.

DeJong GF (1993). *Investigating explanation-based learning*. Boston, MA: Kluwer Academic Press.

Gelman R (1990). First principles organize attention to and learning about relevant data: Number and the animate-inanimate distinction as examples. *Cognitive Science*, 14, 79–106.

Goldberg S (1976). Visual tracking and existence constancy in 5-month-old infants. *Journal of Experimental Child Psychology*, 22, 478–491.

Gopnik A and Wellman HM (1994). The theory theory. In: LA Hirschfeld and SA Gelman, eds. *Mapping the mind: Domain specificity in cognition and culture*, pp. 257–293. New York: Cambridge University Press.

Goubet N and Clifton RK (1998). Object and event representation in 6.5-month-old infants. *Developmental Psychology*, 34, 63–76.

Gratch G (1982). Responses to hidden persons and things by 5-, 9-, and 16-month-old infants in a visual tracking situation. *Developmental Psychology*, 18, 232–237.

Gredebäck G and von Hofsten C (2004). Infants' evolving representations of object motion during occlusion: A longitudinal study of 6- to 12-month-old infants. *Infancy*, 6, 165–184.

Haith MM and Benson JB (1998). Infant cognition. In: W Damon, series ed. and D Kuhn and R Siegler, vol. eds. *Handbook of child psychology*, Vol. 2, pp. 199–254. New York: Wiley.

Hespos SJ and Baillargeon R (2001a). Infants' knowledge about occlusion and containment events: A surprising discrepancy. *Psychological Science*, 12, 140–147.

Hespos SJ and Baillargeon R (2001b). Knowledge about containment events in very young infants. *Cognition*, 78, 204–245.

Hespos SJ and Baillargeon R (in press). Décalage in infants' knowledge about occlusion and containment events: Converging evidence from action tasks. *Cognition*.

Hofstadter M and Reznick JS (1996). Response modality affects human infant delayed-response performance. *Child Development*, 67, 646–658.

Hood B and Willatts P (1986). Reaching in the dark to an object's remembered position: Evidence of object permanence in 5-month-old infants. *British Journal of Developmental Psychology*, 4, 57–65.

Kahneman D, Treisman A and Gibbs BJ (1992). The reviewing of object files: Object-specific integration of information. *Cognitive Psychology*, 24, 174–219.

Kaldy Z and Leslie AM (2003). Identification of objects in 9-month-old infants: Integrating 'what' and 'where' information. *Developmental Science*, 6, 360–373.

Kaufman J, Csibra G and Johnson MH (in press). Oscillatory activity in the infant brain reflects object maintenance. *Proceeding of the National Academy of Science of the United States of America*.

Keil FC (1991). The emergence of theoretical beliefs as constraints on concepts. In: S Carey and R Gelman, eds. *The epigenesis of mind: Essays on biology and cognition*, pp. 237–256. Hillsdale, NJ: Erlbaum.

Keil FC (1995). The growth of causal understandings of natural kinds. In: D Sperber, D Premack and AJ Premack, eds. *Causal cognition: A multidisciplinary debate*, pp. 2342–62. Oxford: Clarendon Press.

Kestenbaum R, Termine N and Spelke ES (1987). Perception of objects and object boundaries by 3-month-old infants. *British Journal of Developmental Psychology*, 5, 367–383.

Lécuyer R (2001). Rien n'est jamais acquis. De la permanence de l'objet … de polemiques. *Enfance*, 55, 35–65.

Lécuyer R and Durand K (1998). Bi-dimensional representations of the third dimension and their perception by infants. *Perception*, 27, 465–472.

Leslie AM (1984). Infant perception of a manual pick-up event. *British Journal of Developmental Psychology*, 2, 19–32.

Leslie AM (1994). ToMM, ToBY, and agency: Core architecture and domain specificity. In: LA Hirschfeld and SA Gelman, eds. *Mapping the mind: Domain specificity in cognition and culture*, pp. 119–148. New York: Cambridge University Press.

Leslie AM (1995). A theory of agency. In: D Sperber, D Premack and AJ Premack, eds. *Causal cognition: A multidisciplinary debate*, pp. 121–149. Oxford: Clarendon Press.

Leslie AM, Xu F, Tremoulet PD and Scholl BJ (1998). Indexing and the object concept: Developing 'what' and 'where' system. *Trends in Cognitive Sciences*, **2**, 10–18.

Li J and Baillargeon R (2005a). Change detection in infancy. Event-category effects. Manuscript in preparation.

Li J and Baillargeon R (2005b). Mapping object representations across successive events in infancy: Positive and negative carry-over effects. Manuscript in preparation.

Luo Y and Baillargeon R (2005a). Development of infants' reasoning about transparent occluders. Manuscript in preparation.

Luo Y and Baillargeon R (2005b). Infants' reasoning about transparent occluders and containers. Manuscript in preparation.

Luo Y and Baillargeon R (2005c). When the ordinary seems unexpected: Evidence for incremental physical knowledge in young infants. *Cognition*, **95**, 297–328.

Luo Y, Baillargeon R, Brueckner L and Munakata Y (2003). Reasoning about a hidden object after a delay: Evidence for robust representations in 5-month-old infants. *Cognition*, **88**, B23–32.

Luo Y, Baillargeon R and Lécuyer R (2005). Young infants' reasoning about height in occlusion events. Manuscript in preparation

McCall D (2001). *Perseveration and infants' sensitivity to cues for containment*. Paper presented at the biennial meeting of the Society for Research in Child Development, Minneapolis, MN, April, 2001.

McDonough L, Choi S and Mandler JM (2003). Understanding spatial relations: Flexible infants, lexical adults. *Cognitive Psychology*, **46**, 229–259.

Meicler M and Gratch G (1980). Do 5-month-olds show object conception in Piaget's sense? *Infant Behavior and Development*, **3**, 265–282.

Mitchell TM (1997). *Machine learning*. New York: McGraw-Hill.

Muller AA and Aslin RN (1978). Visual tracking as an index of the object concept. *Infant Behavior and Development*, **1**, 309–319.

Munakata Y (1997). Perseverative reaching in infancy: The roles of hidden toys and motor history in the AB task. *Infant Behavior and Development*, **20**, 405–416.

Munakata Y (2000). Challenges to the violation-of-expectation paradigm: Throwing the conceptual baby out with the perceptual processing bathwater? *Infancy*, **1**, 471–490.

Munakata Y, McClelland JL, Johnson MH and Siegler R (1997). Rethinking infant knowledge: Toward an adaptive process account of successes and failures in object permanence tasks. *Psychological Review*, **104**, 686–713.

Needham A (2000). Improvements in object exploration skills may facilitate the development of object segregation in early infancy. *Journal of Cognition and Development*, **1**, 131–156.

Newcombe N, Huttenlocher J and Learmonth A (1999). Infants' coding of location in continuous space. *Infant Behavior and Development*, **22**, 483–510.

Piaget J (1952). *The origins of intelligence in children*. New York: International Universities Press.

Piaget J (1954). *The construction of reality in the child*. New York: Basic Books.

Pylyshyn ZW (1989). The role of location indexes in spatial perception: A sketch of the FINST spatial index model. *Cognition*, 32, 65–97.

Pylyshyn ZW (1994). Some primitive mechanisms of spatial attention. *Cognition*, 50, 363–384.

Quinlan JR (1993). *C4.5: Programs for machine learning*. San Mateo, CA: Morgan Kaufmann.

Rensink RA (2002). Change detection. *Annual Review of Psychology*, 53, 245–277.

Rensink RA, O'Regan JK and Clark JJ (1997). To see or not to see: The need for attention to perceive changes in scenes. *Psychological Science*, 8, 368–373.

Rivera SM, Wakeley A and Langer J (1999). The drawbridge phenomenon: Representational reasoning or perceptual preference? *Developmental Psychology*, 35, 427–435.

Roder BJ, Bushnell EW and Sasseville AM (2000). Infants' preferences for familiarity and novelty during the course of visual processing. *Infancy*, 1, 491–507.

Schilling TH (2000). Infants' looking at possible and impossible screen rotations: The role of familiarization. *Infancy*, 1, 389–402.

Scholl BJ and Leslie AM (1999). Explaining the infants' object concept: Beyond the perception/ cognition dichotomy. In: E Lepore and Z Pylyshyn, eds. *What is cognitive science?*, pp. 26–73. Oxford: Blackwell.

Siegler RS (1978). The origins of scientific reasoning. In: RS Siegler, ed. *Children's thinking: What develops?*, pp. 109–149. Hillsdale, NJ: Erlbaum.

Simon T, Hespos SJ and Rochat P (1995). Do infants understand simple arithmetic? A replication of Wynn (1992). *Cognitive Development*, 10, 253–269.

Simons DJ (1996). In sight, out of mind: When object representations fail. *Psychological Science*, 7, 301–305.

Simons DJ (2000). Current approaches to change blindness. *Visual Cognition*, 7, 1–15.

Sitskoorn SM and Smitsman AW (1995). Infants' perception of dynamic relations between objects: Passing through or support? *Developmental Psychology*, 31, 437–447.

Slater A (1995). Visual perception and memory at birth. In: C Rovee-Collier and LP Lipsitt, eds. *Advances in infancy research*, Vol. 9, pp. 107–162. Norwood, NJ: Ablex.

Spelke ES (1982). Perceptual knowledge of objects in infancy. In: J Mehler, E Walker and M Garrett, eds. *Perspectives on mental representation*, pp. 409–430. Hillsdale, NJ: Erlbaum.

Spelke ES (1994). Initial knowledge: Six suggestions. *Cognition*, 50, 431–445.

Spelke ES, Breinlinger K, Macomber J and Jacobson K (1992). Origins of knowledge. *Psychological Review*, 99, 605–632.

Spelke ES and Kestenbaum R (1986). Les origines du concept d'objet. *Psychologie Francaise*, 31, 67–72.

Spelke ES, Phillips A and Woodward AL (1995). Infants' knowledge of object motion and human action. In: D Sperber, D Premack and AJ Premack, eds. *Causal cognition: A multidisciplinary debate*, pp. 44–78. Oxford: Clarendon Press.

Thelen E and Smith LB (1994). *A dynamic systems approach to the development of cognition and action*. Cambridge, MA: MIT Press.

Wang S and Baillargeon R (in press). Infants' physical knowledge affects their change detection. *Development Science*.

Wang S and Baillargeon R (2005a). Can infants' physical knowledge be trained? Manuscript in preparation.

Wang S and Baillargeon R (2005b). Inducing infants to detect a physical violation in a single trial. *Psychological Science*, 16, 542–549.

Wang S, Baillargeon R and Brueckner L (2004). Young infants' reasoning about hidden objects: Evidence from violation-of-expectation tasks with test trials only. *Cognition*, **93**, 167–198.

Wang S, Baillargeon R and Paterson S (2005). Detecting continuity violations in infancy: A new account and new evidence from covering and tube events. *Cognition*, **95**, 129–173.

Wellman HM and Gelman SA (1992). Cognitive development: Foundational theories of core domains. *Annual Review of Psychology*, **43**, 337–375.

Wilcox T (1999). Object individuation: Infants' use of shape, size, pattern, and color. *Cognition*, **72**, 125–66.

Wilcox T and Baillargeon R (1998a). Object individuation in infancy: The use of featural information in reasoning about occlusion events. *Cognitive Psychology*, **17**, 97–155.

Wilcox T and Baillargeon R (1998b). Object individuation in young infants: Further evidence with an event-monitoring task. *Developmental Science*, **1**, 127–142.

Wilcox T and Chapa C (2002). Infants' reasoning about opaque and transparent occluders in an object individuation task. *Cognition*, **85**, B1–10.

Wilcox T and Chapa C (2004). Priming infants to attend to color and pattern information in an individuation task. *Cognition*, **90**, 265–302.

Wilcox T, Nadel L and Rosser R (1996). Location memory in healthy preterm and fullterm infants. *Infant Behavior and Development*, **19**, 309–323.

Wilcox T and Schweinle A (2003). Infants' use of speed information to individuate objects in occlusion events. *Infant Behavior and Development*, **26**, 253–282.

Wilson RA and Keil FC (2000). The shadows and shallows of explanation. In: FC Keil and RA Wilson, eds. *Explanation and cognition*, pp. 87–114. Cambridge, MA: MIT Press.

Yonas A and Granrud CE (1984). The development of sensitivity to kinetic, binocular, and pictorial depth information in human infants. In: D Engle, D Lee and M Jeannerod, eds. *Brain mechanisms and spatial vision*, pp. 113–145. Dordrecht: Martinus Nijhoff.

Chapter 8

The emergence of cognitive specialization in infancy: The case of face preference

Francesca Simion, Chiara Turati, Eloisa Valenza, and Irene Leo

Abstract

Recent studies suggest that newborns' face preference might be explained as the result of the combined effect of non-specific perceptual constraints that stem from the general properties of visual processing shortly after birth (Simion *et al*. 2001, 2003) rather than by an innate mechanism triggered by the specific structure of the face (Johnson and Morton 1991). In particular, it has been demonstrated that a perceptual property, which is defined by the presence of more patterning in the upper than in the lower part of the configuration, determines newborns' preference in the case of both geometric stimuli (Simion *et al*. 2002) and faces (Macchi Cassia *et al*. 2004; Turati *et al*. 2002). Based on these results, the present study was aimed at testing whether the same general biases that induce face preference at birth still operate and explain face preference in 3-month-old infants. In order to address this issue, newborns (Experiment 1) and 3-month-old infants (Experiment 2) were presented with pairs of stimuli composed of a natural face and a scrambled face. The scrambled face had more elements in the top portion than the natural face. Results indicated that, while newborns preferred the scrambled face, at 3 months of age infants preferred the face over the non-face image. These findings appear relevant to the issue of how face processing emerges as a specialized ability during development, suggesting that signs of a process of cognitive specialization for faces are already present in 3-month-old infants.

8.1 **The emergence of cognitive specialization: the case of faces**

Many studies on the development of the face processing system share the idea that the emergence of the ability to process faces is the result of the interaction between innately specified predispositions and the extensive experience everyone has with faces (de Schonen 2002; Johnson 1993; Karmiloff-Smith and Johnson 2004; Le Grand *et al.* 2003; Nelson 2001, 2003; Simion *et al.* 2001, 2003). This perspective contrasts both the idea that the functional and neural distinction that would characterize the adults' face system is 'fully determined prior to any postnatal experience' and 'explicitly specified in the genome' (Farah *et al.* 1998, 2000), and the opposite conviction that places almost exclusive emphasis on the role played by experience in the ontogenetic development of face processing (e.g. Tarr and Gauthier 2000; Gauthier and Lagothethis 2000).

Some authors explain the development of face processing in terms of an experience-*expectant* process. The cortical tissue would have gained, through evolutionary pressure, the potential to become specialized for face processing. However, this specialization would emerge on condition that the critical type of input is provided within the crucial time windows (Nelson 2001, 2003). Face processing, as every other domain-specific cognitive activity, is seen as emerging gradually from the interaction between innate constraints and the structure of input provided by the species-typical environment, with innate constraints having the function of potentiating early learning (Johnson 1993). For instance, deprivation of early visual input to the right hemisphere, as a consequence of unilateral congenital cataract, leads to impaired configural face processing even after years from surgery. On the contrary, comparable deprivation to the left hemisphere has no apparent effect on face processing (Le Grand *et al.* 2003). This suggests that the right hemisphere cerebral tissue is predisposed to process configural information embedded in faces, whereas the left hemisphere is not, and that normal visual input is required in order to convert this predisposition in expert face processing abilities.

The experience-*expectant* perspective on the development of face processing is contingent on a probabilistic epigenesis of cognitive development that views interactions between genes, structural brain changes, and psychological functions as bidirectional (Black *et al.* 1998; Greenough and Black 1992), and is rooted in a neurocostructivist approach to cognitive development that considers brain specialization as the product of gradual developmental processes, rather than as inherently present at birth (Elman *et al.* 1996). Specialization would arise as a product of development under the guidance of genetically specified constraints.

Constraints is a key notion within this framework. Constraints are defined as biases in the information processing due to the properties of brain architecture or perceptual systems in a given period of development. Benefits from these biases are in selectively focusing the cognitive system toward certain aspects of the surrounding environment or facilitating processing of certain kinds of inputs, thus strengthening learning of some categories of stimuli rather than others, and, consequently, guiding and shaping subsequent cognitive development.

Although the general notion that some constraints of infants' neural and perceptual system interact with environmental factors in shaping the emerging cognitive abilities is largely accepted, controversy remains on how these constraints might be implemented, and on a precise specification of what constraints are present in the human system at birth. This issue also appears particularly relevant in the study of the development of face processing, even if that of face processing is an emblematic topic within the neurocostructivistic approach.

In this respect, the well known visual preference that newborns manifest towards faces is of particular interest for our purposes. Using a visual tracking task or measuring the time spent by infants looking at different stimuli, several studies have shown that newborns prefer looking at face configurations, rather than at other, equally complex, non-face stimuli (Goren *et al.* 1975; Johnson and Morton 1991; Macchi Cassia *et al.* 2004; Mondloch *et al.* 1999; Valenza *et al.* 1996). Most authors would agree that this phenomenon is highly adaptive because, by ensuring that infants have visual experience with faces, this initial predisposition would favor the gradual emergence of the specialized cortical circuits that subserve face processing in adults (de Schonen and Mathivet 1989; Johnson and Morton 1991; Simion *et al.* 2001, 2003). However, it is still a matter of dispute as to what the visuoperceptual constraints that induce newborns' face preference are, and how long it takes for them to become effective.

The model of the development of face processing proposed by Johnson and Morton (1991) and de Schonen and Mathivet (1989) refused the existence at birth of *cortical* circuits specifically devoted to faces. It rather explained newborns' preference for faces by hypothesizing the existence of a subcortical face-detecting device, Conspec, which selectively responds to the structure of the face, that is to facedness. Facedness was defined as the spatial disposition of the internal features of the face, that is by the presence of three high-contrast blobs in the correct relative location for eyes and mouth.

Contrary to this proposal, other authors have suggested that the preference for face versus non-face configurations in newborns reflects the activity of general perceptual constraints rather than a content-determined bias toward the face geometry. In this view, newborns would be attracted by certain constellations of general features which sometimes happen to resemble a face (Kleiner and Banks 1987; Maurer 1985; Simion *et al.* 2001, 2003; Turati 2004). These features include a number of dimensions that have been shown to be visually preferred in the first days of life *and* may be found in real faces. Some of them (e.g. high vs. low contrast or luminance, moving vs. stationary) are powerful in infants' daily life, but do not appear sufficient to fully explain experimental evidence, since visual preference for faces has been observed even with static configurations, paired for low-level variables (e.g. Kleiner and Banks

1987; Valenza *et al.* 1996). Other perceptual features have to do with the structural organization of the elements embedded within a visual configuration, but, as the low-level variables listed above, are not specifically tailored for the face domain.

Several studies demonstrated that the limits of the immature visual system at birth do not prevent newborns from detecting and processing high-level perceptual properties. Rather, the available evidence suggests that, since birth, infants are sensible to the organization of the visual information within a stimulus, showing visual preferences for geometric patterns paired in terms of their psychophysical properties (Farroni *et al.* 2000; Slater and Sykes 1977), and being able to discriminate and recognize stimuli that differ exclusively for the arrangement of visual information within configurations (Antell *et al.* 1985; Macchi Cassia *et al.* 2002; Slater *et al.* 1991; Turati *et al.* 2003). For example, when horizontal and vertical gratings are paired newborns prefer the horizontal gratings, thus showing that they prefer a stimulus on the basis of its structural configuration (Farroni *et al.* 2000; Slater and Sykes 1977).

Recent data from our lab showed that at least two non-specific structural properties not only are preferred at birth when embedded in non-face geometric configurations (Macchi Cassia *et al.* 2002; Simion *et al.* 2002), but also play a major role in determining newborns' preference for faces (Acerra *et al.* 2002; Macchi Cassia *et al.* 2004; Turati *et al.* 2002). A first property is defined by the presence of a congruent spatial relationship between the spatial disposition of the inner features and the shape of the outer contour, with more features located in the widest portion of the configuration (i.e. *congruency* Macchi Cassia *et al.* 2002; see also Acerra *et al.* 2002). A second property is defined by the presence of higher stimulus density appearing in the upper than in the lower part of the configuration (i.e. *up–down asymmetry* Simion *et al.* 2002; Macchi Cassia *et al.* 2004; Turati *et al.* 2002).

Evidence revealed that when congruent and non-congruent non-face configurations were compared, a reliable tendency to prefer the congruent pattern was observed in newborns (Macchi Cassia *et al.* 2002). In a similar way, we were able to demonstrate that newborns orient their gaze more frequently to, and look longer at, geometrical stimuli with a higher density of elements in the upper part. These results demonstrate that at birth there is a preference for up–down asymmetrical patterns with more elements in the upper part, that is a pattern is preferred when its more salient part is the upper one (Simion *et al.* 2002). Based on these results, given that faces are up–down asymmetrical stimuli, we hypothesized that a possible reason why newborns prefer a face might be the presence of an up–down asymmetry in the distribution of the face features, with more features placed in the upper part.

Recent studies supported this prediction (Turati *et al.* 2002; Macchi Cassia *et al.* 2004). In particular, manipulating the location of three square elements within a head-shaped contour, Turati and colleagues demonstrated that an upright stimulus with two blobs randomly located in the upper part, and only one blob in the lower, was always preferred over the upside-down stimulus, thus showing that the correct face disposition of the inner elements is not necessary in order to induce a preference. To contrast more directly the hypothesis of a specific built in mechanism that explains face preference at birth (Johnson and Morton 1991) with the alternative hypothesis of the presence of a general mechanism sensitive to up–down asymmetry (Simion *et al.* 2001), a face-like stimulus was paired with a stimulus with the same number of blobs in a different disposition. The results demonstrated that when face-like and non-face-like stimuli are equated for the number of elements placed in the upper part of the configuration face preference disappears (Exp. 2 in Turati *et al.* 2002). Also, newborns showed a visual preference for a non-face-like arrangement of elements located in the upper portion of the stimulus over a face-like arrangement positioned in the lower portion of the pattern (Exp. 3 in Turati *et al.* 2002).

Overall, because newborns' visual behavior was affected by the up–down arrangement of the inner features independently of whether such arrangement was or not face-like, these findings suggest that newborns' preference for faces may be ascribed to a non-specific attentional bias toward top–heavy patterns with a higher density of elements in the upper part, rather than to a specific bias toward the face geometry (i.e. Conspec). Such conclusion was recently strengthened by the finding that a similar pattern of results was obtained using images of real faces and manipulating the position of the inner features within the face, thus extending previous evidence obtained with schematic configurations to veridical stimuli (Macchi Cassia *et al.* 2004).

This evidence indicated that newborns' putatively specific preference for faces may be explained as the result of the cumulative effect of a set of non-specific constraints that stem from the general characteristics of the human visuoperceptual system at birth, rather than by an experience-independent subcortical mechanism specific to the face. Face processing seems to emerge from a broadly-tuned non-specific system, which only through development becomes tuned to faces (Nelson 2001, 2003). The presence at birth of general perceptual biases on visual processing seems sufficient to cause the human face to be a frequent focus of newborns' visual attention, allowing, through experience, the gradual development of brain circuits increasingly specialized for face processing. The face processing system appears thus capable of bootstrapping from minimal information, not requiring highly specific predispositions.

However, a limit of the studies reviewed above is that they do not address the issue of how long these constraints are working during development, because they are focused only on a restricted developmental period, that of the first days after birth. The purpose of the present study was to follow the developmental time course of the face preference phenomenon, investigating the general perceptual constraints that mediate this phenomenon at birth and later during development, by comparing different age levels. More specifically, two experiments were carried out in order to test the biases that induce face preference in newborns (Experiment 1) and in 3-month-old infants (Experiment 2), when the first signs of cortical specialization for faces have been observed (Halit *et al.* 2003; Tzourio-Mazoyer *et al.* 2002). Two alternative predictions can be made. One possibility is that the constraints that underlie face preference at 3 months of age parallel those that mediate the same phenomenon at birth. An alternative hypothesis might suggests that, during the first months of life, infants' preferential response to faces develops from broadly-tuned and non-specific, to increasingly specific and tuned to the human face, showing thus a gradual process of specialization for faces.

8.2 Experiment 1

In a recent study, the role of facedness in triggering newborns' preference for faces was tested using a natural and a scrambled face, which were equated for the number of features appearing in the upper and lower halves of the configurations (Macchi Cassia *et al.* 2004). Because newborns did not show a preference for the face over the non-face stimulus with the same number of elements in the upper portion of the configuration, it was concluded that the face arrangement of the inner features displayed by the natural face did not affect newborns' visual behavior, which seemed to have relied solely on the amount of information appearing in the upper as opposed to the lower portion of the stimuli.

However, two different objections may be raised against this conclusion. First, a lack of visual preference, that is a null result, is not sufficient to support the hypothesis that up–down asymmetry in the distribution of the inner elements plays a crucial role in eliciting newborns' preference for faces. Second, the disappearance of newborns' preference for faces when a natural face is contrasted with a scrambled face equated for the number of features in the upper portion may still be interpreted as reflecting the existence of a face-detecting device such as Conspec. One has just to propose that the template for what constitutes a face is loosely defined. That is, the mechanism that determines face preference at birth would not be as precisely defined as that proposed by Johnson and Morton: 'three high-contrast blobs in the correct relative locations for two eyes and a mouth' (Johnson and Morton 1991, p. 85). However, it would still be especially sensitive to faces. This possibility is strengthened by the consideration that face and non-face top-heavy stimuli might become nearly indistinguishable when filtered at low spatial frequencies through the newborns' poor visual system.

Experiment 1 was designed to test the above objections, providing a direct comparison between up–down asymmetry and facedness in inducing a visual preference at birth. An image of a natural face was presented together with a top-heavy scrambled face in which the number of features placed in the upper portion of the configuration was greater than in the natural face. It was predicted that, if newborns' face preference emerges by virtue of the specific spatial relations between the elements embedded in faces, newborns should prefer the natural face, which preserves this relation. Alternatively, if newborns' visual behavior is governed by the presence of more patterning in the top part, newborns should prefer the top-heavy scrambled face which is more up–down asymmetrical than the natural face.

8.2.1 Method

8.2.1.1 Participants

Fourteen healthy, full-term infants, ranging in age from 1 to 3 days, were recruited in the nursery of the maternity hospital of Padua (Italy). Two infants were removed from the study because they became too fussy or cried. So, the final sample consisted of 12 newborns (four females and eight males) who met the screening criteria of normal delivery – a birth weight between 2550 and 4000 g, and an Apgar score of at least 8 at 5 min. Babies were tested during the hour preceding the scheduled feeding time only if they were awake and in an alert state. Informed consent was obtained from their parents. The ethic committee of the Hospital of Padua, where all of the testing was conducted, granted permission.

8.2.1.2 Stimuli

High-quality black and white photographs of five woman's faces were used. Each photograph was digitally modified, manipulating the position of the inner face features so that a top-heavy scrambled version of each face was generated (Fig. 8.1).

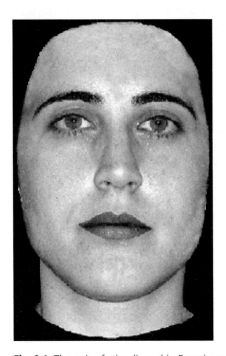
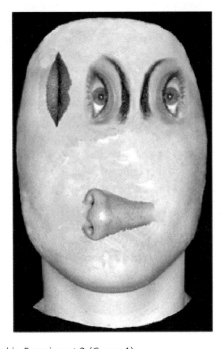

Fig. 8.1 The pair of stimuli used in Experiment 1 and in Experiment 2 (Group 1).

Five pairs of natural and top-heavy scrambled faces were thus created. Each infant was presented with a single pair of stimuli, consisting of a natural face and its corresponding top-heavy scrambled version.

In the scrambled faces, not only the spatial position but also the natural orientation of each face feature was altered, so that the stimulus differed as much as possible from the natural face. The top portion of the scrambled faces contained more patterning than the top portion of natural faces, because not only the eyes and eyebrows but also the mouth were located in the upper part of the configuration. The natural and the scrambled faces within each pair differed exclusively for the orientation and up–down distribution of the inner features, being paired for all low-level variables (i.e. contrast, luminance, number of features within the configuration). Each stimulus was 20.7 cm high (about 39°) and 13 cm wide (about 25°).

8.2.1.3 Apparatus

The infant sat on a student's lap, in front of a black panel, at a distance of about 30 cm. The panel had two square holes where the black screens of two computer monitors appeared. The horizontal midline of the stimuli was aligned with a red flickering LED that was located in the center of the panel, between the screens. At the start of each trial, the LED was used both to attract the infant's gaze and to check that the infant's sight was level with the horizontal midline of the panel during the testing session. Stimuli were projected at a distance of 5 cm from the central LED. To prevent interference from irrelevant distractors, peripheral vision was limited by two black panels placed on both sides of the infant.

8.2.1.4 Procedure

Each trial began with the central flickering LED. As soon as the infant fixated the LED, one of the experimenters started the sequence of the trials by pressing a key on the computer keyboard. This automatically turned off the central LED and activated the stimuli on the screen. When the infant shifted his/her gaze from the display for more than 10 s, the experimenter turned off the stimuli and the central LED automatically started flickering again.

Each infant was presented with a single pair of stimuli, composed of a natural face and its corresponding top-heavy scrambled version. The specific pair of stimuli presented (out of five possible) was counterbalanced between subjects. All infants were submitted to two trials, in which the position (left or right) of the stimuli within the pair was counterbalanced. A coder, who was unaware of the hypotheses being tested and of the stimuli presented, recorded the duration of each fixation by pressing a button that was connected to the computer. At the same time, videotapes of eye movements throughout the trial were recorded and subsequently analyzed frame by frame to the nearest 40 ms by a second coder. Inter-coder agreement (Pearson correlation) was 0.95 for total fixation time and 0.90 for discrete number of looks.

8.2.2 Results and discussion

Preliminary statistical analyses showed no significant effects or interactions involving the factor pair of stimuli. As a consequence, data were collapsed across this factor.

In order to test whether newborns showed a visual preference toward one of the stimuli presented (i.e. the natural face or the top-heavy scrambled face), a paired-sample t-test was carried out on infants' fixation time toward the two configurations. The analysis was statistically significant, $t(11) = 7.20$, $p < 0.001$. Infants looked longer at the top-heavy scrambled face ($M = 111.86$ s, $SD = 20.87$) than at the natural face ($M = 45.50$, $SD = 22.79$). Additional analyses were conducted on preference scores (percentages) for the top-heavy scrambled face. Each infant's looking time at the top-heavy scrambled face was divided by the looking time to both test stimuli and converted into a percentage score. Preference scores for the top-heavy scrambled face were significantly above the chance level of 50 per cent ($M = 71.79$ per cent, $SD = 9.66$, one-sample $t(11) = 7.82$, $p < 0.001$). Finally, examination of the data for individual infants revealed that 11 out of 12 infants looked longer at the top-heavy scrambled face (binomial test, $p < 0.003$).

These findings demonstrated that a scrambled face, with more patterning in the upper half than a natural face, was more able to attract and maintain newborns' gaze than was the image of a real face. When up–down asymmetry and facedness were directly contrasted, the up–down position of the features, rather than their correct positions for eyes and mouth, proved to be the crucial factor in determining newborns' preference. Experiment 1 provides thus clear evidence that, at birth, the human visual processing system is functionally organized to prefer the configuration that displays a higher stimulus density appearing in the upper part. This result is consistent with previous observations obtained with geometric stimuli (Simion *et al.* 2002), highly schematic face-like patterns (Turati *et al.* 2002), and images of real faces (Macchi Cassia *et al.* 2004). In addition to previous evidence, the present experiment indicates that the immature visual system does not prevent newborns discriminating between a face and a scrambled face because a preference toward the top-heavy scrambled face is present. This result contradicts the hypothesis that points to the existence of a specific, although loosely defined, mechanism that selectively responds to all the visual configurations akin to faces. In fact, in Experiment 1, infants preferred the configuration most dissimilar from a natural face, that is the top-heavy scrambled face.

An alternative explanation might be that Conspec responds to facedness, whereas other structural properties not specific to faces attract newborns' gaze as faces do, or even more than faces do. In this perspective our results do not rule out the possibility of an interaction between a preference for visual patterns with more elements in the top half and a separate preference for face-like structures. According to this hypothesis the mechanisms responsible of newborns' preference for up–down asymmetrical configurations would be more powerful than a specific mechanism (i.e. Conspec) in triggering newborns' gaze. However, because one of the structural properties that characterizes face stimuli is precisely up–down asymmetry, a more parsimonious explanation for this outcome is that newborns' visual behavior is governed by general rules that apply indifferently to face or non-face stimuli. One of these rules deals with the up–down distribution of features within the pattern – human infants seem to be born with a visual processing system geared to prefer configurations that display more patterning in the upper half. Faces respond to this rule because they are up–down asymmetrical, therefore they are spontaneously preferred.

8.3 **Experiment 2**

Experiment 2 was carried out in order to test whether the same general biases that induce face preference at birth still operate and explain face preference in 3-month-old infants. Recent evidence indicates that, by 3 months of age, some neuropsychological measures show the first signs of a differential response for human faces, although not comparable with that obtained with older infants or adult subjects (Halit *et al.* 2003; Tzourio-Mazoyer *et al.* 2002). However, signs of a gradual process of specialization have never been demonstrated in 3-month-old infants using behavioral, rather than neuropsychological, measures.

Experiment 2 investigated whether face preference in 3-month-old infants might be ascribed, as in the case of newborns, to a non-specific structural property, namely the up–down asymmetry in the distribution of the inner features within the configuration, or whether, during the first months of life, infants' preferential response becomes more specific to the face category. In order to achieve this purpose, 3-month-old infants were presented with the same stimuli shown to newborns in Experiment 1. One possibility is that older infants, as newborns, would prefer the non-face stimulus that displays, in the upper part, a greater number of elements than faces. This finding would support the notion that similar, basic constraints mediate face preference at birth and at 3 months of age. On the contrary, a preference for the face over the top-heavy non-face pattern would suggest that different processes mediate face preference at different ages during development.

Since face preference has never been tested using images of real faces in 3-month-old infants, the presence of the face preference phenomenon at this age has been verified in a control group that was presented with a face in the canonical upright orientation and an upside-down version of the same face in which the inner portion was 180° rotated.

8.3.1 **Method**

8.3.1.1 Participants

Twenty-eight full-term infants (13 males), assigned to one of two groups (16 to Group 1 and 12 to Group 2), comprised the final sample, ranging in age from 82 to 112 days (mean = 95.46). An additional 12 infants were observed but not included in the analyses, due to a strong position bias (four infants), excessive movement on the part of the infant (two), and an inability to obtain, for unknown reasons, a reliable point of gaze (six). Infants were tested only if awake and in an alert state, after that their parents signed an informed consent.

8.3.1.2 Stimuli

Infants assigned to Group 1 (face vs. scrambled face) were shown the same five pairs of stimuli used in Experiment 1 (Fig. 8.1). Infants assigned to Group 2 (face vs. upside-down face) were presented with five pairs of stimuli, each composed of one of the five images of natural faces shown to Group 1 and an upside-down version of the same face in which only the inner portion of the face was 180° rotated (Fig. 8.2). The upside-down face was thus comparable to that used in a recent study that tested face preference in newborns using veridical face images (Macchi Cassia *et al.* 2004, Exp. 1). Stimuli measured 10 cm in width (about 10°) and 15 cm in height (about 14°) and appeared on a black background. The upright and upside-down face were shown on a computer screen at a distance of 10 cm one from the other.

8.3.1.3 Apparatus

The experiment was run using an apparatus that allows the automatic recording of eye movements direction by virtue of an infra-red camera (i.e. an eye-tracker system

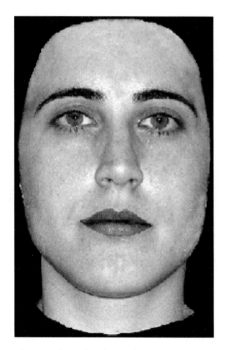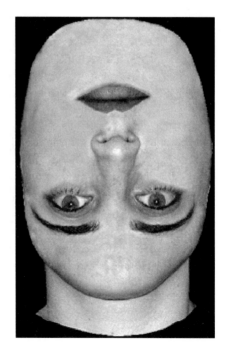

Fig. 8.2 The pair of stimuli used in Experiment 2 (Group 2).

made by the Applied Science Laboratories). A student guided the infra-red camera by means of a remote control, so that the left eye of the infant was always in focus on a TV-monitor. The eye-tracker system was able to detect the position of the pupil and the corneal reflection of the infra-red LEDs in the eye. Because these signals change in relation to infants' gaze direction, the apparatus allows one to register, with a frequency of 50 Hz, the x–y co-ordinates corresponding to the infant fixation point during stimulus presentation. Two crosses of different colors corresponding to the signals coming from infants' pupil and corneal reflection were superimposed on the images of the stimuli, so that the direction of infants' gaze with respect to the stimuli during the experimental session could be videorecorded.

8.3.1.4 Procedure

A visual preference procedure adapted to 3-month-old infants was used. Infants were placed in an infant seat at a distance of about 60 cm from the computer screen where the stimuli were presented. Each trial began with a calibration phase: (1) to adapt the parameters for the detection of the pupil and of the corneal reflection to the characteristics of the eye of each infant; and (2) to detect and memorize the signals of the pupil and of the corneal reflection in the precise moment in which infant gaze is directed toward three different locations of the computer screen (center, top left, and bottom right). In order to attract infants' gaze toward the predetermined locations, an animated cartoon with a musical soundtrack was employed. On the basis of the initial calibration phase, the eye-tracker system was subsequently able to determine the precise direction of infants' gaze during the experimental session.

The experimental session began with the presentation, in the middle of the screen, of a central fixation point particularly attractive for the infant (i.e. a colored moving clown). This central fixation point was used to attract infants' gaze toward the computer screen where stimuli were shown, and to check that the infants' gaze was aligned with the horizontal midline of the screen during the entire experimental session. As soon as the infant looked at the central fixation point, the first pair of stimuli automatically appeared on the computer screen and the central fixation was removed. Each stimulus pair was presented for 8 s. Afterwards, the central fixation point reappeared in the middle of the screen and the trial loop started again.

Each of the five pairs of stimuli was presented four times, in a pseudorandom sequence, for a total of 20 trials. The left vs. right position of the two stimuli within each pair was counterbalanced. A software program processed the raw data coming from the eye-tracker system, calculating infants' total fixation time toward the upright and upside-down faces.

8.3.2 Results and discussion

Given the innovative eye-tracker apparatus employed in Experiment 2, two separate series of statistical analyses were performed. The first series of analyses were concerned with the *overall total looking time* on the stimuli. In this way, the eye-tracker potentials were used to avoid human coders, and data obtained paralleled those classically registered in a visual preference paradigm. So results obtained with 3-month-old infants in Experiment 2 were comparable with those obtained with newborns in Experiment 1. A second series of analyses were run in order to examine which perceptual cues *within* the face and the non-face stimuli attracted infants' gaze, an opportunity allowed by the eye-tracker.

8.3.2.1 Overall total looking time

No significant effects or interactions involving the factor pair of stimuli were found. Data were thus collapsed across this factor.

In order to explore whether 3-month-old infants showed a preference for the face over the non-face image, looking times were investigated with a Group (1, 2) × Stimulus (Face, Non-face) mixed ANOVA. The analysis yielded a significant effect of the factor Stimulus, due to longer fixation time toward the face ($M = 2379$ ms, $SE = 159$) than toward the non-face configuration ($M = 1629$ ms, $SE = 107$), $F(1, 26) = 2.57, p < 0.001$. Also the factor Group reached statistical significance, in that fixation times were longer for infants assigned to Group 1 (face vs. scrambled face) ($M = 2291$ ms, $SE = 165$) than Group 2 (face vs. upside-down face) ($M = 1718$ ms, $SE = 143$), $F(1, 26) = 6.92, p < 0.02$. The interaction between the two factors was not significant.

Additional analyses were performed considering preference scores (i.e. percentage of looking) on the face stimulus, which were computed as in Experiment 1. When computed irrespective of the Group to which infants belonged, the mean preference score was 58.56 per cent ($SD = 9.70$) and differed significantly from chance level of 50 per cent ($t(27) = 4.67, p < 0.001$). To determine whether both infants belonging to Group 1 and infants belonging to Group 2 showed a preference for the face significantly different from chance level, two separate one-sample *t*-tests were applied, one for each Group. Preference scores for the face configuration were significantly above chance for both Group 1 (face vs. scrambled face) ($M = 60.50$ per cent, $SD = 9.26$, $t(11) = 3.93, p < 0.003$) and Group 2 (face vs. upside-down face) ($M = 57.11$ per cent, $SD = 10.06, t(15) = 2.82, p < 0.02$). A *t*-test for independent samples revealed that the mean preference scores for the two Groups did not differ significantly, ($t(26) = -0.9$, $p > 0.35$). Finally, examination of the data for individual infants revealed that 10 out of 12 infants assigned to Group 1 (binomial test, $p < 0.02$) and 13 out of 16 infants assigned to Group 2 (binomial test, $p < 0.009$) looked longer at the face.

Overall, evidence revealed that, at 3 months of age, infants' preference for faces emerged both when the face was contrasted with an upside-down face and when it was contrasted with a scrambled face with more elements in the upper part than a regular face.

Thus, first of all, results demonstrated that the face preference phenomenon persists in 3-month-old infants, corroborating previous evidence obtained with schematic face-like stimuli (Haaf 1974; Haaf and Brown 1976; Johnson *et al.* 1992; Johnson *et al.* 1991; Johnson and Morton 1991). More importantly, at 3 months of age, up–down asymmetry in the distribution of the inner features can not be anymore considered a crucial factor able to induce infants' preference for faces. When presented with the same stimuli shown to newborns in Experiment 1 (i.e. a face configuration and a non-face stimulus with more features than a face in the upper part), an opposite pattern of results was observed. Three-month-old infants did not prefer the stimulus with more patterning in the upper part – as newborns did. They rather preferred the face. Thus, findings disprove the hypothesis that similar general basic constraints mediate face preference during infancy, and suggest that the bias toward up–down asymmetric stimuli at birth acts as an early facilitating factor that leads to an increased specialization for faces later in development.

8.3.2.2 Distribution of looking time

In order to understand which perceptual cues of each stimulus attracted infants' gaze, a series of statistical analyses were performed on percentage of looking toward four selected areas, corresponding to the upper and lower half of each stimulus within a pair. One sample t-tests were applied to verify whether such percentages of looking differed from a chance level of 25 per cent. When the pair of stimuli composed by the upright and upside-down face was presented (Group 2), the following distribution of looking was observed. Three-month-old infants looked at the upper half portion of the face for 47 per cent of total fixation time (i.e. eyes, $M = 46.67$ per cent, $SD = 16.28$, $t(15) = 5.33$, $p < 0.001$), the lower half portion of the face for 10 per cent (i.e. mouth, $M = 10.43$ per cent, $SD = 11.44$, $t(15) = 5.09$, $p < 0.001$), the upper-half part of the upside-down face was looked at for 26 per cent of total looking time (i.e. mouth, $M = 26.31$ per cent, $SD = 10.36$, $t(15) = 0.5$, ns), and, finally, the lower-half part of the upside-down face was looked at for 17 per cent of total looking time (i.e. eyes, $M = 16.58$ per cent, $SD = 11.44$, $t(15) = 2.94$, $p < 0.02$).

A similar pattern of looking was observed for the pair of stimuli composed by the face image and the scrambled face with more features in the upper part than a face (Group 1). The upper half portion of the face was fixated for 49 per cent of total fixation time (i.e. eyes, $M = 49.02$ per cent, $SD = 13.35$, $t(11) = 6.23$, $p < 0.001$), the lower half portion of the face for 11 per cent (i.e. mouth, $M = 11.47$ per cent, $SD = 5.96$, $t(11) = 7.86$, $p < 0.001$), the upper-half part of the top-heavy scrambled face was looked at for 32 per cent of total looking time (i.e. misplaced and misoriented mouth and eyes, $M = 32.34$ per cent, $SD = 7.86$, $t(11) = 3.23$, $p < 0.009$), and, finally, the lower-half part of the top-heavy scrambled face was fixated for 7 per cent of total looking time (i.e. nose, $M = 16.58$ per cent, $SD = 11.44$, $t(15) = 2.94$, $p < 0.02$).

Evidence indicates that the preference for the upright face configuration obtained in Group 1 and Group 2 is mainly due to a higher percentage of looking toward the area of the face that corresponds to eyes, that attracted nearly half of the total looking time toward the stimuli. Interestingly, eyes *per se* did not attract the infants' gaze when misplaced and located in the lower portion of the face: percentage of looking toward the lower-half part of the upside-down face (Group 1) was significantly *lower* than chance level and comparable to percentage of looking toward the mouth in the upright face. A higher percentage of looking was accumulated also in the upper part of the top-heavy scrambled face (Group 2), most probably because in that region there were many features to explore.

8.4 General discussion

This study examined the development of infants' abilities to process a particular class of visual stimuli, that is faces. Although face processing and recognition have been extensively studied in various fields, our knowledge of how face processing skills develop appears still limited. Even when there is a general agreement concerning the presence versus absence of a certain ability at a certain age, controversy remains about the processes underlying such ability.

This is the case of the visual preference that newborns manifest toward faces. Evidence of this phenomenon is frequently cited as favoring the hypothesis that specific mechanisms for face processing are present since birth (de Schonen and Mathivet 1989; Farah *et al.* 2000; Johnson and Morton 1991). However, recent findings challenged this position suggesting that it is not necessary to postulate a built-in mechanism specifically devoted to attract newborns' gaze toward faces. On the contrary, newborns' preference for faces may be explained as determined by general perceptual properties that faces share with other non-face objects. In particular, research was focused on the up–down asymmetry in the distribution of the inner elements within a visual pattern and suggested that it is not the specific configuration of facial features *per se* that infants find attractive but rather having elements positioned in the upper half of the pattern (Macchi Cassia *et al.* 2004; Simion *et al.* 2002, 2003; Turati *et al.* 2002; Turati 2004).

Findings reported in Experiment 1 of the present study strengthened this latter position showing that a scrambled face with more features than a natural face in the top part is preferred over an equally complex veridical face. That is, newborns preferred the top-heavier visual configuration, independently of the face or non-face arrangement of its inner features. This outcome excludes the possibility that a specific mechanism, although loosely defined, is responsible for newborns' preference for faces, since a preferential response was elicited by the stimulus less akin to faces. It is important to note that, although our research was mainly focused on the role of up–down asymmetry in inducing newborns' face preference, it is likely that other structural properties, beside the one investigated in the present study, contribute to the phenomenon, rendering newborns' predilection for faces even more powerful. This point is supported by those studies that show a preference for an attractive over an unattractive face (Slater *et al.* 1998) or for a face with direct rather than averted gaze (Farroni *et al.* 2002). In these studies, a preference was observed even though the stimuli were paired both for up–down asymmetry and for the presence of the specific structure that characterizes a face. Therefore, in our view such newborns' preferences support the notion that a series of non-specific properties, such as the symmetry or congruence of the configuration (in the case of the attractive faces), and the presence of different spatial frequencies (in the case of the direct vs. averted gaze), might be collectively responsible of newborns preferences. In other words, our crucial point is that newborns' putatively specific preference for faces may be explained as the result of the cumulative effect of general, rather than specific, constraints that stem from the general characteristics of the human visual system shortly after birth.

Experiment 2 showed that the general constraints active in newborns are no more sufficient to explain face preference in 3-month-old infants. When the same visual stimuli shown to newborns were presented at 3 months of age, an opposite pattern of results emerged, since infants preferred the face over the top-heavy non-face. Those general visual-processing constraints that directed newborns' gaze toward visual configurations that display more patterning in the upper half did not seem to be effective anymore. Indeed, unpublished evidence that investigated, using geometric patterns, whether up–down asymmetry is capable of producing a preferential re-sponse in 3-month-old infants suggested that, at this age, the general constraints responsible for infants' visual preference for top-heavy patterns are still present but weaker. In fact they are activated only when vertical asymmetry is very pronounced (Turati *et al.* in press).

Overall, the whole pattern of results of the present study is consistent with an experience-expectant perspective on face processing development that emphasizes the relevance of both general biases and exposure to certain experiences to drive the emergence of later-developing systems. This study showed, using behavioral meas-ures, a process of gradual functional specialization of the face processing system in the first months of life. Most probably by virtue of the prolonged exposure to human faces, the processes responsible for infants' face preference shift from broadly-tuned to a wide range of visual stimuli to increasingly tuned to human faces. It is worth noting that such specialization does not have to do solely with eyes detection. In fact, our findings showed that 3-month-old infants manifested a preference for looking at the eyes over other regions of the natural face. However, contrary to the view that an Eye Direction Detector (EDD) would be present from birth (Baron-Cohen 1995), the perceptual information conveyed by eyes lost its importance when eyes were located in the lower rather than in the upper part of the face, as in the upside-down face shown in Experiment 2. Thus, the presence of the eyes *per se* is not sufficient to attract 3-month-old infants' gaze, since infants' visual preference is modulated by the position of eyes within the stimulus, that is by the context in which eyes are located.

The empirical evidence gathered in the present study on the functional specialization of face processing in early infancy raises interesting questions regarding what are the anatomical substrates that mediate face preference at birth and at 3 months of age. Two different hypotheses might be tentatively advanced. One possibility is that, at birth, subcortical circuits, rather than supporting a specific mechanism that responds to a primitive face representation (Johnson and Morton 1991), mediate general processes that ensure a biased input toward up–down asymmetrical visual patterns. Faces would be the patterns most likely to display such an asymmetry in the newborns' visual world. Indeed, in several species, a major role in visual exploration of the upper visual field is played by the superior colliculus (Sprague et al. 1973), which is supposed to affect considerably newborns' visual behavior (Atkinson et al. 1992; Braddick et al. 1992; Bronson 1982; Johnson 1990, 1995). As a consequence of the extensive experience with faces ensured by general perceptual constraints located in the subcortical system, over the first days or weeks of life, increasingly specialized face processing would gradual develop in cortical tissue. According to this dual mechanism hypothesis, not only the visual-processing mechanisms at the basis of face preference would be different in newborns and older infants, but they would be mediated by different anatomical areas.

However, an alternative proposal on the early emergence of face processing has been raised by recent computational models (Bednar 2003) and might be also consistent with our findings. This proposal suggests that a single, rather than multiple, increasingly complex system might be sufficient in order to account for the evidence gathered on the face preference phenomenon in early infancy. More specifically, it may be hypothesized that tuning properties of cells of the visual processing system may act as a general perceptual filtering and amplification device, giving an advantage to up–down asymmetrical stimuli. As a consequence of this biased input, regions within the inferior temporal cortex may become increasingly specialized for the processing of a narrower category of visual stimuli of which infants have extensive experience, that is faces. Further research is thus needed in order to clarify the issue of the anatomical basis of infants' preference for faces, which are certainly one of the most important biological stimuli for humans.

Acknowledgements

The research reported here was supported by a grant from the Ministero dell'Università e della Ricerca Scientifica e Tecnologica (No. 2003112997_004). The authors are deeply indebted to Dr Beatrice Dalla Barba and the nursing staff at the Pediatric Clinic of the University of Padova for their collaboration. We also thank Viola Macchi Cassia for providing some of the stimuli used, Sandro Bettella for writing the software used for testing newborns, and Stefano Massaccesi for his help in assembling the eye-tracker apparatus.

References

Acerra F, Burnod I and de Schonen S (2002). Modeling aspects of face processing in early infancy. *Developmental Science*, 5, 98–117.

Antell SA, Caron AJ and Myers RS (1985). Perception of relational invariants by newborns. *Developmental Psychology*, 21, 942–948.

Atkinson J, Hood B, Wattam-Bell J and Braddick O (1992). Changes in infants' ability to switch visual attention in the first three months of life. *Perception*, 21, 643–653.

Baron-Cohen S (1995). *Mindblindness: An essay on autism and theory of mind.* Cambridge, MA: MIT Press.

Bednar JA (2003). The role of internally generated neural activity in newborn and infant face preferences. In: O Pascalis and A Slater, eds. *The development of face processing in infancy and early childhood: Current perspectives.* New York: Nova Science Publishers.

Black JE, Jones TA, Nelson CA and Greenough WT (1998). Neuronal plasticity and the developing brain. In: NE Alessi JT Coyle SI Harrison and S Eth, eds. *Handbook of child and adolescent psychiatry, Vol. 6: Basic psychiatric science and treatment,* pp. 31–53. New York: Wiley.

Braddick O, Atkinson J, Hood B, Harkness W, Jackson G and Vargha-Cadem F (1992). Possible blindsight in infants lacking one cerebral hemisphere. *Nature*, 360, 461–463.

Bronson GW (1982). Structure, status and characteristics of the nervous system at birth. In: P Stratton, ed. *Psychobiology of the human newborn,* pp. 99–118. New York: Wiley.

de Schonen S (2002). Epigenesis of the cognitive brain: a task for the 21st Century. In: L Backman and C von Hofsten, eds. *Psychology at the turn of the millennium, pp. 55–88.* Hove, UK: Psychology Press.

de Schonen S and Mathivet E (1989). First come, first served: A scenario about the development of hemispheric specialization in face recognition during infancy. *European Bulletin of Cognitive Psychology*, 9, 3–44.

Elman JL, Bates EA, Johnson MH, Karmiloff-Smith A, Parisi D and Plunkett K (1996). *Rethinking innateness. A connectionist perspective on development.* Cambridge, MA: MIT Press.

Farah MJ, Rabinowitz C, Quinn GE and Liu GT (2000). Early commitment of neural substrates for face recognition. *Cognitive Neuropsychology*, 17, 117–123.

Farah MJ, Wilson KD, Drain M and Tanaka JN (1998). What is 'special' about face perception? *Psychological Review*, 105, 482–498.

Farroni T, Csibra G, Simion F and Johnson MH (2002). Eye contact detection in humans from birth. PNAS, 14, 9602–9605.

Farroni T, Valenza E, Simion F and Umiltà C (2000). Configural processing at birth: Evidence for perceptual organization. *Perception*, 29, 355–372.

Gauthier I and Logothetis NK (2000). Is face recognition not so unique after all? *Cognitive Neuropsychology*, 17, 125–142.

Goren C, Sarty M and Wu P (1975). Visual following and pattern discrimination of face-like stimuli by newborn infants. *Pediatrics*, 56, 544–549.

Greenough WT and Black JE (1992). Induction of brain structure by experience: Substrates for cognitive development. In: M Gunnar and CA Nelson, eds. *Behavioral developmental neuroscience, Minnesota symposia on child psychology,* vol. 24, pp. 35–52. Hillsdale, NJ: Erlbaum.

Haaf R (1974). Complexity and facial resemblance as determinants of response to face-like stimuli by 5- and 10-week-old infants. *Journal of Experimental Child Psychology*, 18, 480–487.

Haaf R and Brown C (1976). Infants' response to face-like patterns: Developmental changes between 10 and 15 weeks of age. *Journal of Experimental Child Psychology*, 22, 155–160.

Halit H, de Haan M and Johnson MH (2003). Cortical specialization for face processing: Face sensitive event-related potential components in 3- and 12-month-old infants. *Neuroimage*, 19, 1180–1193.

Johnson MH (1990). Cortical maturation and the development of visual attention in early infancy. *Journal of Cognitive Neuroscience*, 2, 81–95.

Johnson MH (1993). Constraints on cortical plasticity. In: MJ Johnson, ed. *Brain development and cognition. A reader.* Cambridge, US: Blackwell.

Johnson MH (1995). The development of visual attention: A cognitive neuroscience perspective. In: MS Gazzaniga, ed. *The cognitive neuroscience*, pp. 735–747. Cambridge, MA: MIT Press.

Johnson MH and Morton J (1991). *Biology and cognitive development. The case of face recognition.* Oxford, UK: Basil Blackwell.

Johnson MH, Dziurawiec S, Bartrip J and Morton J (1992). The effects of movement of internal features on infants' preferences for face-like stimuli. *Infant Behavior and Development*, 15, 129–136.

Johnson MH, Dziurawiec S, Ellis H and Morton J (1991). Newborns' preferential tracking of face-like stimuli and its subsequent decline. *Cognition*, 90, 1–19.

Karmiloff-Smith A and Johnson MH (2004). Neuroscience perspectives on infant development. In: G Bremner and A Slater, eds. *Theories of infant development.* Oxford, UK: Blackwell.

Kleiner KA and Banks MS (1987). Stimulus energy does not account for 2-month-old infants' face preference. *Journal of Experimental Psychology: Human, Perception and Performance*, 13, 594–600.

Le Grand R, Mondloch CJ, Maurer D and Brent HP (2003). Expert face processing requires visual input to the right hemisphere during infancy. *Nature Neuroscience* 6, 1108–1112.

Macchi Cassia V, Simion F, Milani I and Umiltà C (2002). Dominance of global visual properties at birth. *Journal of Experiment Psychology: General*, 131, 398–411.

Macchi Cassia V, Turati C and Simion F (2004). Can a non specific bias toward top-heavy patterns explain newborns' face preference? *Psychological Science*, 15, 379–383.

Macchi Cassia V, Valenza E, Pividori D and Simion F (2002). Facedness vs. non-specific structural properties: What is crucial in determining face preference at birth. *ICIS Conference.* Toronto, Canada, April 18–21.

Maurer D (1985). Infants' perception of facedness. In: TM Field and NA Fox, eds. *Social perception in infants.* Norwood, NJ: Ablex.

Mondloch CJ, Lewis TL, Budreau DR, Maurer D, Dannemiller JL, Stephens BR and Kleiner-Gathercoal KA (1999). Face perception during early infancy. *Psychological Science*, 5, 419–422.

Nelson CA (2001). The development and neural bases of face recognition. *Infant and Child Development*, 10, 3–18.

Nelson CA (2003). The development of face recognition reflects an experience-expectant and activity-dependent process. In: O Pascalis and A Slater, eds. *The development of face processing in infancy and early childhood: Current perspectives.* New York: Nova Science Publishers.

Simion F, Macchi Cassia V, Turati C and Valenza E (2001). The origins of face perception: Specific vs non-specific mechanisms. *Infant and Child Development*, 10, 59–65.

Simion F, Macchi Cassia V, Turati C and Valenza E (2003). Non-specific perceptual biases at the origins of face processing. In: O Pascalis and A Slater, eds. *The development of face processing in infancy and early childhood: Current perspectives*, pp. 13–25. New York: Nova Science.

Simion F, Valenza E, Macchi Cassia V, Turati C and Umiltà C (2002). Newborns' preference for up-down asymmetrical configurations. *Developmental Science*, 5, 427–434.

Slater A and Sykes M (1977). Newborn infants' responses to square-wave gratings. *Child Development*, 48, 545–553.

Slater A, Mattock A, Brown E and Bremner JG (1991). Form perception at birth: Cohen and Younger (1984) revisited. *Journal of Experimental Child Psychology*, 51, 395–406.

Slater A, Von der Schulenburg C, Brown E, Badenoch M, Butterworth G, Parsons S *et al.* (1998) Newborn infants prefer attractive faces. *Infant Behavior and Development*, 21, 345–354.

Sprague JM, Berlucchi G and Rizzolatti G (1973). The role of the superior colliculus and pretectum in vision and visually guided behavior. In: R Jung, ed. *Handbook of sensory physiology*, vol. 7. Germany: Springer-Verlag.

Tarr MJ and Gauthier I (2000). FFA: a flexible fusiform area for subordinate level visual processing automatized by expertise. *Nature Neuroscience*, 8, 764–769.

Turati C (2004). Why faces are not special to newborns: An alternative account of the face preference. *Current Directions in Psychological Science*, 13, 5–8.

Turati C, Simion F, Milani I and Umiltà C (2002). Newborns preference for faces: What is crucial? *Developmental Psychology*, 38, 875–882.

Turati C, Simion F and Zanon L (2003). Newborns' perceptual categorization for closed and open geometric forms. *Infancy*, 4, 309–325.

Turati C, Valenza E, Leo I and Simion F (in press). Three-month-old visual preference for faces and its underlying visual processing mechanisms. *Journal of Experimental Child Psychology*.

Tzourio-Mazoyer N, de Schonen S, Crivello F, Reutter B, Aujard Y and Mazoyer B (2002). Neural correlates of woman face processing by 2-month-old infants. *Neuroimage*, 15, 454–461.

Valenza E, Simion F, Macchi Cassia V and Umiltà C (1996). Face preference at birth. *Journal of Experimental Psychology: Human Perception and Performance*, 22, 892–903.

Chapter 9

Age-related changes in infant memory retrieval: Implications for knowledge acquisition

Harlene Hayne

Abstract

One of the most consistent findings in the area of infant memory development is that memory retrieval occurs if, and only if, the cues present at the time of retrieval are virtually identical to stimuli encountered during original encoding. The specificity of the cues required to initiate memory retrieval means that infants' ability to use their prior knowledge to solve new problems is very limited, particularly early in development. Over the course of both age and experience, however, infants begin to exploit a wider range of effective retrieval cues, applying potentially useful memories to situations different from those encountered when those memories were originally established. These developmental changes in memory retrieval provide a model for the way in which knowledge accumulates and accrues during the infancy period.

> Events are always unique, they are never repeated. But events may resemble one another, by virtue of the similarity of their settings, focal elements, or both.
>
> Tulving 1984, p. 229

9.1 Introduction

During the course of our normal interactions in the world, we often encounter objects or events that are similar, but not identical, to objects or events that we have encountered before. If there is sufficient overlap between these new objects and events and attributes that are stored as part of a previously established memory representation, the representation will be retrieved and we can apply what we have learned before to a new situation. If this subsequent learning opportunity occurs while the original memory is still accessible to retrieval, the new information may be integrated with existing attributes, thereby increasing the strength or content of the representation. This process is not unique to learning and memory by verbal adults, but rather reflects the way in which the knowledge base is updated throughout the lifespan.

Although the fundamental learning and memory skills that are required for knowledge acquisition are present very early in development (for recent reviews, see Hayne 2004; Rovee-Collier and Barr 2001), a key developmental change in this process is the degree of the match that is required between retrieval cues and memory attributes. Studies of both infants and young children have shown that there are important age-related changes in their ability to exploit cues that were not part of the original learning episode. In this way, age-related changes in memory retrieval play a fundamental role in the development of knowledge acquisition during infancy and early childhood.

The goal of the present chapter is four-fold. First, I will show that early in the infancy period, memory retrieval is highly specific to the conditions of original encoding. Second, I will show that, despite this initial high degree of specificity, older infants begin to exploit cues that are similar, but not identical, to stimuli encountered during original encoding. Third, I will show that, for infants of all ages, experience may increase the range of effective retrieval cues for a particular memory. Finally, I will present new data from my laboratory showing that, under some conditions, infants can use analogy as the basis of memory retrieval – solving a new problem on the basis of its conceptual similarity to a problem that they have encountered before. Taken together, these data provide a model for memory organization and knowledge acquisition during the infancy period.

9.2 Memory retrieval by adults

Most theories of human memory share at least three common assumptions. First, most assume that a memory representation consists of a hypothetical collection of attributes that reflect information that the individual encoded at the time of the original experience. Second, most assume that the attributes that comprise a memory include information about focal elements of the event as well as information about the context in which that event occurred. Finally, most assume that subsequent access to a memory representation requires a match between cues present at the time of retrieval and attributes that are stored as part of the memory representation.

During the early 1970s, Tulving and Thomson published a series of papers in which they argued that the nature of the match between retrieval cues and memory attributes was highly specific and was established at the time of original encoding (Thomson and Tulving 1970; Tulving and Thomson 1973). According to their view, a stimulus would serve as an effective retrieval cue if, and only if, that stimulus had been part of original encoding. This relation between encoding and effective retrieval cues is commonly referred to as the Encoding Specificity Hypothesis (Tulving and Thomson 1973).

At the time of its inception, the Encoding Specificity Hypothesis provided an excellent account of a number of different memory-related phenomena, but it also raised an intriguing paradox. Given that no two events ever occur the same way twice, how could memory retrieval ever occur in situations that differed from those in which the target information was originally encoded? How could prior knowledge be used to solve new problems? At least two sets of findings provided some resolution to this paradox. First, a number of researchers showed that cues that were *not* present at the time of original encoding were sometimes effective in eliciting retrieval of the target memory (Baker and Santa 1977; Kochevar and Fox 1980; Light 1972; Marcel and Steel 1973; Postman 1975). Baker and Santa (1977) and Postman (1975), for example, reported that presentation of a strong associate (e.g. bloom) cued retrieval of a target word (e.g. flower) even when that strong associate had not been part of the original study list. Second, a number of researchers also showed that cues present at the time of original encoding sometimes cued false memories for items that were not present at the time of original encoding. For example Roediger and McDermott (1995) reported that adults who studied lists of words (e.g. bed, rest, awake) often recalled seeing a related target word (e.g. sleep) even when that word had not been part of the study list. This false memory illusion has been replicated in a number of different laboratories using both recognition and recall procedures to test memory.

Taken together, the data reported by Postman (1975), Baker and Santa (1977), Roediger and McDermott (1995), and others illustrate that memory retrieval by adults is not restricted to cues that were actually present during original encoding, but rather extends to cues that match attributes of memory representations that share attributes with the target memory (Tulving 1984). The interconnected nature of multiple memories leads to highly flexible memory retrieval, allowing adults to access their prior memories in situations that are very different from those present at the time of original encoding. Furthermore, the absolute match that is required between effective retrieval cues and memory attributes is sometimes very minimal and may occur on a conceptual, rather than a perceptual, basis in adults (Tulving 1984). In some instances, the interconnected nature of adult memory can also lead to powerful false memory illusions.

The initial finding that stimuli that were not part of the original learning episode could cue memory retrieval by human adults was seen by many as a major blow to the Encoding Specificity Hypothesis. In response to some of his original critics, however, Tulving (1984) argued that, 'Until such time as the encoding specificity hypothesis is shown to be contrary to facts, it seems reasonable to claim that *at some as yet undetermined level of abstraction*, it probably holds for all phenomena of episodic memory...' (pp. 234–235, italics added).

The data presented in this chapter provide a model for the way in which the 'level of abstraction' that Tulving describes might emerge during the course of human development. I will argue that, as a function of both age and experience, an individual's memory representations become more organized and interconnected. As such, the content of the representation becomes more than merely the sum of the individual attributes, allowing older children and adults to consider possibilities and draw conclusions about events for which they have no prior experience. In this way, age-related changes in memory retrieval mark a major achievement in cognitive development.

9.3 Memory retrieval by infants

Although memory retrieval by human adults is highly flexible, memory retrieval by human infants is not. Tulving and Thomson originally developed the Encoding Specificity Hypothesis to account for data collected with verbal adults – little did they know that some of the best evidence for the hypothesis would begin to emerge more than a decade later in studies conducted with preverbal infants. One of the most consistent findings in the area of infant memory development is that memory retrieval occurs if, and only if, the cues present at the time of retrieval are virtually identical to those encountered during original encoding.

The first inkling that encoding specificity played such a fundamental role in infant memory retrieval emerged in the course of studies conducted with infants tested in the mobile conjugate reinforcement paradigm. In this experimental procedure, 2- to 6-month-old infants learn to kick their feet to produce movement in an overhead crib mobile. Mobile movement is made possible by a length of white, satin ribbon; one end of the ribbon is attached to the infant's ankle, and the other is attached to a flexible, metal mobile stand (Fig. 9.1, left panel).

During periods of reinforcement (acquisition), the ribbon is attached to the stand that supports the mobile. During periods of non-reinforcement (baseline and test periods), the ribbon is attached to an empty stand. During periods of reinforcement, kicks of the infant's foot produce corresponding movement in the mobile (i.e. conjugate reinforcement). The mobile conjugate reinforcement task was originally developed for use with 2- to 3-month-old infants (Rovee and Rovee 1969), but the task can also be modified for use with 6-month-olds simply by placing the infant in a sling seat rather than on his or her back and by decreasing the duration of the procedure (Hill *et al.* 1988).

Figure 9.2 provides one example of the highly specific nature of infant memory retrieval that has been documented in the mobile conjugate reinforcement paradigm. These data were collected from 2- and 3-month-old infants who were trained for two consecutive days with a five-object mobile and who were tested 24 h later (Hayne *et al.* 1986). Independent groups of infants at each age were tested with either the training

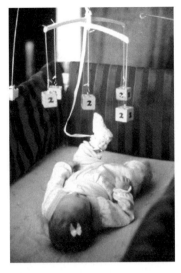

Fig. 9.1 The mobile conjugate reinforcement paradigm (left panel) and the deferred imitation paradigm (right panel) are two tasks that are commonly used to study learning and memory during the infancy period.

mobile (i.e. zero novel test objects) or with a mobile that differed from the training mobile by one to five objects. Retention was calculated by dividing each infant's kick rate during the test by his or her kick rate at the end of training (i.e. Retention Ratio). A retention ratio of 1.00 indicates no decline in performance over the delay; ratios smaller than 1.00 indicate some degree of forgetting. As shown in Fig. 9.2, infants of

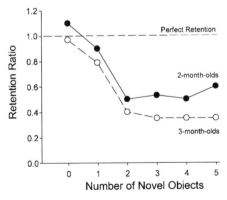

Fig. 9.2 The memory performance of 2- and 3-month-old infants who were tested in the mobile conjugate reinforcement paradigm with a mobile that differed from their training mobile by zero to five novel objects. The retention ratio expresses kick rate during the retention test as a fraction of kick rate at the conclusion of training. These data have been redrawn from Hayne et al. (1986).

both ages exhibited near-perfect retention when they were tested with the training mobile or with a mobile that contained a single novel component. When infants were tested with mobiles that contained more than one novel component, however, their performance declined sharply; their kick rate during the test was not statistically different from their kick rate prior to training (i.e. baseline).

Subsequent research has shown that this high degree of encoding specificity is not unique to the mobile conjugate reinforcement paradigm nor is it restricted to the first 2 to 3 months of life. Figure 9.3 shows data collected from 6-month-old infants who were tested in the mobile conjugate reinforcement or deferred imitation paradigms. In the deferred imitation paradigm, an experimenter demonstrates a series of actions with objects and the infant's ability to reproduce those actions is assessed after a delay (Fig. 9.1, right panel). Although there is ample evidence of imitation of facial gestures by neonates (Meltzoff and Moore 1983, 1989), the earliest age at which infants exhibit deferred imitation with objects is approximately 6 months (Barr *et al.* 1996; Collie and Hayne 1999). The task most commonly used with 6-month-olds is shown in the right panel of Fig. 9.1. In this task, the experimenter removes a mitten from the puppet's hand, shakes the mitten ringing the bell hidden inside, and then replaces the mitten on the puppet's hand. Infants' ability to reproduce these three target actions (i.e. remove, shake, replace) is assessed immediately or after a delay. With modifications to the objects and target actions, the deferred imitation procedure can be used effectively with 6- to 30-month-olds (for review, see Hayne 2004).

The data shown in Fig. 9.3 were collected from independent groups of 6-month-old infants who were tested in one of three conditions: some infants were tested with the

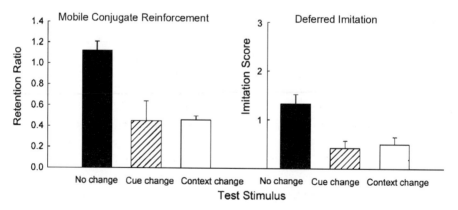

Fig. 9.3 The memory performance of 6-month-old infants who were tested in the mobile conjugate reinforcement or deferred imitation paradigms. Independent groups of infants were tested after a 24-h delay with the original cue in the original context (no change), with a novel cue in the original context (cue change), or with the original cue in a novel context (context change). These data have been redrawn from Borovsky and Rovee-Collier (1990), Hartshorn and Rovee-Collier (1997), Hill *et al.* (1988), and Hayne *et al.* (2000).

same proximal cue (e.g. mobile or puppet) in the original training context (Fig. 9.3, no change), some infants were tested with a different proximal cue in the original training context (Fig. 9.3, cue change), and some infants were tested with the same proximal cue in a different context (Fig. 9.3, context change). The pattern of results across the two procedures is virtually identical – in all cases, 6-month-olds exhibited excellent retention when the cues present at the time of retrieval matched the cues present at the time of original encoding, but they exhibited no retention whatsoever when either the proximal stimulus or the environmental context was altered at the time of the test; that is, performance during the test did not exceed baseline production of the target behavior (Borovsky and Rovee-Collier 1990; Hayne *et al.* 2000; Hill *et al.* 1988).

The effect of contextual change on infant memory retrieval is all the more striking when we consider the nature of the contexts involved. In the mobile conjugate reinforcement paradigm, for example, the context was defined by draping the sides and ends of the infant's crib with a brightly colored cloth liner; at the time of the test, the color of the liner, but not the location of the crib, was altered. In the deferred imitation paradigm, the context was defined by the location of the demonstration and the test sessions (home or laboratory), but both locations included many of the same features including a sofa, a table, and pictures on the wall. In studies conducted with adults, the effect of contextual change on memory retrieval is much more ephemeral and typically occurs only when the contextual change is extremely dramatic (e.g. on land versus under water; Godden and Baddley 1975). In fact, Crowder (1985) has argued that context effects on adult memory retrieval only occur when 'sledgehammer' manipulations in context are included.

The data on infant memory retrieval reviewed thus far clearly show that young infants' memory representations contain highly detailed information about the focal event and about the environmental context in which that event occurred. These data also show that, for memory retrieval to occur, the cues present at the time of retrieval must match stimuli present at the time of encoding almost exactly. If either the target objects or the context is altered at the time of the test, retrieval suffers. By the same token, the data described thus far also suggest that the probability that infants will actually retrieve and use their early memories is extremely limited. Given that memory retrieval only occurs when infants encounter stimuli that are virtually identical to those present during original encoding, developmental changes in perception or selective attention would significantly decrease the probability of retrieval, particularly after very long retention intervals. Furthermore, the specificity of the cues required to initiate memory retrieval indicates that it may be difficult, if not impossible, for potentially useful memories to be retrieved by cues (or in contexts) not previously encountered. Given that events rarely occur the same way twice, the high degree of encoding specificity exhibited by young infants seriously limits their ability to accumulate information over successive learning opportunities.

9.3.1 Age-related changes in memory retrieval

Over the course of development, infants must eventually overcome the high degree of encoding specificity illustrated in Figs 9.2 and 9.3 and begin to exploit retrieval cues that are similar, but not identical, to cues encountered during original encoding. When tested in the deferred imitation paradigm, for example, infants' ability to exploit novel retrieval cues increases gradually between 6 and 30 months of age. When tested in the puppet task shown in Fig. 9.1 (right panel), for example, changes to the test stimuli preclude retrieval by 6- and 12-month-olds, but 18-month-olds exhibit the same level of retention irrespective of the puppet present at the time of the test (Fig. 9.4, left panel; Appendix 9.1, Puppets: Mouse/Rabbit). If the discrepancy between the demonstration and the test puppet is increased (Appendix 9.1, Puppets: Cow/Duck), however, it is not until 21 months of age that infants exhibit the same level of retention irrespective of whether they are tested with the same or a different puppet (Fig. 9.4, right panel, Hayne *et al.* 1997). Finally, if the stimuli and the target actions are made more complex (Appendix 9.1, Animals and Rattles), then changes to the test stimuli disrupt retrieval by infants as old as 24 months; it is not until 30 months of age that infants exhibit the same level of retention irrespective of changes to the test stimuli (Fig. 9.5, Herbert and Hayne 2000). Presumably, further increasing the complexity of the imitation task or further increasing the discrepancy

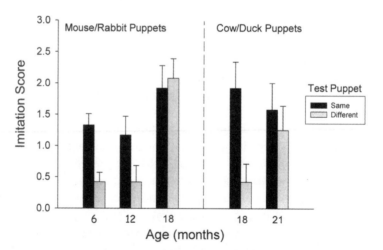

Fig. 9.4 The memory performance of 6- to 21-month-old infants who were tested in the deferred imitation paradigm after a 24-h delay. Independent groups of infants were tested with either the same puppet that was used during the original demonstration or with a different one. The mouse and rabbit puppets were used to test 6- to 18-month-old infants (left panel) and the cow and duck puppets were used to test the 18- and 21-month-old infants (right panel). These data have been redrawn from Hayne *et al.* (1997).

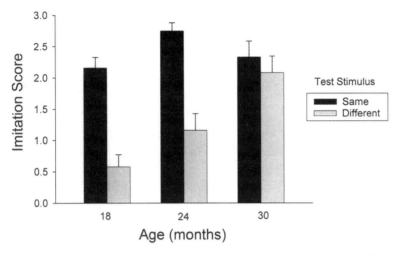

Fig. 9.5 The memory performance of 18- to 30-month-old infants who were tested in the deferred imitation paradigm after a 24-h delay. Independent groups of infants were tested with either the same stimuli that were used during the original demonstration or with different ones. The two versions of the animal (monkey and rabbit) and rattle stimuli are shown in Appendix 9.1. These data have been redrawn from Herbert and Hayne (2000).

between the demonstration and test stimuli would also increase the age at which infants would exhibit retention if they encountered novel stimuli during the test.

The data shown in Figs 9.4 and 9.5 indicate that the range of effective retrieval cues gradually broadens between 6 and 30 months of age. These same findings have also been obtained in studies of operant conditioning (Hartshorn *et al.* 1998) and in studies in which the environmental context, rather than the proximal stimulus, has been altered at the time of the test (Hartshorn *et al.* 1998; Hayne *et al.* 2000). In the deferred imitation paradigm, for example, changes to the environmental context disrupt memory retrieval by 6-month-old infants, but not by infants who are 12 months old and older (Barnat *et al.* 1996; Hanna and Meltzoff 1993; Hayne *et al.* 2000).

In all of the studies described thus far, infants have been tested in simple forgetting paradigms. That is, the test occurred while the memory was still highly accessible. As the retention interval between learning and testing increases, however, infants' performance gradually returns to baseline, suggesting that they have forgotten the target event. In the mobile conjugate reinforcement paradigm, for example, 3-month-olds exhibit excellent retention when they are tested after delays as long as 3 to 6 days, but they exhibit no retention whatsoever if they are tested after a delay of 14 days (for review, see Rovee-Collier and Hayne 1987).

Despite substantial forgetting, performance can be restored if infants are briefly exposed to some component of the original training event prior to the test. In the original demonstration of the reminding phenomenon with human infants, 3-month-olds were given a 3-min exposure to the training mobile that was moved non-contingently by the experimenter. The test occurred 24 h later. Under these conditions, infants exhibited excellent retention; in fact, the level of retention was identical to that typically seen 24 h after original training. Infants who were reminded but never trained or infants who were trained but not reminded responded at baseline during the test (Rovee-Collier *et al.* 1980). Thus, despite changes in accessibility over the retention interval, the target memory remains available for several weeks after the conclusion of training.

Subsequent research on reminding with human infants has shown that, like simple forgetting, memory retrieval by young infants tested in reminder paradigms only occurs when the cues present at the time of reminding match the cues present at the time of original encoding almost exactly (for review, see Rovee-Collier and Hayne 1987). In one study conducted by Hayne *et al.* (1991), for example, infants who were trained in their bedroom, but who were reminded in their kitchen, exhibited no retention whatsoever even though they were reminded and tested with their original training mobile. Apparently, infants did not recognize the training mobile when it was encountered 'out of context' at the time of the reminder. This finding was obtained despite the fact that the reminder context was another, highly familiar location in the infant's own home. Similarly, forgetting is not alleviated by the presentation of a mobile different from the one encountered during original training, even if that mobile is highly familiar, but has never been associated with the contingency (Rovee-Collier *et al.* 1985). Taken together, these findings clearly illustrate that the relation between the conditions present at encoding and at retrieval, rather than novelty *per se*, determine whether a cue will initiate retrieval of the target memory.

Despite the high degree of specificity documented in studies with young infants, studies conducted with older infants have shown that, by 12 months of age, infants can be reminded in a novel context (DeFrancisco 2003). Furthermore, by the end of the infancy period, representational media such as videos and photographs also cue retrieval of the target memory (Decampo and Hudson 2003; Sheffield and Hudson 1994). Taken together, these age-related changes in the range of effective retrieval cues in reminder paradigms are virtually identical to those seen in simple forgetting procedures.

9.3.2 The role of experience in infant memory retrieval

The data shown in Figs 9.4 and 9.5 illustrate that, as infants get older, their ability to exploit novel retrieval cues increases dramatically. As such, the probability that infants will access and use their memories in novel situations increases as a function of age. In addition to these maturational changes, experience also plays an important role in infants' ability to retrieve their prior memories in new situations.

9.3.2.1 Mobile conjugate reinforcement paradigm

The role of experience in infant memory retrieval was originally documented using the mobile conjugate reinforcement paradigm. Despite the high degree of specificity in this procedure (Fig. 9.2), memory retrieval can be cued by novel stimuli under some circumstances. One way to overcome the high degree of specificity that is typically exhibited by very young infants is to expose them to multiple mobiles during original training. For example, in one study conducted with 3-month-olds, some infants were trained with the same mobile during each of three daily sessions (invariant series) and some infants were trained with a different mobile on each day (variable series; Fagen *et al.* 1984). During the test, 24 h after the conclusion of training, all infants were tested with a novel mobile. Infants who had been trained with the invariant series exhibited no retention whatsoever, providing yet another example of the high degree of specificity that is typically exhibited by infants of this age. In contrast, infants who had been trained with multiple mobiles exhibited excellent retention when they were tested with yet another mobile. Similarly, infants who are trained in multiple contexts also exhibit retention when they are tested in yet another context after a 24-h delay (Amabile and Rovee-Collier 1991; Rovee-Collier and DuFault 1991). Under these variable training conditions, the nature of the match required between retrieval cues and memory attributes apparently shifts from the specific (e.g. '*this* mobile,' '*this* context') to the general (e.g. '*a* mobile,' '*a* context'). Despite this shift, however, the retrieval cue present at the time of the test must still match at least some attributes that make up the target memory (i.e. five objects hanging over the crib).

9.3.2.2 Deferred imitation paradigm

Prior experience also plays a key role in the effect of novel retrieval cues on infant retention in the deferred imitation paradigm. Although changes to the proximal test stimulus disrupt memory retrieval, particularly by younger infants, the provision of verbal cues at the time of encoding and again at the time of the test has been shown to improve infants' memory performance when they are tested with novel stimuli. For example Herbert and Hayne (2000) tested 18- and 24-month-olds in a deferred imitation paradigm in which an experimenter performed three target actions to create either a rattle or an animal (Appendix 9.1). During both the demonstration and the test, the experimenter provided the infants with verbal labels for the stimuli. During the demonstration with the rattle stimuli, for example, the experimenter said 'We can use these things to make a *meewa*. The word 'meewa' was used as the novel verbal label for the stimuli that could be used to make a rattle; the word 'thornby' was used as the novel verbal label for the stimuli that could be used to make an animal.

During the test the next day, infants were presented with either the same set of stimuli that had been used during the original demonstration or with a different set that could be used to perform the same target actions and that yielded the same target outcome. If the stimulus set was the same as the set used the day before, the experimenter said, 'Yesterday, I showed you how to make a meewa [thornby]. These are the things that we used to make a meewa. Can you show me how we can use these things to make a meewa?' If the stimulus set was different from the set used the day before, the experimenter said, 'Yesterday I showed you how to make a meewa [thornby]. These are some *other* things that we can use to make a meewa. Can you show me how we can use these things to make a meewa?'

The data collected by Herbert and Hayne (2000) are shown in Fig. 9.6. Consistent with prior research, memory retrieval by 18-month-olds was precluded by a change in the stimuli at the time of the test; the addition of verbal cues did not enhance infants' performance. For 24-month-olds, on the other hand, the provision of verbal cues offset the change in the stimuli at the time of the test. That is, by 24 months of age, infants were able to use verbal information as the basis of the match between encoding and retrieval even when other salient cues were altered at the time of the test.

Although the addition of verbal cues does not facilitate memory retrieval by infants younger than 24 months, another kind of experience has been shown to increase the effect of novel retrieval cues. For example in the standard deferred imitation procedure, an experimenter demonstrates a series of actions with objects and the infant's ability to reproduce those actions is assessed after a delay. The infant is not allowed to touch the objects or to practice the target actions prior to the test. Under these conditions, infant memory retrieval is highly specific to the demonstration stimuli until at least 18 to 30 months of age (Figs 9.3, 9.4, and 9.5). If, on the other hand,

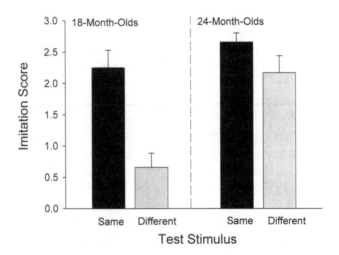

Fig. 9.6 The memory performance of 18- and 24-month-old infants who were tested in the deferred imitation paradigm after a 24-h delay. All infants were provided with a verbal label for the stimulus during the demonstration and again at the time of the test. These data have been redrawn from Herbert and Hayne (2000).

infants are given the opportunity to practice the target actions prior to the retention interval, then they do exhibit retention even when they are tested with novel stimuli (Hayne *et al.* 2003).

The data presented in Fig. 9.7 were obtained from 18-month-old infants who were shown a series of three target actions with either the puppet stimuli (left panel) or the rattle stimuli (right panel) that had been used in prior research with infants of this age. Some infants were given the opportunity to practice the target actions three times at the conclusion of the demonstration (Practice) and some infants were not (No Practice). In order to equate exposure to the stimuli across these two conditions, infants in the No Practice condition were shown the target actions an additional three times.

Twenty-four hours later, infants were tested with either the same stimuli that had been used by the experimenter during the original demonstration or with different stimuli that could be used to perform the same target actions. As before, infants without practice exhibited no evidence of retention during the test. In contrast, infants who had practiced the actions (albeit briefly) exhibited excellent retention even when the test stimuli were different from those present at the time of original encoding.

How might practice alter the accessibility and generality of infants' memories? It is possible that practice influences memory performance by enhancing both the content

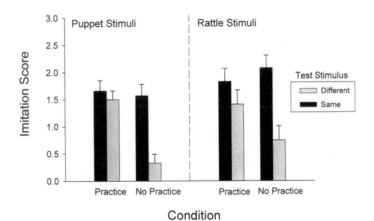

Fig. 9.7 The memory performance of 18-month-old infants who were tested in the deferred imitation paradigm after a 24-h delay. Some infants were provided the opportunity to practice the target actions prior to the test (Practice) and some infants were not (No Practice). Infants were tested with either the same stimuli that were used during the original demonstration or with different ones. Data from infants tested with the cow and duck puppets are shown in the left panel. Data from infants tested with the rattle stimuli are shown in the right panel. These data have been redrawn from Hayne *et al.* (2003).

and the strength of the underlying memory representation much in the same way as other forms of rehearsal. That is, infants without practice presumably encoded information about the visual features of the objects and the experimenter's actions as well as information about the goal or end state of the target event. In addition to this information, infants with practice had the opportunity to encode other information about the characteristics of the stimuli (e.g. the weight and texture of the objects in their hands) and the target actions as well as affective information that may arise in the course of playing with the objects (e.g. joy, interest, or feelings of success). As such, the representation formed by infants who are given the opportunity to practice would contain more total attributes and the connections between individual attributes might also be stronger.

9.3.3 The emergence of highly flexible memory retrieval

In the experiments described thus far, the test stimuli (retrieval cues) have resembled the encoding stimuli, at least in some way. For example when infants were exposed to multiple mobiles during the course of variable training, they were trained with a series of five-object mobiles and tested with yet another five-object mobile. Similarly, in studies of deferred imitation, infants were given the opportunity to practice the target actions with puppets or rattles and were tested with another puppet or rattle. As such, despite the novelty of the test cue, there was still substantial overlap between the cues present at the time of encoding and the cues present at the time of the test. What happens if this degree of physical similarity is eliminated? Can infants strike a match between memory attributes and retrieval cues on a conceptual rather than a perceptual basis?

The concept of *analogy* is often used in the cognitive literature to describe the transfer of problem-solving strategies from one context (or problem) to another (Chen 2002; Chen *et al.* 1997; Gentner 1989). Although we might consider analogy to require highly sophisticated conceptual knowledge, some experts have argued that, like similarity, analogy simply requires a one-to-one mapping between a novel problem and a previously established mental representation (Gentner and Markman 1997). From this perspective, analogy requires the same basic memory retrieval skills described in this chapter. In fact, there is some evidence to suggest that a glimmer of analogical memory retrieval begins to emerge during the infancy period (Chen *et al.* 1997; Greco *et al.* 1990). Furthermore, recent research in my laboratory suggests that there are key age-related changes in infants' ability to extract information from multiple sources, to integrate that information with existing knowledge, and to apply what they have learned to completely novel problems.

In one of the first empirical reports of analogical memory retrieval by infants, 3-month-olds were trained in the mobile conjugate reinforcement paradigm for three consecutive days with a different mobile on each day (Greco *et al.* 1990). Although this kind of variable training has been shown to expand the range of effective retrieval cues in this task (e.g. Fagen *et al.* 1984), there are still some 'mobiles' to which infants will not respond even after variable training. Two of these 'mobiles' – a butterfly wind chime and a cloth rainbow pillow with streamers – were rated by adults as being least similar to the training mobiles (see Greco *et al.* 1990 for photographs of the stimuli). Consistent with the adults' impression, infants who were tested with these objects did not apply what they had learned during variable training even though the object would have moved when the infant kicked.

Although 3-month-old infants do not spontaneously kick when tested with the wind chime, they will kick if they are briefly shown the function of this object prior to the test (i.e. that it is movable). To do this, the experimenter, rather than the infant, pulls the ribbon attached to the mobile stand for a 3-min period, causing the wind chime to move. Following this brief exposure, infants exhibit excellent retention when tested with the wind chime even after a long delay (Greco *et al.* 1990; Rovee-Collier *et al.* 1993). Taken together, these studies show that yet another kind of experience (i.e. passive exposure to functional information) can increase the range of effective retrieval cues for the training memory.

In the analogical version of the mobile task, Greco *et al.* (1990) trained 3-month-old infants with three different mobiles on three consecutive days. At the conclusion of the final training session, the infants were briefly exposed to the wind chime as it was moved passively by the experimenter. Twenty-four hours later, infants were tested with yet another 'mobile' – in this case, the cloth rainbow pillow with streamers. Under these conditions, infants exhibited excellent retention despite the fact that the rainbow test stimulus shared very little in common with either the training stimuli or with the wind chime. Presumably, the integration of one highly dissimilar object into the training memory was sufficient for infants to respond to yet another novel stimulus on the basis of its conceptual (i.e. potentially moveable), rather than its physical, similarity to previously encountered exemplars.

Chen *et al.* (1997) have also provided evidence of analogical transfer by 10- to 13-month-olds. In their means–ends task, infants learned to pull a cloth and then pull a string to retrieve a toy that was beyond their reach. Although infants of both ages could use their prior experience with the task to solve a new problem that involved the same goal, the older infants were more successful overall and were less affected by changes in the physical characteristics of the stimuli across successive problems.

The data reported by Greco *et al.* (1990) and Chen *et al.* (1997) piqued my interest in the issue of age-related changes in analogical memory retrieval during the infancy period. I was particularly interested in two related questions. First, what different kinds of information might infants use to solve an analogical memory retrieval problem? In the Greco *et al.* (1990) study, for example, exposure to functional information increased the range of effective retrieval cues for the target memory. In the Chen *et al.* (1997) study, the similarity of the goal objects and the tools was

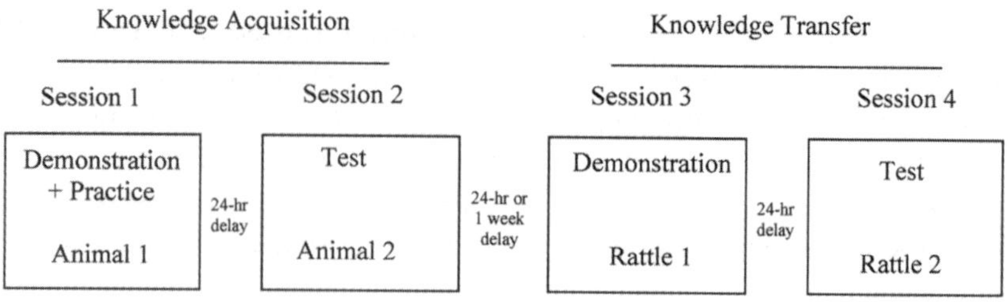

Knowledge Acquisition   Knowledge Transfer

Session 1		Session 2		Session 3		Session 4
Demonstration + Practice Animal 1	24-hr delay	Test Animal 2	24-hr or 1 week delay	Demonstration Rattle 1	24-hr delay	Test Rattle 2

Fig. 9.8 A schematic representation of the analogy (practice) procedure used with 18- and 24-month-old infants.

particularly important for analogical transfer by the 10-month-olds. Second, over what period of time might infants use their prior knowledge to solve new problems? In the Greco *et al.* (1990) study, the delay between successive events was 24 h. Would older infants tolerate even longer delays?

The first hurdle to overcome was to develop a non-verbal task that required infants to use analogy, rather than physical similarity, as the basis for memory retrieval during the test. To do this, we used a procedure that was based on our prior work on deferred imitation but that differed from that prior work in one important way – infants had to use what they had learned with one set of stimuli when they were tested with a completely different set of stimuli that shared no physical or functional similarity with the first set. In our first experiment, 18- and 24-month-old infants participated in four sessions that were separated by at least 24 h (Fig. 9.8). During Session 1, the experimenter performed three target actions using one set of stimuli (e.g. Animal 1 – a white rabbit). Following the demonstration, the infant was allowed to practice the target actions a total of three times. Twenty-four hours later, infants were tested with the other member of the stimulus set (e.g. Animal 2 – a brown monkey). Recall that, after practice of this kind, infants' memory performance is typically outstanding (Fig. 9.7). Twenty-four hours or 1 week later, the experimenter performed three target actions using the other set of stimuli (e.g. Rattle 1 – a square jar made from clear plastic with a wooden bead to place inside). During this session, infants were not allowed to touch the stimuli or practice the target actions prior to the test which occurred 24 h later. Infants were then tested with the other member of the stimulus set (e.g. Rattle 2 – a round ball with a bell to place inside) 24 h later. The question was, would infants apply what they had learned with the animal stimuli during the knowledge acquisition phase in Sessions 1 and 2 (e.g. surface features do not matter) when they were tested with the rattle stimuli during the knowledge transfer test in Session 4?

In addition to the experimental condition, there were two control groups. The procedure for infants in one control group (Con Novel) was identical to that used for infants in the experimental condition except that they were not allowed to practice the target actions at the conclusion of Session 1. In this way, these infants received the same exposure to the demonstration and test stimuli and to the experimenter, but they were not given the critical target experience (i.e. practice). Infants in the other control group (Con Baseline) were simply tested with the stimuli in the absence of any prior demonstration. The performance of these infants provided an estimate of the spontaneous production of the target actions in the absence of any prior experience with the stimuli.

The Session 4 performance for all the groups is shown in Fig. 9.9. Consistent with our prior research with these stimuli, the spontaneous production of the target actions was very low (Con Baseline). Furthermore, the performance of infants who were not allowed to practice the target actions at the conclusion of Session 1 (Con Novel) was impaired when they were tested with a novel stimulus in Session 4. At both ages, the test performance of infants in the Con Novel condition was not significantly different from that of infants in their age-matched baseline control group (Con Baseline). These data, once again, confirm the high degree of specificity that is required for memory retrieval by infants in this age range.

In contrast to this high degree of specificity, infants who were allowed to practice the target actions only briefly during Session 1 applied what they had learned when they were tested with a completely different set of stimuli in Session 4. The 18-month-old infants applied what they had learned when the gap between Session 2 and Session 3 was 1 day, but not 1 week, and 24-month-old infants applied what they had learned when the gap between Session 2 and Session 3 was 1 week. Taken together, these data show that it is possible for infants to establish a memory representation that can be used in situations that are vastly different from those in which the representation was

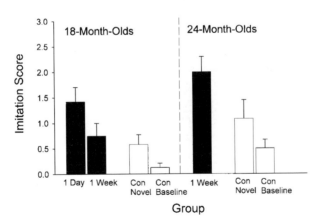

Fig. 9.9 The memory performance of 18- and 24-month-old infants tested in the analogy (practice) version of the deferred imitation paradigm. The dark bars indicate the performance of infants in the experimental group (Fig. 9.8). The open bars indicate the performance of the two control groups.

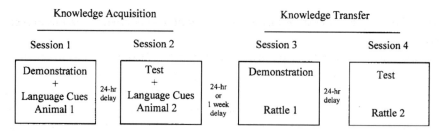

Fig. 9.10 A schematic representation of the analogy (language) procedure used with 24-month-old infants.

initially acquired. These data also show that there is an age-related increase in the period of time over which infants will exploit the contents of their prior representations to solve new problems that they encounter.

In addition to practice, older infants can also use adults' verbal cues to facilitate memory retrieval when other aspects of the test context are altered (Fig. 9.6). In the next experiment, we examined infants' ability to use verbal cues to solve problems that they had never encountered before. The procedure for this experiment is shown in Fig. 9.10. It is virtually identical to the procedure that we used for practice except that 24-month-olds were given verbal cues rather than practice during Session 1 and 2. The procedure for the control groups was identical to that used before.

The results of this experiment are shown in Fig. 9.11. Again, the performance of the two control groups was low and did not differ from each other. In contrast, 24-month-olds exhibited excellent retention when tested with a novel stimulus in Session 4 irrespective of whether the delay between Sessions 2 and 3 was 1 day or

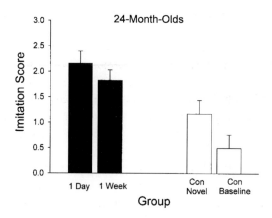

Fig. 9.11 The memory performance of 24-month-old infants who were tested in the analogy (language) version of the deferred imitation paradigm. The dark bars indicate the performance of infants in the experimental group (see Fig. 9.10). The open bars indicate the performance of the two control groups.

1 week. We are currently exploring the upper limit of infants' retention in this procedure.

Taken together, these new data highlight the growing flexibility of infant memory retrieval. On the basis of both age and prior experience, infants begin to exploit the contents of their memories to solve new memory problems that they have never encountered before. These data add to a small but growing body of research illustrating infants' ability to strike a match on a conceptual, rather than a strictly perceptual, basis (see also, Chen *et al.* 1997; Greco *et al.* 1990).

9.4 Summary and conclusions

The accumulation of information across successive learning episodes is dependent on two related skills. First, accumulating information across time requires the ability to remember from one episode to the next. Second, accumulating information from multiple sources requires the ability to retrieve the representation of relevant prior events when faced with cues that may be similar, but not identical, to cues encountered when those representation(s) were originally established. The data reviewed in this chapter show that age-related changes in memory retrieval play a fundamental role in knowledge acquisition during the infancy period. Memory retrieval by young infants is characterized by the principle of encoding specificity; changes to the experimental stimuli or to the environmental context preclude or disrupt retrieval of the target memory. Only when the cues present at the time of retrieval match those present at the time of original encoding almost exactly will infants gain access to the target representation. The high degree of specificity required for infant memory retrieval places severe constraints on infants' ability to retrieve and use their memories in novel situations.

Over the course of development, infants gradually overcome this high degree of specificity and begin to retrieve and use their memories in situations that differ from those present at the time that the memory was initially established. By the age of approximately 18 to 30 months, successful memory retrieval will sometimes occur when retrieval cues and memory attributes match at a '*level of abstraction*' similar to that originally described by Tulving for adult memory retrieval. Despite these initial first steps, age-related changes in the nature of the match between retrieval cues and memory attributes continue to occur throughout childhood (and perhaps throughout the lifetime).

Understanding the variables that influence infant memory retrieval provides new insight into the ways in which memories are organized and used, and sheds light on the way in which knowledge might accumulate and accrue throughout the lifespan. Data collected using both operant conditioning and deferred imitation procedures provide convergent evidence that both maturation and experience play a role in age-related changes in memory retrieval. Although it is often argued that the mobile conjugate reinforcement and deferred imitation tasks measure very different kinds of memory and may be supported by different neural systems (e.g. Nelson 1995), the data obtained with both tasks are virtually identical (for review, see Hayne 2004). Considering these tasks in concert provides a unique opportunity to trace developmental changes in memory retrieval and knowledge acquisition across the infancy period.

Acknowledgments

Some of the data reviewed in this chapter were supported by a Marsden Grant from the Royal Society of New Zealand. I would like to thank Dr Julien Gross and Gayleen Lawson-Washington for their help with data collection.

References

Amabile TA and Rovee-Collier C (1991). Contextual variation and memory retrieval at six months. *Child Development*, 62, 1155–1166.

Baker L and Santa JL (1977). Context, integration, and retrieval. *Memory and Cognition*, 5, 308–414.

Barnat SA, Klein PJ and Meltzoff AN (1996). Deferred imitation across changes in context and object: Memory and generalization in 14-month-old infants. *Infant Behavior and Development*, 19, 241–251.

Barr R, Dowden A and Hayne H (1996). Developmental changes in deferred imitation by 6- to 24-month-old infants. *Infant Behavior and Development*, 19, 159–170.

Borovsky D and Rovee-Collier C (1990). Contextual constraints on memory retrieval at six months. *Child Development*, 61, 1569–1583.

Chen Z (2002). Analogical problem solving: A hierarchical analysis of procedural similarity. *Journal of Experimental Psychology: Learning, Memory, and Cognition*, 28, 81–98.

Chen Z, Sanchez RP and Campbell T (1997). From beyond to within their grasp: The rudiments of analogical problem solving in 10- and 13-month-olds. *Developmental Psychology*, 33, 790–801.

Collie R and Hayne H (1999). Deferred imitation by 6- and 9-month-old infants: More evidence for declarative memory. *Developmental Psychobiology*, 35, 83–90.

Crowder RL (1985). Basic theoretical concepts in human learning and cognition. In: L-G Nilsson and T Archer, eds. *Perspectives on learning and memory*, pp. 19–37. Hillsdale, NJ: Erlbaum.

Decampo JA and Hudson JA (2003). Reinstatement of 2-year-olds' event memory using photographs. *Memory*, 11, 13–25.

DeFrancisco BS (2003). *The effects of cue and context changes on memory reactivation over the first year of life*. Unpublished Doctoral Dissertation, Rutgers University, New Brunswick, NJ.

Fagen J, Morrongiello BA, Rovee-Collier CK and Gekoski MJ (1984). Expectancies and memory retrieval in three-month-old infants. *Child Development*, 55, 936–943.

Gentner D (1989). The mechanisms of analogical reasoning. In: S Vosniadou and A Ortony, eds. *Similarity and analogical reasoning*, pp. 199–241. London: Cambridge University Press.

Gentner D and Markman AB (1997). Structure mapping in analogy and similarity. *American Psychologist*, 52, 45–56.

Godden DR and Baddley AD (1975). Context-dependent memory in two natural environments: On land and underwater. *British Journal of Psychology*, 66, 325–332.

Greco C, Hayne H and Rovee-Collier C (1990). Roles of function, reminding, and variability in categorization by 3-month-old infants. *Journal of Experimental Psychology: Learning, Memory, and Cognition*, 16, 617–633.

Hanna E and Meltzoff AN (1993). Peer imitation by toddlers in laboratory, home, and day-care contexts: Implications for social learning and memory. *Developmental Psychology*, 29, 701–710.

Hartshorn K and Rovee-Collier C (1997). Learning and memory in 6-month-old infants: A confirming analysis. *Developmental Psychobiology*, 30, 71–85.

Hartshorn K, Rovee-Collier C, Gerhardstein PC, Bhatt RS, Klein PJ, Aaron F, *et al.* (1998). Developmental changes in the specificity of memory over the first year of life. *Developmental Psychobiology*, 33, 61–78.

Hayne H (2004). Infant memory development: Implications for childhood amnesia. *Developmental Review*, 24, 33–73.

Hayne H, Barr R and Herbert J (2003). The effect of prior practice on memory reactivation and generalization. *Child Development*, 74, 1615–1627.

Hayne H, Boniface J and Barr R (2000). The development of declarative memory in human infants: Age-related changes in deferred imitation. *Behavioral Neuroscience*, 114, 77–83.

Hayne H, Greco C, Earley LA, Griesler PC and Rovee-Collier C (1986). Ontogeny of early event memory: II. Encoding and retrieval by 2- and 3-month-olds. *Infant Behavior and Development*, 9, 461–472.

Hayne H, MacDonald S and Barr R (1997). Developmental changes in the specificity of memory over the second year of life. *Infant Behavior and Development*, 20, 237–249.

Hayne H, Rovee-Collier C and Borza MA (1991). Infant memory for place information. *Memory and Cognition*, 19, 378–386.

Herbert J and Hayne H (2000). Memory retrieval by 18–30-month-olds: Age-related changes in representational flexibility. *Developmental Psychology*, 36, 473–484.

Hill WH, Borovsky D and Rovee-Collier C (1988). Continuities in infant memory development over the first half-year. *Developmental Psychobiology*, 21, 43–62.

Kochevar JW and Fox PW (1980). Retrieval variables in the measurement of memory. *American Journal of Psychology*, 93, 355–366.

Light LL (1972). Homonyms and synonyms as retrieval cues. *Journal of Experimental Psychology*, 96, 355–362.

Marcel AJ and Steel RG (1973). Semantic cuing in recognition and recall. *Quarterly Journal of Experimental Psychology*, 25, 368–377.

Meltzoff AN and Moore MK (1983). Newborn infants imitate adult facial gestures. *Child Development*, 54, 702–709.

Meltzoff AN and Moore MK (1989). Imitation in newborn infants: Exploring the range of gestures imitated and the underlying mechanisms. *Developmental Psychology*, 25, 954–962.

Nelson C (1995). The ontogeny of human memory: A cognitive neuroscience perspective. *Developmental Psychology*, 31, 723–738.

Postman L (1975). Tests of the generality of the principle of encoding specificity. *Memory and Cognition*, 3, 663–672.

Roediger HL and McDermott KB (1995). Creating false memories: Remembering words not presented in lists. *Journal of Experimental Psychology: Learning, Memory, and Cognition*, 21, 803–814.

Rovee CK and Rovee DT (1969). Conjugate reinforcement of infant exploratory behavior. *Journal of Experimental Child Psychology*, 8, 33–39.

Rovee-Collier C and Barr R (2001). Infant learning and memory. In: G Bremner and A Fogel, eds. *Blackwell handbook of infant development. Handbooks of developmental psychology,* pp. 139–168. Malden, MA: Blackwell Publishers.

Rovee-Collier C and DuFault D (1991). Multiple contexts and memory retrieval at three months. *Developmental Psychobiology,* 24, 39–49.

Rovee-Collier C, Greco-Vigorito C and Hayne H (1993). The time-window hypothesis: Implications for categorization and memory modification. *Infant Behavior and Development,* 16, 149–176.

Rovee-Collier C and Hayne H (1987). Reactivation of infant memory: Implications for cognitive development. In: HW Reese, ed. *Advances in child development and behavior,* vol. 20, pp. 185–238. New York: Academic Press.

Rovee-Collier C, Patterson J and Hayne H (1985). Specificity and the reactivation of infant memory. *Developmental Psychobiology,* 18, 559–574.

Rovee-Collier C, Sullivan M, Enright M, Lucas D and Fagen JW (1980). Reactivation of infant memory. *Science,* 208, 1159–1161.

Sheffield EG and Hudson JA (1994). Reactivation of toddlers' event memory. *Memory,* 2, 447–465.

Thomson DM and Tulving E (1970). Associative encoding and retrieval: Weak and strong cues. *Journal of Experimental Psychology,* 86, 255–262.

Tulving E (1984). Precis of elements of episodic memory. *Behavioral and Brain Science,* 7, 223–268.

Tulving E and Thomson DM (1973). Encoding specificity and retrieval processes in episodic memory. *Psychological Review,* 80, 359–380.

Appendix 9.1 Photographs of the stimuli used in the experiments described in this chapter.

Puppet Stimuli:
During the demonstration the experimenter removed the mitten from the puppet's hand, shook the mitten to ring the bell that was hidden inside, and then replaced the mitten on the puppet's hand.

Mouse/Rabbit

Cow/Duck

Rattle Stimuli:
During the demonstration, the experimenter put the wooden bead (or the bell) in the jar (or the ball), attached the handle to the top, and then shook the handle to make a noise.

Animal Stimuli:
During the demonstration, the experimenter raised the lever on the side lifting the ears into place, attached the eyes with Velcro, and then inserted the carrot (rabbit) or the banana (monkey) into the mouth.

Chapter 10

Learning how to be flexible with words

Kim Plunkett

Abstract

Eight-month-old infants are able to recognize words, whether they hear them in isolation or in fluent speech (Jusczyk and Aslin, 1995). Yet, they fail to attach meaning to words until around their first birthday (Benedict, 1979; Stager and Werker, 1997; Bates, 1979; Huttenlocher, 1974). It is shown that 17-month-old children still have difficulty in recognizing words in continuous speech in the service of identifying a referent. They fare better if the word is presented in isolation. In contrast, 24-month-olds have no such difficulty in recognizing words. They identify the referent of a word equally well if it is presented in isolation or in continuous speech. Furthermore, 24-month-olds demonstrate a flexibility in the face of systematic distortions that linguistic context imposes upon a word, even when the word is stripped of its surrounding context. This flexibility may play an important role in the dramatic changes that take place in children's vocabulary during the second year of life, while younger children may benefit from parental naming practices that package words as unambiguous labels for objects (Brent and Siskind, 2001).

10.1 Introduction

Dramatic changes occur in children's vocabularies during the second year of life. From producing a mere trickle of words around 15 months of age, the average 24-month-old commands a repertoire of hundreds (Bloom, 1973; Dromi and Berman, 1986; Nelson, 1973; Plunkett, 1993). The capacity to understand words also exhibits dramatic growth during this period (Goldfield and Reznick, 1992). Yet a considerable body of recent research has shown that prelinguistic infants already know a great deal about words. By 10 months of age, infants demonstrate that they can recognize words that they have heard earlier in isolation or continuous speech (Jusczyk and Aslin, 1995), they can detect sound patterns which disobey the phonotactics of their language (Jusczyk, et al. 1993b), they can identify the sound contrasts which constitute the phonemic repertoire of their language (Werker and Tees, 1984), and they know whether the stress patterns of words are typical of their mother tongue (Jusczyk, et al. 1993a). Why then do infants take so much time to exploit this knowledge in meaningful linguistic communication with others? One explanation is that the ability to identify and remember word forms is not enough for linguistic communication. The child must also establish a referential association between word and object. The dramatic linguistic developments that occur during the second year of life may reflect the extra work that the child has to do in establishing a meaningful referential function for words.

More recent research indicates that the ability of infants to recognize words in continuous speech is sensitive to the position of the word in the sentence and the speed of presentation of the acoustic signal: using the familiarization headturn preference procedure, Aslin (2000) found that 8-month-olds listen longer to a set of previously familiarized words when tested in sentence-final position than in sentence-medial position. Using a similar procedure, Morgan et al. (2002) found that infants listened longer to passages containing familiarized words, compared with unfamiliar words, when presented in sentence-medial position as well as sentence-final position, provided the presentation was in slowed infant-directed speech. Morgan et al. (2002) argue that processing speed is a significant bottleneck in early spoken word recognition.

What kind of work does the infant have to do in order to understand speech? We know that infants do not experience difficulty in associating a novel spoken word with a novel object and they can retain that information for several days without further exposure (Schafer and Plunkett, 1998; Woodward, et al. 1994; Werker, et al. 1998). However, infants were not required in these experiments to recognize the novel word in continuous speech. The ability to do so may be compromised when the infant is confronted simultaneously with the task of identifying referents for words. Indeed, Brent and Siskind (2001) have argued that exposure to isolated words may significantly facilitate vocabulary development during its earliest stages. They show that the caregivers of normally developing early language learners are more likely to deliver words in their citation forms (words presented in isolation) than was previously supposed.

Brent and Sisking (2001) point out that citation forms offer the young language learner some valuable clues to solving the problem of lexical segmentation. Moreover, Fernald, Pinto, Swingley, Weinberg, and McRoberts (1998) have shown that infants make rapid gains in the speed with which they recognize words in continuous speech. Using an eye-tracking procedure, Fernald et al. (1998) found that 15-month-old infants did not shift their gaze towards a target picture until after the word had been spoken, whereas 24-month-old infants already began to shift their gaze towards the target picture before the end of the word. In a related study, Fernald, Swingley, and Pinto (2001) found that 18-month-old infants were able to identify the referent of a word presented in continuous speech on the basis of word-initial information alone, and that their accuracy of identification improved with increasing productive vocabulary size. On the basis of these findings, the authors argue that lexical growth is associated with increased speed and efficiency in understanding spoken language.

What factors contribute to the increasing speed and efficiency of spoken word recognition during the second year? Evidence from habituation tasks suggests that the phonological representations of *novel* words that infants use to refer may suffer from under-specification relative to the adult state. For example, 14-month-olds don't seem to distinguish between /Dih/ and /Bih/ when listening to meaningful expressions even though they readily do so in a simple discrimination task (Stager and Werker, 1997).

Phonological under-specification may exacerbate the problem of word recognition in continuous speech when confronted simultaneously with the task of identifying a referent, though it should be kept in mind that a certain amount of *variability* has to be tolerated when listening to continuous speech due to coarticulation effects, speaker identity, speech register, etc. On the other hand, evidence from a preferential look task (Swingley and Aslin, 2002) indicates that 14-month-olds are able to detect slight mispronunciations of *familiar* words, suggesting that 14-month-olds have relatively detailed phonological representations for familiar words.

Using a similar task, Ballem and Plunkett (2005) have shown that 14-month-olds can detect slight mispronunciations of novel words which they have just learned, though not so reliably as for familiar words. Word familiarity may, therefore, play an important role in the ease with which infants can identify words in continuous speech. Furthermore, when vocabularies are small and the mental space of words is sparsely populated, phonological under-specification is unlikely to pose a problem for the young language learner. However, as vocabularies grow, discriminating small differences between words can be critical for successful communication.

The *memory load* associated with processing continuous speech compared to isolated words may also create difficulties in segmenting words and subsequently identifying the target referent. Fernald, McRoberts, and Herrera (1992) (cited in Fernald *et al.* 1998) found that 15-month-olds recognized a familiar word in sentence-final position but failed to recognize the word in sentence-medial position. Nineteen-month-olds were equally adept at recognizing the word in either sentence position. The authors argue that this result indicates an increased *flexibility* of speech processing in the 19-month-olds. However, the performance of the 15-month-olds in the sentence-medial position may also have arisen from the additional memory load imposed by the auditory material following the target words. These findings would suggest that the joint requirement of segmenting a word from continuous speech and of identifying the referent of the segmented word may be a constraining factor in early lexical development.

The main aim of the current study was to determine whether presentation of words in citation form, where lexical segmentation is not required, as opposed to continuous speech facilitates recognition of a target referent. It was supposed that citation form presentation would be particularly efficacious during the earliest stages of vocabulary development. The study uses an adapted version of the intermodal preferential looking task (Bailey and Plunkett, 2002; Meints, *et al.* 1999). Seventeen- and twenty four-month-olds were given the opportunity to identify the referents of familiar spoken words presented in isolation or in continuous speech. It was predicted that the younger infants would be more adept at identifying the referent of a familiar word presented in its citation form as compared to continuous speech, whereas the older infants would be less sensitive to the manner in which the words are presented. In addition, the impact of the acoustic distortions (coarticulation effects) introduced by continuous speech for infants' ability to identify the referents of words when those words are removed from their acoustic context was evaluated. This manipulation reduced the memory load on the infants to that of citation form presentation, thereby permitting an memory-neutral evaluation of coarticulation effects on word recognition outside of a sentential context.

10.2 **Method**

10.2.1 **Participants**

Fifteen 17-month-olds (seven boys, eight girls, mean age=17.7 months, min=16.4m, max=18.2m) and 15 24-month-olds (seven boys, eight girls, mean age=24.4 months, min=23.9m, max=25.2m) participated in the experiment. Three additional infants (two 17-month-olds and one 24-month-old) did not complete all the experimental trials and were excluded from the analysis. Caregivers were asked to complete a communicative development inventory to assess vocabulary size before arrival at the test center (Hamilton *et al.* 2000). Median productive vocabulary for the 17-month-old group was 29 words (min=5, max=62) and 269 words for the 24-month-old group (min=165, max=324). Participants were recruited by parental response to leaflets sent to doctors and nurseries or distributed by health visitors. Expenses were paid for participation. All of the infants were learning English as their first language, and none were regularly exposed to another language. They were all in good health at the time of testing.

10.2.2 **Auditory and visual stimuli**

Twenty-six object words were selected from a list of the earliest words that are reported to be understood and/or produced by infants. These words are listed in Table 10.1.

Table 10.1 Set of 26 words from which 18 auditory stimuli were selected for each child

apple	brush	cow	flower	shoe	tree
ball	bunny	cup	hat	sock	
banana	car	dog	house	spoon	
bird	cat	duck	mouse	table	
bottle	chair	dish	plate	train	

Infants heard recordings only of words that their parents reported they could understand. The auditory stimuli were recorded as single, citation words and fluent sentences spoken by a female voice, using infant directed speech. Fluent sentences were of the form 'Look at the dog over there', so that the target word was always in sentence-medial position and received primary stress. Single, coarticulated words were created by splicing target words from their fluent sentences and isolating them. Only tokens of spliced words that sounded acceptable to the adult ear were included in the study. Six adult native speakers of British English were asked to identify the spliced words in the absence of any visual support. No errors were made. Single word stimuli (citation and coarticulated) were combined with identical tokens of the alerting word *look* to yield the prompt 'Look! ... <*target word*>'. In each auditory condition, the onset of the target word occurred 2500 ms after the beginning of an experimental trial. The auditory stimuli were digitally recorded at 22.05 kHz into signed, 16-bit files. Each utterance was edited to remove head- and tail-clicks. The visual images were chosen from a CD-ROM children's dictionary. Each image matched one of the 26 auditory labels.

10.2.3 Procedure

Infants sat on a parent's lap facing two monitors. A target and a distracter image were displayed on the monitors at the beginning of each trial. Shortly after the onset of a trial (500 ms), infants heard the auditory stimulus directing them to look at the target image. The monitors were at a distance of about 80 cm. The screen of each monitor measured 30 cm diagonally, and the screens were horizontally aligned 44 cm apart from each other (center to center). The loudspeaker presenting the auditory stimulus was positioned centrally above the monitors. The infant's attention was drawn to the center by a flashing light. The experimenter, who remained out of sight during the experiment, controlled this light and used it between trials if the infant's gaze left the monitors. Parents were asked to close their eyes and listen to instructions played over headphones. These instructions reminded parents to sit quietly and to keep the infant seated in a central position. The instructions were recorded using the same female voice in the auditory stimuli presented to the infants, and played against a background of white noise. Two miniature cameras were used to record the infant's eye and head movements. The miniature cameras were placed immediately above each monitor and were connected to a video mixer that permitted recording of a split screen 'twin-image' of the infant during the experimental session.

10.2.4 Experimental design

Each infant was presented with 30 trials, 10 trials for each auditory condition (citation words, fluent sentences, coarticulated words). Each trial lasted 5 s. For the whole trial, the child was shown a pair of images. The auditory label always matched one image, and the onset of the target word always occurred 2500 ms into the trial, irrespective of auditory condition. The side of presentation (left or right) of the target image was randomized. Target images could appear as distracters, and *vice versa*. Across the 30 trials, each infant heard 18 different words, randomized across conditions, but subject to the constraints that no word was repeated within an auditory condition and no word was repeated more than once across auditory conditions. Across infants, all images were presented with approximately equal frequency and each object appeared as both target and distracter with approximately equal frequency. The ordering of the trials was randomized by the computer at run-time. The experimenter was blind to this order. The procedure lasted about 5 minutes.

10.2.5 Data analysis

The assessment of the video recording was carried out after data collection was completed. The scorer used a button box to trigger a data-registration program, syncronized with the video recording. This apparatus was used to determine the total amount of looking at the target (T) and at the distracter (D), and the length of the infant's longest look at the target (t) and distracter (d) images for the two phases of each trial; before and after the onset of the target word. Trials in which infants did not fixate on both images were excluded from the analysis. This constraint led to a total of eight trials being eliminated from the analysis. No infant had more than two trials excluded.

The difference between the longest looks at target and distracter ($t - d$) images before target word onset was used as an index of the child's baseline preference for the target image. Systematic increments in this difference after the onset of the target word can be interpreted as a measure of the child's understanding of the target word. A difference measure is used to calculate the target preference during each phase of the trial because the longest looks involve only single fixations on target and distracter.

It is also common practice to calculate the *proportion* of time looking at the target compared to time looking at both the target and distracter ($T/(T + D)$), for both phases of the trial. Again, increments in this proportional measure can be interpreted as an index of the child's understanding of the target word. A proportional measure is used in this case because the total amount of looking at both target and distracter may involve different numbers of fixations during each phase of the trial.

Previous work suggests that the longest look measure is a more sensitive index of comprehension than the proportional measure. However, both measures tend to reveal a similar *pattern* of looking behavior (Schafer and Plunkett, 1998; Meints *et al.*, 1999; Bailey and Plunkett, 2002).

10.3 Results

10.3.1 Longest look measure

The pattern of longest looking at the images in the preferential looking task is depicted in Fig. 10.1 for each of the three auditory conditions during each phase of the trial for both age groups.

Figure 10.1 shows the averages for the longest look at the target minus the longest look at the distracter $(t - d)$ for each condition and trial phase. In all conditions for both age groups, the difference in amount of looking at the target and distracter images prior to the onset of the target word is small ($\pm$ 100 ms). However, after the

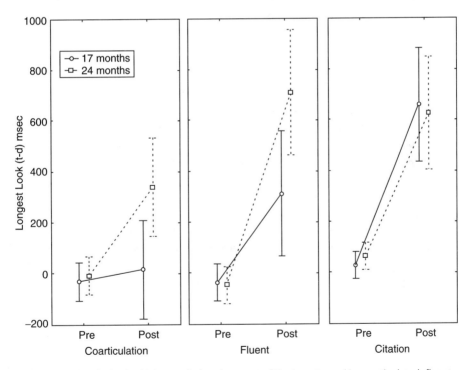

Fig. 10.1 Looking behavior before and after the onset of the target word in coarticulated, fluent, and citation conditions for 17- and 24-month-olds, measured as the difference between the longest look at the target and the distracter $(t - d)$ for each phase of the trial. Whiskers indicate 95 per cent confidence intervals.

onset of the target word, the amount of looking at the target image (relative to the distracter) increases substantially ($\approx$ 600 ms) for both age groups across all conditions, except for the coarticulated condition for the 17-month-olds. A three-way mixed model ANOVA with age (two levels), auditory condition (three levels), and trial phase (two levels) as factors indicated that this pattern of findings was statistically significant. There were main effects of age ($F(1,28)=5.39$, p<0.03), trial phase ($F(1,28)=60.94$, p $\ll$0.001) and condition ($F(2,56)=15.43$, p$\ll$0.001). There was a significant interaction between trial phase and condition ($F(2,56)=9.04$, p<0.001) and a near-significant three-way interaction between age, condition, and trial phase ($F2,56)=2.99$, p<0.058). Planned comparisons of the effects of trial phase were highly significant (p$\ll$0.008) for both age groups under all conditions, except for the 17-month-olds in the coarticulated condition (p=0.66). This analysis demonstrates that the children were able to identify the correct referent upon hearing the target word in all conditions bar one, namely when 17-month-olds were presented with the coarticulated form of the target word in isolation. No items analysis is offered since each participant heard a different subset of the 26 vocabulary items used in the experiment. Test materials were tailored to the comprehension of each infant as reported by their parents.

In order to compare the impact of age and auditory condition on target identification, the trial phase effect was calculated for each age and auditory condition, defined as the longest look difference after naming minus the longest look difference before naming: $(t-d)_{post}-(t-d)_{pre}$. The increment in fixation on the referent after hearing the target word is listed by age and auditory condition in Table 10.2.

The table indicates that 24-month-olds show a greater increment in target looking than the 17-month-olds in the fluent condition. However, in the citation condition 17- and 24-month-olds seem to show similar increments in target looking behavior. Not surprisingly, given the lack of a naming effect for the 17-month-olds demonstrated in the previous analysis, 24-month-olds show a greater increment in target looking than the 17-month-olds for the coarticulated condition. A two-way mixed model ANOVA with age (two levels) and auditory condition (three levels) confirmed these observations. The analysis revealed a non-significant trend of age ($F(1,28)=3.44$, p<0.075) and a significant effect of auditory condition ($F(2,56)=9.04$, p<0.001). There was a near-significant interaction between age and condition ($F(2,56)=2.99$, p<0.06). As predicted, 24-month-olds showed a significantly greater target preference than 17-month-olds after the onset of the target word in the fluent condition ($F(1,28)=5.67$, p<0.025). Likewise, 24-month-olds showed near-significant greater target preference than the 17-month-olds in the coarticulated condition ($F(1,28)=3.60$, p<0.068). However, no such difference was observed between the two age groups in preference for the target image after naming in the citation condition ($F(1,28)=0.17$, p=0.68). Within age groups, the 17-month-olds showed a significant increment in target looking between the coarticulated and the fluent

Table 10.2 Increment (SE ms.) in target fixation $(T–D)_{post}–(T–D)_{pre}$ for 17- and 24-month-olds in the three auditory conditions

Age	Auditory Condition		
	Coarticulated	Fluent	Citation
17 Months	49 (111)	349 (121)	630 (117)
24 Months	350 (112)	758 (122)	562 (117)

conditions (F(1,28)=4.10, p=0.05), and a trend to increment target looking across the fluent and citation conditions (F(1,28)=3.49, p<0.073). The 24-month-olds showed a marked increase in relative target looking between the coarticulated and the fluent conditions (F(1,28)=7.61, p<0.01), but not between the fluent and the citation conditions (F(1,28)=1.69, p=0.2).

10.3.2 Proportional looking measure

The pattern of proportional looking at the images in the preferential looking task is depicted in Fig. 10.2 for each of the three auditory conditions during each phase of the trial for both age groups.

Figure 10.2 shows the averages for the proportion of time looking at the target compared to the time looking at the target and distracter combined $(T/(T + D))$, for each condition and trial phase. The pattern of looking behavior is very similar to that reported for the longest look measure depicted in Fig. 10.1: for both age groups across all three conditions, the proportion of time fixating the target image increases after hearing the target word, except for the coarticulated condition for the 17-month-olds. A three-way mixed model ANOVA with age (two levels), auditory condition (three levels), and trial phase (two levels) as factors indicated that this pattern of findings was statistically significant. There were main effects of age (F(1,28)=6.9, p<0.02), trial phase (F(1,28)=33.5, p≪0.001), and condition (F(2,56)=30.56, p≪0.001). There was a significant interaction between trial phase and condition (F(2,56)=11.45, p<0.001). Planned comparisons of the effects of trial phase were significant (p≪0.01) for both age groups in the fluent speech and citation conditions. In the coarticulation condition, effects of trial phase were significant for the 24-month-olds (p=0.029) but not the 17-month-olds (p=0.085). However, the difference between ages was not significant; possible reasons are considered in the Discussion.

The increment in proportional fixation $((T/(T + D))_{post}–(T/(T + D))_{pre})$ on the referent after hearing the target word is listed by age and auditory condition in Table 10.3.

Table 10.3 indicates that 24-month-olds show a greater increment in target looking than the 17-month-olds in the fluent condition. However, in the citation and coarticulation conditions, 17- and 24-month-olds show similar increments in target looking behavior. A two-way mixed model ANOVA with age (two levels) and auditory

Table 10.3 Increment (SD) in target fixation $(T/(T–D))_{post}–(T/(T–D))_{pre}$ for 17- and 24-month-olds in the three auditory conditions

Age	Auditory Condition		
	Coarticulated	Fluent	Citation
17 Months	0.037 (0.101)	0.104 (0.093)	0.204 (0.072)
24 Months	0.047 (0.051)	0.167 (0.082)	0.205 (0.074)

condition (three levels) confirmed these observations. The analysis revealed a highly significant effect of auditory condition (F(2,56)=20.04, p≪0.001). There were no other significant main effects or interactions. Within age groups, the 17-month-olds showed significant increments in target looking between the coarticulated and the fluent conditions (F(1,28)=12.63, p=0.0013), and between the fluent and citation conditions (F(1,28)=18.6, p<0.002). The 24-month-olds showed a marked increase in relative target looking between the coarticulated and the fluent conditions

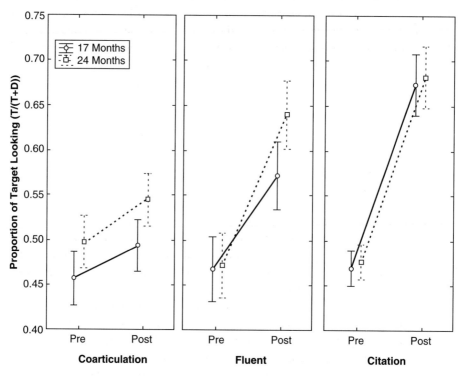

Fig. 10.2 Looking behavior before and after the onset of the target word in coarticulated, fluent, and citation conditions for 17- and 24-month-olds, measured as a proportion $T/(T + D)$ of looking at the target compared to the distracter, for each phase of the trial. Whiskers indicate 95 per cent confidence intervals.

(F(1,28)=18.67, p<0.001), but not between the fluent and the citation conditions (F(1,28)=2.6, p=0.12). Across age groups, 24-month-olds showed a marginally significant greater increment in target preference than 17-month-olds (F(1,28)=3.95, p<0.056) in the fluent condition. However, no significant differences were observed between the two age groups in either of the other two auditory conditions.

10.4 **Discussion**

This study set out to investigate whether infants' early word comprehension benefits from the presentation of words in their citation form as compared to continuous speech. The assumption underlying this investigation was that the joint requirement of segmenting a word from continuous speech and of identifying the referent of the segmented word may be a constraining factor in early lexical development. The pattern of results indicates that 17-month-olds are adept at identifying the referent of a target word, when that word is presented in citation form or in fluent speech. However, 17-month-olds show evidence of enhanced target looking when the referent's label is uttered in isolation compared to when it is embedded in fluent speech. Furthermore, 17-month-olds show little evidence of understanding the coarticulated form of the word when spoken in isolation. The only evidence that they may have understood the coarticulated form of the word is found in a marginal tendency to increase the *proportion* of target looking in the coarticulated condition (Fig. 10.2).

These findings are consistent with the view that although infants may be able to understand words in continuous speech, they find it easier to relate those words to objects in the world, if the words are spoken in isolation. The current experiment offers additional empirical support to the claim that exposure to isolated words may significantly facilitate vocabulary development during its earliest stages (Brent and Siskind, 2001). The finding that 17-month-old infants can identify the referents of words embedded in continuous speech indicates that they have already internalized knowledge regarding the systematic distortions that linguistic context imposes on an embedded word. However, their performance in the coarticulated condition indicates that without this contextual information, the embedded word is difficult to recognize as a meaningful token of that word.

In contrast, 24-month-olds are equally adept at identifying the referent of a target word in citation form or in fluent speech. Furthermore, they show evidence of adult-like recognition of the coarticulated form of the word when spoken in isolation, though target looking was less pronounced than in the citation or fluent speech conditions. This result indicates that 24-month-olds represent the phonological form of a word in a sufficiently flexible form that they can tolerate systematic distortions of the word, even in the absence of compensatory, linguistic contextual cues.

When presented with isolated citation forms of words, 17-month-olds are indistinguishable from 24-month-old children in identifying the target referent in the preferential looking task. However, 24-month-olds show a much stronger preference than 17-month-olds for the target image when its label is embedded in fluent speech. To the extent that degree of target preference reflects the ease with which young children identify and comprehend a meaningful label, this result indicates that 24-month-olds are better equipped to identify meaningful labels in fluent speech than are 17-month-olds. This finding corroborates those of Fernald *et al.* (1998) and Fernald *et al.* (2001) who argue that lexical growth is associated with increased speed and efficiency in understanding spoken language.

It is noteworthy that the difference in target preference between the 17- and 24-month-olds was only marginally significant in the fluent speech condition when evaluated using the proportional looking measure (Table 10.3), whereas the longest look measure revealed a clear difference between the two age groups (Table 10.2). The discrepancy between these two findings may reflect the greater sensitivity of the longest look measure that has been reported in previous studies (Schafer and Plunkett, 1998; Meints *et al.*, 1999; Bailey and Plunkett, 2002). However, it is also possible that the proportional measure, which is a composite of looking time throughout the 5-second trials, also permits the slower speech processing abilities of the 17-month-olds to reveal themselves.

Twenty four-month-olds' superior performance in the fluent speech condition may reflect an increased speed and efficiency and improved phonological memory span which aids word recognition or referent identification under increased cognitive load. However, this interpretation by itself cannot explain the differences between the two age groups in the coarticulated condition where a difference in target preference is also observed but where the memory load is the same as the citation condition in which both age groups performed equally well. Indeed, the 24-month-olds' higher level of target preference in the coarticulated condition compared to the 17-month-olds ($\approx$ 300 ms) accounts for much of the discrepancy between the two age groups in the fluent condition ($\approx$ 400 ms)—see Table 10.2. The 17-month-olds' comparative difficulty in comprehending words in the fluent speech condition does not appear to be attributable to memory overload. Rather, the fact that 17-month-olds are impaired in the coarticulated condition, makes it more likely that the specific problem they have with distorted words can explain why they are also poor at understanding fluent speech.

The difference in target preference between the 17- and 24-month-olds disappears in the coarticulated speech condition when evaluated using the proportional looking measure (Table 10.3). Again, this may reflect the greater sensitivity of the longest look measure. However, the proportional measure may also permit the slower speech processing abilities of the 17-month-olds to reveal themselves, thereby masking any differences to the 24-month-olds. Nevertheless, on both measures, 24-month-olds show a significant effect of naming in the coarticulated condition whereas 17-month-olds do not (Fig 10.1 and 10.2).

Some studies have demonstrated that 10-month-old infants are sensitive to the allophonic variation introduced by surrounding linguistic context at particular word boundaries (Hohne and Jusczyk, 1994; Jusczyk et al., 1999). However, these studies do not require the infant to show any comprehension of the speech signal. In the present study, the requirement that the infant demonstrate comprehension of the speech signal seems to interfere with 17-month-olds' recognition of the disembedded, coarticulated form of the word. In a similar vein, Stager and Werker (1997) have demonstrated that 14-month-olds don't seem to distinguish between two words that form a minimal pair when listening to meaningful expressions, even though they readily do so in a simple discrimination task. Unlike Stager and Werker (1997) who argue that 14-month-old infants' phonological representations may be under-specified, the current findings suggest that the acoustic stimuli that infants are willing to accept as tokens of meaningful words are over-specific, even at 17-months-old. Furthermore, the findings of the current study suggest that infants become increasingly flexible in their interpretation of systematically distorted words as development proceeds. Note that the coarticulation effects investigated here are not the same as the phonemic manipulations investigated by Stager and Werker (1997). The possibility that the allophonic variations introduced by coarticulation are easier to detect than phonemic variations seems unlikely but cannot be excluded.

The finding that 17-month-olds have detailed representations of word tokens is consistent with a number of recent studies investigating phonological specificity in early words (Bailey and Plunkett, 2002; Ballem and Plunkett, 2005; Swingley and Aslin, 2000, 2002; Werker et al. 2002). However, the claim that infants become *more* flexible in their interpretation of word tokens would, at first blush, seem to contradict findings showing that the forms labels can take become more *constrained* with age. For example younger infants will map gestures or non-linguistic tones to object categories, but older children will not (Woodward and Hoyne, 1999; Namy and Waxman, 1998).

It seems plausible to suppose that the increasing flexibility of *linguistic* word tokens and the exclusion of gestures and non-linguistic tones may be part of the same process of learning: as vocabulary development progresses, the overwhelming number of label tokens accumulated by the normally developing child are *phonotactically legal* sequences. These are the type of labels that are most widely and consistently used in the community. The language-learning infant can infer the privileged status of phonotactically legal sequences by paying attention to the type and distribution of labels used for object categories by her caregivers. Likewise, once the infant has recognized the privileged status of phonotactically legal sequences, she is then in a better position to evaluate the degrees of acoustic variation associated with these sequences. The type and distribution of variability when listening to continuous speech due coarticulation effects, speaker identity, speech register, pitch, etc., provides the infant with just the evidence needed to identify acceptable limits of tolerance. The ability of 24-month-olds in the current experiment to identify the target referent in the coarticulation condition highlights their improving flexibility when confronted with systematically distorted speech signals.

10.5 Conclusion

The findings of this study support the hypothesis that infant word comprehension benefits from the presentation of words in their citation form as compared to continuous speech, particularly during the early stages of lexical development. The results indicate that 17-month-olds (but not 24-month-olds) benefit from the presentation of words in isolation. The results also indicate that 24-month-olds are more flexible in their ability to recognize words, tolerating the systematic distortions that are characteristic of fluent speech, even when the contextual cues signaling those distortions are removed. This study also corroborates previous demonstrations (Fernald *et al.*, 1998, 2001) that substantial improvements occur during the second year in the ease with which infants can recognize a word in continuous speech and identify it with a referent. The results indicate that these changes occur at the same time that infants exhibit an increased flexibility in their capacity to accept speech sounds as meaningful tokens of words.

This emergent flexibility in phonological representations may be closely related to the dramatic changes observed in children's vocabulary development during the second year. New words entering children's vocabularies can function as phonological and semantic landmarks to assist in the problem of lexical segmentation (Plunkett, 1993). As vocabulary grows and word recognition skills develop, children are afforded the opportunity to identify the range of variations that different linguistic contexts impose upon the spoken word, leading to a more flexible appreciation of the systematic variability of individual words. Likewise, a more flexible basis for identifying meaningful words in continuous speech may facilitate the process of lexical acquisition. It is possible that exposure to variable input itself (*dog, look at the dog over there, what a big dog that is*) may lay the foundations for a more flexible approach to word comprehension.

The study also offers experimental support for the claim that labeling practices emphasizing the use of citation forms may facilitate early development in normal and delayed language learners (Brent and Siskind, 2001). Brent and Siskind (2001) argued that caregivers of normally developing early language learners are more likely to deliver words in their citation forms than was previously supposed and that citation forms offer the language learner some valuable clues to solving the problem of lexical segmentation. The current study is consistent with the view that exposure to *both* citation forms and systematically variable input may be important to establish anchor points and flexibility in speech processing for word comprehension in the second year of life.

Acknowledgement

My thanks to Stephanie Somerville who collected most of the data for this study and to two anonymous reviewers who provided very helpful feedback on an earlier draft of this manuscript.

References

Aslin RN (2000). Interpretation of infant listening times using the headturn preference procedure. In: *Paper presented at the International Conference on Infant Studies*. Brighton, UK.

Bailey TM and Plunkett K (2002). Phonological specificity in early words. *Cognitive Development*, 17, 1267–1284.

Ballem KD and Plunkett K (2005). Phonological specificity in children at 1;2. *Journal of Child Language*, 32, 159–173.

Bates E (1979). *The emergence of symbols*. New York: Academic Press.

Benedict H (1979). Early lexical development: Comprehension and production. *Journal of Child Language*, 6, 183–200.

Bloom L (1973). *One word at a time: The use of single word utterances*. The Hague: Mouton.

Brent MR and Siskind JM (2001). The role of exposure to isolated words in early vocabulary development. *Cognition*, 81, B33–B44.

Dromi E and Berman R (1986). Language-specific and language-general in developing syntax. *Journal of Child Language*, 13, 371–387.

Fernald A, McRoberts GW and Herrera C (1992). Prosodic features and early word recognition. In: *Paper presented at the 8th International Conference on Infant Studies*. Miami, FL.

Fernald A, Pinto JP, Swingley D, Weinberg A and McRoberts GW (1998). Rapid gains in speed of verbal processing by infants in the second year. *Psychological Science*, 9, 228–231.

Fernald A, Swingley D and Pinto JP (2001). When half a word in enough: Infants can recognize spoken words using partial phonetic information. *Child Development*, 72, 1003–1015.

Goldfield B and Reznick JS (1992). Rapid change in lexical development in comprehension and production. *Developmental Psychology*, 28, 406–413.

Hamilton A, Plunkett K and Schafer G (2000). Infant vocabulary development assessed with a British communicative development inventory. *Journal of Child Language*, 27, 689–705.

Hohne EA and Jusczyk PW (1994). Two-month-old infants' sensitivity to allophonic differences. *Perception and Psychophysics*, 56, 613–623.

Huttenlocher J (1974). The origins of language comprehension. In: R Solso, Ed. *Theories in cognitive psychology: The loyola symposium*. pp. 331–368 Potomac, Maryland: Lawrence Erlbaum.

Jusczyk PW and Aslin RN (1995). Infant's detection of sound patterns of words in fluent speech. *Cognitive Psychology*, 29, 1–23.

Jusczyk PW, Cutler A and Redanz N (1993a). Preference for the predominant patterns of English words. *Child Development*, 64, 675–687.

Jusczyk PW, Friederici AD, Wessels J, Svenkerud VY and Jusczyk AM (1993b). Infant's sensitivity to the sound patterns of native language words. *Journal of Memory and Language*, 32, 402–420.

Jusczyk PW, Hohne EA and Baumann A (1999). Infant sensitivity to allophonic cues for word segmentation. *Perception and Psychophysics*, **61**, 1465–1476.

Meints K, Plunkett K and Harris, PL. (1999). When does an ostrich become a bird: The role of prototypes in early word comprehension. *Developmental Psychology*, **35**, 1072–1078.

Morgan J, Singh L, Bortfeld H, Rathbun K, White K and Anderson J (2002). Infant word recognition: Sentence position and processing time. In: *Paper presented at the International Conference on Infant Studies*. Atlanta, GA.

Namy LL and Waxman SR (1998). Words and gestures: Infants' interpretations of different forms of symbolic reference. *Child Development*, **69**, 295–308.

Nelson K (1973). Structure and strategy in learning how to talk. *Monographs of the Society for Research in Child Development*, **38**, Whole Nos. 1–2.

Plunkett K (1993). Lexical segmentation and vocabulary growth in early language acquisition. *Journal of Child Language*, **20**, 1–19.

Schafer G and Plunkett K (1998). Rapid word learning by 15-month-olds under tightly controlled conditions. *Child Development*, **69**, 309–320.

Stager CL and Werker JF (1997). Infants listen for more phonetic detail in speech perception than word learning tasks. *Nature*, **388**, 381–382.

Swingley D and Aslin RN (2000). Spoken word recognition and lexical representation in very young children. *Cognition*, **76**, 147–166.

Swingley D and Aslin RN (2002). Lexical neighborhoods and the word-form representations of 14-month-olds. *Psychological Science*, **13**, 480–484.

Werker J, Cohen LB, Lloyd VL, Casasolo M and Stager CL (1998). Acquisition of word-object associations by 14-month-olds. *Developmental Psychology*, **34**, 1289–1309.

Werker J and Tees R (1984). Cross-language speech perception: Evidence for perceptual reorganisation during the first year of life. *Infant Behaviour and Development*, **7**, 49–63.

Werker JF, Fennell CT, Corcoran KM and Stager CL (2002). Infants' ability to learn phonetically similar words: Effects of age and vocabulary size. *Infancy*, **3**, 1–30.

Woodward AL and Hoyne KL (1999). Infants' learning about words and sounds in relation to objects. *Child Development*, **70**, 65–70.

Woodward AL, Markman EM and Fitzsimmons CM (1994). Rapid word learning in 13- and 18-month-olds. *Developmental Psychology*, **30**, 553–566.

Chapter 11

Social learning and social cognition: The case for pedagogy

Gergely Csibra and György Gergely

Abstract

We propose that humans are adapted to transfer knowledge to, and receive knowledge from, conspecifics by teaching. This adaptation, which we call 'pedagogy', involves the emergence of a special communication system that does not presuppose either language or high-level theory of mind, but could itself provide a basis for facilitating the development of these human-specific abilities both in phylogenetic and ontogenetic terms. We speculate that tool manufacturing and mediated tool use made the evolution of such a new social learning mechanism necessary. However, the main body of evidence supporting this hypothesis comes from developmental psychology. We argue that many central phenomena of human infant social cognition that may seem puzzling in the light of their standard functional explanation can be more coherently and plausibly interpreted as reflecting the adaptations to receive knowledge from social partners through teaching.

11.1 Introduction

One way to highlight the merits of a new theory is by making explicit previously largely unnoticed inconsistencies in the standard functional explanations for some of the central phenomena in its domain, and then to demonstrate how the novel theoretical approach can shed new explanatory light on such phenomena, successfully resolving the puzzles inherent in their previously accepted interpretations. In what follows, we shall follow this strategy in presenting our new hypothesis on human adaptation for pedagogy. Therefore, we shall start by discussing a few salient examples of early competences in the domain of infant social cognition and show why their standard functional interpretations involve puzzling inconsistencies when one scrutinizes them in the light of the available data.

We shall then outline our new theoretical proposal about human pedagogy as an evolutionary adaptation for efficient knowledge transfer. We shall explicate our theory in three ways: (a) by providing a speculative hypothesis – a just-so story – about the possible evolutionary conditions that could plausibly account for the selection of pedagogy as a special type of social learning mechanism; (b) by describing the design specifications of pedagogical communication in humans; and (c) by reviewing evidence from the developmental psychology of infant social cognition that supports our hypothesis of the existence of this dedicated system of pedagogical knowledge transfer during human ontogeny. This review will reveal how the application of our theory of human pedagogy to the puzzling phenomena of infant social cognition can clear up the inconsistencies that are inherent in their standard functional interpretations. We shall argue that the phenomena in question receive a more satisfactory and coherent alternative explanation when viewed as the results or manifestations of the basic human evolutionary adaptation to receive knowledge from conspecifics through specialized forms of pedagogical interactions.

11.2 Some puzzles in infant social cognition

11.2.1 Face preference in newborns

Newborns are more likely to follow, and more persistent in following, geometric patterns that resemble faces than other similar geometric patterns, including upside-down faces (Johnson and Morton 1991). Newborns also show this preference when presented with static images on the visual periphery: they tend to look first, and longer, at the face-like pattern (Valenza *et al.* 1996). The standard functional explanation for this behavior is that it reflects an adaptive orientation mechanism that ensures that infants will fixate and learn about the most relevant social stimuli in their environment. This functional interpretation, however, does not explain why newborns' face preference is orientation-specific; in other words, why it is restricted to upright faces. Adults and children perform much better with upright than upside-down faces in face recognition tasks, and this finding can be plausibly explained by the fact that the subjects have had more experience with seeing, and have acquired more expertise in recognizing, upright than inverted face orientation. Newborns, however, see faces, including their mother's face, in many different orientations (importantly, during breast feeding the mother's face does not appear in the canonical orientation). Thus, if the function that the newborn face preference system were selected for were indeed that of identifying faces of conspecifics, evolution could have equipped neonates with a more efficient face recognition mechanism whose design included no orientation constraints. Clearly, such a mechanism could serve its dedicated function to find and learn about faces of conspecifics better as it could also exploit the many naturally occurring opportunities provided by the presence of non-canonically oriented faces in the infant's visual environment. A further relevant aspect of newborns' face preference, which we have recently demonstrated (Farroni, Johnson, and Csibra, unpublished data), is that it disappears if the contrast polarity of the stimuli is reversed from black-on-white to white-on-black. White spots on a black background form as good of a facial pattern as black spots on white background and could, therefore, also be used successfully to identify conspecifics. Why does face preference in newborns not exploit this possibility either?

11.2.2 Gaze-following

Our second example of a puzzling standard explanation is the functional interpretation of the phenomenon of gaze following by infants. In the second half of their first year, infants start to look where an interactive social partner is looking, establishing what is called a joint-attention situation with the adult (Moore and Dunham 1995). In fact, in laboratory situations, younger infants and even newborns also tend to look in the same direction as the eyes of a face in front of them have moved moments before (Hood *et al.*1998). The standard explanation for this behavior is that the eyes provide privileged access to the mind of others: looking at the gaze target of another person will inform the infant about what the other person is attending to, and allows him to share her experience. The problem with this functional interpretation is that infants are hopelessly inaccurate in locating objects targeted by the gaze direction of others (Butterworth and Jarrett 1991). In well-controlled laboratory experiments, young infants manage to identify the object the other is looking at only in the simplest situations (for example, 6-month-olds, who turn their gaze towards the general direction of the other's visual focus, will stop at and explore the first salient object found in that direction irrespective of whether that is the actual target of the other's gaze or not), and it is not until they are about 18 months old that they can accurately zero in on the target of the other's attention. This, however, implies that in real-life situations infants will be much more likely to mistakenly identify the object of the other's attention than to succeed in sharing her mental experience. How could the hypothesized function of mental sharing be facilitated by being engaged in a behavior that would regularly mislead the child about the other's attentional focus? And how could the frequently resulting misattributions help the development of understanding others in terms of mental states?

11.2.3 Imitation of novel actions

In a classic study, Meltzoff demonstrated to 14-month-old infants a rather unusual action: he bent forward from waist and lit up a box by touching it with his head (Meltzoff 1988). A week later the infants came back to the laboratory and most of them spontaneously performed the same action: they touched the box with their head. Why? According to the standard functional explanation, imitation allows the child to learn how to achieve certain goals, for example new and interesting effects, like lighting up this box (Tomasello 1999). This explanation is puzzling, however, because infants do not need to imitate to achieve this goal. They do not have to imitate the novel head action, because they have a simpler means at their disposal to bring about the same end: they could simply touch the box with their hand. Why do they imitate then?

11.3 The 'pedagogy' hypothesis

The puzzle in all three phenomena lies in a mismatch between the assumed function and the characteristic pattern of infant behavior it purports to explain. The behavior is either suboptimal with respect to the attributed function (as in the case of newborns' face preference), or is simply unnecessary to fulfill it (as with imitation), or it can downright defeat its stated function (as in gaze-following). Here we propose a hypothesis that attempts to resolve these puzzles. The hypothesis simply states that humans are adapted to transfer knowledge to, and receive knowledge from, conspecifics *through teaching*, and we claim that these phenomena, as well as many other central phenomena of early social cognition, reflect this adaptation.

We are, of course, not the first to realize the importance of teaching in the evolution and ontogenesis of human cognition; several theorists have pointed this out before (e.g. Barnett 1973; Caro and Hauser 1992; Kruger and Tomasello 1996; Premack 1984; Premack and Premack 2003; Tomasello *et al*. 1993; Tomasello 1999). Nevertheless, our proposal differs from those of others in at least two significant respects.

First, teaching is usually described as a secondary derivative of some more fundamental human-specific adaptation, such as language (Dunbar 1996), theory of mind (Tomasello 1999), aesthetics (Premack and Premack 2003), or culture itself. In contrast, we believe that the ability to teach and to learn from teaching is a primary, independent, and possibly phylogenetically an even earlier adaptation than either language or the ability to attribute mental states. Having language and a theory of mind would no doubt assist both teaching and learning from teaching but, as we shall argue, they are not necessary prerequisites for pedagogical knowledge transmission. On the contrary, it seems to us equally possible that the cognitive mechanisms that had independently evolved to support pedagogy may have contributed to the subsequent evolution of language and theory of mind.

Second, while several theorists have developed specific proposals about what abilities a 'teacher' needs to successfully transmit cultural information (e.g. Olson and Bruner 1996; Strauss *et al*. 2002), the complementary cognitive mechanisms that make someone able to benefit from teaching have so far been largely ignored (for an exception, see Tomasello *et al*. 1993). In fact, there is a long history of discussing the facilitative effects of cultural environment on early human social and cognitive development in terms of 'scaffolding' (Wood *et al*. 1976; Whiten 1999). These approaches are typically based on the implicit assumption that what is 'scaffolded' by parents' educational practices is the child's general-purpose learning mechanisms. In contrast, we propose and emphasize that human parental inclination for manifesting cultural knowledge in teaching contexts is complemented by dedicated cognitive mechanisms on the infant's part that ensure that he will benefit from his parents' teaching efforts.

11.4 Just a just-so story

As our hypothesis asserts that pedagogy is a primary, human-specific adaptation that does not necessarily rely on other (arguably human-specific) abilities such as language or theory of mind, the question of evolutionary origin would inevitably be raised. How and why did pedagogy evolve? Because of the scarcity of hard facts about human cognitive evolution, any attempt to reconstruct prehistoric processes would necessarily be a 'just-so story'. Nevertheless, whenever evolutionary adaptation is claimed to play a role in human cognition, it is important to demonstrate that there exists at least one story (even if it is a just-so story) that could plausibly explain the emergence of the new trait/behavior/cognitive mechanism. Below we shall outline our, admittedly, just-so story that puts pedagogy in an evolutionary context, relates it to the emergence of other cognitive abilities, and drives our intuitions about the possible phylogenetic conditions that could have provided selective pressure for the evolution of this dedicated cognitive system.

11.4.1 'Simple' teleology

Our story starts with early hominids, who, just like some primate species living today, most notably chimpanzees, occasionally resorted to using tools. Simple tool use certainly requires the understanding that a given object is 'good for' achieving a specific goal. However, 'seeing' the object in terms of its goal-related affordance properties is being maintained only until the goal is achieved (or abandoned). In fact, chimpanzees tend to choose functionally suitable objects from the immediate surroundings as temporary tools to achieve a specific goal. Sometimes they even modify them on the spot to improve their affordance properties to enable them to harness the concrete goal in the situation. However, after having used the object to attain their goal, they tend to simply discard it and move on. This can be considered evidence for a goal-activated, situationally restricted and temporally fleeting 'teleological mode' of object construal. It does not imply a more permanent categorization of such objects *as* tools or representing them as having stable functional properties.

11.4.2 'Inverse' teleology

We know, though, that several million years ago our ancestors had already surpassed or qualitatively modified their 'simple' teleology, when they started to view the tools that they created as having *permanent functions*. As evidenced in the archaeological record, this new level of more stable teleological conceptualization of objects *as* tools was manifested in routine behaviors such as keeping tools instead of discarding them after use, storing them at specific locations, or prefabricating the tools at one location and carrying them for long distances for later application at a different place. We suggest that this momentous change in the application of teleological reasoning about tools required a *reversal of perspective* in the way our ancestors were thinking about tool–goal relations. While 'simple' teleology, being always triggered by the activation of a desire for a concrete goal, raises the question, 'Which object could I use to achieve this specific goal?', 'inverse' teleological reasoning is triggered when the sight of an object activates the question: 'What purpose could I use this object for?'

11.4.3 'Recursive' teleology

By allowing tools to be conceived of as desirable goals, 'inverse' teleology opened up the way to attaching functions to tools that did not directly involve outcomes that enhance the adaptive fitness of the individual (such as food). This, in turn, made it possible to apply teleological reasoning in a 'recursive' manner by looking at objects as potential tools to create desired tools as their goals. Therefore, the emerging ability to conceive tools with useful functions as themselves being the goal objects of desire led to the capacity of thinking in terms of chains or hierarchies of means and ends. The archaeological record, in fact, provides evidence of the early use of tools to make other tools, manifesting the presence of 'recursive' teleological competence early on in hominid history.

11.4.4 Learnability of 'recursive' tool use

Now, consider the situation that children find themselves in when growing up in a hominid group that has already gone through these transformations of teleological thinking and that relies on tool use extensively. The children themselves will expect that objects (and especially artifacts) have functions, because they are equipped with the cognitive mechanisms that had been selected to support teleological thinking. How can they figure out the function of an object? First, they can try various actions with it to find out the object's affordances. Human infants (unlike infants of most other primates) are indeed fascinated with objects and enjoy manipulating them. Figuring out artifact functions by such trial-and-error methods, however, is slow and very limited. Trial-and-error procedures would not reveal, for example, functions that have their useful effects through multiple mediations (tool use on tools), or in the future.

Alternatively, they can rely on various social learning mechanisms, from stimulus enhancement through emulation to imitation, that have been observed in many species (e.g. Whiten 2000). They can observe, for example, when another individual uses a tool, and can infer its function from the visible outcome achieved. However, this kind of observational learning of function is also restricted to simple tool use that leads to immediately interpretable effects, and not easily applicable to mediated tool use that creates tools. This is because any behavior has multiple effects, and unless the range of desired outcomes is predefined, no behavior is transparent to its goal. If, for example, an individual observes another using a tool to peel away the skin of a hard fruit, it may be obvious that the tool is used in order to get to the edible parts of the fruit and not in order to obtain bits of fruit skin, but this inference is based on a pre-existing knowledge of the desirability of the food, and is reinforced by observing the subsequent consumption of the fruit. In contrast, imagine the child observing some-one using a tool to carve away bits of a piece of wood, which results in a smaller piece of wood and shavings (not to mention sound effects, etc.). In this case there is no way for the child to know which of these outcomes is the desired effect, and hence the function of the tool, unless he can rely on further pre-existing knowledge about the tool, the material, or the observed individual's immediate goal.

This difficulty does not imply that acquiring tool use by observational learning is impossible. When the actual goal of the behavior is opaque, one can acquire the use of a tool by *blind imitation* (Want and Harris 2002), hoping that he will learn later the useful function of the tool. Indeed, humans, and especially human children, tend to imitate apparently meaningless actions much more readily than other species. Imita-tion is not necessary, however, when the goal of the to-be-learned behavior and the causal affordance properties of the tool are transparent: in such cases the child can acquire the tool use by emulation (Tomasello 1996).

Blind imitation, however, solves only one side of the problem. Mediated tool use conceals not only the ultimate goal of the behavior but it is also opaque with respect to the background knowledge that governs the observed actions. Without this back-ground knowledge, one would not know what conditions are appropriate to use the tool, which aspects of its observed use are essential and relevant, and which are superfluous. A blind imitator runs the risk of repeating the observed action when it is not appropriate, and replicating many elements of the action that are idiosyncratic to the observed individual or situation, but are irrelevant with respect to the func-tional use of the tool. Even if one has a good guess about the goal of an action, it does not imply that he would know which elements of the observed actions are relevant for goal achievement, unless he also possesses the whole package of causal knowledge to grasp the connection between action and its effects.

This is the critical point of our story. Generally, the observable behavior of indi-viduals is never transparent either with respect to the background knowledge that governs their actions or with respect to the ultimate goal of the action (if it were transparent, cognitive psychology would not exist as a scientific discipline). Thus, to acquire the relevant knowledge through observation sets an ill-posed *inverse problem*: a behavior can always be generated and explained by an infinite number of different mental state combinations, representing diverse goals and/or different types of back-ground knowledge. This difficulty is just multiplied when observing mediated (recursive) tool use, where no perceptible reward would inform the observer about the tool's function and, in the absence of that, there is no way to assess the relevance of any element of the behavior observed. If at least some information about the immediate goal of the tool user and the knowledge that she applies were made explicit, the observer would have a much better chance to extract functionally relevant knowledge from his observation. This information can only be made explicit by the user himself, the individual who knows both the function and the relevant usage of the tool. If she not only applies but also *manifests* some of this knowledge in her behavior, and the observer is receptive to these manifestations, knowledge transfer becomes much easier. (This is, of course, not a direct knowledge transfer, and, as we shall see, it relies heavily on inferential processes. Nevertheless, these inferences, as we shall argue later, are constrained much more than the inferences one has to use in simple observation.) In the case of tool use, manifestation of knowledge may be achieved by demonstrations: emphasizing some, while ignoring other, aspects of tool use, separating products from by-products, contrasting suitable and unsuitable conditions of use, etc.

In sum, we hypothesize that the 'birth of pedagogy' was necessitated by extensive tool use by early hominid groups, and especially by the appearance of mediated tool use generated through 'recursive' teleology that decoupled means and ends in such a way that made these functional aspects opaque and uninferable for the uninformed observer. In fact, proliferation of tool use, and the emergence of a rich artifact culture, would have probably been impossible without an efficient social learning mechanism that enabled transmission of not just observable behaviors but also unobservable knowledge. At the same time, as soon as this mechanism evolved, it opened up new territories for evolutionary selection, both in biological and in cultural evolution. First, when the mechanism became available, it could be applied to domains outside tool use as well. In other words, pedagogical knowledge transfer may have extended to knowledge domains that are not strictly related to tool use. Second, the very fact that pedagogical knowledge acquisition can work without observing immediate, or even delayed, rewards gained by the teacher, implies that the relevance of the acquired knowledge is presumed and not verified by the learner. Consequently, it allows for the acquisition of knowledge contents that are not only functionally non-transparent, but that do not seem to (or actually do not) have any direct and perceivable adaptive value at all. This aspect of pedagogical knowledge transmission enables the development, transmission, and stabilization of arbitrary conventions and traditions that are uniquely characteristic of human cultures. Third, pedagogy essentially created a new way of information transfer among individuals through the use of ostensive communication (see later). This might have facilitated, or even provided a precondition for, the evolution of linguistic communication. And fourth, an active inclination for pedagogical knowledge transfer implies seeing each other not just in terms of kinship, as sexual partners, sources of protection, and members of a social hierarchy, but also as repositories and consumers of knowledge, which might have had profound effects on the further evolution of human social cognition.

Let us emphasize again that the above story is *just* a just-so story. The main body of evidence for our claim that pedagogy is a primary human-specific adaptation comes not from evolutionary history but from developmental psychology. Even if the above historical reconstruction were shown to be flawed, the theory may prove to be the best explanation of the developmental evidence we have.

11.5 The design specifications of pedagogy

We define *pedagogy* as: (1) explicit manifestation of generalizable knowledge by an individual (the 'teacher'); and (2) interpretation of this manifestation in terms of knowledge content by another individual (the 'learner'). In other words, pedagogy, in the sense that we use this term, is a specific type of social learning achieved by a specific type of communication. It is important to realize the distinctive nature of pedagogy both as a particular type of social learning, and as a particular type of communication.

On the one hand, pedagogy, as a form of social learning mechanism – similarly to all types of social learning (imitation, emulation, stimulus enhancement, etc.) – conveys generalizable knowledge that is valid beyond the actual situation. However, unlike most other social learning mechanisms that rely on mere observation, pedagogy requires active participation by the source of knowledge (the teacher), which is achieved by a type of communication involving manifestation of relevant knowledge. The fact that pedagogy requires an active participation by the source of knowledge implies that it may incur costs for the teacher. We would therefore expect that this kind of social learning mechanism, unlike most other types of social learning that predominantly spread behaviors horizontally (Laland *et al.* 2000), would be selected primarily to support vertical (parent to offspring) transmission of knowledge. Indeed, vertical transmission seems to be the dominant mode of diffusion of cultural traits among humans (Hewlett and Cavalli-Sforza 1986; Guglielmino *et al.* 1995).

On the other hand, pedagogy is also a type of communication, but unlike any other forms of communication in non-human animals, it conveys generalizable knowledge rather than factual information. All types of communication in non-human animals transmit information about the 'here and know', or about particular individuals, that does not generalize to other situations or to other individuals.

Our definition of pedagogy is both wider and narrower than others' use of this or similar terms. Many theorists (e.g. Barnett 1973; Premack 1984; Premack and Premack 1996) see the instructor's feedback and monitoring efforts, which can be called training or 'coaching' (Caro and Hauser 1992), as integral and essential parts of the teaching process. Although evaluative feedback, as modern educational theories indicate, can obviously facilitate teacher-guided learning, we do not restrict pedagogy to such practices. Our notion of pedagogy is also broader than the notion of *instructed learning* developed by Tomasello, Kruger, and Ratner (1993), which requires the learner to internalize the teacher's instructions and rehearse them later. We treat any knowledge transmission, as long as it is based on explicit manifestation of knowledge, as evidence for pedagogy, irrespective of whether it involves later rehearsal of internalized instructions or not. On the other hand, we do not consider any behavior that aims to facilitate the emergence of new knowledge in another individual as pedagogical teaching. Behavioral conditioning by rewards or punishment, or supervised learning in connectionist models, can assist the generation of knowledge, but it does so without explicit communication and knowledge manifestation.

How does pedagogy work then? As we have argued, pedagogy involves a special type of communication, and in order to understand its workings, we have to describe the design specifications of this communication system. Here we shall define the minimum requirements that are necessary for pedagogical knowledge transmission. There are three of them: ostension, reference, and relevance. (We borrowed these terms from the philosophy of language to emphasize the analogy with basic aspects of linguistic communication.)

11.5.1 Ostension

Pedagogy is costly for the teacher; it requires her to engage in an activity (knowledge manifestation, over and above simple functional knowledge use) that benefits someone else (the learner), but not herself. If she simply *uses* her knowledge, it does not allow others to extract its content from her behavior – otherwise there would be no need for pedagogy. Therefore the teacher has to make sure that she does not waste her time with manifestations when the intended learner is not in a recipient state. On the other side, the learner has to be able to distinguish whether another individual simply applies her knowledge or demonstrates it for him, because only this latter kind of activity will give him a good chance to extract knowledge from her behavior. Thus, the teacher has to manifest not only her knowledge to be transmitted to the learner, but also the fact *that* she is manifesting her knowledge, in other words, that she is teaching. This requirement also entails that it is not sufficient for the teacher to make manifest that she is about to teach something; her signals also have to specify the addressee of her teaching attempt (i.e. her intended pupil). In other words, the teacher has to explicitly mark her behavior as being a pedagogical manifestation, and has to make sure that the intended recipient has received her signals. This requirement is directly analogous, if not identical, to the Gricean view of ostensive communication, which holds that normal human communication makes manifest not just the intended message content but also the communicative intent of the speaker. We call this aspect of pedagogy, after Sperber and Wilson (1986), *ostension*. From an evolutionary point of view, the strong claim here is that ostensive communication, which, according to several theorists, emerged before linguistic communication during human evolution, originally evolved to assist pedagogy.

The most common way to provide an ostensive stimulus by humans is to talk to each other, but this is not the only way. Making eye contact, for example, is a very powerful communicative signal, and it also specifies the addressee of the concurrent and subsequent message unambiguously. In fact, an ostensive context can be achieved entirely by relatively low-level mechanisms. Teachers and learners can establish a teaching context by emitting and picking up ostensive signals. As these signals are essential for ensuring that the participants mutually recognize that they are in a teaching context, the sensitivity to at least some of these signals must be innate.

11.5.2 **Reference**

Pedagogy involves communication of generalizable knowledge that can be used outside the current situation; therefore the teacher also has to specify *what* she is teaching about. Specifying the referent of the to-be-transmitted knowledge content is essential because this will determine for the learner the scope of the acquired knowledge by anchoring the starting point of such generalizations. We shall call this aspect of pedagogy *reference*. Note that our point here is *not* that it is only pedagogy that requires referential communication – many examples of non-human animal communication are also referential (Seyfarth and Cheney 2003). However, referential messages in animal communication systems (e.g. in monkey alarm calls) are holistic: they do not have to, and they do not, specify the referent separately from the message, because there is no knowledge conveyed by the message that would be generalizable to other referents. The strong evolutionary claim following from this analysis would be that the predicate–argument (knowledge–referent) structure of human communication predates the emergence of language and originates in pedagogical communication.

Reference assignment can take a symbolic, iconic, or indexical format. However, interpreting symbolic reference entails knowledge of symbols, acquired by earlier learning processes, and iconic reference may also require familiarity with the referent. In contrast, indexical referent assignment, especially in terms of spatial indices, can be achieved without prior knowledge about the referent. We assume that the earliest forms of referent assignment in pedagogy, both in phylogenetic and ontogentic timescales, are deictic gestures, like gaze-shift or pointing, and other behaviors that can serve as spatial indices. Note also that while knowledge content is assumed to be asymmetrical in pedagogical contexts, ostensive and referential signals are not, as they could be produced by either or both participants equally. Thus, setting up the pedagogical context can be initiated by the learner through emitting ostensive signals towards the teacher, and he can also assign reference by deictic gestures for the teacher. If the person to whom these ostensive gestures are addressed interprets these signals as requests for teaching (which is not guaranteed), these ostensive and referential behaviors would function as non-verbal questions to induce transfer of relevant knowledge about the deictically identified referent.

11.5.3 Relevance

Pedagogy requires the teacher to make manifest the knowledge content to be transmitted to the learner (which is essentially a predicate that holds the referent as (one of) its argument(s)). However, there is no predefined code system that could unambiguously represent any new knowledge. Thus, interpretation of manifestations, just like interpretation of observed behaviors, is always *inferential*. Pedagogy solves the inverse problem of action interpretation that we described in Section 11.4 *not* by eliminating inference, but by providing extra information for the learner, which can constrain and channel his inferences towards the appropriate interpretation. There is, however, an important aspect of pedagogy that may help both parties in achieving successful knowledge transfer. Manifesting knowledge content and disambiguating such manifestation can rely on the mutually shared understanding between teacher and learner that what is going on is pedagogical knowledge transfer, in other word, that the teacher's communication conveys *novel and relevant* knowledge to the learner. This aspect of pedagogy, which we call *relevance*, is analogous to the communicative principle of relevance in verbal communication (Sperber and Wilson 1986) in that it provides guidance for the learner in figuring out the knowledge content that he is supposed to acquire by the teacher's communication.

In order to provide new and relevant knowledge, the teacher has to be able to recognize what knowledge the learner lacks. It is often emphasized that teachers will have to monitor what their pupils understand and adjust their teaching efforts accordingly (e.g. Strauss *et al.* 2002). However, this function can, most of the time, be fulfilled without actually reading the pupil's mind. If, for example, the teacher, as in a typical parent–offspring setting, can track more or less permanently what knowledge the learner has already acquired, she will be able to identify what would constitute novel knowledge for the learner. It is also important to realize that the teacher does not have to solve the hard inverse problem in order to assess the learner's knowledge state. She does not have to understand what (insufficient or inadequate) knowledge makes the learner behave in a certain way (the inverse problem) – she only has to check if he behaves in accordance with the knowledge that is relevant in the given situation (the forward problem). If he does not, manifesting the relevant knowledge will likely to be beneficial for him.

At the same time, the teacher also has to recognize what it is that she herself knows, and has to be able to analyze this knowledge in terms of its relevance for the learner. This is far from being a trivial achievement. Generally, one does not need to be aware of the content of one's knowledge in order to use that knowledge to generate appropriate behavior effectively. (This becomes evident when we try to teach a well-practiced skill of ours, e.g. how to ride a bike, to someone else. Chicken sex-typers are also famous for typically not being able either to describe or to accessibly demonstrate their amazing skill to others.) Teaching therefore requires a certain amount of *metacognitive* access to one's own knowledge content (Karmiloff-Smith 1986), to single out and emphasize in her demonstration those aspects of her knowledge that are relevant and novel for the learner, while ignoring others. In other words, a teacher needs to be able to create metarepresentations of her own knowledge (Sperber 2000). Thus, maybe somewhat paradoxically, this leads us to conclude that while teaching, at least in its initially selected form, does not necessarily require the ability to create metarepresentations of other individuals' representations (i.e. a theory of mind), it does, however, require the ability to develop metarepresentations of one's own knowledge.

On the learner's side, interpreting the teacher's communicative acts in terms of novel knowledge content is not a trivial task either. Such inferences are guided by the assumption that the teacher's acts convey novel and relevant knowledge, but, just like the inferential interpretation of goal-directed acts (Csibra *et al.* 2003), they must rely on the learner's already accumulated background knowledge. In fact, the assumption of relevance requires the learner to decode the teacher's manifestation with respect to his *own* knowledge. This implies that while the outcome of the learner's inferential interpretation of the teacher's communicative manifestation will provide him with the teacher's knowledge, the inferential process itself whereby he arrives at this new knowledge content will be based on and constrained by his own, already existing knowledge. In other words, the pedagogical question driving the learner's inferential interpretation of the teacher's demonstration is this: 'What is the new information in this manifestation that I don't yet know and would not be able to figure out myself?' To successfully answer this question it will therefore be necessary for the learner to consult and be guided by the contents of his own existing knowledge. As a result, however, the ensuing output of his inferential interpretation of the teacher's demonstration will enrich his knowledge with the new and relevant information that he was supposed to acquire.

11.6 Evidence of adaptation for pedagogy in human infants

The design specifications of pedagogy suggest that this adaptation would not be achieved by the emergence of a unitary, single ability that would miraculously solve the problem of knowledge transfer across individuals. Instead, pedagogy works as a well-organized package of biases, tendencies, and skills, many of which are implemented in low-level processes. Considering only the receptive side of pedagogy, such an adaptation should make human infants: (1) be sensitive to ostensive stimuli; (2) be biased to follow directional cues in ostensive contexts to identify referents; and (3) be able to extract novel information from manifestations provided by sources in these contexts and learn this information quickly.

11.6.1 **Ostension**

An ostensive stimulus is a signal that indicates communication as well as specifies the addressee of the to-be-achieved communication. Human infants are sensitive to at least three kinds of ostensive stimuli from the moment they are born: eye contact, contingent responsivity, and infant-directed speech.

Eye contact is the fastest way to establish and re-establish a communicative link between people. Mutual looking into each other's eyes confirms that the other is 'on line', that she is the intended addressee of the other's communicative message. When they can choose, newborns prefer to look at a face directly looking at them, whether that face is a realistic photograph (Farroni *et al.* 2002) or a schematic drawing (Farroni *et al.* 2004). This effect disappears when the faces are presented upside down (Farroni, Johnson, Csibra, and Zulian, unpublished data), which implies that the preferred stimulus for newborns is not simply two eyes with the pupils in their centre, but two eyes with the pupils in their centre in the context of a face that is in a canonical (i.e. upright) position.

Recognizing that an upright face with direct gaze not only signals the presence of a conspecific, but also acts as an ostensive stimulus may provide us with a solution to the puzzle described in Section 11.2.1. If newborns' preference is directed towards ostensive stimuli, they should not be interested in inverted faces, whether or not these involve a direct or an averted gaze, because only faces in the canonical orientation indicate a possible communicative context. In other words, if we interpret the phenomena in question as reflecting 'eye-contact preference' rather than 'face-preference', the puzzle disappears. When looking around in the world, newborns are searching not simply for faces, but for potential 'teachers'. Note that mothers always make sure that their baby's head is aligned with their own when they initiate interactions with their offspring (Watson 1972).

Another aspect of newborns' preference for faces confirms further that this innate ability is based on more than a geometric face template to be matched. Gaze perception in humans is extremely sensitive to contrast polarity (Ricciardelli *et al.* 2000) because our perceptual system tries to read gaze direction by identifying the location of a darker spot (pupil) within a lighter area (sclera). Human eyes have a unique morphology with large areas of the white sclera visible (Kobayashi and Koshima 1997). It is possible that this unique morphology serves a human specific function, namely, to make the identification of gaze direction easier for our conspecifics. If 'gaze' is identified by the location of a dark spot on a light background, than a figure that does not have such spots cannot be seen as having a 'gaze' and cannot be identified as a stimulus with mutual gaze (i.e. eye contact). Whether newborns' preference is directed towards stimuli with a specific geometric face configuration, or is determined by the number of elements in the upper and lower parts of the stimuli (Turati *et al.* 2002; Cassia *et al.* 2004), they should show preference for upright face configurations even if the contrast polarity of these stimuli are inverted. If, however, their preference is directed to potential eye contact stimuli, where eyes are defined as dark spots on light background in the context of a canonically oriented face, they should not show any preference, because neither of those stimuli satisfies this definition. A recent study (Farroni, Johnson, and Csibra, unpublished data) confirmed this latter prediction.

Another ostensive stimulus is contingency. If a source repeatedly appears to remain silent during your actions but start to emit signals as soon as you have stopped your actions, it gives you the strong impression that the source is communicating with you. In fact, this kind of turn-taking temporal contingency is a characteristic feature of normal human communication. Newborns are known to be sensitive to such temporal contingency, as it is shown by the fact that they can be subjected to operant conditioning (e.g. Floccia *et al.* 1997). Although their behavioral repertoire is very limited, they nevertheless use those of their actions that they can control voluntarily relatively well, like sucking, to test if they receive contingent responses from their mother (Masataka 2003).

Contingent turn taking remains a very important factor in mother–infant communication during the first months of life. These types of early interactions received a lot of attention, and were hailed as providing evidence for the innate sociability of human infants. These contingent interactions are sometimes called 'proto-conversation' (Bateson 1979), 'dyadic interaction' (Stern 1977) or 'primary intersubjectivity' (Trevarthen 1979), and it has been attributed various functions, such as 'sharing mental states' (Trevarthen 1979), 'affect attunement' (Stern 1977), 'mutual affect regulation' (Gianino and Tronick 1988), or serving identification (Tomasello 1999) or attachment purposes (e.g. Watson 2001). While we agree that some of these processes may indeed be assisted by early conversation-like interactions, we do not believe that the primary function of human infants' innate sensitivity to contingent turn taking is the fulfillment of any of these functions (see Gergely 2002). For example, filial attachment is established in many mammalian and avian species without extended proto-conversational routines. It also seems to be an overstatement that mothers and infants are both motivated to and subjectively aware of 'sharing' each other's mental or emotional states in these interactions. No doubt, they both enjoy these situations, and one can say that they, in fact, 'share' this positive hedonic experience, at least in the sense of being simultaneously in a similar affective state. Also, apart from generating simultaneous enjoyment, what aspect of the evidence would indicate that any other, more differentiated discrete emotional states are shared during turn taking? Do mothers and babies share sadness, fear, anger, disgust, or distress? Infants may be able to recognize the expressions of these emotional states, and mothers will certainly react to these emotions if their child expresses them. But this reaction will hardly be an initiation of a turn-taking interchange: she is much more likely to just pick the child up and establish close bodily contact with him. Engaging in proto-conversational turn taking is neither a typical nor an effective response when the baby is in need of soothing.

The fact that young infants enjoy contingent interactions even in the absence of another human being (for example, with a mobile, see Watson 1972) also suggests that the sensitivity to contingent responsivity does not imply a sharing of emotional states or identification with the source of contingency. We believe that these early dyadic interactions serve an ultimately epistemic function: identifying teachers and teaching situations, and practicing this process. It is adaptive to seek out such situations because they indicate the potential to acquire a commodity that has survival value: socially transmitted and culturally relevant knowledge.

Perhaps the most obvious communicative signal in humans is the most used form of communication itself: speech. Unlike the other two communication signals, however, speech itself is not necessarily an ostensive stimulus, as it does not directly specify the addressee of a communicative act. To figure out if one is being addressed by a speech signal, one can look for the presence of other ostensive stimuli, like eye contact or contingency, or can try to disambiguate the situation from the content of the speech. This latter method of disambiguation, however, is not available to preverbal infants. Nevertheless, speakers can provide additional cues in the auditory domain to indicate that they are talking to an infant. Adults, and especially mothers, instinctively alter their prosody when they talk to preverbal infants. The prosody of infant-directed speech, often termed as 'motherese', is characterized by higher pitch, broader pitch and amplitude variation, and lower speed than adult-directed speech.

Several functions have been attributed to this distinctive type of speech pattern addressed to infants: it captures infants' attention (Fernald 1985), it regulates affects (Werker and McLeod 1989), it may play a causal role in language acquisition (Furrow *et al.* 1980), or it is just a by-product of the fact that infants are talked to in emotionally charged contexts (Trainor *et al.* 2000; Singh *et al.* 2002). We propose that the primary function of motherese is much simpler: it merely *makes it manifest that the speech is infant-directed*. In other words, the special prosody associated with motherese indicates to the baby that he is the one to whom the given utterance is addressed. This signaling function turns motherese into the sibling of eye contact and contingent responsivity, as it will also indicate to the child that he is in a potential pedagogical context. If this is the case, we should see that infant-directed speech elicits the same responses as do the other two cues: easy and fast detection of, preferential orientation to, and positive affect towards the source of such stimuli.

Indeed, 2-day-old newborns pay more attention to a source talking to them in infant-directed speech than to a source speaking in an adult-directed way (Cooper and Aslin 1990), even if they are born to congenitally deaf parents who could not have trained them in special speech patterns prenatally (Masataka 2003). Older infants prefer motherese even if the speech represents a foreign language never heard before (Werker *et al.*1994), and are more likely to extract motherese than adult-directed speech from acoustic noise (Colombo *et al.* 1995). Infants' responses to motherese, just like their responses to eye contact and contingency, also have an affective component. When they attend to infant-directed speech, babies smile more and appear to be more attractive to adults than when they are listening to adult-direct speech (Werker and McLeod 1989). This shows that infants' response to motherese, just like their response to eye contact, fulfils its function: it makes adults repeat their actions and prolong the (potentially pedagogical) interaction with them.

Finally, we have to mention that the earliest word that infants recognize at 4.5 months of age is an ostensive stimulus: their own name (Mandel *et al.* 1995). Of course, sensitivity to their own name is not inborn, but it is also unlikely that their name at this age would function as a lexical item referring to the self. Instead, this word must have acquired a special status via strong associations with other ostensive stimuli, like eye contact or motherese, and its 'meaning' for an infant is entirely defined by pragmatic rather than semantic factors. From about 6 months, infants spontaneously turn their head when their name is called, showing that they interpret this word as a vocative.

11.6.2 Reference

The widespread view among students of infant communication is that referential communication does not exist before the second half of the first year of life. Young infants are restricted to affective communication, and only some time after 6 months of age can they change over from dyadic to triadic interactions, from primary to secondary intersubjectivity, and from affective to referential communication (e.g. Adamson and McArthur 1995; Butterworth 2004; Masataka 2003; Tomasello 1999; Trevarthen and Aitken 2001). This developmental stage is characterized by the emergence of episodes of 'joint attention', where the infant and another person (usually a caregiver) simultaneously attend to the same object, while they are mutually aware that they share their experience. Joint attention can be initiated by either party, especially after the infant has started to point to objects at the end of the first year.

While we agree that infants' receptive and productive communicative abilities extend enormously during the first year, we think that this two-stage view of early communication has to be revised in the light of recent results. In particular, several studies have shown that young infants are sensitive to gaze shifts in faces that they observe. If 4-month-old infants see that the gaze direction of a person suddenly shifts to one side, they will be more likely, and faster, to detect and localize a target stimulus on the same side than on the other side (Farroni *et al.* 2000; Hood *et al.* 1998). They do not necessarily follow the gaze (while sometimes they do; gaze-following cannot be reliably triggered by eye-movement alone until 18 months of age), but their attention is sensitized to events in the indicated direction. In fact, the same effect of gaze-triggered attentional shift is also present in newborns (Farroni *et al.* 2004). If the adult turns her head as well, and the target objects are close enough, overt gaze following can also be elicited in young infants (D'Entremont *et al.* 1997).

These phenomena are usually interpreted as reflecting infants' sensitivity to the attentional state of others. There is an important aspect of these results, however, that calls this interpretation into question. Infants shift their attention to the direction of the gaze of the observed person only if: (1) they can see the eyes moving to the side position (Farroni *et al.* 2000); and (2) the eyes are departing from central, that is eye-contact position (Farroni *et al.* 2003). If what infants are interested in is the direction of attention of the other person, they should not care about where she was looking before; her attention, or her shift of attention, could be read out from her final eye position in any case. This pattern of results, however, is consistent with an alternative interpretation, which claims that infants follow others' gaze, or are at least sensitized to the visual field of the direction of gaze shifts of others, because they conceive gaze shifts as referential acts (Csibra 2003). Directional stimuli from another person will only be interpreted as referential actions if they occur in an ostensive situation, established, for example, by eye contact. In fact, if the communicative situation has been established by eye contact, infants seem to be sensitized by any motion coming from the ostensive stimulus, even if it is not a gaze shift (Farroni *et al.* 2000). Further, 'gaze following' could also be elicited without a face, if the ostensive stimulus is provided by contingency, rather than eye contact, information (Johnson *et al.* 1998; Movellan and Watson 2002).

The fact that young infants tend to interpret the actions of the source of an ostensive stimulus as referential does not guarantee that they will also be able to identify the referent. Studies have shown that the accuracy of finding the target object of a referential act, whether it is looking or pointing, is developing slowly during the first 18 months (Butterworth and Jarrett 1991), especially if the referent is in a distal position or it is outside of the baby's visual field (Flom *et al.* 2004). If the function of gaze following were to allow the infant to 'share' the attentional state of another person (e.g. Tomasello 1999), this inaccuracy would be puzzling (see Section 11.2.2). Why would such a response survive if it failed to achieve successful 'sharing' and would lead to a misinterpretation of what the object of the other's mental experience is most of the time? If, however, gaze following reflects a communicative-referential expectation, this is not a problem: an infant can confidently expect that his communicative partner (the 'teacher') would specify the referent in a way that he could decode it, or that she would repeat and extend the referential cues if the baby has not succeeded in locating it. And if he still failed to find the referent, he would only run into the risk of missing an opportunity to learn something from his teacher rather than misattributing a mental state to her.

It is also important that infants expect that a referential action would specify something that they can learn about, for example, an object. When infants make a mistake in studies on gaze following, their gaze never stops at an empty surface, but always lands on an object (Butterworth and Jarrett 1991). Similarly, if reference is specified by jiggling and moving an object in front of the infant after making eye contact with him, a 3- or 4-month-old baby's gaze will stick to the object even after the hand has been withdrawn from it (Amano *et al.* 2004). And when they can identify the referred location but not the referent because it is behind a barrier, they will locomote to get a view of the referred object (Moll and Tomasello 2004). Infants therefore have a strong expectation that the actions of a person (or, in fact, any source) that emits ostensive stimuli towards them will highlight an object (or event), which they are supposed to attend to. While it is true that this tendency will, most of the time, establish 'joint attention' between the infant and the source, we believe that the function of this outcome is neither to uncover others' mental states for the infants, nor to share experience between them, but to specify for the infant what it is that he is going to be taught about some new and relevant information. Infants are prepared from birth to interpret actions as referential. The impression of stage-like development of communication is simply created by the fact that while ostensive stimuli are innately specified (and elicit strong affective responses), the mechanisms of indexical referent identification are only crudely defined at birth, and have to be tuned by slow perceptual learning during early development.

11.6.3 **Relevance**

The function of pedagogy is to allow transfer of culturally accumulated knowledge to new members of the community. The actual content of this knowledge can fall into various domains: function and use of tools, valence of objects or animals, some aspects of language (primarily words), non-linguistic symbols (for example gestures), cultural conventions, and even abstract beliefs expressing the world view of the community. Learning in all these domains can rely on some specialized cognitive mechanisms, and never depends exclusively on explicit teaching. Nevertheless, teaching would accelerate learning by warranting the relevance of the acquired knowledge. This is achieved if the learner assumes that the teacher's communication will increase his knowledge by novel elements. Infants and children indeed apply this assumption when they are subject to teaching and this can be demonstrated in all the domains we listed above. Here we illustrate the functioning of this assumption in the domain of tool use.

If one assumes that a certain unfamiliar object has a function to serve, he can try to figure out what it is without assistance. He can take the 'design stance' (Dennett 1987) and look for the intended use of the artifact. Young children and infants are unlikely to be able to go down this route (Matan and Carey 2001), but that does not imply that they would not be able to understand and reason about functions (Kemler Nelson *et al.* 2004) or that they would be helpless in finding out what an artifact is for. They could, for example, try out various actions with it to find out the object's affordances.

Human infants (unlike infants of most other animals) are indeed fascinated by objects and enjoy manipulating them. Trial-and-error methods, however, as we discussed in Section 11.4, can only have a limited use in discovering artifact functions. We hypothesized that pedagogy might have originally developed to transmit knowledge about non-obvious artifact functions and usage. When a learner is taught how to use a tool, he does not have to understand either the ultimate function of the object or the rationale that justifies a particular procedure applied to the tool. In accordance with this purpose, and perhaps counter-intuitively at first sight, the relevance assumption will dictate to the learner to attend to those aspects of a demonstrated tool use that he would not be able to infer from his existing knowledge (i.e. those aspects that do not make sense for him), and conclude that he has been taught these novel aspects.

In a well-known study on infant imitation, Meltzoff (1988) demonstrated a novel action on a novel object to 14-month-old infants. The model made eye contact with the infant and then conspicuously leaned forward and touched a box with his forehead, lighting it up. One week later, when they came back to the laboratory and had a chance to approach the object, the majority of the infants replicated the action that they had seen performed only once before. This is a textbook example of pedagogical learning: the teacher (the model) (1) established a teaching context by an ostensive stimulus (eye contact); (2) identified the referent object (the magic box) by looking at it and touching it; and (3) demonstrated a novel action (touching the box with his forehead) that created a novel effect (lighting up the box). In response, infants learned in a single trial both the function of the novel object and the special way it should be operated, and retained this knowledge for a relatively long time. The answer to the question raised in Section 11.2.3, 'Why do infants imitate a novel action even when they have access to a more efficient means to achieve the same end?' is simply, 'Because they have been taught to perform that action'.

This interpretation of Meltzoff's study is markedly different from what he and others (e.g. Tomasello 1999) offered. Meltzoff (and Tomasello) reasoned that infants imitated the model's unusual action because they identified with him, and this made them copy his action when they had the same goal as the model had had before. Thus, according to this interpretation, infants' imitative behavior does not depend on either the teaching context or the novelty aspect of the demonstration. Recent studies tested some differential predictions of these contradicting interpretations. Gergely, Bekkering, and Király (2002) modified Meltzoff's situation in a way that rendered the same action understandable, hence removing its relevance. Before demonstrating the head-touch action, the model – pretending to be chilly – covered her shoulders with a blanket that she had to hold on to by her hands to keep it on. In this situation, where the hands are no longer available, the head-touch action seems to be the most efficient way to touch an object in front of the model. By 14–months of age infants are known to understand that agents normally act efficiently to achieve their goals (Csibra et al. 1999; Gergely et al. 1995); therefore the model's action in this situation did not represent any novel information for them. If infants conceived the situation as a teaching attempt, they would learn the function of the novel object, but they would not learn the particular action the object was operated by because it did not represent new and relevant knowledge. This prediction was confirmed when the infants returned to the laboratory a week later; hardly any of them imitated the head-touch action in this 'hands-occupied' demonstration condition, while all of them operated the box using their hand.

The pedagogical account of Meltzoff's study also suggests that the ostensive stimuli before the demonstration might have played a critical role in defining the context as teaching. Király, Csibra, and Gergely (2004) replicated Meltzoff's study with the single modification that the model never made any eye contact with the infants, who therefore observed the same actions outside of a teaching context. Despite the fact that these infants saw exactly the same demonstration, only a minority of them imitated the novel action. Imitation is a ubiquitous phenomenon in human social learning (whether or not it is exclusive to humans); however, it is not an end but a means. It subserves a more general human-specific adaptation of acquiring relevant knowledge from teachers who are willing to manifest such knowledge (for a more thorough discussion of the role of imitation in human development see Gergely and Csibra, in press).

11.7 Pedagogy and social cognition

Just like the general learning mechanisms that implement individual knowledge acquisition, the design of pedagogical knowledge acquisition also relies on implicit assumptions about the world. Associationist learning, for example, assumes stable or permanent relations between the associated events, and food avoidance learning assumes a causal link between the consumption of a new food item and the subsequent sickness. In case these assumptions were false, the learning mechanisms would not yield valid and adaptive knowledge. Similarly, pedagogical learning makes assumptions about the social world without which the adaptivity of such a knowledge acquisition system would collapse. These assumptions determine fundamentally the picture that we create about our conspecifics, and they form the core of our social cognitive development.

The first assumption that an infant must hold in order to take advantage of pedagogy is that there will be 'teachers' around who will transmit relevant knowledge to him. Teaching is a co-operative activity that incurs no immediate benefit for the teacher while it may be costly for her (cf. Caro and Hauser 1992). Note also that the advantages of pedagogical knowledge transfer over other types of observational social learning (i.e. rapid acquisition, unrestricted content) arise only if the learner trusts the teacher unconditionally, without verifying the relevance of the acquired knowledge. This *co-operativity* assumption seems to apply not only to family members, since infants are happy to learn new skills from experimenters in hundreds of developmental psychology laboratories around the world. As this is a core assumption, it is applied 'by default' to everyone in every situation, and (probably in contrast to other animals) what human children have to learn by experience is when to suspend this assumption.

The second general assumption of pedagogical knowledge acquisition is that mature members of the community store valuable knowledge in themselves that they can manifest any time, even when they do not need to use the knowledge themselves. Note that this assumption is not equivalent to rendering other people's minds as representational devices because the existence and validity of their knowledge is presumed. Indeed, this assumption implies that infants will see other people (or at least adults) as *omniscient*, whose knowledge is available to tap at any time (for an opposite view, see Baldwin and Moses 1996). Thus, what children have to learn by experience is not the conditions that make people knowledgeable but the conditions that make people ignorant.

Finally, a corollary of the omniscience assumption is that the knowledge that the child acquires is public, shared, and universal. If someone knows something, everyone knows it; otherwise the assumption of omniscience would be violated. This assumption is analogous to the similar assumption about words: a child can plausibly assume that a word learned from a certain person is not her specific way to express a certain concept, but part of a shared sign system. The assumption of *universality* implies that whatever the child knows (especially if it was taught to him) will be known by everyone. Though this will be a valid inference most of the time, children eventually have to learn the conditions under which this assumption should be suspended to overcome the erroneous conclusions that have recently been dubbed as the 'curse of knowledge' (Birch and Bloom 2004).

If our hypothesis about the fundamental role that pedagogy has played during human evolution and plays during human development is correct, this would then also imply that seeing each other as co-operative and omniscient individuals is also part of our nature. And though one aspect of social cognitive development will necessarily be to learn when to overcome (suspend or inhibit) these default assumptions, we would never get rid of them. We expect that many people will resist the idea that important aspects of human social cognition and co-operation are derived from an originally epistemic function (i.e. knowledge acquisition). In our view, however, discovering that the evolutionary design of a basic human adaptation, such as pedagogy, involves built-in assumptions about the social world would not degrade but rather strengthen our understanding and appreciation for the inherent sociability of humans.

Acknowledgements

This work was supported by the UK Medical Research Council (G9715587) and the Guggenheim Foundation. We thank Paul Bloom, Deb Kelemen, Jean Mandler, Csaba

Pléh, Dan Sperber, Victoria Southgate, John S. Watson, and two anonymous reviewers for their valuable comments on an earlier version of this paper.

References

Adamson L and McArthur D (1995). Joint attention, affect, and culture. In: C Moore and PJ Dunham, eds. *Joint attention: its origins and role in development*, pp. 205–221. Hillsdale: Lawrence Erlbaum.

Amano S, Kezuka E and Yamamoto A (2004). Infant shifting attention from an adult's face to an adult's hand: a precursor of joint attention. *Infant Behavior and Development*, 27, 64–80.

Baldwin DA and Moses LJ (1996). The ontogeny of social information gathering. *Child Development*, 67, 1915–1939.

Barnett SA (1973). Homo docens. *Journal of Biosocial Science*, 5, 393–403.

Bateson MC (1979). The epigenesis of conversational interaction: a personal account of research development. In: M Bullowa, ed. *Before speech: the beginning of interpersonal communication*, pp. 63–77. New York: Cambridge University Press.

Birch AJ and Bloom P (2004). Understanding children's and adults' limitations in mental state reasoning. *Trends in Cognitive Sciences*, 8, 255–260.

Butterworth G (2004). Joint visual attention in infancy. In: G Bremner and A Slater, eds. *Theories of infant development*, pp. 317–354. Oxford: Blackwell.

Butterworth G and Jarrett N (1991). What minds have in common is space: Spatial mechanisms serving joint visual attention in infancy. *British Journal of Developmental Psychology*, 9, 55–72.

Caro TM and Hauser MD (1992). Is there teaching in nonhuman animals? *Quarterly Journal of Biology*, 67, 151–174.

Cassia VM, Turati C and Simion F (2004). Can a nonspecific bias toward top-heavy patterns explain newborns' face preference? *Psychological Science*, 15, 379–383.

Colombo J, Frick JE, Ryther JS, Coldren JT and Mitchell DW (1995). Infants' detection of analogs of 'motherese' in noise. *Merrill-Palmer Quarterly*, 41, 104–113.

Cooper RP and Aslin RN (1990). Preference for infant-directed speech in the first month after birth. *Child Development*, 61, 1584–1595.

Csibra G (2003). Teleological and referential understanding of action in infancy. *Philosophical Transactions of the Royal Society, London, B*, 358, 447–458.

Csibra G, Bíró S, Koós S and Gergely G (2003). One-year-old infants use teleological representations of actions productively. *Cognitive Science*, 27, 111–133.

Csibra G, Gergely G, Bíró S, Koós O and Brockbank M (1999). Goal attribution without agency cues: The perception of 'pure reason' in infancy. *Cognition*, 72, 237–267.

Dennett D (1987). *The intentional stance*. Cambridge: MIT Press.

D'Entremont B, Hains SMJ and Muir DW (1997). A demonstration of gaze following in 3- to 6-month-olds. *Infant Behavior and Development*, 20, 569–572.

Dunbar R (1996). *Grooming, gossip and the evolution of language*. London: Faber and Faber.

Farroni T, Csibra G, Simion F and Johnson MH (2002). Eye contact detection in humans from birth. *Proceedings of the National Academy of Sciences of the USA*, 99, 9602–9605.

Farroni T, Johnson MH, Brockbank M and Simion F (2000). Infants' use of gaze direction to cue attention: The importance of perceived motion. *Visual-Cognition*, 7, 705–718.

Farroni T, Mansfield EM, Lai C and Johnson MH (2003). Infants perceiving and acting on the eyes: tests of an evolutionary hypothesis. *Journal of Experimental Child Psychology*, **85**, 199–212.

Farroni T, Massaccesi S, Pividori D, Simion F and Johnson MH (2004). Gaze following in newborns. *Infancy*, **5**, 39–60.

Fernald A (1985). Four-month-old infants prefer to listen to motherese. *Infant Behavior and Development*, **8**, 181–195.

Floccia C, Christophe A. and Bertoncini J (1997). High-amplitude sucking and newborns: The quest for underlying mechanisms. *Journal of Experimental Child Psychology*, **64**, 175–189.

Flom R, Deák GO, Phill CG and Pick AD (2004). Nine-month-olds shared visual attention as a function of gesture and object location. *Infant Behavior and Development*, **27**, 181–194.

Furrow D, Nelson K and Benedict H (1980). Mothers' speech to children and syntactic development: Some simple relationships. *Journal of Child Language*, **6**, 423–442.

Gergely G (2002). The development of understanding self and agency. In: U Goshwami, ed. *Blackwell handbook of childhood cognitive development*, pp. 26–46. Oxford: Blackwell.

Gergely G, Bekkering H and Király I (2002). Rational imitation in preverbal infants. *Nature*, **415**, 755.

Gergely G and Csibra G (in press). Sylvia's recipe: Human culture, imitation, and pedagogy. In: NJ Enfield and SC Levinson, eds. *Roots of human sociality: culture, cognition, and human interaction*. London: Berg Press.

Gergely G, Nádasdy Z, Csibra G and Bíró S (1995). Taking the intentional stance at 12 months of age. *Cognition*, **56**, 165–193.

Gianino A and Tronick EZ (1988). The mutual regulation model: The infant's self and interactive regulation and coping and defensive capacities. In: TM Field, PM McCabe and N Schneiderman, eds. *Stress and coping across development*, pp. 47–68. Hillsdale: Lawrence Erlbaum.

Guglielmino CR, Viganotti C, Hewlett B and Cavalli-Sforza LL (1995). Cultural variation in Africa: Role of mechanisms of transmission and adaptation. *Proceedings of the National Academy of Sciences of the USA*, **92**, 7585–7589.

Hewlett BS and Cavalli-Sforza LL (1986). Cultural transmission among Aka pygmies. *American Anthropologist*, **88**, 922–934.

Hood BM, Willen JD and Driver J (1998). Adult's eyes trigger shifts of visual attention in infants. *Psychological Science*, **9**, 131–134.

Johnson MH and Morton J (1991). *Biology and cognitive development: the case of face recognition.* Oxford: Blackwell.

Johnson SC, Slaughter V and Carey S (1998). Whose gaze will infants follow? The elicitation of gaze-following in 12-month-olds. *Developmental Science*, **1**, 233–238.

Karmiloff-Smith A (1986). From meta-processes to conscious access: Evidence from children's metalinguistic and repair data. *Cognition*, **23**, 95–147.

Kemler Nelson DG, Egan LC and Holt MB (2004). When children ask, 'What is it' what do they want to know about artifacts? *Psychological Science*, **15**, 384–389.

Király I, Csibra G and Gergely G (2004). The role of communicative-referential cues in observational learning during the second year. Poster presented at the *14th Biennial International Conference on Infant Studies, May 2004, Chicago, IL, USA.*

Kobayashi H and Kohshima S (1997). Unique morphology of the human eye. *Nature*, **387**, 767–768.

Kruger A and Tomasello M (1996). Cultural learning and learning culture. In: D Olson and N Torrance, eds. *The Handbook of education and human development*, pp. 369–387. Oxford: Blackwell.

Laland KN, Odling-Smee J and Feldman MW (2000). Niche construction, biological evolution, and cultural change. *Behavioral and Brain Sciences*, 23, 131–146.

Mandel DR, Jusczyk PW and Pisoni DB (1995). Infants' recognition of the sound patterns of their own names. *Psychological Science*, 6, 314–317.

Masataka N (2003). *The onset of language*. New York: Cambridge University Press.

Matan A and Carey S (2001). Developmental changes within the core of artifact concepts. *Cognition*, 78, 1–26.

Meltzoff AN (1988). Infant imitation after a 1-week delay: Long-term memory for novel acts and multiple stimuli. *Developmental Psychology*, 24, 470–476.

Moll H and Tomasello M (2004). 12- and 18-month-old infants follow gaze to spaces behind barriers. *Developmental Science*, 7, F1–F9.

Moore C and Dunham PJ (1995). *Joint attention. Its origins and role in development*. Hillsdale, NJ: Lawrence Erlbaum.

Movellan JR and Watson JS (2002). *The development of gaze following as a Bayesian systems identification problem*. UCSD Machine Perception Laboratory Technical Reports 2002.01.

Olson DR and Bruner JS (1996). Folk psychology and folk pedagogy. In: DR Olson and N Torrance, eds. *The handbook of education and human development*, pp. 9–27. Oxford: Blackwell.

Premack D (1984). Pedagogy and aesthetics as sources of culture. In: MS Gazzaniga, ed. *Handbook of cognitive neuroscience*, pp. 15–35. New York: Plenum Press.

Premack D and Premack AJ (1996). Why animals lack pedagogy and some cultures have more of it than others. In: DR Olson and N Torrance, eds. *The handbook of education and human development*, pp. 302–323. Oxford: Blackwell.

Premack D and Premack A (2003). *Original intelligence. Unlocking the mystery of who we are*. New York: McGraw-Hill.

Ricciardelli P, Baylis G and Driver J (2000). The positive and negative of human expertise in gaze perception. *Cognition*, 77, B1–B14.

Seyfarth RM and Cheney DL (2003). Signalers and receivers in animal communication. *Annual Review of Psychology*, 54, 145–173.

Singh L, Morgan JL and Best CT (2002). Infants' listening preferences: Baby talk or happy talk? *Infancy*, 3, 365–394.

Sperber D (2000). Metarepresentations in an evolutionary perspective. In: D Sperber, ed. *Metarepresentations: A multidisciplinary perspective*, pp. 117–137. Oxford: Oxford University Press.

Sperber D and Wilson D (1986). *Relevance: communication and cognition*. Oxford: Blackwell.

Stern D (1977). *The first relationship: infant and mother*. London: Fontana Books.

Strauss S, Ziv M and Stein A (2002). Teaching as a natural cognition and its relations to preschoolers' developing theory of mind. *Cognitive Development*, 17, 1473–1487.

Tomasello M (1996). Do apes ape? In: CM Heyes and BG Galef, eds. *Social learning in animals: the roots of culture*. New York: Academic Press.

Tomasello M (1999). *The cultural origins of human cognition*. Cambridge, MA: Harvard University Press.

Tomasello M, Kruger A. and Ratner H (1993). Cultural learning. *Behavioral and Brain Sciences*, 16, 495–511.

Trainor LJ, Austin CM and Desjardins RN (2000). Is infant-directed speech prosody a result of vocal expression of emotion? *Psychological Science*, **11**, 188–195.

Trevarthen C (1979). Communication and cooperation in early infancy: a description of primary intersubjectivity. In: M Bullowa, ed. *Before speech: the beginning of interpersonal communication*, pp. 321–347. New York: Cambridge University Press.

Trevarthen C and Aitken KJ (2001). Infant intersubjectivity: research, theory, and clinical applications. *Journal of Child Psychology and Psychiatry*, **42**, 3–48.

Turati C, Simion F, Milini I and Umiltà C (2002). Newborns' preference for faces: What is crucial? *Developmental Psychology*, **38**, 875–882.

Valenza E, Simion F, Cassia VM and Umiltà C (1996). Face preference at birth. *Journal of Experimental Psychology: Human Perception and Performance*, **22**, 892–903.

Want SC and Harris PL (2002). How do children ape? Applying concepts from the study of non-human primates to the developmental study of 'imitation' in children. *Developmental Science*, **5**, 1–41.

Watson JS (1972). Smiling, cooing, and "the game". *Merrill-Palmer Quarterly*, **18**, 323–339.

Watson JS (2001). Contingency perception ad misperception in infancy: Some potential implications for attachment. *Bulletin of the Menninger Clinic*, **65**, 296–320.

Werker JF and McLeod PJ (1989). Infant preference for both male and female infant-directed talk: a developmental study of attentional and affective responsiveness. *Canadian Journal of Psychology*, **43**, 320–346.

Werker JF, Pegg JE and McLeod PJ (1994). A cross-language investigation of infant preference for infant-directed communication. *Infant Behavior and Development*, **17**, 323–333.

Whiten A (1999). Parental encouragement in *Gorilla* in comparative perspective: implications for social cognition and the evolution of teaching. In: ST Parker, RW Mitchell and HL Miles, eds. *The mentalities of gorillas and orangutans in comparative perspective*, pp. 342–466. New York: Cambridge University Press.

Whiten A (2000). Primate culture and social learning. *Cognitive Science*, **24**, 477–508.

Wood D, Bruner J and Ross G (1976). The role of tutoring in problem solving. *Journal of Child Psychology and Psychiatry*, **17**, 89–100.

Chapter 12

Constraints on the acquisition of specialization for face processing

Isabel Gauthier

Abstract

The domain-specificity of the mechanisms supporting face perception is debated both for early preferences observed in the newborn and later skills found in adults. However, an even more complex question is that of the relationship between newborns' face preference and adult face expertise. Here, I review the evidence addressing the question of the necessity of early constraints for the development of expertise with objects or faces. These results suggest little reason to postulate that newborn's face preferences constrain the acquisition of face recognition in adults, beyond conjectures of an evolutionary benefit. However, more work is needed to uncover other roles for an early face bias, as well as to understand how general biases constrain the visual system so that expertise in individuating similar objects tends to recruit the same neural regions across individuals.

12.1 Introduction

Be they students of development or not, psychologists are fascinated by what newborn babies know, how they learn, and what innate biases they may possess that constrain how and what they eventually learn. Over the last decades, it has become clear that early infancy is a much more exciting time than previously thought for the study of perceptual and cognitive abilities. Exciting debates over the necessity of more than general-purpose learning mechanisms abound, ranging from discussions over word learning (Markson, Chapter 5, this volume) to social learning (Csibra and Gergerly, Chapter 11, this volume). The general issue discussed here, the importance of understanding how these early biases relate to and constrain skills observed later in life, applies across a wide range of domains. However, face processing is a particularly interesting domain in which to address this question. First, numerous studies provide evidence for the specialization of the mechanisms for face processing in both the newborn and the adult. Second, there are indications that the early and late mechanisms differ in nature. And finally, claims have been made (and have been questioned) about innate constraints playing a role in both of these cases. After a brief and selective review of some of this evidence, I will argue that a very difficult challenge lies in understanding the relation between these two mechanisms.

12.2 Constraints on the early (subcortical) face processing system

The newborn is capable of discriminate relatively complex visual stimuli and shows evidence of grouping according to Gestalt principles (Farroni *et al.* 2000). Newborns also demonstrate interesting and sometimes surprising preferences for some patterns over others. For instance, they prefer stimuli with high amplitude and spatial frequency information falling within their peak contrast sensitivity (Banks and Salapatek 1981), novel stimuli over familiar ones (Slater *et al.* 1985), and horizontal over vertical gratings (Farroni *et al.* 2000). Among all such biases, the preference to look at face-like stimuli over scrambled or inverted controls has perhaps received the most attention (Goren *et al.* 1975; Johnson *et al.* 1991). The face preference present in newborns is thought to arise from a subcortical system. This is suggested by findings that the preference is present only when objects are presented in the temporal (and not the nasal) hemifield (Simion *et al.* 1998), an index of extrageniculate mediation, and disappearance of the preference at 6 weeks of age (Mondloch *et al.* 1999), consistent with the timing of a switch from subcortical to cortical influences. This subcortical subsystem is thought to possess a very simple representation of a face, three high-contrast blobs arranged in a triangular formation within a bounded contour. This representation would be suitable only for directing the newborn gaze towards face-like objects, but is insufficient for more elaborate face discrimination. However, newborns demonstrate surprisingly fine visual discrimination skills. For instance, although they show a general bias for global configuration in hierarchical patterns (face-like or not), newborns can also process their local properties, for instance whether the inner features are closed or open-shaped (Cassia *et al.* 2002; Turati and Simion 2002). In addition, there is some evidence that newborns prefer to look at attractive rather than at unattractive faces, and that they do so for upright but not for inverted faces (Slater *et al.* 2000). This later finding in particular suggests a much more complex face recognition apparatus than that which would support only face detection. But whether it reflects a system that is dedicated to faces *per se* is debatable: it may be possible to explain this result using more general biases. This will be discussed below, together with accounts for newborn visual skills that do not require the existence of an innate face template.

There is little dispute over the existence of a preference for face-like stimuli in newborns – the debate concerns what the preference is 'about'. On the one hand, this preference could reflect the action of an innate mechanism (termed CONSPEC by

Morton and Johnson 1991) whose function is to provide the newborn with a template of what a face looks like. On the other hand, it is possible that a number of general biases that have *a priori* nothing to do with faces converge to give faces an advantage in preference studies. Such an idea is often dismissed because it appears implausible that a number of general biases would happen to conspire to produce a face detector. However, this may reflect an attribution error, reflecting the larger saliency (for scientists) of face preferences relative to other types of biases present in the newborn.

As is sometimes forgotten, the newborn visual system can rapidly learn about stimuli that are not faces (Slater *et al.* 1985) and faces do not always win against other types of stimuli: for instance a checkerboard tends to be preferred over a face-like configuration (Morton and Johnson 1991). Therefore, in addition to comparisons between face-like and control stimuli, it is important to also compare different types of non-face stimuli. Such comparisons between non-face stimuli can yield unexpected preferences for non-face stimuli, some of which appear relevant to the interpretation of face preferences. For instance, newborns prefer patterns with more elements in the upper part of a configuration: they prefer elements organized into a T rather than into an inverted T, or into an inverted U than into an upright U (Simion *et al.* 2002). When this top–down bias is pitted against the putative face preference, as in comparing an upright face with a scrambled face that has more elements on top than a normal face, the top–down bias wins (Simion *et al.*, Chapter 8, this volume). These sorts of findings are consistent with a theory accounting for the newborn face preference in terms of a number of domain-general constraints, including both low-level (e.g. contrast and spatial frequency content) and higher-level variables (e.g. top–down bias, congruency between the internal and external elements) (Simion *et al.*, Chapter 8, this volume). In contrast, one may salvage a face-specific explanation by suggesting that a crude face template leads to some of these biases. Do infants prefer upright to inverted faces because they have a top–down bias (a more parsimonious, although seemingly arbitrary, explanation) or do they show a top-heavy bias because of a CONSPEC mechanism (an account that may seem more meaningful)?

One criterion in evaluating the plausibility of a general bias account for face processing is whether such general biases can account for something as high level as newborns' preference for attractive upright, but not inverted, faces (Slater *et al.* 2000). Crucially, newborns can learn very rapidly: they have been shown to develop a preference for a morph of four briefly flashed faces (400 ms each), after only a few repetitions (Walton and Bower 1993). The faces used in the Slater *et al.* experiments were deemed attractive based on ratings by adults, so the attractive faces were likely more symmetrical and average than the unattractive ones (Rhodes *et al.* 2001). The newborns in these experiments were on average over 2 days old, and so would have had enough time, according to the Walton and Bower's (1993) findings, to learn from the few faces they would have seen. The early top-heavy bias may lead to more attention to top-heavy patterns so that a preference for symmetrical and/or average faces only develops for upright faces. Although this is speculative, it illustrates the difficulty of interpreting newborns' skills as innate constraints when placed in the context of the very powerful learning mechanisms they possess. We need to better understand these mechanisms, for instance does the ability to learn faces rapidly rely on domain-specific or on general skills? Unfortunately, studies such as Walton and Bower's have not been conducted with non-face stimuli.

To be fair, there is currently no definitive evidence on whether newborn face perception requires an innate bias for the face geometry. Indeed, this may be mainly a question of interpretation. Even the most conclusive evidence that a face preference arises from a combination of general biases may also be interpreted as Nature's economical way of evolving a face detector. Therefore, I turn to a slightly different question that may be more tractable: whether the early mechanism postulated in the infant (CONSPEC) has an influence on the later development and workings of face specialization in the adult. In the next section I go over some of the evidence for face-selective mechanisms in the adult and go on to argue that there is currently surprisingly little evidence linking these early and late mechanisms.

12.3 Constraints on the adult (cortical) face processing system

Building on a long history of neuropsychological findings suggesting specialization in the human brain for face processing, brain imaging techniques such as PET and fMRI have localized face-selective regions in the ventral temporal lobe (Kanwisher *et al.* 1997; Sergent *et al.* 1992), and more temporally-sensitive techniques such as ERPs and MEGs have revealed early face-sensitive responses arising from the same general visual areas (although the specific match between areas visualized by fMRI and given ERP components is not entirely known (Horovitz *et al.* 2004). The evidence for specialization for faces in the human fusiform gyrus (fusiform face area or FFA) has been reviewed elsewhere and is generally not questioned. Unlike the idea of CONSPEC, this specialization (and the proposed mechanism for its acquisition, CONLERN (Morton and Johnson 1991)) appears to supports the discrimination of individual faces (Gauthier *et al.* 2000b; Grill-Spector *et al.* 2004). Here again, debate centers on the interpretation for this specialization and what its origins may be. I focus on some evidence that bears on possible innate constraints over the development of cortical specialization for faces in humans.

Perhaps the most radical claim about the origin of this cortical mechanism was made on the basis of a single case study (Farah *et al.* 2000). The patient suffered from prosopagnosia acquired as a result of damage to ventral temporo-occipital cortex at 1 day of age (although the exact regions damaged at the time remain unknown). He showed profound impairments with faces and a more moderate deficit with common objects, when tested as a 16-year-old. The authors concluded that 'The distinction between face and object recognition, and the anatomical localization of face recognition, are explicitly specified in the genome' (Farah *et al.* 2000). However, since there is clear evidence for specialization for faces in a consistent region of the adult brain, damaging this region should be expected to impair the development of face recognition even if it is only because this is the best possible part of the visual system for the processing necessary to discriminate faces. An analogy is that abnormalities in parts of the brain that are important for acquiring reading skills may cause developmental dyslexia, without reading being explicitly specified in the genome (Jenner *et al.* 1999).

This idea, that brain areas observed in adults which respond maximally to faces may reflect the recruitment of the neural substrates best suited to the computational requirements posed by face recognition, has been tested in studies of perceptual expertise with other objects. One prediction is that the mere presentation of an object from the expert category would automatically recruit the neural substrates that support the task(s) strongly associated with the category. Therefore, given extensive experience with a category that is homogeneous in a similar way to faces (i.e. all objects share the same number of parts in roughly the same configuration), this account predicts that face recognition mechanisms will be recruited for these objects. Indeed, individuals who are experts with cars or birds show increased FFA activity for objects in their domain of expertise (Gauthier *et al.* 2000a; Xu, 2005). In the best car experts, car activity can even be found to be equivalent or superior to that for faces (Gauthier *et al.* in press). Such specialization can also be obtained for novel objects (called 'greebles'), using a training procedure that is about 8 h long over the course of a couple of weeks (Gauthier *et al.* 1999). ERPs reveal face-like electrophysiological components for both novel objects following training (Rossion *et al.* 2002) and for categories of extant expertise (Gauthier *et al.* 2003; Tanaka and Curran 2001). Importantly, neural effects of expertise are accompanied by, and correlated with, behavioral changes whereby non-face objects are progressively treated in a configural and holistic manner (Gauthier and Tarr 2002). There is disagreement in the literature on whether specialization for objects of expertise arises from *exactly* the same area or neurons as the face-selective responses (Carmel and Bentin 2002; Xu *et al.* 2004). However, for the purpose of elucidating whether face specialization in adults requires an innate predisposition to process the face geometry, these findings are telling. That is, while they may not by themselves refute the domain-specificity of a given marker (e.g. the FFA), they demonstrate that the FFA and/or nearby areas can develop a category specialization without any bias for a specific geometry. The same argument can be made on the basis of specialization for letter strings in the left fusiform cortex (McCandliss *et al.* 2003; Polk *et al.* 2002). For sure, there appear to be constraints that dictate which part of the visual system will be recruited for a given skill or object category – but at least in some cases (e.g. cars, letter strings, houses) these constraints do not include a 'template' of what the objects in a category will look like.

12.4 **The link between the newborn and adult systems**

The demonstration that some specialized mechanisms in the ventral visual cortex can develop without domain-specific constraints offers a proof of existence for one account of how face specialization could develop, and this account makes no use of an early mechanism such as CONSPEC. Turning more directly to developmental evidence, what do we know about the relationship, if any, between the early and late sorts of specialization for faces? Morton and Johnson (1991) raised this question of the interaction between early CONSPEC and the later CONLERN mechanism, useful to learn to discriminate between individual faces. They suggested that there may be no direct interaction between the two systems, and that they may interact indirectly through the environment. That is, 'CONLERN [...] is a nonspecialized learning mechanism. Effectively it learns about the characteristics of faces because the infant pays a lot of attention to them. The role of CONSPEC is to direct this attention.' (p. 175). Interestingly, this account would make it possible for CONLERN to acquire expertise for two domains in exactly the same way even if the motivation to attend to these objects came from very different sources, for instance an innate headstart for faces and a later interest for cars. Many different types of motivations (picking up the skills for a job, hobbies, computer games, performing as well as possible in an experiment) could play the same role as early biases, focusing one's attention on complex stimuli for which a lot of experience is necessary to extract the diagnostic information that allows rapid and efficient processing. But the question arises, why postulate innate bias at all if evidence suggests that it is not necessary? A possibility is that relying on environmental sources of motivation to learn faces (e.g. pairing of faces with familiar voices, or sources of warmth and food) could be too slow or too variable among individuals.

If CONSPEC plays a special role in jumpstarting CONLERN, then a dysfunctional CONSPEC system should lead to problems with CONLERN. This proves to be a difficult question to answer. One may hope to find a relationship in autism, a developmental disorder in which individuals show abnormal face processing (Klin *et al.* 1999) and a lack of specialization for faces in the fusiform gyrus (Pierce *et al.* 2001; Schultz *et al.* 2000). But the idea is difficult to test: autism cannot be diagnosed with any certainty before language develops, and provisional diagnosis is generally not done before 2 years of age. Retrospective studies of home videotapes at 1 year of age suggests a lack of interest in looking at others, but this is more likely to reflect a failure in CONLERN than in CONSPEC, as the later is thought to disappear by 6 weeks of age (Mondloch *et al.* 1999; see also Simion *et al.*, Chapter 8, this volume). Another way to investigate the relationship between CONSPEC and CONLERN would be to study the relationship between individual differences in the CONSPEC preference early in life and later skills at face recognition. Up to now, early preferences have not been related to performance in other tasks.

We thus lack evidence that a problem with a face CONSPEC leads to abnormal face processing later in life. In addition, some results suggest that within the adult visual system, specialization for faces does not necessarily precede specialization for other types of objects. Most people start acquiring face expertise before using similar skills with other objects (in our society, the first non-face expertise may be devoted to homogeneous categories of toys, TV characters, or dinosaurs). But special interests in individuals with autism allow for the possibility of studying specialization for objects of expertise before specialization for faces. Grelotti *et al.* (2004) used fMRI to study a boy (DD) with autism who happened to be an expert with Digimon characters. Like other individuals with autism, DD did not show a response for faces over objects in his fusiform gyrus (Schultz *et al.* 2000). However, Digimon engaged DD's fusiform gyrus more than objects and faces, even if the Digimon faces were blanked. Neither an expertise effect for objects in the fusiform gyrus or the lack of fusiform activity to faces in people with autism are new findings, but the combination of the two in the same individual demonstrates that specialization for objects in the visual system does not require prior specialization for faces. This evidence adds to that from several studies indicating that normal individuals can acquire expertise with objects such as birds, cars, greebles, or fingerprints, and demonstrate behavioral and neural effects similar to those obtained with faces, without a headstart from a CONSPEC-like mechanism. In fact, the same argument holds for other proposed biases such as the top–down bias (Simion *et al.*, Chapter 8, this volume): there is at the present time no evidence that such biases influence the later acquisition of expertise for faces or any other object.

12.5 Looking in other directions

I have argued that we are limited in our understanding of the constraints placed on the development of face processing by a lack of data that speaks to the causal relationship between the functions of early biases such as CONSPEC and later mechanisms such as CONLERN. I would like to end by suggesting that perhaps CONSPEC is necessary for some adult functions, just not for CONLERN, and that CONLERN is constrained by early biases, but perhaps not by CONSPEC or even the top-heavy bias. We may be fooled by the superficial similarity of these mechanisms (which both seem to be 'about' faces) into forgetting that they are part of a much more complex system: there are many unexplored avenues for how these mechanisms may relate to other ways in which faces are processed. For instance, one piece of evidence that CONLERN is constrained by early experiences is that deprivation of patterned visual input to the right hemisphere in early infancy results in an impairment in configural processing for faces (and possibly other objects, this has not been tested (Le Grand *et al.* 2003)). Likewise, CONSPEC could be a necessary trigger for the development of skills other than recognition of individual faces, including emotional face processing or social learning (Csibra and Gergely, Chapter 11, this volume). Therefore, instead of debating whether a given skill is constrained or not by early biases, more important challenges exist: that of investigating the constraining effects of specific early preferences and of figuring out which combination of all the mechanisms present in the newborn influence any given skill observed later in life.

References

Banks MS and Salapatek P (1981). Infant pattern vision: a new approach based on the contrast sensitivity function. *Journal of Experimental Child Psychology*, 31, 1–45.

Baron-Cohen S (1994). How to build a baby that can read minds: Cognitive mechanisms in mind-reading. *Current Psychology of Cognition*, 13, 513–552.

Carmel D and Bentin S (2002). Domain specificity versus expertise: factors influencing distinct processing of faces. *Cognition*, 83, 1–29.

Cassia VM, Simion F, Milani I and Umilta C (2002). Dominance of global visual properties at birth. *Journal of Experimental Psychology: General*, 131, 398–411.

de Schonen S, Mancini J and Leigeois F (1998). About functional cortical specialization: The development of face recognition. In: F Simion and G Butterworth, eds. *The development of sensory, motor, and cognitive capacities in early infancy*, pp.103–120. East Sussex, UK: Psychology Press.

Diamond R and Carey S (1986). Why faces are and are not special: An effect of expertise. *Journal of Experimental Psychology: General*, 115, 107–117.

Farah MJ, Rabinowitz C, Quinn GE and Liu GT (2000). Early commitment of neural substrates for face recognition. *Cognitive Neuropsychology*, 17, 117–124.

Farroni T, Valenza E, Simion F and Umilta C (2000). Configural processing at birth: evidence for perceptual organisation. *Perception*, 29, 355–372.

Gauthier I, Curby KM, and Epstein RA (in press). Activity of spatial frequency channels in the fusiform face-selective area relates to expertise in ear recognition. *Cognitive and Affective Behavioural Neuroscience*.

Gauthier I, Curran T, Curby KM and Collins D (2003). Perceptual interference supports a non-modular account of face processing. *Nature Neuroscience*, 6, 428–432.

Gauthier I and Nelson CA (2001). The development of face expertise. *Current Opinion in Neurobiology*, 11, 219–224.

Gauthier I, Skudlarski P, Gore JC and Anderson AW (2000). Expertise for cars and birds recruits brain areas involved in face recognition. *Nature Neuroscience*, 3, 191–197.

Gauthier I and Tarr MJ (1997). Becoming a "Greeble" expert: exploring mechanisms for face recognition. *Vision Research*, 37, 1673–1682.

Gauthier I and Tarr MJ (2002). Unraveling mechanisms for expert object recognition: Bridging brain activity and behavior. *Journal of Experimental Psychology: Human Perception and Performance*, 28, 431–446.

Gauthier I, Tarr MJ, Anderson AW, Skudlarski P and Gore JC (1999). Activation of the middle fusiform 'face area' increases with expertise in recognizing novel objects. *Nature Neuroscience*, 2, 568–573.

Gauthier I, Tarr MJ, Moylan J, Anderson AW, Skudlarski P and Gore JC (2000). The fusiform "face area" is part of a network that processes faces at the individual level. *Journal of Cognitive Neuroscience*, 12, 495–504.

Goren C, Sarty M and Wu P (1975). Visual following and pattern discrimination of face-like stimuli by newborn infants. *Pediatrics*, 56, 544–549.

Grelotti DJ, Klin AJ, Gauthier I, Skudlarski P, Cohen DJ, Gore JC, *et al.* (2005). fMRI activation of the fusiform gyrus and amygdala to cartoon characters but not to faces in a boy with autism. *Neuropsychologia*, 43, 373–385.

Grill-Spector K, Knouf N and Kanwisher N (2004). The fusiform face area subserves face perception, not generic within-category identification. *Nature Neuroscience*, 7, 555–562.

Horovitz SG, Rossion B, Skudlarski P and Gore JC (2004). Parametric design and correlational analyses help integrating fMRI and electrophysiological data during face processing. *Neuroimage*, 22, 1587–1595.

Jenner AR, Rosen GD and Galaburda AM (1999). Neuronal asymmetries in primary visual cortex of dyslexic and nondyslexic brains. *Annals of Neurology*, 46, 189–196.

Johnson MH, Dziurawiec S, Ellis H and Morton J (1991). Newborns' preferential tracking of face-like stimuli and its subsequent decline. *Cognition*, 40, 1–19.

Kanwisher N, McDermott J and Chun MM (1997). The fusiform face area: A module in human extrastriate cortex specialized for face perception. *Journal of Neuroscience*, 17, 4302–4311.

Klin A, Sparrow SS, de Bildt A, Cicchetti DV, Cohen DJ and Volkmar FR (1999). A normed study of face recognition in autism and related disorders. *Journal of Autism and Developmental Disorders*, 29, 499–508.

Le Grand R, Mondloch CJ, Maurer D and Brent HP (2003). Expert face processing requires visual input to the right hemisphere during infancy. *Nature Neuroscience*, 6, 1108–1112.

McCandliss BD, Cohen L and Dehaene S (2003). The visual word form area: expertise for reading in the fusiform gyrus. *Trends in Cognitive Science*, 7, 293–299.

Mondloch CJ, Lewis TL, Budreau DR, Maurer D, Dannemiller JL, Stephens BR, *et al.* (1999). Face perception during early infancy. *Psychological Science*, 10, 419–422.

Morton J and Johnson MH (1991). CONSPEC and CONLERN: A two-process theory of infant face recognition. *Psychological Review*, 98, 164–181.

Pierce K, Muller RA, Ambrose J, Allen G and Courshenes E (2001). Face processing occurs outside the fusiform 'face area' in autism: evidence form functional MRI. *Brain*, 124, 2059–2073.

Polk TA, Stallcup M, Aguirre GK, Alsop DC, D'Esposito M, Detre JA, *et al.* (2002). Neural Specialization for Letter Recognition. *Journal of Cognitive Neuroscience*, 14, 145–159.

Rhodes G, Yoshikawa S, Clark A, Lee K, McKay R and Akamatsu S (2001). Attractiveness of facial averageness and symmetry in non-western cultures: in search of biologically based standards of beauty. *Perception*, 30, 611–625.

Rossion B, Gauthier I, Goffaux V, Tarr MJ and Crommelinck M (2002). Expertise training with novel objects leads to left lateralized face-like electrophysiological responses. *Psychological Science*, 13, 250–257.

Rubin N, Nakayama K and Shapley R (1996). Enhanced perception of illusory contours in the lower versus upper visual hemifields. *Science*, 271, 651–653.

Schultz RT, Gauthier I, Klin A, Fulbright RK, Anderson AW, Volkmar F, *et al.* (2000). Abnormal ventral temporal cortical activity during face discrimination among individuals with autism and Asperger syndrome. *Archives of General Psychiatry*, 37, 331–340.

Sergent J, Ohta S and MacDonald B (1992). Functional neuroanatomy of face and object processing: A positron emission tomography study. *Brain*, 115, 15–36.

Simion F, Valenza E, Macchi Cassia V, Turati C and Umiltà C (2002). Newborns' preference for up-down asymmetrical configurations. *Developmental Science*, 5, 427–434.

Simion F, Valenza E, Umilta C and Dalla Barba B (1998). Preferential orienting to faces in newborns: a temporal-nasal asymmetry. *Journal of Experimental Psychology: Human Perception and Performance*, **24**, 1399–1405.

Slater A, Earle DC, Morison V and Rose D (1985). Pattern preferences at birth and their interaction with habituation-induced novelty preferences. *Journal of Experimental Child Psychology*, **39**, 37–54.

Slater A, Quinn PC, Hayes R and Brown E (2000). The role of facial orientation in newborn infant's preference for attractive faces. *Developmental Science*, **3**, 181–185.

Tanaka JW and Curran T (2001). A neural basis for expert object recognition. *Psychological Science*, **12**, 43–47.

Turati C and Simion F (2002). Newborns' recognition of changing and unchanging aspects of schematic faces. *Journal of Experimental Child Psychology*, **83**, 239–261.

Walton GE and Bower TGR (1993). Newborns form "prototypes" in less than 1 minute. *Psychological Science*, **4**, 203–205.

Xu Y (2005). Revisiting the role of the fusiform face area in visual expertise. *Cerebral Cortex*, **15** (8), 1234–1242.

Xu Y, Liu J and Kanwisher N (2004). The M170 is selective for faces, not for expertise. *Neuropsychologia*, in press.

Part 3

Representational change

Chapter 13

Different profiles of plasticity within human cognition

Helen J. Neville

Abstract

Behavioral, event related potentials (ERP), and magnetic resonance imaging (MRI) studies of the development and plasticity of visual processing, auditory processing, attention, and language are reviewed. The results show that within each domain of processing there is considerable variability in the degree to which, and the time periods when, different subsystems are modifiable by experience. Some subsystems appear highly constrained and are not different even when experience is very different. Others are dependent on, and modified by, experience but only during specific time periods in human development. Still other subsystems appear to be changeable throughout life. Taken together these data raise testable hypotheses about the mechanisms of neuroplasticity.

13.1 Introduction

One of the questions that has occupied the minds of parents, educators, and philosophers for millennia, is at the heart of the research I describe here: the nature of, and the interactions between, biological constraints and the role of experience (i.e. input from the environment) in human cognitive and neural development. Although this issue has long been central in philosophical and societal debate, it has only been systematically researched over the past 40 years. It began, of course, with the work of Hubel and Weisel and their followers, who reported marked effects of visual experience on the development of visual cortex and related functions (Wiesel and Hubel 1965). Until recently, most of this research had been performed with non-human animals and was concerned with sensory development. With the advent of non-invasive methods for imaging the human brain, we can now more directly seek answers to the following questions about the human mind/brain: to what extent do different brain systems possess intrinsic constraints that make them capable of processing some but not other types of information? What is the role of inputs from the environment in specifying the functional properties of the brain regions they contact?

These are fundamental questions about who we are and where we come from. On a practical level, answers to these questions can contribute information important to the design of educational and rehabilitative programs in that they will help us identify the functional brain systems that are most modifiable and the time periods when they are most modifiable.

Over the past several years, we have approached these questions in two ways. In the first, we have compared cerebral organization in normally hearing, seeing, monolingual, speaking adults with that observed in individuals who have had altered sensory and/or language experience. This latter group includes deaf and blind adults, bilinguals who learned English at different ages, and those who have learned a visual/manual language. The second approach has been to compare brain organization in children of different ages and stages of cognitive development, as well as before and after various intervention programs. In these studies we have used both ERPs and MRI methods. We have studied the development of perceptual/attentional systems, as well as the development of the language systems of the brain.

In this chapter, I first review the structural development of the human brain, relevant literatures on sensory plasticity, as well as our newer studies of sensory plasticity and development. Second, I review literature relevant to the plasticity and development of the language systems, as well as our newer studies along these lines.

13.2 **Structural development of the human brain**

The structural development of the human brain displays a protracted timecourse of postnatal development that in some regions does not reach maturity until the third decade of life. There is great variability in the rate of maturation of different neural systems and subsystems, as indexed by the extent of dendritic branching, number of dendritic spines, neuronal size and density, number and type of synapses, pharmacological composition, grey to white matter ratios, and cortical volumes (Chugani *et al.* 1987; Huttenlocher and Dabholkar 1997; Neville 1998). Following this protracted development, the mature human brain is a complex mosaic of systems and subsystems that display considerable specificity in their functional properties. A burgeoning literature has identified several molecular and genetic factors important in specifying aspects of the initial anatomy and physiology of developing brain systems in animals (Kahn and Krubitzer 2002; Krubitzer and Huffman 2000; Silver *et al.* 2001; Taha and Stryker 2002). The overarching goals of the research summarized in this chapter are to characterize both biological constraints, and the degree to which, and the time periods during which, the functional specializations of different neural systems are dependent on, and modifiable by, experience in human development.

13.3 Intra- and intermodal plasticity

During the past 30 years, research with animals has documented marked and specific effects of both sensory deprivation and training on the organization of cortical areas that represent a particular sensory system and on the development of remaining sensory modalities (Frost *et al.* 2000; Metin and Frost 1989; Roe *et al.* 1992; Sur and Garraghty 1986; von Melchner *et al.* 2000). These studies have shown that some neural systems and associated behavioral capabilities are affected by such experience only during specific time periods (sensitive periods) and that different systems have different sensitive periods. For example within the visual system, the development of acuity, orientation preferences, ocular dominance columns, stereopsis, and photoptic and scotopic vision display different sensitive periods (Harwerth *et al.* 1986; Horton and Hocking 1997; Hubel and Wiesel 1977; Mitchell 1990). This variability in the timing of experience-dependent modifiability likely arises in part from subsystem differences in rate of maturation, extent and timing of redundant connectivity and presence of chemicals and receptors known to be important in plasticity. By contrast, some neural systems appear not to be constrained by sensitive periods. For example, remapping of the representation of the visual fields following retinal lesions can occur throughout life (Kaas *et al.* 1990), as can remapping of the primary cortical representation of the digits following amputation or training (Merzenich and Jenkins 1993).

Recent studies support the view that in humans, as in other animals, there is considerable variability in experience-dependent plasticity. For example if cataracts are not removed by 5 months of age, visual acuity never reaches normal values, and if convergent input to the two eyes is not achieved by 11 months of age, stereopsis is not acquired (Maurer *et al.* 1999; Tychsen 2001). In addition, lack of patterned visual input during the first 2 to 6 months of age results in permanent deficits in configural but not featural aspects of face processing (Le Grand *et al.* 2001), and visual deprivation occurring as late as 6 years of age leads to deficits in the ability to orient to peripheral visual information (Kovacs *et al.* 2000). In contrast, other systems appear not to show sensitive period effects in humans: for example amputation in adults results in reorganization of cortical areas that formerly represented the lost limb (Elbert *et al.* 1994; Ramachandran *et al.* 1992).

13.4 Plasticity within the visual system after auditory deprivation

13.4.1 Motion and color

Anatomical, physiological, and psychophysical evidence from several lines of investigation has defined the distinction between the dorsal visual pathway, projecting from V1 to parietal cortex, that includes structures important for the processing of spatial location and motion, and the ventral visual pathway, projecting from V1 to anterior inferior temporal cortices, that includes systems important for processing color and form information (Tootell *et al.* 1995; Ungerleider and Mishkin 1982). Further evidence confirmed that the central visual field is largely represented along the ventral pathway while the peripheral visual fields are largely represented along the dorsal pathway (Baizer *et al.* 1991). Consistent with this, in several early studies we observed that sensory and attentional processing of visual information presented to the central and peripheral visual fields elicits activity in different neural systems in normally hearing adults. Furthermore, we observed that congenital auditory deprivation – but not the acquisition of American Sign Language (ASL) – results in enhanced detection of motion and enhanced ERPs in the peripheral (but not the central) visual fields (Neville *et al.* 1983; Neville and Lawson 1987a, 1987b, 1987c; Neville 1995). These results suggested the hypothesis that the dorsal visual pathway might be more modified following auditory deprivation than the ventral pathway. To test this, we used stimuli designed to selectively activate either the parvocellular neurons that project strongly (but not solely, see, Sawatari and Callaway 1996; Stoner and Albright 1993) to the ventral pathway or the magnocellular system that projects strongly to the dorsal pathway. The parvo system is highly responsive to color information and to stimuli of high spatial frequency, while the magno system is very responsive to motion and to stimuli of low spatial frequency and low contrast (Livingstone and Hubel 1988; Merigan and Maunsell 1993).

We tested normal hearing and congenitally deaf participants. Peripheral stimuli were presented 8° from the central (foveal) stimulus in the upper and lower left and right visual fields. The parvo stimuli were isoluminant blue and green high spatial frequency gratings (adjusted for the cortical magnification factor) continuously visible at all locations. The eliciting stimulus was a color change: randomly at one location, the blue bars changed to red for 100 ms. The magno stimuli consisted of low spatial frequency gratings of light and dark gray bars with a low luminance contrast. The eliciting stimulus consisted of the bars at one location (random) moving transversely to the right for 100 ms. Research participants fixated centrally and monitored all locations for the rare occurrence of a black square (Armstrong *et al.* 2002).

In normal hearing adults the color and motion stimuli elicited ERPs that differed in their componentry, latencies, and distributions, and were consistent with the hypothesis that these stimuli activated distinct neural systems. An early positivity (100 ms) focal to medial occipital regions was largest in response to motion, and a later, lateral (130 ms) positivity was larger in response to color changes. In addition, the latency of the negativity around 170 ms (N170) was faster to motion stimuli. The earliest responses (P100, P130) were similar in deaf and hearing participants, suggesting that processing within early visual cortical areas may be unaffected by auditory deprivation. The N170 component was similar in response to color changes in deaf and hearing participants, but in response to motion it was significantly larger and was distributed more anteriorly in deaf than hearing participants (Fig. 13.1). These results

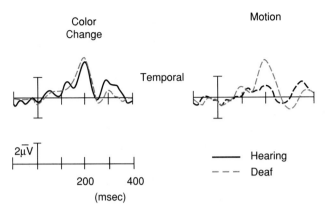

Fig. 13.1 ERPs to color and motion in normally hearing and congenitally deaf adults.

were more pronounced for peripheral than central motion. These results are consistent with the hypothesis that early auditory deprivation has more pronounced effects on the functions of the dorsal than the ventral visual pathway.

13.4.2 **Motion processing**

Too more precisely identify the visual areas that might underlie the enhanced behavioral and ERP responses to motion in deaf participants we employed the functional magnetic imaging (fMRI) technique (details in Bavelier *et al.* 2000). In particular, we tested the hypothesis that the middle temporal areas (MT/MST), shown in previous studies to be responsive to motion and attention to motion, displays enhanced activation in deaf as compared to hearing individuals. Participants included hearing and congenitally, genetically deaf individuals who viewed alternating blocks of static dots and flow fields of moving dots. Motion flow fields strongly recruit the motion pathway, including the motion-selective area MT/MST (O'Craven *et al.* 1997; Tootell and Taylor 1995). On separate runs, participants attended the center or the periphery (6–8°) of the display to detect luminance changes.

MT/MST was identified individually for each participant and the data were analyzed for each participant by computing the temporal correlation between the magnetic resonance (MR) signal and a reference function for each voxel. Analyses of the extent of activation in MT/MST revealed that whereas MT/MST recruitment was comparable across populations when the center of the visual field was monitored, deaf individuals displayed greater MT/MST activation than hearing participants when the peripheral visual field was monitored. This finding indicates a specific modulation of attention to peripheral moving stimuli in the deaf and suggests that changes in MT may have contributed to the behavioral and ERP effects described in our previous research (Neville and Lawson 1987b).

To further characterize the altered MT activation in the deaf, we used structural equation modeling to estimate the strength of cortical connections between early visual areas (V1/V2), area MT/MST, and part of the posterior parietal cortex (PPC) (Beauchamp and DeYoe 1996; Buchel and Friston 1997; McIntosh and Gonzalez-Lima 1994). During attention to the center the connectivity was comparable across groups but during the attend-periphery condition the effective connectivity between MT/MST and PPC was increased in the deaf as compared with the hearing participants. This finding suggests that the enhanced responsiveness to peripheral motion in deaf individuals may be specifically linked to attention.

13.4.3 Motion velocity

In this study we further characterized the effects of auditory deprivation on several motion sensitive areas and separated them from the effects of the acquisition of ASL (Bavelier *et al.* 2001). Congenitally deaf and hearing native signers and normally hearing controls attended either the center or periphery of a moving flow field to detect a transient acceleration of the dots. Cortical areas V1/V2, MT/MST, V3A, PPC, and posterior superior temporal sulcus (pSTS) were delineated separately for each individual on the basis of functional and anatomical criteria. We observed marked and specific differences in the recruitment of motion related areas as a function of sensory and language experience. Both of the hearing populations displayed better behavioral performance and greater recruitment of MT/MST under central than peripheral attention, whereas the opposite pattern was observed in deaf signers, indicating enhanced peripheral attention following early deafness *per se*. In addition, deaf signers, but neither of the hearing populations, displayed an overall increase in the activation of the PPC, supporting the view that parietal functions are significantly modified after early auditory deprivation. Finally, only in deaf signers did attention to motion velocity result in enhanced recruitment of the pSTS, establishing for the first time functionally specific compensatory plasticity in this polymodal area following altered sensory experience. These results add further support to the proposal that experience-dependent plasticity in humans can be highly specific and is likely constrained both by features of the biological substrates involved and by functionally driven processes.

In these studies, as in every other study mapping the visual field and visual attention in humans, the stimuli did not extend past 20° eccentricity, which is considered the beginning of the periphery. Recently (Scott *et al.* 2003), we have employed fMRI to map cortical areas sensitive to visual stimuli presented from the center of the visual field to the far periphery (2–80° eccentricity) (Scott *et al.* 2003). Mapping was performed along a single radial direction in four visual field quadrants, in each of four adult participants (Fig. 13.1a). A V1 mapping was clearly identified for 16 of 16 quadrants. A V2 mapping was found for 12 of 16 quadrants, though not always to the most peripheral locations. In all participants, several other occipital-parietal areas also showed retinotopic or non-retinotopic visual activation. Some of these only contained representations of the far periphery. These maps were used to estimate cortical distance as a function of eccentricity (cortical magnification factor). The cortical magnification estimate was about 20 per cent more shallow than previous estimates using other mapping techniques in the central visual field ($<20°$) (Engel *et al.* 1997). Our retinotopic mapping was performed with focused attention at the stimulus location. However, we also repeated a portion of the experiments with attention focused at the fixation point or with two or four simultaneously attended stimuli (always in different visual field quadrants). In each of these cases, the magnitude of activity was decreased or absent for more eccentric locations ($>20°$). As the stimulation was identical across these experiments, this result suggests that the cortical representation of space was modulated with attention and, further, that this effect increased with increasing eccentricity. Indeed this modulation with attention could have altered the cortical magnification estimate with respect to previous mapping studies that have not manipulated focused spatial attention. In ongoing research we are explicitly testing this hypothesis. In addition, we are testing the hypothesis that the effects of attention, and the extent of plastic changes in the deaf, increase with increasing eccentricity.

13.5 Plasticity and vulnerability

We are also conducting studies to assess the hypothesis that the same subsystems that display the greatest plasticity and are enhanced in deaf individuals are more vulnerable in development and will display the greatest deficits in developmental disorders, including dyslexia. A considerable body of research has reported selective deficits among at least some individuals with dyslexia in functions mediated by the magnocellular, but not parvocellular, visual pathway (Cornelissen *et al.* 1995; Everatt *et al.* 1999; Hansen *et al.* 2001; Lovegrove *et al.* 1986; Sperling *et al.* 2003; Talcott *et al.* 1998, 2000). Individuals with dyslexia also show reduced (Demb *et al.* 1998) or even non-significant (Eden 1996) activations in motion-sensitive areas MT/MST when processing motion stimuli, and evidence from post mortem autopsies reveal abnormalities in the magnocellular, but not parvocelluar, layers of the lateral geniculate nucleus (LGN) of adults with dyslexia (Livingstone *et al.* 1991).

This pattern of results has been taken to support the hypothesis that the deficits observed in visual M-pathway functions are reflective of a more general deficit in magnocellular pathways throughout the brain, including those in the medial geniculate nucleus that subserve auditory processing (Stein and Talcott 1999). An impairment in fast-processing streams could result in poor temporal integration of stimuli from the two modalities during reading, which requires both visuo-orthographic and auditory-phonological representations of letters (Breznitz and Maya 2003). However, previous research on M- versus P-pathway visual deficits has been criticized on the grounds that the tasks used to assess M-pathway function are typically more attentionally and cognitively demanding than those used to assess P-pathway function (Newport *et al.* 2002). It remains unclear whether the selective M-pathway deficits observed could be explained by attentional differences in individuals with dyslexia. Preliminary data from our laboratory suggests that the visual deficit in adults with dyslexia persists even for 'simple' tasks of M-pathway function. In this study, participants indicated at which point in the far periphery (~50°) they detected a dot moving along a straight trajectory to the center of vision. Whereas deaf participants detected the moving dots significantly sooner (i.e. at greater eccentricity) than controls, participants with dyslexia detected them significantly later than controls. By contrast, both groups performed within normal limits on a detection task in the center of the visual field (Darves and Neville 2004). These data together with other lines of evidence (Atkinson *et al.* 1997; Bellugi *et al.* 2000) support the hypothesis that more modifiable systems may be more vulnerable in developmental disorders.

13.6 Development of visual pathways

As noted, many investigators have documented greater vulnerability of the dorsal pathway in developmental disorders including dyslexia (Eden 1996; Galaburda and Livingstone 1993; Lovegrove *et al.* 1990, Lovegrove 1993; Livingstone *et al.* 1991) and Williams syndrome (Atkinson *et al.* 1997; Bellugi *et al.* 2000). In recent experiments, we tested the hypothesis that the greater modifiability/vulnerability may arise in part from a longer maturational period of the dorsal system, since the available evidence (largely psychophysical) on this is currently conflicting (Dobkins and Teller 1996; Hickey 1977; Hollants-Gilhuijs *et al.* 1998a, 1998b; Johnson *et al.* 2001). We recently tested 30 children, aged 6 to 10, on the same paradigm that we used in studies of deaf and hearing adults (Armstrong *et al.* 2002; Mitchell and Neville in press). ERPs were recorded to the same stimuli employed in the study of ERPs to color and motion in adults described above and in Armstrong and colleagues (2002). Whereas in adults the latency of the N100 responses to the motion stimuli were significantly earlier than the N100 latencies to the color stimuli (consistent with studies of single neurons in the two pathways), all of the children displayed the opposite pattern: responses to motion were slower than those to color (Fig. 13.2). Moreover, latencies to the color changes were equivalent in the children and adults, but the children's responses to motion were slower than those of adults (Fig. 13.2).

Additional evidence for the relative immaturity of the motion responses was evident in the amplitudes: whereas the color and motion responses were of equivalent amplitude in the adults, in children the ERP amplitudes to motion were considerably smaller than were those to color. Thus these data are consistent with the hypothesis that the greater vulnerability/modifiability of the dorsal stream may be due in part to its more protracted development.

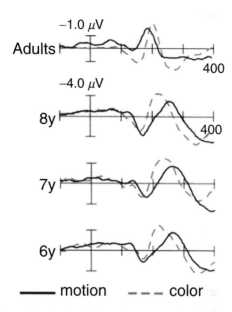

Fig. 13.2 ERPs to motion and color in adults and 6-, 7-, and 8-year-old children.

13.7 Plasticity within the auditory system after visual deprivation

To test the generality of the results from our studies of the effects of auditory deprivation, we conducted studies of the effects of visual deprivation on the development of remaining sensory systems. Although relatively little is known about the organization of the auditory system, as in the visual system there are larger (magno) cells in the medial geniculate nucleus that conduct faster than the smaller parvo cells, and recent evidence suggests that there may be dorsal and ventral processing streams with different functional specializations (Rauschecker 1995). Furthermore, animal and human studies of blindness have reported changes in parietal cortex (i.e. dorsal pathway). To determine whether parallel patterns of plasticity occur following auditory and visual deprivation we developed two auditory paradigms that are parallel to visual paradigms that we had previously employed in studies of the deaf.

In the first paradigm, participants detected infrequent pitch changes in a series of tones that were preceded by different interstimulus intervals (Röder *et al.* 1999a). Congenitally blind participants were faster at detecting the targets and displayed ERPs that were less refractory, that is, recovered amplitude faster than normally sighted research participants. These results are parallel to those from our study showing faster amplitude recovery of the visual ERP in deaf than hearing participants (Neville *et al.* 1983) and suggest that rapid auditory and visual processing may show specific enhancements following sensory deprivation.

In a second experiment, we tested the generality of our finding of a specific enhancement of the representation of the visual periphery in deaf participants. We first developed a paradigm to compare attention to central and peripheral auditory space in normal controls (Teder-Salejarvi *et al.* 1999a). Participants attended selectively to brief noise bursts delivered in free-field via central and peripheral arrays of speakers extending from midline to 90° right of center. In separate runs, participants selectively attended to the center or rightmost speaker to detect infrequent 'target' stimuli occurring at that location. Behavioral detection rates and concurrently recorded ERPs indicated that attentional gradients were steeper for the central than the peripheral array, indicating that attention can be more sharply focused on sound sources directly in front of the listener. In the study of congenitally blind participants, we observed that, when attending central auditory space, blind and sighted participants displayed similar localization abilities and ERP attention effects. In contrast, blind participants were superior to sighted controls at localizing sounds in peripheral auditory space and ERPs revealed sharper tuning of early spatial attention mechanisms in the blind individuals only when attending the periphery (Röder *et al.* 1999b). Differences in the scalp distribution of brain electrical activity between the two groups suggested a compensatory reorganization of visual areas in the blind that may contribute to the improved spatial resolution for peripheral sound sources.

13.8 Development of sustained attention

The results showing increased auditory attention in the blind suggest that auditory attention may also be a system displaying a long developmental timecourse. Behavioral studies have indicated that auditory selective attention skills develop throughout childhood at least until adolescence. Both the abilities to selectively attend to relevant stimuli and to successfully ignore irrelevant stimuli improve progressively with increasing age across childhood (Doyle 1973; Geffen and Sexton 1978; Geffen and Wale 1979; Hiscock and Kinsbourne 1980; Lane and Pearson 1982; Maccoby and Konrad 1966; Sexton and Geffen 1979; Zukier and Hagen 1978). The ability to shift attention quickly and effectively also develops across childhood, at least until adolescence (Andersson and Hugdahl 1987; Geffen and Wale 1979; Hiscock and Kinsbourne 1980; Pearson and Lane 1991). Furthermore, there is some evidence that background noise creates greater masking effects for younger children as compared to adolescents or adults (Elliott 1979).

Although behavioral studies offer evidence for the development of selective auditory attention in school-age children, there is little comparable electrophysiological evidence from children in this age range. One published study employed a typical ERP dichotic listening attention paradigm using tones and syllables with young participants (groups with mean age 8 and 14 years) (Berman and Friedman 1995). The expected effect of attention (increased NI amplitude or Nd) was observed in all participants, with Nd amplitude increasing with age, more so for syllables than for tones. The primary effect of age appeared to be smaller negative ERPs elicited by stimuli in the unattended channel, which the authors suggested might reflect a narrowing of attentional focus or greater facility in suppressing unattended inputs with age (Berman and Friedman 1995).

Moreover, in the selective auditory attention paradigm, the expected N100 attention effect was observed in control adolescents aged 12 to 14 (Loiselle *et al.* 1980). Other studies have reported similar attention effects in adolescent boys (Lovrich *et al.* 1983; Zambelli *et al.* 1977).

Recently we developed a dichotic listening task to characterize the development of sustained auditory attention across the early school age years. Our paradigm was modeled after those that we and many others have employed in adults (Hillyard *et al.* 1973; Röder *et al.* 1999b; Spezio *et al.* 2000; Teder-Salejarvi *et al.* 1999a, Teder-Salejarvi *et al.* 1999b; Woods *et al.* 1984) and was designed to be difficult enough to demand and switch focused selective attention alone, while keeping the physical stimuli, arousal levels, and task demands constant (Coch *et al.* in press; Woods *et al.* 2002a, 2002b). Two children's stories (one read by a man, one by a woman) were presented concurrently from speakers to the left and right of a central monitor. Participants were asked to attend to one story and ignore the other. Every so often the stories switched sides and a pointing cartoon character on the monitor reminded research participants to follow the attended story to the other side. Superimposed on the stories were linguistic and non-linguistic 'probe' stimuli to which ERPs were recorded: these were a 100 ms token of the syllable *ba* and a 100 ms 'buzz' created by scrambling 6 ms segments of the *ba* so that the frequency spectra and other acoustic characterizations of the two stimuli were the same. After the experiment, participants were asked questions about the attended and unattended stories.

We first tested 16 adults on this paradigm. ERPs to the attended and unattended probes elicited the classic effects of auditory attention including enhanced negativity to the probes when attention was directed toward as compared to away from them (Fig. 13.3). We then tested 24 6-year-olds, 24 7-year-olds, and 24 8-year-olds. Behaviorally, all groups performed well; however, the percent of correctly answered questions increased with age for the attended story and decreased for the unattended story. The ERPs from each age group showed clear and significant attention effects, however, these were opposite in polarity to those in the adults; that is, when attended, probes elicited greater positivity than when unattended (Fig. 13.3). However, the attention effect to the non-linguistic probes displayed an anterior bilateral distribution in all groups. The attention effect to the linguistic probes displayed a different distribution in the children and adults. These results indicate that slowly developing, non-identical neural systems mediate aspects of linguistic and non-linguistic auditory attention.

13.9 **Plasticity within the language systems**

It is reasonable to propose that the principles and mechanisms that govern the development of sensory systems also guide the development of neural systems important for language processing. In particular, to the extent that different subsystems within language depend on non-identical neural substrates with different developmental time courses, it is likely that they display different patterns of experience-

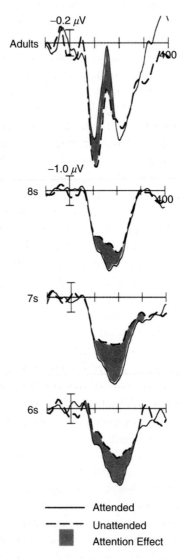

Fig. 13.3 Effects of selective auditory attention on ERPs from adults and 6-, 7-, and 8-year-old children.

dependent plasticity. One way this question has been investigated is to compare cerebral organization in adults who learned language at different times in development.

13.9.1 Delayed second language acquisition

Changes in several postnatal maturational processes during neural development have been implicated as potential mechanisms underlying sensitive period phenomena. Lenneberg (1967) hypothesized that maturational processes similar to those that govern sensory and motor development may also constrain capabilities for normal language acquisition. In this study, we investigated the hypothesis that maturational constraints may have different effects upon the development of the functional specializations of distinct subsystems within language (Weber-Fox and Neville 1996a). Research participants were Chinese/English bilinguals who were exposed to English at different points in development. ERPs and behavioral responses were obtained as participants read sentences that included semantic anomalies, three types of syntactic violations (phrase structure, specificity constraint, and subjacency constraint), and their controls. Accuracy in judging the grammaticality of the different types of syntactic sentences and their associated ERPs were affected by delays in second language exposure as short as 4 to 6 years. By comparison, the N400 response and the behavioral accuracy in detecting semantic anomalies were altered only in participants who were exposed to English after 11 to 13 and 16 years of age, respectively. Furthermore, the type of ERP changes concomitant with delays in exposure were qualitatively different for semantic and syntactic processing. All groups displayed a significant N400 effect in response to semantic anomalies. However, the peak latencies of the N400 elicited in bilinguals who were exposed to English between 11 and 13 and greater than 16 years occurred later, suggesting a slight slowing in processing. For syntactic processing, ERP differences associated with delays in exposure to English were observed in the morphology and distribution of components. Our findings are consistent with the view that maturational changes significantly constrain the development of neural systems relevant for language, and, in addition, that subsystems specialized for processing different aspects of language display different sensitive periods (Weber-Fox and Neville 1996b).

In similar groups of monolingual and Chinese/English bilinguals we compared responses to open- and closed-class words embedded in normal, written sentences to further explore the hypothesis that there are different effects of delays in language exposure on the processing of words that carry different amounts of semantic and grammatical information (Weber-Fox and Neville 1999). Whereas the latencies and distributions of the N350 response to open-class words were similar in all groups of research participants, the peak latency of the N280 response to closed-class words was significantly delayed in all groups exposed to English after 7 years of age. In both of these studies we were able to separately assess the contributions of age of exposure and years of experience. The results clearly show that delays in L2 acquisition have more pronounced effects on grammatical than on lexical–semantic aspects of language processing.

13.9.2 Sentence processing in American Sign Language

The study of ASL provides a rare opportunity to determine which of the language-relevant aspects of cerebral organization are independent of the modality of language production and perception and so therefore may be candidates for biological universals of language. It also provides the opportunity to isolate those modality-specific effects that are determined by the nature of language experience. In several studies we have attempted to extend to ASL our findings from studies of English that suggest that different subsystems mediate aspects of grammatical and semantic processing and that subsystems have different sensitive periods. In addition, we investigated different hypotheses that could account for why, in earlier studies (Neville *et al.* 1992), our deaf participants did not display evidence for specialization within the left hemisphere when processing English. It could be, as has been proposed by several investigators, that the left hemisphere is specifically specialized for the auditory encoding of language and for the visual to auditory or 'phonological' decoding that characterizes reading by hearing, but not deaf, individuals. However, if grammatical recoding is an important variable in the development of left hemisphere specialization for a language (Liberman 1974), then deaf participants should display left hemisphere specialization when processing ASL. In fact, a sizeable literature has accumulated during the past 100 years that suggests lesions to the left hemisphere impair the use of signed languages in much the same way as is the case for spoken languages (Corina 2002; Hickok *et al.* 1996; Poizner *et al.* 1987). Less is known about the contribution of the right hemisphere (RH) to sign language, as fewer right hemisphere damaged deaf patients have been studied systematically, and the results are not consistent. However, language comprehension deficits have been reported following right hemisphere damage (Corina 2002; Poizner *et al.* 1987; Poizner and Tallal 1987).

In one study, ERPs were recorded from deaf and hearing native signers as they viewed ASL signs that formed sentences. The results suggest that there are constraints on the organization of the neural systems that mediate formal languages and that these are independent of the modality through which language is acquired. These include different specializations of anterior and posterior cortical regions for aspects of grammatical and semantic processing and a bias for the left hemisphere to mediate aspects of mnemonic functions in language. In addition, the results suggest that the nature and timing of sensory and language experience significantly impacts the development of the language systems of the brain. Effects of early acquisition of ASL include an increased role for the right hemisphere and parietal cortex that occurs in both hearing and deaf native signers. An increased role of posterior temporal and occipital areas occurs only in deaf native signers and thus may be attributable to auditory deprivation (Neville *et al.* 1997).

Because our ERP evidence for right hemisphere activation in ASL was unexpected given previous clinical studies, we began a series of fMRI studies to more precisely specify and compare the brain areas active in processing ASL and English. Effects of deafness, age of language acquisition, and bilingualism were assessed by comparing results from: (a) normally hearing, monolingual, native speakers of English; (b) congenitally, genetically deaf, native signers of ASL who learned English late and through the visual modality; and (c) normally hearing bilinguals who were native signers of ASL and speakers of English. All groups, hearing and deaf, processing their native language, English or ASL, displayed strong and repeated activation within classical language areas of the left hemisphere. Deaf native signers reading English did not display activation in these regions, suggesting that the early acquisition of a natural language is important in the expression of the strong bias for these areas to mediate language, independently of the form of the language. In addition, native signers (hearing and deaf) processing ASL (but not English) displayed extensive activation of homologous areas within the right hemisphere, indicating that the specific processing requirements of the language also, in part, determine the organization of the language systems of the brain (Bavelier *et al.* 1998; Neville *et al.* 1998). Since our publication, other groups have performed related studies and report evidence of left and right temporal lobe activation during ASL processing (Petitto *et al.* 2000; Soederfeldt *et al.* 1997).

To assess the possibility that the increased right hemisphere activation to signed as compared to written sentences might be attributable to factors including the presence of prosody in ASL (but not in written sentences), we compared activation for written and signed sentences with that for sentences spoken by a person that was both heard and viewed. Activations for spoken and written sentences were both strongly left-lateralized, in contrast to the activations for ASL sentences, which were bilateral or larger over the right hemisphere (Capek *et al.* 1998, 2004).

In a recent study we assessed the hypothesis that for ASL, like other natural languages, there may be a sensitive period beyond which exposure to the language is associated with deficits in acquisition and altered brain organization (Newman *et al.* 2002). As described above, when native learners of ASL view ASL sentences, in addition to LH activation, they show a unique pattern of extensive RH activation. In this study, we demonstrated that one of these RH regions, the angular gyrus, is active when hearing native signers process ASL, but not when late learners, who acquired ASL after puberty, do so. This suggests the existence of a sensitive period, during which, but not after, the acquisition of ASL results in the recruitment of the angular gyrus for language processing. This result has implications both for language acquisition, and more broadly for an understanding of age-related changes in neuroplasticity (Newman *et al.* 1998, 2002).

As noted above, studies of written and spoken language suggest that non-identical neural subsystems mediate semantic and syntactic processing. While these effects have been found for a variety of semantic and syntactic permutations in spoken languages, there is a paucity of research investigating semantic and syntactic processing in sign languages. The evidence reviewed above suggests that ASL depends upon many of the same neural systems as spoken language, but also recruits additional brain regions, primarily in the right hemisphere. In this study, we recorded ERPs from congenitally deaf native signers of ASL as they viewed semantically or syntactically appropriate and anomalous ASL sentences. As with written/spoken sentence processing, semantic violations elicited a central posterior N400 ERP response, while syntactic violations elicited an early anterior negativity followed by a broadly distributed posterior late positive shift. This pattern of results closely parallels results for spoken language and suggests modality independent universals in the language systems of the brain. However, in contrast to spoken/written language, the lateral distribution of the early negativity varied as a function of the type of syntactic agreement violation, suggesting that both biological constraints and experience shape the development of neural systems important for language.

13.9.3 Delay in first language acquisition

As noted above, many investigations of the critical or sensitive period for language have examined the effects of delays in second language acquisition on proficiency and brain organization for that language. Although effects of such delays have been reported it has been difficult to determine whether these are the result of changes in cortical maturation that limit the time periods when a language can be optimally acquired or whether they are due to interference from the first language. The deaf population provides a rare and powerful opportunity to address this issue because more than 90 per cent of deaf people are born to hearing parents who try to teach their children to speak and/or lip read. Understandably, many fail and thus the acquisition of a first language is delayed until they are exposed to ASL.[1] Behavioral studies of such individuals indicate that with increasing age of acquisition, proficiency decreases (Newport 1990; Mayberry and Eichen 1991; Mayberry 1993; Mayberry et al. 2002; Mayberry 2003), however there have not been studies of brain organization of delayed first language acquisition. We have recently studied groups of deaf individuals who acquired ASL either from birth, from 2 to 10 years or between 11 and 21 years of age (Capek et al. 2003; Capek 2004; Capek et al. in prep). We employed the ERPs paradigm described above to separately assess the effects of delayed acquisition of a first language on semantic and syntactic processing. The results clearly show that the N400 index of semantic processing displayed the same amplitude, latency and cortical

---

[1] While some deaf people communicate with their families using common gestures, such systems are not full languages.

distribution in all three groups of participants. However, the early anterior negativity thought to index more automatic aspects of syntax was only evident in those who acquired ASL before the age of 10 years. These results strongly indicate that interference effects from a first language are not necessary in order to observe the effects of delayed language acquisition and supports the hypothesis that there are maturational constraints that determine the optimal time period for the acquisition of a first language.

13.9.4 Language processing following visual deprivation

Individuals blind since birth provide another important opportunity to assess the effects of altered sensory and language experience on the development of language-relevant brain systems. We employed ERPs to test the hypothesis that auditory language processing occurs more rapidly in blind than sighted adults. We confirmed this hypothesis in two experiments, one of sentence processing and the other of auditory memory (Röder *et al.* 2000; Röder *et al.* 2001). In addition, we hypothesized that, in the absence of visuospatial input to the right hemisphere (which in normal development gradually becomes less responsive to auditory language (Neville and Mills 1997)), the right hemisphere may retain the capacity for processing auditory language, resulting in a more bilateral pattern of activation in blind individuals. This hypothesis was strongly confirmed, suggesting that many factors, including age of acquisition, modality of the language acquired, and the presence of other specialized brain systems operate together to determine the mature pattern of hemispheric specialization for language.

We also recently used fMRI to map language-related brain activity in congenitally blind adults (Röder *et al.* 2002). Participants listened to sentences, with either an easy or a more difficult syntactic structure, which were either semantically meaningful or meaningless. Results show that blind adults not only activate classical LH perisylvian language areas during speech comprehension, as did a group of sighted adults, but that they additionally display an activation in the homologous RH structures and in extrastriate and striate cortex. Both the perisylvian and occipital activity varied as a function of syntactic difficulty and semantic content. The results demonstrate that the cerebral organization of complex cognitive systems such as the language system is significantly shaped by the input from the environment.

13.9.5 Individual differences in semantic and grammatical processing

In studying the development and role of experience in the differentiation of the semantic and syntactic subsystems described above, we adapted the stimuli we have used in studies of adults for use with children. In the course of validating this new sentence set we demonstrated that it elicited effects comparable to those we have previously reported in adults and that, in addition, there were considerable individual

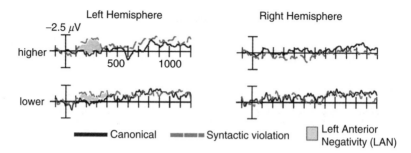

Fig. 13.4 Adult native English speakers: individuals scoring high and low on tests of grammar. ERPs to syntactically canonical and anomalous auditory sentences.

differences in the data from adult participants (Pakulak *et al.* 2002; Yamada *et al.* 2002). In follow-up studies we compared responses to these sentences in normal, monolingual adults who scored high and low on a standardized test of grammatical knowledge (Test of Adolescent and Adult Language-3, Hammil *et al.* 1994). The results clearly show the typical left-lateralized effects for closed-class words and grammatical anomalies in high scoring individuals, but significant reductions of these effects in low scoring individuals. These results were replicated in the visual and auditory modalities (Fig. 13.4).

We have also tested 30 children aged 32 to 38 months on these sentences. Whereas semantic anomalies elicited a clear N400 response with a bilateral posterior distribution similar to adults, the grammatical anomalies elicited an anterior negativity that tended to be larger over the left hemisphere (LAN). However, the onset of this effect was 200 ms later than that seen in adults. (Adamson 2000; Adamson-Harris *et al.* 2000; Fig. 13.5).

We observed considerable individual variability in these effects in the children. To assess the hypothesis that differences in language knowledge might account for this variability we compared responses from children of the same age (35 months) who scored high (84th percentile) on tests of language (Dunn and Dunn 1997; Semel *et al.* 1995) and those scoring lower (but well within normal limits – approximately 50th percentile). These analyses clearly show that the LAN effect to the grammatical anomalies is present in the high scoring children but is not reliably present in the lower scoring children (Fig. 13.6).

In ongoing studies, we are employing this paradigm in larger groups of 3-, 4- and 5-year-old children to determine when these systems are reliably present and distinct. In addition we are exploring the different factors that may determine the large individual differences in language knowledge and rate of maturation of these systems. Considerable behavioral data show that children with more talkative parents have higher language proficiencies than those with less talkative parents (Hart and Risley 1999; Huttenlocher *et al.* 1991; Huttenlocher *et al.* in press). These results can be (and have been) interpreted

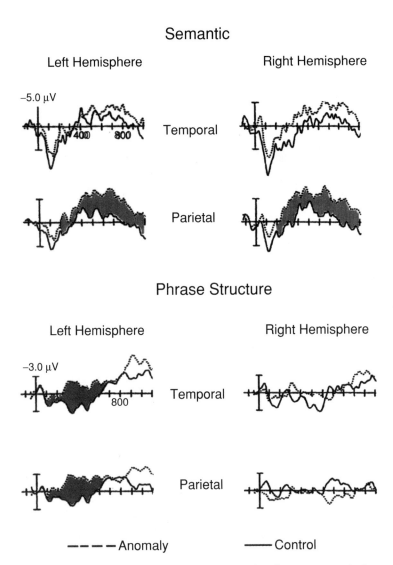

Fig. 13.5 ERPs to semantically and grammatically canonical auditory sentences in 3-year-old children.

either as showing: (a) that experience drives neural development (Hart and Risley 1999); or (b) that genetic factors shared by parents and children determine individual differences in language proficiency and brain organization (Pinker 2002). The problem of course is that children and parents share both genes and environment.

Although it is widely accepted that language acquisition depends in part on innate, intrinsic structures and in part on environmental input, few behavioral studies have

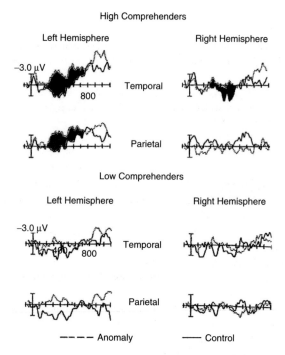

Fig. 13.6 ERPs to grammatically canonical and anomalous auditory sentences in 3-year-old children scoring high or low on tests of grammar and comprehension.

separately assessed the contribution of intrinsic and extrinsic variables to language proficiency, and none have directly assessed the effects of language input on the development of language-relevant neural systems in the developing child. Therefore, in ongoing studies, we are assessing the hypothesis that normal variation in language input from children's teachers and specific interventions drive change in these systems in normal children.

Acknowledgement

I am grateful to my current and former students and post-doctoral fellows whose research is summarized here and to Linda Heidenreich, Ean Huddleston, and Courtney Darves Stevens for help in manuscript preparation. This research is supported by National Institutes of Health, DC00128 and DC00481.

This paper is adapted from one entitled Development and Plasticity of Human Cognition to appear in Mayr *et al.* (eds), *Developing Individuality in the Human Brain: A Tribute to Mike Posner.* APA Books

References

Adamson A (2000). *Processing semantic and grammatical information in auditory sentences: Electrophysiological evidence from children and adults.* Unpublished Doctoral Dissertation, University of Oregon, Eugene, OR.

Adamson-Harris AM, Mills DL and Neville HJ (2000). Children's processing of grammatical and semantic information within sentences: Evidence from event-related potentials. Abstract, *Cognitive Neuroscience Society*, 7, 58.

Andersson B and Hugdahl K (1987). Effects of sex, age, and forced attention on dichotic listening in children: A longitudinal study. *Developmental Neuropsychology*, 3, 191–206.

Armstrong B, Hillyard SA, Neville HJ and Mitchell TV (2002). Auditory deprivation affects processing of motion, but not color. *Cognitive Brain Research*, 14, 422–434.

Atkinson J, King J, Braddick O, Nokes L, Anker S and Braddick F (1997). A specific deficit of dorsal stream function in Williams' Syndrome. *NeuroReport*, 8, 1919–1922.

Baizer JS, Ungerleider LG and Desimone R (1991). Organization of visual inputs to the inferior temporal and posterior parietal cortex in macaques. *Journal of Neuroscience*, 11, 168–190.

Bavelier D, Brozinsky C, Tomann A, Mitchell T, Neville H and Liu G (2001). Impact of early deafness and early exposure to sign language on the cerebral organization for motion processing. *Journal of Neuroscience*, 21, 8931–8942.

Bavelier D, Corina D, Jezzard P, *et al.* (1998). Hemispheric specialization for English and ASL: Left invariance-right variability. *NeuroReport*, 9, 1537–1542.

Bavelier D, Tomann A, Hutton C, *et al.* (2000). Visual attention to the periphery is enhanced in congenitally deaf individuals. *Journal of Neuroscience*, 20, 1–6.

Beauchamp M and DeYoe E (1996). Brain areas for processing motion and their modulation by selective attention. *NeuroImage*, 3, S245.

Bellugi U, Lichtenberger L, Jones W, Lai Z and George MS (2000). The neurocognitive profile of Williams Syndrome: A complex pattern of strengths and weaknesses. *Journal of Cognitive Neuroscience*, 12, 7–29.

Berman S and Friedman D (1995). The development of selective auditory attention as reflected by event-related brain potentials. *Journal of Experimental Child Psychology*, 59, 1–31.

Breznitz Z and Maya M (2003). Speed of processing of the visual-orthographic and auditory-phonological systems in adult dyslexics: The contribution of "asynchrony" to word recognition deficits. *Brain and Language*, 85, 486–502.

Buchel C and Friston KJ (1997). Modulation of connectivity in visual pathways by attention: Cortical interactions evaluated with structural equation modelling and fMRI. *Cerebral Cortex*, 7, 768–778.

Capek C (2004). *The cortical organization of spoken and signed sentence processing in adults.* Unpublished Doctoral Dissertation, University of Oregon, Eugene, OR.

Capek CM, Bavelier D, Corina D, Newman AJ, Jezzard P and Neville HJ (2004). The cortical organization for audio-visual sentence processing: A fMRI study at 4 Tesla. *Cognitive Brain Research*, 20, 111–119.

Capek CM, Corina D, Grossi G, *et al.* (2003). American Sign Language sentence processing: ERP evidence from adults with different ages of acquisition. Abstract, *Cognitive Neuroscience Society*, 10, 105.

Capek CM, Corina D, Grossi G, *et al.* (in prep). American Sign Language sentence processing: ERP evidence from adults with different ages of acquisition.

Capek C, Newman A, Murray S, *et al.* (1998). Cortical organization of auditory sentence comprehension: A functional magnetic resonance imaging (fMRI) study. Abstract, *Society for Neuroscience*, 24, 1174.

Chugani HT, Phelps ME and Mazziotta JC (1987). Positron emission tomography study of human brain functional development. *Annals of Neurology*, 22, 487–497.

Coch D, Sanders L and Neville H (in press). An ERP study of selective linguistic auditory attention in children and adults. *Journal of Cognitive Neuroscience*.

Corina DP (2002). Sign language aphasia. In: SE Petersen, ed. *Aphasia in atypical populations*, pp. 261–310. Hillsdale, NJ: Erlbaum.

Cornelissen P, Richardson A, Mason A, Fowler S and Stein J (1995). Contrast sensitivity and coherent motion detection measured at photopic luminance levels in dyslexics and controls. *Vision Research*, 35, 1483–1494.

Darves C and Neville H (2004). Two sides of neural plasticity in the dorsal visual pathway: Evidence from deaf, dyslexic, and control adults. Abstract, *Cognitive Neuroscience Society*, 11, 117.

Demb JB, Boynton GM, Best M and Heeger DJ (1998). Psychophysical evidence for a magnocellular pathway deficit in dyslexia. *Vision Research*, 38, 1555–1559.

Dobkins KR and Teller DY (1996). Infant motion: Detection (*M-D*) ratios for chromatically defined and luminance-defined moving stimuli. *Vision Research*, 36, 3293–3310.

Doyle AB (1973). Listening to distraction: A developmental study of selective attention. *Journal of Experimental Child Psychology*, 15, 100–115.

Dunn LM and Dunn LM (1997). *Peabody picture vocabulary test*. Circle Pines, MN: American Guidance Services.

Eden G (1996). Abnormal processing of visual motion in dyslexia revealed by functional brain imaging. *Nature*, 382, 66–69.

Elbert T, Flor H, Birbaumer N, *et al.* (1994). Extensive reorganization of the somatosensory cortex in adult humans after nervous system injury. *NeuroReport*, 5, 2593–2597.

Elliott LL (1979). Performance of children aged 9 to 17 years on a test of speech intelligibility in noise using sentence material with controlled word predictability. *Journal of the Acoustical Society of America*, 66, 651–653.

Engel SA, Glover GH and Wandell BA (1997). Retinotopic organization in human visual cortex and the spatial precision of functional MRI. *Cerebral Cortex*, 7, 181–192.

Everatt J, Bradshaw MF and Hibbard PB (1999). Visual processing and dyslexia. *Perception*, 28, 243–254.

Frost DO, Boire D, Gingras G and Ptito M (2000). Surgically created neural pathways mediate visual pattern discrimination. *Proceedings of the National Academy of Science, USA*, 97, 11068–11073.

Galaburda A and Livingstone M (1993). Evidence for a magnocullular defect in developmental dyslexia. In: P Tallal, AM Galaburda, RR Llinas and C von Euler, eds. *Temporal information processing in the nervous system*, pp. 70–82. New York: New York Academy of Sciences.

Geffen G and Sexton MA (1978). The development of auditory strategies of attention. *Developmental Psychology*, 14, 11–17.

Geffen G and Wale J (1979). Development of selective listening and hemispheric asymmetry. *Developmental Psychology*, 15, 138–146.

Hammil DD, Brown VL, Larsen SC and Wiederholt JL (1994). *Test of adolescent and adult language*, 3rd edn. Austin, Tx: pro-ed.

Hansen PC, Stein JF, Orde SR, Winter JL and Talcott JB (2001). Are dyslexics' visual deficits limited to measures of dorsal stream function? *NeuroReport*, 12, 1527–1530.

Hart B and Risley TR (1999). *The social world of children: Learning to talk.* Balitmore, MD: Brookes Publishing Co.

Harwerth R, Smith E, Duncan G, Crawford M and von Noorden G (1986). Multiple sensitive periods in the development of the primate visual system. *Science*, 232, 235–238.

Hickey TL (1977). Postnatal development of the human lateral geniculate nucleus: Relationship to a critical period for the visual system. *Science*, 198, 836–838.

Hickok G, Bellugi U and Klima ES (1996). The neurobiology of sign language and its implications for the neural basis of language. *Nature*, 381, 699–702.

Hillyard SA, Hink RF, Schwent VI and Picton TW (1973). Electrical signs of selective attention in the human brain. *Science*, 182, 177–179.

Hiscock M and Kinsbourne M (1980). Asymmetries of selective listening and attention switching in children. *Developmental Psychology*, 16, 70–82.

Hollants-Gilhuijs MAM, Ruijter JM and Spekreijse H (1998a). Visual half-field development in children: Detection of colour-contrast-defined forms. *Vision Research*, 38, 645–649.

Hollants-Gilhuijs MAM, Ruijter JM and Spekreijse H (1998b). Visual half-field development in children: Detection of motion-defined forms. *Vision Research*, 38, 651–657.

Horton JC and Hocking DR (1997). Timing of the critical period for plasticity of ocular dominance columns in macaque striate cortex. *Journal of Neuroscience*, 17, 3684–3709.

Hubel DH and Wiesel TN (1977). Functional architecture of macaque monkey visual cortex. *Proceedings of the Royal Society of London*, 198, 1–59.

Huttenlocher J, Haight W, Byrd A, Seltzer M and Lyons T (1991). Early vocabulary growth: Relation to language input and gender. *Developmental Psychology*, 27, 236–248.

Huttenlocher J, Vasilyeva M, Cymerman E and Levine S (in press). Language input and child syntax. *Cognitive Psychology*.

Huttenlocher PR and Dabholkar AS (1997). Regional differences in synaptogenesis in human cerebral cortex. *Journal of Comparative Neurology*, 387, 167–178.

Johnson MH, Mareschal D and Csibra G (2001). The functional development and integration of the dorsal and ventral visual pathways: A neurocomputational approach. In: CA Nelson and M Luciana, eds. *Handbook of developmental cognitive neuroscience*. Cambridge, MA: MIT Press.

Kaas J, Krubitzer L, Chino Y, Langston A, Polley E and Blair N (1990). Reorganization of retinotopic cortical maps in adult mammals after lesions of the retina. *Science*, 248, 229–231.

Kahn DM and Krubitzer L (2002). Massive cross-modal cortical plasticity and the emergence of a new cortical area in developmentally blind mammals. *Proceedings of the National Academy of Science, USA*, 99, 11429–11434.

Kovacs I, Polat U, Pennefather PM, Chandna A and Norcia AN (2000). A new test of contour integration deficits in patients with a history of disrupted binocular experience during visual development. *Vision Research*, 40, 1775–1783.

Krubitzer L and Huffman KJ (2000). A realization of the neocortex in mammals: genetic and epigenetic contributions to the phenotype. *Brain, Behavior and Evolution*, 55, 322–335.

Lane D and Pearson D (1982). The development of selective attention. *Merrill-Palmer Quarterly*, 28, 317–337.

Le Grand R, Mondloch CJ, Maurer D and Brent HP (2001). Early visual experience and face processing. *Nature*, 410, 890.

Lenneberg E (1967). *Biological foundations of language*. New York: Wiley.

Liberman AM (1974). The specialization of the language hemisphere. In: FO Schmitt and FG Worden, eds. *The neurosciences third study program*, pp. 43–56. Cambridge, MA: MIT Press.

Livingstone M and Hubel D (1988). Segregation of form, color, movement and depth: Anatomy, physiology, and perception. *Science*, **240**, 740–749.

Livingstone MS, Rosen GD, Drislane FW and Galaburda AM (1991). Physiological and anatomical evidence for a magnocellular defect in developmental dyslexia. *Proceedings of the National Academy of Science, USA*, **88**, 7943–7947.

Loiselle DL, Stamm JS, Maitinsky S and Whipple SC (1980). Evoked potential and behavioral signs of attentive dysfunctions in hyperactive boys. *Psychophysiology*, **17**, 193–201.

Lovegrove W (1993). Weakness in the transient visual system: A causal factor in dyslexia. In: P Tallal, AM Galaburda, RR Llinas and C von Euler, eds. *Temporal information processing in the nervous system*, pp. 57–69. New York: New York Academy of Sciences.

Lovegrove W, Garzia R and Nicholson S (1990). Experimental evidence for a transient system deficit in specific reading disability. *Journal of the American Optometric Association*, **61**, 137–146.

Lovegrove W, Martin F and Slaghuis W (1986). A theoretical and experimental case for a visual deficit in specific reading disability. *Cognitive Neuropsychology*, **3**, 225–267.

Lovrich DL, Stamm JS, Maitinsky S and Whipple SC (1983). Event-related potential and behavioral correlates of attention in reading retardation. *Journal of Clinical Neuropsychology*, **5**, 13–37.

Maccoby E and Konrad K (1966). Age trends in selective listening. *Journal of Experimental Child Psychology*, **3**, 113–122.

Maurer D, Lewis TL, Brent HP and Levin AV (1999). Rapid improvement in the acuity of infants after visual input. *Science*, **286**, 108–110.

Mayberry R (1993). First-language acquisition after childhood differs from second-language acquisition: The case of American Sign Language. *Journal of Speech and Hearing Research*, **36**, 1258–1270.

Mayberry R and Eichen E (1991). The long-lasting advantage of learning sign language in childhood: Another look at the critical period for language acquisition. *Journal of Memory and Language*, **30**, 486–512.

Mayberry RI (2003). Age constraints on first versus second language acquisition: Evidence for linguistic plasticity and epigenesis. *Brain and Language*, **87**, 369–384.

Mayberry RI, Lock E and Kazmi H (2002). Linguistic ability and early language exposure. *Nature*, **417**, 38.

McIntosh AR and Gonzalez-Lima F (1994). Structural equation modelling and its application to network analysis of functional brain imaging. *Human Brain Mapping*, **2**, 2–22.

Merigan W and Maunsell J (1993). How parallel are the primate visual pathways? *Annual Review of Neuroscience*, **16**, 369–402.

Merzenich MM and Jenkins WM (1993). Reorganization of cortical representations of the hand following alterations of skin inputs induced by nerve injury, skin island transfers, and experience. *Journal of Hand Therapy*, **6**, 89–104.

Metin C and Frost D (1989). Visual responses of neurons in somatosensory cortex of hamsters with experimentally induced retinal projections to somatosensory thalamus. *Proceedings of the National Academy of Science, USA*, **86**, 357–361.

Mitchell DE (1990). Sensitive periods in visual development: Insights gained from studies of recovery of function in cats following early monocular deprivation or cortical lesions. In: C Blakemore, ed. *Vision: Coding and efficiency*, pp. 234–246. Cambridge: Cambridge University Press.

Mitchell TV and Neville HJ (in press). Asynchronies in the development of electrophysiological responses to motion and color. *Journal of Cognitive Neuroscience.*

Neville HJ (1995). Developmental specificity in neurocognitive development in humans. In: M Gazzaniga, ed. *The cognitive neurosciences,* pp. 219–231. Cambridge, MA: MIT Press.

Neville HJ (1998). Human brain development. In: M Posner and L Ungerleider, eds. *Fundamental neuroscience,* pp. 1313–1338. New York: Academic Press.

Neville HJ, Bavelier D, Corina D, *et al.* (1998). Cerebral organization for language in deaf and hearing subjects: Biological constraints and effects of experience. *Proceedings of the National Academy of Science, USA,* **95,** 922–929.

Neville HJ, Coffey SA, Lawson DS, Fischer A, Emmorey K and Bellugi U (1997). Neural systems mediating American sign language: Effects of sensory experience and age of acquisition. *Brain and Language,* **57,** 285–308.

Neville HJ and Lawson D (1987a). Attention to central and peripheral visual space in a movement detection task: An event-related potential and behavioral study. I. Normal hearing adults. *Brain Research,* **405,** 253–267.

Neville HJ and Lawson D (1987b). Attention to central and peripheral visual space in a movement detection task: An event-related and behavioral study. II. Congenitally deaf adults. *Brain Research,* **405,** 268–283.

Neville HJ and Lawson D (1987c). Attention to central and peripheral visual space in a movement detection task. III. Separate effects of auditory deprivation and acquisition of a visual language. *Brain Research,* **405,** 284–294.

Neville HJ and Mills D (1997). Epigenesis of language. *Mental Retardation and Developmental Disabilities Research Reviews,* **3,** 282–292.

Neville HJ, Mills D and Lawson D (1992). Fractionating language: Different neural subsystems with different sensitive periods. *Cerebral Cortex,* **2,** 244–258.

Neville HJ, Schmidt A and Kutas M (1983). Altered visual-evoked potentials in congenitally deaf adults. *Brain Research,* **266,** 127–132.

Newman A, Corina D, Tomann A, *et al.* (1998). Effects of age of acquisition on cortical organization for American Sign Language (ASL): An fMRI study. *NeuroImage,* **7,** 5194.

Newman AJ, Bavelier D, Corina D, Jezzard P and Neville HJ (2002). A critical period for right hemisphere recruitment in American Sign Language processing. *Nature Neuroscience,* **5,** 76–80.

Newport E (1990). Maturational constraints on language learning. *Cognitive Science,* **14,** 11–28.

Newport EL, Bavelier D and Neville H (2002). Critical thinking about critical periods: Perspectives on a critical period for language acquisition. In: E Dupoux, ed. *Language, brain and cognitive development,* pp. 481–502. Cambridge, MA: MIT Press.

O'Craven K, Rosen B, Kwong K, Triesman A and Savoy R (1997). Voluntary attention modulates fMRI activity in human MT-MST. *Neuron,* **18,** 591–598.

Pakulak E, Harris AM, Yamada Y, Coch D, Schachter J and Neville H (2002). Syntactic processing without semantic cues in adult monolinguals of varying proficiency: An ERP study. Abstract, *Cognitive Neuroscience Society,* **9,** 135.

Pearson DA and Lane DM (1991). Auditory attention switching: A developmental study. *Journal of Experimental Child Psychology,* **51,** 320–334.

Petitto LA, Zatorri RJ, Gauna K, Nikelski EJ, Dostie D and Evans AC (2000). Speech-like cerebral activity in profoundly deaf people processing signed languages: Implications for the neural basis of human language. *Proceedings of the National Academy of Science, USA,* **97,** 13961–13966.

Pinker S (2002). *The blank slate: The modern denial of human nature.* New York: Viking.

Poizner H, Klima ES and Bellugi U (1987). *What the hands reveal about the brain.* Cambridge, MA: MIT Press.

Poizner H and Tallal P (1987). Temporal processing in deaf signers. *Brain and Language,* 30, 52–62.

Ramachandran VS, Rogers-Ramachandran DR and Stewart M (1992). Perceptual correlates of massive cortical reorganization. *Science,* 258, 1159–1160.

Rauschecker J (1995). Compensatory plasticity and sensory substitution in the cerebral cortex. *Trends in Neurosciences,* 18, 36–43.

Röder B, Rösler F and Neville HJ (1999a). Effects of interstimulus interval on auditory event-related potentials in congenitally blind and normally sighted humans. *Neuroscience Letters,* 264, 53–56.

Röder B, Rösler F and Neville HJ (2000). Event-related potentials during auditory language processing in congenitally blind and sighted people. *Neuropsychologia,* 38, 1482–1502.

Röder B, Stock O, Neville H, Bien S and Rösler F (2002). Brain activation modulated by the comprehension of normal and pseudo-word sentences of different processing demands: A functional magnetic resonance imaging study. *NeuroImage,* 15, 1003–1014.

Röder B, Stock O, Rösler R, Bien S and Neville H (2001). Plasticity of language functions in blind humans: An fMRI study. Abstract, *Cognitive Neuroscience Society,* 8, 119.

Röder B, Teder-Sälejärvi W, Sterr A, Rösler F, Hillyard SA and Neville HJ (1999b). Improved auditory spatial tuning in blind humans. *Nature,* 400, 162–166.

Roe AW, Pallas SL, Kwon YH and Sur M (1992). Visual projections routed to the auditory pathway in ferrets: Receptive fields of visual neurons in primary auditory cortex. *Journal of Neuroscience,* 12, 3651–3664.

Sawatari A and Callaway EM (1996). Convergence of magno- and parvocellular pathways in layer 4B of macaque primary visual cortex. *Nature,* 380, 442–446.

Scott GD, Dow MW and Neville HJ (2003). Human retinotopic mapping of the far periphery. Abstract, *Society for Neuroscience,* 29, 776.

Semel E, Wiig EH and Secord WA (1995). *Clinical evaluation of language fundamentals.* San Antonio, TX: Psychological Corporation, Harcourt Brace and Company.

Sexton MA and Geffen G (1979). Development of three strategies of attention in dichotic monitoring. *Developmental Psychology,* 15, 299–310.

Silver MA, Fagiolini M, Gillespie DC, *et al.* (2001). Infusion of nerve growth factor (NGF) into kitten visual cortex increases immunoreactivity for NGF, NGF receptors, and choline acetyltransferase in basal forebrain without affecting ocular dominance plasticity or column development. *Neuroscience,* 108, 569–585.

Soederfeldt B, Ingvar M, Roennberg J, Eriksson L, Serrander, B. and Stone-Elander, S. (1997). Signed and spoken language perception studied by positron emission tomography. *Neurology,* 49, 82–87.

Sperling AJ, Lu Z-L, Manis FR and Seidenberg MS (2003). Selective magnocellular deficits in dyslexia: A "phantom contour" study. *Neuropsychologia,* 41, 1422–1429.

Spezio ML, Sanders LD and Neville HJ (2000). Covert audiospatial attention using virtual sound sources. Abstract, *Cognitive Neuroscience Society,* 7, 81.

Stein J and Talcott JB (1999). Impaired neuronal timing in developmental dyslexia: The magnocellular deficit hypothesis. *Dyslexia,* 5, 59–77.

Stoner GB and Albright TD (1993). Image segmentation cues in motion processing: Implications for modularity in vision. *Journal of Cognitive Neuroscience,* 5, 129–149.

Sur M and Garraghty P (1986). Experimentally induced visual responses from auditory thalamus and cortex. Abstract, *Society for Neuroscience,* 12, 592.

Taha S and Stryker MP (2002). Rapid ocular dominance plasticity requires cortical but not geniculate protein synthesis. *Neuron*, **34**, 425–436.

Talcott JB (2000). Visual motion sensitivity in dyslexia: Evidence for temporal and energy integration deficits. *Neuropsychologia*, **38**, 935–943.

Talcott JB, Hansen PC, Willis-Owens C, W. MI, Richardson A and Stein J (1998). Visual magnocellular impairment in adult developmental dyslexics. *Neuro-Opthalmology*, **20**, 187–201.

Teder-Salejarvi WA, Hillyard S, Röder B and Neville HJ (1999a). Spatial attention to central and peripheral auditory stimuli as indexed by event-related potentials (ERPs). *Cognitive Brain Research*, **8**, 213–227.

Teder-Salejarvi WA, Munte TF, Sperlich F-J and Hillyard SA (1999b). Intra-modal and cross-modal spatial attention to auditory and visual stimuli. An event-related brain potential (ERP) study. *Cognitive Brain Research*, **8**, 327–343.

Tootell R and Taylor J (1995). Anatomical evidence for MT and additional cortical visual areas in humans. *Cerebral Cortex*, **1**, 39–55.

Tootell RB, Reppas JB, Kwong KK, *et al.* (1995). Functional analysis of human MT and related visual cortical areas using magnetic resonance imaging. *Journal of Neuroscience*, **15**, 3215–3230.

Tychsen L (2001). Critical period of development of visual acuity, depth perception and eye tracking. In: DBJ Bailey, JT Bruer, FJ Symons and JW Lichtman, eds. *Critical thinking about critical periods: Perspectives from biology, psychology and education*, pp. 67–80. Baltimore, MD: Brookes Publishing.

Ungerleider LG and Mishkin M (1982). Two cortical visual systems. In: DJ Ingle, MA Goodale and RJ Mansfield, eds. *Analysis of visual behavior*, pp. 549–586. Cambridge, MA: MIT Press.

von Melchner L, Pallas SL and Sur M (2000). Visual behavior mediated by retinal projections directed to the auditory pathway. *Nature*, **404**, 871–876.

Weber-Fox C and Neville HJ (1996a). Effects of delays in second-language immersion on functional neural subsystems. Abstract, *AAAS Symposium: The brain, cognition, and education: Exploring the bridge between research and practice*.

Weber-Fox C and Neville HJ (1996b). Maturational constraints on functional specializations for language processing: ERP and behavioral evidence in bilingual speakers. *Journal of Cognitive Neuroscience*, **8**, 231–256.

Weber-Fox C and Neville HJ (1999). Functional neural subsystems are differentially affected by delays in second-language immersion: ERP and behavioral evidence in bilingual speakers. In: D Birdsong, ed. *New perspectives on the critical period for second language acquisition*, pp. 23–38. Hillsdale, NJ: Lawrence Erlbaum.

Wiesel T and Hubel D (1965). Comparison of the effects of unilateral and bilateral eye closure on cortical unit responses in kittens. *Journal of Neurophysiology*, **28**, 1003–1017.

Woods D, Hillyard S and Hansen J (1984). Event-related brain potentials reveal similar attentional mechanisms during selective listening and shadowing. *Journal of Experimental Psychology*, **10**, 761–777.

Woods J, Coch D, Sanders L, Skendzel W, Capek C and Neville H (2002b). The development of selective auditory attention to linguistic and non-linguistic sounds. Abstract, *Cognitive Neuroscience Society*, **9**, 122.

Woods J, Coch D, Sanders L, Skendzel W and Neville H (2002a). *The development of selective auditory attention to linguistic and non-linguistic stimuli*. Unpublished Master's Thesis, University of Oregon, Eugene, OR.

Yamada Y, Harris AM, Pakulak E, Schachter J and Neville H (2002). Language proficiency in monolinguals and bilinguals reflected in ERPs during sentence processing. Abstract, *Cognitive Neuroscience Society*, **9**, 135.

Zambelli AJ, Stamm JS, Maitinsky S and Loiselle DL (1977). Auditory evoked potentials and selective auditory attention in formerly hyperactive adolescent boys. *American Journal of Psychiatry*, **134**, 742–747.

Zukier H and Hagen JW (1978). The development of selective attention under distracting conditions. *Child Development*, **49**, 870–873.

Chapter 14

Atypical representational change: Conditions for the emergence of atypical modularity

Michael S. C. Thomas and Fiona M. Richardson

Abstract

Where do functional modules come from? This question is particularly pertinent for developmental disorders, where some researchers have argued that apparently domain-specific behavioural deficits (e.g., in language) correspond to the failure of an isolated module to develop normally. Such a view requires that modules are pre-specified and develop independently. By contrast, other researchers argue that functional modules are emergent, the product of development rather than a precursor to it. If this is true, the emergence of specialized structures (as exhibited, for example, in patterns of lateralization) might be disrupted in developmental disorders, where the process of development is itself atypical. In this chapter, we take a neurocomputational approach to this question. We explore separately the origin of functional specialisation for self-organizing learning systems and for error-driven learning systems, and address three key issues: (1) What neurocomputational parameters drive normal specialization? (2) To what extent do atypical parameter settings disrupt behavioural performance and/or regional specialization of function? (3) How are systems with pre-specified modularity, emergent specialization, or multiple redundancy related at a computational level — and how robust is each type of solution to damage? We conclude that two factors drive the specialisation observed in normal development: (a) differential computational properties of regions of the substrate and (b) competition between regions. Before we can evaluate the extent to which atypical modularity will figure in explanations of developmental disorders, we must understand the relative weighting of these two factors in achieving specialization across normal development.

14.1 **Introduction**

There are a number of developmental disorders that display uneven cognitive profiles in their developmental endstates, exhibiting areas of relative strength and relative weakness. For example in Specific Language Impairment and developmental dyslexia, a relative weakness is observed in various aspects of language compared with relative strength in non-verbal abilities. Disorders that show differential performance in numerical cognition, face recognition, and motor co-ordination have also been identified. Neurogenetic developmental disorders can display more complex patterns of uneven performance affecting multiple domains, such as the cases of Williams syndrome (relatively stronger language, face recognition, and social cognition, relatively weaker visuospatial cognition, numerical cognition, and problem solving, against a background of low IQ) and autism (a central triad of deficits in communication, imagination, and socialization). However, the theoretical implication of these uneven cognitive profiles remains a matter for debate. One of the central issues concerns the origin of cognitive modules that are specialized for functions such as language, visuospatial cognition, and face recognition. Where do these modules come from and can they be selectively disrupted in developmental disorders?

One theoretical standpoint, which we will call *innate modularity*, argues that evidence of uneven cognitive profiles in genetic developmental disorders points to an innate basis for functional specialization. High-level cognitive structures are taken to be prespecified during normal development, preceding the influence of experience. Developmental disorders represent a case of differential perturbations to different innate modules. Such a proposal need not invoke innate knowledge within the modules, since a developmental process could serve to put in place the content of each component. If an innate module were atypical, this would lead to a differential deficit in the adult endstate for that domain, while initially normal components would lead to domains with normal endstate performance. However, initially normal components might be compromised by attempting to compensate for the faulty one(s) across development. The uneven cognitive profile is in both cases explained with reference to the functional (modular) structure of the normal adult system (since this is prespecified). Proponents of this position do not rule out the possibility that qualitatively atypical functional structures could occur in developmental disorders. Instead they argue that the empirical evidence has not supported it. Thus, Temple and Clahsen (2002, p. 770) argued on behavioral grounds that 'there remains no empirical evidence in any developmental disorder that the ultimate functional architecture has fundamentally different organization from normal, rather than merely lacking or having reduced development of components of normal functional architecture'. Tager-Flusberg (2000, p. 33) commented that 'despite some variation in size (either smaller or larger) and other surface features, in fact, across a wide range of disorders it is actually quite remarkable how similar the brains of different populations are to one another and to normally developing children... To be sure, there is some functional variation, but not much beyond the degree that is observed in normal people... We need to view the brain as a dynamic system that develops along flexible but fairly bounded and directed pathways'. More recently, Tager-Flusberg *et al.* (2003, p. 22) added that 'there is much less deviance in the developmental processes and neuro-cognitive organization in people with genetically based disorders than has been portrayed in the literature'.

A second theoretical standpoint, called *neuroconstructivism*, argues that assump-tions of innate modularity are inconsistent with what is known about early brain and cognitive development (Elman *et al.* 1996; Karmiloff-Smith 1998). For example Karmiloff-Smith (1998) pointed out that current evidence indicates that there is no region-specific gene expression in the areas of cortex that come to underlie higher cognitive functions in adults. Moreover, brain imaging of infants suggests that modu-lar structure may be emergent, in that it is a product of the developmental process rather than a precursor to it. For example, both localization and specialization of event related potential (ERP) waveforms increase in response to faces and spoken words across the first 2 years of life (De Haan 2001; Mills *et al.* 1997). In Karmiloff-Smith's view, the uneven cognitive profiles found in adults with developmental disorders are due to subtle differences in the neurocomputational properties of neonate brain, constraints that are both less detailed and less domain-specific than the processing structures involved in higher-level cognitive functions. A cascade of developmental processes then attenuates or exaggerates these initial differences, so that the process of modularization may be disrupted. The result could be an atypical modular structure in which even the cognitive processes underlying the relative cognitive *strengths* are atypical. Karmiloff-Smith (1998) suggested that the absence of overt evidence for atypical modularity stems from the poor sensitivity of stand-ardized cognitive tests used to verify normal performance and the restricted research attention paid to areas of strength in disorders. Reviewing evidence for face processing and language development in Williams syndrome, both areas of relative strength, she argued that behavioral and brain evidence are consistent with atypical processing underlying performance. Her conclusion was that abnormal cognitive phenotypes should not automatically be described with reference to normal adult functional structure because the structure itself may be atypical.

In assessing the relative merits of these two positions, evidence from functional brain development in infancy does appear to support the idea that modularity is emergent rather than prespecified, with functional specialization of brain areas increasing with age and expertise. Proponents of innate modularity typically de-emphasize the developmental process in their explanatory models and therefore do not offer accounts of existing infant data in terms of prespecified structures. However, one could defend the innate modularity position in at least two ways. First, one could express skepticism that we know enough about brain development to rule out the possibility that specialization occurs via intrinsic factors (representing the maturation of prespecified modules), or argue that brain-imaging evidence, as it stands, holds little relevance to the development of cognitive structures *per se*. Thus Dudek (2001, p.146) predicted that 'a unique gene will be found for each and every distinct cortical area'; and Fodor (1998, p.130) argued that 'nobody knows whether the infant's brain is plastic *in respects that affect cognitive architecture*' (italics in original). Second, one could claim that the modules present in the infant are less abstract than those found in the adult and that development serves to glue these together into higher-level modules. Thus Baron-Cohen (1999) proposes a 'minimalist' innate modularity to explain theory-of-mind deficits in autism.

However, the neuroconstructivist and innate modularity positions could converge if it were the case that the emergence of modularity was difficult to disrupt. That is, modularity could be a product of development as neuroconstructivism suggests, but the neurocomputational properties that guide the emergence of large-scale functional structure might not be altered by the kinds of genetic mutations found in developmental disorders so that normal patterns of specialization emerge. By contrast, if the constraints that shape the properties of the eventual functional components are irrevocably tied to the constraints that drive the emergence of modularity, then neuroconstructivism and innate modularity must represent opposing and empirically distinguishable theories.

The aim of this article, then, is to address whether there can be common ground between the two approaches, given what we currently know about the principles that guide the emergence of functionally specialized neurocomputational structures. Ultimately, we will introduce a set of computational simulations to investigate the constraints that would disrupt or preserve the emergence of functional architecture. However, to get to that point we need to do some groundwork. First, we need to unpack the theoretical claims of neuroconstructivism regarding the emergence of modularity. We will illustrate the relevant issues using the example of the lateralization of language in the brain. Second, we need to review current computational approaches to the emergence of modularity in order to identify the constraints that guide specialization in the normal case. Third, we need to identify a set of architectures and sample cognitive domains through which we can investigate the effects of disruption to these constraints. Specifically, to explain uneven cognitive profiles in an emergent framework, we need to ask whether different parameters guide the emergence of specialized functional components versus the computational properties within the eventual components themselves.

14.1.1 The emergence of modularity

The proposal that functional structure is emergent (i.e. formed as a product of development) sits between two more extreme positions that contribute to current theories of functional modularity (Bates and Roe 2001). The first is *equipotentiality*, which proposes that all areas of cortex are equally able to perform all cognitive functions at birth. The second is *innate modularity* (which Bates and Roe refer to as 'irreversible determinism'). This states that areas of cortex are innately and irreversibly specialized for certain cognitive functions. The emergentist position seeks to reconcile two empirical facts: (1) at a broad scale, there is reasonable uniformity of outcome in the assignment of cortical areas to functions in normal adults; and (2) there appears to be flexibility after early brain damage – following focal lesions, otherwise healthy children often show recovery to within the normal range of cognitive abilities. However, the exact extent both of uniformity and the completeness of recovery are still matters for debate. The constraints that guide the emergence of specialized structure must be strong enough to explain the uniformity but weak enough to accommodate the recovery. Once flexibility is added, it is also necessary to explain why the outcome should be an array of specialized systems rather than multiple redundant systems: if a component can aid in the recovery of a function, why did it not take on this function in the first place?

The emergentist proposal is that two factors explain specialization: (1) *domain-relevance* and (2) *competition between areas for functional specialization* (e.g. Elman *et al.* 1996; Karmiloff-Smith *et al.* 1998). Domain-relevance means that some brain areas are more suited to carrying out the computations for a given cognitive domain than others, without encoding any specific details of that domain. An area will bear differing degrees of computational relevance to a range of possible domains. Competition refers to a process where the activity of one component tends to increase at the expense of other components. To the extent that representational change is activity dependent, such change will occur differentially in the 'winning' component.

Specialization then occurs as follows. The initial substrate of the cortex is computationally heterogeneous. Different areas are more or less able to perform the computations required for different cognitive domains. These areas compete with each other to acquire the various cognitive domains, a competition biased by the information to which various areas are initially exposed by global connectivity. (For example auditory areas would tend to beat visual areas to compute audition since they are biased by the rich connectivity that delivers auditory input to this area. This is independent of the relative ability of these areas to perform the computations.) The winners of the competition come to specialize in a given domain, modifying their structures to represent the regularities of each domain and thereby becoming domain specific. Importantly, areas may be able to process alternative domains but less efficiently. Following damage, the less-suited areas are then able to acquire, or develop a partial specialization for, an alternative domain, so long as they can access the relevant information. This explains recovery. Overall, the account produces two candidate constraints to guide specialization: (1) the set of domain relevancies present in the initial state (that is, the default set of mechanisms present at the onset of development); and (2) the (biased) competition that drives eventual specialization.

14.1.2 The example of language

The domain of language and in particular the phenomenon of language lateralization, serves to illustrate the type of data that support theories of specialized functional structure. In adults, the processing of syntax and semantics is mostly left lateralized, implying that language is specialized to structures in this hemisphere. However, this conclusion emerges more strongly from lesion data (where left-hemisphere damage produces aphasia but right-hemisphere damage does not) than from brain-imaging data (where homologous areas of the right hemisphere show activation in some comprehension and production tasks, albeit at lower levels; see Price 2003). The left-dominance of syntax and semantics exhibits *uniformity of outcome*. It is found in around 95 per cent of adults, irrespective of handedness (Bates and Roe 2001). Brain-imaging data suggest that left lateralization for word recognition emerges in infancy. Mills *et al.* (1997) found bilateral ERP patterns in response to single words in 13 to 17 month olds, but left lateralized and more focal patterns in 20 month olds. The restriction to the left hemisphere was more closely associated with comprehension ability than chronological age, arguing against a maturational effect strictly linked to age.

The parameters that drive this emergent specialization are as yet unknown. There are anatomical differences in brain structure between the hemispheres, for instance a larger left temporal plane, but in one study, this was found in only 65 per cent of individuals, somewhat short of the 95 per cent that exhibit left lateralization of language (Reggia and Schulz 2002). Indeed, structural hemispheric differences have been argued to dissociate from functional differences, since rare individuals with *situs inversus* (left–right reversed internal organs) nevertheless still show left-lateralized language (Kennedy *et al.* 1999; Walker 2003). Bates and Roe (2001) argued for a functional difference that might pull language development to the left side, specifically that left temporal areas are better than right temporal areas in the fine perceptual discrimination required to recognize (and later produce) speech sounds. Huttenlocher (2002) noted that the development of synapses in the auditory cortex precedes that in Wernicke's area, which in turn precedes synaptogenesis in Broca's area. This reflects the sequence of functional development found in these regions of cerebral cortex (perception of speech sounds precedes language comprehension which precedes language production), implying a possible role for plasticity in mediating specialization.

Despite evidence of left lateralization at 20 months, the *flexibility* of the system is illustrated by the fact that if unilateral brain damage occurs prior to the age of 5 to 7 years, children recover to acquire language in the normal range. Although the side of damage predicts the profile of recovery, eventually, as adults, there is no obvious effect of side of damage, or a disadvantage for initial left-sided damage that can only be revealed by subtle psycholinguistic measures (Bates and Roe 2001; Huttenlocher 2002). Following early left-sided damage, then, the greater plasticity of the child's brain may permit the right hemisphere to acquire language. To do so, it is possible that the right hemisphere constructs a *de novo* language system. However, it is also possible that language development exploits derelict right-hemisphere structures remaining from the earlier phase of bilateral processing (Huttenlocher 2002); or even that recovery takes advantage of existing *redundant* right-hemisphere systems that are suppressed during normal performance. Certainly in normal adults, homologous right-hemisphere areas appear to be inhibited by the left hemisphere during language production and released from that inhibition after left hemisphere damage (for left and right pars opercularis: Blank *et al.* 2003). A similar effect has been observed in the perception of same-species vocalizations in rhesus monkeys: right-hemisphere inhibition in the temporal pole in the normal adult, followed by greater right hemisphere activation after disconnection from the left hemisphere (Poremba *et al.* 2004). Thus the brain's position on a scale between *specialization* and *redundancy* is not settled.

Moreover, it has recently been claimed that specialization is not fixed in adulthood, with the balance of left vs. right contributions changing across the life span. Szaflarski *et al.* (2004) used fMRI to assess regions of interest in 121 right-handed children and adults between 5 and 63 years of age in a verb generation task. They reported that language became more left lateralized with age in children and young adults, reaching a maximum lateralization between 25 and 35, and then started to become more bilateral again. These researchers suggested that the increase in specialization reflects improved linguistic skills, maturation of the central nervous system, and pruning of synaptic connections, while the later reduction reflects compensation for age-related loss of functional capacity.

Although specialization has often been associated with expertise, the functional significance of left-sided language specialization is not clear-cut. It has been suggested that women demonstrate more bilateral patterns of activation than men (e.g. in a reading task: Shaywitz *et al.* 1995), while performing better on language-related tasks (Kimura 1992) and exhibiting better recovery from unilateral left-sided damage (Strauss *et al.* 1992). Atypical language lateralization is not necessarily associated with language pathology (Knecht *et al.* 2001), suggesting that different individuals may utilize different patterns of cortical organization to process the same information and to produce normal behavior (weakening claims of uniformity of outcome). Specialization to a single hemisphere is therefore not necessarily associated with better performance and may be associated with greater vulnerability to damage.

If emergent language lateralization can stand as a proxy for specialization, answers to the following questions remain unclear: (1) What are the neurocognitive factors that drive specialization? (2) When does specialization fully occur (if at all)? (3) To what extent does specialization become fixed with age or experience? (4) Is recovery better explained by reorganization or by bilateral redundancy? and (5) Does specialization necessarily convey an (externally observable) behavioral advantage? To investigate these questions further, the process of specialization must be specified in greater detail and for this we turn to computational modeling.

14.1.3 Computational approaches to emergent modularity

Three principal types of computational account have been put forward to account for emergent functional specialization (Jacobs 1999). In the *mixture-of-experts* approach (Jacobs 1997; Jacobs *et al.* 1991), the initial system is comprised of components that have different computational properties. A separate mechanism gates the contribution of these components to the output. When the overall system is presented with a task, the gating mechanism mediates a competition between the set of components, allowing the most successful component for each training pattern both to drive output performance and to update its weights to become better at that pattern. Across training, certain mechanisms come to specialize on sets of patterns, by virtue of having an initial (perhaps small) advantage in processing those patterns. In *the neural selectionism* or *parcellation* approach, the initial computational system has a surplus of connections. However, during learning, many of these connections are weeded out (pruned), whereas others are stabilized depending on usage. In addition, a locality constraint favors the stabilization of connections between nearby processing units. The result is that nearby units communicate with each other and come to perform the same functions, whereas those far apart do not communicate and come to specialize in different functions (Jacobs and Jordan 1992; Johnson and Karmiloff-Smith 1992). In the *wave of plasticity* approach, the initial computational system experiences differential responsiveness to learning, both spatially and temporally. Plasticity is reduced over time across a sheet of computational units, so that one side of the sheet loses its plasticity earlier than the other. The result is that later maturing units can employ the functions computed by the earlier maturing units as input, thereby computing more abstract functions from them. The later maturing units effectively specialize in more abstract aspects of the problem domain (Shrager and Johnson 1996).

To date, the majority of computational modeling approaches to atypical development have focused on processing anomalies within prespecified functional modules. For example, parameter variations have been used to explain characteristics of autism in categorization networks, characteristics of dyslexia in reading networks, or characteristics of Williams syndrome and Specific Language Impairment in inflectional morphology networks (see Thomas and Karmiloff-Smith 2002a, for a review). One model has offered a preliminary insight to atypical specialization. Oliver *et al.* (2000) explored the parameters that affect the successful emergence of topographic maps in a self-organizing network. In this model, the network was presented with four bars on an input retina and had to learn a map with four regions, one specialized to recognize each bar. Oliver *et al.* found that several computational parameters disrupted the organization of the map, including reducing the length of lateral inhibitory connections in the output layer and altering the relative similarity of the four input patterns. They suggested that the simulations might offer a model of 'encapsulation' and the emergence of information-processing modules. The parameter variations could therefore represent atypical modularization via a disrupted parcellation process. However, the functional significance of the disrupted networks was hard to evaluate given the simple problem domain.

Three other computational models are also relevant in that they establish some of the conditions under which specialization can occur. Dailey and Cottrell (1999) used a mixture-of-experts model to capture the emergence of specialized structures for face recognition in a system also trained to recognize images of books, cups, and cans. The model had two components that competed to classify the images. In one version of the model, there was no processing difference between the two components other than their initial random connection weights. Partial specialization of the faces to one mechanism did occur but the effect was not particularly strong. Nevertheless, this condition demonstrated that with very low domain relevance, competition is sufficient to produce specialization. In a second version, one component was fed high spatial frequency information from the visual input while the other was fed low spatial frequency information. The result was much more reliable emergent specialization for face recognition to the low spatial frequency component.

Monaghan and Shillcock (2004) employed a similar approach to capture hemispheric asymmetries in a model of unilateral visual neglect. The hidden layer of a three-layer network was split so that the left side had gaussian units with narrow receptive fields, while the right side had gaussian units with wide overlapping receptive fields. This manipulation implemented the assumption that the two hemispheres have different spatial scales at which they prefer to operate. The model was trained to recognize the location and length of lines presented on an input retina. When the network was given a unilateral lesion after training, its performance on a line bisection task replicated a number of asymmetries found after cases of human brain damage. These included larger displacements of the centre of the line following damage to the coarse-coded right side than to the left side of the hidden layer and faster recovery after left damage than right damage. In this model, there was no explicit competition process, yet domain relevance led to specialization.

Finally, Reggia and Schulz (2002) reviewed a number of their models designed to explore the computational conditions under which two cerebral regions that communicate via a simulated corpus callosum produce emergent specialization between the two hemispheres. Using both self-organizing and back propagation networks, they examined the effect of using excitatory vs. inhibitory connections between the hemispheres, as well as a range of other parameter variations. Their results demonstrated that specialization can occur in the absence of competition between the hemispheres or even in the presence of excitation, so long as the parameter settings of the two hemispheres are different enough. However, specialization effects were stronger with inhibitory connections implementing a competitive process.

14.1.4 The current simulations

In the following sections, we report the results of new computational work designed to investigate possible disruptions to the emergence of functionally specialized structures. We focused on four issues:

♦ What are the computational parameters that affect emergent specialization in associative (task-driven) systems?

♦ What are the relative contributions of domain relevance and competition, the two features of the emergentist approach, in driving emergent specialization?

♦ Are there computational parameters that determine whether a system with multiple components will exhibit prespecified modularity, emergent modularity, or redundancy?

♦ When a normally developed system with specialized components experiences damage, how do parameter settings alter the patterns of recovery? In particular, under what conditions do side-of-lesion effects persist after recovery (consistent with innate modularity) and under what conditions do side-of-lesion effects eventually disappear (consistent with emergentism), as in the case of language development after early unilateral brain damage (Bates and Roe 2001)?

14.1.4.1 Architectures, cognitive domains, and parameters

Previous modeling work has drawn a distinction between two types of neurocomputational learning systems (O'Reilly 1998). In *self-organizing* systems, the emergence of functional structure is based upon patterns of similarity in the input. Self-organizing systems are normally used to learn categories within input sets. In *error-driven* systems, the emergence of functional structure is guided through an error signal. The error signal is normally used to allow the system to learn input–output transformations. It is possible that the key parameters guiding specialization differ between the two types of system and we therefore consider them separately. While the models are greatly simplified from neurobiological and behavioral reality, they are nevertheless based on some basic principles of biological neural elements, circuits, and synaptic plasticity (Reggia and Schulz 2002). We take two exemplar cognitive domains, one appropriate to a self-organizing system, one to an error-driven system, both of which demonstrate emergent specialization of functional structure in our chosen architectures. The two cognitive domains are relatively rich, facilitating evaluation of possible decrements on behavioral task performance caused by different parameter settings. The self-organizing domain is a feature-based set of semantic representations. The error-driven domain is English past tense. As in previous simulations of developmental deficits, parameter manipulations are carried out prior to training the various models, and subsequent developmental trajectories and endstate deficits are then assessed (Thomas and Karmiloff-Smith 2002b). The parameters we consider are the amount of processing resources for both self-organizing and error-driven systems, the level of plasticity and the nature of the learning rule in the error-driven system, competition mechanisms in both systems, and changes in input frequency in both systems.

14.2 Simulations

14.2.1 Simulation 1: specialization in self-organizing systems

In this simulation, we consider the effects of parameter manipulations on the emergence of specialized structures in a self-organizing feature map (Kohonen 1995), one example of a self-organizing system. This architecture is relevant to basic sensory development, for example, of topographic maps. Our model is similar to that employed by Oliver *et al.* (2000) described previously, in that the relationship between inputs is reflected in the topography of the map formed on the cortical layer. The architecture we used had simpler activation dynamics but was exposed to a richer cognitive domain, permitting a consideration of the quality of the learned representations for driving categorization. The example categories were drawn from semantics and included humans, animals, vegetables, fruit, dairy produce, kitchen utensils, tools, and vehicles, defined over a set of features. Our interest was to explore two constraints in the model: (1) a domain-relevant constraint – the level of resources available in the output layer (that is, the number of output units available to represent the categories); and (2) the competition process occurring in the network. To alter conditions of competition, we either reduced the neighborhood size of the units that would update their weights for a given pattern (i.e. the size of the region of units affected when a given unit became associated with a given pattern), or we altered the balance of the input set to favor some categories over others. The final self-organizing maps were evaluated with regard to whether they maintained the same regions of specialization and whether they permitted the same degree of discrimination within each semantic category.

14.2.1.1 Simulation details

Architecture: We employed the Self-organizing feature map (SOFM) available in the Matlab Neural Networks toolbox (Demuth and Beale 2002). The SOFM is a two-layer network with full connectivity between the layers. When a pattern is presented to the network, the output unit with the weight vector closest to the input vector becomes the winner. The weights for this unit and for those in a given neighborhood surrounding it are then updated. The result is a topological arrangement of the SOFM, with neighboring regions of the input space coming to be represented by neighboring units on the map. The network was trained in two phases. The first 'ordering' phase defined the broad topology (with a large but reducing neighborhood size and large but reducing learning rate). The second 'tuning' phase refined the topology (smaller fixed neighborhood size and smaller and slowly declining learning rate). Six parameters defined training: the number of presentations of the training set in the ordering phase, the total number of presentations, the ordering phase learning rate, the tuning phase learning rate, and the final neighborhood size. In the normal condition, the following values were used, respectively: 1000 presentations, 3000 presentations, 0.9, 0.02, and a size of 1. Two atypical parameter sets were used to disrupt competition: we either set the neighborhood size to zero throughout training (the 'No neighborhood' condition); or we allowed a brief ordering phase of ten presentations of the training set before setting the neighborhood to zero (the 'Fast commitment' condition). The output layer used a hexagonal topology and a box-distance function to calculate the distance between two units. In the normal condition, a 14×14 output layer was used. These resources were progressively reduced to 12×12, 10×10, and 7×7 maps. The input layer comprised 154 units. Each network was run three times with different random seeds for the initial weights.

Training set: We exposed the network to a training set comprising semantic representations for 58 concepts. The concept set was based on that used by Small *et al.* (1996), who constructed an item set from concepts employed in neuropsychological tests of semantic deficits. Our training set comprised eight major categories: humans, animals, vegetables, fruit, dairy produce, kitchen utensils, tools, and vehicles. Concepts were defined over 154 meaningful semantic features (such as 'has legs', 'is food'). Each concept activated on average 19 of these features. An individual input pattern consisted of 154 binary digits, indicating the presence or absence of each semantic feature. From the set of 58 prototypes, multiple exemplars (variations on a given prototype) were generated from each prototype to produce a final training set of 185 items (for example if 'apple' was the prototype, 'green apple' and 'red apple' might be two exemplars). A single random order of the items was created and this was used in all conditions, to ensure that any variability stemmed from internal rather than external constraints. To investigate the effect of altering the balance of inputs from different categories, two Altered Input Competition conditions were created. One combined the exemplars for Living concepts with the prototypes of Non-living (A) for a training set of 143 items. The other combined the prototypes for Living concepts with the exemplars for Non-living concepts (B) for a set of 100 items.

14.2.1.2 Results

The maps produced in each condition are presented in Fig. 14.1 (a color version of this diagram is available at http://www.psyc.bbk.ac.uk/people/academic/thomas_m/). To plot these diagrams, we used a cluster analysis of the similarity structure in the training set to assign a gray scale to each pattern. This color was then assigned to the unit(s) that became activated on presentation of this pattern to the trained network. If

Plate 1 Biological screening-off (Schulz and Gopnik 2004). (Fig. 15.3 in text.)

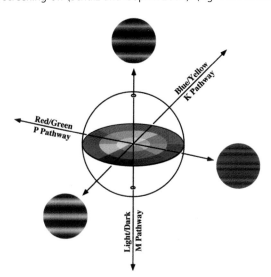

Plate 2 Three fundamental dimensions of color presented in three-dimensional color space: light/dark (luminance), red/green (chromatic), and blue/yellow (chromatic). Detection of light/dark, red/green, and blue/yellow grating stimuli (depicted by the icons at the end of the axes) is thought to be mediated by three subcortical pathways, the magnocellular (M), parvocellular (P), and koniocellular (K) pathways, respectively. (Reprinted from Dobkins, 2000 with permission from *Neuron*.) (Fig. 17.1 in text.)

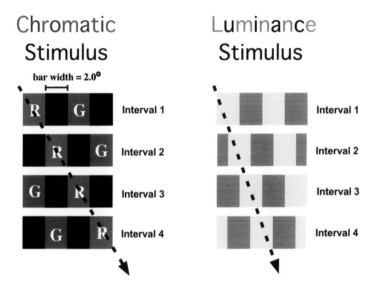

Chromatic Stimulus

bar width = 2.0°

R G	Interval 1
R G	Interval 2
G R	Interval 3
G R	Interval 4

Luminance Stimulus

	Interval 1
	Interval 2
	Interval 3
	Interval 4

Plate 3 Schematic depiction of stimuli used to test the P pathway retraction hypothesis. Left panel: moving chromatic stimulus. Right panel: moving luminance stimulus. For both, the position of a slice through the stimulus is shown at four consecutive time intervals. Motion based on chromatic matches (left panel) or luminance matches (right panel) is rightward in these examples. Note that, because the luminance stimulus necessarily employed a smaller displacement per time interval (half the width of one stripe), the displacement occurred twice as frequently for the luminance stimulus as for the chromatic stimulus, in order to create identical speeds in the two conditions (i.e. 35°/s). Reprinted from Dobkins and Anderson (2002) with permission from *Psychological Science*. (Fig. 17.5 in text.)

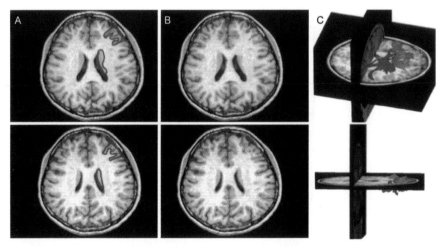

Plate 4 Illustration of most common MR methods used in study of development and learning. MRI-based brain morphometry (Panel A), fMRI-based patterns of brain activity (Panel B) and DTI-based fiber tracking (Panel C) of frontostriatal connections shown in two representative axial slices. (Fig. 22.1 in text.)

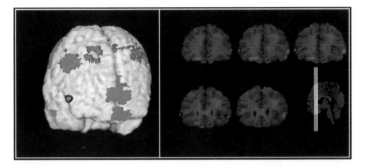

Plate 5 Illustration of fMRI-based changes in MR signal observed with development longitudinally. Blue areas indicate decreases in activity in these regions with age and red areas are those that show increase in activation with age. (Fig. 22.4 in text.)

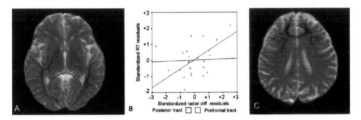

Plate 6 DTI-based anterior (A) and posterior (C) fiber tracts and the correlation with performance of the go/nogo task with prefrontal tracts, but not posterior tracts (B). (Fig. 22.5 in text)

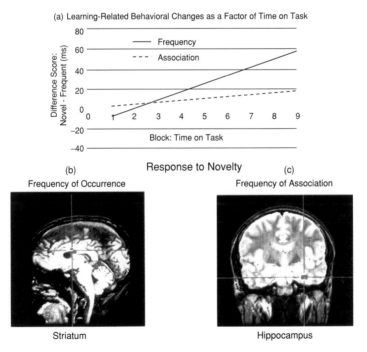

Plate 7 Behavioral performance (A), striatal activity (B), and hippocampal activity (C) to infrequently presented target stimuli and stimuli associations. (Fig. 22.9 in text.)

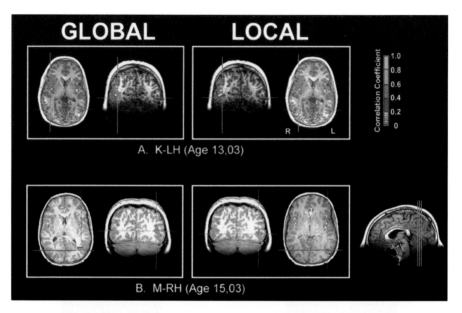

Plate 8 See Fig. 23.4 in text for full caption. Adapted with permission from Stiles *et al.* (2003)

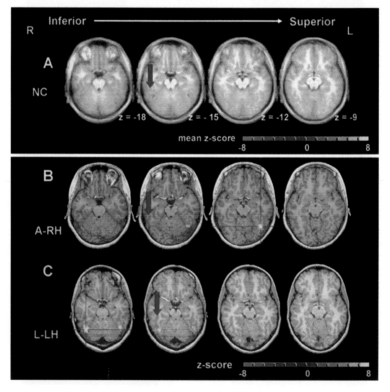

Plate 9 See Fig. 23.6 in text for full caption.

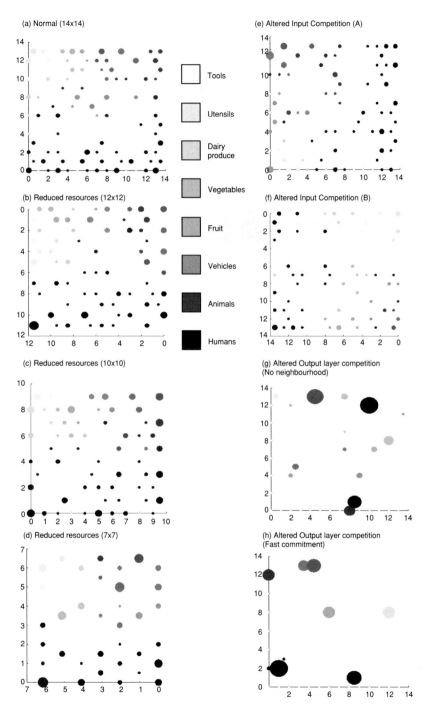

Fig. 14.1 Self-organizing maps for variations in map size (a to d), variations in input (e to f), and variations in competition within the output layer (g to h).

several patterns activated the same unit, the colors were averaged. The number of patterns activating each unit determined the size of the circle representing that unit. Fig. 14.1a depicts the normal condition for the 14 × 14 map. The systematic change of shading across the map indicates that the network formed separate areas representing the major semantic categories. Of the network's 196 output units, on average 78 (40 per cent) were activated by one or more inputs. Figure 14.1b to d illustrate the effect of reducing the map size. Three points are of note. First, for smaller maps, a similar organization of specialized areas still emerged. Replications revealed some instability in whether fruit/vegetables or people/animals were to the right of vehicles, but Living patterns were always separate from Non-living. Second, for the smaller maps, the circles became progressively larger. That is, each unit came to respond to more input patterns. As a result, these maps were less able to discriminate between items *within* each category. Third, as the maps became smaller, they progressively filled up: on average the 12 × 12 activated 70 of its 144 units (48 per cent), the 10 × 10 activated 58 of its 100 units (58 per cent) and the 7 × 7, 36 of its 49 units (72 per cent).

Figure 14.1e and f demonstrate the effect of altering the balance of input patterns from each category. These networks demonstrated comparable use of units and broadly similar organization of the maps, although the location of areas could be different. The effects of altering the inputs were sometimes subtle, with expansion of areas for over-represented categories and reduction of areas for under-represented categories, but little change in the discrimination that the maps offered within categories (at least with reference to the altered training sets). In the normal condition, Living occupied 60 per cent of the active map space and Non-living 40 per cent. For Competition A, where the Living category was considerably larger, Living items occupied 73 per cent of the active map space and Non-living 27 per cent. For Competition B, where the proportion of Non-living items was larger, Non-living items occupied 72 per cent of the active map space and Living 28 per cent. Figure 14.1g demonstrates the effect of eliminating neighborhoods. The result is a very disordered map, sparsely filled (16 of 196 units), an absence of specialized regions defined by similarity and very poor discrimination. Figure 14.1h demonstrates the result of quickly shrinking the neighborhoods. The result is an organization that reflects the similarity structure of the input, but again, a sparsely filled network (9/196) and very poor (indeed absent) discrimination within categories.

14.2.1.3 Discussion

When the domain-relevant parameter of resource level was varied in the SOFM, the functional specialization of regions was retained but within-category discrimination was lost. When competition was changed at the input level, regions for each category changed their relative sizes whilst retaining many of the features of overall organization. When competition was altered at output (represented by changes in the neighborhood function), both organization and discrimination were lost. This finding reflects observations from the empirical literature. Huttenlocher (2002) notes that healthy infants suffering either focal or diffuse damage to the cerebral cortex tend to exhibit an impairment in the overall efficiency of cortical functions (reflected in a decrease in IQ) rather than patterns of differential cognitive deficits. There are also parallels with much lower level functioning in the research on sensory map formation in the animal literature. In comparative studies of cortical field development in marsupials (the short-tailed opossum), it was found that reducing the size (processing resources) of the cortical neuroepithelial sheet unilaterally at an early stage of development nevertheless led to the normal spatial relationships between visual, somatosensory, and auditory cortical fields in the reduced cortical sheet, but an increase in neurons responding to multiple inputs (Huffman *et al.* 1999). By contrast, changing the competition between inputs by peripheral innervation of vision early in development led to a subsequent alteration in the organization of adult cortical areas, with auditory and somatosensory systems expanding to capture the usual visual area (Kahn and Krubitzer 2002). In sum, this simulation suggests that the level of processing resources is a parameter that can be disrupted (and lead to performance decrements) without compromising functional specialization in self-organizing systems. By contrast, functional specialization is more readily altered when the parameter of competition is atypical.

14.2.2 Simulation 2: the emergence of functional specialization in error-driven systems

In this simulation, we consider the effects of parameter manipulations on the emergence of specialized structures in an error-driven system. We employed a base model that was required to learn the transformations for a quasiregular domain, which is characterized by a predominant rule along with a smaller set of exceptions to the rule. The problem domain was drawn from work on language development, specifically the acquisition of English past tense within inflectional morphology. In this task, the model is required produce the past tense form of a word when presented with its present tense at input (for example regular: 'part-parted', exception: 'go-went'). This domain is useful for two reasons. First, it has a bipartite organization of regular versus exception mappings. We have previously shown that in a type of a mixture-of-experts model, those two classes of mapping can show emergent specialization to two processing mechanisms (Thomas and Karmiloff-Smith 2002b). Second, there has been an extensive debate within the field of language development on whether the cognitive system deploys *a priori* separate mechanisms to learn the two parts of the past tense domain (Pinker 1994, 1999), or whether acquisition proceeds via a single undifferentiated system (Rumelhart and McClelland 1986). Researchers supporting the former theory have already speculated on the competitive processes necessary to control the two prespecified mechanisms during development, which will become relevant in Simulation 3. In the meantime, this training set again provides a relatively rich cognitive domain against which we can assess both performance and functional specialization. In this simulation, we took the base model of Thomas and Karmiloff-Smith (2002b) and explored the effect on emergent specialization of varying four computational parameters determining the domain-relevant computational properties of the system. (We consider variations in competition in the following simulation.) The four parameters were: (1) processing resources, (2) plasticity, (3) the nature of the associative learning rule, and (4) input frequency.

14.2.2.1 Simulation details

Architecture: The base model was a back propagation network in which input and output layers are connected by two routes: either by direct connections (the Direct route) or via a set of hidden units (the Indirect route). The normal condition of the model was trained using the back propagation algorithm with a cross entropy error measure, learning rate of 0.1 and momentum of 0, for 500 presentations of the training set (random order without replacement). The network had 90 input units and 100 output units, with 20 hidden units in the Indirect route. Processing resources were varied by including 100 hidden units in the Indirect route. Plasticity was varied by multiplying the learning rate by a factor of four either in the Direct route (the '41' conditions) or the Indirect route (the '14' condition). The learning rule was varied by changing the back propagation to employ root mean square (RMS) error to the target (BP-RMS), producing a network more vulnerable to entrenchment (Thomas and Karmiloff-Smith 2003). Six replications of each network were run using different random seeds. In all figures, error bars portray the standard error of the means across the six replications.

Training: The training set comprised 508 training items, with a further set of 410 test items assessing regular generalization. Performance was assessed on five categories of items: *Regular* mappings (410 items within the training set); generalization of the regular *Rule* to 410 novel items similar to the regular items in the training set; and three types of exception patterns. Exception patterns varied in their level of inconsistency with regular items, which might alter the extent to which they are driven to use alternate processing mechanisms. *EP1* exceptions (20) were most consistent with the regular training items. *EP2* exceptions (68) were less consistent with the regular training items. *EP3* exception items (10) were most inconsistent, sharing input similarity with regular items but requiring a qualitatively different transformation. Training items were split into high and low frequency groups. To ensure the acquisition of the EP3 items, these were given a higher token frequency that all other patterns, hence they are labeled *EP3f*. This training set therefore permits assessment of the effects of mapping type on specialization, including: (1) a continuum of consistency and (2) the effect of token frequency. Performance was measured at 1, 2, 5, 10, 25, 50, 100, 200, and 500 epochs of training (full details can be found in Thomas and Karmiloff-Smith 2002b).

14.2.2.2 Results

All parameter conditions led to successful acquisition of this quasiregular domain, albeit with developmental trajectories that could be accelerated or delayed and relative rates of acquisition of regulars and exceptions that could be altered. Figure 14.2a demonstrates the developmental trajectories for the five pattern types in the base model and includes the effect of token frequency on acquisition. The base model contains two processing routes (Direct and Indirect) and the problem domain contains two types of problem (Regular / Rule vs. Exceptions). Figure 14.2b demonstrates the specialization of function of the problem types to the two routes. Specialization was assessed by measuring the differential impairment of a unilateral lesion to each route, at a level that did not cause performance to stay at ceiling or hit floor (this corresponded to a loss of 50 per cent of connections). Using the standard logic of

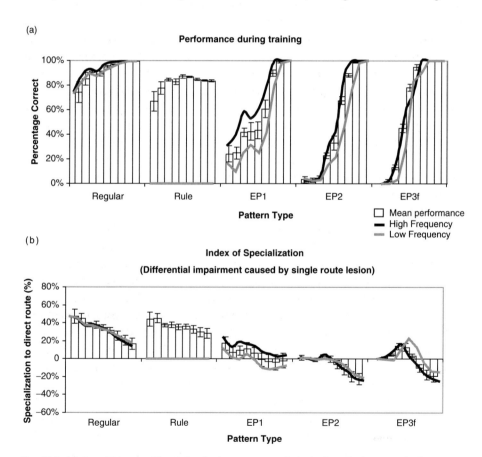

Fig. 14.2 (a) Acquisition profile of the dual-route network, including the impact of token frequency. (b) Specialization of the patterns to each route. The black line represents high frequency items, the gray line represents low frequency items.

neuropsychology, if a pattern type was impaired more by damage to the Direct mechanism than to the Indirect mechanism, it was assumed to be more specialized to the Direct mechanism. Figure 14.2b indicates that partial specialization of this system emerged across training, with Regulars and Rule-based generalization preferring the Direct mechanism, EP1 relying equally on both routes, and both the more inconsistent EP2 and EP3f patterns preferring the Indirect route. Technically, this partial specialization occurs because the model requires hidden units in order to learn exception patterns, since the mapping problem is linearly inseparable and cannot be solved with only one layer of weights. More broadly, the exceptions form the harder part of the problem that requires the power of the hidden units to solve. However, the one layer of weights in the Direct route is more plastic than the two layers of weights in the Indirect route, so most mappings are initially acquired by the Direct route and then progressively move over to the Indirect route with further training. Importantly, Fig. 14.2 demonstrates that the token frequency of mappings modulates the pattern of specialization, tending to accelerate the shift from Direct to Indirect routes – that is, the relatively frequency of items in the training set itself is sufficient to alter patterns of specialization.

Figure 14.3a depicts the developmental trajectories for the increased resources, BP-RMS, and differential plasticity conditions, while Fig. 14.3b illustrates the emergent specialization for these conditions. Altering the learning algorithm has a subtle effect on specialization, changing the ability of the Direct route to accommodate both EP1 and EP3f patterns early in training and driving EP1 across to the Indirect route. However, both resource changes and plasticity changes have marked effects on specialization. Provision of extra resources in the hidden layer pulls all functions across to this route. The relative plasticity of the two routes is able to override structure–function correspondences (i.e. how well the two routes are suited to computing the two parts of the problem domain) and impose functional specialization by a method that might be called the 'who gets there first' approach. However, all conditions achieved only partial rather than full specialization by the end of training.

14.2.2.3 Discussion

This model demonstrates that structure–function correspondences can lead to emergent specialization of function in an error-driven system, but that resources and relative plasticity of the processing routes play a significant role in driving specialization. More subtle effects were produced by modifications to the learning rule. Even the token frequency of the patterns could modulate trajectories of specialization. The influential role of plasticity reproduces similar findings by Reggia and Schulz (2002) in their simulations of hemispheric asymmetry. It is also consistent with proposals by Huttenlocher (2002) that the differential rates of plasticity in different cortical areas (indexed by synaptogenesis) may play a role in driving functional specialization. However, differential plasticity can only have an effect when the relation between

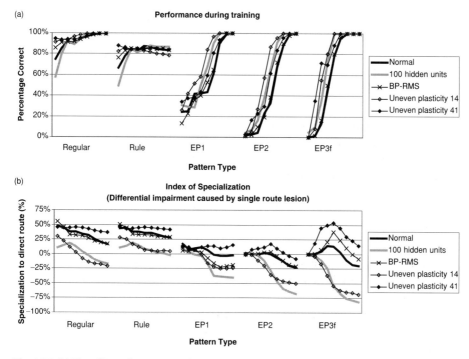

Fig. 14.3 (a) The effect of parameter changes on acquisition profiles. (b) The effect of parameter changes on emergent specialization.

mechanisms and domains is 'relevant' rather than specific; that is, each mechanism must have at least some ability to process each domain.

Returning to the broader picture, inappropriate levels of resources or region-specific changes of plasticity appear as constraints that would alter emergent functional structure in error-driven systems. However, importantly, the outward behavioral consequences of these alterations were subtle, producing little more than uneven or delayed development. On the other hand, the results *did not* point to any parameters that would allow the emergence of normal functional structure while showing circumscribed performance decrements. If anything, they pointed in the opposite direction: performance similar to normal could be achieved by an atypical underlying functional structure.

14.2.3 Simulation 3: varieties of competition

In this simulation, we consider variations to the competition process in error-driven systems. To foreshadow the results, it turned out that competition alone could mediate between a developmental system with *prespecified modularity*, one with *emergent modularity*, and one with multiple *redundant* components. To understand this, we need to take a brief step backwards: a question one might ask of the preceding simulation is why specialization occurred *at all*. While the architecture included two processing mechanisms like a traditional mixture-of-experts model, there was no gating mechanism to force the two routes to compete. Why did they specialize? Why didn't each route attempt to compute all the patterns to the best level it could, thereby producing redundancy of function?

Further analysis revealed that a different form of competition was operating in this network, one that we will call 'Update' competition. For each input, both routes generate a contribution to the output layer. The difference between this output and the target leads to an error signal that allows weights to be changed in both routes. However, if one route is producing the correct answer before the other route has figured out its contribution, there will be no disparity between output and target and therefore no error signal to drive further weight change in the non-contributing route. This form of competition is sufficient to drive specialization. However, Update competition does not prevent weaker routes from making a contribution *per se*, it merely freezes the contribution when the error at output has been eliminated. As a result, Update competition encourages *co-operation and partial emergent specialization*. Monaghan and Shillcock's (2004) model of hemispheric asymmetries in unilateral visual neglect provides an example of specialization through update competition.

Update competition contrasts with two other forms of competition: (1) 'Input' competition and (2) 'Output' competition. In 'Input' competition, each mechanism is only presented with the patterns that it must learn. Because Input competition can ensure that each component is exposed only to patterns from a single cognitive domain, it is a way to implement *prespecified modularity*. One might envisage at least three ways to implement Input competition: (1) it might stem from the initial prewiring of the system, what Elman *et al.* (1996) call the global architecture. Certain areas of the cortex receive certain inputs and not others by virtue of their location. (2) It might be the outcome of a self-organizing process, whereby connections from certain inputs may be pruned as a function of learning. For example when the self-organizing map learns, strengthening the weights from the input layer to the winning area of the map means that connections to other areas are weakened. Eventually, areas distant from the winning location will simply stop receiving the signal for a given input and therefore can no longer compete to be activated by it. (3) Input competition might be achieved by some kind of intelligent 'gatekeeper' that directs the input patterns to various mechanisms depending on their identity. Fodor (2000) argues that to support this form of Input competition, the gatekeeper, would have to be a (rather powerful) domain-general processing mechanism. Such a gatekeeper figures in a recent proposal by Pinker (1999) for a dual-component cognitive system for acquiring the English past tense. Construed in terms of our base model, Pinker's proposal amounts to training the Direct route only on Regular patterns. A gatekeeper would need to identify these from exception mappings, even though the two are fairly similar at input.

The third form of competition is 'Output' competition. In this case, all mechanisms are allowed to compute an answer for a given input. However, only the 'best' output will drive behavior, while the other mechanisms are either ignored or potentially inhibited. For instance, in the example of language, we saw earlier that activation of left-sided language areas causes inhibition of homologous right-sided areas, consistent with some bilaterally of language function that is silenced by Output competition (Blank *et al.* 2003). Pinker's (1994) model of past tense formation also includes Output competition, whereby (in terms of our current architecture) the Indirect route would overrule the Direct mechanism and drive output under certain circumstances. One complication with Output competition is how to decide which mechanism is providing the 'best' output, particularly if the overall system is presented with a novel pattern where neither mechanism necessarily has a 'correct' answer. One possibility is to take something like the highest activation level. Finally, the use of Output competition is consistent with producing *multiple redundant systems* where all components attempt to learn all parts of the problem.

Although we have identified three different types of competition, combinations of these three types are possible. For example, within this scheme the traditional mixture-of-experts model is a combination of Update and Output competition. In this simulation, we explore the implications of all combinations of Input, Update, and Output competition on the emergence of specialized or redundant structures, as well as on the external developmental trajectories exhibited by each type of overall system. The domain-relevant computational properties of the system are held constant.

14.2.3.1 Simulation details

Architecture and training: We employed the same architecture as in Simulation 2. For simplicity, competition types were treated dichotomously, as present or absent. Update competition was implemented by training both Direct and Indirect routes in tandem, so that both contributed simultaneously to the output and error was propagated back to both routes. Input competition was implemented by training the Direct route in isolation on the Regular patterns and the Indirect route in isolation on the Exception patterns. It was thus implemented in an absolute form. The output layer was common to both and therefore the routes were constrained to use the same threshold settings on the output units. Output competition was implemented by training both routes in isolation as above but now on the whole training set. During testing, the output activations were computed separately for each route. To determine the 'best' output, a thresholded version of each was created, with values set to 1 if a unit was activated above 0.5, and 0 if it was activated below 0.5. The Euclidean distance between each actual output vector and its thresholded version was then calculated. The route with the smallest distance reflected the most 'binary' output. Since all targets in the training set were 0 or 1, a more binarized output could be judged a more confident response. The most binary output vector from the two routes was assigned the winner and therefore the output from the whole system. Again, this is an absolute implementation of Output competition. Note that traditional the mixture-of-experts architecture permits weighted combinations of each route (see Dailey and Cottrell 1999).

Input, Update, and Output competition could each be employed in the network, providing eight combinations. However, Update competition is meaningless if both routes are not being supplied with the input (i.e. if Input competition is on), since a route without input cannot contribute to the output during training. This leaves six combinations. The network was trained using the parameters of Simulation 2 for these six combinations. When the Indirect route was trained in isolation, its 20 hidden units risked making it underpowered to learn a given set of mappings. An additional condition using 100 hidden units in the Indirect route was therefore also assessed. Since generalization to novel inputs was one of the performance metrics, networks trained with Input competition were tested by presenting the input to both routes, as in Pinker's (1994) instantiation of Input competition.

14.2.3.2 Results

Figure 14.4 shows the developmental trajectories for the six conditions. Where acquisition was only successful with 100 hidden units in the Indirect route, only this trajectory is plotted. Two of the combinations were unsuccessful in acquiring the quasiregular domain. Otherwise, competition decisions tended to modulate developmental trajectories, sometimes differentially across regulars and exceptions.

The two unsuccessful combinations failed for the following reasons. The network trained without Input competition but with Update and Output competition (NYY) was unsuccessful because the mechanisms that had co-operated in reducing the error on the output layer were now required to function in isolation and in competition. The division of labor meant neither had enough labor on its own. The network trained with Input competition but without Update and Output competition (YNN) was unsuccessful because two mechanisms trained in isolation were not co-ordinated at output and therefore interfered with each other's responses.

The network with Input competition, Output competition, but no Update competition (YNY100) captures the combination proposed by Pinker (1994) for how the child acquires this domain of grammar (a modification of this model proposed by Pinker 1999, was also explored, however the results are not reported here). Two things are notable here. First, this combination produced a *prespecified modular* system that successfully acquired the domain. One mechanism was prespecified for regulars, the other for exceptions and they competed to drive the response. Second, the conditions under which acquisition was successful were rather circumscribed. First, the hidden layer of the Indirect route required 100 hidden units. But even in this case, performance (as selected by Output competition) was mostly driven by the Direct route. This is

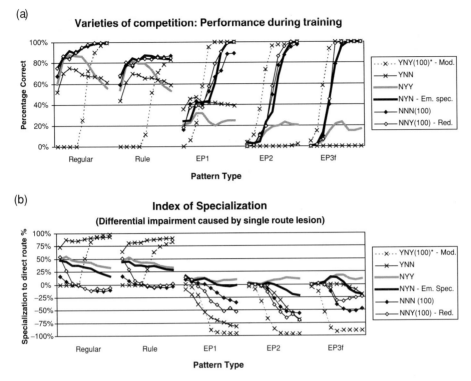

Fig. 14.4 (a) Acquisition profiles for different combinations of competition. (b) Specialization profiles. The first letter indicates the presence of Input competition (Y or N), the second letter indicates the presence of Update competition (Y or N) and the third Output competition (Y or N). 100 indicates the use of 100 hidden units in the Indirect layer. Mod. = Prespecified modularity, Em. Spec. = Emergent specialization, Red. = Redundancy. * = Indirect route had to be biased during Output competition to permit successful acquisition.

because the Exception patterns were learnt by a mechanism with two layers of weights rather than one. The two layers take more training to produce an equivalent level of binarization of output values. Thus, even when the Indirect route had the correct answer, the Direct route was more confident of the incorrect answer. Only by biasing the output competition (increasing the 'confidence' measure of the Indirect route by a factor of 200, a value determined via a parameter search) was the Indirect route successfully able to drive the output for its set of patterns. It is possible that such a calibration could have been acquired by learning, for example by gradually biasing the Output competition each time a route produced the correct answer but did not win the output competition. Nevertheless, under the conditions used here, prespecified modularity to drive performance at a common output was not a robust solution for acquisition.

As we saw in Simulation 2, the sole use of Update competition produced *emergent specialization* (NYN, NYN100). Successful acquisition was achieved with only 20 hidden units, implying that emergent specialization represents an efficient use of resources. Use of additional resources (Fig. 14.3b) also produced partial specialization, but now with the heavily resourced route playing the dominant role.

When neither Input nor Update competition was used (NNN100, NNY100), acquisition was successful with or without Output competition, so long as additional resources were used in the Indirect route. As we shall see in the next simulation, these combinations produced *redundant* systems. The system performed better with Output competition, since the routes did not have to shout over each other to drive performance – the most confident route could produce behavior. At the end of training, 90 per cent of Regulars were produced by the Indirect route, 100 per cent of Exceptions and 50 per cent of Rule generalizations. The main contribution of the Direct device was therefore in generalization (see Taatgen and Anderson 2002, for a similar result with a hybrid symbolic-associative model acquiring the past tense domain implemented in the ACT-R cognitive architecture). A summary of the outcomes of competition combinations can be found in Table 14.1.

14.2.3.3 Discussion

This simulation demonstrated that in error-driven systems, competition is exceedingly important in driving functional specialization because, for a given set of domain–relevancies or structure–function correspondences, it can differentiate between pre-specified modularity, emergent specialization, and redundancy. For example, one could have an otherwise equipotential system segregated by Input and Output competition into a prespecified modular system. In this case, the equipotentiality could be demonstrated by taking a processing element from, say, the vision component and placing it in the audition component, where it would be equally at home and start to be conditioned by the input/output mappings of that domain. Such equipotentiality of function would, however, be fully consistent with prespecified modularity. Therefore the theoretical distinction between innate modularity and equipotentiality that we encountered in the Introduction is not necessarily a dichotomy – in this case the two exist as different settings of a competition parameter.

Although the conceptual outcome of the combinations of competition might have been anticipated in advance, implementation demonstrated that: (1) emergence was a

Table 14.1 The effect of varying types of competition on specialization in a dual route network

Input competition	Update competition	Output competition	
		Yes	**No**
Yes	Yes	N/A	N/A
	No	Prespecified modularity	Unsuccessful acquisition
No	Yes	Unsuccessful acquisition	Emergent specialization
	No	Redundancy	Redundancy

resource-efficient form of acquisition; (2) competition decisions nevertheless had implications for developmental trajectories even when acquisition was successful; and (3) prespecified modularity required a more delicate balance of parameters than the other combinations to learn this particular problem domain. Overall, the implication of this simulation is that if the conditions of competition are not perturbed, modular architecture should not be disrupted.

14.2.4 Simulation 4: recovery patterns of systems with different functional structure

In the Introduction, we noted the challenge of trying to reconcile uniformity of outcome in functional specialization with the flexibility implied by recovery after damage. This simulation sought to assess the implications of the specialization induced by competition for recovery after damage. It did so with particular reference to: (1) the possibility of redundant systems aiding recovery (e.g. for language, see Blank *et al.* 2003); and (2) whether systems produced side-of-damage effects, either during recovery or once recovery was complete (e.g. for language, see Bates and Roe 2001). The combinations of competition from Simulation 3 that successfully acquired the problem domain were given either a bilateral lesion to both routes, unilateral damage to the Direct route, or unilateral damage to the Indirect route, and their patterns of recovery observed. Note that these models assume unchanging plasticity with age.

14.2.4.1 Simulation details

Architecture and training: For the successful networks in Simulation 3, a probabilistic lesion of 75 per cent of network connections was applied either to both routes, to the Direct route alone, or to the Indirect alone. Networks were then retrained for 500 epochs, using the same parameter settings as in Simulation 3. Performance was measured after 1, 2, 5, 10, 25, 50, 100, 200, and 500 epochs of training after damage.

14.2.4.2 Results

Figure 14.5 demonstrates the recovery profiles following a *bilateral* lesion, for the *prespecified modular* system, for the *emergent specialization* systems with 20 and 100 hidden units, and for the *redundant* system with 100 hidden units and Output competition. For Regular and Rule patterns, only the prespecified modular system failed to show strong recovery. For Exception patterns, recovery was weaker in the emergent system with limited resources and the redundant system, and stronger in the rich emergent and modular networks. Rich resources aided recovery. Interestingly, the rich emergent system was more successful in recovering from overall damage than the redundant system. This was because it could use its remaining resources co-operatively. In most cases, recovery was aided by frequency, either the higher type frequency of Regulars or the higher token frequency of the EP3f exceptions.

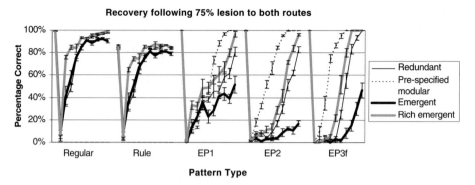

Fig. 14.5 Recovery profiles for different dual route systems following a lesion to both routes.

Figure 14.6a to c contrast recovery patterns following *unilateral* lesions to each route for the prespecified modular, emergent, and redundant systems. For the two conditions with Output competition (modular and redundant), Fig. 14.6c indicates which route was driving performance across recovery.

The emergent systems (Fig. 14.6a) exhibited differential vulnerability for the two types of damage. Direct damage caused a decrement across the board and Indirect damage targeted Exceptions. Recovery after Direct damage was fast for the resource rich version and slow and incomplete for the resource poor version. Recovery after Indirect damage was slower for both versions and complete only for the resource rich version. Overall, the resource-rich emergent system, with co-operation between its routes, demonstrated the strongest recovery. The trajectories of recovery differed depending on the side of damage, but, notably, following recovery, no there was *no evidence of the initial side of damage.* By contrast, the prespecified modular system (Fig. 14.6b) revealed extreme side of lesion effects and poor recovery. Damage to the Direct route produced complete and irrecoverable loss of Regular and Rule patterns, because the Indirect route now dominated the output competition. Damage to the Indirect route produced Exception impairments with slow and incomplete recovery, as the Direct route now tended to dominate the output. The redundant system (Fig.14.6b) was robust to Direct route damage but showed vulnerability of Exception mappings to Indirect damage and incomplete recovery.

Finally Fig. 14.6c demonstrates how the presence of Output competition causes a system to shift to driving behavior from an intact mechanism following unilateral damage. This is adaptive only if the intact mechanism possesses the appropriate knowledge for correct performance. The recovering mechanism may later start to influence behavior once more. In the current case the recovering mechanism primarily drove the (limited) recovery of Exception performance in the modular and redundant systems.

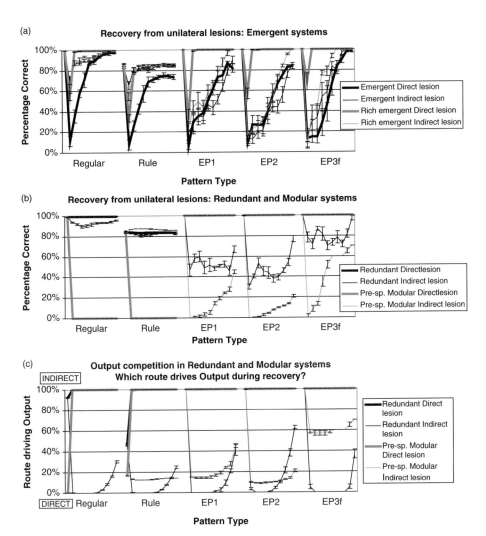

Fig. 14.6 Recovery profiles for unilateral lesions. (a) Systems with emergent specialization. Rich = use of 100 hidden units in the Indirect route. (b) Redundant and prespecified modular systems (c) The route that drives behavior during recovery for the redundant and modular systems.

14.2.4.3 Discussion

The redundant system was robust to damage but did show some unilateral vulner-ability. This stemmed from the different domain relevancies of the two processing routes in the network. The Direct route was less able to learn both parts of the domain than the Indirect route, therefore loss of the Indirect route was more serious. Unless the two routes are equipotential, even redundant systems will show unilateral vulner-ability under some circumstances.

The system with emergent specialization and rich computational resources demonstrated the strongest recovery. It illustrated the importance of having abundant computational resources available to relearn the problem domain, but also the ability to exploit remaining resources in a co-operative fashion. Most notably, this system reproduced the pattern found in the recovery of language after early unilateral damage (Bates and Roe 2001). Recovery patterns were conditioned by side of damage but final performance levels were independent of side of damage.

The emergentist position is therefore an account that may be able to explain both uniformity of outcome (driven by initial domain relevancies) and recovery from early injury (because structure–function correspondences are relevant rather than specific). By contrast, prespecified modularity appears only able to explain uniformity of outcome. However, its strong side-of-damage effects and limited recovery is characteristic of adult aphasia. If the emergent system best explains developmental damage and the prespecified modular system best explains the adult state, this suggests some qualitative change of the system with age, presumably in its effective plasticity or available resources.

14.3 Conclusion

We first summarize the main findings with regard to the specific aims of the simulation work. We then relate these to our wider theoretical questions. The modeling work indicated the following: (1) For self-organizing systems, changes in competition tended to disrupt specialization, with changes to intrinsic competition in the output layer more powerful than changes to the input (for the parameter variations we considered). Reductions in resources led to the same functional structure but poorer categorical discrimination. (2) For error-driven systems, we evaluated a version of the mixture-of-experts model. This revealed that differential properties of areas of heterogeneous computational substrate (i.e. the experts) could mediate patterns of functional specialization. Differential settings of plasticity and levels of resources between areas were particularly powerful modifiers of emergent specialization. (3) In error-driven systems, once again, competition was a powerful factor. Indeed the choice of competition settings was sufficient to mediate between outcomes with prespecified modularity, emergent specialization, and redundancy in a system with otherwise identical domain-relevant computational properties. (4) Consideration of recovery after damage indicated that systems with emergent specialization (defined by Update competition) were best positioned for recovery so long as they were sufficiently resourced, because this form of emergent specialization arises from conditions encouraging co-operative processing. The system with emergent specialization demonstrated a recovery profile found in language development in children experiencing early unilateral brain damage. This supports the idea that the emergentist position can reconcile normal uniformity of outcome with flexibility after early damage, by specifying suitable constraints in learning. Prespecified modularity could account for uniformity of outcome but (as implemented here) it was not a robust solution for successful acquisition. Moreover, it showed greater vulnerability and poorer recovery after damage than either emergent or redundant systems, a pattern more in common with deficits after adult focal brain damage.

We now return to our broader theoretical questions regarding the origins of specialized functional structures. First, of the neurocomputational factors that drive specialization, can separate parameters affect specialization versus functioning within the subsequent individual components? The answer is a qualified 'yes'. In self-organizing systems, resources could affect within-component processing but leave emergent structure untouched. However, this did not lead to uneven performance across components. In error-driven systems, competition was a parameter that altered specialization without changing the functioning of components. However, changes to the computational properties of individual components led to an alteration in specialization. In short, we did not find conditions where uneven profiles of performance arose at the same time as normal functional structure.

Second, we asked when does full specialization occur, if at all? Self-organization appeared to drive fairly complete specialization. In the error-driven system, when the competition parameter guided the system to emergent modular structure or redundancy, specialization was only partial. In this case, complete specialization required prespecification of functional modules.

Third, we asked if specialization becomes fixed. We did not consider alterations to plasticity across the 'age' of the system. However, the recovery data suggested that emergent modularity captured recovery after focal damage in childhood, while prespecified modularity was more reminiscent of more limited adult recovery. These two findings would be reconciled if there were a change of state with age in the parameters affecting functional specialization.

Fourth, we asked whether recovery (such as in the case of language and unilateral brain damage in children) might be better explained by bilateral redundancy rather than reorganization. The results indicated that a resource rich emergent model captured the data better than a redundant system. Notably, however, in systems with Output competition, focal damage could immediately cause a different mechanism to drive behavior. Depending on whether the alternate mechanism could support normal behavior, this could represent robustness or an immediate source of errors. In both cases, the damaged component could take over driving performance if it later recovered. This finding demonstrates the difficulty of drawing inferences from deficits, since behavior after damage may reflect the functioning of a different component.

Fifth, we asked whether specialization necessary conveys a behavioral advantage. The results indicated that prespecified modularity was not a robust solution for acquisition where both components were required to drive the same output, since their competition needed to be calibrated. Both the emergent modular system and the redundant system were flexible after damage, the emergent system more so. The emergent modular system had the additional advantage of being resource efficient. However, prespecified modularity may be advantageous where the modules must drive separate outputs – see Calabretta *et al.* (2003) for a model where prespecified modules are a superior solution for learning to output the identity versus the location of an object on an input retina.

Evidence of more bilateral brain activation patterns in some developmental disorders (for example in face processing in Williams syndrome; see Karmiloff-Smith 1998) might be taken as evidence for *reduced* specialization. This could be explained as less competition operating in the cognitive system, either an absence of Input competition (via initial over-connectivity or insufficient pruning) or an absence of Update competition. However, reduced specialization may also be a consequence of reduced processing resources. When we carried out severe startstate lesions to both routes of the base model (Thomas and Karmiloff-Smith 2002b), the result was poorer acquisition and an absence of specialization. In effect, the system exhibited an all-hands-to-the-pump approach, because both mechanisms were necessary to produce any kind of correct performance. Emergent specialization and redundancy are a luxury born of sufficient resources.

Finally, what do the simulation results tell us about the possible causes of uneven cognitive profiles in developmental disorders? They point to two possible sources: (1) Focal changes in the domain-relevant computational properties of different areas of the initial substrate (i.e. changes restricted to a subset of future specialized components) or focal changes in connectivity modifying the input to a restricted subset of future components. For either of these initial differences not to affect the emergence of other modular structures, the atypical area of substrate must either be self-organizing or not interact/compete with unaffected regions during normal development. (2) The uneven profile is caused by an atypical overall structure, where shifts in the conditions of competition or the domain-relevant properties cause different specialization to emerge. Importantly, the simulations suggested that variations in functional architecture might only modulate the external behavioral trajectories of development in subtle ways. Sensitive empirical measures may be necessary to discriminate between different possible functional architectures underlying variations in development.

In conclusion, the indication is that the emergence of normal modularity despite focal problems in a subset of functionally specialized components could only occur under circumscribed conditions. This implies that *innate modularity* and *neuroconstructivism* represent diverging explanations of uneven cognitive profiles in developmental disorders. The key question remains the extent to which the functional structure varies in atypical development, either for disorders with wide-ranging cognitive deficits such as autism and Williams syndrome, or for disorders in which the deficits are apparently narrower, such as Specific Language Impairment and dyslexia. The answer to this question will tell us much about the origins of modular structure in the human cognitive system.

Acknowledgements

This work was supported by UK Medical Research Council Grant G0300188 to Michael Thomas. We thank to two anonymous reviewers for their helpful comments.

References

Baron-Cohen S (1999). Does the study of autism justify minimalist innate modularity? *Learning and Individual Differences*, **10**, 179–191.

Bates E and Roe K (2001). Language development in children with unilateral brain injury. In: CA Nelson and M Luciana, eds. *Handbook of developmental cognitive neuroscience*, pp. 281–307. Cambridge, MA: MIT Press.

Blank SC, Bird H, Turkheimer F and Wise RJS (2003). Speech production after stroke: The role of the right pars opercularis. *Annals of Neurology*, **54**, 310–320.

Calabretta R, Di Ferdinando A, Wagner GP and Parisi D (2003). What does it take to evolve behaviorally complex organisms? *Biosystems*, **69**, 245–262.

Dailey MN and Cottrell GW (1999). Organization of face and object recognition in modular neural network models. *Neural Networks*, **12**, 1053–1073.

De Haan M (2001). The neuropsychology of face processing during infancy and childhood. In: CA Nelson and M Luciana, eds. *The handbook of developmental cognitive neuroscience*, pp. 381–398. Cambridge, MA: MIT Press.

Demuth H and Beale M (2002). *Neural network toolbox for use with Matlab: User's guide, Version 4.* The Mathworks.

Dudek SM (2001). Multidimensional gene expression in cortical space. *Developmental Science*, **4**, 145–146.

Elman JL, Bates EA, Johnson MH, Karmiloff-Smith A, Parisi D and Plunkett K (1996). *Rethinking innateness: A connectionist perspective on development.* Cambridge, MA: MIT Press.

Fodor JA (1998). *In critical condition: polemic essays on cognitive science and the philosophy of mind.* Cambridge, MA: MIT Press.

Fodor JA (2000). *The mind doesn't work that way: the scope and limits of computational psychology.* Cambridge, MA: MIT Press.

Huffman KJ, Molnar Z, Van Dellen A, Kahn DM, Blakemore C and Krubitzer L (1999). Formation of cortical fields on a reduced cortical sheet, *Journal of Neuroscience*, **19**, 9939–9952.

Huttenlocher PR (2002). *Neural plasticity.* Cambridge, MA: Harvard University Press.

Jacobs RA (1997). Nature, nurture and the development of functional specializations: a computational approach. *Psychonomic Bulletin Review*, **4**, 229–309.

Jacobs RA (1999). Computational studies of the development of functionally specialized neural modules. *Trends in Cognitive Science*, **3**, 31–38.

Jacobs RA. and Jordan MI (1992). Hierarchical mixtures of experts and the EM algorithm. *Neural Computation*, **6**, 181–214.

Jacobs RA, Jordan MI, Nowlan SJ and Hinton GE (1991). Adaptive mixtures of local experts. *Neural Computation*, **3**, 79–87.

Johnson MH and Karmiloff-Smith A (1992). Can neural selectionism be applied to cognitive development and its disorders? *New Ideas in Psychology*, **10**, 35–46.

Kahn DM and Krubitzer L (2002). Massive cross-model cortical plasticity and the emergence of a new cortical area in developmentally blind mammals. *Proceedings of the National Academy of Science, USA*, **99**, 11429–11434.

Karmiloff-Smith A (1998). Development itself is the key to understanding developmental disorders. *Trends in Cognitive Sciences*, **2**, 389–398.

Karmiloff-Smith A, Plunkett K, Johnson MH, Elman JL and Bates EA (1998). What does it mean to claim that something is 'innate'? Response to Clark, Harris, Lightfoot and Samuels. *Mind and Language*, **13**, 558–597.

Kennedy DN, O'Craven KM, Ticho BS, Goldstein AM, Makris N and Henson JW (1999). Structural and functional brain imaging brain asymmetries in human situs inversus totalis. *Neurology*, **53**, 1260–1265.

Kimura D (1992). Sex differences in the brain. *Scientific American*, **267**, 118–125.

Knecht S, Drager B, Floel A, Lohmann H, Breitenstein C, Deppe M, *et al.* (2001). Behavioural relevance of atypical language lateralisation in healthy subjects. *Brain*, **124**, 1657–1665.

Kohonen T (1995). *Self-organizing maps*. New York: Springer.

Mills DL, Coffey-Corina S and Neville HJ (1997). Language comprehension and cerebral specialization from 13 to 20 months. *Developmental Neuropsychology*, **13**, 397–445.

Monaghan P and Shillcock RC (2004). Hemispheric asymmetries in cognitive modelling: Connectionist modelling of unilateral visual neglect. *Psychological Review*, **111**, 283–308.

Oliver A, Johnson MH, Karmiloff-Smith A and Pennington B (2000). Deviations in the emergence of representations: A neuroconstructivist framework for analysing developmental disorders. *Developmental Science*, **3**, 1–23.

O'Reilly RC (1998). Six principles for biologically based computational models of cortical cognition. *Trends in Cognitive Sciences*, **2**, 455–462.

Pinker S (1994). *The language instinct*. Penguin books.

Pinker S (1999). *Words and rules*. London: Weidenfeld and Nicolson.

Poremba A, Malloy M, Saunders RC, Carson RE, Herscovtich P and Mishkin M (2004). Species-specific calls evoke asymmetric activity in the monkey's temporal poles. *Nature*, **427**, 448–451.

Price CJ (2003). An overview of the functional anatomy of speech comprehension and production. In: RSJ Frackowiak, ed. *Human brain function*. USA: Elsevier Science.

Reggia JA and Schulz R (2002). The role of computational modelling in understanding hemispheric interactions and specializations. *Cognitive Systems Research*, **3**, 87–94.

Rumelhart DE and McClelland JL (1986). On learning the past tense of English verbs. In: JL McClelland, DE Rumelhart and the PDP Research Group, eds. *Parallel distributed processing: explorations in the microstructure of cognition, vol. 2: Psychological and biological models*, pp. 216–271. Cambridge, MA: MIT Press.

Shaywitz BA, Shaywitz SE, Pugh KR, Constable RT, Skudlarski P, Fulbright RK, *et al.* (1995). Sex differences in the functional organization of the brain for language. *Nature*, **373**, 607–609.

Shrager J and Johnson MH (1996). Dynamic plasticity influences the emergence of function in a simple cortical array. *Neural Networks*, **9**, 1119–1129.

Small SL, Hart J, Nguyen T and Gordon B (1996). Distributed representations of semantic knowledge in the brain: Computational experiments using feature based codes. In: J Reggia, E Ruppin and RS Berndt, eds. *Neural modelling of brain and cognitive disorders.* New Jersey: World Scientific.

Strauss E, Wada J and Hunter M (1992). Sex-related differences in the cognitive consequences of early left-hemisphere lesions. *Journal of Clinical and Experimental Neuropsychology,* 14, 738–748.

Szaflarski JP, Holland SK, Schmithorst VJ and Weber-Byars A (2004). *An fMRI study of cerebral language lateralisation in 121 children and adults.* Paper presented to the American Academy of Neurology 56th Annual Meeting, April 24 2004, San Francisco.

Taatgen NA and Anderson JR (2002). Why do children learn to say 'broke'? A model of learning the past tense without feedback. *Cognition,* 86, 123–155.

Tager-Flusberg H (2000). Differences between neurodevelopmental disorders and acquired lesions. *Developmental Science,* 3, 33–34.

Tager-Flusberg H, Plesa-Skwerer D, Faja S and Joseph RM (2003). People with Williams syndrome process faces holistically. *Cognition,* 89, 11–24.

Temple C and Clahsen H (2002). How connectionist simulations fail to account for developmental disorders in children. *Behavioral and Brain Sciences,* 25, 769–770.

Thomas MSC and Karmiloff-Smith A (2002a). Modelling typical and atypical cognitive development. In: U Goswami, ed. *Handbook of childhood development,* pp. 575–599. Oxford: Blackwells.

Thomas MSC and Karmiloff-Smith A (2002b). Are developmental disorders like cases of adult brain damage? Implications from connectionist modelling. *Behavioural and Brain Sciences,* 25, 727–780.

Thomas MSC and Karmiloff-Smith A (2003). Modelling language acquisition in atypical phenotypes. *Psychological Review,* 110, 647–682.

Walker SF (2003). Misleading asymmetries of brain structure. *Behavioural and Brain Sciences,* 26, 240–241.

Chapter 15

A brand new ball game: Bayes net and neural net learning mechanisms in young children

Alison Gopnik and Clark Glymour

Abstract

We outline a new computational account of learning in children using the causal Bayes net formalism. We also present evidence that children as young as 2 years old use something like causal Bayes net learning mechanisms to infer the causal structure of the world around them. This kind of learning may play an important role in the development of intuitive theories. Finally, we contrast causal Bayes net and neural net learning mechanisms.

15.1 Introduction

Over the past 30 years we have discovered an enormous amount about what children know and when they know it. That research has completely transformed the traditional Piagetian view of young children's cognition. Even the youngest infants seem to have abstract representations of the world and are not restricted to 'sensorimotor' schemas. Similarly, preschool children are far from being the illogical, egocentric, 'precausal' creatures Piaget envisioned.

In particular, young children, and even infants, seem to have intuitive theories of the physical, biological, and psychological world (for reviews see Gopnik and Meltzoff 1997; Gelman and Raman 2002; Flavell 1999; Wellman and Inagaki 1997). These theories, like scientific theories, are complex, coherent, abstract representations of the causal structure of the world. Even the youngest preschoolers can use these intuitive theories to make causal predictions, provide causal explanations, and even reason about causation counterfactually (Harris *et al.* 1996; Hicking and Wellman 2001; Sobel 2004; Wellman *et al.* 1997). As with scientific theories, children's theories are much more than just summaries of the evidence – they allow children to draw novel conclusions and provide novel explanations. Moreover, there is extensive evidence for changes in intuitive theories as children grow older.

Are these changes the result of maturation or are they the result of learning? Several recent findings suggest the latter alternative. First, natural variations in the kinds of evidence children receive can influence the development of intuitive theories. For example, rich city-dwelling children who are relatively deprived of biological experience have a less elaborated view of biology than children growing up on Native American reservations (Ross *et al.* 2003). Similarly, children with older siblings, who have a wider range of psychological experiences, seem to have an accelerated understanding of intuitive psychology (Ruffman *et al.* 1998). Moreover, training studies show that providing children with specific kinds of evidence relevant to biological or psychological theories can accelerate the development of those theories (Slaughter and Gopnik 1996; Slaughter *et al.* 1999; Slaughter and Lyons 2003). Even providing a child with a pet fish can influence their folk biology (Inagaki and Hatano 2004).

But the real question for developmental cognitive science is not so much what children know, when they know it, or even whether they learn it. The real question is HOW they learn it and WHY they get it right. In the past 'theory theorists' have suggested that children's learning mechanisms are analogous to scientific theory formation. However, what we would really like is a more precise computational specification of the mechanisms that underlie both types of learning.

The traditional candidates for learning mechanisms in psychology have been variants of associationism, either the mechanisms of classical and operant conditioning in behaviorist theories (e.g. Rescorla and Wagner 1972) or, more recently, the mechanisms of dynamical systems theories (e.g. Thelen and Smith 1994) and connectionist theories (e.g. Rumelhart and McLelland 1986; Elman *et al.* 1996; Shultz 2003; Rogers and McLelland 2004). Of these, only connectionist models really offer computational mechanisms: behaviorism eschews them altogether, while dynamical systems theories claim that learning is the result of direct physical interactions between the organism and the environment, with no internal computations at all.

Such theories have had great difficulty explaining how apparently rich, complex, abstract, rule-governed representations, the sorts of representations encoded in everyday theories, could be derived from evidence. Typically, associationist theories, both the earlier behaviorist theories and their recent connectionist and dynamic inheritors, denied that such representations really exist. Although children might appear to have rule-governed abstract representations of the world, these theorists argue that, in fact, they have a collection of much more specific learned associations between inputs and outputs.

Connectionists often qualify this denial by appealing to the notion of 'distributed' representations, concepts, and categories, or any psychological process that relates inputs to outputs. The distributed representation is whatever features of the connectionist system produce the relevant outputs from the relevant inputs. On this view, however, the representations are not independent accounts of the external world that are responsible for input–output relations. Instead, they are summaries of those input–output relations

Conversely, more nativist theories endorse the existence of abstract, rule-governed representations but deny that they are learned. Modularity or 'core knowledge' theorists, for example, suggest that there are a few innate causal schemas designed to fit particular domains of knowledge, such as a belief–desire schema for intuitive psychology or a teleological schema for intuitive biology. Development is either a matter of enriching those innate schemas, or else involves quite sophisticated and culture-specific kinds of learning like those of the social institutions of science (e.g. Spelke *et al.* 1992).

This has left empirically-minded developmentalists, who seem to see both abstract representation *and* learning in even the youngest children, in an unfortunate theoretical bind. There appears to be a vast gap between the kinds of knowledge that children learn and the mechanisms that could allow them to learn that knowledge. The attempt to bridge this gap dates back to Piagetian ideas about constructivism, of course, but simply saying that there are constructivist learning mechanisms is a way of restating the problem rather than providing a solution. Is there a more precise computational way to bridge this gap?

To take the computationalist conception seriously, think for a moment of children as very, very complex natural robots. We psychologists want to explain how those robots learn, much as a computer scientist might want to know how a chess playing computer works. The right answer for the computer scientist is a description of an algorithm, perhaps in a high level computer language. Something like that is what is needed for the developmental psychology of learning as well. But that is not what the traditional approaches offer. Behaviorists tell us not to even try to explain – just summarize the input–output regularities. Dynamical systems theorists tell us to describe the physics of the process – which is much like telling a computer scientist who wants to know how a chess playing computer manages to play chess that she should study the physics of silicon chips. Connectionists tell us to try to model the neural connections and dependencies that produce children's remarkable learning capacities – but to do it without biological data about how individual cells act and interact when learning takes place. That is very much like telling the computer scientist that to understand how the computer plays chess, she needs to reconstruct the machine code – not the high level chess playing program.

Computer scientists learned very quickly that computational understanding has levels, and the physical level is useful for building machines but not for understanding the details of their behavior, and the machine code level is typically unintuitive and unrevealing. But there have been few promising theories of learning at the higher computational level that is typically revealing in computer science – that is at the level of representations and algorithms acting on those representations.

Several recent theoretical and empirical developments suggest that this situation may be changing. In particular, recent theoretical advances suggest computational learning procedures which allow abstract, coherent, structured representations to be derived from patterns of evidence, given certain assumptions. These procedures relate structured representations such as graph structures, grammars, or representations of three-dimensional space to patterns of input, particularly patterns of conditional probabilities among events. These computational accounts take the kinds of evidence that have been considered in traditional learning accounts – such as evidence about contingencies among events or evidence about the consequences of actions – and use it to learn structured representations of the kind that have been proposed in traditional nativist accounts. Accounts like these have become increasingly dominant in artificial intelligence and machine learning. In this paper we will focus on one such computational account, the causal directed graphical model or causal Bayes net account of causal knowledge and learning.

15.1.1 Causal Bayes nets

Causal directed graphical models, or causal Bayes nets, have been developed in the philosophy of science and statistical literature over the last 15 years (Glymour 2001; Pearl 2000; Spirtes *et al.* 1993). 'Theory theorists' in cognitive development point to an analogy between learning in children and learning in science. Causal Bayes nets provide a formal account of a kind of inductive inference that is particularly important in scientific theory formation. Scientists infer causal structure by observing the patterns of conditional probability among events (as in statistical analysis), by examining the consequences of interventions (as in experiments), or, usually, by combining the two types of evidence.

In causal Bayes nets, causal relations are represented by directed acyclic graphs. The graphs consist of variables, representing types of events or states of the world, and directed edges (arrows) representing the direct causal relations between those variables (Fig. 15.1). The variables can be discrete (like school grade) or continuous (like weight), they can be binary (like 'having eyes' or 'not having eyes') or many valued (like color). Similarly, the direct causal relations can have many forms; they can be deterministic or probabilistic, generative or inhibitory, linear or non-linear. The exact specification of the nature of these relations is called the 'parameterization' of the graph.

The structure of a causal graph constrains the conditional probabilities among the variables in that graph, no matter what the variables are or what the parameterization of the graph is. In particular, it constrains the conditional independencies among those variables. Given a particular causal structure, only some patterns of conditional independence will occur among the variables.

Conditional and unconditional dependence and independence can be precisely defined mathematically. Two variables X and Y are unconditionally independent in

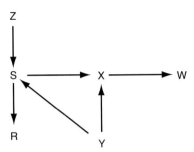

Fig. 15.1 A causal graph.

probability if, and only if, for every value x of X and y of Y the probability of x and y occurring together equals the unconditional probability of x multiplied by the unconditional probability of y. That is p (x and y) = p (x) * p (y). Two variables are independent in probability conditional on some third variable Z if, and only if, p (x, y | z) = p (x | z) * p (y | z). That is for every value x, y, and z of X, Y and Z the probability of x and y given z equals the probability of x given z multiplied by the probability of y given z.

The structure of the causal graph puts constraints on these patterns of probability among the variables. These constraints can be captured by a single formal assumption, the causal Markov assumption as follows.

15.1.2 The causal Markov assumption

For any variable X in a causal graph, X is independent of all other variables in the graph (except for its own direct and indirect effects) conditional on its own direct causes.

Causal Bayes nets also allow us to determine what will happen when we intervene from outside to change the value of a particular variable. When two variables are genuinely related in a causal way then, holding other variables constant, intervening to change one variable should change the value of the other. Indeed, philosophers have recently argued that this is just what it means for two variables to be causally related (Woodward 2003). Given a causal graph, particular interventions will only have effects on some variables and not others. The Bayes net formalism captures these relations through a second assumption, an assumption about how interventions should be represented in the graph.

15.1.3 The intervention assumption

A variable I is an intervention on a variable X in a causal graph if, and only if, (1) I is exogenous (that is, it is not caused by any other variables in the graph); (2) directly fixes the value of X to x; and (3) does not affect the values of any other variables in the graph except through its influence on X.

Given this assumption, we can accurately predict the effects of interventions on particular variables in a graph on other variables. In causal Bayes nets, interventions systematically alter the nature of the graph they intervene on, and these systematic alterations follow directly from the formalism itself. In particular, when an external intervention fixes the value of a variable it also eliminates the causal influence of other variables on that variable. This can be represented by replacing the original graph with an altered graph in which arrows directed into the intervened upon variable are eliminated (Judea Pearl vividly refers to this process as graph surgery (Pearl 2000)). The conditional dependencies among the variables after the intervention can be read off from this altered graph. This same inferential apparatus can be used to generate counterfactual predictions.

A central aspect of causal Bayes nets, indeed the thing that makes them causal, is that they allow us to freely go back and forth from evidence about observed probabilities to inferences about interventions and *vice versa.*

These two assumptions, then, allow us to take a particular causal structure and accurately predict the conditional probabilities of events, and also the consequences of interventions on those events, from that structure.

To illustrate this, consider three simple causal graphs: (1) a chain $X \rightarrow Y \rightarrow Z$, (2) a common effect structure $Z \leftarrow X \rightarrow Y$. and (3) a common cause structure $X \rightarrow Z \leftarrow Y$. Suppose, for example, that I notice that I often can't sleep when I've been to a party and drunk lots of wine, partying (X) and insomnia (Z) covary, and so do wine (Y) and insomnia (Z). This covariation by itself is consistent with all three of the structures above. Maybe parties lead me to drink and wine keeps me up, maybe parties both keep me up and lead me to drink, maybe parties don't affect my wine drinking but parties keep me up and wine independently keeps me up.

However, each structure will lead to a different pattern when I intervene on wine and partying, if, for example, I experiment by intentionally sitting in my room alone and drinking one night, and then partying dead sober the next. I can calculate the effects of such interventions on each of the three causal structures, using 'graph surgery' and predict the results. I will get different results from these experiments depending on the true causal structure (solitary drinking will lead to insomnia, and sober partying won't for graph 1, sober partying will lead to insomnia and solitary drinking won't for graph 2, and both experiments will lead to insomnia for graph 3).

Even if I can't experiment, however, I can still discriminate these three graphs by looking at the patterns of conditional probability among the three variables. If graph 1 is right, and there is a causal chain that goes from parties to wine to insomnia, then $Y \perp Z \mid X$ – the probability of insomnia occurring is independent (in probability) of the probability of party-going occurring conditional on the occurrence of wine-drinking. If graph 2 is right, and parties are a common cause of wine and insomnia, then $X \perp Y \mid Z$ – the probability of wine-drinking occurring is independent (in probability) of the probability of insomnia occurring conditional on the occurrence of party-going.

Insomnia might also be a common effect of both wine-drinking and parties (X →Y←Z). In this case, X is *not* independent of Z conditional on Y. The intuitions here are less obvious, but they reflect the fact that, in this case, knowing about the effect and about one possible cause gives us information about the other possible cause. We can illustrate this best with a different example. Suppose X is a burglar, Y is the burglar alarm sounding, and Z is the neighboring cat tripping the alarm wire, so that Y is a common effect of X and Z. If we hear the alarm sound and see the cat tripping the wire, we are less likely to conclude that there was a burglar than if we simply hear the alarm sound by itself. Similarly, if partying and wine-drinking really were completely independent – if we were just as likely to drink wine at home, then if someone else just knew that we had insomnia and that we had been at a party that would actually lessen the probability that we had also been drinking wine. This effect is called 'explaining away' (see Pearl 2000; Spirtes *et al.* 1993, for discussion).

These systematic relations between causation, intervention, and conditional probability allow a range of systematic predictions. We can also use the formalism to work backwards and learn the causal graph from patterns of conditional probability and intervention. This type of learning requires an additional assumption – the faithfulness assumption.

15.1.4 **The faithfulness assumption**

In the joint distribution on the variables in the graph, all conditional independencies are consequences of the Markov assumption applied to the graph.

Given the faithfulness assumption, it is possible to infer complex causal structure from patterns of conditional probability and intervention (Glymour and Cooper 1999; Spirtes *et al.* 1993). Computationally tractable learning algorithms have been designed to accomplish this task and have been extensively applied in a range of disciplines (e.g. Ramsey *et al.* 2002; Shipley 2000). In some cases, it is also possible to accurately infer the existence of new unobserved variables that are common causes of the observed variables (Silva *et al.* 2003; Richardson and Spirtes 2003).

These learning algorithms typically take two forms. In Bayesian learning, a prior probability for various causal graphs is calculated first (Heckerman *et al.* 1999). Then these prior probabilities are updated given the evidence about the actual conditional probabilities in the data, using Bayes rule. In constraint-based learning the graphs are constructed from the probabilities directly, step by step in a more bottom–up way (Spirtes *et al.* 1993). These two types of learning can also be combined.

Causal Bayes net representations and learning algorithms allow learners to accurately predict patterns of evidence from causal structure and to accurately learn causal structure from patterns of evidence. They constitute a kind of inductive causal logic. It is possible to prove that only certain patterns of evidence will follow from particular causal structures, given the Markov, intervention and faithfulness assumptions, just as only certain conclusions follow from particular logical premises, given the axioms of logic.

Causal Bayes nets are also analogous to the representations and algorithms that allow the visual system to accurately infer spatial structure from retinal patterns – the kinds of representations and deductions captured in 'ideal observer' theories in vision (Gopnik *et al.* 2004). The visual system implicitly assumes that there is a world of three-dimensional moving objects and then makes assumptions about how those objects lead to particular patterns on the retina. By making the further assumption that the retinal patterns were, in fact, produced by the objects in this way, the system can work backwards and infer the structure of objects from those patterns (e.g. Palmer 1999). Causal Bayes net inferences involve similar assumptions and allow similar deductions. Just as the visual system assumes that the patterns at the retina were produced by three-dimensional objects in a particular way and then uses those assumptions to infer the objects from the retinal patterns, causal Bayes net assume that causal structure produced patterns of evidence and uses those assumptions to learn the structure from the evidence.

Causal Bayes nets, then, provide a way of formally specifying accurate inductive causal inferences, just as logic provides a way of formally specifying accurate deductive inferences and 'ideal observer' theories in vision provide a way of formally specifying accurate visual inferences.

15.2 Causal Bayes nets as a model of children's causal learning: empirical results

This leads to a further question. Do human beings use these kinds of ideal rational computations to learn about the world? In vision there is extensive evidence that human visual systems are close to ideal observers, and, although people sometimes make logical errors, there is also extensive evidence that they use logic to draw everyday conclusions. Recently, several investigators have suggested that adults' causal knowledge might involve implicit forms of Bayes nets representations (Gopnik and Glymour 2002; Rehder and Hastie 2001; Steyvers *et al.* 2003; Waldmann 2001). In particular, it turns out that Patricia Cheng's causal power model of human causal learning (Cheng 1997) is a special case of Bayes net learning, with a particular constrained set of graph structures and a particular parameterization (Glymour 2001; Glymour and Cheng 1999). However, Steyvers *et al* (2003) have shown that adults can learn more complex structures, which go well beyond the causal power model, particularly if they are allowed to perform interventions.

Of course, adults have extensive experience and often explicit tuition in causal inference. If young children could use versions of Bayes nets assumptions and computations they would have a powerful tool for making causal inferences. They might, at least in principle, use such methods to uncover the kind of causal structure involved in everyday intuitive theories.

In recent work we have been exploring this possibility by seeing how young children use conditional probability and intervention to make judgments about causation (Gopnik 2000; Gopnik and Sobel 2000; Gopnik and Schulz 2004; Gopnik *et al.* 2001, 2004; Schulz and Gopnik 2004; Sobel *et al.* 2004). Our basic technique is to present children with novel causal relationships, relationships they have never experienced or heard about before. Then we present children with carefully controlled information about conditional probabilities and interventions and see what causal conclusions they draw.

Two-and-a-half year olds can discriminate conditional independence and dependence even with controls for frequency, and can use that information to make judgments about causation, at least when the causal relations are generative, deterministic, and non-interactive. In these experiments we showed children various combinations of objects placed on a new machine, 'the blicket detector'. The blicket detector is a square box which lights up and plays music when some combinations or objects, but not others are placed on it. The children were told that 'blickets make the machine go' and were asked to identify which objects were blickets.

For example, in Gopnik *et al.* 2001, children saw the sequence of events depicted in Fig. 15.2a, and the control sequence depicted in Fig. 15.2b. In Fig. 15.2a the effect E (the detector lighting up) is correlated with both A and B. However, E is independent in probability of B conditional on A, but E remains dependent on A conditional on B. In Fig. 15.2b each block activates the detector the same number of times as in Fig. 15.2a but the conditional independence patterns are the same for A and B. Children consistently choose A rather than B as the blicket, in the first condition, and choose equally between the two blocks in the second condition. Assuming that the causal relations are deterministic, generative, and non-interactive, a Bayes net account would generate a similar prediction.

The experiments with 2-year-olds, however, only required that children discriminate between conditional probabilities of 1 and <1. Moreover, the paradigms could also be explained by the use of a causal form of the Rescorla–Wagner associative learning procedure. In fact, you could think of the Rescorla–Wagner rule precisely as a procedure that approximates the conditional independencies among events in the world that indicate causal structure in certain very simple cases.

In similar experiments, however, 4-year-old children also used principles of Bayesian inference to combine prior probability information with information about the conditional probability of events. Moreover, they did this in a backwards blocking paradigm that is not easily explained by the Rescorla–Wagner rule (Sobel *et al.* 2004).

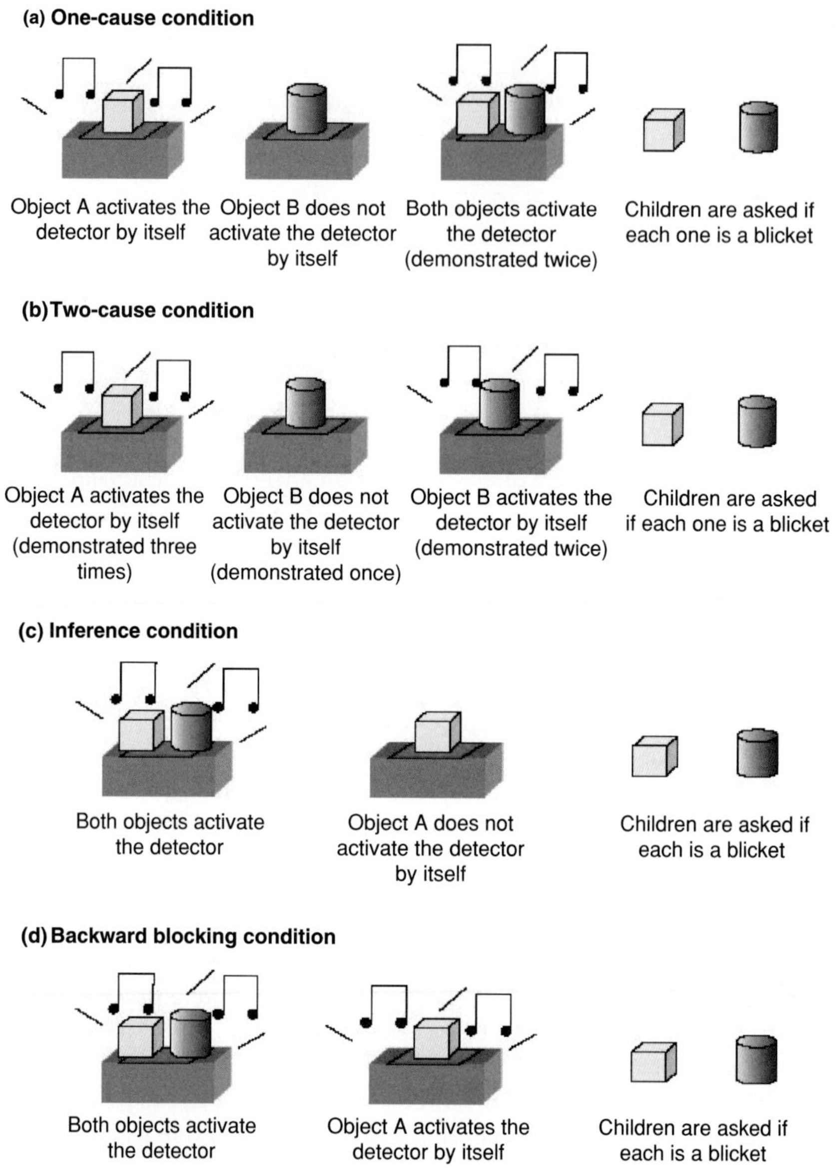

(a) One-cause condition

Object A activates the detector by itself Object B does not activate the detector by itself Both objects activate the detector (demonstrated twice) Children are asked if each one is a blicket

(b) Two-cause condition

Object A activates the detector by itself (demonstrated three times) Object B does not activate the detector by itself (demonstrated once) Object B activates the detector by itself (demonstrated twice) Children are asked if each one is a blicket

(c) Inference condition

Both objects activate the detector Object A does not activate the detector by itself Children are asked if each is a blicket

(d) Backward blocking condition

Both objects activate the detector Object A activates the detector by itself Children are asked if each is a blicket

Fig. 15.2 (a) and (b) Screening-off procedure (Gopnik *et al.* 2001); (c) and (d) backwards blocking procedure (Sobel *et al.* 2004).

For example suppose children see the sequence of events in Fig. 15.2c and d. On a Bayes net account, the causal structure of Fig. 15.2c is plain, A does not cause the effect and B does, and the children also say this. However, the causal structure of Fig. 15.2d is ambiguous, it could be that A and B both make the detector go, but it is also possible that only A does. Note that, in contrast, on a Rescorla–Wagner account the associations between B and the detector should be the same in both these cases – the independent association or lack of association of A and the detector should have no influence. However, the backward blocking result is predicted by Cheng's model. (Note that this is a case of 'explaining away', knowing that the effect was caused by A makes it less likely that it was also caused by B.)

Indeed, children say that B is a blicket much less often in the Fig. 15.2d condition than the Fig. 15.2c condition. However, we can increase the prior probability of the 'A only' structure by telling the children beforehand that almost none of the blocks are blickets. Children who are told that blickets are rare are more likely to choose the 'A only' structure – that is to say that A is a blicket but B is not. This is not predicted by either Rescorla–Wagner or Cheng models.

Four-year-olds can also perform even more complex kinds of reasoning about conditional dependencies, and they do so in many domains, biological and psychological as well as physical. In one experiment children were shown a monkey puppet and various combinations of flowers in a vase (Fig. 15.3) (Schulz and Gopnik 2004). They were told that some flowers made the monkey sneeze and others didn't. Then they were shown the following sequence of events: Flowers A and B together made monkey sneeze. Flowers A and C together made monkey sneeze. Flowers B and C together did not make monkey sneeze. Children correctly concluded that A would make the monkey sneeze by itself, but B and C would not. In a control condition they saw each flower make the monkey sneeze with the same frequency, and they chose between the flowers at chance. This result can be explained by Rescorla–Wagner as well as Bayes net models with suitable assumptions, but cannot be explained by Cheng's causal power model.

15.3 Learning from interventions

Conditional probability is one basic type of evidence for causation. The other basic type of evidence involves understanding interventions and their consequences. Look again at the intervention assumption.

15.3.1 The intervention assumption

A variable I is an intervention on a variable X in a causal graph if, and only if, (1) I is exogenous (that is, is not caused by any other variables in the graph); (2) directly fixes the value of X to x; and (3) does not affect the values of any other variables in the graph except through its influence on X.

The technical definition of intervention in this assumption may look formidable but it actually maps well onto our everyday intuitions about intentional goal-directed human actions. We assume that such actions are the result of our freely-willed mental intentions, and so unaffected by the variables they act on (Clause 1). Clause 2 is basic to understanding goal-directed action. When actions are genuinely

Fig. 15.3 Biological screening-off (Schulz and Gopnik 2004). See Plate I in the centre of this book for a full colour version.

goal-directed we can tell whether our actions are effective: that is whether they determine the state of the variables we act upon, and we modify the actions if they are not. Clause 3 is essential to understanding means–ends relations. When we act on means to gain an end we assume that our actions influenced other variables (our ends) through, and only through, the influence on the acted-upon variable (the means).

Moreover, we assume that these features of our own interventions are shared by the interventions of others. This is an important assumption because it greatly increases our opportunities for learning about causal structure – we learn not only from our own actions but also from the actions of others.

There is evidence that this conception of intervention, as freely-willed, goal-directed actions that may be performed by oneself or others, is in place in children at least by the time they are 18 months old (Meltzoff 1995). In addition, children can clearly learn from interventions in simple cases. For example they can learn which effects directly follow from their actions in trial and error learning.

15.4 Learning from combinations of conditional probabilities and interventions

The crucial aspect of causal Bayes nets, however, is that intervention and conditional probability information can be coherently combined and inferences can go in both directions. Animals have at least some forms of the ability to infer conditional probabilities, and even conditional independencies, among events – as in the phenomenon of blocking in classical conditioning (Rescorla and Wagner 1972; Shanks 1985; Shanks and Dickinson 1987). They also have at least some ability to infer causal relations between their interventions and the events that follow them, as in operant conditioning and trial and error learning. However, there is, at best, only very limited and fragile evidence of non-human animals' ability to combine these two types of learning in a genuinely causal way. Why is it that when Pavlov's dogs associate the bell with food, they don't just spontaneously ring the bell when they are hungry? The animals seem able to associate the bell ringing with food, and if they are given an opportunity to act on the bell and that action leads to food, they can replicate that action. Moreover, there may be some transfer from operant to classical conditioning. However, there is no evidence that animals can go directly from learning novel conditional independencies to designing a correct novel intervention. Moreover, surprisingly, primates show only a very limited and fragile ability to learn by directly imitating the interventions of others, an ability that is robustly present in 1-year-old humans (Povinelli 2000; Tomasello and Call 1997).

In contrast, we've shown that very young children solve causal problems in a way that suggests just this co-ordination of observation and action. Preschool children, for instance, can use contingencies, including patterns of conditional independence, to design novel interventions to solve causal problems. Three-year-olds in the blicket detector experiments use information about conditional independence to produce appropriate interventions (such as taking a particular object off the detector to make it turn off) that they have never seen or produced before (Gopnik *et al.* 2001).

Even more dramatically, 4-year-olds used patterns of conditional dependence to craft new interventions that required them to cross domain boundaries, and overturn earlier knowledge (Schulz and Gopnik 2004). For example children were asked beforehand whether you could make a machine light up by flicking a switch or by saying 'Machine, please go'. All of the children said that flicking the switch would work but talking to the machine would not. Then children saw that the effect was unconditionally dependent on saying 'Machine, please go', but was independent of the switch conditional on the spoken request. When children were then asked to make the machine stop 75 per cent said 'Machine, please stop'. Moreover, these children were more likely to predict that a new machine could be activated by talking to it than a control group of children.

Note that this cross-domain result is particularly difficult to explain using the apparatus of either associationist or nativist theories. Children clearly had built up very strong associations and had extensive experience with the within-domain causal relations. On nativist accounts one of the most characteristic aspects of core knowledge is that inferential principles are restricted to particular domains. Yet children overrode these associations and principles after only a few presentations of the relevant causal evidence – evidence that definitively pointed to cross-domain causal relations.

Most crucially, however, 4-year-olds can also combine patterns of conditional dependence and intervention to infer causal structure and do so in a way that recognizes the special character of intervention (Gopnik *et al.* 2004). This kind of inference is naturally done by Bayes nets and is not a feature of either associationist or causal power accounts of causal learning. Children can even do this when the relations between the events are probabilistic rather than deterministic. And children can use such combinations of information to infer the existence of unobserved variables.

For example, we showed 4-year-olds a novel 'puppet machine' in which two stylized puppets moved simultaneously. They were told that some puppets almost always, but not always, made others go. In one condition they saw the experimenter intervene to move puppet X, and puppet Y also moved simultaneously on five of six trials. On one trial the experimenter moved X and Y did not move. In the other condition they simply observed the puppets move together simultaneously five times, while on one trial the experimenter intervened to move X and Y did not move. The covariation between X and Y was the same in both cases. However, children accurately concluded that X made Y move in the first case, while Y made X move in the second. Again these results would not be predicted either on an associationist or causal power account, but follow directly from Bayes net assumptions.

Similarly, children could use the pattern of interventions and covariation to normatively infer an unobserved variable that was a common cause of two observed variables. Children were again shown the puppet machine but now they saw the two objects move together several times, and then saw the experimenter intervene to move the puppets. In one condition, like the condition described above, the experimenter moved X and Y did not move. When asked to explain why the puppets moved together children said they did so because Y moved X. In the unobserved condition the experimenter intervened on both puppets. When she intervened on X, Y did not move, when she intervened on Y, X did not move. When children were asked to explain why the objects moved together they said that they did so because of some hidden factor. Moreover, adults referred to a hidden structure even when the relations between the puppets were probabilistic, and they discriminated among different hidden structures (Kushnir *et al.* 2003). We have some preliminary evidence that children may behave similarly.

In even more recent work, we have shown that 4-year-old children could also use a pattern of interventions and covariation to normatively infer more complex structures, in particular, to distinguish a causal chain from a common effects structure from a causal conjunction (Schulz and Gopnik 2003). We showed children another new machine – the gear toy. The gear toy consisted of two gears with a switch on the side. When you flicked the switch the gears moved together. This simple machine could involve (at least) four different causal relations between the gears: the switch could make A go which could make B go; the switch could make B go which could make A go; the switch could independently make A go and make B go; or the switch and A together could make B go and *vice versa*. We showed children different patterns of intervention on the gears and the switch, and pictures representing the different causal relationships (basically cuter versions of causal graphs with smiling gears pushing each other instead of letters and arrows). Children appropriately picked the right picture from the evidence, and, given the pictures, they could correctly infer what pattern of evidence would result.

Our empirical work so far has looked at a relatively limited range of causal inferences. Our causal structures involved at most three variables and the variables were simple, discrete, two-valued variables. Children only had to discriminate between conditional probabilities of 1 vs < 1. The causal relations were generative and for the most part (with the exception of the gear toy conjunctions) they were not interactive.

In other experiments, we have shown that 4-year-old children will infer inhibitory relations between two variables, and they will discriminate more finely among different degrees of probabilistic strength between two variables. In particular, children say that an a object that sets off the blicket detector two out of three times has stronger causal powers than one that sets off the detector only one out of three times (Kushnir and Gopnik, in press). We have not yet shown whether children can infer more complex causal structure when the causal relations have these sorts of parameterizations.

Causal Bayes nets do allow such inferences, and allow inferences about much more complex structures involving multiple variables with multiple parameterizations. Moreover, they allow inferences from pure covariation as well as from interventions. Most of our experiments involved a combination of observation and intervention, rather than just observations *per se*. Children's causal learning mechanisms almost certainly involve a more restricted subset of the general causal Bayes nets methods, though we don't yet know the limit of that subset.

For example it may be that children assume that causal relations are fundamentally deterministic with a single 'error term', an assumption that requires interventions to infer complex structure. They may be more closely analogous to, say, experimental chemists who can infer causal structure from a single experiment, than to epidemiologists who infer causal structure from big statistical databases.

Moreover, the youngest children in our experiments were 2 1/2 years and most of the children were 3 or 4^years old. We don't know how far back these learning capacities go, and whether, for example, they are present in infancy.

Nevertheless the learning capacities we have demonstrated in children extend well beyond those predicted by any other theory of causal learning, In our experiments we carefully controlled the apparatus so that were no spatiotemporal or mechanical cues that discriminated causal structure. And, as we note above, although individual experiments might be explained by associationist or causal power theories, many of the experiments (the prior knowledge backwards blocking experiment and the puppet machine and gear toy experiments, in particular) are not easily explicable by either of these theories.

15.5 Causal Bayes nets and connectionism

How are causal Bayes nets related to other theories of children's learning, particularly connectionist or neural net theories?

Neural nets and Bayes nets are very similar as formal mathematical structures, but they have been developed and are typically applied to different purposes in conjunction with quite different algorithms (Table 15.1). Formally, Bayes nets are akin to a kind of feed-forward neural net, but there are differences as well. Both Bayes nets and neural nets have the same graphical structure, they consist of nodes (units) that are connected by arrows (connections). The characteristic Markov property (or the extended version of that property called d-separation) is shared by both Bayes nets

Table 15.1 Comparison of neural and Bayes networks

Feature	Neural network	Bayes network
Graph	Directed graph	Directed graph
Vertices	Random variables	Random variables
Vertex function	Of parent variables in the graph	Of parent variables in the graph
Constraints on the joint probability distribution on the vertices	None	D-separation
Cyclic graphs allowed	Yes	Yes
Distinguished input and output variables	Yes	No
Associated theory of interventions	No	Yes
Graph structure	Heuristic pruning	Asymptotically correct search (Bayesian or constraint based)
Estimation by parameter	Variety of iterative methods, e.g. back-propagation	Maximum likelihood or Bayesian posteriors
Estimation by interpretation of vertices	None, or as representations of 'internal' objects (e.g. nerve cells)	Representations of variable properties of 'external' systems
Usual data application	Classification	Causal and statistical modeling

and neural nets. However, not all Bayes nets assign weights to individual node-to-node connections (arrows), and, in Bayes nets, unlike neural nets, different weights may be assigned for different values of the parent nodes. Some recurrent neural nets that satisfy the d-separation property (Pearl 1988) are likewise cyclic Bayes nets, and *vice versa* (Spirtes *et al.* 2000).

The most important differences involve the semantics of the models, differences that also influence the accompanying algorithms. Nodes in Bayes nets almost always have an external reference; representation is not distributed. Instead, the individual nodes in Bayes nets represent individual variables in the external world, and the individual connections represent individual causal links among those variables. Even the hidden nodes that represent unobserved variables in Bayes nets denote external properties, features, or relations that could be observed in principle.

This contrasts with typical neural net models. In these models input and output variables refer to entities outside the network, but individual hidden nodes and connection weights do not. A group of hidden nodes, their connections and weights, may indirectly represent some aspect of the external world, but these representations are distributed. Nodes and arrows (that is, neural units and connections) do not directly map to individual variables and causal relations in the world, as they do in causal Bayes nets.

Also, unlike typical neural net models, Bayes nets do not distinguish input from output nodes – they are all on the same footing. This enables them to flexibly account for inferences in many directions, including inferences from outputs to inputs as well as the other way around. In this way Bayes net algorithms can not only generate predictions, they can also use the same apparatus to generate counterfactuals and explanations.

There are several different kinds of algorithms for inference and learning associated with Bayes nets. One set of algorithms presuppose a fixed, parameterized Bayes net. The algorithms can be used to update the probability of all nodes given values of any subset of nodes, and thus to predict the values of some nodes from the values of others. Feed-forward neural nets typically provide a more restricted form of such updating, confined to predicting output from input values.

A second set of algorithms updates probabilities for all nodes given external interventions. As noted above, interventions in causal Bayes nets force variables to take a particular value or force a probability distribution on one or more nodes. The same set of algorithms can be used to generate certain kinds of counterfactual claims. At least as currently formulated, neural net models do not distinguish interventions and counterfactuals from predictions in this way.

Similarly, unlike neural net models of the kind developed so far, the links in causal Bayes nets have an intervention interpretation. Assume we know the network and the joint probability distribution in the objective system the network models. Then we can compute the probability distribution that will result from an external manipulation of a variable represented in the network – we can compute what will happen if we intervene on that system in a particular way. In fact, this is precisely what makes causal Bayes nets *causal*. Neural net models do not interpret the connections between nodes in this way.

In a nutshell, in a neural net psychological model, the hidden nodes, linkages, and weights are about psychology or, were the model biologically serious, about specific nerve cells or complexes and their connections. But they are not directly about the world outside the organism – they do not individually represent variables in the world or causal relations between them. The functional input–output relations and the 'distributed representations' are about the world and about psychology. In a causal Bayes net, everything is about the world (right or wrong). As a psychological model, Bayes nets represent what the subject thinks about the world.

Given this basic semantic difference, there are several ways in which Bayes nets modeling and classical neural net modeling might be considered as complementary rather than competitive. Perhaps the most obvious is that, as we are applying them here at least, the two formalisms involve different levels of description. We think of Bayes nets as what Marr (1982) called a 'computational' level of description, in the same way that in vision science the geometric relations between two-dimensional projections and three-dimensional objects involve a computational levels of representation. In principle, these sorts of computations might be implemented at a lower level by a neural net.

In our work, Bayes net models are intended to describe what and how children think as they learn about causal relations and use that knowledge. We have no doubt that ultimately children do this by means of neural synaptic connections, though we have little idea how the brain performs this or other high-level computations. What is needed is a kind of neural compiler – in the computer science sense – which would show how these representations and algorithms could be carried out by specific, actual nerve cells or complexes through their synaptic connections. That kind of problem seems fundamental for a unified account of brain and mind, and will depend on interdisciplinary work by computer scientists, neuroscientists, and psychologists (e.g. O'Reilly and Munakata 2000).

Part of the appeal of neural net models is the sense that the 'ultimate' theory must be such a model – but such a theory will need to be accompanied by a compilation theory for higher order cognitive functions. One way of viewing contemporary neural net models of psychological functions is that they are surmises about features of such a compiler. So understood, explaining how the causal inferences revealed in our experiments and captured by the causal Bayes net formalism could be implemented in the brain represents a challenge to neural net modeling.

Recently, Rogers and McLelland (Rogers and McLelland 2004) have taken up this challenge to model several features of our data with particular types of neural net simulations. One thing that children (and adults) do in causal inference is to make predictions about novel patterns of contingencies among events, based on their experience of past contingencies. In our first studies, for example, children predict that the yellow but not the blue block will now make the detector go. Rogers and McLelland show that these predictions can be modeled by a sequential neural net, and they suggest ways in which such a net could be derived from a particular set of learning experiences. One might interpret these simulations as a hypothetical implementation of at least some aspects of Bayes net computations.

On the other hand, these models do not, as yet, capture several other important features of Bayes net inferences and of our data. Our experiments show that children distinguish passive associations between variables from associations produced by external interventions on one or more variables, and in simple cases use that different information in a way that accords with causal Bayes net principles. They show that children will, from such data, correctly infer the existence of unobserved common causes acting on two variables. They show that children will, from learned causal relations, correctly (both objectively correctly and correctly according to causal Bayes net representations) infer the effects of interventions they have never before seen. Further, they do all of these things from a quite small collection of samples.

It would be a step forward if neural net theorists were able to further extend models of the kind described in Rogers and McLelland smoothly to accommodate these phenomena. Such models could be thought of in both Bayes net and neural net terms and the explanatory power of such models could come from both sources.

A second way in which the two types of theories may be complementary concerns the developmental trajectory and origins of Bayes net learning mechanisms. As we noted above the youngest subjects in our studies so far were 2 1/2 years old. We suggest that the learning mechanisms we have discovered are responsible, at least in part, for the sort of developmental changes in intuitive theories that we see in the preschool years. But this leaves open the question of where the learning mechanisms themselves come from.

It is possible that the learning mechanisms we see in these children, with their characteristic links between contingency, causation, intervention, and explanation, are in place innately. On the other hand it is also certainly possible that these mechanisms are themselves derived from an earlier history of experience. A neural net that could be extended to implement the full set of Bayes net predictions would presumably be derived from some particular set of experiences – some learning history. Again, Rogers and McLelland suggest some ways that a net might be constructed from a certain learning history that could simulate some, though not all, of the causal inferences a Bayes net system would make and our children do make. The further empirical question becomes whether children, in fact, experience that kind of learning history.

A third way that the two systems may be complementary is simply that they model different types of knowledge and learning. The kinds of causal learning that are well-modeled by causal Bayes nets are powerful and general but they are still specific to the domain of causality. There are many other kinds of learning, and there may be many kinds of learning mechanisms, just as the algorithms involved in vision are very different from those in audition.

Consider, for example, the contrast between the baseball knowledge of Billy Beane, the general manager of the Oakland A's and that of Barry Bonds, the star hitter of the rival San Francisco Giants. Even Noam Chomsky and Steven Pinker would agree that baseball knowledge is not likely to be the result of a dedicated innate module, so it must have been learned. Both Billy and Barry have complex motor representations that allow them to take the input of a ball pitched in a certain location with a certain velocity, and translate that information into muscle output that will have a particular effect on the ball. Both also have basic causal knowledge of how baseball works.

Barry, over literally hundreds of thousands of trials, has honed and perfected that motor knowledge to the point where he can hit (or decide not to hit) virtually any kind of pitch that is thrown at him. The computations that allow him to make these decisions in a split second must be of staggering complexity and subtlety. Billy, in contrast, never made it to the majors.

Billy, however, understands the full, complex, causal structure that relates the various skills and actions of a roster of 40 or so players to a particular outcome variable – winning pennants. Billy's causal knowledge allows him to predict the outcomes of particular decisions and interventions (encouraging walks, avoiding steals, hiring college rather than high-school players, trading players as they become stars) on winning. It also allows him to provide explanations of those outcomes (over a long season on-base percentage causes the maximum number of wins), and to consider the outcomes of counterfactuals (if only Jeremy Giambi had slid they would have won the playoff against the Yankees, if they had retained Miguel Tejada they would have done no better this year).

Barry can modulate his motor output to fit his perceptual input better than anyone who has ever lived. But when it comes to explanations and counterfactuals, about the best he can come up with is the classic baseball restatement of phenomenology 'I was seeing the ball well' or 'I'd have hit better if I'd been seeing the ball well'. Similarly, while Barry can adjust his swing to changing circumstances he is unlikely to know before-hand what the consequences of interventions on that swing are likely to be. He may be able to experience a change of stance, say, and adjust to its effects, but he won't be able to say beforehand what that effect will be. In so far as Billy's representation of the causal structure of baseball is indeed accurate, he will be able to plan effective interventions *a priori*. His most important decisions, in fact, are made before each season starts.

Barry, aside from what must be staggering natural neural connectivity, has learned his skill the Carnegie Hall way, practice, practice, practice, by taking on feedback from thousands of trials. Note that unlike Barry, however, Billy has only had a few trials to predict the outcome, and he can't afford to make adjustments only after the play-off feedback has been provided. Instead he infers causal structure by collecting massive amounts of statistical data and considering the results of experiments (such as the failed five closer rotation in Boston).

Similarly, there is no matter of fact about whether Barry Bonds neural representations are wrong or right, Barry's sensorimotor knowledge doesn't seem accurately described as being true or false and it 'represents' the causal structure of baseball only in a very indirect way. Billy's causal claims about baseball do have that character (and many have been hotly debated).

It should be obvious by now that Barry's skills seem well suited to a process of connectionist modeling, while Billy's seem more suited to a causal Bayes net representation. This is consistent with the applications of connectionism, and dynamic modeling more generally. These ideas have been most effectively applied to the learning of such classification skills as handwriting recognition or indeed to skilled motor learning in adults or in children.

This contrasts with learning the kind of causal knowledge that underwrites intuitive theories. That kind of learning allows explanation, intervention, and counterfactuals as well as prediction. It can be learned in a few trials rather than hundreds or thousands. It seems better modeled by the new formalisms. At least when they are constructing intuitive theories children seem more like Billy than Barry.

Until recently, it has seemed that connectionist learning was the only computational game in town – the alternative was some form of innate triggering, a faintly mystical faith in constructivism, or a vague analogy to scientific induction. Causal Bayes nets and related learning mechanisms may supplement rather than replacing connectionist ones. But they still make it a whole new ball game.

Acknowledgments

The research reported in this paper was supported by National Science Foundation Grant DLS0132487, the McDonnell Foundation, and a Hewlett Foundation Grant to the Center for Advanced Studies in the Behavioral Science to the first author. This chapter was written during AG's fellowship year at the Center and she thanks the staff and administration of that wonderful institution. The paper also benefited greatly from discussion with Jay McClelland, Thomas Shultz, Denis Mareschal, Michael Thomas, Thomas Richardson, and John Campbell and comments from two anonymous reviewers.

References

Cheng PW (1997). From covariation to causation: A causal power theory. *Psychological Review*, 104, 367–405.

Elman Jeffrey L, Bates EA, Johnson MH and Karmiloff-Smith A (1996). *Rethinking innateness: A connectionist perspective on development*. Cambridge, MA: MIT Press.

Flavell JH (1999). Cognitive development: Children's knowledge about the mind. *Annual Review of Psychology*, 50, 21–45.

Gelman SA and Raman L (2002). Folk biology as a window onto cognitive development. *Human Development*, 45, 61–68.

Glymour C (2001). *The mind's arrows: Bayes nets and graphical causal models in psychology.* Cambridge, MA: MIT Press.

Glymour C and Cheng P (1999). Causal mechanism and probability: a normative approach. In: K Oaksford and N Chater, eds. *Rational models of cognition*, pp. 215–313. Oxford: Oxford University Press.

Glymour C and Cooper G (1999). *Computation, causation, and discovery.* Menlo Park, CA: AAAI/MIT Press.

Gopnik A (2000). Explanation as orgasm and the drive for causal understanding: The evolution, function and phenomenology of the theory-formation system. In: F Keil and R Wilson, eds. *Cognition and explanation*, pp. 290–323. Cambridge, Mass: MIT Press.

Gopnik A. and Glymour C (2002). Causal maps and Bayes nets: A cognitive and computational account of theory-formation. In: P Carruthers, S Stich and M Siegal, eds. *The cognitive basis of science*, pp. 117–132. Cambridge: Cambridge University Press.

Gopnik A, Glymour C, Sobel D, Schulz L, Kushnir T and Danks D (2004). A theory of causal learning in children: Causal maps and Bayes nets. *Psychological Review*, 111, 1–31.

Gopnik A and Meltzoff AN (1997). *Words, thoughts and theories.* Cambridge, MA: MIT Press.

Gopnik A and Schulz L (2004). Mechanisms of theory-formation in young children. *Trends in Cognitive Science*, 8(8), 371–377.

Gopnik A, Sobel DM, Schulz LE and Glymour C (2001). Causal learning mechanisms in very young children: Two-, three- and four-year-olds infer causal relations from patterns of variation and covariation. *Developmental Psychology*, 37, 620–629.

Gopnik A and Sobel DM (2000). Detecting blickets: How young children use information about causal properties in categorization and induction. *Child Development*, 71, 1205–1222.

Harris PL, German T and Mills P (1996). Children's use of counterfactual thinking in causal reasoning. *Cognition*, 61, 233–259.

Heckerman D, Meek C and Cooper G (1999). A Bayesian approach to causal discovery. In: C Glymour and G Cooper, eds. *Computation, causation and discovery*, pp. 143–167. Cambridge, MA: MIT Press.

Hickling AK and Wellman HM (2001). The emergence of children's causal explanations and theories: Evidence from everyday conversation. *Developmental Psychology*, 5, 668–683.

Inagaki K and Hatano G (2004). Vitalistic causality in young children's naive biology. *Trends in Cognitive Sciences*, 8, 356–362.

Kushnir T and Gopnik A (in press). Young children infer causal strength from probabilities and interventions. *Psychological Science*.

Kushnir T, Gopnik A, Schulz L and Danks D (2003). Inferring hidden causes. In: R Alterman and D Kirsch, eds. *Proceedings of the Twenty-Fourth Annual Meeting of the Cognitive Science Society*, pp. 1–5. Boston, MA: Cognitive Science Society.

Marr D (1982). *Vision: a computational investigation into the human representation and processing of visual information.* San Francisco: W.H. Freeman.

Meltzoff AN (1995). Understanding the intentions of others: Re-enactment of intended acts by 18-month-old children. *Developmental Psychology*, 31, 838–850.

O' Reilly R and Munakata Y (2000). *Computational explorations in cognitive neuroscience.* Cambridge, MA: MIT Press.

Palmer S (1999). *Vision science: From photons to phenomenology.* Cambridge, MA: MIT Press.

Pearl J (1988). *Probabilistic learning in intelligent systems*. San Mateo, CA: Kaatman Press.

Pearl J (2000). *Causality*. New York: Oxford University Press.

Povinelli D (2000). *Folk physics for apes: The chimpanzee's theory of how the world works*. New York: Oxford University Press.

Ramsey J, Roush T, Gazis P and Glymour C (2002). Automated remote sensing with near-infra-red reflectance spectra: Carbonate recognition. *Data Mining and Knowledge Discovery*, 6, 277–293.

Rehder B and Hastie R (2001). Causal knowledge and categories: The effects of causal beliefs on categorization, induction and similarity. *Journal of Experimental Psychology: General*, 3, 323–360.

Rescorla RA and Wagner AR (1972). A theory of Pavlovian conditioning: Variations in the effectiveness of reinforcement and nonreinforcement. In: AH Black and WF Prokasy, eds. *Classical conditioning II: Current theory and research*, pp. 64–99. New York: Appleton-Century-Crofts.

Richardson T and Spirtes P (2003). Causal inference via ancestral graph models. In: P Green, N Hjort and S Richardson, eds. *Highly structured stochastic systems*. Oxford: Oxford University Press.

Rogers T and McLelland J (2004). *Semantic cognition: A parallel distributed approach*. Cambridge, MA: MIT Press.

Ross N, Medin D, Coley JD, Atran S (2003). Cultural and experimental differences in the development of folkbiological induction. *Cognitive Development*, 18(1), 25–47.

Ruffman T, Perner J, Naito M, Parkin L and Clements WA (1998). Older (but not younger) siblings facilitate false belief. *Developmental Psychology*, 34, 161–174.

Rumelhart D and McLelland J (1986). *Parallel distributed processing: Explorations in the microstructure of cognition*. Cambridge, MA: MIT Press.

Schulz L and Gopnik A (2004). Causal learning across domains. *Developmental Psychology*, 40, 162–176.

Schulz L and Gopnik A (2003). Causal learning in children. Paper presented at the *Society for Research in Child Development*, Tampa, Florida.

Shanks DR (1985). Forward and backward blocking in human contingency judgement. *Quarterly Journal of Experimental Psychology: Comparative and Physiological Psychology*, 37, 1–21.

Shanks DR and Dickinson A (1987). Associative accounts of causality judgment. In: GH Bower, ed. *The psychology of learning and motivation: Advances in research and theory*, vol. 21, pp. 229–261. San Diego, CA: Academic Press.

Shipley B (2000). *Cause and correlation in biology*. Oxford, England: Oxford University Press.

Shultz TR (2003). *Computational developmental psychology*. Cambridge, MA: MIT Press.

Silva R, Scheines R, Glymour C and Spirtes P (2003). Learning measurement models for unobserved variables. In C Meek, ed. *Proceedings of the 18th Conference on Uncertainty in Artificial Intelligence*, pp. 543–550. AAAI Press.

Slaughter V and Gopnik A (1996). Conceptual coherence in the child's theory of mind: Training children to understand belief. *Child Development*, 67, 2967–2988.

Slaughter V, Jaakkola R and Carey S (1999). Constructing a coherent theory: Children's biological understanding of life and death. In: M Siegal and C Peterson, eds. *Children's understanding of biology and health*, pp. 71–96. Cambridge, MA: Cambridge University Press.

Slaughter V and Lyons M (2003). Learning about life and death in early childhood. *Cognitive Psychology*, 46, 1–30.

Sobel DM (2004). Exploring the coherence of young children's explanatory abilities: Evidence from generating counterfactuals. *British Journal of Developmental Psychology*, 22(1), 37–58.

Sobel DM, Tenenbaum JB and Gopnik A (2004). Children's causal inferences from indirect evidence: Backwards blocking and Bayesian reasoning in preschoolers. *Cognitive Science.* **28**, 3.

Spelke ES, Breinlinger K, Macomber J and Jacobson K (1992). Origins of knowledge. *Psychological Review,* **99**, 605–632.

Spirtes P, Glymour C and Scheines R (1993). *Causation, prediction and search* (Springer Lecture Notes in Statistics). New York: Springer-Verlag.

Steyvers M, Tenenbaum JB, Wagenmakers E and Blum B (2003). Inferring causal networks from observations and interventions. *Cognitive Science,* **27**(1), 453–480.

Thelen E and Smith LB (1994). *A dynamic systems approach to the development of cognition and action.* Cambridge, MA: MIT Press.

Tomasello M and Call J (1997). *Primate cognition.* London: Oxford University Press.

Waldmann MR and Hagmayer Y (2001). Estimating causal strength: The role of structural knowledge and processing effort. *Cognition,* **1**, 27–58.

Wellman HM, Hickling AK and Schult CA (1997). Young children's psychological, physical and biological explanations. In: HM Wellman, and K Inagaki, eds. *The emergence of core domains of thought: Children's reasoning about physical, psychological and biological phenomena. New directions for child development,* No. 75, pp. 7–25. San Francisco, CA: Jossey-Bass/Pfeiffer.

Wellman HM and Inagaki K, eds (1997). *The emergence of core domains of thought: Children's reasoning about physical, psychological and biological phenomena. New directions for child development,* No. 75. San Francisco, CA: Jossey-Bass/Pfeiffer.

Woodward J (2003). *Making things happen: a theory of causal explanation.* Oxford: Oxford University Press.

Part 4

Representational integration and dissociation

Chapter 16

Modeling integration and dissociation in brain and cognitive development

Randall C. O'Reilly

Abstract

Over the course of development, brain areas can become increasingly dissociated in their functions, or increasingly integrated. Computational models can provide insights into how and why these opposing effects happen. This paper presents a computational framework for understanding the specialization of brain functions across the hippocampus, neocortex, and basal ganglia. This framework is based on computational tradeoffs that arise in neural network models, where achieving one type of learning function requires very different parameters from those necessary to achieve another form of learning. For example we dissociate the hippocampus from cortex with respect to general levels of activity, learning rate, and level of overlap between activation patterns. Similarly, the frontal cortex and associated basal ganglia system have important neural specializations not required of the posterior cortex system. Taken together, these brain areas form an overall cognitive architecture, which has been implemented in functioning computational models, and provides a rich and often subtle means of explaining a wide range of behavioral and cognitive neuroscience data. The developmental implications of this framework, and other computational mechanisms of dissociation and integration, are reviewed.

16.1 Introduction

The brain is not a homogeneous organ: different brain areas are specialized for different cognitive functions. On the other hand, it is also clear that the brain does not consist of strictly encapsulated modules with perfectly segregated contents. This paper reviews one approach to understanding the nature of specialized functions in terms of the logic of *computational tradeoffs* in neural network models of brain areas.

The core idea behind this approach is that different brain areas are specialized to satisfy fundamental tradeoffs in neural network's performance of different kinds of learning and memory tasks. This way of characterizing the specializations of brain areas is generally consistent with some other theoretical frameworks, but it offers a level of precision and subtlety suitable for understanding complex interactions between different brain areas.

Countering these specialization pressures is the need to integrate information to avoid the well-known *binding problem* that arises with completely segregated representations. For example if color and shape information are encoded by distinct neural populations, it then becomes difficult to determine which color goes with which shape when multiple objects are simultaneously present in the stimulus input. One popular solution to this problem is to invoke the mechanism of synchronous neural firing, such that stimulus features corresponding to the same object fire together, and out of phase with those for other objects (e.g. von der Malsburg, 1981; Gray *et al.*, 1992; Engel *et al.* 1992; Zemel, *et al.* 1995; Hummel and Biederman, 1992). However, there are a number of problems with this approach, as elaborated below. One alternative is to use conjunctive representations, where individual neural representations encode multiple stimulus features (e.g. one unit might encode the conjunction of 'blue' and 'triangle'). This solution, in its simple form, is also highly problematic, producing a combinatorial explosion of different representations for each possible conjunction, and the inability to generalize knowledge across different experiences. There is a more subtle and powerful form of conjunctive representations, however, known as distributed coarse-coded conjunctive representations, which avoid these problems (Hinton *et al.* 1986; Wickelgren, 1969; Seidenberg and McClelland, 1989; St John and McClelland, 1990; Mozer, 1991; Mel and Fiser, 2000; O'Reilly and Soto, 2002; O'Reilly, *et al.* 2003). Individual units in such representations encode multiple subsets of conjunctions (i.e. coarse-coding), and the distributed pattern of activation across many such units serves to distinguish different stimulus configurations. This type of representation is ubiquitous in the brain, and its computational features are explored later in this paper.

Taking these two forces of integration and dissociation together, a clear reconciliation emerges. Instead of viewing brain areas as being specialized for specific *representational content* (e.g. color, shape, location, etc.), areas are specialized for specific *computational functions* by virtue of having different neural parameters. Within each area, many types of representational content are intermixed in distributed coarse-coded conjunctive representations, to avoid the binding problem. This framework flies in the face of the pervasive tendency to associate brain areas with content (e.g. the fusiform face area (Kanwisher, 2000); the ventral what pathway vs. the dorsal where pathway (Ungerleider and Mishkin, 1982); the hippocampus as a spatial map (O'Keefe and Nadel, 1978), etc.). Instead it is aligned with alternative frameworks that focus on function. For example the dorsal 'where' pathway has been reinterpreted as 'vision for action', which integrates both 'what' and 'where' information in the service of performing visually-guided motor actions (Goodale and Milner, 1992). Similarly, the fusiform face area has been characterized instead as an area suitable for subordinate category representations of large numbers of similar items, which includes faces but also birds in the case of bird experts, for example (Tarr and Gauthier, 2000). Below, the case for understanding the hippocampus as a system specialized for the general function of rapid learning of arbitrary conjunctive information, including but not restricted to spatial information, is reviewed (O'Reilly and McClelland, 1994; McClelland *et al.*, 1995; O'Reilly and Rudy, 2001; Norman and O'Reilly, 2003).

This 'functionalist' perspective has been instantiated in a number of neural network models of different brain areas, including posterior (perceptual) neocortex, hippocampus, and the prefrontal cortex/basal ganglia system. We are now in the process of integrating these different models into an overall biologically-based cognitive architecture (Fig. 16.1). Each component of the architecture is specialized for a different function by virtue of having different parameters and neural specializations (as motivated by computational tradeoffs), but the fundamental underlying mechanisms are the same across all areas. Specifically, our models are all implemented within the Leabra framework (O'Reilly, 1998; O'Reilly and Munakata, 2000), which includes a coherent set of basic neural processing and learning mechanisms that have been developed by different researchers over the years. Thus, many

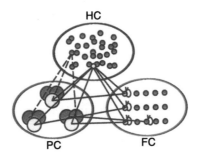

Fig. 16.1 Tripartite cognitive architecture defined in terms of different computational tradeoffs associated with Posterior Cortex (PC), Hippocampus (HC) and Frontal Cortex (FC) (with motor frontal cortex constituting a blend between FC and PC specializations). Large overlapping circles in PC represent overlapping distributed representations used to encode semantic and perceptual information. Small separated circles in HC represent sparse, pattern-separated representations used to rapidly encode ("bind") entire patterns of information across cortex while minimizing interference. Isolated, self-connected representations in FC represent isolated stripes (columns) of neurons capable of sustained firing (i.e. active maintenance or working memory). The basal ganglia also play a critical role in the FC system by modulating ("gating") activations there based on learned reinforcement history.

aspects of these areas work in the same way (and on the same representational content), and in many respects the system can be considered to function as one big undifferentiated whole. For example any given memory is encoded in synapses distributed throughout the entire system, and all areas participate in some way in representing most memories. Therefore, this architecture is much less modular than most conceptions of the brain, while still providing a principled and specific way of understanding the differential contributions of different brain areas. These seemingly contradictory statements are resolved through the process of developing and testing concrete computational simulations that help us understand the ways in which these areas contribute differentially, and similarly, to cognitive and behavioral functions.

In the remainder of the paper, the central computational tradeoffs underlying our cognitive architecture are reviewed, along with a more detailed discussion of the binding problem and the distributed coarse-coded representations solution to it. In each case, these ideas are applied to relevant developmental phenomena, where they may have some important implications, despite the fact that these ideas have been largely based on considerations from the adult system (though across multiple species). There are also some important computational mechanisms of integration and dissociation that do not emerge directly from this computational tradeoff framework, which are briefly reviewed.

16.2 Specializations in hippocampus and posterior neocortex

One of the central tradeoffs behind our approach involves the process of learning novel information rapidly without interfering catastrophically with prior knowledge. This form of learning requires a neural network with very sparse levels of overall activity (leading to highly separated representations), and a relatively high learning rate (i.e. high levels of synaptic plasticity). These features are incompatible with the kind of network that is required to acquire general statistical information about the environment, which needs highly overlapping, distributed representations with relatively higher levels of activity, and a slow rate of learning. The conclusion we have drawn from this mutual incompatibility (see Fig. 16.2a for a summary) is that the brain must have two different learning systems to perform these different functions (O'Reilly and McClelland, 1994; McClelland *et al.*, 1995; O'Reilly and Rudy, 2001; Norman and O'Reilly, 2003). This computational tradeoff idea fits quite well with a wide range of existing theoretical ideas and converging cognitive neuroscience data on the properties of the hippocampus and posterior neocortex, respectively (Scoville and Milner, 1957; Marr, 1971; Grossberg, 1976; O'Keefe and Nadel, 1978; Teyler and Discenna, 1986; McNaughton and Morris, 1987; Sherry and Schacter, 1987; Rolls, 1989; Sutherland and Rudy, 1989; Squire, 1992; Eichenbaum *et al.*, 1994; Treves and Rolls, 1994; Burgess and O'Keefe, 1996; Wu, *et al.*, 1996; Moll and Miikkulainen, 1997; Hasselmo and Wyble, 1997; Aggleton and Brown, 1999; Yonelinas, 2002).

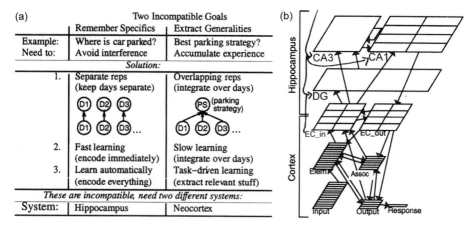

Fig. 16.2 a) Computational motivation for two complementary learning and memory systems in the brain: There are two incompatible goals that such systems need to solve. One goal is to remember specific information (e.g. where one's car is parked). The other is to extract generalities across many experiences (e.g. developing the best parking strategy over a number of different days). The neural solutions to these goals are incompatible: memorizing specifics requires separate representations that are learned quickly, and automatically, while extracting generalities requires overlapping representations and slow learning (to integrate over experiences) and is driven by task-specific constraints. Thus, it makes sense to have two separate neural systems separately optimized for each of these goals. **b)** Our hippocampal/cortical model (O'Reilly and Rudy, 2001, Norman and O'Reilly, 2003). The cortical system consists of sensory input pathways (including elemental (Elem) sensory coding and higher-level association cortex (Assoc)) and motor output. These feed via the entorhinal cortex (EC_in, superficial layers of EC) into the hippocampus proper (dentate gyrus (DG), the fields of Ammon's horn (CA3, CA1), which in turn project back to cortex via EC_out (deep layers of EC). The DG and CA3 areas have particularly sparse representations (few neurons active), which enables rapid learning of arbitrary conjunctive information (i.e. "episodic learning") by producing pattern separation and thus minimizing interference.

We have instantiated our theory in the form of a computational model of the hippocampus and neocortex (Fig. 16.2b). This same model has been extensively tested through applications to a wide range of data from humans and animals (O'Reilly *et al.*, 1998; O'Reilly and Rudy, 2001; Norman and O'Reilly, 2003; Rudy and O'Reilly, 2001; Frank *et al.*, 2003) (see O'Reilly and Norman, 2002 for a concise review). The hippocampal model performs encoding and retrieval of memories in the following manner: during encoding, the hippocampus develops relatively non-overlapping (pattern-separated) representations of cortical inputs (communicated via entorhinal cortex, EC) in region CA3 (strongly facilitated by the very sparse dentate gyrus (DG) inputs). Active units in CA3 are linked to one another (via Hebbian learning), and to a sparser but stable re-representation of the EC input pattern in region CA1. During retrieval, presentation of a partial version of a previously encoded memory representation leads to reconstruction of the complete original CA3 representation (supported by Hebbian-strengthened connections within CA3, and other synaptic modifications throughout the hippocampus). This is *pattern completion*, which is essentially cued recall, where an entire representation is completed or filled-in based on a partial cue. As a consequence of this pattern completion in CA3, the entire studied pattern on the EC output layer is reconstructed (via area CA1), which then spreads out to cortex to fully represent the recalled information. As reviewed in Norman and O'Reilly (2003) and O'Reilly and Rudy (2001), our hippocampal model closely resembles other neural network models of the hippocampus (Treves and Rolls, 1994; Touretzky and Redish, 1996; Burgess and O'Keefe, 1996; Wu *et al.*, 1996; Moll and Miikkulainen, 1997; Hasselmo and Wyble, 1997). There are differences, but the family resemblance between these models far outweights the differences. Recent data comparing neural activation patterns in CA3 and CA1 clearly supports the model's distinctions between these two areas, where CA3 is subject to more pattern completion and separation, while CA1 is a more stable but sparser encoding of the current inputs (Lee *et al.*, 2004; Vazdarjanova and Guzowski, 2004).

In contrast with the rapid, conjunctive learning supported by the hippocampus, our cortical model can support generalization across a large number of experiences, as a result of two neural properties. First, our simulated cortical neurons have a slow learning rate (i.e. small changes in synaptic efficacy after a single presentation of a stimulus). That property insures that any single event has a limited effect on cortical representations. It is the gradual accumulation of many of these small impacts that shapes the representation to capture things that are reliably present across many experiences (i.e. the general statistical structure or regularities of the environment). Second, our model employs representations that involve a relatively large number of neurons (e.g. roughly 15–25 per cent). This property increases the probability that similar events will activate overlapping groups of neurons, thereby enabling these neurons to represent the commonalities across many experiences. More discussion of cortical learning and development is presented later.

16.2.1 Hippocampal and cortical contributions to recall and recognition memory

To flesh out some of the implications of this approach, we briefly review the application of this model to human memory, where we can understand the distinction between recall and recognition memory (Norman and O'Reilly, 2003). The key result is that the ability of the hippocampus to rapidly encode novel conjunctive information with minimal interference is critical for supporting recall of detailed information from prior study episodes. In contrast, the cortex, even with a slow learning rate, can contribute to the recognition of previously experienced stimuli by providing a global, scalar *familiarity* signal. This familiarity-based recognition does not require the ability to pattern-complete missing elements of the original study episode. Instead, it simply requires some kind of ability to match the current input with an existing representation, and report something akin to the 'global-match' between them (e.g. Hintzman, 1988; Gillund and Shiffrin, 1984). It turns out that our cortical network can support this recognition function as a result of small 'tweaks' to the weights of existing representations in the network. These small weight changes cause a recently-activated cortical representation to be somewhat 'sharper' than before (i.e. the difference between active and inactive units is stronger; the contrast is enhanced). This difference in sharpness can be reliably used to distinguish 'old' from 'new' items in recognition memory tests.

This distinction between hippocampal recall and cortical recognition is consistent with many converging sources of data, as reviewed in Yonelinas (2002). One of the interesting novel predictions that arose from our model is that input stimulus similarity and recognition test format should critically impact the cortical system, but not the hippocampal system. Specifically, as the similarity of input stimuli increases, the corresponding cortical representations will also increase in overlap, and this will cause the cortical recognition signal (sharpness) to also overlap. Thus, on a recognition memory test using novel test stimuli that overlap considerably with studied items (e.g. study 'CAT' and test with 'CATS'), the cortical system would be much more likely to false alarm to these similar lures. In contrast, the pattern separation property of the hippocampal system will largely prevent this similarity-based confusion, by encoding the patterns with relatively less overlapping internal representations. However, if both the studied item and the similar lure were presented together at test in a forced-choice testing paradigm, then the cortical system can still provide good performance. This is because although the similar lure will activate an overlapping cortical representation, this representation will nevertheless be reliably less sharpened than that of the actual studied item.

These predictions from the computational model have been tested in experiments on a patient (YR) with selective hippocampal damage, and matched controls (Holdstock *et al.*, 2002). YR is a 61-year-old woman that had focal hippocampal damage due to a painkiller overdose. The damage did not extend to the surrounding medial temporal lobe cortex. On the yes/no recognition task, images were presented one at a time, and the subjects had to respond 'yes' if the image was seen in the previous study phase. On the forced-choice recognition task, a studied image was presented with two novel ones, and the subjects were asked to find the studied one. YR was impaired relative to controls only on the yes/no recognition test with similar lures, and not on the forced-choice test with similar lures, or either test with dissimilar lures. Furthermore, she was impaired at a recall test matched for difficulty with the recognition tests in the control group. This pattern matches exactly the predictions of the model with respect to the impact of a selective hippocampal lesion.

There are numerous other examples where the predictions from our computational models have been tested in both humans and animals (O'Reilly *et al.*, 1998; O'Reilly and Rudy, 2001; Norman and O'Reilly, 2003; Rudy and O'Reilly, 2001; Frank *et al.*, 2003). In many ways, the understanding we have achieved through these computational models accords well with theories derived through other motivations. For example there is broad agreement among theorists that a primary function of the hippocampus is the encoding of episodic or spatial memories (e.g. Vargha-Khadem *et al.*, 1997; Squire, 1992; O'Keefe and Nadel, 1978). This function emerges from the use of sparse representations in our models, because these representations cause the system to develop conjunctive representations that bind together the many different features of an episode or location into a unitary encoding (e.g. O'Reilly and Rudy, 2001; O'Reilly and McClelland, 1994). However, the models are also often at variance with existing theorizing. For example the traditional notions of 'familiarity' and 'recall' do not capture all the distinction between neocortical and hippocampal contributions, as we showed in a number of cases in Norman and O'Reilly (2003). For example neocortical representations can be sensitive to contextual information, and even to arbitrary paired associates, which is not well accounted for by traditional notions of how the familiarity system works.

16.2.2 Developmental Implications

Some implications of this overall framework for understanding various developmental phenomena were described by Munakata (2004). One intriguing application is to the phenomenon of infantile amnesia, where most people cannot remember any experiences prior to the age of about 2–3 years (Howe and Courage, 1993). As with many accounts of this phenomenon, she argues that representational change in the cortex during this formative period can result in the inability to retrieve hippocampal episodic representations later in life (e.g. McClelland *et al.*, 1995). However, this general account does not explain why it is that this representational change does not render all forms of knowledge inaccessible; why does it seem to specifically affect hippocampal episodic memories? Munakata (2004) argues that the pattern separation property of the hippocampus makes it especially sensitive to even relatively small changes in cortical representations. By contrast, the cortex itself would be much less sensitive to such changes, because it tends to generalize across similar patterns to a much greater extent.

Another potential application of this framework is in the domain of so-called 'fast-mapping' phenomena, where children are capable of rapid (e.g. one-trial) learning of novel information (Hayne, Chapter 9, this volume; Hayne *et al.*, 2000; Markson, Chapter 5, this volume; Bloom and Markson, 1998). In the case of the mobile-conjugate reinforcement learning and deferred imitation studies of Hayne and colleagues, infants and children exhibit one-trial learning that is highly sensitive to the study/test stimulus overlap, for both task-relevant and irrelevant stimulus features. This sensitivity to pattern overlap (and fast learning) is highly suggestive of hippocampal function, where the sparse activity levels result in units that are sensitive to stimulus conjunctions (O'Reilly and Rudy, 2001)—only if the study and test environments have sufficient similarity will pattern completion be triggered to produce successful recall. Otherwise, pattern separation will result in an inability to recall the study episode. Nevertheless, there is some question as to when the hippocampus becomes functional in human development, and it is also possible that the high degree of plasticity in the infant neocortex could support rapid learning of this sort. However, the apparently highly conjunctive nature of this fast learning, which fits so well with the hippocampal mechanisms, remains to be explained under this account. Computational models of the detailed behavioral results would be useful to explore these alternative hypotheses.

The fast mapping phenomena studied by Markson and colleagues in the context of early word learning may reflect a more complex interaction between cortical and hippocampal learning mechanisms. This is because this form of learning appears to support considerable generalization and inference, which are hallmarks of cortical representations. Thus, the hippocampus in this case may be only responsible for linking a word with otherwise fairly well-developed cortical representations of the underlying perceptual world. As we saw in the case of recognition memory, the cortical system can exhibit behaviorally-measurable one-trial learning, as long as this learning involves small changes to largely existing representations. Therefore, word-learning fast mapping may be best explained as relatively small changes in the landscape of existing semantic representations, which serve to bring some latent representations 'over threshold', while the hippocampus helps in the linking of these semantic representations with an associated arbitrary verbal label. Again, this is a rich domain that is just waiting to be explored from this hippocampus/cortex computational modeling framework.

16.3 The prefrontal cortex/basal ganglia system

The same tradeoff logic applied to the hippocampal/cortical system has been applied to understanding the specialized properties of the frontal cortex (particularly focused on the prefrontal cortex, PFC) relative to the posterior neocortex and hippocampal systems. The tradeoff in this case involves specializations required for maintaining information in an active state (i.e. maintained neural firing) relative to those required for performing semantic associations and other forms of inferential reasoning. Specifically, active maintenance (often referred to by the more general term of working memory) requires relatively isolated representations so that information does not spread out and get lost over time (O'Reilly and Munakata, 2000; O'Reilly, Braver, and Cohen, 1999). In contrast, the overlapping distributed representations of posterior cortex support spreading associations and inference by allowing one representation to activate aspects of other related representations (e.g. McClelland and Rogers, 2003;

(a)　　　　　　　　　　(b)　　　　　　　　　　(c)

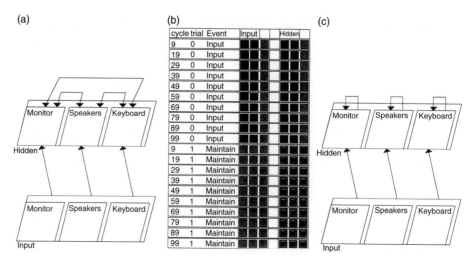

Fig. 16.3 Demonstration of the tradeoff between interconnected and isolated neural connectivity and inference vs. active maintenance. (**a**) Interconnected network: weights (arrows) connect hidden units that represent semantically related information. Such connectivity could subserve semantic networks of posterior cortical areas. (**b**) Input and hidden unit activity as the interconnected network is presented with two inputs (top half of figure) and then those inputs are removed (bottom half of figure). Each row corresponds to one time step of processing. Each unit's activity level is represented by the size of the corresponding black square. The network correctly activates the corresponding hidden units when the inputs are present, but fails to maintain this information alone when the input is removed, due to interactive representations. (**c**) Network with isolated representations: each hidden unit connects to only itself, rather than to other semantically-related units, and thus information does not spread over time, supporting robust active maintenance abilities associated with prefrontal cortical areas. Adapted from O'Reilly and Munakata (2000).

Lambon-Ralph *et al.*, 2003). This tradeoff is illustrated and described further in Fig. 16.3. Neural anatomy and physiology data from prefrontal cortex in monkeys is consistent with this idea. Specifically, prefrontal cortex has relatively isolated 'stripes' of interconnected neurons (Levitt *et al.*, 1993), and neurons located close by each other all maintain the same information according to electrophysiological recordings of 'iso-coding microcolumns' (Rao *et al.*, 1999).

In addition to relatively isolated patterns of connectivity, the prefrontal cortex may be specialized relative to posterior cortex by virtue of its need for an adaptive gating mechanism. This mechanism dynamically switches between rapidly updating new information (gate open) and robustly maintaining other information (gate closed) (Fig. 16.4a). (Cohen *et al.*, 1996; Braver and Cohen, 2000; O'Reilly *et al.*, 1999; O'Reilly and Munakata, 2000). This adaptive gating also needs to be selective, such that some information is updated while other information is maintained. This can be achieved through the parallel loops of connectivity through different areas of the basal ganglia and frontal cortex (Fig. 16.4b) (Alexander *et al.*, 1986; Graybiel and Kimura, 1995; Middleton and Strick, 2000). We postulate that these parallel loops also operate at the finer level of the isolated anatomical stripes in prefrontal cortex, and provide a mechanism for selectively updating the information maintained in one stripe, while robustly maintaining information in other stripes.

A detailed computational model of how such a system would work, and how it can learn which stripes to update when, has been developed (O'Reilly and Frank, in press). This model avoids the 'homunculus problem' that arises in many theories of prefrontal cortex, where it is ascribed powerful 'executive functions' (e.g. Baddeley, 1986) that remain mechanistically unspecified. In effect, these theories rely on unexplained human-like intelligence in the PFC, amounting to a 'homunculus' (i.e. a small man inside the head). In contrast, our model learns to solve complex working memory tasks starting with no pre-existing knowledge whatsoever, demonstrating that they are capable of developing powerful forms of intelligence autonomously.

16.3.1 Development of rule-like PFC representations

We have begun to explore some of the developmental implications of the above specialized PFC/BG mechanisms. In particular, the presence of a adaptive gating mechanism can impose important constraints on the types of representations that form in the PFC system, which in turn can impact the overall behavior of the system in important ways. We recently showed that a network having an adaptive gating mechanism developed abstract, rule-like representations in its simulated PFC, whereas models lacking this mechanism did not (Rougier *et al.* 2005). Furthermore,

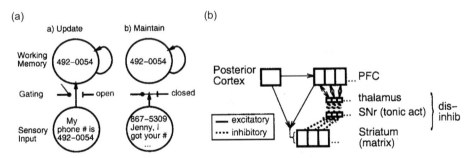

Fig. 16.4 (a) Illustration of adaptive gating. When the gate is open, sensory input can rapidly update working memory (e.g. encoding the cue item A in the 1-2-AX task), but when it is closed, it cannot, thereby preventing other distracting information (e.g. distractor C) from interfering with the maintenance of previously stored information. (b) The basal ganglia (striatum, globus pallidus and thalamus) are interconnected with frontal cortex through a series of parallel loops. Striatal neurons disinhibit prefrontal cortex by inhibiting tonically active substantia nigra pars reticulata (SNr) neurons, releasing thalamic neurons from inhibition. This disinhibition provides a modulatory or gating-like function.

the presence of these rule-like representations resulted in greater flexibility of cognitive control, as measured by the ability to generalize knowledge learned in one task context to other tasks. As elaborated below, these results may have important implications for understanding the nature of development in the PFC, and how it can contribute to tasks in ways that are not obviously related to working memory function (e.g. by supporting more regular, rule-like behavior).

Rougier *et al.* (2005) trained a range of different models on a varying number of related tasks operating on simple visual stimuli (e.g. *name* a 'feature' of the stimulus along a given 'dimension' such as its color, shape, or size; *match* two stimuli along one of these dimensions; *compare* the relative size of two stimuli). Though simple, these tasks also allowed us to simulate benchmark tasks of cognitive control such as Wisconsin card sorting (WCST) and the Stroop task. The generalization test for the cognitive flexibility of the models involved training a given task on a small percentage (e.g. 30 per cent) of all the stimuli, and then testing that task on stimuli that were trained in other tasks. To explore the impact of the adaptive gating mechanism and other architectural features, a range of models having varying numbers of these features were tested.

The model with the full set of prefrontal working memory mechanisms (including adaptive gating) achieved significantly higher levels of generalization than otherwise comparable models that lacked these specialized mechanisms. Furthermore, this benefit of the prefrontal mechanisms interacted with the breadth of experience the network had across a range of different tasks. The network trained on all four tasks generalized significantly better than one trained on only pairs of tasks, but this was only true for the full PFC model. These results were strongly correlated ($r = 0.97$) with the extent to which the model developed abstract rule-like representations of the stimulus dimensions that were relevant for task performance. Thus, the model exhibited an interesting interaction between nature (the specialized prefrontal mechanisms) and nurture (the breadth of experience): both were required to achieve high levels of generalization.

There are numerous points of contact between this model and a range of developmental and neuroscience data. For example the need for extensive breadth of experience in the model to develop more flexible cognitive function may explain the why the prefrontal cortex requires such an extended period of development (up through late adolescence; Casey *et al.* 2001; Morton and Munakata, 2002b; Lewis, 1997; Huttenlocher, 1990). That is, the breadth of experience during that time enables the PFC to develop systematic representations that support the flexible reasoning abilities we have as adults. This model is also consistent with data showing that damage to prefrontal cortex impairs abstraction abilities (e.g. Dominey and Georgieff, 1997), and that prefrontal cortex in monkeys develops more abstract category representations than those in posterior cortex (Wallis *et al.*, 2001; Freedman *et al.* 2002; Nieder *et al.*, 2002). Furthermore, the growing literature on developing task switching abilities in children should prove to be a useful domain in which to explore the developmental properties of this model (e.g. *et al.*, 1996; Munakata and Yerys, 2001; Morton and Munakata, 2002a, 2002b).

In our current research with this PFC/BG model, we are expanding the range and complexity of cognitive tasks, and in the process undertaking an exploration of the 'educational curriculum' that we present to the model. Specifically, we are trying to build up to a wide range of tasks through the training of a smaller set of core competencies. We are starting with a simple sensory/motor domain where the tasks involve focusing on subsets of the visual inputs, and producing appropriate verbal and/or motor outputs. For example the network is being trained to name, match, point, etc. according to different stimulus dimensions or locations. We plan to take this process one step further in the course of developing the full tripartite cognitive architecture, which will involve a more sophisticated perceptual system capable of operating on raw bitmap images, to perform more complex tasks such as visual search in cluttered environments, and real-world navigation. This developmental approach to constructing our models is a necessary consequence of the fact that they are fundamentally learning models. They start out with only broad parametric preconfi-guration, and then must develop their sophisticated abilities through experience-driven learning. Thus, these models should provide an interesting test-bed for under-standing how such parametric variations across different areas of the network lead to differentiations in mature function (e.g. Elman *et al.*, 1996).

16.4 **The need for integration: binding**

To this point, we have focused on the ways in which neural systems need to be specialized to carry out different computational functions. However, there are oppos-ing pressures that force the integration of information processing functions within a single brain area. In particular, as noted earlier, the binding problem places important demands on how information is represented within a given brain area, requiring information to be integrated. As shown in Fig. 16.5, the binding problem arises whenever different aspects of a stimulus input (e.g. color and shape) are encoded by separate neural units. When you have two or more inputs, then you cannot recover from the internal representation which color goes with which shape: was it a red triangle or a blue triangle out there in the world? Although the discussion below focuses on the domain of posterior cortical sensory representations, these binding issues are important for virtually all brain areas.

One trivial solution to the binding problem is to use conjunctive representations to represent each binding that the system needs to perform. In the example shown in Fig. 16.5, there would be a particular unit that codes for a blue square and another that codes for a red triangle. While it is intuitively easy to understand how such conjunct-ive representations solve the binding problem, they are intractable because they

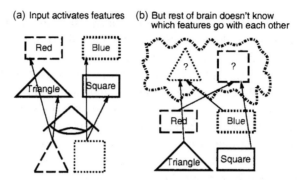

Fig. 16.5 Illustration of the binding problem. (a) Visual inputs (red triangle, blue square) activate separate representations of color and shape properties. (b) However, just the mere activation of these features does not distinguish for the rest of the brain the alternative scenario of a blue triangle and a red square. Red is indicated by dashed outline and blue by a dotted outline.

produce a combinatorial explosion in the number of units required to code for all possible bindings as the number of features to be bound increases. As an example, assume that all objects in the world can be described by 32 different dimensions (e.g. shape, size, color, etc.), each of which contains 16 different feature values. To encode all possible bindings using the naive approach, 16^{32}, or 3.5×10^{38} units would be needed. If the system needed to bind features for four objects simultaneously, four times as many units would be needed. Of course, the brain binds many more types of features and does so with far less units.

Temporal synchrony is a popular alternative to simple conjunctive approach to binding (e.g. von der Malsburg, 1981; Gray *et al.*, 1992; Engel *et al.*, 1992; Zemel *et al.*, 1995; Hummel and Biederman, 1992). This account holds that when populations of neurons that represent various features fire together, those features are considered bound together. To encode multiple distinct sets of bindings, different groups of neurons fire at different phase offsets within an overall cycle of firing, using time to separate the different representations. In the example of Fig. 16.5, the 'red' and 'triangle' units would fire together, and out of phase with the 'blue' and 'square' units. This temporal interleaving is appealing in its simplicity, and the many reports of coherent, phasic firing of neurons in the brain appear to lend it some credibility (e.g. Gray *et al.*, 1992; Engel *et al.*, 1992; Csibra *et al.*, 2000).

However, the temporal synchrony account has several problems, as detailed in several existing critiques (O'Reilly *et al.*, 2003; Cer and O'Reilly, in press; Shadlen and Movshon, 1999). For example the transience of temporal synchrony causes problems when bound information needs to be encoded in long-term memory. One proposal is that there is a separate conjunctive representation system for everything that is encoded into long-term memory (Hummel and Holyoak, 1997), with the idea that this is a small enough set that the combinatorial explosion of such conjunctions is not a problem. However, there is considerable evidence that just about every activation state in our brains produces a lasting trace in the synaptic connections that can later be measured in priming or perceptual learning studies (e.g. Furmanski and Engel, 2000; Gilbert, *et al.*, 2001; Adini *et al.*, 2002; Aslin *et al.*, 2002; Wagner *et al.*, 2000; Stark and McClelland, 2000)—this would suggest that combinatorial explosion is a problem. Furthermore, the process of actually using ('decoding') the temporal synchrony binding information is problematic as shown in Fig. 16.6. In addition, the data showing synchronous neural firing falls well short of demonstrating the interleaved phase-offset synchrony necessary for binding. Instead, this data may just be an epiphenomenon of spike-based neural firing dynamics.

Fortunately, there is another alternative way of solving the binding problem, which involves a more efficient way of implementing conjunctive representations using distributed coarse-coded conjunctive representations (DCC) (Cer and O'Reilly, in press; Mel and Fiser, 2000). A DCC representation encodes binding information via a number of simultaneously active units (i.e. a distributed representation; Hinton *et al.*, 1986), where each unit is activated by multiple different conjunctions. For example, a given unit might respond to red+circle *or* green+square *or* blue+triangle. By getting more conjunctive mileage out of each unit, and leveraging the combinatorial power of distributed representations across multiple units, this solution can be much, much more efficient than naive conjunctive representations (Table 16.1). For example for the case mentioned above of 32 dimensions with 16 features each, only 512 units would be required under an optimal binary distributed representation (see Cer and O'Reilly (in press) for details). The numbers for more realistic neural networks would

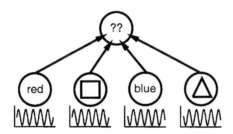

Fig. 16.6 Decoding problem for temporal synchrony. Two sets of features are each firing in phase with each other, and out of phase with the other set (as indicated by the sine wave plots below the features). Without additional mechanisms, it is unclear how a downstream neuron can decode this information to determine what is actually present: it is being uniformly driven by synaptic input at all phases, and its activation would be the same for any combination of synchrony in the input features. Also, even though it looks like the synchronous firing is discriminable, both sets of units have synchronous firing, so there is no basis to choose one over another. One solution is to build in preferential weights for one set of features (e.g. 'red square') but this amounts to a conjunctive representation, which the temporal synchrony approach is designed to avoid in the first place.

Table 16.1 Solution to the binding problem by using representations that encode combinations of input features (i.e. color and shape), but achieve greater efficiency by representing multiple such combinations. Obj1 and obj2 show the features of the two objects. The first six columns show the responses of a set of representations that encode the separate color and shape features: R = Red, G = Green, B = Blue, S = Square, C = Circle, T = Triangle. Using only these separate features causes the binding problem: observe that the two configurations in each pair are equivalent according to the separate feature representation. The final unit encodes a combination of the three different conjunctions shown at the top of the column, and this is enough to disambiguate the otherwise equivalent representations.

obj1	obj2	R	G	B	S	C	T	RC GS BT
RS	GC	1	1	0	1	1	0	0
RC	GS	1	1	0	1	1	0	1
RS	GT	1	1	0	1	0	1	0
RT	GS	1	1	0	1	0	1	1
RS	BC	1	0	1	1	1	0	0
RC	BS	1	0	1	1	1	0	1
RS	BT	1	0	1	1	0	1	1
RT	BS	1	0	1	1	0	1	0
RC	GT	1	1	0	0	1	1	1
RT	GC	1	1	0	0	1	1	0
RC	BT	1	0	1	0	1	1	1
RT	BC	1	0	1	0	1	1	0
GS	BC	0	1	1	1	1	0	1
GC	BS	0	1	1	1	1	0	0
GS	BT	0	1	1	1	0	1	1
GT	BS	0	1	1	1	0	1	0
GC	BT	0	1	1	0	1	1	1
GT	BC	0	1	1	0	1	1	0

certainly be higher than this, but nowhere near the 3.5×10^{38} units of the simple conjunctive approach. In addition to this efficiency, virtually every neural recording study ever performed supports these DCC representations, in that individual neurons inevitably encode conjunctions of different stimulus/task features (e.g. Tanaka, 1996; Rao *et al.*, 1997; Barone and Joseph, 1989; Ito *et al.*, 1998; Walker *et al.*, 1999).

16.4.1 Spatial relationship binding model

The ability of a neural network to learn these DCC representations, and to systematically generalize to novel input patterns, was explored by O'Reilly and Busby (2002). This model demonstrates both that distributed, coarse-coded conjunctive representations can systematically perform binding relationships, and that not all mechanisms for developing such relationships are equivalent. The network (Fig. 16.7a) was trained to encode and report the spatial relationship between two items presented on its

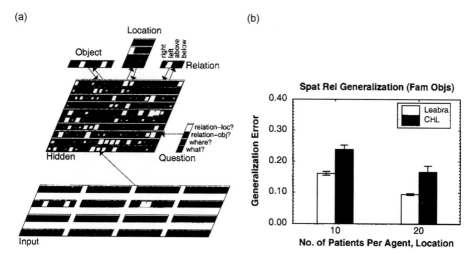

Fig. 16.7 (a) Spatial relationship binding model, representing posterior visual cortex (O'Reilly and Busby, 2002). Objects are represented by distributed patterns of activation over 8 feature values in each location, with the input containing a 4 × 4 array of object locations. Input patterns contain two different objects, arranged either vertically or horizontally. The network answers different questions about the inputs based on the activation of the Question input layer. For the "what?" question, the location of one of the objects is activated as an input in the Location layer, and the network must produce the correct object features for the object in that location. For the "where?" question, the object features for one of the objects are activated in the Object layer, and the network must produce the correct location activation for that object. For the "relation-obj?" question, the object features for one object are activated, and the network must activate the relationship between this object and the other object, in addition to activating the location for this object. For the "relation-loc?" question, the location of one of the objects is activated, and the network must activate the relationship between this object and the other object, in addition to activating the object features for this object (this is the example shown in the network, responding that the target object is to the left of the other object). Thus, the hidden layer must have bound object, location, and relationship information in its encoding of the input. (b) Generalization results for different algorithms on the spatial relationship binding task (testing on familiar objects in novel locations; similar results hold for novel objects as well). Only the 400 Agent, Location × 10 or 20 Patient, Location cases are shown. It is clear that Leabra performed roughly twice as well as the CHL algorithm, consistent with earlier results on other tasks (O'Reilly, 2001).

inputs, in addition to the identity and location of one of these items. Thus, the need for binding was taxed in two ways. First, the mere presence of two stimulus items demanded the ability to bind the features associated with one stimulus as distinct from the other. Second, and perhaps more challenging, the need to encode the spatial relationship information between objects required a kind of *relational* binding that has often been discussed in the context of complex structured knowledge representations (e.g. Touretzky, 1986; Hummel and Biederman, 1992; Hummel and Holyoak, 1997; Smolensky, 1990; Shastri and Ajjanagadde, 1993; Gasser and Colunga, 1998; Plate, 1995). Specifically, the network needed to be able to identify one of the two inputs as the 'agent' item (i.e. the focus of attention), and report the relationship of the other 'patient' item relative to it, and not the other way around.

The model is a very simplified rendition of the early visual system. During training the model is presented with a pair of input items in a simulated visual field, and is 'asked' one of four corresponding questions (via the activation of a question input unit) (see Fig. 16.7a for details). The model was implemented as a recurrent neural network using the Leabra framework (O'Reilly and Munakata, 2000), and it achieved very high levels of generalization based on relatively limited amounts of experience (e.g. 95 per cent correct after training on only 25 per cent of the training space, and 80 per cent correct after training on only roughly 10 per cent of the space). In addition, a model using only contrastive Hebbian (CHL) error-driven learning, and another using the Almedia–Pineda recurrent backpropagation algorithm, were also run. Of these, it was found that Almedia–Pineda was not able to learn to successfully perform the task. While both the Leabra and CHL networks were able to learn, the additional constraints in Leabra (Hebbian learning and inhibitory competition) produced nearly twice as good generalization as CHL (Fig. 16.7b).

Thus, by incorporating additional, biologically motivated constraints on the development of internal representations in the network, the Leabra model is able to achieve more systematicity in its representations, which subsequently give rise to better generalization performance. Importantly, we analyzed the internal representations of the Leabra network, and found that it developed both specialized representations of separable stimulus features (i.e. just representing what or where separately) and distributed coarse-coded conjunctive representations that integrated across features. This is typically what is observed in neural recording studies of the visual pathway, where many neurons encode strange conjunctions of stimulus features (Tanaka, 1996), while others have relatively more featural selectivity.

16.5 Other mechanisms of integration and dissociation

There are numerous other neural mechanisms that can give rise over development to integration and dissociation of function within the cortex. These mechanisms are generally compatible with the above framework, but do not emerge directly from the overall computational tradeoffs behind it. A selection of such mechanisms are briefly reviewed here (see Jacobs, 1999 for a more detailed review).

It is well established that synapses proliferate early in development, and are then pruned as the brain matures (e.g. Huttenlocher, 1990). This process of refining the connectivity of neurons can lead to the development of more clearly delineated functional specializations in different brain areas (Johnson and Vecera, 1996), as has been demonstrated in computational models (Jacobs and Jordan, 1992; Miller, 1995).

This process has been termed 'parcellation'. For example, Jacobs and Jordan (1992) showed that a network with a bias toward strengthening connections to physically proximal neurons produced a topographic organization of specialized functions within an initially homogeneous network. Although a focus on pruning is prevalent, others have emphasized the importance of the ongoing growth of new synapses, which can support continued plasticity of the system (Quartz and Sejnowski, 1997). As Jacobs (1999) points out, both pruning and synaptic growth behave functionally very similar to standard forms of Hebbian learning used in many different neural network models. Thus, it remains to be seen whether including these mechanisms in a broader range of models will result in fundamentally new computational properties. It could well be that these processes are a pragmatic physical necessity of wiring up the huge numbers of neurons in the mammalian cortex, whereas most small-scale models 'cheat' and use full connectivity with Hebbian learning mechanisms, possibly with similar effect.

In both the parcellation models and Hebbian learning, competition plays a critical role in forcing the specialization of different neurons and brain areas. This competition can take place at many different scales, from synapses to neurons to larger-scale brain areas. This latter form of competition has been exploited in the *mixture of experts* models (Jacobs et al., 1991; Jordan & Jacobs, 1994; Jacobs and Kosslyn, 1994). These models posit that learning is somehow gated by the relevance of a given group or pool of neurons (an 'expert') for a given trial of learning. Experts that are most relevant get to learn the most from the feedback on a trial, and this causes further specialization of these experts for particular types of trials. Due to competition, experts for one set of trials typically lose out to other experts for other types of trials, resulting in an overall dissociation or specialization of function across these experts. This may provide a reasonable computational model for specialization of function across different cortical areas. However, as noted in Jacobs (1999), it is unclear if the requisite large-scale competition between areas exists in the brain. Thus, it may make more sense to consider competition to operate fundamentally at the level of individual neurons (which is relatively well accepted), but to also allow for positive excitatory interactions among neurons. These excitatory interactions can cause neurons to group together and act as a more coherent whole. In effect, these excitatory grouping effects, together with pervasive inhibition mediated by local inhibitory interneurons, may result in emergent learning dynamics that resemble those captured in the mixture of experts models. This dynamic is present in several existing models of parcellation, for example in the development of ocular dominance columns (Miller, 1995).

In addition, these kinds of emergent competitive dynamics may have an overlay of more biologically-determined changes in plasticity over development. For example one model explored the effects of 'trophic waves' of plasticity that spread from simulated primary sensory areas to higher-level association areas (Shrager and Johnson, 1996). This trophic wave effect led to greater levels of neural specialization, in particular to the development of more complex higher-order representations in the higher-level association cortex.

These mechanisms are compelling and should be included more widely into neural network learning models. It will be interesting to explore in future work the possible interactions between these types of mechanisms and the general tradeoff principles articulated earlier.

16.6 General discussion

The general conclusions from the computational tradeoffs described above are summarized in the tripartite cognitive architecture pictured back in Fig. 16.1. This architecture is composed of posterior cortex (PC), hippocampus (HC), and frontal cortex/basal ganglia (FC), with each component specialized for a specific computational function. The posterior cortex is specialized for slowly developing rich, overlapping distributed representations that encode the general structure of the world, and for using these representations to support inferential reasoning through spreading activation dynamics, among other functions. The hippocampus uses sparse distributed representations to avoid interference while rapidly learning about arbitrary novel conjunctions (e.g. episodes), and recurrent connectivity in CA3 of the hippocampus supports pattern completion (recall) of previously encoded patterns. The frontal cortex/basal ganglia system uses relatively isolated representations and intrinsic bistability to robustly maintain information in an active state, and the basal ganglia provides adaptive gating to selectively update these representations according to task demands.

These distinctions between functional areas do not align with stimulus content dimensions. In contrast, each area encodes largely the same kinds of content (e.g. different stimulus dimensions and abstractions, language representations, etc.), but does so in a different way, with different computational affordances. This allows the binding problem to be avoided, as each area can use distributed coarse-coded representations to efficiently and systematically cover the space of bindings that need to be distinguished.

This architecture lies between the extremes of modularity and equipotentiality—it has elements of both. However, it is not just any kind of both, but rather a very particular kind of both that focuses on some factors as critical for driving specialization, and not others. This approach can be summarized with the following 'recipe' for 'discovering' dissociated functional areas:

1. Identify essential functions.

2. Identify their requisite neural mechanisms (using computational models).

3. If they are incompatible, separate brain areas are required.

Of course, each of these steps requires considerable elaboration and judgment to be applied successfully, but this at least serves to highlight the core of the logic behind the present work.

This recipe can be applied within posterior cortex, for example to help understand the nature of the specialization in the fusiform face area (FFA) (Kanwisher, 2000; Tarr and Gauthier, 2000). From the hippocampal modeling work, we know that sparse activity levels lead to pattern separation, and thus the ability to distinctly represent a large number of similar input patterns. The apparent ability of the FFA to support identification of highly similar subordinate category members (e.g. faces) would certainly be greatly facilitated by this kind of sparse activity. Thus, it may be that this is what is unique about this brain area relative to other areas of posterior cortex. Note that because this area does not need to also support pattern completion from partial cues in the same way that the hippocampal system does, it therefore does not require the full set of neural specializations present in the hippocampus. In any case, this view of FFA specialization is appealing in its biological simplicity (it is easy to see how such a simple parametric variation could be genetically coded, for example), and is consistent with the notion that this area can also be co-opted for other forms of subordinate category representation (Tarr and Gauthier, 2000).

In conclusion, this paper has hopefully stimulated some interest in the notion that a cognitive architecture defined in terms of computational tradeoffs, with each area integrating information using distributed coarse-coded conjunctive representations to avoid binding problems, may provide some useful understanding of complex patterns of behavior from development to the mature system.

Acknowledgement

Supported by ONR grant N00014-03-1-0428, and NIH grants MH069597 and MH64445.

References

Adini Y, Sagi D and Tsodyks M (2002). Context-enabled learning in the human visual system. *Nature*, 415, 790–792.

Aggleton JP and Brown MW (1999). Episodic memory, amnesia, and the hippocampal-anterior thalamic axis. *Behavioral and Brain Sciences*, 22, 425–490.

Alexander GE, DeLong MR, and Strick PL (1986). Parallel organization of functionally segregated circuits linking basal ganglia and cortex. *Annual Review of Neuroscience*, 9, 357–381.

Aslin C, Blake R and Chun MM (2002). Perceptual learning of temporal structure. *Vision Research*, 42, 3019–3030.

Baddeley AD (1986). *Working memory*. New York: Oxford University Press.

Barone P and Joseph JP (1989). Prefrontal cortex and spatial sequencing in macaque monkey. *Experimental Brain Research*, 78, 447–464.

Bloom P and Markson L (1998). Capacities underlying word learning. *Trends in Cognitive Science*, 2, 67–73.

Braver TS and Cohen JD (2000). On the control of control: The role of dopamine in regulating prefrontal function and working memory. In: S Monsell and J Driver, eds. *Control of cognitive processes: Attention and performance XVIII*, pp. 713–737. Cambridge, MA: MIT Press.

Burgess N and O'Keefe, J (1996). Neuronal computations underlying the firing of place cells and their role in navigation. *Hippocampus*, **6**, 749–762.

Casey BJ, Durston S and Fossella JA (2001). Evidence for a mechanistic model of cognitive control. *Clinical Neuroscience Research*, **1**, 267–282.

Cer DM and O'Reilly, RC (in press). Neural mechanisms of binding in the hippocampus and neocortex: Insights from computational models. In: HD Zimmer, A Mecklinger and U Lindenberger, eds. *Binding in memory*. Oxford: Oxford University Press.

Cohen JD, Braver TS and O'Reilly RC (1996). A computational approach to prefrontal cortex, cognitive control, and schizophrenia: Recent developments and current challenges. *Philosophical Transactions of the Royal Society (London) B*, **351**, 1515–1527.

Csibra G, Davis G and Johnson MH (2000). Gamma oscillations and object processing in the infant brain. *Science*, **290**, 1582.

Dominey PF and Georgieff N (1997). Schizophrenics learn surface but not abstract structure in a serial reaction time task. *Neuroreport*, **8**, 2877.

Eichenbaum HH, Otto T and Cohen NJ (1994). Two functional components of the hippocampal memory system. *Behavioral and Brain Sciences*, **17**, 449–518.

Elman JL, Bates EA, Johnson MH, Karmiloff-Smith A, Parisi D and Plunkett K (1996). *Rethinking innateness: A connectionist perspective on development*. Cambridge, MA: MIT Press.

Engel AK, Konig P, Kreiter AK, Schillen TB and Singer, W (1992). Temporal coding in the visual cortex: New vistas on integration in the nervous system. *Trends in Neurosciences*, **15**, 218–226.

Frank MJ, Rudy JW and O'Reilly RC (2003). Transitivity, flexibility, conjunctive representations and the hippocampus: II. a computational analysis. *Hippocampus*, **13**, 341–354.

Freedman DJ, Riesenhuber M, Poggio T and Miller EK (2002). Visual categorization and the primate prefrontal cortex: Neurophysiology and behavior. *Journal of Neurophysiology*, **88**, 929–941.

Furmanski CS and Engel SA (2000). Perceptual learning in object recognition: Object specificity and size invariance. *Vision Research*, **40**, 473.

Gasser M and Colunga E (1998). *Where do relations come from?* (Technical Report 221). Bloomington, IN: Indiana University Cognitive Science Program.

Gilbert CD, Sigman M and Crist RE (2001). The neural basis of perceptual learning. *Neuron*, **31**, 681–697.

Gillund G and Shiffrin RM (1984). A retrieval model for both recognition and recall. *Psychological Review*, **91**, 1–67.

Goodale MA and Milner AD (1992). Separate visual pathways for perception and action. *Trends in Neurosciences*, **15**, 20–25.

Gray CM, Engel AK, Konig P and Singer, W (1992). Synchronization of oscillatory neuronal responses in cat striate cortex—temporal properties. *Visual Neuroscience*, **8**, 337–347.

Graybiel AM and Kimura M (1995). Adaptive neural networks in the basal ganglia. In: JC Houk, JL Davis and DG Beiser, eds. *Models of information processing in the basal ganglia*, pp. 103–116. Cambridge, MA: MIT Press.

Grossberg S (1976). Adaptive pattern classification and universal recoding I: Parallel development and coding of neural feature detectors. *Biological Cybernetics*, **23**, 121–134.

Hasselmo ME and Wyble B (1997). Free recall and recognition in a network model of the hippocampus: Simulating effects of scopolamine on human memory function. *Behavioural Brain Research*, **89**, 1–34.

Hayne H, Boniface J and Barr R (2000). The development of declarative memory in human infants: Age-related changes in deferred imitation. *Behavioural Neuroscience*, 114, 77.

Hinton GE, McClelland JL and Rumelhart DE (1986). Distributed representations. In: DE Rumelhart, JL McClelland and PDP Research Group, eds. *Parallel distributed processing. Volume 1: Foundations*, pp. 77–109. Cambridge, MA: MIT Press.

Hintzman DL (1988). Judgments of frequency and recognition memory in a multiple-trace memory model. *Psychological Review*, 95, 528–551.

Holdstock JS, Mayes AR, Roberts N, Cezayirli E, Isaac CL, O'Reilly RC *et al.* (2002). Under what conditions is recognition spared relative to recall after selective hippocampal damage in humans? *Hippocampus*, 12, 341–351.

Howe ML and Courage ML (1993). On resolving the enigma of infantile amnesia. *Psychological Bulletin*, 113, 305–326.

Hummel JE and Biederman I (1992). Dynamic binding in a neural network for shape recognition. *Psychological Review*, 99, 480–517.

Hummel JE and Holyoak KJ (1997). Distributed representations of structure: A theory of analogical access and mapping. *Psychological Review*, 104, 427–466.

Huttenlocher PR (1990). Morphometric study of human cerebral cortex development. *Neuropsychologia*, 28, 517–527.

Ito M, Westheimer G and Gilbert CD (1998). Attention and perceptual learning modulate contextual influences on visual perception. *Neuron*, 20, 1191.

Jacobs RA (1999). Computational studies of the development of functionally specialized neural modules. *Trends in Cognitive Sciences*, 3, 31–38.

Jacobs RA and Jordan MI (1992). Computational consequences of a bias toward short connections. *Journal of Cognitive Neuroscience*, 4, 323–336.

Jacobs RA, Jordan MI, Nowlan SJ and Hinton GE (1991). Adaptive mixtures of local experts. *Neural Computation*, 3, 79–87.

Jacobs RA and Kosslyn SM (1994). Encoding shape and spatial relations: The role of receptive field size in coordinating complementary representations. *Cognitive science*, 18, 361–386.

Johnson MH and Vecera SP (1996). Cortical differentiation and neurocognitive development: the parcellation conjecture. *Behavioral Processes*, 36, 195–212.

Jordan MI and Jacobs RA (1994). Hierarchical mixtures of experts and the EM algorithm. *Neural Computation*, 6, 181–214.

Kanwisher N (2000). Domain specificity in face perception. *Nature Neuroscience*, 3, 759–763.

Lambon-Ralph MA, Patterson K, Garrard P and Hodges JR (2003). Semantic dementia with category specificity: A comparative case-series study. *Cognitive Neuropsychology*, 20, 307–326.

Lee I, Yoganarasimha D, Rao G and Knierim JJ (2004). Comparison of population coherence of place cells in hippocampal subfields CA1 and CA3. *Nature*, 430, 456–459.

Levitt JB, Lewis DA, Yoshioka T and Lund JS (1993). Topography of pyramidal neuron intrinsic connections in macaque monkey prefrontal cortex (areas 9 and 46). *Journal of Comparative Neurology*, 338, 360–376.

Lewis DA (1997). Development of the prefrontal cortex during adolescence: Insights into vulnerable neural circuits in schizophrenia. *Neuropsychopharmacology*, 16, 385–398.

Marr D (1971). Simple memory: A theory for archicortex. *Philosophical Transactions of the Royal Society (London) B*, 262, 23–81.

McClelland JL, McNaughton BL and O'Reilly RC (1995). Why there are complementary learning systems in the hippocampus and neocortex: Insights from the successes and failures of connectionist models of learning and memory. *Psychological Review*, 102, 419–457.

McClelland JL and Rogers TT (2003). The parallel distributed processing approach to semantic cognition. *Nature Reviews Neuroscience*, 4, 310–322.

McNaughton BL and Morris RGM (1987). Hippocampal synaptic enhancement and information storage within a distributed memory system. *Trends in Neurosciences*, 10, 408–415.

Mel BA and Fiser J (2000). Minimizing binding errors using learned conjunctive features. *Neural Computation*, 12, 731–762.

Middleton FA and Strick PL (2000). Basal ganglia and cerebellar loops: Motor and cogntive circuits. *Brain Research Reviews*, 31, 236–250.

Miller KD (1995). Receptive fields and maps in the visual cortex: Models of ocular dominance and orientation columns. In: E Domany, JL van Hemmen and K Schulten, eds. *Models of neural networks, III*, pp. 55–78. New York, NY: Springer Verlag.

Moll M and Miikkulainen R (1997). Convergence-zone episodic memory: Analysis and simulations. *Neural Networks*, 10, 1017–1036.

Morton JB and Munakata Y (2002a). Active versus latent representations: A neural network model of perseveration and dissociation in early childhood. *Developmental Psychobiology*, 40, 255–265.

Morton JB and Munakata Y (2002b). Are you listening? Exploring a knowledge action dissociation in a speech interpretation task. *Developmental Science*, 5, 435–440.

Mozer MC (1991). *The perception of multiple objects: A connectionist approach*. Cambridge, MA: MIT Press.

Munakata Y (2004). Computational cognitive neuroscience of early memory development. *Developmental Review*, 24, 133–153.

Munakata Y and Yerys BE (2001). All together now: When dissociations between knowledge and action disappear. *Psychological Science*, 12, 335–337.

Nieder A, Freedman DJ and Miller EK (2002). Representation of the quantity of visual items in the primate prefrontal cortex. *Science*, 298, 1708–1711.

Norman KA and O'Reilly RC (2003). Modeling hippocampal and neocortical contributions to recognition memory: A complementary learning systems approach. *Psychological Review*, 110, 611–646.

O'Keefe J and Nadel L (1978). *The hippocampus as a cognitive map*. Oxford, England: Oxford University Press.

O'Reilly RC (1998). Six principles for biologically-based computational models of cortical cognition. *Trends in Cognitive Sciences*, 2, 455–462.

O'Reilly RC, Braver TS and Cohen JD (1999). A biologically based computational model of working memory. In: A Miyake and P Shah, eds. *Models of working memory: Mechanisms of active maintenance and executive control*, pp. 375–411. New York: Cambridge University Press.

O'Reilly RC and Busby RS (2002). Generalizable relational binding from coarse-coded distributed representations. In: TG Dietterich, S Becker and Z Ghahramani, eds. *Advances in Neural Information Processing Systems (NIPS) 14*. Cambridge, MA: MIT Press.

O'Reilly RC, Busby RS and Soto R (2003). Three forms of binding and their neural substrates: Alternatives to temporal synchrony. In: A Cleeremans ed. *The unity of consciousness: Binding, integration, and dissociation*, pp. 168–192. Oxford: Oxford University Press.

O'Reilly RC and Frank MJ (in press). Making working memory work: A computational model of learning in the frontal cortex and basal ganglia. *Neural Computation*.

O'Reilly RC and McClelland JL (1994). Hippocampal conjunctive encoding, storage, and recall: Avoiding a tradeoff. *Hippocampus*, 4, 661–682.

O'Reilly RC and Munakata Y (2000). *Computational explorations in cognitive neuroscience: Understanding the mind by simulating the brain.* Cambridge, MA: MIT Press.

O'Reilly RC and Norman KA (2002). Hippocampal and neocortical contributions to memory: Advances in the complementary learning systems framework. *Trends in Cognitive Sciences*, 6, 505–510.

O'Reilly RC, Norman KA and McClelland JL (1998). A hippocampal model of recognition memory. In: MI Jordan, MJ Kearns and SA Solla, eds. *Advances in neural information processing systems* 10, pp. 73–79. Cambridge, MA: MIT Press.

O'Reilly RC and Rudy JW (2001). Conjunctive representations in learning and memory: Principles of cortical and hippocampal function. *Psychological Review*, 108, 311–345.

O'Reilly RC and Soto R (2002). A model of the phonological loop: Generalization and binding. In: TG Dietterich, S Becker and Z Ghahramani, eds. *Advances in neural information processing systems (NIPS) 14.* Cambridge, MA: MIT Press.

Plate TA (1995). Holographic reduced representations. *IEEE Transactions on Neural Networks*, 6, 623–641.

Quartz SR and Sejnowski TJ (1997). The neural basis of cognitive development: a constructivist manifesto. *Behavioral and Brain Sciences*, 20, 537.

Rao SC, Rainer G and Miller EK (1997). Integration of what and where in the primate prefrontal cortex. *Science*, 276, 821–824.

Rao SG, Williams GV and Goldman-Rakic PS (1999). Isodirectional tuning of adjacent interneurons and pyramidal cells during working memory: Evidence for microcolumnar organization in PFC. *Journal of Neurophysiology*, 81, 1903.

Rolls ET (1989). Functions of neuronal networks in the hippocampus and neocortex in memory. In: JH Byrne and WO Berry, eds. *Neural models of plasticity: Experimental and theoretical approaches*, pp. 240–265. San Diego, CA: Academic Press.

Rougier NP, Noelle D, Braver TS, Cohen JD and O'Reilly RC (2005). Prefrontal cortex and the flexibility of cognitive control: Rules without symbols. *Proceedings of the National Academy of Sciences*, 102, 7338–7343.

Rudy JW and O'Reilly RC (2001). Conjunctive representations, the hippocampus, and contextual fear conditioning. *Cognitive, Affective, and Behavioral Neuroscience*, 1, 66–82.

Scoville WB and Milner B (1957). Loss of recent memory after bilateral hippocampal lesions. *Journal of Neurology, Neurosurgery, and Psychiatry*, 20, 11–21.

Seidenberg MS and McClelland JL (1989). A distributed, developmental model of word recognition and naming. *Psychological Review*, 96, 523–568.

Shadlen MN and Movshon JA (1999). Synchrony unbound: A critical evaluation of the temporal binding hypothesis. *Neuron*, 24, 67–77.

Shastri L and Ajjanagadde V (1993). From simple associations to systematic reasoning: A connectionist representation of rules, variables, and dynamic bindings using temporal synchrony. *Behavioral and Brain Sciences*, 16, 417–494.

Sherry DF and Schacter DL (1987). The evolution of multiple memory systems. *Psychological Review*, 94, 439–454.

Shrager J and Johnson MH (1996). Dynamic plasticity influences the emergence of function in a simple cortical array. *Neural Networks*, 9, 1119.

Smolensky P (1990). Tensor product variable binding and the representation of symbolic structures in connectionist networks. *Artificial Intelligence*, 46, 159–216.

Squire LR (1992). Memory and the hippocampus: A synthesis from findings with rats, monkeys, and humans. *Psychological Review*, 99, 195–231.

St John MF and McClelland JL (1990). Learning and applying contextual constraints in sentence comprehension. *Artificial Intelligence*, 46, 217–257.

Stark CEL and McClelland JL (2000). Repetition priming of words, pseudowords, and nonwords. *Journal of Experimental Psychology: Learning, Memory, and Cognition*, 26, 945.

Sutherland RJ and Rudy JW (1989). Configural association theory: The role of the hippocampal formation in learning, memory, and amnesia. *Psychobiology*, 17, 129–144.

Tanaka K (1996). Inferotemporal cortex and object vision. *Annual Review of Neuroscience*, 19, 109–139.

Tarr MJ and Gauthier I (2000). FFA: a flexible fusiform area for subordinate-level visual processing automatized by expertise. *Nature Neuroscience*, 3, 764–770.

Teyler TJ and Discenna P (1986). The hippocampal memory indexing theory. *Behavioral Neuroscience*, 100, 147–154.

Touretzky DS (1986). BoltzCONS: Reconciling connectionism with the recursive nature of stacks and trees. In: C. Clifton ed. *Proceedings of the 8th Annual Conference of the Cognitive Science Society*, pp. 522–530. Hillsdale, NJ: Lawrence Erlbaum Associates.

Touretzky DS and Redish AD (1996). A theory of rodent navigation based on interacting representations of space. *Hippocampus*, 6, 247–270.

Treves A and Rolls ET (1994). A computational analysis of the role of the hippocampus in memory. *Hippocampus*, 4, 374–392.

Ungerleider LG and Mishkin M (1982). Two cortical visual systems. In: DJ Ingle, MA Goodale and RJW Mansfield, eds. *The analysis of visual behavior*, pp. 549–586. Cambridge, MA: MIT Press.

Vargha-Khadem F, Gadian DG, Watkins KE, Connelly A, Van Paesschen W and Mishkin M (1997). Differential effects of early hippocampal pathology on episodic and semantic memory. *Science*, 277, 376–380.

Vazdarjanova A and Guzowski JF (2004). Differences in hippocampal neuronal population responses to modifications of an environmental context: Evidence for distinct, yet complementary, functions of CA3 and CA1 ensembles. *Journal of Neuroscience*, 24, 6489–6496.

von der Malsburg C (1981). The correlation theory of brain function. MPI Biophysical Chemistry, Internal Report 81–2. In: E Domany JL van Hemmen and K Schulten, eds. *Models of neural networks, II*. Berlin: Springer.

Wagner AD, Koutstaal W, Maril A, Schacter DL and Buckner RL (2000). Task-specific repetition priming in left inferior prefrontal cortex. *Cerebral Cortex*, 10, 1176–1184.

Walker GA, Ohzawa I and Freeman RD (1999). Asymmetric suppression outside the classical receptive field of the visual cortex. *Journal of Neuroscience*, 19, 10536.

Wallis JD, Anderson KC and Miller EK (2001). Single neurons in prefrontal cortex encode abstract rules. *Nature*, 411, 953–956.

Wickelgren WA (1969). Context-sensitive coding, associative memory, and serial order in (speech) behavior. *Psychological Review*, 76, 1–15.

Wu X, Baxter RA and Levy WB (1996). Context codes and the effect of noisy learning on a simplified hippocampal CA3 model. *Biological Cybernetics*, 74, 159–165.

Yonelinas AP (2002). The nature of recollection and familiarity: A review of 30 years of research. *Journal of Memory and Language*, **46**, 441–517.

Zelazo PD, Frye D and Rapus T (1996). An age-related dissociation between knowing rules and using them. *Cognitive Development*, **11**, 37–63.

Zemel RS, Williams CK and Mozer MC (1995). Lending direction to neural networks. *Neural Networks*, **8**, 503.

Chapter 17

Enhanced red/green color input to motion processing in infancy: Evidence for increasing dissociation of color and motion information during development

Karen R. Dobkins

Abstract

Early in postnatal development, the brain produces exuberant connections, some of which are later retracted. This retraction process is thought to play a role in the formation of functionally segregated modules in the brain. In the case of visual development, retraction between visual areas might underlie the known psychophysical and neural segregation of processing for different aspects of vision (e.g. color, motion, form, depth) known to exist in adults. The segregation between color and motion processing is a particularly interesting case to study, since in adults a wealth of psychophysical and neural data has documented the limited contribution of chromatic information to motion processing, which is thought to arise from minimal cross-talk between neural areas encoding object color vs. object motion. In this chapter, studies investigating the development of chromatic (red/green) contribution to motion processing in human infants are summarized and discussed. The results of these studies demonstrate that, compared to adults, infants exhibit a relatively enhanced ability to use chromatic information for motion processing. Such findings suggest the possibility of greater connectivity between color and motion areas early in life. Presumably, motion areas must then specialize to the adult-like state by reweighting or selectively pruning their chromatic inputs over the course of development.

17.1 **Introduction**

The basic task confronting a visual motion processor is that of detecting the continuity of image features as they are displaced in time and space. This process, referred to as the *motion correspondence* problem, involves 'matching' features at one moment in time with the same features, displaced in space, at a later moment in time. Color might be expected to play an important role in this process, as this aspect of vision provides one of the most reliable means for discerning the boundaries of objects. Despite the appeal of this argument, numerous psychophysical and neurophysiological studies in adults have demonstrated that chromatic information provides only limited contribution to motion processing. This effect is accounted for by *segregated processing* in the visual system, that is, areas of the brain encoding object motion do not encode object color, and *vice versa*. The current chapter addresses whether this strong color/motion dichotomy can be seen very early in infancy or, rather, whether it is an emergent property of the developing visual system.

Before discussing the development of color input to motion processing, the three fundamental dimensions of color vision – light/dark, red/green, and blue/yellow, and the neural substrates thought to detect modulation along these dimensions – the Magnocellular (M), Parvocellular (P), and Koniocellular (K) pathways, respectively, will be introduced. This will be followed by a brief summary of psychophysical data in human adults demonstrating impoverished motion perception when stimuli are defined solely by red/green chromatic contrast. The neural mechanisms mediating these perceptual effects will be addressed by presenting data obtained from adult macaque monkeys, whose visual systems are known to the very similar, in both structure and function, to that of humans (e.g. De Valois *et al.* 1974; Golomb *et al.* 1985; Newsome and Paré 1988; Newsome *et al.* 1989). In the last part of the chapter, results from several psychophysical studies conducted in human infants will be discussed. These studies demonstrate that red/green chromatic input to motion processing is stronger early in infancy than in adulthood, suggesting that the color/motion dichotomy seen in adults is an emergent property of the developing visual system.

17.2 **Three fundamental dimensions of color: light/dark, red/green, and blue/yellow**

The ability of humans to perceive color arises from the existence of three types of cone photoreceptors in the eye, which are maximally sensitive to long (*l*), medium (*m*) and short (*s*) wavelengths of light. The signals from the *l*-, *m*- and *s*-cone photoreceptors are thought to be combined to form three independent color pathways in the brain. The 'luminance' pathway, also referred to as the light/dark pathway, signals a weighted sum of *l*- and *m*-cones (i.e. *l*+*m*). Two 'chromatic' pathways signal weighted sums and differences of the cones. The red/green chromatic pathway signals differences between *l*- and *m*-cones (i.e. *l*−*m* or *m*−*l*). The blue/yellow chromatic pathway signals differences between *s*-cones and the sum of *l*- and *m*-cones (i.e. $s-(l+m)$ or $(l+m)-s$). The stimuli that isolate these three pathways are referred to as the three fundamental dimensions of color space (Fig. 17.1) (see Kaiser and Boynton 1996 for review).

There are several things to note about color space, which are relevant throughout this chapter. First, stimuli varying along either the red/green or blue/yellow axis (or any axis within the plane of the two) vary only in chromaticity and not in luminance. For this reason, stimuli modulated within this plane are referred to as 'equiluminant'. Second, in the world of color science, any point along the light/dark axis (including 'black' and 'white', which are the end points) are considered 'colors', although, importantly, points along this axis do not vary in chromaticity. Accordingly, throughout the chapter, the word 'color' is used to refer to stimuli along any of the three axes,

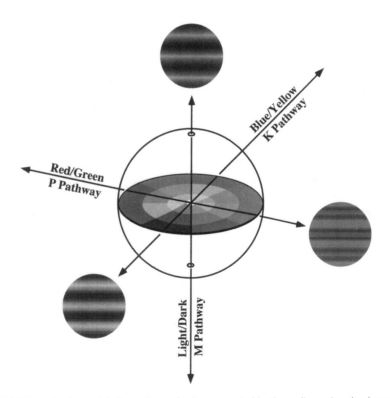

Fig. 17.1 Three fundamental dimensions of color presented in three-dimensional color space: light/dark (luminance), red/green (chromatic), and blue/yellow (chromatic). Detection of light/dark, red/green, and blue/yellow grating stimuli (depicted by the icons at the end of the axes) is thought to be mediated by three subcortical pathways, the magnocellular (M), parvocellular (P), and koniocellular (K) pathways, respectively. (Reprinted from Dobkins, 2000 with permission from *Neuron*.) See Plate 2 in the centre of this book for a full colour version.

whereas 'chromatic' is reserved for the red/green and blue/yellow axes. Finally, note that for the remainder of the chapter, only the light/dark and red/green pathways are discussed, since much more is known about these pathways and it is only these pathways that are relevant to the infant psychophysical data presented below.

17.3 Magnocellular (M) vs. parvocellular (P) subcortical pathways

In the primate visual system, there are actually more than a half dozen pathways from the eye to the brain, each likely to have its own specialized function. The two considered in the current chapter – the magnocellular (M) and parvocellular (P) pathways – are only those that provide input to visual cortex, which are called the 'retino-geniculo-cortical' pathways and constitute the bulk of the projections from the eye. (Because this chapter does not address the blue/yellow dimension of color, encoded by the K pathway, this pathway will not be discussed further here, see Dobkins 2000; Hendry and Reid 2000 for reviews.) Details of the anatomy and physiology of the M and P pathways can be found in several reviews (e.g. Merigan and Maunsell 1993; Dobkins and Albright 1998, 2003). In brief, the terms parvocel-lular and magnocellular were first adopted to describe anatomically-distinguishable layers within the lateral geniculate nucleus (LGN) of the thalamus in monkeys; four LGN layers contain densely packed, small ('parvo') neurons, and two contain more sparsely placed, large ('magno') neurons. However, the separation between the path-ways originates within the eye, in two morphologically-distinct types of retinal ganglion cells, referred to as 'midget' and 'parasol' cells. Midget ganglion cells project selectively to the P layers of the LGN, which, in turn, project selectively to layer 4Cβ of primary visual cortex (area V1). In a parallel fashion, parasol cells project selectively to the M layers of the LGN, which, in turn, send their projections to layer 4Cα of area V1.

Neurophysiological studies investigating color responses of M and P neurons have demonstrated that P neurons receive opponent input from l- and m-cones (either $l-m$ or $m-l$). As expected based on this pattern of input, P neurons respond preferentially to stimuli modulated along the red/green dimension of color, and moreover, are *selective* for red vs. green. For example, a P neuron receiving $l-m$ cone input will be excited by red light yet inhibited by green light (and *vice versa* for a P cell receiving $m-l$ cone input). This chromatic selectivity allows P neurons to signal the chromatic *identity* of an object ('red' vs. 'green'). By contrast, neurons within the M pathway receive additive (i.e. $l+m$) signals. This input makes M neurons unselect-ive for red vs. green, yet very responsive to light/dark modulation (e.g. Derrington *et al.* 1984; see Dacey 1999 for review).

Although these findings suggest that the red/green and light/dark dimensions of color map directly onto the P and M pathways, respectively, an under-appreciated fact is that both M and P cell types respond to *both* luminance and red/green chromatic stimuli, but with different contrast sensitivities. Neurons in the M pathway are more sensitive to (i.e. they have lower thresholds for) luminance contrast than are those in the P pathway. Conversely, neurons in the P pathway are more sensitive to red/green contrast than are those in the M pathway (e.g. Lee *et al.* 1989a; Shapley 1990; see Dobkins and Albright, 2003 for review). Based on these neural sensitivity data, psychophysically-derived contrast sensitivity for luminance and red/green chromatic stimuli can be attributed to the M and P pathways, respectively (e.g. Lee *et al.* 1990; Shapley 1990; Smith *et al.* 1995; but see Lennie and D'Zmura 1988 for an opposing point of view). And it is for this reason that the M and P pathways are often called the 'luminance mechanism' and 'chromatic mechanism', respectively. Accordingly, in this chapter, the terms 'luminance mechanism' and 'chromatic mechanism' are used to refer to the neural mechanisms most sensitive to (i.e. with the lowest contrast thresholds for) luminance and chromatic contrast, respectively.

Because this chapter focuses on the use of red/green information for motion processing, it is important to elaborate on how neurons of the M pathway, despite their lack of *selectivity* for red vs. green, can nonetheless respond to red/green contrast. First, M neurons can respond to borders defined by red/green contrast and to temporal changes between red and green, without regard for the *sign* of chromatic contrast (e.g. Schiller and Colby 1983; Lee *et al.* 1988; Kaiser *et al.* 1990; Valberg *et al.* 1992), an ability that arises from non-linear summation of *l*- and *m*-cone inputs (see Lee *et al.* 1989b for discussion). A second way in which M neurons can signal red/green contrast arises from the fact that the red/green luminance 'balance point' – the contrast for which red and green phases of a stimulus elicit responses of equal magnitude – varies across the population of M neurons. This variability assures that, even at a psychophysically-determined equiluminance point, M neurons as a population can never be fully silenced by red/green stimuli (see Logothetis *et al.* 1990).

In sum, both the M and the P pathways in adults can signal red/green chromatic information, although there are two important differences to keep in mind. First, the P pathway is far more sensitive to chromatic contrast than is the M pathway. Second, the nature of the chromatic signal differs significantly between the two pathways. P neurons exhibit selectivity for the *sign* of chromatic contrast (i.e. they are excited by one color and inhibited by another), a property that allows them to signal the chromatic *identity* of an object (i.e. red vs. green). M neurons signal chromatic contrast, but because they are unselective for the sign of chromatic contrast, cannot convey information about chromatic identity. Still, the fact that both P and M neurons can respond to red/green chromatic contrast means that both pathways hold the potential to contribute to chromatic motion processing, an issue that is returned to throughout this chapter.

17.4 Chromatic motion processing in adults: psychophysics and neural underpinnings

At the cortical level, starting in area V1, other response properties begin to emerge, such as selectivity for orientation, depth, and direction-of-motion. The cortical area thought to play a key role in motion processing is the middle temporal (MT) area. This region of extrastriate visual cortex, which receives direct input from layer 4B of area V1 as well as indirect input from V1 via the second visual area (V2), contains a high proportion (~90 per cent) of directionally selective neurons (see Albright 1993 for a review). Based on results from studies investigating the effects of LGN layer inactivation on area MT responsivity in adult monkeys, it appears that MT receives predominantly M pathway-driven input, and only a small amount of P pathway-driven input (Maunsell *et al.* 1990). These findings lead to the prediction that red/green chromatic information (carried mainly in the neurons of the P pathway) should exert lesser effects on motion processing than light/dark information (carried mainly in the neurons of the M pathway).

One of the most direct *psychophysical* ways to investigate this hypothesis has been to simply determine whether the direction of a chromatic (i.e. equiluminant, red/green) moving stimulus can be accurately discriminated. In general, the results from such studies demonstrate an ability to discriminate the motion of red/green stimuli, however, as would be predicted, this motion appears slower and less discernable than the motion of light/dark stimuli (for detailed reviews see Gegenfurtner and Hawken 1996; Dobkins and Albright 1998, 2003). Attempts to explore the *neural substrates* of chromatic contribution to motion perception have focused on motion area MT in macaque monkeys. Mirroring the psychophysical effects, several neuro-physiological studies in monkeys have shown that MT neurons are able to signal the direction of moving red/green equiluminant gratings, although responses are significantly weaker than for moving light/dark gratings (see Dobkins and Albright, 2003 for a review of studies in monkeys and see Ffytche *et al.* 1995; Tootell *et al.* 1995; Wandell *et al.* 1999 for similar results obtained using brain imaging techniques in humans). It is important to point out that this (impoverished) ability of MT neurons to use chromatic information for signaling direction does not necessitate *selectivity* for object color. In fact, all neurophysiological studies addressing this question have reported a lack of color selectivity in MT neurons (Zeki 1974; Baker *et al.* 1981; Van Essen *et al.* 1981; Maunsell and Van Essen 1983; Albright 1984), and it is precisely this finding that has contributed to the notion of segregated processing for color and motion in adults.

That motion processing (both psychophysically and neurophysiologically) exists, but is impoverished, for moving chromatic (red/green) gratings can be accounted for by the fact that neurons of the M pathway, which provide the bulk of the input to area MT, can signal chromatic red/green borders yet have relatively weak chromatic sensitivity. (And, the fact that neither M neurons nor MT neurons possess chromatic *selectivity*, i.e. their responses are *unsigned*, is consistent with this account). However, the other logical alternative is that impoverished chromatic motion processing reflects weak input from the more chromatically (red/green) sensitive neurons of the P pathway (see Dobkins and Albright 1998, 2003 for reviews of adult experiments designed to isolate the contribution of M vs. P pathway-based chromatic contribution to motion processing). These two hypotheses are discussed in further detail below.

17.5 Separating out sensitivity of mechanisms supplying input to motion detectors vs. efficacy of input

When interpreting the results of studies measuring the degree of chromatic contribution to motion processing, either psychophysically or neurophysiologically, it is necessary to consider two factors: (1) *Sensitivity*: the *chromatic sensitivity* of the mechanism(s) that provide input to motion detectors; and (2) *input to motion detectors*: the *extent* or *efficacy* of input from these mechanisms. One classical way these factors have been parceled out in adult psychophysics, and one that is particularly relevant to the infant psychophysical studies discussed below, has been to employ a 'motion/detection' (*MOT/DET*) paradigm. In these experiments, contrast thresholds for *detection* of a moving stimulus (*DET*) are compared to contrast thresholds for *direction-of-motion discrimination* (*MOT*), for the same moving stimulus (see Fig. 17.2 for stimuli and methodological details used in Dobkins and Teller, 1996). The results of these *MOT/DET* studies in adults yield qualitatively different findings for luminance (light/dark) vs. chromatic (equiluminant, red/green) moving stimuli. For luminance stimuli, *MOT/DET* ratios are typically near 1.0, indicating that the amount of luminance contrast needed to detect a moving stimulus is also sufficient to permit discrimination of direction (e.g. Watson *et al.* 1980; Green 1983; Graham 1989). For chromatic stimuli, however, *MOT/DET* ratios are significantly larger (ranging from 2.0 to 4.0), indicating that chromatic contrast levels sufficient for detection are *not* sufficient for discriminating direction (e.g. Lindsey and Teller 1990; Dobkins and Teller 1996; see Dobkins and Albright, 2003 for review). Example data from adult subjects tested in Dobkins and Teller (1996) are presented in the *left* panel of Fig. 17.3.

These *MOT/DET* results allow us to parcel out the two factors contributing to motion processing (sensitivity vs. input to motion detectors) as follows. For the case of luminance stimuli, the *DET* threshold will be mediated by a *luminance mechanism* at an early stage of visual processing, defined as the mechanism most sensitive to, that is, with the lowest threshold for, luminance contrast. The *MOT* threshold relative to the *DET* threshold reflects how well that early luminance mechanism transmits information (i.e. provides input) to motion detectors. Accordingly, equal *DET* and *MOT* thresholds (i.e. an *MOT/DET* ratio near 1.0) for luminance stimuli suggests that there exists highly efficient input from the luminance mechanism to motion detectors.

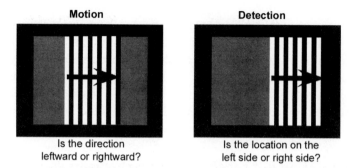

Motion   **Detection**

Is the direction   Is the location on the
leftward or rightward?   left side or right side?

Fig. 17.2 Stimuli and methods for obtaining *MOT/DET* threshold ratios (from Dobkins and Teller, 1996). Left panel: The *MOT* threshold was obtained by presenting a moving grating in the center of the video monitor. Adult subjects were asked to report its direction. For infant subjects, direction discrimination was obtained using a directional eye movement (DEM) technique. Right panel: The *DET* threshold was obtained by presenting a moving grating on the left or right side of the video monitor (stimulus direction counterbalanced across trials). Adult subjects were asked to report its location. For infant subjects, detection was measured using the forced-choice preferential looking (FPL) technique. Stimuli were either light/dark (as shown here) or chromatic red/green (not shown) and the contrast of both types of stimuli was varied across trials. For both infants and adults, eye movements were unregulated and the stimuli remained present until a decision was made.

In an analogous fashion, chromatic *MOT/DET* ratios greater than 1.0 suggest inefficient input from an early *chromatic mechanism* (i.e. defined as that most sensitive to chromatic contrast) to motion detectors. Given that luminance and chromatic mechanisms map onto the M and P pathways, respectively (as is thought to be the case in adults, see above), these *MOT/DET* findings suggest a lesser extent of, or less efficient, input from the P pathway to cortical motion detectors. This, in fact, is perfectly in line with studies demonstrating greater M- vs. P-driven input to motion area MT (Maunsell *et al.* 1990).

Note, however, that this neural explanation still leaves open the question of what, specifically, accounts for the elevated *MOT*, with respect to *DET*, chromatic threshold. The first possibility is that the chromatic *MOT* threshold, like the chromatic *DET* threshold, is mediated by (the most chromatically sensitive) P pathway. Here, the chromatic *MOT* threshold is elevated because P pathway input to motion detectors is inefficient, and thus the chromatic contrast in the motion stimulus must be increased in order for motion detectors to respond. A second possibility is that the chromatic *MOT* threshold is mediated by (the less chromatically sensitive) M pathway, which supplies efficient input to motion detectors. Here, *MOT/DET* ratios are greater than 1.0 simply because the chromatic threshold of M neurons (which mediate the *MOT* threshold) is higher than that of P neurons (which mediate the *DET* threshold). Either way, chromatic *MOT/DET* ratios greater than 1.0 in adults indicate that chromatic input to cortical motion detectors is limited.

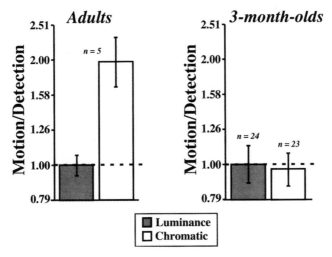

Fig. 17.3 MOT/DET threshold ratios. Mean ratios are shown for adults (left panel) and 3-month-old infants (right panel), separately for luminance stimuli (grey bars) and chromatic stimuli (white bars). Error bars denote standard errors of the means. For adults, but not infants, there is a significant difference between *MOT/DET* ratios for luminance vs. chromatic stimuli. For both age groups, note that the *MOT/DET* ratios were normalized so that the mean *MOT/DET* ratio was 1.0, the purpose of which was to facilitate comparison between the two ages. This is justified because the *MOT* task (which relies on detecting very small eye movements) tends to be inherently more difficult than the *DET* task (which is typically based on detecting large head movements), and this difference likely biases the *MOT/DET* ratio. Thus, the most fundamental outcome measurement is the comparison of *MOT/DET* ratios *between* chromatic and luminance stimuli, and not the absolute value of *MOT/DET* ratios *per se*. The data in this figure are adapted from Dobkins and Teller, 1996. Non-normalized *MOT/DET* ratios as well as absolute threshold values can be found in this earlier manuscript.

17.6 Development of chromatic motion processing in human infants

In infants, only a handful of psychophysical studies have investigated the development of chromatic (red/green) motion processing. Before reviewing these studies, it is worthwhile reiterating the important point (described above for adults) that the degree of chromatic contribution to motion processing will be governed by two factors: (1) *Sensitivity:* the *chromatic sensitivity* of the mechanism(s) that provide input to motion detectors; and (2) *input to motion detectors:* the *extent* or *efficacy* of input from these mechanisms. Thus, when charting out the course of development for chromatic motion processing, it is important to parcel out these two factors, considering how each might change with age.

17.6.1 Development of chromatic (red/green) motion discrimination

In one of the earliest psychophysical studies to investigate the development of chromatic motion processing, Teller and Palmer (1996) used a directional eye movement (DEM) technique to measure infants' ability to discriminate the direction of motion of equiluminant red/green gratings (see Teller and Lindsey 1993 for an earlier version of this work). The DEM technique relies on the fact that infants (and adults) make directionally-appropriate eye movements in response to moving stimuli (e.g. Kremenitzer *et al.* 1979; Hainline *et al.* 1984). More importantly, previous studies in adults have shown that eye movements can be used as a reliable indicator of perceived motion direction (e.g. Kowler and McKee 1987; Beutter and Stone 1998, 2000), and thus it is assumed that this is likely to be true in infants as well (see Dobkins *et al.* 2004 for discussion). On each trial, a stimulus is presented moving either leftward or rightward, and an adult experimenter uses the subject's eye movements to judge the stimulus direction (two-alternative forced-choice). Above chance (i.e. >50 per cent correct) performance indicates an ability of the subject to discriminate direction of motion.

The DEM stimulus in the Teller and Palmer (1996) study consisted of red/green gratings (spatial frequency = 0.15 or 0.3 cyc/deg, depending on the subject age) moving leftward or rightward (25°/s) across the entire video display (54° × 46°). Because equiluminance is known to vary across subjects, subjects were tested with red/green gratings containing varying levels of luminance contrast (including photometric, i.e. V_λ, equiluminance), with the notion that one of these values would capture each subject's personal equiluminance point. Further, given that chromatic information provides limited contribution to motion processing (as is known to be the case in adults), it was assumed that the minimum DEM performance for an individual subject would be generated at that subject's personal equiluminance point. Most importantly, if the per cent correct performance at this equiluminance point was greater than chance, this was taken as positive evidence for chromatic contribution to motion processing.

The results of this study demonstrated minimum performance values that were above chance for adults and 2-month-olds, but not 1-month-olds (and see Brown *et al.* 1995 for positive results in 3-month-olds). Although, at first glance, the negative result in 1-month-olds would suggest a lack of chromatic input to motion detectors, it is equally likely to reflect poor chromatic sensitivity of the mechanism(s) that supply input to motion detectors. In other words, for 1-month-olds, the amount of chromatic contrast in the moving red/green gratings may simply have not been visible (a point that is also raised in Teller and Palmer, 1996). In fact, this is likely to be the case, since chromatic contrast sensitivity – outside the domain of motion – is known to be quite low in 1-month-olds (see Brown 1990 for review). Unfortunately, without an independent estimate of chromatic contrast sensitivity at this age, using the same stimuli (i.e. gratings at the same spatial and temporal frequency) and preferably the same set of infants, this negative result in 1-month-olds does not allow us to distinguish between the two alternatives; weak chromatic sensitivity vs. weak chromatic input to motion detectors.

17.6.2 Development of motion/detection (MOT/DET) threshold ratios

As a way of directly parceling out the sensitivities of the mechanisms that provide input to motion detectors vs. the efficacy of input from those mechanisms, Dobkins and Teller (1996) used the motion/detection (*MOT/DET*) paradigm described earlier in this chapter for adults. As a reminder, these experiments involve comparing contrast thresholds for *detection* of a moving stimulus *(DET)* to contrast thresholds for *direction-of-motion discrimination (MOT)*, for the same moving stimulus. For both 3-month-old infants and adults, *MOT/DET* ratios were obtained for chromatic (equiluminant[1], red/green) gratings and luminance (light/dark) gratings (0.25 cyc/deg, moving at 22°/s). (Due to the limited number of trails that can be obtained from a given infant, separate infants were tested on chromatic vs. luminance stimuli. Adults were tested with both types of stimuli).

For infants, contrast thresholds for direction-of-motion discrimination (*MOT*) were obtained using the directional eye movement (DEM) technique described above. On a DEM trial, a grating appeared in the center of the video monitor (size = 27° by 40°) moving leftward or rightward and an adult experimenter used the infant's eye movements to judge the stimulus direction (see Fig. 17.2, left panel). Infant contrast thresholds for detection (*DET*) were obtained using forced-choice preferential looking (FPL). The FPL technique relies on the fact that infants prefer to look at a patterned stimulus on one side of a display rather than a blank field on the other side. On an FPL trial, the moving grating appeared on the left or the right side of the video display and an adult experimenter used the infant's eye gaze and head direction to judge the stimulus location (see Fig. 17.2, right panel). Above chance (i.e. >50 per cent correct) performance indicated an ability of the subject to detect the stimulus. The two different trial types were intermixed across trials (with beeps

---

[1] For infants, we used the mean equiluminance point value obtained from adult subjects using a 'minimally-distinct motion' technique, and the same stimulus conditions (spatial and temporal frequency) as in the main study. The use of adult settings for infants is justified because infant equiluminance values are known to be indistinguishable from those of adults (Brown *et al.* 1995; Dobkins *et al.* 2001; Pereverzeva *et al.* 2002). Moreover, we have previously shown that the amount of luminance error that could arise due to variability in equiluminance points across infant subjects is about 2 per cent, which is far below the contrast threshold of, that is, will be undetectable by, young infants (Dobkins *et al.* 1997). In other words, the low luminance contrast sensitivity of infants allows for some error in the red/green stimulus used as the equiluminant point. Adults were tested at their own equiluminance point.

alerting the experimenter as to which type of decision needed to be made), and the contrast of the stimuli was varied in order to determine contrast thresholds (i.e. the contrast yielding 75 per cent correct experimenter performance). In the end, both a *MOT* and a *DET* threshold were obtained for each infant subject. This infant protocol is directly analogous to that previously employed in adult *MOT/DET* studies, that is identical stimulus conditions, yet *different* tasks.

For adults in the current study, the stimuli used to obtain contrast thresholds were identical to those employed for infants, but the data were collected using conventional 2-AFC psychophysical methods, that is, adults reported the direction of the *MOT* stimuli and the location of the *DET* stimuli. In addition to these conventional self-report methods, for each adult subject a *MOT* threshold was also determined by the DEM technique. This latter measure was obtained to ensure that any differences between infant and adult data could not be attributable to the use of eye movements as an indicant of perceived direction in infants vs. direct perceptual reports in adults. The results from the adult DEM analysis mirror those obtained from their perceptual reports and therefore will not be discussed further here.

The results of these *MOT/DET* studies are shown in Fig. 17.3. As expected, adult *MOT/DET* threshold ratios (left panel, n = 5) were close to 1.0 for luminance gratings, and significantly elevated (roughly doubled) for chromatic gratings (p <0.05). As described earlier in this chapter, this result suggests that in adults, there exists efficient input from the luminance mechanism (i.e. defined as the mechanism most sensitive to luminance contrast, which is the M pathway) to motion detectors (presumably in area MT), but inefficient input from the chromatic mechanism (i.e. defined as the mechanism most sensitive to chromatic contrast, which is the P pathway). For infants, a qualitatively very different pattern was observed; infant *MOT/DET* ratios for luminance and chromatic gratings were statistically indistinguishable and close to 1.0 (Fig. 17.3, right panel, n = 23 for chromatic data, n = 24 for luminance data). In contrast to adults, this result in infants suggests that luminance and chromatic mechanisms provide strong and equally efficient input to motion detectors (and see Lia *et al.* 1999 for a replication of these *MOT/DET* results using slightly different stimuli).

There are two competing hypotheses that could account for the difference observed between infant and adult data. The first, referred to as the '*P pathway retraction hypothesis*' supposes that the P pathway in infants is the chromatic mechanism (as is thought to be the case in adults) and that the extent or efficacy of input from the P pathway to motion detectors (in area MT) is strong early in infancy, but then decreases over the course of development (see Fig. 17.4, left panel). This possibility is consistent with the general principle that developing brains produce exuberant connections or branching patterns, some of which are later retracted (e.g. Dehay *et al.* 1988; Huttenlocher 1990; Rodman and Consuelos 1994; see Johnson and Vecera 1996 for an in-depth review). In fact, data from Florence and Casagrande (1990) have

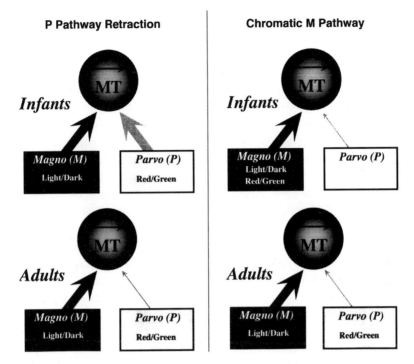

Fig. 17.4 Two competing hypotheses for relatively enhanced chromatic motion processing in infants. Left panel: P pathway retraction hypothesis. The extent of parvo pathway (subserving red/green chromatic sensitivity) vs. magno pathway (subserving light/dark sensitivity) input to motion detectors is greater in infancy than in adulthood. Right panel: chromatic M pathway hypothesis. In infancy, the magno pathway subserves both red/green and light/dark sensitivity, with red/green sensitivity switching over to the P pathway by adulthood.

shown that P pathway (but not M pathway) projections into area V1 of infant galago monkey are dramatically larger than those of adults, suggesting selective retraction of P pathway inputs over the course of development.

The second hypothesis, referred to as the 'chromatic M pathway hypothesis', supposes that (opposite to the case for adults) the chromatic mechanism in infants is the M, rather than the P, pathway. (As a reminder, in adults, both M and P neurons signal red/green chromatic contrast, although the P neurons are far more sensitive.) This could occur if the development of contrast sensitivity (both chromatic and luminance) is much faster for the M, than for the P, pathway, with the result that the infant's M pathway is more sensitive to chromatic (and luminance) contrast than is the infant's P pathway. Given that the M pathway in infants provides the bulk of the input to motion detectors in area MT (as is thought to be the case in adults), this could account for infant *MOT/DET* ratios for luminance and chromatic stimuli that are close to 1.0 and indistinguishable from one another (see Fig. 17.4, right panel). Although the chromatic M pathway hypothesis may seem unlikely, data from other studies in our laboratory (investigating the development of temporal contrast sensitivity functions for luminance and chromatic stimuli) have led us to propose that, early in development, chromatic sensitivity may be mediated by the M, rather than the P, simply because the M pathway develops faster than the P pathway (see Dobkins *et al.* 1997, 1999). The possibility of faster M, with respect to P, pathway development is generally supported by studies of anatomical growth and synapse formation in infant primates (*macaques*: Mates and Lund 1983; Lund and Harper 1991; Lund and Holbach 1991; Distler *et al.* 1996; but cf. Chalupa *et al.* 1996 for prenatal data; *galagos*: Lachica and Casagrande 1988; Florence and Casagrande 1990; *humans*: Burkhalter *et al.* 1993; but cf. Hickey 1977). The faster development of the M pathway suggests that aspects of vision known to involve the M pathway (like motion processing) are more crucial for early developmental interactions with the environment (for example, to avoid collision with, or reach for, moving objects) than are those involving the P pathway (like color vision, which enhances, but is often not necessary, for object recognition).

In sum, *MOT/DET* data from infants can be explained by either the chromatic M pathway hypothesis, which supposes a developmental change in the neural substrate for the putative chromatic mechanism (i.e. a switchover from the M to the P pathway) or the P pathway retraction hypothesis, which supposes a change in the efficacy of P vs. M pathway input to motion detectors. To distinguish between the two hypotheses, one must be ruled out. There are two possible ways to rule out the chromatic M pathway hypothesis. The first way would be to show that, as is the case in the adult visual system, infant's P neurons are more sensitive to chromatic contrast than are their M neurons, that is, the P pathway in infants is the putative chromatic mechanism. Unfortunately, there are currently no neurophysiological data on the chromatic sensitivities of M and P neurons in infant monkeys that would bear on this issue. (Note, however, that there do exist neurophysiological data on luminance sensitivities of M and P pathways in infant monkeys, which show the adult pattern of higher sensitivity in the M than P pathway (Hawken *et al.* 1997; Movshon *et al.* 1997)). The second way would be to employ stimuli that eliminate activity in the M pathway and/or eliminate the contribution of the M pathway to chromatic motion processing. This was not achieved in the above-described *MOT/DET* studies, since the use of conventional chromatic (red/green) moving gratings allowed either the M or P pathway to provide chromatic signals to be used for motion processing. In other words, because M neurons could signal chromatic contrast in the *MOT/DET* stimulus, and given the possibility that, in infants, the M pathway might be the neural substrate for the chromatic mechanism, we specifically could not rule out the chromatic M pathway hypothesis.

17.6.3 Investigating the P pathway retraction hypothesis

In the next set of studies, we directly investigated the P pathway retraction hypothesis by using a novel chromatic stimulus designed to isolate the contribution of the P pathway to chromatic motion processing (Dobkins and Anderson 2002). This stimulus consisted of moving red/black/green/black (R/B/G/B) sinusoidal gratings (subtending $59° \times 45°$), for which the red and green stripes were equiluminant with each other (see Fig. 17.5, left panel). The stimulus was displaced the width of one stripe ($2.0°$) at each successive time interval, with the result that a consistent leftward vs. rightward direction of motion could be discerned only if chromatic identity was employed, that is matching red to red and green to green over time (stimulus speed $= 35°/s$).

Using the DEM technique, we measured the ability of infant subjects (ages 2, 3 and 4 months) and adults to discriminate direction of motion in this chromatic stimulus. Since encoding chromatic identity is a property of neurons in the P, and not the M, pathway, this direction discrimination task was expected to rely on P pathway input to motion areas. Note that the intervening black stripes, which were dimmer than the red

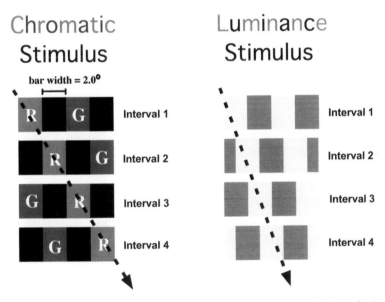

Fig. 17.5 Schematic depiction of stimuli used to test the P pathway retraction hypothesis. Left panel: moving chromatic stimulus. Right panel: moving luminance stimulus. For both, the position of a slice through the stimulus is shown at four consecutive time intervals. Motion based on chromatic matches (left panel) or luminance matches (right panel) is rightward in these examples. Note that, because the luminance stimulus necessarily employed a smaller displacement per time interval (half the width of one stripe), the displacement occurred twice as frequently for the luminance stimulus as for the chromatic stimulus, in order to create identical speeds in the two conditions (i.e. $35°/s$). Reprinted from Dobkins and Anderson (2002) with permission from *Psychological Science*. See Plate 3 in the centre of this book for a full colour version.

and green stripes by 90 per cent, provided an important function. Namely, their presence was expected to saturate the responses of M neurons (adult M neuron saturation range: 10–20 per cent, Shapley 1990; infant M neuron saturation range: 20–30 per cent, Movshon *et al.* 1997), meaning that M neurons were expected to respond the same amount to the luminance contrast between the red and black stripes as between the green and black stripes. Thus, the signals arising in M neurons could not be used for matching red to red (or green to green) over time, rendering them useless in this task. This manipulation is crucial because, as discussed above, without the intervening black stripes, a conventional equiluminant red/green chromatic grating will produce residual (and usable) activity within the M pathway (based on responses to red/green borders and/or variability in the red/green luminance 'balance point' across the population of M neurons). In addition, at the perceptual level, the intervening black stripes have the advantage of making any small luminance mismatch between the red and green stripes extremely difficult to notice. This is because luminance discrimination is quite poor at high contrasts, in adults and especially in infants (Brown 1994).

For each subject, as a comparison to performance on the chromatic stimulus, we also measured the ability to discriminate the leftward vs. rightward direction of a moving light/dark luminance grating presented at varying levels of luminance contrast (same stripe width and speed as the chromatic stimulus, see Fig. 17.5, right panel). The effectiveness of this luminance stimulus was expected to reflect M pathway input to motion areas, since the neurons of this pathway are thought to underlie sensitivity to light/dark stimuli, in adults (e.g. Lee *et al.* 1990; Shapley 1990; Smith *et al.* 1995) and infants (Hawken *et al.* 1997; Movshon *et al.* 1997). The main purpose of the luminance grating was to obtain, for each subject, an *equivalent luminance contrast* (*EqLC*), defined as the contrast in the luminance stimulus required to yield the same per cent correct performance as that elicited by the chromatic stimulus. This EqLC value, which is a relative measure, is expected to reflect the strength of chromatic-based motion with respect to luminance-based motion, with higher values indicating relatively more effective P pathway, as compared to M pathway, contribution to motion processing.

Results from this study are presented in Fig. 17.6. Shown are individual (open circles) and group mean (open triangles) EqLC values for 2-month-olds (n = 12), 3-month-olds (n = 13), 4-month-olds (n = 10), and adults (n = 6). As can be seen in this plot, EqLC values decreased significantly with age (p <0.0001). Specifically, mean EqLC values were 8.8, 2.5, 1.0, and 0.02 per cent for 2-, 3-, 4-month-olds, and adults, respectively. While the extremely low EqLC values observed for adults are to be expected – since motion processing areas in adults, like area MT, are known to receive substantial input from luminance sensitive M neurons, yet only minimal input from chromatically-selective P neurons – the surprisingly high EqLC values for infants suggest that the contribution of chromatic (P pathway-based) vs. luminance (M pathway-based) signals to motion processing is greater in the immature visual system.

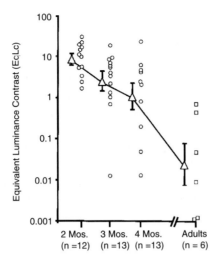

Fig. 17.6 EqLCs plotted as a function of age. Data are shown for individual subjects (open circles) and group means for each age (open triangles). Error bars denote standard errors of the means. These data reveal a significant decrease in EqLC with age. Mos. = months. Reprinted from Dobkins and Anderson (2002), with permission from *Psychological Science*.

However, because EqLC is a relative measure, is does not allow us to independently measure the contribution of chromatic (P pathway-based) vs. luminance (M pathway-based) signals to motion processing as a function of age. Does the decrease in EqLC with age reflect a decrease in chromatic motion (P pathway-based) processing with age, an increase in luminance motion (M pathway-based) processing with age, or both? And, returning to the issue of sensitivity, can changes in either chromatic motion or luminance motion processing with age be accounted for by developmental changes in the sensitivity of chromatic and luminance mechanisms that supply input to motion detectors?

To address these questions, we looked at absolute per cent correct performance on the chromatic-motion vs. luminance-motion task as a function of age, and compared these data to known developmental changes in chromatic vs. luminance contrast sensitivity (contrast sensitivity being the inverse of contrast detection threshold). Data for ages 2 to 4 months are plotted in Fig. 17.7. (Adult data are not included in this analysis, since adult subjects had to be tested under slightly different testing conditions that did not allow for a fair comparison of absolute per cent correct data between adults and infants[2]). Absolute per cent correct performance for the

---

[2] Adult data were obtained using the same DEM technique (rather than obtaining direct reports from subjects), to ensure that differences observed between infants and adults could not be attributable to differences in response measure. However, we modified the adult paradigm slightly to keep per cent correct performance below ceiling (i.e. 100 per cent correct), which was required in order to calculate EqLC. To this end, adults were tested with limited-duration stimuli (460 ms), which differed from infants who were tested with unlimited-duration stimuli.

chromatic-motion and luminance-motion tasks are shown in the left panel of Fig. 17.7. Because for the luminance-motion stimulus several different contrasts were tested, here, per cent correct data from only one contrast are plotted, 8.8 per cent luminance contrast. This value was chosen because it yielded a mean per cent correct performance at 2 months of age that matched that obtained in the chromatic-motion task at the same age, and because at all ages performance obtained for 8.8 per cent luminance contrast was neither at ceiling nor floor. The results of this analysis show a clear increase in luminance-motion performance between 2 and 4 months of age (black circles, from 74.3 per cent to 90.2 per cent, p <0.005). The results for chromatic-motion are strikingly different, however; if anything, there is a slight decrease in performance between 2 and 4 months of age (open circles, from 74.7 per cent to 68.3 per cent, although this effect was not statistically significant).

How can these results be reconciled with what is known about changes in contrast sensitivity with age? To address this question, chromatic and luminance contrast

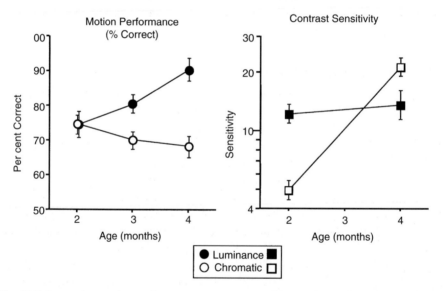

Fig. 17.7 Comparing motion performance to contrast sensitivity. Left panel: absolute per cent correct performance on the luminance-motion task (black circles) and the chromatic-motion task (open circles) as a function of age. Luminance-motion data were obtained for gratings that contained 8.8 per cent contrast. Right panel: contrast sensitivities for luminance (black squares) and chromatic (open squares) stimuli as a function of age. Error bars denote standard errors of the means. These data show that changes in motion performance with age cannot simply be accounted for by changes in contrast sensitivity with age.

sensitivities obtained using the FPL technique and stimulus parameters nearly identical to those of the current study (i.e. same spatial frequency, although the speed of the stimuli was slower, 15.4°/s, Dobkins *et al.* 2001), are plotted as a function of age in the right panel of Fig. 17.7. Luminance contrast sensitivity (black squares) shows only a minimal increase between 2 and 4 months of age, even though there is a clear increase in the luminance-motion task over the same developmental time period. These results suggest that developmental increases in luminance sensitivity are probably insufficient to account for developmental increases in luminance-motion performance. Given that both luminance sensitivity and luminance-motion performance in these studies rely on the M pathway, these results hint at an increase in the extent or efficacy of M pathway input to motion detectors with age. In an opposite fashion, chromatic contrast sensitivity (open squares) shows a robust increase between 2 and 4 months, while performance on the chromatic-motion task shows no change (or even a decrement) over the same developmental period. These results clearly demonstrate that developmental changes in chromatic sensitivity cannot account for chromatic-motion performance in infants. Given that both chromatic sensitivity and chromatic-motion performance in these studies rely on the P pathway, one can reconcile the two data sets by supposing a decrease in the extent or efficacy of P pathway input to motion detectors with age.

17.7 **Concluding remarks**

Together, the results of these psychophysical studies in infants point to the P pathway retraction hypothesis, that is, the efficacy of P pathway input to motion detectors (presumably in area MT) is relatively strong in infants and then decreases with age. This change could occur either through a decrease in the synaptic strength of P pathway connections to MT, or anatomical pruning of those connections. This possibility is consistent with the general principle that developing brains produce exuberant connections or branching patterns, some of which are later retracted. In fact, pruning of anatomical connections during development has been suggested as necessary for the proper development of other aspects of vision, specifically, the processing of depth from stereo cues (Atkinson 1984; Held 1993).

But in the case of motion processing, what purpose might retraction of P pathway input serve? In general, retraction may help to eliminate redundancy, a notion that has been previously discussed in the literature. But why retraction of the P, rather than the M, pathway to motion areas? At first glance, it is tempting to speculate that the selective retraction of P vs. M pathway input is related to the different color properties of neurons in these pathways. That is, one could argue that, for motion processing, the chromatic (red/green) aspects of an object (encoded in the P pathway) are less reliable or informative than the luminance (light/dark) aspects (encoded in the M pathway). However, a more likely explanation for the selective retraction of P pathway input is based on another, hitherto unmentioned in this chapter, difference in response properties between the two pathways. It is well established that P neurons have lower temporal and higher spatial resolution than M neurons (see Merigan and Maunsell, 1993). These differences are expected to make the responses of P neurons less reliable for aiding in motion detection (see Galvin et al. 1996). In turn, these differences in reliability may be responsible for the rewiring or reweighting of inputs to motion areas over the course of development, with the ultimate result of segregated color and motion processing in the adult brain.

References

Albright TD (1984). Direction and orientation selectivity of neurons in visual area MT of the macaque. *Journal of Neurophysiology*, 52, 1106–1130.

Albright TD (1993). Cortical processing of visual motion. In: J Wallman and FA Miles, eds. *Visual motion and its use in the stabilization of gaze*, 177–201. Amsterdam: Elsevier.

Atkinson J (1984). Human visual development over the first 6 months of life: a review and a hypothesis. *Human Neurobiology*, 3, 61–74.

Baker JF, Petersen SE, Newsome WT and Allman JM (1981). Visual response properties of neurons in four extrastriate visual areas of the owl monkey (Aotus trivirgatus): a quantitative comparison of medial, dorsomedial, dorsolateral, and middle temporal areas. *Journal of Neurophysiology*, 45, 397–416.

Beutter BR and Stone LS (1998). Human motion perception and smooth eye movements show similar directional biases for elongated apertures. *Vision Research*, 38, 1273–1286.

Beutter BR and Stone LS (2000). Motion coherence affects human perception and pursuit similarly. *Visual Neuroscience*, 17, 139–153.

Brown AM (1990). Development of visual sensitivity to light and color vision in human infants: a critical review. *Vision Research*, 30, 1159–1188.

Brown AM (1994). Intrinsic contrast noise and infant visual contrast discrimination. *Vision Research*, 34, 1947–1964.

Brown AM, Lindsey DT, McSweeney EM and Walters MM (1995). Infant luminance and chromatic contrast sensitivity: optokinetic nystagmus data on 3-month-olds. *Vision Research*, 35, 3145–3160.

Burkhalter A, Bernardo KL and Charles V (1993). Development of local circuits in human visual cortex. *Journal of Neuroscience*, 13, 1916–1931.

Chalupa LM, Meissirel C and Lia B (1996). Specificity of retinal ganglion cell projections in the embryonic rhesus monkey. *Perspectives on Developmental Neurobiology*, 3, 223–231.

Dacey DM (1999). Primate retina: cell types, circuits and color opponency. *Progress in Retinal and Eye Research*, 18, 737–763.

Dehay C, Kennedy H and Bullier J (1988). Characterization of transient cortical projections from auditory, somatosensory, and motor cortices to visual areas 17, 18, and 19 in the kitten. *Behavioural Brain Research*, 29, 237–244.

Derrington AM, Krauskopf J and Lennie P (1984). Chromatic mechanisms in lateral geniculate nucleus of macaque. *Journal of Physiology (London)*, 357, 241–265.

De Valois RL, Morgan HC, Polson MC, Mead WR and Hull EM (1974). Psychophysical studies of monkey vision. I. Macaque luminosity and color vision tests. *Vision Research*, 14, 53–67.

Distler C, Bachevalier J, Kennedy C, Mishkin M and Ungerleider LG (1996). Functional development of the corticocortical pathway for motion analysis in the macaque monkey: a 14C-2-deoxyglucose study. *Cerebral Cortex,* **6,** 184–195.

Dobkins KR (2000). Moving colors in the lime light. *Neuron,* **25,** 15–18.

Dobkins KR and Albright TD (1998). The influence of chromatic information on visual motion processing in the primate visual system. In: T Watanabe, ed. *High-level motion processing-computational, neurobiological and psychophysical perspectives, pp.* 53–94. Cambridge: MIT Press.

Dobkins KR and Albright TD (2003). Merging processing streams: color cues for motion detection and interpretation. In: L Chalupa and JS Werner, eds. *The visual neurosciences.* Cambridge: MIT Press, pp. 1217–1228.

Dobkins KR and Anderson CM (2002). Color-based motion processing is stronger in infants. *Psychological Science,* **13,** 75–79.

Dobkins KR, Anderson CM and Kelly JP (2001). Development of psychophysically-derived detection contours in L- and M- cone contrast space. *Vision Research,* **41,** 1791–1807.

Dobkins KR, Anderson CM and Lia B (1999). Infant temporal contrast sensitivity functions (tCSFs) mature earlier for luminance than for chromatic stimuli: Evidence for precocious magnocellular development? *Vision Research,* **39,** 3223–3239.

Dobkins KR, Fine I, Hsueh AC and Vitten C (2004). Pattern motion integration in infants. *Journal of Vision,* **4,** 144–155.

Dobkins KR, Lia B and Teller DY (1997). Infant color vision: temporal contrast sensitivity functions (tCSFs) for chromatic (red/green) stimuli in 3-month-olds. *Vision Research,* **37,** 2699–2716.

Dobkins KR and Teller DY (1996). Infant motion:detection (M:D) ratios for chromatic-defined and luminance-defined moving stimuli. *Vision Research,* **36,** 3293–3310.

Ffytche DH, Skidmore BD and Zeki S (1995). Motion-from-hue activates area V5 of human visual cortex. *Proceedings of the Royal Society London, B Biological Science,* **260,** 353–358.

Florence SL and Casagrande VA (1990). Development of geniculocortical axon arbors in a primate. *Vision Neuroscience,* **5,** 291–309.

Galvin SJ, Williams DR and Coletta NJ (1996). The spatial grain of motion perception in human peripheral vision. *Vision Research,* **36,** 2283–2295.

Gegenfurtner KR and Hawken MJ (1996). Interaction of motion and color in the visual pathways. *Trends in Neurosciences,* **19,** 394–401.

Golomb B, Andersen RA, Nakayama K, MacLeod DI and Wong A (1985). Visual thresholds for shearing motion in monkey and man. *Vision Research,* **25,** 813–820.

Graham NVS (1989). *Visual pattern analyzers.* New York: Oxford University Press.

Green M (1983). Contrast detection and direction discrimination of drifting gratings. *Vision Research,* **23,** 281–289.

Hainline L, Lemerise E, Abramov I and Turkel J (1984). Orientational asymmetries in small-field optokinetic nystagmus in human infants. *Behavioural Brain Research,* **13,** 217–230.

Hawken MJ, Blakemore C and Morley JW (1997). Development of contrast sensitivity and temporal frequency in primate lateral geniculate nucleus. *Experimental Brain Research,* **114,** 86–98.

Held R (1993). Two stages in the development of binocular vision and eye alignment. In: K Simons, ed. *Infant vision: basic and clinical research,* pp. 250–257. New York: Oxford University Press.

Hendry SHC and Reid RC (2000). The koniocellular pathway in primate vision. *Annual Review of Neuroscience,* **23,** 127–153.

Hickey TL (1977). Postnatal development of the human lateral geniculate nucleus: relationship to a critical period for the visual system. *Science, 198,* 836–838.

Huttenlocher PR (1990). Morphometric study of human cerebral cortex development. *Neuropsychologia, 28,* 517–527.

Johnson MH and Vecera SP (1996). Cortical differentiation and neurocognitive development: The parcellation conjecture. *Behavioural Processes, 36,* 195–212.

Kaiser PK and Boynton RM (1996). *Human color vision.* Washington, D.C.: Optical Society of America.

Kaiser PK, Lee BB, Martin PR and Valberg A (1990). The physiological basis of the minimally distinct border demonstrated in the ganglion cells of the macaque retina. *Journal of Physiology (London), 422,* 153–183.

Kowler E and McKee SP (1987). Sensitivity of smooth eye movement to small differences in target velocity. *Vision Research, 27,* 993–1015.

Kremenitzer JP, Vaugham HGJ, Kutzberg D and Dowling K (1979). Smooth-pursuit eye movements in the newborn infants. *Child Development, 50,* 442–448.

Lachica EA and Casagrande VA (1988). Development of primate retinogeniculate axon arbors. *Vision Neuroscience, 1,* 103–123.

Lee BB, Martin PR and Valberg A (1988). The physiological basis of heterochromatic flicker photometry demonstrated in the ganglion cells of the macaque retina. *Journal of Physiology (London), 404,* 323–347.

Lee BB, Martin PR and Valberg A (1989a). Sensitivity of macaque retinal ganglion cells to chromatic and luminance flicker. *Journal of Physiology (London), 414,* 223–243.

Lee BB, Martin PR and Valberg A (1989b). Nonlinear summation of M- and L-cone inputs to phasic retinal ganglion cells of the macaque. *Journal of Neuroscience, 9,* 1433–1442.

Lee BB, Pokorny J, Smith VC, Martin PR and Valberg A (1990). Luminance and chromatic modulation sensitivity of macaque ganglion cells and human observers. *Journal of the Optical Society of America [a], 7,* 2223–2236.

Lennie P and D'Zmura M (1988). Mechanisms of color vision. *Critical Reviews in Neurobiology, 3,* 333–400.

Lia B, Dobkins KD, Palmer J and Teller DY (1999). Infants code the direction of chromatic quadrature motion. *Vision Research, 39,* 1783–1794.

Lindsey DT and Teller DY (1990). Motion at isoluminance: discrimination/detection ratios for moving isoluminant gratings. *Vision Research, 30,* 1751–1761.

Logothetis NK, Schiller PH, Charles ER and Hurlbert AC (1990). Perceptual deficits and the activity of the color-opponent and broad-band pathways at isoluminance. *Science, 247,* 214–217.

Lund JS and Harper TR (1991). Postnatal development of thalamic recipient neurons in the monkey striate cortex: III. Somatic inhibitory synapse acquisition by spiny stellate neurons of layer 4C. *Journal of Comparative Neurology, 309,* 141–149.

Lund JS and Holbach SM (1991). Postnatal development of thalamic recipient neurons in the monkey striate cortex: I. Comparison of spine acquisition and dendritic growth of layer 4C alpha and beta spiny stellate neurons. *Journal of Comparative Neurology, 309,* 115–128.

Mates SL and Lund JS (1983). Developmental changes in the relationship between type 2 synapses and spiny neurons in the monkey visual cortex. *Journal of Comparative Neurology, 221,* 98–105.

Maunsell JH, Nealey TA and DePriest DD (1990). Magnocellular and parvocellular contributions to responses in the middle temporal visual area (MT) of the macaque monkey. *Journal of Neuroscience, 10,* 3323–3334.

Maunsell JH and Van Essen DC (1983). Functional properties of neurons in middle temporal visual area of the macaque monkey. I. Selectivity for stimulus direction, speed, and orientation. *Journal of Neurophysiology*, 49, 1127–1147.

Merigan WH and Maunsell JH (1993). How parallel are the primate visual pathways? *Annual Review of Neuroscience*, 16, 369–402.

Movshon JA, Kiorpes L, Hawken MJ, et al. (1997). *Sensitivity of LGN neurons in infant macaque monkey*. Ft. Lauderdale, Florida: Investigative Ophthalmology and Vision Science.

Newsome WT, Britten KH and Movshon JA (1989). Neuronal correlates of a perceptual decision. *Nature*, 341, 52–54.

Newsome WT and Paré EB (1988). A selective impairment of motion perception following lesions of the middle temporal visual area (MT). *Journal of Neuroscience*, 8, 2201–2211.

Pereverzeva M, Hui-Lin Chien S, Palmer J and Teller DY (2002). Infant photometry: are mean adult isoluminance values a sufficient approximation to individual infant values? *Vision Research*, 42, 1639–1649.

Rodman HR and Consuelos MJ (1994). Cortical projections to anterior inferior temporal cortex in infant macaque monkeys. *Vision Neuroscience*, 11, 119–133.

Schiller PH and Colby CL (1983). The responses of single cells in the lateral geniculate nucleus of the rhesus monkey to color and luminance contrast. *Vision Research*, 23, 1631–1641.

Shapley R (1990). Visual sensitivity and parallel retinocortical channels. *Annual Review of Psychology*, 41, 635–658.

Smith VC, Pokorny J, Davis M and Yeh T (1995). Mechanisms subserving temporal modulation sensitivity in silent-cone substitution. *Journal of the Optical Society of America A*, 12, 241–249.

Teller DY and Lindsey DT (1993). Infant color vision: OKN techniques and null plane analysis. In: K Simons, pp. 143–162. *Early visual development, normal and abnormal*. New York: Oxford University Press.

Teller DY and Palmer J (1996). Infant color vision: motion nulls for red/green vs luminance-modulated stimuli in infants and adults. *Vision Research*, 36, 955–974.

Tootell RB, Reppas JB, Kwong KK, et al. (1995). Functional analysis of human MT and related visual cortical areas using magnetic resonance imaging. *Journal of Neuroscience*, 15, 3215–3230.

Valberg A, Lee BB, Kaiser PK and Kremers J (1992). Responses of macaque ganglion cells to movement of chromatic borders. *Journal of Physiology (London)*, 458, 579–602.

Van Essen DC, Maunsell JH and Bixby JL (1981). The middle temporal visual area in the macaque: myeloarchitecture, connections, functional properties and topographic organization. *Journal of Comparative Neurology*, 199, 293–326.

Wandell BA, Poirson AB, Newsome WT, et al. (1999). Color signals in human motion-selective cortex. *Neuron*, 24, 901–909.

Watson AB, Thompson PG, Murphy BJ and Nachmias J (1980). Summation and discrimination of gratings moving in opposite directions. *Vision Research*, 20, 341–347.

Zeki SM (1974). Functional organization of a visual area in the posterior bank of the superior temporal sulcus of the rhesus monkey. *Journal of Physiology (London)*, 236, 549–573.

Chapter 18

When do 4-month-olds remember the 'what' and 'where' of hidden objects?

Denis Mareschal and Andrew J. Bremner

Abstract

The dual stream hypothesis is one of the most important heuristic frameworks for understanding the development of early human infant–object interactions. Electrophysiological evidence suggests that both dorsal and ventral streams are at least partially functional from a very young age. However, the two streams may not be functionally integrated until well into the second year of life (DeLoache et al. 2004). In this chapter, we present evidence from early infancy that the two streams are initially poorly integrated. We begin by describing a series of five experiments showing a dissociation in 4-month-olds' short-term object memory following occlusion. Depending on the target's affordance for action, infants are found to remember either only the object's identity or only the object's location. We then describe a dual stream connectionist model that captures many aspects of early infant object-directed behaviors. The model uses a temporal-synchrony mechanism to bind object information processed separately within simplified dorsal and ventral streams. It suggests a putative functional role for 40 Hz (gamma) oscillations found in electrophysiological recordings of infant neural activity during object occlusion tasks (Kaufman et al. 2003a).

18.1 Introduction

The 'dual stream hypothesis' – the idea that visual object information is processed down two largely independent cortical streams – has been around for over 20 years now (e.g. Ungerleider and Mishkin 1982; Livingston and Hubel 1988; Milner and Goodale 1995). While there continues to be some controversy surrounding the exact functionality of the two streams (e.g. Glover, 2004; Jeannerod 1997), it is generally agreed that they process and compute different kinds of information. Perhaps the most widely cited description of visual stream specialization comes from Milner and Goodale (1995). Milner and Goodale have argued that the ventral stream is implicated in the processing of information that subserves the identification of objects and people, information that is largely view invariant (e.g. surface features (SF) such as color: Zeki 1980; Tanaka 1993). In contrast, they argue that the dorsal stream processes information that is relevant to the action affordances of visual stimulation (i.e. the information that is relevant to action such as spatial and temporal information (ST)).

More recently, however, the degree of independence of these two streams has been challenged (e.g. Merigan and Maunsell 1993; Humphreys and Riddoch 2003). Indeed, there is substantial cross connection between the two streams (Felleman and Van Essen 1991; Van Essen et al. 1992) and evidence of supposedly dorsal processing (e.g. motion sensitivity) in the ventral stream (e.g. Puce and Alison 1998; Puce and Perret 2003).

Nevertheless, several authors invoke the dual stream hypothesis as one of the most important heuristic frameworks for understanding early human infant–object interactions (e.g. Atkinson 2000; Johnson et al. 2001; Kaldy and Sigala 2004; Xu et al. 1999; Leslie et al. 1998; Berthenthal 1996). Albeit in different ways, these authors have appealed to the notion of dual stream processing in order to explain odd paradoxes of object-directed behaviors in early infancy. In particular, a dissociation between the two streams has been invoked to explain the problems infants have when dealing with *briefly occluded objects*: across the first year of life young infants appear unable to retain aspects of both surface feature (e.g. identity) and spatial–temporal (e.g. location) object information (e.g. Wilcox and Schweinle 2002; Wilcox and Chapa, 2004; Xu and Carey 1996; Kaldy and Leslie 2003; Kaufman et al. 2003b). It is important to note that occlusion plays a key role in eliciting these behavioral dissociations, indicating that such problems arise in the absence of direct perception to sustain the two classes of representations.

Recent evidence suggests that early dissociations between dorsally and ventrally processed visual information subserving object-directed behaviors may even persist into the third year of life. Deloache et al. (2004) documented a number of striking scale errors in 2-year-olds' action selection. When presented with miniature replicas of object such as chairs or cars, 2-year-olds occasionally engaged in behaviors that were appropriate for the life-sized version of the object but not the miniature (e.g. trying to climb into a 15-cm car). For example, Deloache et al. interpret these findings in terms of a dissociation between a visual recognition systems and a motor control or motor planning system (see also Glover, in press).

In the rest of this chapter, we will examine evidence suggesting that young infants do not retain both dorsal- and ventral-specific information during occlusion. We then examine whether this is a target/stimulus driven phenomenon, or whether it is due to some kind of general capacity limitation. (Indeed, some studies have concluded that short-term memory is limited to a span of one item in infants less than 5 months old (Ross-Sheehy *et al.* 2003)). Finally, we describe an initial computational model of dual-stream object processing that attempts to build a bridge between the observed behavioral data and recent neurological evidence of object processing in the infant brain.

18.2 The 'what' and 'where' of infant object representation

Mareschal and Johnson (2003) recently explored the conditions under which infants would process or retain visual information about objects characteristic of dorsal processing, and those under which they would retain information characteristic of ventral processing. In this study, 4-month-olds were first familiarized with two objects moving in and out from behind two separate occluders (Fig. 18.1, top four panels). During testing, the infants first saw both objects move behind the occluders. There was then a 5-second retention interval following which the occluders were raised to reveal four possible outcomes (see Fig. 18.1, bottom four panels): (1) the original two objects in their expected locations (baseline condition; Baseline); (2) the same two familiar objects behind a single location (location violation condition; ST); (3) one familiar object and one novel object (identity violation condition; SF); and (4) the same two familiar objects, but in switched locations (binding violation condition; Binding).

Infants were familiarized under four different conditions. The four conditions differed in the kind of target that was used. In the 'Faces' condition, infants viewed female faces moving in and out from behind the occluders. In the 'Asterisks'

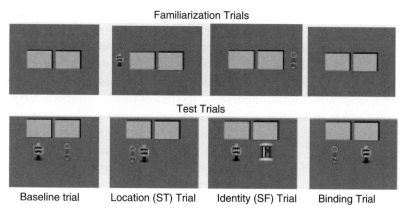

Familiarization Trials

Test Trials

Baseline trial   Location (ST) Trial   Identity (SF) Trial   Binding Trial

Fig. 18.1 Examples of test and familiarization trials in Mareschal and Johnson (2003). The top four panels illustrate a single familiarization event whereas the bottom four panels illustrate the four possible test trials.

conditions, they viewed monochromatic colored asterisks moving in and out from behind the occluders. In the 'Toys with manipulations' condition infants were first shown three toys and then viewed the images of these toys moving in and out from behind the occluders. Finally, in the 'Toy as without manipulation condition', the infants simply viewed images of toys moving in and out from behind the occluders (without prior exposure to the actual toys).

They found that when the test objects were images of faces or monochromatic asterisks, the infants responded to an identity violation only and *not* to a violation of location. In contrast, when images of infant toys were used, the infants responded to violations of location only and *not* to a change in identity as they had when presented with faces or colored asterisks (Fig. 18.2). In addition, the infants did not respond to the binding violation, whatever stimuli were used. Thus, it appears that 4-month-olds can maintain either identity (color or face – ventral features) or location (a dorsal feature) following a brief occlusion, but not both. Moreover, they do not maintain the binding of the dorsal and ventral features (e.g. the link between a particular color and its location when there is more than one object present). Mareschal and Johnson proposed that stimuli that potentially support actions (e.g. images of baby toys) lead to the selective retention of location (dorsal) information whereas stimuli that do not support actions (e.g. monochromatic color stars) lead to the selective retention of identity (ventral) information.

It is notable that the stimuli for which infants appear to retain ventrally processed information (colors and identity) hold rather less potential for manual action than those for which they retain dorsally processed information (location). Thus, Mareschal and Johnson hypothesized that features in the visual stimuli that specify the target's potential for action mediate the information that is retained during occlusion. Gibson (1979) has suggested that there is structure in visual information that directly specifies an object's potential for action in terms of its relation to the perceived self. He terms such sensory information 'affordances'. The idea that infants' behavior may be influenced by such information is consistent with other studies suggesting that infant reaches can be triggered by a target's affordance (e.g. Yonas and Hartman 1993).

However, it is still unclear from the finding above whether the selective maintenance of identity or location information is target specific, or whether 4-month-olds simply cannot remember two different kinds of information. Indeed, Ross-Sheehey *et al.* (2003) have suggested that short-term memory in infants less than 5 months of age is limited to one item. If the latter case is true, then perhaps the infants are remembering the location of the toys and not their identity on test because the repeated familiarization trials have selectively tuned their attention (and limited memory capacity) to location information only. Conversely, perhaps the infants are only remembering the identity of faces because the familiarization phase has biased them to selectively attend to and retain identity only. According to this argument, the dissociation identified by Mareschal and Johnson (2003) does not reflect the outcome of *stimulus specific*

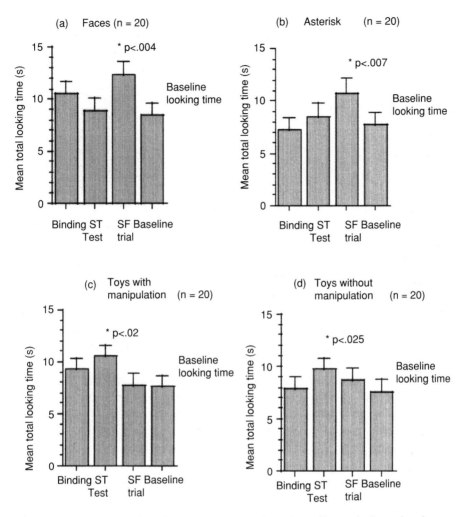

Fig. 18.2 Infants in the Mareschal and Johnson (2003) study looked longer in the surface feature change (SF) trial than baseline when tested with faces and color, and longer at the location change (ST) than baseline when tested with images of toys (after Mareschal and Johnson, 2003).

retention of dorsal and ventral information during occlusion, but rather, it reflects a kind of 'attentional bias' that the infants develop during the familiarization trials.

We examined this possibility in the experiment below by assessing infants' memory for location and identity information when both identity or location violations occurred within the same test sessions (as before), but this time with two different kinds of targets. One target was selected to elicit identity retention (a face) and the other was selected to elicit location retention (a toy). That is, the same infant was assessed for both their memory of location (with respect to toys) and identity (with respect to female faces) within one test session. Mareschal and Johnson (2003) found that infants demonstrated retention of either location *or* identity, when only *one* stimulus type was used. However, in the experiment below, we present both 'dorsal' and 'ventral' stimulus types in the same event. This kind of presentation gives us differential predictions according to the alternative explanations outlined above. If the selective maintenance found by Mareschal and Johnson is due to some kind of selective attention bias set up during the familiarization phase (perhaps as a result of an inability to maintain two different kinds of information), then we would predict that under these conditions the infants would notice changes in one *but not both* of the identity of the face or the location of the toy. On the other hand, if the selective maintenance is linked to whether or not the individual stimuli hold a spatially specific affordance for action and not a processing limitation, then we would expect infants to notice the changes to both the toy and the face stimuli.

18.3 Behavioral experiment

18.3.1 Method

18.3.1.1 Participants

Twenty-eight 4-month-olds took part in this study (14 girls and 14 boys). The mean age of the whole sample was 120.2 days (SD = 4.7). The mean age of the males was 120.4 days (SD = 5.2), and the mean age of the females was 119.9 days (SD = 4.3). A further eight infants were tested but were not included in the analyses because of fussiness (five), experimental error (one), or because they failed to complete all four test trails (two).

18.3.1.2 Procedure

Infants were tested at the Centre for Brain and Cognitive Development. Parents were led into a reception/play room in which the study was explained to them and they signed consent forms. They were then led into a special purpose testing room painted grey, and illuminated from above. The infants were sat in a car seat facing a 40 × 30 cm computer monitor located 60 cm in front of them. The monitor was encased in a black curtain. The experiment was run from a control station in a separate room. All events were computer controlled and presented on this monitor. This ensured that stimulus characteristics such as target velocities and occlusion rates were constant across all infants and in all experimental conditions.

As in the original Mareschal and Johnson (2003) study, the familiarization phase consisted of five repetitions of the same events sequenced automatically by the computer, in which a digital target image moved out from behind an occluder, moved towards the edge of the monitor, remained stationary for 5 s, then moved back behind the occluder. As soon as the first target had disappeared, a second target moved out from behind the second occluder, moved towards the opposite edge of the monitor, remained stationary for 5 s, then returned behind the occluder. The appearance and disappearance of both targets constituted a complete familiarization trial (Fig. 18.1, top four panels).

During the familiarization phase, no object ever passed in the gap between the occluders. Moreover, the disappearance of one target and the appearance of another target were temporally contiguous. This provided an additional cue to rule out the possibility that a single target was traversing the distance behind the occluders. During motion, all targets moved at a constant 9 cm/s. In addition, black shading along the outer boarder of the occluders provided some further evidence of depth in the image.

Following the familiarization trials, the test trial *per se* began. Each infant saw four different test trials. Presentation order was determined by one of four different latin-square designs, three of which were run in both directions. A test trial began when the infant was fixating a green flashing centering cue between the two yellow occluders (the flashing cue disappeared as soon as the trial began). Between trials, a noise was made to help reorient the infant to the center of the monitor. Each test trail began with one familiarization trial (i.e. one target moving in and out from behind each occluder). At the end of familiarization (i.e. once the second target had returned behind its original occluder) there was a 5-s pause. After the pause, both yellow occluders shifted upwards towards the top of the monitor at 5 cm/s, and revealed what lay behind them (Fig. 18.1, bottom four panels).

In the *Baseline* test trial, the occluders moved up to reveal the two targets from the familiarization phase, each behind the occluder from which it had appeared during the familiarization phase. Looking times at this event provides a baseline for how engaging the event is when there has been no violation of feature or location information. All looking times during other test trials were compared to this baseline value.

In the *Surface Feature* (SF) test trial, the occluders moved up to reveal one target behind each occluder. However, on this occasion, the face was novel while the other target was the familiar toy. This event contains a violation of feature information (a novel face), but not location information (there is one target behind each occluder). Increased looking times to this event (over and above looking times in the baseline condition) would suggest that the infants encoded the features of the face, remembered the features of the face during the occlusion period, and responded to the novelty of the new face.

In the *Spatial–Temporal* (ST) test trial, the occluders moved up to reveal no toy behind one occluder and both the toy and the face behind the other occluder. Moreover, it was always the toy that moved to the occluder initially occupied by the face alone. This event contains a violation of spatial–temporal (location) information but no violation of feature information (same targets). Increased looking to this event (over and above looking times in the baseline condition) would suggest that the infants encoded the location of the toy, remembered the location of the toy during the occlusion period, and responded to the novelty of the toy's location.

In the *Binding* test trial the occluders moved up to reveal one of the targets from the familiarization phase behind each occluder. However, the targets had been switched around such that each target was behind the occluder from which it had never appeared. This condition contains a violation of the binding (conjunction) between surface-feature and spatial–temporal (location) information. The separate components in this display (surface features and location) are identical to those in the baseline condition but the feature–location compounds have changed. Increased looking times to this event (over and above looking times in the baseline test trial) would suggest that the infants encoded the locations of targets, processed the features of targets, remembered the location and features of the targets, remembered which target was at which location during the occlusion period, and responded to the novelty of the feature–location compound.

In all test trials, the occluding screens remained raised and stationary for a maximum of 15 s after which they descended to their original positions, thereby reoccluding the targets. Test trials were terminated if infants looked away from the event for more than 3 s consecutively. To terminate a trial, the experimenter pushed a computer key that lowered the occluding screens as though the trial was terminating naturally. The left–right location of the face was counter-balanced across infants, and independently of one another. Thus, half the infants experienced an identity violation on the left and half experienced an identity violation on the right. Conversely, half the infants saw the toy on the right unexpectedly appear on the left and half the infants saw the toy on the left unexpectedly appear on the right.

The monitor viewing area was 38.5 × 29.5 cm and of a dull grey color (RGB: 153, 153, 153). The yellow occluders (RGB: 255, 204, 0) were 11 × 7cm with a 1-cm gap between them. The target images varied in size slightly depending on the object, but were constrained to be within a 6 × 4 cm rectangle. For each infant, one toy and two female face images (one familiar and one novel face) were randomly selected from the sets displayed in Fig. 18.3. During the familiarization phase, the targets moved to a position where their closest edge was 3 cm from the closest edge of the occluder.

18.3.1.3 Coding

Infant looking time to the display was coded off-line. During the familiarization trials the scoring interval started as soon as a the first target was fully revealed from behind an occluder and finished as soon as the occluder began to cover the second target. During the test trials, the scoring interval began as soon as the occluders had fully revealed the occluded objects and ended as soon as the descending occluders began to occlude the targets (a maximum total of 15 s). To provide interobserver reliability, a second experienced coder recoded 25 per cent of the trials from the video records. The Pearson correlation of looking times between the two coding sessions was 0.89.

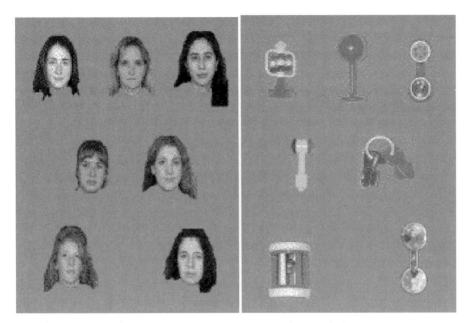

Fig. 18.3 Female face and toy stimuli used during familiarization and testing.

18.3.2 **Results**

18.3.2.1 Familiarization trials

The mean total looking time (and standard deviations) in the first five familiarization trials was: 4.53 (1.53), 5.01 (0.53), 4.97 (1.02), 4.83 (1.01), and 4.69 (1.06) seconds respectively. Comparison of the looking times in the second and third trials versus the fourth and fifth trials revealed a significant decrement between the mean of the second and third and the mean of the fourth and fifth trials (Wilcoxon signed rank test, $Z = 2.1$, $N = 28$, $p < 0.04$). Thus, there was a general decrease in looking across the last four familiarization trials, suggesting that infants are encoding some aspect of the display during familiarization. Lower looking times in the initial familiarization trial are also consistent with the encoding of complex stimuli by young infants. In such cases, infants usually shows an initial increase in looking at the stimulus while the infant builds a representation of that stimulus, followed by a decrease in looking (Sirois and Mareschal 2002).

18.3.2.2 Test trials

Figure 18.4 shows the mean total looking time in each of the four possible test trials. Examination of the variances in each condition revealed substantial differences between conditions. For example the variance in the baseline trial was three times as large as that in the ST trial. Therefore, to homogenize variances, looking time scores were transformed using a $\ln(1+x)$ transformation prior to analysis. The transformed

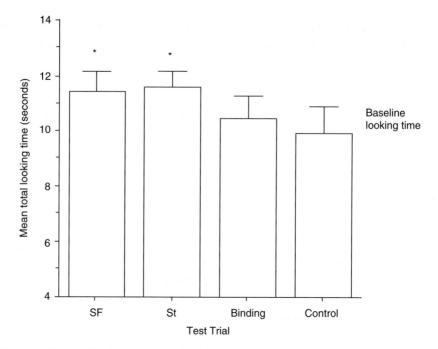

Fig. 18.4 Mean total looking time in each of the four test trials (raw scores and standard errors). SF = surface features; St = spatial and temporal.

scores were subjected to an analysis of covariance with Trial (SF, ST, Binding and Baseline) as a repeated factor, Location of face (left or right) as a between subject factor, and Total looking time at test as a covariate. The Location factor is introduced to identify if there is a side bias in responding to violations of location or identity information. The covariate is introduced to account for the fact that infants with near ceiling total looking times may not be able to demonstrate a discrimination between test trials as well as infants with looking times in the middle of the allowable range.

This ANCOVA revealed a significant effect of Trial ($F(3, 72) = 6.93$, $p < 0.001$), a significant effect of Total looking time ($F(1, 24) = 3.71$, $p < 0.001$) and a significant Trial × Total looking time interaction ($F(3, 72) = 5.19$, $p < 0.006$). The main effect of Total looking time is neither surprising nor interesting, and is essentially an artifact of the analyses used. Effectively, it indicates that when one collapses the transformed looking time scores across all the test scores, the resulting sum of transformed scores covaries very strongly with the sum of raw looking time scores. The Trial × Total looking time interaction can be interpreted as an indication that the significant main effect of Trial is modulated by the total amount of time infants spent looking at the test events. Inspection of the raw looking times suggests that several infants had near ceiling looking times in all test conditions. In these infants, the differential effect of trial is therefore reduced. Analyses with the untransformed data led to the very similar pattern of results.

The main effect of Trials was further examined by comparing the looking times in each of the SF, ST, and Binding trials to that in the Baseline trial. Looking times were significantly longer in the SF ($t(27) = 2.01$, $p < 0.05$) and ST ($t(27) = 2.43$, $p < 0.02$) trials than in the Baseline trials. The looking times in no other pairs of trials were differed significantly from one another. In particular, the looking times in the SF and ST trials did not differ from one another, nor did the looking times in the Binding and Baseline trials.

18.3.3 Discussion of behavioral experiment

Mareschal and Johnson (2003) had suggested that 4-month-olds maintain different kinds of information depending on the target encountered. From this earlier work, we conclude that when encountering events involving images of faces the infants will maintain identity information but not location information during occlusion. In contrast, when encountering with events containing images of toys, they will maintain location information and not identity information. However, because the original study involved events that contained either only faces or only toys, it is difficult to conclude whether infants can, in fact, retain both kinds of information within one test session. The results of the current study show that 4-month-olds can retain both location and identity information within the same session – although not for the same target. This result replicates the original Mareschal and Johnson (2003) finding, and further strengthens the conclusion that it is the action affordance of the target that modulates what kind of information is retained.

It is also worth noting that the effect sizes are smaller here than they were in the original Mareschal and Johnson (2003) study. A comparison with the previous data suggested that this is due to a slightly higher average looking at the Baseline condition. In the previous study infants looked around 7.5 s at the baseline condition (Fig. 18.2), whereas they look around 10 s in the current study. This difference could be due to the reduced habituation during the familiarization trials arising, perhaps, from the intrinsically more attractive stimulus events consisting of both toys and faces rather than the events using only one kind of object as in the previous work. Indeed, there was a smaller decrement in looking time during familiarization in the current study than in the previous studies. This may have led several babies to exhibit ceiling, or nearly ceiling, looking times in several test trials, including the control baseline trial. In the current study, five of the 28 infants showed total looking times of 14.5 s or above on all four test trials.

An alternative and less interesting explanation is that the difference in looking in the Baseline trial reflects changes in the experimental setup. This study was run in a cubicle normally used for EEG experiments that, although similar, was not identical to the cubicle used previously. In particular, the lighting conditions can be extremely well controlled in these EEG cubicles. In an initial pilot study with 10 infants, we found that if the light in the room was too low (i.e. nothing could possibly be seen other than the illuminated monitor) then the infants would simply stare at the monitor for the full possible duration in all test events.

18.4 Combining dorsal–ventral representations

Processing information about multiple objects down two independent pathways leads to a *binding problem* (Sougné 1998). In the tasks above, there is a need to keep track of which SF (e.g. identity) representation corresponds to which ST (e.g. location) representation. Neural networks with pulsing activation rather than continuous activation can simultaneously encode information about more than one object (Shastri and Ajjanagandde 1993; Sougné 1998; MacKay 1997; Mass and Bishop 1999; Gerstner and Kistler 2002). Such networks pulse (or spike) at regularly spaced intervals. The activation of the network at the different pulses encodes information relevant to distinct objects. Since the same network is used to compute information for all objects (at each of the pulses), the connection weights encode information that is true across all objects. Thus a single network can encode general object knowledge while simultaneously representing and keeping separate the information arising from two distinct objects (Henderson 1996). The binding problem can then be solved by synchronizing activations (or correlating the firing of spikes) across multiple subnetworks that carry information about the same object.

This concept of dynamic binding by synchronization of neural discharges has been developed mainly in the context of perceptual processing; especially visual processing which shows a highly distributed organization. To solve the binding problem in such a system, neurons that respond to the same sensory object fire their action potentials in synchrony (e.g. Singer and Gray 1995; Singer 1999). Such mechanism have been used to model grouping and segmentation in visual processing (e.g. Horn *et al.* 1992; Tononi *et al.*1992; Schillen and Koonig 1994) but also with recent applications in cognitive psychology (Hummel and Biedermann 1992; Shastri and Ajjanagadde 1993; Hummel and Holyoak 1997) and object memory (Raffone and Wolter 2001).

In the modeling work described below, we begin to explore the possibility that temporal synchrony could be used as a mechanisms for binding and or retaining the information that is independently processed in the dorsal and ventral streams. Indeed, electrophysiological evidence suggests that oscillatory synchrony could be used to establish dynamic links between various cortical areas or during short-term memory maintenance tasks (Tallon-Baudry, 2003; Ward 2003). Perhaps the limitations of young infants on task such as those described above are a result of the immature development of such a mechanisms.

18.5 A developmental model

To address these questions, we propose to build a connectionist computational model. These are computational models that are loosely based on neural information processing. However, they are not models of individual neurons, but, rather, models of simplified functional systems (e.g. Elman *et al.* 1996; Quinlan 2003). An important question for this project is to explore how a temporal synchrony binding mechanism will interact with learning (within task adaptation) and development (ontogenetic adaptation).

Mareschal *et al.* (1999) had originally proposed a simple neural network model of dorsal/ventral function to explain early infant object-directed behaviors (Fig. 18.5). The model 'existed' in a microenvironment in which there were four kinds of objects that moved back and forth either horizontally or vertically. In the middle of this world was an occluder. Horizontally moving objects would occasionally pass behind the occluder, giving the model experience of occlusion events. In the model, one stream (the Object Recognition Network) used an unsupervised competitive algorithms (Foldiak 1991) to develop spatially-invariant object representations (the 'ventral' component of the model). A second stream used self-supervised backpropagation to learn to track a moving object predictively (the 'dorsal' component of the model). Finally, information that was processed independently down the two streams was

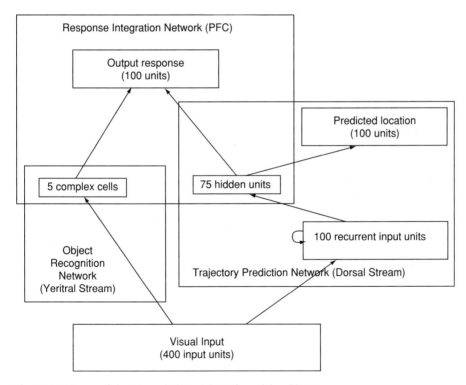

Fig. 18.5 Schema of the Mareschal *et al.* (1999) model architecture.

integrated by the Response Integration module when this was required to complete a response (a function attributed to the prefrontal cortex (PFC; Rao *et al.* 1997). This model successfully captured a number of developmental phenomena such as the ability to track a moving object during the occlusion period, the ability to maintain a representation of the object's features during occlusion, and to respond to unexpected changes in those feature. Finally, as with infants, the model showed a developmental lag between its ability to predict an objects location and its ability to act on that information (for example in producing a retrieval reach towards the object's predicted location).

However, this model could not deal with more than one object at a time. This is a common problem in connectionist networks. The internal representation that arise from the presence of each object are superimposed across the internal units. This can lead to interference effects, or, even if the representations do not interfere with one another, it becomes impossible for units further upstream to identify which internal representation corresponds to which object. Thus, to augment the functionality of this model, we now introduce here a temporal synchrony mechanism that enables the representation of information from multiple object simultaneously. We do this by introducing pulsing activation in the network (Mass and Bishop 1999). That is, instead of having a single sweep of activation passing through the network, bursts with several pulses were propagated through the different streams of the network (Fig. 18.6).

Each burst consists of four peaks of activation. In connectionist networks, information about the current object is encoded in the patterns of activation across the nodes in the network whereas information about the networks experiences as a whole is encoded in the connection weights between nodes. Consequently, information related to multiple current objects can be kept separate by associating a different activation peak with each object. For example the first activation peak may encode information about object 1, whereas the second peak may encode information about object 2, and so on. However, the network weights are adapted in response to all activation patterns and therefore encode regularities that are true of all objects encountered. In this way, the network can learn things that are true across classes of objects and yet maintain individual object representations separate (Henderson 1996).

The activation bursts that flow down the dorsal and ventral streams in the model do not need to be synchronized or correlated when the object information is originally encoded. So long as information about different objects is encoded on different peaks, that information will be kept separate. Thus, for example, it is possible to encode the location of object 1 on peak 3 and that of object 2 on peak 1, down the dorsal stream while encoding the identity information of object 1 on peak 2 and that of object 2 on peak 4, down the ventral stream (Fig. 18.6). However, when the network needs to access which object is at which location (perhaps to reach towards a desired object

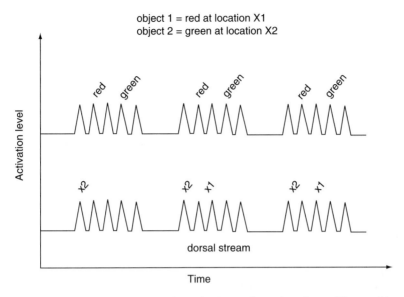

Fig. 18.6 Illustration of a pulsing network mechanism. Information about different objects is encoded on separate spikes within repeated pulses of activation that flow through the two network streams.

amongst several other targets), then the separate identity and location representations encoded within the two streams need to be realigned.

The integration of object information across the dorsal and ventral streams was accomplished by aligning (correlating) the firing patterns of the dorsal and the ventral bursts such that the peaks coding the feature information fired in phase with those encoding the corresponding spatial information. In the current model, the alignment took place in the response integration (PFC) module. This module takes as its input the output of the object recognition module (complex cells in Fig. 18.5) and the hidden units of the trajectory prediction module (the internal spatial-temporal representation). As a pulse of activation moved through the two network streams, the network simply cycled through the activation peaks that arrive through the two streams and performed a pairwise comparison of each possible location-feature binding. The family of feature–location pairs that produced the least error was used to produce an output response.

The idea behind this scheme is that direct perception provides clues that enable a system to solve the binding problem. Imagine that the network is tracking three different objects. When all objects are visible, direct perception can solve the problem of which features correspond to which location. Now suppose that one object becomes occluded. Knowing what the other two bindings are allows the system to recover what the third (occluded) binding is. If two objects are occluded, the remaining visible object provides some constraints on what the possible feature location bindings are for the two occluded objects, but there is no longer any certainty.

Although this model is still in the early stages of development, a number of key behaviors have emerged. First, even though the weights are updated after every peak (effectively interleaving information about different objects) it can still learn to track predictively and respond appropriately to multiple moving objects (as had the original Mareschal *et al.* model but with only a single object at a time).

Secondly, although in this implementation the synchronization mechanism (in the PFC) is in place from the onset of development (thereby theoretically enabling the network to form correct bindings from the onset), the model initially fails to form correct location–identity bindings. This is because the binding mechanism is based on selecting the feature–location pair that results in the network best reconstructing the current perceptual input. However, until the network (specifically the object tracking and object recognition modules) has learned to encode sufficient information, none of the possible bindings will lead to an accurate reconstruction of perceptual input. As the separate feature and location representations become more reliable (in terms of their information content), the synchronization mechanisms starts to pick out which feature–location pairs lead to better performance.

Thirdly, while there is an overall improvement in the model's ability to identify the correct feature–location bindings with increased training, this interacts with the number of objects being tracked and the duration of the occlusion. The more objects are present, the more likely the network makes a binding error. Similarly, the longer the occlusion, the more likely it is that the network will make a binding error.

Of special note is the fact that periods of realignment (synchronization) occur when the network is required to produce a response towards one of several objects, each at different locations. It also happens when there are unexpectedly changes in object properties following brief occlusions. This is because the network needs to update its internal representation of the feature or location information of objects that it is tracking.

18.6 A potential fit with electrophysiological data?

Event related oscillatory brain activity (ERO) allows investigations at an additional level of organization than is typically obtained from ERP data (Ward 2003). It allows the examination of the internal co-ordination of spike timing and covariation in neuronal firing patterns (Singer 1999; Gerstner and Kistler 2002). Increased activity in the gamma band range (40-Hz oscillations) has been linked with focused attention, visual object processing, and short-term memory maintenance (Ward 2003; Tallon-Baudry, 2003).

Kaufman and colleagues (Kaufman *et al.* 2003a; Kaufman, Csibra, Volein, and Johnson, submitted) have suggested that ERO in the gamma band range may be a marker of object retention during occlusion, events in 6-month-olds. They recorded the brain electrical activity (EEG) while infants watched a video of a toy train passing through a tunnel. On some trials, the train unexpectedly disappeared while in the tunnel They found that there was: (1) *early and sustained* gamma-band activity during a period of time in which the train was occluded; and (2) a *late increased* gamma-band activity following the presentation of an event in which the train had unexpectedly disappeared. This latter period of increased gamma band activity (synchronization on the 40-Hz range) seems to occur in similar conditions under which the model enters a phase of trying to synchronize bursts of activation down its dorsal and ventral streams (i.e. following a surreptitious change in object features during an occlusion). This suggests that the gamma-band activity observed infants may reflect a process of trying to realign neural representations of location and identity with the now inconsistent perceptual information.

18.7 **General discussion**

In this chapter, we have reviewed evidence of dorsal–ventral dissociations in early development. The dissociation is manifested in occlusion tasks that require infants to maintain object information in short-term memory. The evidence suggests that 4-month-olds are limited in the information that they will retain during such tasks. For targets that afford action, they retain information characteristic of dorsal processing (e.g. location). In contrast, for targets that do not afford action, they will retain information characteristic of ventral processing (identity). Moreover, the new experiment reported here replicates the findings of Mareschal and Johnson (2003), and suggests that 4-month-olds can, in fact, retain both location and identity information within a single session – albeit not for the same object. What information is retained appears to be truly target specific.

What we have described is a retention issue and not a failure to encode one kind of information or the other. Indeed, there is ample evidence that both dorsal and ventral pathways are at least partially functional from a very young age (Johnson *et al.* 2001). Even within the task described above, the infants have to encode at least some aspect of object features for the action affordance to have any impact on retention. Again, the final experiment shows that both location and identity are encoded within a single test session. However, it is the infants' failure to hold in mind more than *just* spatial or *just* featural information about an object, and consequently bind such information together within a unified representation of the object, that is so striking.

The view that the 4-month-olds were sensitive to the affordance of the targets raises an interesting question about the ontogeny of visual affordances. Tucker and Ellis (2001) argue that these visual–motor associations reflect a participant's previous experience and interactions with objects. However, infants begin reaching towards an object only round 3.5 months and do not do so systematically until 4.5 months (Gordon 2001). So, how could our 4-month-olds have acquired a sensitivity to action affordances in objects?

One possibility is through simple observation. Although 4-month-olds do not reliably reach yet, they are on the cusp of reaching. The toys photographed for use in this experiment were common, commercially available infant toys. They may have recognized the objects as members of the category of objects that they routinely encounter and observe being used in particular ways. Certainly, adults can categorize visually presented objects on the basis of the actions that they afford (Klatsky *et al.* 1993; Tucker and Ellis, 2001). This suggests that infants may initially acquire crude object–action associations through observation alone. These initial associations may underpin early efforts to engage in purposeful action with an object. Clearly, further work is required to tease these possibilities apart. One interesting possibility would be to see whether the amount of time that infants had been reaching (rather than just their age) predicted the probability that they would retain location information when presented with images of toys. This would allow us to test the extent to which motor experience was necessary for the emergence of the dissociation in short-term memory.

An alternative way to strengthen our conclusions would be to test infants with real objects that were located in proximal or distal space (Kaufman *et al.* 2003b). Although the appearance of the object would not change, its potential to be grasped would differ depending on whether it was within or out of reach. Under these circumstances, we might predict that infants would retain the location information when the objects were within proximal space, but only retain the identity information when the objects were in distal space.

To help understand how the behavioral dissociations might relate to the underlying neural information processing, we also described a connectionist computational model that learns to track the location and identity of moving objects that undergo occlusions. To enable the model to track more than one object at a time, it is augmented with a temporal synchrony mechanism. Information about separate objects is kept separate by encoding it on separate peaks of activation bursts that travel down the model's two pathways. Information that is true of all objects is encoded in the network's connection weights. The model successfully learns to track the identity and location of multiple objects simultaneously. It also shows an increased probability of making a binding error with increased number of objects that it is a tracking and increased duration of occlusion. Following a binding error, the model attempts to realign object identity and location information. This may correspond to the bursts of increased gamma band activity found in infants following unexpected disappearances of temporarily hidden objects.

The model is still in its preliminary stages of development and needs much more work. However, it promises to provide a mechanistic tool for relating observations at the behavioral level with observations at the electrophysiological level and brain functional systems. There are also several ways in which the current model does not fit with the behavioral data reported above. In particular, there is no mechanism in the model for differentially retaining location or feature information. Thus, this model should, in principle, be able remember both the location and identity information of the object's that it is tracking. In addition, there is no way that the current model could use object features to modulate the kind of information that is retained. Before we adapt the model, we need to understand better what triggers this process in infants. Are there bottom–up cues (micro-affordances as Tucker and Ellis (1998) call them) in the targets that prime the selective retention of location, or is this the outcome of top–down feedback? Once we understand this, we can get a better idea of how the model will need to be extended to provide a fuller account of infants' developing interactions with occluded objects.

Acknowledgements

We thank the parents and infants who participated in these studies. We are also grateful to the members of the Centre for Brain and Cognitive Development, and especially Agnes Volein for assistance in running the studies. We also thank Mark H. Johnson and Jordy Kaufman for helpful discussions, and Marko Nardini who programmed the model described in the second half of this chapter. Finally, funding for the work reported here was obtained from Birkbeck College, the ESRC (UK) Postdoctoral Fellowship T026271357 and grant R00023911, and European Commission grant HPRN-CT-1999–00065.

References

Atkinson J (2000). *The developing visual brain.* Oxford, UK: Oxford University Press.

Bertenthal BI (1996). Origins and early development of perception, action, and representation *Annual Review of Psychology,* **47**, 431–459.

DeLoache JS, Uttal D and Rosengren KS (2004). Scale errors offer evidence for a perception-action dissociation early in life. *Science, 304,* 1027–1029.

Elman JL, Bates EA, Karmiloff-Smith A, Johnson MH, Parisi D and Plunkett K (1996). *Rethinking innateness: Connectionism in a developmental framework.* Cambridge, MA: MIT Press.

Felleman DJ and Van Essen DC (1991). Distributed hierarchical processing in primate cerebral cortex. *Cerebral Cortex,* **1**, 1–47.

Foldiak P (1991). Learning invariance from transformation sequences. *Neural Computation,* **3**, 194–200.

Gerstner W and Kistler WM (2002). *Spiking neuron models.* Cambridge, UK: Cambridge University Press.

Gibson JJ (1979). *The ecological approach to visual perception.* Boston, MA: Houghton-Mifflin.

Glover S (2004). What causes scale errors in children? *Trends in Cognitive Sciences,* **8**, 440–443.

Gordan AM (2001). Development of hand motor control. In: AF Kalverboer and A Gramsbergen, eds. *Handbook of brain and behaviour in human development,* pp. 513–538. Kluwer Academic Press.

Henderson J (1996). A connectionist architecture with inherent systematicy. In: GW Cottrell, ed. *Proceedings of the eighteenth annual conference of the Cognitive Science Society,* pp. 574–580. Mahwah, NJ: Lawrence Erlbaum Associates.

Horn D, Sagi D and Usher M (1992). Segmentation binding and illusory conjunctions. *Neural Computation,* 3, 509–524.

Hummel JE and Biederman I (1992). Dynamic binding in a neural network for shape recognition. *Psychological Review,* 99, 480–517.

Hummel JE and Holyoak KJ (1997). Distributed representations of structure: A theory of analogical access and mapping. *Psychological Review,* 104, 427–466.

Humphreys GW and Riddoch M (2003). From what to where. *Psychological Science,* 14, 487–492.

Jeannerod M (1997). *The cognitive neuroscience of action.* Oxford, UK: Blackwell.

Johnson MH, Mareschal D and Csibra G (2001). The development and integration of the dorsal and ventral visual pathways: A neurocomputational approach. In: CA Nelson and M Luciana, eds. *The Handbook of Developmental Cognitive Neuroscience,* pp. 339–351. Cambridge, MA: MIT Press.

Kaldy Z and Leslie AM (2003). Identification of objects in 9-month-old infants: integrating 'what' and 'where' information. *Developmental Science,* 6, 360–373.

Kaldy Z and Sigala N (2004). The neural mechanisms of object working memory: what is where in the infant brain? *Neuroscience and Biobehavioural Reviews,* 28, 113–121.

Kaufman J, Csibra G and Johnson MH (2003a). Representing occluded objects in the human infant brain. *Proceedings of the Royal Society London, B (Suppl.) Biology Letters,* 270/S2, 140–143.

Kaufman J, Mareschal D and Johnson MH (2003b). Graspability and object processing in infants, *Infant Behavior and Development,* 26, 516–528.

Klatzky RL, Pellegrino JW, McCloskey BP and Ledereman SJ (1993). Cognitive representations of functional interactions with objects. *Memory and Cognition,* 21, 253–270.

Leslie A, Xu F, Tremoulet P and Scholl B (1998). Indexing and the object concept: 'what' and 'where' systems in infancy. *Trends in Cognitive Sciences,* 2, 10–18.

Livingstone M and Hubel D (1988). Segregation of form, color, movement, and depth – anatomy, physiology, and perception. *Science,* 240, 740–749.

MacKay WA (1997). Synchronised neuronal oscillations and their role in motor processes. *Trends in Cognitive Sciences,* 1, 176–183.

Mareschal D and Johnson MH (2003). The 'What' and 'Where' of infant object representations in infancy. *Cognition* 88, 259–276.

Mareschal D, Plunkett K and Harris P (1999). A computational and neuropsychological account of object-oriented behaviours in infancy. *Developmental Science,* 2, 306–317.

Mass W and Bishop C (1999). *Pulsed neural networks.* Cambridge, MA: MIT Press.

Merigan WH and Maunsell JHR (1993). How parallel are the primate visual pathways. *Annual Review of Neuroscience,* 16, 369–402.

Milner A.D and Goodale MA (1995). *The visual brain in action.* Oxford, UK: Oxford University Press.

Puce A and Alison J (1998). Temporal cortex activation in humans viewing eye and mouth movements. *Journal of Neuroscience,* 18, 2188–2199.

Puce A and Perret D (2003). Electrophysiology and brain imaging of biological motion. *Philosophical Transactions of the Royal Society of London B,* 358, 435–445.

Quinlan P (2003). *Connectionist models of development.* Hove, UK: Psychology Press.

Raffone A and Wolter G (2001). A cortical mechanism for binding in visual working memory. *Journal of Cognitive Neuroscience,* 13, 766–785.

Rao SC, Rainer G and Miller E (1997). Integration of 'what' and 'where' in the primate prefrontal cortex. *Science,* 276, 821–824.

Ross-Sheehy S, Oakes LM and Luck SJ (2003). The development of visual short-term memory capacity in infants. *Child Development*, 74, 1807–1822.

Schillen TB and Koonig P (1994). Binding by temporal structure in multiple feature domains of an oscillatory neuronal network. *Biological Cybernetics*, 70, 397–405.

Shastri L and Ajjanagadde V (1993). From simple associations so systematic reasoning: A connectionist representation of rules, variables, and dynamic bindings using temporal synchrony. *Behavioral and Brain Sciences*, 16, 417–494.

Singer W (1999). Neural synchrony: A versatile code for the definition of relations. *Neuron*, 24, 49–65.

Singer W and Gray CM (1995). Visual feature integration and the temporal correlation hypothesis. *Annual Review of Neuroscience*, 18, 555–586.

Sirois S and Mareschal D (2002). Models of infant habituation *Trends in Cognitive Sciences*, 6, 293–298.

Sougné J (1998). The problem of multiple instantiation. *Trends in Cognitive Sciences*, 2, 183–189.

Tallon-Baudry, C (2003). Oscillatory synchrony and human visual cognition. *Journal of Physiology*, 97, 355–363.

Tanaka K (1993). Neuronal mechanisms of object recognition. *Science*, 262, 685–688.

Tononi GO, Sporns ON and Edelman GM (1992). Reentry and the problem of integrating multiple cortical areas: Simulation of dynamic integration in the visual system. *Cerebral Cortex*, 2, 310–335.

Tucker M and Ellis R (1998). On the relation of seen objects and components of potential actions. *Journal of Experimental Psychology: Human Perception and Performance*, 24, 830–846.

Tucker M and Ellis R (2001).The potentiation of grasp types during visual object categorization. *Visual Cognition*, 8, 769–800.

Ungerleider LG and Mishkin M (1982). Two cortical visual systems. In: DL Ingles, MA Goodale, & RJ Maugfield (Eds.) *Analysis of visual behavior*, pp. 549–586. Cambridge, MA: MIT Press.

Van Essen DC, Anderson CH and Felleman DJ (1992). Information processing in the primate visual system: an integrated systems perspective. *Science*, 255, 419–423.

Ward LM (2003). Synchronous neural oscillations and cognitive processes. *Trends in Cognitive Sciences*, 7, 553–559.

Wilcox T and Chapa C (2004). Priming infants to attend to color and pattern information in an individuation task, *Cognition*, 90, 265–302.

Wilcox T and Schweinle A (2002). Object individuation and event mapping: developmental changes in infants' use of featural information. *Developmental Science*, 5, 132–150.

Xu F and Carey S (1996). Infants' metaphysics: the case of numerical identity. *Cognitive Psychology*, 30, 111–153.

Xu F, Carey S and Welch J (1999). Infants' ability to use object kind information for object individuation. *Cognition*, 70, 137–166.

Yonas A and Hartman B (1993). Perceiving the affordance of contact in four- and five-month-olds infants. *Child Development*, 64, 298–308.

Zeki S (1980). The representation of colours in the cerebral cortex. *Nature*, 284, 412–418.

Chapter 19

The infant as synesthete?

Daphne Maurer and Catherine J. Mondloch

Abstract

The hypothesis that newborns' perception is synesthetic holds up well in light of recent evidence on the neural basis of synesthesia, on developmental plasticity, and on cross-modal interactions in non-synesthetic adults and children. The starting point for this paper is our previous proposal that newborns' perception is synesthetic: that their undifferentiated sensory pathways lead to cross-modal influences on their perception resulting in perceptual experiences that resemble, in some respects, the perception of adults with synesthesia (Maurer 1993; Maurer and Maurer 1988; Maurer and Mondloch 1996, 2004; see Johnson and Vecera 1996, for a similar argument they called the parcellation conjecture). Adult synesthetes report that stimulation in one modality (or along one dimension) causes percepts not only in the original modality but also in a second sensory modality (or along a second dimension). For example the taste of chicken may induce the feeling of a sharply pointed figure, or the grapheme A may induce the percept of red. In this paper we re-evaluate the hypothesis of neonatal synesthesia, beginning with a consideration of evidence in the last decade on the nature of synesthetic perception and its neural basis. We then consider the similarities between the neural immaturity of infants' brains and the neural substrate for synesthesia in adults, and from those similarities derive predictions for the forms that neonatal synesthesia might take. We end the paper with a consideration of the match between those predictions and empirical findings on the development of cross-modal perception.

19.1 **Synesthesia**

Although the existence of synesthetic perception is based on subjective reports from adults, its reality has been confirmed by the consistency of those reports across time and by documented interactions between the reported synesthetic percepts and controlled stimuli presented in the laboratory. When synesthetic adults in whom the sight of letters and digits or the sound of words induces a colored percept are asked to match the induced color to an extensive palette of real colors, their matches are almost identical when they are given a surprise retest many months or even years later, much higher than the consistency shown by non-synesthetes asked to pick and remember the best color match to each stimulus and retested after much shorter intervals (Baron-Cohen *et al.* 1993; Laeng *et al.* 2004; Mattingley *et al.* 2001; Mills *et al.* 2002; Ward and Simner 2003; but see Elias *et al.* 2003). Synesthetic color and objective color interact in a fashion analogous to the Stroop effect: when adults with color grapheme synesthesia are asked to name the ink color in which a letter is printed, they are faster if the objective and synesthetically induced colors are congruent (e.g. both red) than if they are incongruent (e.g. one green, one red) (e.g. Dixon, *et al.* 2000; Mattingley *et al.* 2001; Mills *et al.* 2002; Myles *et al.* 2003; Palermi *et al.* 2002; Smilek *et al.* 2003; but see Elias *et al.* 2003). In one study, subjects reported that they could not suppress the synesthetic color, and that it took 'overwhelming mental effort' to name the ink color on incongruent trials (Mattingley *et al.* 2001). Similarly, the speed with which an adult with color grapheme synesthesia reads a black letter or reports the answer to an arithmetic problem is affected by the congruency of the background with the color induced by the letter or digit: if they are contrasting (red synesthetic color on green background), performance is faster than if they are similar (red synesthetic color on red background) (Dixon *et al.* 2000; Smilek *et al.* 2001). Unlike adults without synesthesia, their visual search for a target among a large number of similarly shaped distracters is also faster when the target and distracters have different synesthetic colors and their reaction times are not affected by the addition of distracters, as if the target is 'popping out' because of a difference in synesthetic color (although the slope of the function relating reaction time to number of distracters is not as flat as expected for pop out; Laeng *et al.* 2004; Palermi *et al.* 2002; Smilek *et al.* 2003). These demonstrations that synesthetically induced colors interact in predictable ways with objective stimuli establish the reality of the color percepts reported by adults with color grapheme synesthesia and support their impression that it is triggered automatically. Additional evidence of automaticity comes from the finding that synesthetically induced colors can act as facilitory primes in a color naming task (when they are presented for 500 ms but not when they are presented for 56 ms; Mattingley *et al.* 2001) and from a study using hierarchical shapes (e.g. a big A formed from small Bs): even when told to ignore the local level and to report the objective color at the global level, the presence of a letter at the local level evoking an incongruent color interfered with performance (Rich and Mattingley 2003). Finally, when a target letter presented in the periphery is surrounded by flanker letters, non-synesthetic adults have difficulty identifying the target; in contrast, synesthetic adults are able to guess the identity of the target because the appropriate synesthetic color (e.g. red for the letter 'A') is induced (Ramachandran and Hubbard 2001).

19.1.1 Neural mechanisms

One candidate neural mechanism for synesthesia is unusual functional connections between neighboring sensory cortical areas. Evidence comes from imaging studies with adults with colored word hearing, in whom the sight or sound of a specific letter evokes the percept of a specific color. In such synesthetes, hearing the inducing letter produces neural activity not only in the 'normal' areas of auditory sensory cortex but also in extrastriate visual cortex (Gray *et al.* 1997; Nunn *et al.* 2002; Winawer and Witthoft 2004; see also Elias *et al.* 2003), in a number of higher visual areas (Paulesu *et al.* 1995), and, in one study, even in the primary visual cortex (Aleman *et al.* 2001). Similarly, in a case of gustatory synesthesia in which words induce specific tastes, the presentation of words, but not tones, evokes activity in the primary gustatory cortex that abuts cortical areas involved in phonological decoding (Ward and Simner 2003).

An alternative hypothesis is that such connections exist in all adult brains, but are normally inhibited; synesthesia represents a release from that inhibition (Grossenbacher and Lovelace 2001; see Cytowic 1989 for evidence that synesthesia can result from more general cortical inhibition). This hypothesis is supported by evidence that some transient connections present in early development remain after infancy but are inhibited (see Section 19.1.2) and fMRI evidence for suppression of some areas of sensory visual cortex during colored hearing or grapheme synesthesia (Paulesu *et al.* 1995; see also Schiltz *et al.* 1999).

19.1.2 The newborn brain

There is ample evidence that the cortex of the human newborn is immature (e.g. Johnson 1997) and that it contains transient connections between cortical areas that will later be pruned or inhibited. In the neonatal hamster there are transient connections between the retina and the main somatosensory and auditory nuclei of the thalamus (Frost 1984) and in the kitten there are transient connections between the visual, auditory, somatosensory, and motor cortices (Dehay *et al.* 1984; Dehay *et al.* 1988). A similar pattern of exuberant connections followed by pruning has been documented in both human and non-human primates, including projections from the monkey's auditory cortex to area V4, the color-form region of extrastriate cortex that is active during colored hearing synesthesia (Huttenlocher 1994; Kennedy *et al.* 1997). Neuroimaging data from human infants suggest that those transient connections are functional. EEG studies have documented an influence of auditory input on the responses of the somatosensory and visual cortices and an influence of visual input on the auditory cortex. For example stimulation of the newborn's wrist evokes a response over the somatosensory cortex, as it does in non-synesthetic adults, but only in newborns is the magnitude of the response increased when wrist stimulation is accompanied by white noise (Wolff *et al.* 1974). Spoken language elicits large event-related potentials (ERPs) over the infant's temporal cortex, as it does in non-synes-thetic adults, but only in infants does it also elicit a large response over the visual cortex (Neville 1995; Neville, Chapter 13, this volume), a pattern analogous to the fMRI activity in response to spoken words over both temporal and visual cortices in adults with synesthesia (e.g. Aleman *et al.* 2001; Nunn *et al.* 2002; Paulesu *et al.* 1995). Faces also evoke more widespread activity whether it is measured by ERPs (e.g. de Haan *et al.* 2002) or positron-emission tomography (PET) (Tzourio-Mazoyer *et al.* 2002). At 2 months of age, PET activation in response to faces, compared to illumin-ated diodes, includes areas that are differentially activated in non-synesthetic adults, namely, an area within the right inferior temporal gyrus that is homologous to the adult fusiform face area (FFA) and bilateral activation of inferior occipital cortex. In the infants, unlike non-synesthetic adults, faces also activate the left inferior frontal and superior temporal gyri – areas that will become specialized for language. A similar lack of specificity occurs among the visual pathways: infants, unlike adults, are as sensitive to motion when it is defined by chromatic stimuli as by achromatic stimuli. The most straightforward explanation is that during infancy there is functional input from the parvocellular pathway to the magnocellular pathway, including the medial temporal area (V5), input that will later be retracted by pruning (see Dobkins, Chapter 17, this volume). Collectively, the neuroimaging and behavioral results indicate less specificity of cortical areas during early infancy, as would be expected if the transient connections are functional.

19.1.3 Neural plasticity: evidence from sensory deprivation

Specificity increases postnatally, such that by 36 months the ERP recorded over the visual cortex in response to spoken language has declined to the negligible adult level (Neville 1995). The increasing specificity is driven, at least in part, by the type of sensory input received by each cortical area. The most striking evidence comes from studies in which retinal axons in the infant ferret are induced to replace the normal auditory innervation of the medial geniculate nucleus (MGN). Neurons in the auditory cortex, to which the rewired MGN projects, become sensitive to visual orientation, direction of motion, and velocity and mediate *visual* percepts (reviewed in Sur and Leamey 2001). Mere removal of the normal input to the visual cortex in the cat – by enucleation of the eyes at birth – is sufficient to induce neurons in the primary visual cortex to respond to auditory stimuli (Yaka *et al.* 1999; reviewed in Bavelier and Neville 2002). These unusual responses are thought to reflect the stabilization of transient connections through Hebbian competition and/or the unmasking of silent inputs that would normally be ineffective or inhibited (reviewed in Bavelier and Neville 2002; Rauschecker 1995). An intriguing report on the fMRI responses of synesthetes with colored hearing suggest that such competitive interactions may explain what happens in the brain development of individuals who become synesthetic adults: seeing colors activated an area of the extrastriate visual cortex called V4 in both hemispheres in the control group, but only in the right hemisphere in the synesthetic group; their left V4 responded instead to hearing words – as if auditory input had captured the left V4 through Hebbian competition to the detriment of the normal visual input (Nunn *et al.* 2002).

Evidence from humans who are congenitally blind or congenitally deaf also indicates that transient connections between cortical areas that are present in early infancy are modified postnatally by the type of input received, such that input from the 'wrong' modality can stabilize the connections if the 'right' input is missing. Importantly for understanding neonatal perception, the stabilized connections influence perception. For example in adults blind from an early age, tactile input from reading Braille or discriminating complex tactile patterns (Gizewksi *et al.* 2003) activates the visual cortex, including much of extrastriate visual cortex, and, in most studies, the primary visual cortex as well, with the level of activation nearly as strong as that over the sensorimotor cortex (Burton *et al.* 2002; Melzer *et al.* 2001; Sadato *et al.* 2002; Sadato *et al.* 1998; but see Büchel *et al.* 1998). When the visual cortical activity is temporarily disrupted by transcranial magnetic stimulation (TMS), adults blind from an early age report that Braille dots do not make sense, that some are missing, and that they feel extraneous phantom dots; their error rates also increase significantly (Cohen *et al.* 1997; Cohen *et al.* 1999). TMS over other cortical areas has no effect. Additional evidence that the visual cortex play a functional role in the blind's ability to decode the tactile signals from Braille dots comes from the report of a congenitally blind woman who suddenly lost her ability to read Braille when she suffered a bilateral occipital stroke at age 63, despite intact peripheral tactile sensitivity (Hamilton *et al.* 2000).

The visual cortex of adults blind from an early age responds not only to tactile stimulation from Braille dots or non-linguistic tactile dot patterns but also to sound: in addition to activity over the normal auditory areas, spoken sentences cause fMRI activation of primary and extrastriate visual areas (Röder *et al.* 2002) and deviant sounds (an infrequent frequency or location or incongruous word) elicit ERPs (or magnetoencephalographic responses) over the visual cortex (Kujala *et al.* 1995; Leclerc *et al.* 2000; Liotti *et al.* 1998; Röder *et al.* 2000; Röder *et al.* 1999; see also Neville, Chapter 13, this volume). Overall, the responses to spoken language are more bilateral than in sighted adults, a pattern suggesting that transient connections for language in the right hemisphere that are present during infancy have not been pruned (Röder *et al.* 2000, 2002).

Similar effects have been documented for the congenitally deaf: in studies using PET and fMRI, presentation of moving dots, visual sign language, and vibrotactile stimulation have activated auditory cortical areas, including activation of primary auditory cortex. Those who learn sign language at an early age show activation of language areas both in the left hemisphere *and* in homologous areas in the right hemisphere (Finney *et al.* 2001; Levänen *et al.* 1998; Nishimura *et al.* 1999; Nishimura *et al.* 2000; see Neville 1995 for ERP evidence; see also Neville, Chapter 13, this volume). Combined with the evidence from the congenitally blind, these studies suggest that transient connections between cortical areas are shaped postnatally by the type of input received.

Recent studies of the congenitally blind suggest that normal development may involve more than the pruning of transient connections via Hebbian competition. In addition, some of the putatively transient connections may be preserved during normal development but functionally silenced, probably by inhibitory feedback from higher cortical areas, including the frontal cortex. Thus, there is robust V1 activation during tactile discrimination even in adults who became blind during early adolescence, long after transient connections would have been pruned by normal visual input (Cohen *et al.* 1999; Sadato *et al.* 2002). In higher levels of the visual cortical pathway, there is some activity during tactile discrimination even when the onset of blindness occurred in adulthood (e.g. Burton *et al.* 2002) and even when the individual has not learned Braille (Sadato *et al.* 2004) – as if tactile responses from visual cortical neurons have been released following the abolition of visual signals. Consistent with that interpretation is evidence that normally sighted adults improve in discriminating Braille characters after 5 days of training while blindfolded and begin to show fMRI activation of the visual cortex in response to tactile stimulation of the fingertips, activation which disappears within a day of sight being restored (Kauffman *et al.* 2002). Similarly, the increased activation in visual cortex when the congenitally blind process tactile or auditory stimuli contrasts with *decreased* activation in some of these areas in normally sighted subjects doing the same tasks (Laurienti *et al.* 2002; Sadato *et al.* 1998; Weeks *et al.* 2000). In adult monkeys, anatomical tracing studies have identified substantial inputs from the auditory cortex to parts of the primary visual cortex representing the peripheral visual field and, to a much smaller extent, the central visual field (Falchier *et al.* 2002; see Wallace *et al.* 2004, for evidence for intermixed auditory/visual, auditory/somatosensory, and visual/somatosensory neurons at borders between domains in the brain of the adult rat).

Thus, in addition to the pruning of many transient connections during development through Hebbian competition among inputs, some 'unusual' connections between sensory cortical areas may not be eliminated but rather come to be inhibited and retain the potential to be activated and influence perception. (See Thomas and Richardson, Chapter 14, this volume, for evidence of language representations in the right hemisphere that become inhibited during development and that can be released after left hemisphere damage.) There is evidence from cats for relatively slow development of the phasic inhibition that is efficacious in changing synaptic strength (reviewed in Berardi *et al.* 2003) and evidence that the human frontal cortex undergoes protracted development (e.g. Sowell *et al.* 1999). In the absence of effective inhibitory influences, the visual cortex of the young infant would be expected to respond to auditory input, as has been demonstrated with ERPs (Neville 1995), and to tactile input as well. Similar cross-modal influences would be expected on other sensory cortical areas.

Less effective inhibition than normal, possibly accompanied by abnormally little pruning, could underlie synesthetic perception in adults. The lack of inhibition would explain why adults with synesthesia are able to acquire new synesthetic connections as they learn the letters of the alphabet, new foods, or a new language (Mills *et al.* 2002; Ward and Simner 2003; Winawer and Witthoft 2004). Although these individuals report being synesthetic all their lives, it is obvious that a synesthetic color for the letter *a*, or the association between words like *phillip* and the taste *oranges not quite ripe* must be based on a connection learned after infancy. In fact, following lab testing, one synesthete reported acquiring synesthetic colors for symbols that were previously neutral and those new colors persisted for weeks (Mills *et al.* 2002). Thus, what is different about the brain of a synesthete may be cross-modal inter-actions in primary sensory cortical areas that are not suppressed and that allow automatic cross-modal connections to be formed readily. Because of transient con-nections and immature inhibitory mechanisms, the same is likely to be true of the normal infant. Below we demonstrate that the perceptual world of the newborn infant may resemble that of the adult synesthete and then demonstrate how these inter-sensory associations influence perception and language in non-synesthetic children and adults.

19.2 Synesthesia in human newborns

According to one form of our hypothesis, the perceptual world of newborn infants resembles that of synesthetic adults in whom stimulation of one sensory modality evokes a percept not only in that modality (such as hearing the presented sound or seeing the achromatic letter) but also a specific percept in a second modality (or along a second dimension, such as color). Thus, when the baby is habituated to an auditory stimulus, he/she simultaneously perceives and is habituated to the corresponding visual stimulus. According to this form of the hypothesis, a stimulus such as a tone induces more than one percept for the baby – one in the inducing modality (hearing the tone) and one or more in other modalities (e.g. seeing a red color or tasting a sweet substance induced by the tone). In the strongest form of the hypothesis, unlike synesthetic adults, the baby is unable to differentiate real from synesthetically induced percepts (e.g. seeing a red object versus 'seeing' a red-inducing tone; tasting sweet milk versus 'tasting' a sweet-inducing tone). Of course, because of cortical immaturity, none of the baby's percepts are as richly differentiated as those of adults: red will not look as saturated and sweet will not taste as complex.

19.2.1 A special neonatal form of synesthesia

Another form of the hypothesis is that, largely because of an immature cortex, the baby does not differentiate stimuli from different modalities, but rather responds to the total amount of energy, summed across all modalities. The baby is aware of changes in the pattern of energy—and recognizes some patterns that were experienced before—but is unaware of which modality produced the pattern. As a result, the baby will appear to detect cross-modal correspondences when stimuli from different modalities produce common patterns of energy change. When presented with a human voice, the baby may experience a pattern of changing oscillations, and recognize their similarity to patterns experienced before from the same voice. Although aware of the oscillations, the baby does not yet perceive them as sound *per se*. As a result the baby may not differentiate between the pattern of oscillations created by the voice and by a stimulus from another modality – a bouncing ball or rhythmic stroking that creates the same frequency of oscillations. As would be predicted from this form of the hypothesis, the newborn's visual preferences and sleeping patterns are related to total amount of stimulation, with equivalent effects of increasing stimulation within one modality and adding a moderate level of stimulation from another modality (e.g. Brackbill 1970, 1971, 1973, 1975; Gardner *et al.* 1986; Greenberg and Blue 1977; Lewkowicz 1991; Lewkowicz and Turkewitz 1981; Turkewitz *et al.* 1984).

This form of the hypothesis resembles Zelazo's (1996) claim that the young infant has only first-level minimal consciousness in which the baby perceives objects but is unaware of whether he or she is seeing or feeling them. Newborns' perception may be analogous to the mandatory fusion of information from different visual cues that occurs in adults' perception of depth (Hillis *et al.* 2002). Adults can perceive the slant of an object based on the changes in the texture on its surface or from binocular disparity and they perceive it more accurately when those cues are consistent. However, when those cues are made inconsistent in the laboratory, adults' pattern of errors indicates that they cannot access information from the separate visual cues: they appear to perceive slant but not the visual cues specifying that slant. In adults, no such mandatory fusion occurs between visual and tactile cues to depth: performance is better if the cues are consistent, but does not deteriorate if the cues are inconsistent, a pattern indicating fused cross-modal perception without loss of information from each modality. A type of mandatory fusion may occur across modalities for infants, such that they perceive an object, but lose access to information about the modality supplying the information. Unlike synesthetic adults who experience two percepts – one in the inducing modality and a second in the synesthetic modality – the baby may experience just one percept for a given pattern of energy change, a percept that is the same whether the pattern is heard, seen, or tasted. Alternatively, the baby may experience different percepts when the energy change is heard rather than seen or tasted but be less aware than adults of the modality of input and much more sensitive than adults to similarities across modalities in the pattern of energy change. That enhanced sensitivity will diminish as transient connections are pruned (or inhibited) and a more specialized cortex exerts more control. Thereafter the baby learns to interrelate differentiated senses, but remnants of the synesthesia persist in cross-modal influences (see Section 19.3.3).

19.3 **Predictions**

19.3.1 **U-shaped development of cross-modal integration**

The neonatal synesthesia hypothesis grew out of, and predicts, the paradoxical evidence of U-shaped development of cross-modal perception (see Johnson and Vecera 1996 for similar predictions). During the second half of the first year of life, infants demonstrate veridical cross-modal transfer (reviewed in Rose and Ruff 1987); after being habituated to an object in one modality (e.g. haptic) they recognize that object when it is presented in a second modality (e.g. visual). Recognition is demonstrated by their looking longer at a novel object when it is paired with the familiar object.

Consistent with the evidence from neuroimaging studies (see Section 19.1.2), several studies provide evidence of cross-modal integration near birth. For example 1-month-olds who saw a patch of white light repeatedly for 20 trials showed evidence of habituation to that light *and* to a sound at a level identified by adults as best matching the intensity of the light. When another group was shown a more intense light, evidence of habituation shifted to a more intense sound (Lewkowicz and Turkewitz 1980). Evidence of the young infant's ability to link auditory and visual information extends beyond intensity matching to synchrony – the synchrony of sound to the visual impact of a dropped object (Bahrick 2001) and the synchrony of a spoken passage to lip movements of a stranger's face (Pickens *et al.* 1994). There is also evidence of links between touch and vision: after being habituated to one of two shapes tactually, newborns look longer at a novel shape, at least if familiarized with their right hand (Streri and Gentaz 2004). Likewise, after a familiarization period during which they mouthed a hard pacifier, 1-month-olds preferred to look at a novel soft deforming pacifier (and *vice versa*) (Gibson and Walker 1984), and after tactual habituation to one object (e.g. a six-pointed star or a plain square), 2 to 3-month-olds demonstrated a similar preference to look at the novel shape (e.g. a six-pointed flower or a square with a central hole) (Streri 1987). Apparent imitation of tongue protrusion also suggests integration between vision (e.g. the sight of a model sticking out his/her tongue or of *any* looming visual stimulus (Jacobson 1979)) and proprioception (i.e. the feeling of sticking out the tongue or of making similar movements with *other* appendages (Gardner and Gardner 1970)). (Note that some interpretations of the phenomenon do not involve cross-modal integration, for example the baby 'reaches' with the tongue toward an interesting visual stimulus (Jones 1996)).

It is unlikely, however, that cross-modal integration near birth is mediated by the same mechanisms underlying cross-modal transfer later in the first year of life. Several studies report surprising failures at intermediate ages and evidence of the baby's subsequently learning to integrate differentiated senses. The most striking evidence comes from three studies that used the same procedure at different ages and found success at younger ages followed by failure later in infancy. For example Pickens *et al.* (1994) found that 5 to 6-month-old full-term infants looked randomly at the adult reciting the passage they were hearing when that was paired with an adult reciting a different passage, while younger (3 to 4-month-old) and older (7 to 8-month-old) infants looked preferentially at the adult reciting the matching passage. Similarly, unlike younger infants (Streri 1987), 4 to 5-month-olds fail to look differentially at two objects following tactile habituation to one of them (Streri and Pêcheux 1986). The frequency with which babies stick out their tongue in response to a visual model also decreases systematically after the first month (Abravanel and Sigafoos 1984; Fontaine 1984; Heimann *et al.* 1989), and gradually re-emerges later in infancy as the baby appears to learn the connection between movements of his/her own face and those of a visual model (e.g. Piaget 1952).

19.3.2 Lack of specificity in cross-modal connections

Details of the findings from behavioral studies of cross-modal correspondences during infancy also reveal the lack of specificity predicted by the hypothesis (see Johnson and Vecera 1996 for similar predictions). Molina and Jouen (2001) measured the frequency with which newborns squeezed smooth and granular objects and found that they squeezed smooth stimuli more frequently than granular stimuli. During the test period, the newborns were presented with the same tactile stimulus and a visual stimulus. The visual stimulus either matched (e.g. smooth–smooth) or did not match (e.g. smooth–granular) the tactile stimulus. Frequency of squeezing did not change when a matching visual stimulus was presented. However, frequency of squeezing increased when the granular tactile stimulus was accompanied by the smooth visual stimulus and decreased when the smooth tactile stimulus was accompanied by the granular visual stimulus. Molina and Jouen (2001) conclude that newborns are able 'to compare texture density information across modalities' (p. 123). An alternative interpretation is that these results indicate newborns' failure to differentiate the senses; newborns' handling of the tactile stimulus varies with the overall pattern of energy rather than the texture of the tactile stimulus *per se*. Thus, the smooth – smooth and granular – granular combinations simply supply reflections of the same pattern of energy experienced in the first part of the study. The combined pattern of energy evoked by the smooth tactile – granular visual combination represents an increase in energy over smooth tactile alone and evokes the same frequency of squeezing as a granular texture. The combination of granular texture with a smooth visual pattern represents a reduction in energy in the synesthetic compound and hence yields the increased frequency of squeezing evoked by a smooth texture alone. Indeed, similar changes in frequency of squeezing might be observed if the tactile stimulus was accompanied by a pulsating versus a continuous tone.

Newborns do show evidence of learning some cross-modal correspondences that are not arbitrary, that is, that occur naturally in the world based on properties like common location and synchronous change (*amodal* correspondences in Gibsonian terms). The reported successes are consistent with the neonatal synesthesia hypothesis because they occur in situations where the baby could be treating two inputs as the same based on similar patterns of neural firing in two sensory areas that are not yet differentiated. For example after being habituated to a single toy that was both colocated and synchronous with a sound, newborns' looking time increased (i.e. they showed a novelty response) when the toy was presented on the opposite side of the midline from the sound (Morrongiello *et al.* 1998). Furthermore, following habituation to two objects, only one of which was colocated with sound, newborns looked longer when the sound was located with the other toy. Likewise, Bahrick (2001) showed that 4-week-old infants are sensitive to synchrony: they dishabituate when they see an asynchronous auditory–visual event after being habituated to a synchronous event. By 7 weeks of age, infants also show sensitivity to composition – another amodal relationship. After being habituated to a single object that was synchronous with a single impact sound and to a cluster of objects that was synchronous with a multiple impact sound, 7-week-olds looked longer when the sound–object pairings were reversed.

According to the *intermodal redundancy* hypothesis (Bahrick and Lickliter 2000; Gogate *et al.* 2001), infants' sensitivity to amodal characteristics such as tempo/rhythm/composition is enhanced when that characteristic is presented bimodally (e.g. through vision and audition) and the stimulation is synchronous relative to when it is presented in only one modality: 5-month-olds discriminate a novel rhythm if the rhythm is presented bimodally, but not if is presented in only one modality (Bahrick and Lickliter 2000) and 3-month-olds discriminate a novel tempo, as long as the tempo is presented bimodally (Bahrick *et al.* 2002). Likewise, Bobwhite quail embryos require more than 2 hours of exposure to an individual maternal call to prefer that call over another if the exposure is unimodal; 1 hour of exposure is sufficient if the call is accompanied by a synchronously flashing light (Lickliter *et al.* 2002). The neonatal synesthesia hypothesis suggests one possible mechanism underlying the benefits of intermodal redundancy: sensitivity to amodal correspondences may be based on shared patterns of neural stimulation (e.g. timing, spatial representation, proportion of fibers activated (Cytowic 2002; Marks,1987)) across undifferentiated senses and facilitate the infant's learning of more arbitrary relations (e.g. shape-pitch (Bahrick 1994, 2001; Fernandez and Bahrick 1994; see also Reardon and

Bushnell 1988)). The later development of sensitivity to arbitrary correspondences also is consistent with the neonatal synesthesia hypothesis because such correspondences (e.g. pitch–shape) are unlikely to be mediated by the common patterns of neural firing across undifferentiated senses characteristic of early infancy. Whether neonatal synesthesia is a tenable explanation for the effects of intermodal redundancy could be evaluated by determining whether infants' sensitivity to redundancy decreases after birth and gradually re-emerges (see Section 19.3.1).

19.3.3 Synesthetic correspondences in children and adults

Although individuals with normal perception do not experience visual percepts in response to auditory stimuli, they provide evidence of correspondences that may be remnants of the initial wiring that was not pruned or is not completely inhibited. Some of these correspondences do not match statistical properties of the environment and hence could not be learned from a specific teaching signal. Adults' perceptual judgments are influenced by seemingly irrelevant input from other sensory modalities, with a pattern of correspondences similar to those reported by synesthetic adults. For example, adults report that odors presented in colored solutions smell stronger than odors presented in colorless solutions (Zellner and Kautz 1990) and the more saturated the color, the stronger the effect – regardless of whether or not the color is appropriate: red mint smells stronger than pink mint. Similarly, although the specific correspondences vary across synesthetes (e.g. whether 'p' is green or blue), there is general agreement that high-frequency sounds produce smaller, brighter percepts than low-frequency sounds (e.g. a higher pitched *p* is a brighter green or a brighter blue; Marks 1974; Marks *et al.* 1987). Non-synesthetic adults match higher-pitched tones with smaller, brighter lights (Marks *et al.* 1987) and the lighter of two gray squares (Marks 1974). They also match louder tones with brighter lights (Marks *et al.* 1987) and larger objects (Smith and Sera 1992). Likewise, non-synesthetic adults' discrimination of visual stimuli is influenced by auditory distracters: their performance is better if there is a synesthetic match (bright light/high pitch) than if the match is opposite (Marks 1987; Melara 1989). We contend that such cross modal influences in adults arise from remnants of the initial wiring of the nervous system that gave rise to neonatal synesthesia and not all of which was pruned (or inhibited).

Some of these cross-modal correspondences can be attributed to intensity matching. This explanation can be invoked whenever subjects are asked to match stimuli that vary along dimensions we describe in more-end terms (i.e. 'prothetic' dimensions), such as size, loudness, and brightness (Smith and Sera 1992; Stevens 1957): 'big', 'loud', and 'bright' are more than 'small', 'quiet', and 'dim', respectively. Thus a match of the bigger of two objects or the brighter of two lights to the louder of two sounds could be based on intensity matching. However, intensity matching cannot be invoked if one of the dimensions is 'metathetic' and cannot be described in more-end terms. Although 'loud' is more than 'quiet', and 'bright' is more than 'dim', adults do not describe either achromatic color (surface lightness) or pitch in more-end terms. Dark gray, for example, is not 'more than' light gray and 'treble tones' are not 'more than' bass tones. Thus, although adults match 'large' with 'bright' (Marks *et al.* 1987) they do not match 'large' with either dark or light gray (Smith and Sera 1992). Thus the correspondences that both synesthetes and non-synesthetic adults report between pitch and surface lightness and between pitch and size cannot be attributed to intensity matching. Some correspondences may be learned (e.g. larger objects do make louder sounds than smaller objects when dropped, and smaller musical instruments, such as a violin, do make higher frequency sounds than larger musical instruments, such as a cello). At least some of these learned correspondences are slow to develop. Unlike adults, 2-year-olds do not match size and loudness; it is not until 3 years of age that children match the larger of two objects with the louder sound (Smith and Sera 1992).

Other metathetic correspondences are not learned through experience of the cross-modal correspondence in the environment. It is hard to imagine a learned basis for the correspondence between surface lightness and pitch—lighter objects do not make higher-pitched sounds in the real world. We hypothesize that these correspondences are remnants of cross-modal neural connections that are present at birth and that influence the development of perception and language even in adults and children without synesthesia. Consequently, some cross-modal correspondences (e.g. pitch/ brightness) may be evident in young children before they acquire sophisticated language (e.g. metaphors), providing the environment with which they interact supports normal sensory and cognitive development. That environment, however, does not supply a specific teaching signal about the pitch/brightness correspondence.

We have tested correspondences between pitch and both size and surface lightness in young children (Mondloch and Maurer 2004). We showed 30- to 36-month-olds a movie of two balls bouncing in synchrony with each other and with a central sound that varied in frequency. The balls differed in size and/or surface lightness. Each child was asked to point to the ball that was 'making' the sound. Based on correspondences reported both by synesthetic (Marks 1974) and non-synesthetic adults (Marks *et al.* 1987), we predicted that young children would associate the lighter and/or smaller ball with the higher-pitched sound. In Experiment 1, the balls differed in both size and surface lightness. Eleven of the 12 children said that the smaller, white ball was making the higher-pitched sound or that the larger, gray ball was making the lower-pitched sound ($p < 0.01$). In Experiment 2 both balls were the same size, but they differed in surface lightness. Every child ($n = 12$) said that the white ball was making the higher-pitched sound. In Experiment 3 both balls were white, but they differed in size. Only nine of the 12 children matched the smaller ball with the higher-pitched sound ($p = 0.07$). We tested an additional 12 children; 10 of these children matched in the expected direction ($p < 0.05$).

Thus, when a 'child-friendly' procedure is used, children as young as 30 to 36 months tend to matcher higher-pitched sounds with smaller objects – perhaps as a result of learning. However, this correspondence may be weaker than that between pitch and surface lightness, a result that is consistent with results from a different procedure showing that 9-year-olds matched higher pitch with a brighter, but not a smaller light (Marks *et al.* 1987). Because both pitch and surface lightness are metathetic, the pitch–surface lightness correspondence shown by the toddlers cannot be attributed to intensity matching. Furthermore, pitch and surface lightness are not reliably related in the real world, and so this correspondence cannot be attributed to learning. Rather, our results support the hypothesis that some cross-modal correspondences in non-synesthetic children and adults may be remnants of the neural mechanisms underlying neonatal perception.

19.4 **The evolution and development of language**

Language – both its adult form and its development – provides an excellent example of how early intermodal correspondences influence and are influenced by a complex system. Evidence of natural correspondences in non-synesthetic adults abounds in human language – as evidenced by the preponderance of cross-modal metaphors, such as 'soft light' and 'loud colors'. Systematic investigations of the role of language in cross-modal correspondences have demonstrated that words denoting loudness, brightness, pitch, and surface lightness act in much the same way as sensory stimuli that vary on these dimensions. Adults rate sunlight as louder than moonlight and violins as brighter than thunder (Marks 1974, 1982, 1987). The use of metaphors also parallels synesthesia in that metaphors in which a visual noun is modified by an auditory word (e.g. 'a loud tie') are much more common both in English and German literature than are metaphors in which an auditory noun is modified by a visual word (e.g. 'bright thunder') (Day 1996). Language can influence perception in ways predicted by synesthesia: in perceptual classification tasks, reaction times are reduced not only when the to-be-classified stimuli (e.g. tones that vary in pitch) are accompanied by congruent stimuli (e.g. higher pitch with brighter light) but also when accompanied by congruent words (e.g. SHARP rather than DULL (Martino and Marks 1999; Walker and Smith 1984)).

Ramachandran and Hubbard (2001) suggest that synesthetic correspondences not only facilitate the production and understanding of cross-modal metaphors, but may have 'boot-strapped' the very evolution of language. Adults rate angular nonsense figures as more aggressive, more tense, stronger, and noisier than rounded shapes (Marks 1996); they also are more likely to label angular shapes 'takete' or 'kiki' and rounded shapes 'maluma' or 'bouba' – perhaps because of a correspondence between the visual percept of the shape, the phonemic inflections, and movement of the tongue that are produced when one says the words, and the appearance of the speaker's lips when someone else says the words, all of which result from the same cortical connections among contiguous cortical areas that underlie synesthesia (Kohler 1947; Ramachandran and Hubbard 2001). For example movements made to produce words conveying large objects frequently involve widening the vocal tract and lips (e.g. LARGE, HUGE) whereas words describing small objects often involve narrowing the vocal tract and lips (e.g. TEENY, TINY) (Nuckolls 1999; Ramachandran and Hubbard 2001; see also Tanz 1971). This tendency may be the result of natural constraints on sensory and motor maps, which are in turn linked in non-arbitrary ways to an object's appearance. The role of natural correspondences in the evolution of language is evident in the finding that speakers of one language (English) performed above chance when asked whether words in a novel language (Huambisa) were the name of a bird or a fish (Berlin 1994). Likewise, Hebrew speaking adults match Chinese characters to their corresponding Hebrew words with an accuracy that is above chance (Koriat and Levy 1979) and judge both Hindi and Japanese orthographic characters that represented vowel sounds such as 'i' as smaller in size than those characters that represented vowels such as 'a' or 'u' (Koriat and Levy 1977).

In a recent study with children aged 30 to 33 months, we demonstrated that these same correspondences bias children's assignment of nonsense labels to novel objects (Pathman 2004). Children (n = 20) were given a hand-puppet 'Mr Mouse' that interacted with the experimenter's 'Mr Bear', who they were told could not see very well and needed his friend, Mr Mouse, to help him find some things. On four control trials, children were asked to find one of two objects (e.g. the green rabbit with a striped shirt) where the correct word–object mapping was objective. On four experimental trials the child was asked to make a selection between an angular and a rounded shape, with the shapes based on the known form preferences of neurons in area V4, one of the visual cortical areas that is active during colored grapheme synesthesia (Kobatake and Tanaka 1994; Gallant *et al.* 1996; Nunn *et al.* 2002). On each trial the experimenter provided the child with two labels and then asked the child to make a choice: '*I have to look for a friend. He's a yellow dog named Pluto. But I think he is hiding.*' The experimenter then took out a box with two shapes cut out. '*He is hiding inside one of these holes. I'll give you a clue to help you find him. One of these holes is called Bouba and the other is called K[ej]ki. I think he's hiding in the K[ej]ki. Which hole should I look in?*' On each experimental trial, one nonsense word was comprised of voiceless consonants (e.g. 'k') and non-rounded vowels (e.g. [ej]); the other nonsense word was comprised of a voiced consonant (e.g. 'm') and a rounded vowel (e.g. 'o') (see Table 19.1).

All children met the inclusion criterion on control trials: correct on at least three of the four trials. Consistent with Ramachandran and Hubbard's hypothesis, like adults (n = 20), children reliably matched words with voiceless consonants and non-rounded vowels with angular shapes and words with voiced consonants and rounded vowels with rounded shapes (p <0.001). This pattern was consistent across exemplars

Table 19.1 Word pairings used to test toddlers and adults

(1) bamu and k[ ]t[ej]	(pronounced 'baa-moo' and 'kut-eh')
(2) bouba and k[ej]ki	(pronounced 'boo-baa' and 'keh-key')
(3) goga and tit[ej]	(pronounced 'go-ga' and 'tee-teh')
(4) mabuma and tikete	(pronounced 'ma-boo-ma' and 'te-kee-tee')

in adults and consistent across all but one exemplar (goga and tit[ej]) in children. Thus natural correspondences between visual percepts, phonemic inflections, and movement of the tongue on the palate appear to influence language very early in its development.

The relationship between natural correspondences and language development is one of mutual influence: natural correspondences bias language development (see above), but vocabulary growth also influences perceptual matching. Smith and Sera (1992) asked preschoolers (2 to 5-year-olds) and undergraduate students to match stimuli varying in size, loudness, or surface lightness to a perceptual or verbal model that represented an extreme value on one of the other dimensions. For example they were asked which of two mice, one large and one small, was most like a dark grey model. Two-year-olds matched the larger mouse with the dark grey model, a match that is consistent with adult synesthetes who match lower-pitched sounds with both larger and darker lights (Marks 1974). In contrast, they did not match 'loud' with 'big', a correspondence for which the environment does provide a specific training signal: when asked which of two mice – one emitting a quiet noise, one a louder noise – was most like a large mouse or the word 'BIG', 2-year-olds performed randomly. Increased vocabulary comprehension altered the pattern of matching. Unlike 2-year-olds, 3-year-olds showed comprehension of the adjectives big, little, loud, and quiet; they also matched 'loud' with 'big'. Three-year-olds also showed comprehension of the words underlying the polar dimension of surface lightness – dark and light. In this case, increased comprehension produced perceptual disorganization: like adults, some of whom matched dark with big while others matched dark with small, 3-year-olds no longer matched the larger of two mice with the dark grey model.

19.5 Summary

Our current knowledge of infant behavior, cortical plasticity, cross-modal matching, language, and synesthesia suggests that connections – either direct (e.g. Ramachandran and Hubbard 2001) or indirect (e.g. Cytowic 2002) – between brain regions typically associated with distinct modalities may underlie each of these phenomena. According to the neonatal synesthesia model, newborns fail to differentiate input from different senses – because of connections between cortical areas that are pruned or inhibited later in development. Because of more widespread cortical activation, newborns nevertheless sometimes behave as if they are able to relate input between distinct modalities. The remnants of this unspecialized cortex are most clearly evident in synesthetic adults who experience, for example, visual percepts in response to sound, and in adults with abnormal sensory experiences, such as the congenitally blind or deaf who have unusual patterns of activation in cortical areas deprived of typical input. However, remnants also are observed in normal children and adults, remnants that are similar to the connections present in synesthetic adults and that are most likely between contiguous brain areas. That young children match lower pitched sounds with darker gray objects (Mondloch and Maurer 2004), words containing voiced consonants and rounded vowels with smoother shapes (Pathman 2004), but not larger objects with louder sounds (Smith and Sera 1992), is consistent with the hypothesis that some correspondences observed in non-synesthetic adults are not the result of specific training by the environment. Rather, they may reflect the preservation of neural connections between sensory areas that were present at birth and that were not pruned: those connections continue to influence perception (e.g. cross-modal matching) and come to influence language, as demonstrated in biases evident in early language development, and in the prevalence of cross-modal metaphors (e.g. 'loud colors') in everyday speech.

Acknowledgement

The preparation of this paper was supported by a grant from the National Sciences and Engineering Research Council (Canada) to Daphne Maurer.

References

Abravanel E and Sigafoos AD (1984). Exploring the presence of imitation during early infancy. *Child Development*, **55**, 381–392.

Aleman A, Rutten GJ, Sitskoorn MM, Dautzenberg G and Ramsey NF (2001). Activation of striate cortex in the absence of visual stimulation: an fMRI study of synaesthesia. *Neuroreport*, **12**, 2827–2830.

Bahrick L (1994). The development of infants' sensitivity to arbitrary intermodal relations. *Ecological Psychology*, **6**, 111–123.

Bahrick L (2001). Increasing specificity in perceptual development: Infants' detection of nested levels of multimodal stimulation. *Journal of Experimental Child Psychology*, **79**, 253–270.

Bahrick LE, Flom R and Lickliter R (2002). Intersensory redundancy facilitates discrimination of tempo in 3-month-old infants. *Developmental Psychobiology*, **41**, 352–363.

Bahrick LE and Lickliter R (2000). Intersensory redundancy guides attentional selectivity and perceptual learning in infancy. *Developmental Psychology*, **36**, 190–201.

Baron-Cohen S, Harrison J, Goldstein L and Wyke M (1993). Coloured speech perception: Is synaesthesia what happens when modularity breaks down? *Perception*, **22**, 419–426.

Bavelier D and Neville H (2002). Cross-modal plasticity: Where and How? *Nature Reviews Neuroscience*, **3**, 443–452.

Berardi N, Pizzorusso T, Ratto G and Maffei L (2003). Molecular basis of plasticity in the visual cortex. *Trends in Neurosciences*, **26**, 369–378.

Berlin B (1994). Evidence for pervasive synaesthetic sound symbolism in ethnozoological nomenclature. In: L Hinton, J Nichols and J Ohala, eds. *Sound symbolism*, pp. 76–93. New York: Cambridge University Press.

Brackbill Y (1970). Acoustic variation and arousal level in infants. *Psychophysiology*, 6, 517–525.

Brackbill Y (1971). Cumulative effects of continuous stimulation on arousal level in infants. *Child Development*, 42, 17–26.

Brackbill Y (1973). Continuous stimulation and arousal level: Stability of the effect over time. *Child Development*, 44, 43–46.

Brackbill Y (1975). Continuous stimulation and arousal level in infancy: Effects of stimulus intensity and stress. *Child Development*, 46, 364–369.

Büchel C, Price C, Frackowiak R and Friston K (1998). Different activation patterns in the visual cortex of late and congenitally blind subject. *Brain*, 121, 409–411.

Burton H, Snyder A, Conturo T, Akbudak E, Ollinger J and Raichle M (2002). Adaptive changes in early and late blind: a fMRI study of Braille reading. *Journal of Neurophysiology*, 87, 589–607.

Cohen L, Weeks R, Sadato N, Celnik P, Ishii, K and Hallett M (1999). Period of susceptibility for cross-modal plasticity in the blind. *Annals of Neurology*, 45, 451–460.

Cohen LG, Celnik P, Pascual-Leone A *et al.* (1997). Functional relevance of cross-modal plasticity in blind humans. *Nature*, 389, 180–183.

Cytowic RE (1989). *Synesthesia: A union of the senses.* New York: Springer-Verlag.

Cytowic RE (2002). *Synesthesia: A union of the senses,* 2nd edn. New York: MIT Press.

Day S (1996). Synaesthesia and synaesthetic metaphor. *Psyche: An Interdisciplinary Journal of Research on Consciousness*, 2. http: //psyche.cs.monash.edu.au/v2/psyche-2-32-day.html.

de Haan M, Pascalis O and Johnson M (2002). Specialization of neural mechanisms underlying face recognition in human infants. *Journal of Cognitive Neuroscience*, 14, 199–209.

DeHay C, Bullier J and Kennedy H (1984). Transient projections from the fronto-parietal and temporal cortex to areas 17, 18, and 19 in the kitten. *Experimental Brain Research*, 57, 208–212.

DeHay C, Kennedy H and Bullier J (1988). Characterization of transient cortical projections from auditory, somatosensory and motor cortices to visual areas 17, 18, and 19 in the kitten. *Journal of Comparative Neurology*, 230, 576–592.

Dixon M, Smilek D, Cudahy C and Merikle P (2000). Five plus two equals yellow. *Science*, 406, 365.

Elias L, Saucier D, Hardie C and Sarty G (2003). Dissociating semantic and perceptual components of synaesthesia: behavioural and functional neuroanatomical investigations. *Cognitive Brain Research*, 16, 232–237.

Falchier A, Clavagnier S, Barone P and Kennedy H (2002). Anatomical evidence of multimodal integration in primate striate cortex. *Journal of Neuroscience*, 22, 5749–5759.

Fernandez M and Bahrick LE (1994). Infants' sensitivity to arbitrary object-odor pairings. *Infant Behavior and Development*, 21, 745–760.

Finney E, Fine I and Dobkins K (2001). Visual stimuli activate auditory cortex in the deaf. *Nature Neuroscience*, 4, 1171–1173.

Fontaine R (1984). Imitative skills between birth and six months. *Infant Behavior and Development*, 7, 323–333.

Frost B (1984). Axonal growth and target selection during development: retinal projections to the ventrobasal complex and other 'nonvisual' structures in neonatal Syrian hamsters. *Journal of Comparative Neurology*, 230, 576–592.

Gallant J, Connor C, Rakshit S, Lewis J, Van Essen D (1996). Neural responses to polar, hyberbolic, and Cartesian gratings in Area V4 of the macaque monkey. *Journal of Neurophysiology*, 76, 2718–2739.

Gardner J and Gardner H (1970). A note on selective imitation by a six-week old human infant. *Child Development*, 41, 1209–1213.

Gardner J, Lewkowicz D, Rose S and Karmel B (1986). Effects of visual and auditory stimulation on subsequent visual preferences in neonates. *International Journal of Behavioural Development*, 9, 251–263.

Gibson EJ and Walker AS (1984). Development of knowledge of visual-tactual affordances of substance. *Child Development*, 55, 453–460.

Gizewski E, Gasser T, de Greiff A, Boehm A and Forsting M (2003). Cross-modal plasticity for sensory and motor activation patterns in blind subjects. *NeuroImage*, 10, 968–975.

Gogate LJ, Walker-Andrews AS and Bahrick LE (2001). The intersensory origins of word comprehension: an ecological-dynamic systems view. *Developmental Science*, 4, 1–37.

Gray J, Williams S, Nunn J and Baron-Cohen S (1997). Possible implications of synaesthesia for the hard question of consciousness. In: S Baron-Cohen and J Harrison, eds. *Synaesthesia: Classic and contemporary readings, pp.* 173–181. Blackwell: Oxford.

Greenberg DJ and Blue SZ (1977). The visual preference technique in infancy: Effect of number of stimuli presented upon experimental outcome. *Child Development*, 48, 131–137.

Grossenbacher P and Lovelace G (2001). Mechanisms of synaesthesia: cognitive and physiological constraints. *Trends in Cognitive Sciences*, 5, 36–41.

Hamilton R, Keenan J, Catala M and Pascual-Leone A (2000). Alexia for braille following bilateral occipital stroke in an early blind woman. *Neuroreport*, 11, 237–240.

Heimann M, Nelson KE and Schaller J (1989). Neonatal imitation of tongue protrusion and mouth opening: Methodological aspects and evidence of early individual differences. *Scandinavian Journal of Psychology*, 30, 90–101.

Hillis JM, Ernst MO, Banks MS and Landy MS (2002). Combining sensory information: mandatory fusion within, but not between, senses. *Science*, 298, 1627–1630.

Huttenlocher P (1994). Synaptogenesis in human cerebral cortex. In: G Dawson and K Fischer, eds. *Human behaviour and the developing brain*, pp. 137–152. New York: Guildford.

Jacobson SW (1979). Matching behavior in the young infant. *Child Development*, 50, 425–430.

Johnson M (1997). *Developmental cognitive neuroscience*. Oxford: Blackwell.

Johnson M and Vecera S (1996). Cortical differentiation and neurocognitive development: the parcellation conjecture. *Behavioural Processes*, 36, 195–212.

Jones S (1996). Imitation or exploration? Young infants' matching of adults' oral gestures. *Child Development*, 67, 1952–1969.

Kauffman T, Théoret H and Pascual-Leone A (2002). Braille character discrimination in blindfolded human subjects. *NeuroReport*, 13, 571–574.

Kennedy H, Batardiere A, Dehay C and Barone P (1997). Synaesthesia: implications for developmental neurobiology. In: S Baron-Cohen and J Harrison, eds. *Synaesthesia: Classic and contemporary readings*, pp. 243–256. Oxford: Blackwell.

Kobatake E and Tanaka K (1994). Neuronal selectivities to complex object features in the ventral visual pathway of the macaque cerebral cortex. *Journal of Neurophysiology*, 71, 856–867.

KohlerW (1947). *Gestalt psychology*, 2nd edn. New York: Liveright.

Koriat A and Levy I (1977). The symbolic implications of vowels and of their orthographic representations in two natural languages. *Journal of Psycholinguistic Research*, 6, 93–103.

Koriat A and Levy I (1979). Figural symbolism in Chinese ideographs. *Journal of Psycholinguistic Research*, 8, 353–365.

Kujala T, Huotilainen M, Sinkkonen J, *et al.* (1995). Visual cortex activation in blind humans during sound discrimination. *Neuroscience Letters*, 183, 143–146.

Laeng B, Svartdal F and Oelmann H (2004). Does color synaesthesia pose a paradox for early-selection theories of attention? *Psychological Science*, 15, 277–281.

Laurienti P, Burdette J, Wallace M, Yen YF, Field A and Stein B (2002). Deactivation of sensory-specific cortex by cross-modal stimuli. *Journal of Cognitive Neuroscience*, 14, 420–429.

Leclerc C, Saint-Amour D, Lavoie M, Lassonde M and Lepore F(2000). Brain functional reorganization in early blind humans revealed by auditory event-related potentials. *Neuroreport*, 11, 545–550.

Levänen S, Jousmäaki V and Hari R (1998). Vibration-induced auditory-cortex activation in a congenitally deaf adult. *Current Biology*, 8, 869–872.

Lewkowicz DJ (1991). Development of intersensory functions in human infancy: auditory/visual interactions. In: MJ Weiss and PR Zelazo, eds. *Newborn attention*, pp. 308–338. Norwood, NJ: Ablex.

Lewkowicz D and Turkewitz G (1980). Cross-modal equivalence in early infancy: auditory-visual intensity matching. *Developmental Psychology*, 16, 597–607.

Lewkowicz DJ and Turkewitz G (1981). Intersensory interaction in newborns: Modification of visual preferences following exposure to sound. *Child Development*, 52, 827–832.

Lickliter R, Bahrick LE, Honeycutt H (2002). Intersensory redundancy facilitates prenatal perceptual learning in Bobwhite Quail (*Colinus virginianus*) embryos. *Developmental Psychology*, 38, 15–23.

Liotti M, Ryder K and Woldoff M (1998). Auditory attention in the congenitally blind: where, when, and what gets recognized. *Neuroreport*, 9, 1007–1012.

Marks LE (1974). On associations of light and sound: The mediation of brightness, pitch, and loudness. *American Journal of Psychology*, 87, 173–188.

Marks LE (1982). Bright sneezes and dark coughs, loud sunlight and soft moonlight. *Journal of Experimental Psychology: Human Perception and Performance*, 8, 177–193.

Marks LE (1987). Auditory-visual interactions in speeded discrimination. *Journal of Experimental Psychology: Human Perception and Performance*, 13, 384–394.

Marks LE (1996). On perceptual metaphors. *Metaphor and Symbolic Activity*, 11, 39–66.

Marks LE, Hammeal R and Bornstein M (1987). Perceiving similarity and comprehending metaphor. *Monographs of the Society for Research in Child Development*, 52, (Serial No. 215).

Martino G and Marks LE (1999). Perceptual and linguistic interactions in speeded classification: tests of the semantic coding hypothesis. *Perception*, 28, 903–923.

Mattingley J, Rich A, Yelland G and Bradshaw J (2001). Unconscious priming eliminates automatic binding of colour and alphanumeric form in synaesthesia. *Nature*, 410, 580–582.

Maurer D (1993). Neonatal synaesthesia: implications for the processing of speech and faces. In: B Boysson-Bardies, S de Schonen, P Jusczyk, P McNeilage and J Morton, eds. *Developmental neurocognition: speech and face processing in the first year of life.* pp. 109–124. Dordrecht: Kluwer.

Maurer D and Maurer C (1988). *The world of the newborn.* New York: Basic Books.

Maurer D and Mondloch C (1996). Synaesthesia: A stage of normal infancy? In S Masin, ed. *Proceedings of the 12th meeting of the International Society for Psychophysics, pp.* 107–112. Padua.

Maurer D and Mondloch C (2004). Neonatal synaesthesia: A re-evaluation. In: L Robertson and N Sagiv, eds. *Synesthesia: Perspectives from cognitive neuroscience*, pp. 193–213. Oxford University Press, New York.

Melara RD (1989). Dimensional interactions between color and pitch. *Journal of Experimental Psychology: Human Perception and Performance*, 15, 69–79.

Melzer P, Morgan V, Pickens D, Price R, Wall R and Ebner F (2001). Cortical activation during Braille reading is influenced by early visual experience in subjects with severe visual disability: a correlational fMRI study. *Human Brain Mapping*, 87, 589–607.

Mills C, Viguers M, Edelson S, Thomas A, Simon-Dack S and Innis J (2002). The color of two alphabets for a multilingual synaesthete. *Perception*, 31, 1371–1394.

Molina M and Jouen F (2001). Modulation of manual activity by vision in human newborns. *Development Psychobiology*, 38, 123–132.

Mondloch CJ and Maurer D (2004). Do small white balls squeak? Pitch-object correspondences in young children. *Cognitive Affective and Behavioral Neuroscience*, 4, 133–136.

Morrongiello B, Fenwick KD and Chance G (1998). Cross-modal learning in newborn infants: Inferences about properties of auditory-visual events. *Infant Behaviour and Development*, 21, 543–554

Myles K, Dixon M, Smilek D and Merikle P (2003). Seeing double: The role of meaning in alphanumeric-colour synaesthesia. *Brain and Cognition*, 53, 342–345.

Neville H (1995). Developmental specificity in neurocognitive development in humans. In: M Gazzaniga, ed. *The cognitive neurosciences*, pp. 219–231. Cambridge, MA: Bradford.

Nishimura H, Doi K, Iwuki T, Hashikawa K, Nishimura T and Kubo T (2000). Sign language activated the auditory cortex of a congenitally deaf subject: revealed by positron emission tomography. In: C Kim, S Chang and D Lim (Eds). *Updates in cochlear implantation. Advances in Otorhinolaryngology*, 57, 60–62.

Nishimura H, Hashikawa K, Doi K *et al.* (1999). Sign language 'heard' in the auditory cortex. *Nature*, 367, 116.

Nuckolls J (1999). The case for sound symbolism. *Annual Reviews of Anthropology*, 28, 225–252.

Nunn JA, Gregory LJ, Brammer M *et al.* (2002). Functional magnetic resonance imaging of synaesthesia: activation of V4/V8 by spoken words. *Nature Neuroscience*, 5, 371–375.

Palmeri T, Blake R, Marois R, Flanery M and Whetsell W (2002). The perceptual reality of synaesthetic colors. *Proceedings of the National Academy of Science*, 99, 4127–4131.

Pathman T (2004). *Sound/shape correspondences in children and adults.* Unpublished undergraduate thesis. McMaster University.

Paulesu E, Harrison J, Baron-Cohen S *et al.* (1995). The physiology of coloured-hearing: a PET activation study of colour-word synaesthesia. *Brain*, 118, 661–676.

Piaget J (1952). *The origins of intelligence in children.* New York: International University Press.

Pickens J, Field T, Nawrocki T, Martinez A, Soutollo D and Gonzalez J (1994). Full-term and preterm infants' perception of face-voice synchrony. *Infant Behavior and Development*, 17, 447–455.

Ramachandran VS and Hubbard EM (2001). Synaesthesia – A window into perception, thought and language. *Journal of Consciousness Studies*, 8, 3–34.

Rauschecker J (1995). Compensatory plasticity and sensory substitution in the cerebral cortex. *Trends in Neuroscience*, 18, 36–43.

Reardon P and Bushnell E W (1988). Infants' sensitivity to arbitrary pairings of color and taste. *Infant Behavior and Development*, 11, 245–250.

Rich A and Mattingley J (2003). The effects of stimulus competition and voluntary attention on colour-graphemic synaesthesia. *NeuroReport*, 14, 1793–1798.

Röder B, Rösler F and Neville H (2000). Event-related potentials during auditory language processing in congenitally blind and sighted people. *Neuropsychologia*, 38, 1482–1502.

Röder B, Sock O, Bien S, Neville H and Rösler F (2002). Speech processing activates visual cortex in congenitally blind humans. *European Journal of Neuroscience*, 16, 930–936.

Röder B, Teder-Sälejärvi W, Sterr A, Rösler F, Hillyard S and Neville H (1999). Improved auditory spatial tuning in blind humans. *Nature*, 400, 162–166.

Rose S and Ruff H (1987). Cross-modal abilities in human infants. In: J Osofsky, ed. *Handbook of infant development, pp.* 318–362. New York: Wiley.

Sadato N, Okado ,T, Honda M and Yonekura Y (2002). Critical period for cross-modal plasticity in blind humans: A functional MRI study. *NeuroImage*, 16, 389–400.

Sadato N, Okado T, Kubota K and Yonekura Y (2004). Tactile discrimination activates the visual cortex of the recently blind naïve to Braille: a functional magnetic resonance imaging study in humans. *Neuroscience Letters*, 359, 49–52.

Sadato N, Pascual-Leone A, Grafman J, Deiber M-P, Ibañez, V and Hallett M (1998). Neural networks for Braille reading by the blind. *Brain*, 121, 1213–1229.

Schiltz K, Trocha K, Wieringa BM, Emrich HM, Johannes S and Münte T (1999). Neurophysiological aspects of synaesthetic experience. *Journal of Neuropsychiatry and Clinical Neurosciences*, 11, 58–65.

Smilek D, Dixon MJ, Cudahy C. and Merikle PM (2001). Synesthetic photisms influence visual perception. *Journal of Cognitive Neuroscience*. 13, 930–936.

Smilek D, Dixon M and Merikle P (2003). Synaesthetic photisms guide attention. *Brain and Cognition*, 53, 364–367.

Smith LB and Sera MD (1992). A developmental analysis of the polar structure of dimensions. *Cognitive Psychology*, 24, 99–142.

Sowell E, Thompson P, Holmes C, Jernigan T and Toga A (1999). *in vivo* evidence for post-adolescent brain maturation in frontal and striatal regions. *Nature Neuroscience*, 2, 859–861.

Stevens SS (1957). On the psychophysical law. *Psychological Review*, 64, 153–181.

Streri A (1987). Tactile discrimination of shape and intermodal transfer in 2- to 3-month-old infants. *British Journal of Developmental Psychology*, 5, 213–220.

Streri A and Gentaz E (2004). Cross-modal recognition of shape from hand to eyes and handedness in human newborns. *Neuropsychologia*, 42, 1365–1369.

Streri A and Pêcheux MG (1986). Vision-to-touch and touch-to-vision transfer of form in 5-month-old infants. *British Journal of Developmental Psychology*, 4, 161–167.

Sur M and Leamey C (2001). Development and plasticity of cortical areas and networks. *Nature Reviews Neuroscience*, 2, 251–262.

Tanz C (1971). Sound symbolism in words relating to proximity and distance. *Language and Speech*, 14, 266–276.

Turkewitz G, Gardner J and Lewkowicz DJ (1984). Sensory/perceptual functioning during early infancy: The implications of a quantitative basis for responding. In: G Greenberg and E Tobach, eds. *Behavioral evolution and integrative levels*, pp.167–195. Hillsdale, NJ: Erlbaum.

Tzourio-Mazoyer N, de Schonen S, Crivello F, Reutter B, Aujard Y and Mazoyer B (2002). Neural correlates of woman face processing by 2-month-old infants. *NeuroImage*, 15, 454–461.

Walker P and Smith S (1984). Stroop interference based on the synaesthetic qualities of auditory pitch. *Perception*, **13**, 75–81.

Wallace M, Ramachandran R and Stein B (2004). A revised view of sensory cortical parcellation. *Proceedings of the National Academy of Sciences*, **101**, 2167–2172.

Ward J and Simner J (2003). Lexical-gustatory synaesthesia: linguistic and conceptual factors. *Cognition*, **89**, 237–261.

Weeks R, Horwitz B, Aziz-Sultan A, *et al*. (2000). A positron emission tomographic study of auditory localization in the congenitally blind. *Journal of Neuroscience*, **20**, 2664–2672.

Winawer J and Witthoft N (2004). Anticolors: Early visual mechanisms in color-grapheme synaesthesia.. Poster presented at the meeting of the Cognitive Neuroscience Society, San Francisco.

Wolff P, Matsumiya Y, Abrohms IF, van Velzer C and Lombroso CT (1974). The effect of white noise on the somatosensory evoked responses in sleeping newborn infants. *Electroencephalography and Clinical Neurophysiology*, **37**, 269–274.

Yaka R, Yinon U and Wollberg Z (1999). Auditory activation of cortical visual areas in cats after early visual deprivation. *European Journal of Neuroscience*, **11**, 1301–1312.

Zelazo PD (1996). Towards a characterization of minimal consciousness. *New Ideas in Psychology*, **14**, 63–80.

Zellner DA and Kautz MA (1990). Color affects perceived odor intensity. *Journal of Experimental Psychology: Human Perception and Performance*, **16**, 391–397.

Chapter 20

The development of human conceptual representations: A case study

Susan Carey and Barbara W. Sarnecka

Abstract

This chapter discusses a uniquely human learning mechanism – conceptual-role bootstrapping – whereby external symbolic systems (especially language) enable the creation of new, internal representational resources. The process is described in general terms and is also illustrated with a specific case: the acquisition of concepts for positive integers (one, two, three, etc.). First, the core knowledge systems that have numerical content are described and it is shown that none of these systems alone is capable of representing the positive integers. Next, children's typical pattern of acquisition of the positive integers is described. Finally, conceptual-role bootstrapping is argued to be the best explanation for the attested pattern of acquisition and several types of evidence for this argument are reviewed.

20.1 The problem

Human adults can think thoughts formulated over hundreds of thousands of concepts, concepts such as *dog, banana, water, quark, George W. Bush, sidewalk, fourteen, pi*.... Non-human animals represent only the tiniest fraction of the human repertoire. The problem, then, is accounting for the difference. Where do human concepts come from?

20.1.1 Some terminology

Concepts are mental representations with conceptual content, as opposed to perceptual or sensory content. Mental representations are characterized by their extensions (the entities in the world they pick out) and by their computational role (the inferences they support, the rules of combination that yield new representations, and so on).

20.1.2 **Overview of the argument**

Logically, accounting for the adult human conceptual repertoire has two components: a characterization of innate representational resources and a characterization of the mechanisms that underlie developmental change. Here we are concerned only with learning mechanisms, although maturationally driven processes undoubtedly also play a role in early development.

With respect to innate conceptual representations, we endorse the core knowledge hypothesis. With respect to the mechanisms that underlie developmental change, we focus on bootstrapping processes – processes whereby the new representational resources created are more than the sum of their parts. They transcend, in some qualitative way, the representational resources that were their input. Thus, we take on Fodor's challenge to cognitive science – accounting for the construction of concepts more powerful than those the infant begins with.

20.1.3 **Core knowledge**

Along with Baillargeon *et al.* (Chapter 7, this volume), Carey and Spelke (1994), Leslie (1994), and many others, we endorse the existence of core knowledge. That is, we agree with the empirical claim that there are systems of representations with the following properties: (1) the real-world entities in the domains of core knowledge systems are identified by innate input analyzers; (2) acquisition of knowledge of these entities is supported, at least partially, by innate, domain specific, learning mechanisms; (3) core knowledge systems are often evolutionarily ancient; and (4) core knowledge systems operate throughout the whole life span, even in adulthood.

The ethological literature provides many examples of core knowledge systems in non-human animals. Lorenzian imprinting, for example, is an innately-given learning mechanism that enables geese and many other birds to identify conspecifics. Mark Johnson and colleagues showed that identifying conspecifics is so important that evolution has provided two separate mechanisms for it. In addition to Lorenzian imprinting, chickens are also endowed with an innate schematic representation of what a chicken looks like. The two distinct entity identification systems (one based on movement, one based on a static schema of a bird-shaped entity) support the chick's learning to identify its mother (or the entity it should stay close to). The two input analyzers have distinct neural substrates, with distinct critical periods and a complex interaction during development (Johnson and Morton 1991).

Another famous example of a non-human core knowledge system is the learning mechanism through which Indigo buntings learn to identify the North Star and then use it for celestial navigation for the rest of their lives. In a series of elegant studies culminating in planetarium experiments with arbitrary arrangements of the stars, Emlen and colleagues (Emlen 1975; Emlen *et al.*1976) showed that nestlings analyze the rotation of the night sky, extracting the center of rotation as north. The representation that is the output of this domain-specific learning process then guides direction of flight when the bird's hormones indicate that it's time to fly north (in the spring) or south (in the fall).

We note these examples from ethology for two reasons. First, they illustrate what is meant by core knowledge. Second, they show that there is nothing theoretically problematic about the core-knowledge hypothesis. It would be astounding if human beings were the only animals without core knowledge systems. Indeed, there is good empirical evidence for human core knowledge of objects, causality, number, and intentional agency (Carey and Spelke 1994; Gergely *et al.* 1995; Johnson 2003; Leslie 1994; Woodward 1998; Woodward *et al.* 2001, see also Baillargeon *et al.* Chapter 7, this volume).

20.1.4 Fodor's challenge to cognitive science

Although we endorse the core-knowledge hypothesis, we also hold that human beings have the capacity to create representational resources that transcend core knowledge. That is, we believe that human beings can create systems of representation that allow for concepts not expressible by the core systems. This is precisely what Fodor (1975) famously argued was impossible. Fodor's argument was simple. All known learning mechanisms, he claimed, are forms of hypothesis testing and one can't test a hypothesis if one cannot represent it. Thus, such mechanisms cannot be responsible for the creation of new representational resources.

In the famous Chomsky/Piaget debate (Piatelli-Palmarini 1980), Piaget offered an equally simple counter-argument to Fodor's. All that is needed is a counter-example – if new representational capacities *do* arise in the course of development (either on individual or historical time scales) then this must be *possible*. Piaget's examples were from the history of mathematics. Early in the cultural history of mathematics, the concept of number included only the positive integers; later development expanded the concept to include zero, negative integers, rational and irrational numbers, and so on. Before the construction of the rationals, thoughts involving *14/15* could not be entertained. Similarly, before the construction of the irrationals, propositions about $\sqrt{2}$ or π could not be represented.

Thus, Fodor's challenge first requires that we describe successive conceptual systems, spelling out what is qualitatively new in the second. But we can also address the explanatory part of Fodor's challenge. It is not the case that no known learning mechanisms create new representational resources. Learning in some kinds of connectionist architectures yields emergent representations (see Shultz, Chapter 3, this volume) and the learning mechanisms that discover Bayes net causal representations (see Gopnik and Glymour, Chapter 15, this volume) also are capable of positing previously unrepresented variables. Additionally, bootstrapping processes of many different kinds have been described (Block 1986; Nersessian 1992; Quine 1960). Here we characterize a type of bootstrapping process, called *conceptual-role bootstrapping*, that we believe to be uniquely human – one that underlies the creation of new representational resources.

20.2 **The case study**

We fill out the picture sketched above through a particular case study: The acquisition of positive-integer concepts (i.e. 1, 2, 3, and so forth.). We describe two systems of core knowledge with numerical content: (1) analog magnitude representations of number – Dehaene's 'number sense' (Dehaene 1997); and (2) a system of parallel individuation of small sets of individuals. When the individuals are objects, this system of representation encompasses the object-indexing and short-term memory mechanisms of mid-level vision – Pylyshyn's FINSTs (Pylyshyn 1994; Pylyshyn and Storm 1998) or Triesman's object files (Treisman 1998) (See Feigenson *et al.* 2004, for a much more complete account of these two core systems.) We then show that although these systems of representation have numerical content, they do not have the power to represent the positive integers and we characterize the bootstrapping process through which, at around age $3\frac{1}{2}$, children create a new representational system with the power to do so.

A system of representation can express the positive integers if it represents the cardinal values of sets and also represents the successor relation among adjacent cardinal values. The numeral lists of natural language provide such a system, as long as numerals are deployed in a counting routine that assigns one numeral to each individual in a set and in which the last numeral reached in a count corresponds to the cardinal value of the set. In other words, counting routines must respect the 'cardinal principal' described by Gelman and Gallistel (1978). In this paper, we use 'integer' or 'positive integer' to refer to such representations. But is important to note that representations can have numerical content and still fall short of being representations of the integers. Any representations of discrete quantity that are sensitive to numerical identity of individuals (sameness in the sense of *the same individual*) *and* over which computations with numerical content are defined (e.g. numerical comparison, addition, subtraction), have numerical *content* – even if these representations capture cardinal values only roughly or even not at all. In this paper, we characterize representational systems in terms of both their format and the computations they enter into, thus specifying the type of numerical content they have.

20.2.1 **Core system 1: analog magnitude representations**

Core system 1 is described by Stanislas Dehaene in his delightful book *The Number Sense* (Dehaene 1997). Analog magnitudes are representations of the approximate cardinal values of large sets of individuals (at least up through several hundred). The representational tokens are neural magnitudes monotonically related to the number of individuals in a set (linearly on some formulations; logarithmically on others). Because the symbols themselves get bigger as the represented entity gets bigger, they are called *analog* magnitudes. Figure 20.1 provides a sample analog magnitude representation of number, where the symbol is a line and the dimension

Fig. 20.1 Analog magnitude representations of 1, 2, 3, 7, and 8; line length represents number.

varying with set size is length. Mental analog magnitude number representations support numerical computations of many types, including comparison, addition, and subtraction (Barth *et al.* 2003; Barth *et al.* in press; Dehaene 1997).

Number is not the only dimension of experience represented by analog magnitudes – other examples include brightness, loudness, and temporal duration. In each case, as the physical magnitudes get bigger, it becomes increasingly harder to discriminate values that are the same absolute distance apart. You can see in Fig. 20.1 that is harder to tell the symbols for seven and eight apart than it is to tell the symbols for two and three apart. In other words, the discriminability of any two values is a function of their ratio, as described by Weber's law.

To demonstrate Weber's law for yourself, tap out as fast as you can without counting (you can prevent yourself from counting by thinking the word 'the' with each tap) the following numbers of taps: 4, 24, 7 and 27. If you did this several times, you'd find your mean numbers of taps to be 4, 24, 7 and 27, with the range of variation very tight around 4 (usually 4, occasionally 3 or 5) and very great around 27 (from 14 to 40 taps, for example). Although the absolute difference separating 4 and 7 is the same as that separating 24 and 27, the distributions of taps around 4 and 7 will overlap much less than the distributions around 24 and 27. This happens because your ability to discriminate values depends not on their absolute numerical difference, but on their ratio, as characterized by Weber's law. This discriminability function is one of the psychophysical signatures of analog magnitude representations.

Space precludes our reviewing the elegant evidence for analog magnitude representations of number in non-human animals and human infants, but let us give just one example. Fei Xu and Elizabeth Spelke showed infants arrays of dots, one array at a time. Total array size, total volume of dots, density of dots, and so on were controlled in these studies, such that the only possible basis for the infants' discrimination was numeric. Seven-month-old infants were habituated either to arrays of 8 or 16 dots. After habituation they were presented with new displays, alternating between arrays of the same number of dots to which they had been habituated and arrays of the other number. Xu and Spelke found that the infants recovered interest to the new number

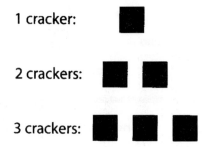

Fig. 20.2 Representation of sets of 1, 2, and 3 crackers. One symbol for each individual, no summary symbol for cardinal value of sets.

and also found evidence for Weber's law. The infants could discriminate 8 from 16 and 16 from 32 (both ratios of 1:2), but not 8 from 12 or 16 from 24 (both ratios of 2:3) (Xu and Spelke 2000).

Lipton and Spelke (2003) reported parallel findings when the individuals were streams of discrete sounds; the Weber fraction threshold of success at 7 months was 1:2, just as for dots in the Xu and Spelke studies. In addition, by 9 months of age, the ratio at which infants succeed is 2:3 in both modalities. Finally, Wood and Spelke (in press) extended these findings to streams of puppet jumps.

In sum, infants and animals (Dehaene 1997; Gallistel 1989) form numerical analog magnitude representations of fairly large sets of quite different types of individuals, but these representations are only approximate. Analog magnitude representations of number fall short of representing the positive integers. In this system one cannot represent *exactly* 15, or 15 *as opposed to* 14. Nonetheless, analog magnitude representations clearly have numerical content: they refer to cardinal values of sets discrete individuals and number-relevant computations are defined over them.

20.2.2 **Core system 2: parallel individuation of small sets**

A second system of representation with numerical content works very differently. Infants and non-human primates have the capacity to form mental representations of individuals and to create mental models of ongoing events in which each individual is represented by a single representational token. Figure 20.2 shows how, in this system, sets of one, two, or three crackers might be represented. In this figure, the format of representation of each cracker is iconic. However, the representations could certainly have other formats. What is important is that there is one representational token for each individual cracker in the set. Number is implicitly represented; the representational tokens in the model stand in one-to-one correspondence with the objects in the world.

To get a feel for the evidence that infants do indeed deploy such models, consider the following experiment. Ten- to 14-month-old infants are shown a box they can

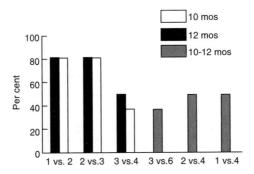

Fig. 20.3 Performance in Infant Ordinal Choice task: percentage of infants who approach the box with more crackers. n = 16 infants per condition, one trial each; 10-month-old group on 3 vs. 4 comparison n = 12 infants.

reach into, but cannot see into. If you show an infant three objects being placed (one at a time or all at once) into this box and then allow her to reach in to retrieve them one at a time, she shows by her pattern of reaching that she expects to find exactly three objects there. That is, after she has reached in and retrieved one object, if you have surreptitiously removed the other two, she searches persistently for more. Similarly, if she has retrieved two objects, but you have absconded with the third, she searches for the remaining one. So far, this is just another demonstration that infants represent number. However, an exploration of the limits on infants' performance of this task implicates a different system of representation from the analog magnitude system sketched above. In the box-reach task, performance breaks down at four objects. If the infant sees four objects being placed into the box and is allowed to retrieve two of them, or even just one of them, she does not keep reaching for the remaining objects. Remember that in the analog magnitude system of representation, success at numerical comparison is a function of the ratios of the numbers being compared and that infants' system of representation can handle sets of objects at least as big as 32. But in this reaching task, infants succeed at ratios of 2:1 and 3:2, but fail at 4:2 and even 4:1 (Feigenson and Carey 2003, in press). This result makes sense in terms of the limits on parallel attention and short-term memory that characterize mid-level, object-based attention (see Scholl 2001 for review).

A second paradigm provides convergent evidence of the breakdown of performance at set sizes above three (Feigenson *et al.* 2002a; Hauser *et al.* 2000). Ten- and 12-month-olds watch as crackers are placed, one at a time, into each of two tall, opaque boxes. For example three crackers are placed into the leftmost box and two crackers into the rightmost. Infants are then are allowed to crawl toward one of the boxes. As Fig. 20.3 shows, when the choices are 1 vs. 2 or 2 vs. 3 crackers, infants overwhelmingly approach the box with more crackers. But when the choices are 3 vs. 6, 2 vs. 4 or even 1 vs. 4, performance falls to chance. The comparison of 2 vs. 3 and 1 vs. 4 is particularly informative. Both events involve a total of five cracker placements, so they take equally long overall. In terms of Weber ratios 1 vs. 4 is clearly easier to discriminate than 2 vs. 3. But children succeed on the latter and fail at the former. Again, as soon as either set exceeds three items, children fail.

To recap: When representing small sets, infants reveal the set-size limit characteristic of parallel individuation rather than the Weber ratio signature of analogue magnitude representations. This is the best evidence that the parallel individuation system depicted in Fig. 20.2 underlies performance on the box-reach task and cracker-choice task (and indeed, performance on most infant tasks involving small sets, including Wynn's infant addition and subtraction studies and simple habituation studies; see Feigenson *et al.* 2004 for a review). See Carey and Xu (2001) for other evidence supporting the identification of infant representations of small sets of objects with the object-files of mid-level, attentional parallel individuation.

Unlike the system of analog magnitude number representations, the core knowledge system implicated in these studies is not dedicated to representing the cardinal values of sets. Rather, it represents each individual in the set separately. *Individual* is a deeply numerical concept; infants make use of a wide variety of information in establishing whether a given individual is the same one or a different one from another (*numerical identity*). The computations carried out over these representations include summing the total spatial extent of the individuals in the set (e.g. computing total volume, surface area, contour) and comparing sets on the basis of these magnitudes (Clearfield and Mix 1999; Feigenson *et al.* 2002a; Feigenson *et al.* 2002b). But models of small sets of individuals can also be compared on the basis of one–one correspondence, establishing numerical equality or inequality, numerical more or less (Feigenson, in press; Feigenson and Carey 2003). Thus, although not a dedicated number representation system, Core System 2 has rich numerical content.

20.2.3 Detour: infants seem to lack the singular/plural distinction

In both the cracker-choice and box-reach paradigms, infants failed at 1 vs. 4 comparisons. These are striking failures. If a 12-month old infant sees one cracker placed in a box and four crackers placed in another box, the infant chooses at random between the boxes. If a 12- or 14-month-old infant sees four objects placed in a box into which the infant can reach but cannot see, she is satisfied after retrieving only one of them. We offer these data to support the conclusion that when tracking individuals, infants do not represent numbers beyond 3. But to succeed at these 1 vs. 4 tasks, infants need not represent *exactly 4* or even *approximately 4*; they need only represent the set of 4 as a plurality and hence as more than 1. In other words, all they need is a singular/plural distinction. But they appear to have none.

We found these data so puzzling that we extended the box-reach task to older infants. Infants were either shown three or four balls, first displayed on top of the box and then placed inside it. All balls but one were surreptitiously removed, so when the infants reached in, they found only one ball. At all ages tested, when three balls had been placed in the box, infants persistently searched for further balls after retrieving just 1. But at 12, 14, 18, and 20 months of age, infants who had seen four balls placed into the box stopped searching after retrieving four. Their behavior on these trials was the same as when they saw just one ball placed in the box and had retrieved it. It is not until 22 months of age that infants succeed, as a group, on this non-verbal singular/plural task (Barner *et al.* 2005).

Perhaps it should not be so surprising that non-verbal infants do not represent the singular/plural distinction. Neither of the core systems with numerical content includes a computationally relevant break between single individuals, on the one hand, and sets of more than one individual, on the other. The analog magnitude system distinguishes among all sets whose ratio exceeds the Weber threshold of discriminability. It does not treat 8 and 16 as equivalent to each other, in contrast to 1. Similarly, the system of parallel individuation tracks each individual in sets of 1, 2, or 3 and does not lump 2 and 3 together as principally different from 1.

Interestingly, 20-month-old English and French learners also have not yet learned the linguistic markers of the singular/plural distinction, whereas 24-month-old French and English speaking children have (Kouider *et al.* 2005, in press; Wood *et al.* 2005). Ongoing work in our laboratory shows that mastery of the singular/plural distinction in English is correlated with success on the non-verbal 1 vs. 4 comparison task (Barner *et al.* 2005). Furthermore, preliminary work from Kouider's lab in Paris shows that French-learning infants both master singular/plural morphology in French several months earlier than do English-learning children, and also succeed at the non-verbal 1 vs. 4 comparison task several months earlier.

These data hint at another source of representational resources relevant to the acquisition of number concepts – the semantic distinctions that underlie number marking in natural-language syntax and in natural-language quantifier systems.

20.2.4 A third developmental source of number representations: natural-language semantics

Linguists such as Chierchia (1998) and Link (1983) have provided unified treatments of the linguistically universal quantificational resources that underlie the singular/plural distinction, the count/mass distinction, quantification in classifier languages and quantifiers themselves ('none,' 'some,' 'all,' 'each,' etc.). These treatments rest on the semilattice of *sets* that can be constructed from a universe of *individuals* (the atoms, At, of Fig. 20.4.) These linguistically universal devices require an explicit conceptual distinction between individuals and sets; having such a distinction available for hypothesis testing might help the child construct a representation of integers.

Notice that in the two core systems with numerical content, there are no representational tokens with 'individual' or 'set' as their content, although there are attentional mechanisms that pick out sets of individuals for which one token for each individual is created (parallel individuation) or for which a summary representation of approximate

$$\{a, b, c, d, \ldots\}$$

$$\{a, b, c\} \ \{a, b, d\} \ \{b, c, d\} \ \{a, c, d\} \ \ldots$$

$$\{a, b\} \ \{a, c\} \ \{a, d\} \ \{b, c\} \ \{b, d\} \ \{c, d\} \ \ldots$$

$$a \quad b \quad c \quad d \quad \ldots \ = At$$

Fig. 20.4 The semilattice structure underlying natural language quantifier semantics (Chierchia 1998).

numerosity is computed (analog magnitudes). The third system of representation, explicit natural language quantification, is also on-line before age 2, at least in languages with singular/plural distinctions.

20.2.5 Transcending core knowledge

We have described three systems of mental representations with numerical content that are available to children before age 2. The analog magnitude system and the system of parallel individuation of small sets meet the criteria for core knowledge: they are evolutionarily ancient, supported by domain-specific input analyzers, have content that goes beyond sensorimotor primitives, support domain-specific learning, and continue to articulate our mental models of the world throughout the life span. On some views of language acquisition, which we share, acquisition of cross-linguistically universal quantificational devices is also likely to be supported by innate domain-specific constraints within a language-acquisition device, but for present purposes, all that matters is that these quantificational devices are available at the outset of the learning process that constructs the positive integers. Importantly, none of the three systems alone has the power to represent the positive integers.

The system of parallel individuation has no symbols for integers – no summary symbols for the cardinal values of sets. And it has a set-size limit of 3 or 4. A person cannot think a thought formulated over the concept *7* using this system of representation alone. The analog magnitude system comes closer to a representation of the positive integers. At least it contains representational tokens for the approximate cardinal values of sets. However, it too cannot represent exactly *7*, or exactly *15*, or exactly *32*... Furthermore, because quantities are compared via their ratios, analog magnitude representations of number obscure the successor relation. The difference between 2 and 3 is not experienced as is the difference between 8 and 9 (indeed, the latter cannot be discriminated at all). Finally, the number-marking systems of natural language distinguish singular (1), dual (2), sometimes triple or paucal (3 or few) and have quantifiers like 'many' or 'some' that pick out relative numerical magnitudes. However, barring numeral lists themselves, natural language quantification includes no representations of exact cardinal values above 3.

20.2.6 **Interim conclusion**

We must be very careful when we interpret a researcher's claim that prelinguistic infants represent number. This is true, but which numbers can they represent? Not rational or real numbers and not even the positive integers. When we specify the representational systems available to infants, characterizing the format and content of the symbols therein and the computations they support, we can be precise about what numerical content they include. This cashes out what we mean when we say prelinguistic infants represent number.

We have met the descriptive part of Fodor's challenge. Children in cultures where counting is salient create a representation of the positive integers by age $3\frac{1}{2}$ to 4 (Fuson 1988, 1992; Wynn 1992). We have characterized how representations of positive integers transcend (qualitatively) the three systems of representation that are universally available to human beings and that are evident in children under 2 years of age.

The claim that integer representations transcend core knowledge has implications for development, both over historical time and in the individual child. Whereas the representations given by core knowledge systems should be easily and universally accessible, representations of positive integers should be relatively difficult to create. And indeed, whether we consider cultures evolving number concepts in historical time, or individual children acquiring the number concepts available in their culture, the process is a slow one.

Gordon (2004) has described an isolated Amazonian culture – the Piraha – in which the adults demonstrate (on non-verbal tasks) normal analog magnitude and parallel individuation representations. The Piraha language also has quantifiers (including 'one,' 'two' and 'many.') However, the particular history of this people is such that they have not developed or imported, as most of the world's cultures now have, a numeral list. And Gordon shows that Piraha adults fail at a wide variety of non-verbal tasks requiring the mental representation of exact numbers above 3 or 4, although they do perfectly well on tasks tapping analog magnitude representations of sets above 4 (see Pica *et al.* 2004, for convergent evidence from the Munduruku, another isolated Amazonian culture). The Piraha case demonstrates the importance of cultural input (i.e. a culturally transmitted system of external symbols, like numeral words) in individuals' development of positive-integer concepts. Similarly, Hurford (1987) reviews ethnographic studies of partial systems of number representation that historically precede (in any given language) the construction of a full, base-system, numeral-list representation of the positive integers.

Turning to individual development, many psychologists (e.g. Fuson 1992; Schaeffer *et al.* 1974; Siegler and Robinson 1982; Wynn 1992) have noted how difficult it is for toddlers to come to understand the numerical meaning of counting. Of course, this difficulty is to be expected on the view that core knowledge lacks the resources to represent the positive integers.

20.3 Wynn's difficulty-of-learning argument

If concepts for the exact numbers 1, 2, 3, 4, and 5 were available from infancy, then identifying the words to label those concepts should be a relatively simple matter. Consider the challenge that you, the reader, would face if you suddenly found yourself in a foreign country where you didn't speak the language. You know what numerals are – you just wouldn't know the local words for them. But if you saw people counting (at a market, for example) you would be able to figure out the numeral words quite easily. Let's say you heard and saw people counting, using the sequence *ash, naz, gim, batul, thropp*. Then, you noticed people asking for *gim* this or *gim* that and getting three things in return. You would conclude that *gim* meant 3. And once you knew that, it would take you no time at all to match 1, 2, 4 and 5 with *ash, naz, batul* and *thropp*.

If representations of the positive integers were given by any one core knowledge system, (e.g. via a preverbal, mental list of numeral-like symbols, Gelman *et al.* 1978) we should expect children to learn the numerals of their native language the same way that adults learn the numerals of a foreign language. That is to say, once one numeral is learned, the other numerals should follow almost immediately. But children's numeral learning is actually quite a lengthy process (e.g. Fluck and Henderson 1996; Fuson 1992; Siegler and Robinson 1982; Wynn 1990, 1992). As Karen Wynn has argued, the pattern of numeral learning that children actually show suggests that they are doing something much more difficult than simply labeling pre-existing number concepts. They seem actually to be constructing new number representations as they go along.

By about age 3, most children can recite the numeral sequence (count out loud) up to 'ten' (Fuson 1988; Miller *et al.* 1995). They can also 'count' sets of 5 or 6 objects – that is, they recite the number sequence while pointing to each object in turn (Fuson 1988; Sarnecka and Gelman 2004; Wynn 1990, 1992). However, children this age don't understand that the last numeral used in counting reveals the number of items in the whole set; that is they have not yet mastered Gelman and Gallistel's (1978) 'cardinal principle.'

Several observations show that children count without understanding how counting represents number. For example if you ask a 2- or 3-year-old to count (or watch you count) a row of 5 apples ('one, two, three, four, five') and then ask her 'So, how many apples are there?' she will probably respond by recounting. It is virtually impossible to induce a young child to produce a cardinal response after a count, but if you succeed, she responds by guessing ('Um ... two! No, wait – three!')

Clearly, 3-year-olds do not connect counting and numeral meanings in the same way that adults do. But it's not that young preschoolers know nothing about numerals. They do use numerals as quantifiers, although without regard to the actual set sizes each numeral denotes. (The second author's 2-year-old son once demanded more M and M's by saying 'I like some *plenty*! I like some *too much*! I like some *lot*! I like some

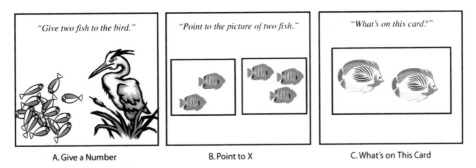

Fig. 20.5 Tasks measuring exact-numeral knowledge.

eight!') So the question is: what exactly do preschoolers know about numerals? To answer that question, Wynn and others came up with a variety of ways to probe numeral knowledge. Three such tasks are described below.

The *Give-a-Number task* (Schaeffer *et al.* 1974; Wynn 1990, 1992) – in this task, children are given a pile of small objects (e.g. 15 toy fish) and are asked to give a certain number of them to a puppet. For example, the child might be asked 'Can you give *two* fish to the bird' (Fig. 20.5, Part A). The dependent measure is how many items the child actually gives.

The *Point-to-X task* (Wynn 1992) – in this task the child is shown a pair of pictures (e.g. a picture of 2 fish next to a picture of 3 fish). The child is asked to choose one. For example 'Point to the picture of *two* fish.' (Fig. 20.5, Part B). The dependent measure is which picture the child chooses.

The *What's-on-This-Card task* (Gelman 1993; LeCorre 2003) – in this task, the child is shown a picture of one or more objects and asked simply 'What's on this card?' Children typically respond with just the object name at first (e.g. 'fish'). So feedback is given on the first trial, modeling a numeral response ('That's right! It's *two fish!*'). On subsequent trials, no feedback is given, but most children give numeral responses, as modeled. The dependent measure is what numeral the child says (Fig. 20.5, Part C).

20.3.1 The pattern of numeral learning

Data from the tasks above have uncovered a systematic pattern to numeral learning – a pattern that has now been replicated in many studies and with child speakers of Japanese, Mandarin, and Russian as well as English (LeCorre *et al.* 2003; Li *et al.* 2003; Sarnecka *et al.* 2005).

The pattern is as follows. The child begins as a no-numeral-knower, meaning that she makes no distinctions among numerals. On the Give-a-Number task, she gives either 1 item for every request or a handful for every request. On the Point-to-X task, she points at random; on the What's-on-This-Card task, she usually produces no numerals, answering with nouns alone. The no-numeral-knower level is followed by a series of intermediate levels – the 'one'-knower, 'two'-knower *and* 'three'-knower levels; children at any of these levels are called 'subset-knowers,' for they know the exact meaning of only a subset of the numerals in their count list. We illustrate the pattern of responses of subset-knowers by describing a 'two'-knower. On the Give-a-Number task, a 'two'-knower gives the correct number asked for if it is 'one' or 'two,' but for all other numerals grabs and handful that is more than 2. On the Point-to-X task, a 'two'-knower is correct for any pair of items that includes a set of 1 or 2 (i.e. presented with a set of 2 and 5, chooses correctly when asked for 'two' or 'five', but is random on every pair involving sets greater than 2, e.g. chooses randomly when asked for the set of 'three' between cards with 3 and 6). On the What's-on-this-Card task, a 'two'-knower says 'one' for cards with 1, 'two' for cards with 2 and then uses larger numerals randomly (often 'three' for all sets) for cards containing 3 through 10 items. One of the striking findings in this body of literature is the within-child consistency on these three tasks – diagnosis as a 'two'-knower on the basis of Give-a-Number predicts knower-level on the other two tasks, in spite of the widely different perform-ance demands of the tasks (LeCorre *et al.* 2005, in press; Wynn 1992). These studies also show that subset-knowers use counting differently from children who understand how counting represents number. They do not spontaneously count to solve the Give-a-Number or What's-on-this-Card tasks and when they have given a wrong number on Give-a-Number and are asked to fix it, they usually leave the set unchanged or fix it in the wrong direction.

Between $3\frac{1}{2}$ and $4\frac{1}{2}$ years of age a qualitative change occurs: the child becomes a *high-numeral-knower*. She solves all three tasks in Fig. 20.5 for all numerals in her count list, using counting to do so for large numbers. If counting to check reveals she has made a mistake on Give-a-Number, she adjusts the set correctly, without recount-ing. She has figured out how counting represents number; she has induced the cardinality principle.

20.3.2 Interim conclusions

The data on subset-knowers supports our conclusions from the description of the two core systems of numerical content. The pattern of slow, piece-by-piece numeral learning and the qualitative differences between subset-knowers and high-numeral-knowers are evidence for discontinuity in number-concept development. If integer representations were part of core knowledge, then numeral learning would be a simple mapping problem, as it is for adults learning the numerals of a foreign language. Instead, the data reviewed above indicate that children learn the numeral list and as soon as they are 'one'-knowers, they understand that numerals encode something having to do with number (e.g. they use numerals other than 'one' as plural markers, as quantifiers meaning 'some.') They then take months to figure out what 'two' means. Why should this be so, given that children can certainly *perceive* the difference between 1, 2, and 3 items even before they learn to talk? We submit that numeral learning takes so long because learning numerals requires children to construct *summary* representations of exact numbers – single representational tokens with content different from any in a core knowledge system.

We turn now to the second part of Fodor's challenge to cognitive science – sketching a learning process that might underlie the creation of a representational resource with more power than its input.

20.4 A bootstrapping proposal

To explain how children construct the positive integers, we appeal to 'conceptual-role bootstrapping.' Many psychologists, historians, and philosophers of science have used the metaphor of bootstrapping to describe learning processes whose endpoints transcend in some qualitative way their starting points. The choice of metaphor may seem puzzling, because pulling oneself up by one's own bootstrap is clearly impossible, whereas the learning we seek to explain actually occurs and thus is certainly possible. We keep the term because of its historical credentials and because it seeks to explain cases of learning that many have argued *are* impossible.

We use the term 'bootstrapping' in its original sense from the literature in the philosophy of science, not as it has come to be used in the language acquisition literature. 'Semantic bootstrapping' and 'syntactic bootstrapping' are processes hypothesized to help the child construct a mapping between innately specified syntactic and semantic categories. Conceptual-role bootstrapping is a process that underlies the construction of new representational resources. In the bootstrapping process we propose, a set of symbols (and the relations among them) are first learned in terms of each other. At this point, the symbols have meaning in relation to the other symbols in the set, but are not yet interpreted (or at most are only partially interpreted) in terms of antecedent mental representations. Once the symbols and the relations among them are learned, they serve as placeholders, waiting to be filled in with richer and richer meanings. These richer meanings are connections between the placeholder symbols and representations in other parts of the mind (for example the outputs of core knowledge systems). These connections are gradually made through analogical reasoning, inductive leaps, and inference to best explanation.

The resulting system has greater power than core knowledge systems for two reasons. First, part of a symbol's meaning comes from its place in the set – its relation to the other symbols with which it was learned. The symbols thus have content they could not have if each were learned on its own, defined completely in terms of meanings from the core systems. Second, bootstrapping allows representations from previously distinct representational systems to be combined and integrated. This allows for the formation of representations that could not be produced by any one of the original systems alone. Thus, bootstrapping is not just a way of acquiring knowledge, it is a way of acquiring new representational resources. To use a computer analogy, bootstrapping is to some other kinds of learning as software installation is to data entry. It doesn't just add more information, it enables new kinds of thinking.

20.4.1 Bootstrapping exact-number concepts

How does bootstrapping explain the pattern of numeral learning described above? First, let's consider what children have to learn:

- The numeral list (i.e. the words and their order).
- The meaning of each numeral ('three' = 3, 'seven' = 7, etc.).
- How the numeral list represents exact numbers (for any word 'X' on the list whose cardinal meaning N is known, the next word on the list has a cardinal meaning $N+1$).

Next, let's consider some of the knowledge systems that children have available at the outset of learning:

- The parallel individuation system (tracks up to three individuals at the same time).
- Analog magnitude representations of number (yields large, approximate numbers).
- The quantificational semantics of natural language (providing the distinctions of individual vs. set, discrete vs. continuous quantification, singular vs. plural, etc.).
- The capacity for explicit symbols – the capacity to create lexical entries and to search for meanings.
- The capacity to represent serial order, including ordered lists of lexical items (e.g. to learn nonsense strings like 'eenie, meenie, minie, mo').

Now let's consider how a bootstrapping process might occur. Our proposal draws on many others (e.g. Bloom 2000; Bloom and Wynn 1997; Fuson 1992; Hurford 1987; Klahr and Wallace 1976; Spelke and Tsivkin 2001).

20.4.1.1 Numerals in a list

In the earliest phase of the learning process, two things happen independently. On the one hand, children learn a meaningless string of numeral words ('one, two, three...') just as they learn other meaningless strings ('eenie, meenie, minie, mo...'). At this point, the counting routine may be associated with particular situations (e.g. with pointing, with reading particular books that involve counting, etc.), but the only meaning the numerals have are the relations that hold between them within the list (e.g. 'five' is just the word after 'four' and before 'six'). This list – meaningless except for its internal order – is the placeholder structure.

20.4.1.2 Numerals in sentences

Separately, children encounter the numerals as quantifiers – appearing in sentences without the other members of the list ('You can take *two* cookies. No, *two* is plenty... I said *two*! Hey! Come back here!'). Eventually, children learn the exact meanings of some of them (first 'one,' then 'two,' then 'three,' in the pattern described above.) From the very start, children's knowledge of grammar constrains the hypotheses they entertain about what the numerals might mean. Imagine yourself at age 2, hearing the sentence 'We have two cats' (or its equivalent in your native language). Suppose you understand this whole sentence (words, syntax, morphology) except for the word 'two'. The rest of the sentence gives you lots of hints about what 'two' might mean. First of all, you can tell that 'two' is an adjectival form. And you already know that adjectival forms pick out properties, not individuals. So you know that 'two' refers to some property (let's call it *twoness*). Thereafter, your question is not 'What is a *two*?' but rather, 'What is *twoness*?' and 'What sorts of things have *twoness*?' Next, you can tell by how it interacts with other words that 'two' is a quantifier (rather than a plain old adjective). For example, in English, only quantifiers can appear in the partative construction: 'A lot of sunny weather,' 'five hundred of our closest friends,' etc. Other languages also have special constructions in which only quantifiers can appear. For example, in Japanese, only quantifiers can appear in classifier constructions (Downing 1996). Once you recognize the constructions that are typical of quantifiers in your language, you can infer that the numerals are quantifiers – words that explicitly refer to quantity – because they appear in these constructions (Bloom and Wynn 1997).

After children figure out that numerals are quantifiers, they begin to learn exact meanings for some of them just as they would learn the meanings of other quantifiers. 'One' is learned like the singular determiner 'a(n)' – as an explicit marker of sets containing 1 individual (indeed, in many languages, the numeral 'one' and the indefinite article 'a(n)' are the same lexical item). If the structure indicated in Fig. 20.4 is available to support the meanings of quantifiers, it is the source of explicit concepts of *individual* and *set*. The plural morpheme '-s' is learned as an explicit marker of sets containing more than 1 individual. At this point, the other numerals ('two,' 'three,' 'four,' etc.) are treated simply as quantifiers that mark sets of more than 1 individual.

Next, 'two' is learned just as dual markers are learned in languages that have singular/dual/plural morphology – that is, as a marker for pairs of individuals, for sets in the first level above the atoms in Fig. 20.4. Higher numerals are seen as quantifiers referring to sets of more than 2. Finally 'three' is learned just as trial markers are in the rare languages that have singular/dual/trial/plural morphology – that is, as a marker of triplets of individuals. Higher numerals are seen as quantifiers referring to sets of more than 3. The child can integrate these representations with outputs of the parallel individuation system, which are also representations of individuals (one individual file open), pairs (two individual files open), and triplets (three individual files open).

20.4.1.3 The contribution of language

The question arises: If children do not have the concepts *exactly 1*, *exactly 2*, and *exactly 3* beforehand, then how do they learn the singular/plural distinction, the dual marker, and the trial marker? This is the very crux of our argument. We believe that the concepts of *set* and *individual* actually come neither from the parallel individuation system nor from the analog magnitude system, for although attentional mechanisms pick out sets and individuals as input to both systems, neither has representations with the content *set*. Rather, these concepts become available in the course of language acquisition; they are part of LAD (the language acquisition device). It is language that requires the notion of a set and language that draws a singular/plural distinction – that is, a special distinction between sets of 1 (individuals) and all other sets.

Similarly, we argue that although the parallel individuation system is what allows children to keep track of 1, 2, or 3 objects a time, it is language that induces children to create a summary representation with the content '2.' In other words, it is language that spurs the creation of an internal symbol whose meaning is *that which is common to all situations where a pair of individuals are being tracked at the same time.* Associating linguistic markers with unique states of the parallel individuation system is only possible for up to three objects, because the parallel individuation system can only keep track of up to three individuals at once. This is why the piecemeal learning described above must end upon learning the exact meaning of 'three' (or 'four,' if parallel individual extends to 4 items in the preschool years, as it does for adults).

20.4.1.4 The leap from low- to high-numeral knowledge

Once these two senses (quantifier meaning and list position) of 'one,' 'two,' and 'three' have been learned, the child is in a position to notice that the first three syllables in the counting list ('one, two, three') are the same as the singular, dual and trial markers 'one,' 'two,' and 'three.' Having noticed this, the child draws an analogy based on two very different 'follows' relations – the relation of words in the count list ('one' is followed by 'two', which is followed by 'three') and the relation of sets denoted by the singular, dual, and trial markers (a single plus an individual makes a pair; a pair plus an individual makes a triple). This numerical meaning derives from the system of parallel individuation (remember, the infant represents the numerical relations between models containing 1, 2, and 3 individuals). So, moving forward a word in the count list can be likened to adding 1 individual to a set.

This idea (one word forward equals one more individual) captures the successor principle. On this basis, the child can assign meanings to numerals in the list beyond 'three'. The new insight also gives meaning to the object-counting routine – object counting, after all, is the very act of co-ordinating steps forward in the list with the addition of individuals to a set. So the child can finally understand what counting has to do with the question of how many – the logic of the cardinality principle becomes clear.

Thus, the child learns the integer meanings of 'two' and 'five' in different ways. (The *list* meanings of 'two' and 'five' would be something like *follows 'one,' precedes 'three'* and *'follows 'four,' precedes 'six,'* respectively. These are both learned the same way – by memorizing the ordered list.) Returning to the integer meanings, 'two' (i.e. *dual*) uses notions inherent in natural language (such as *individual* and *set*) plus the system of parallel individuation. The meaning of 'five' (i.e. *'four' plus 1*) is given by the successor principle – a rule the child has induced by integrating the quantifier meanings and list meanings of the words 'one,' 'two,' and 'three.'

20.4.2 Evidence for the bootstrapping proposal

Several types of evidence support this bootstrapping proposal. First, many studies have now shown that children initially learn the numeral list as a meaningless string (Fuson 1992; LeCorre *et al.* 2005, in press; Schaeffer *et al.* 1974). Second, the morphosyntactic cues that constrain numeral meanings are part of the speech children hear and use (Bloom 2000; Bloom and Wynn 1997). Third, as discussed above, the partial meanings children assign to large numerals before inducing the successor principle are quantifier-like meanings. For example one-knowers interpret numerals higher than 'one' to mean *plural*, two-knowers interpret numerals higher than 'two' to mean *some, larger than 2*, etc. Fourth, children learning languages that do not obligatorily mark singular/plural (e.g. Mandarin and Japanese) learn the meaning of 'one' many months later than English- and Russian-speaking children (Li *et al.* 2003; Sarnecka *et al.* 2005). This is true even though the English and Russian speakers are *not* better at counting objects and even though the word 'one' is used just as often in Japanese as in Russian (Sarnecka *et al.* 2005).

Our bootstrapping proposal contains one conspicuous omission: We assign no role to the analog magnitude system. We realize that this omission may be viewed with alarm. First and foremost, magnitudes are a critical component of numeral meaning for adults and they may be essential to the representation of numerical order (Dehaene 1997; Lemer *et al.* 2003). Second, the analog magnitude system can represent larger numerosities than can the parallel individuation system. So it could allow children to assign approximate numerical meanings to numerals beyond 'three' before inducing the cardinal principle. It's not hard to imagine a bootstrapping proposal that would build on magnitudes rather than (or in addition to) the system of parallel individuation.

Despite the plausibility of these arguments, research using several different tasks has shown that it is not until *after* children work out how the numeral list represents number that they learn which analog magnitudes correspond to which words in the list (LeCorre 2003). Thus, magnitudes (at least analog magnitude representations of sets greater than 4) do not play a role in the initial construction of exact-number concepts. Rather, the bootstrapping process seems to rely exclusively on information yielded by the parallel individuation system and natural language.

20.5 **Conclusions**

We offer the bootstrapping process in answer to Fodor's explanatory challenge. Of course, new representational capacities cannot come from nowhere; on this we agree with Fodor. Many distinct representational systems with numerical content are drawn upon. The new representational power derives from two sources – the capacity to interrelate symbols directly, in terms of each other, and the capacity to combine representations from distinct systems of core knowledge by creating mappings between them. Through this process, aspects of representations implicit in one system and explicit in another, such as the notion of 'set' needed to create a summary representation of cardinal values of pairs, enrich understanding of both systems.

Our sketch is, by necessity, only a caricature of the bootstrapping process under-lying the construction of the count list. In other work, we have filled in more of the details (e.g. LeCorre and Carey 2005; Sarnecka and Gelman 2004; Sarnecka *et al.* 2005) but many of the relevant details simply are not yet known. For example in the bootstrapping process as we've laid it out, only the serial order of the memorized count is hypothesized to function as the essential placeholder, but it is likely that the initially meaningless counting routine (learned like the gestures in 'patty-cake, patty-cake . . .') may also play a role in working out the numerical meaning of the numeral list. Or, for another example, the account leaves open whether it is *necessary* that the numerals be learned in order, 'one' first, 'two' second and 'three' next, or whether this is merely a matter of input frequency. It is interesting that language typologies find a similar ordering of quantifier systems; a language with a dual marker also has singular/plural markers, but not *vice versa*; a language with a trial marker also always has a dual marker, but not *vice versa* (Corbett 2000). We are currently engaged in a series of training studies that address these and other questions and that test details of the bootstrapping proposal.

Language has two roles to play in this bootstrapping story. Unique to this case, the role of numerals as quantifiers helps the child begin to construct meanings for them. And like all bootstrapping of the sort we describe here (see Block 1986, for a general characterization of this process from the point of view of conceptual role semantics), the numeral list is learned directly, with serial order its only meaning-relevant property and serves as a placeholder to scaffold the construction of a representation of natural number. In all cases of conceptual-role bootstrapping, a set of explicit, external symbols (words or mathematical symbols) is learned directly, with their meanings initially characterized only, or mainly, in terms of the conceptual roles given by their interrelations. These symbols serve as placeholders and model-manipulation mechanisms (analogical mapping, limiting case analyses and so on) serve to fill in those placeholders by relating these symbols to antecedent mental representa-tions. Bootstrapping mechanisms of this sort have been posited to underlie the creation of new conceptual resources in the history of science and in the construction of intuitive theories in childhood. See, for some examples, Nersessian's (1992) analysis of Maxwell's construction of electromagnetic theory, Smith and colleagues' (Smith *et al.* 1992) analysis of conceptual change within elementary-school-aged children's theories of matter and Carey's (1999) analysis of the construction of a vitalist biology in early childhood.

Because of its dependence on explicit, external, symbols, conceptual-role bootstrapping is a uniquely human learning mechanism. It differs, in this regard, from other learning mechanisms sketched in these pages (e.g. connectionist learning algorithms). It also makes salient another aspect of human learning absent from the most of the other chapters in this book – human learning is not exhausted by mechanisms in which the individual confronts statistical data in the world (as in algorithms for constructing Bayes net representations of causal structure, or again, as in connectionist learning algorithms). Undoubtedly, human beings, like other animals, make use of a huge variety of learning algorithms, but only humans culturally create new representational resources and only human children make use of language to build these anew for themselves. The construction of the integer list is offered here as an example of this uniquely human process.

References

Barner D, Thalwitz D, Wood J and Carey S (submitted). On the relation between the acquision of singular-plural morpho-syntax and the conceptual distinction between one and more than one. Manuscript submitted for publication.

Barth HC, Kanwisher N and Spelke ES (2003). The construction of large number representation in adults. *Cognition*, **86**, 201–221.

Barth HC, La Mont K, Lipton JS, Dehaene S, Kanwisher N and Spelke ES (in press). Nonsymbolic arithmetic in adults and young children. *Cognition*.

Block N (1986). Advertisement for a semantics for psychology. *Midwest Studies in Philosophy*, **10**, 615–678.

Bloom P (2000). *How children learn the meanings of words*. Cambridge, MA: MIT Press.

Bloom P and Wynn K (1997). Linguistic cues in the acquisition of number words. *Journal of Child Language*, **24**, 511–533.

Carey S (1999). Sources of conceptual change. In: EK Scholnick, KE Nelson, SA Gelman and P Miller, eds. *Conceptual development: Piaget's legacy*, pp. 293–326. Hillsdale, NJ: Erlbaum.

Carey S and Spelke ES (1994). Domain-specific knowledge and conceptual change. In: LA Hirschfeld and SA Gelman, eds. *Mapping the mind: Domain specificity in cognition and culture*, pp. 169–201. New York: Cambridge University Press.

Carey S and Xu F (2001). Infants' knowledge of objects: Beyond object files and object tracking. *Cognition*, **80**, 179–213.

Chierchia G (1998). Plurality of mass nouns and the notion of 'semantic parameter'. In: S Rothstein, ed. *Events and grammar*, pp. 53–103. London: Kluwer Academic Publishers.

Clearfield MW and Mix KS (1999). Number versus contour length in infants' discrimination of small visual sets. *Psychological Science*, **10**, 408–411.

Corbett GG (2000). *Number*. Cambridge, UK: Cambridge University Press.

Dehaene S (1997). *The number sense: How the mind creates mathematics.* New York: Oxford University Press.

Downing P (1996). *Numeral classifier systems: The case of Japanese.* Philadelphia: John Benjamins Pub.

Emlen ST (1975). The stellar orientation system of a migratory bird. *Scientific American,* **233**, 102–111.

Emlen ST, Wiltschko W, Demong NJ, Wiltschko R and Berian S (1976). Magnetic direction finding: Evidence for its use in migratory indigo buntings. *Science,* **193**, 505–508.

Feigenson L (in press). A double dissociation in infants' representation of object arrays. *Cognition.*

Feigenson L and Carey S (2003). Tracking individuals via object files: Evidence from infants' manual search. *Developmental Science,* **6**, 568–584.

Feigenson L and Carey S (in press). On the limits of infants' quantification of small object arrays. *Cognition.*

Feigenson L, Carey S and Hauser MD (2002a). The representations underlying infants' choice of more: Object files versus analog magnitudes. *Psychological Science,* **13**, 150–156.

Feigenson L, Carey S and Spelke ES (2002b). Infants' discrimination of number vs. continuous extent. *Cognitive Psychology,* **44**, 33–66.

Feigenson L, Dehaene S and Spelke ES (2004). Core systems of number. *Trends in Cognitive Sciences,* **8**, 307–314.

Fluck M and Henderson L (1996). Counting and cardinality in English nursery pupils. *British Journal of Educational Psychology,* **66**, 501–517.

Fodor J (1975). *The language of thought.* Cambridge, MA: Harvard University Press.

Fuson KC (1988). *Children's counting and concepts of number.* New York: Springer-Verlag.

Fuson KC (1992). Relationships between counting and cardinality from age 2 to age 8. In: J Bideaud, C Meljac and JP Fischer, eds. *Pathways to number: Children's developing numerical abilities,* pp. 127–149. Hillsdale, NJ: Lawrence Erlbaum Associates.

Gallistel CR (1989). Animal cognition: The representation of space, time and number. *Annual Review of Psychology,* **40**, 155–189.

Gelman R (1993). A rational-constructivist account of early learning about numbers and objects. In: D Medin, ed. *Learning and motivation,* pp. 61–96. New York: Academic Press.

Gelman R and Gallistel CR (1978). *The child's understanding of number.* Cambridge, MA: Harvard University Press.

Gergely G, Nadasdy Z, Csibra G and Biro S (1995). Taking the intentional stance at 12 months of age. *Cognition,* **56**, 165–193.

Gordon P (2004). Numerical cognition without words: Evidence from Amazonia. *Science,* **306**, 496–499.

Hauser MD, Carey S and Hauser LB (2000). Spontaneous number representation in semi-free-ranging rhesus monkeys. *Proceedings of the Royal Society of London Series B: Biological Sciences,* **267**, 829–833.

Hurford JR (1987). *Language and number : The emergence of a cognitive system.* New York: Blackwell.

Johnson MH and Morton J (1991). *Biology and cognitive development: The case of face recognition.* Cambridge, MA: Blackwell.

Johnson SC (2003). Detecting agents. *Philosophical Transactions of the Royal Society, London,* **358**, 549–559.

Klahr D and Wallace JG (1976). *Cognitive development: An information-processing view.* Hillsdale, NJ: Erlbaum Associates.

Kouider S, Halberda J and Feigenson L (2005). Acquisition of French number marking: The singular/plural distinction. Manuscript in preparation.

Kouider S, Halberda J, Wood J and Carey S (in press). Acquisition of English number marking: The singular/plural distinction. *Language Learning and Development.*

LeCorre M (2003). *On the role of analog magnitudes in learning how counting represents number.* Paper presented at the biennial meeting of the Society for Research in Child Development, Tampa, Florida.

LeCorre M, Brannon EM, Van de Walle GA and Carey S (in press). Re-visiting the performance/competence debate in the acquisition of the counting principles. *Cognitive Psychology.*

LeCoree M, Brannon EM, Van de Walle GA and Carey S (2005). Why learning to count is hard: Performance vs. competence. Manuscript submitted for publication.

Le Corre M, and Carey S (submitted). The roles of analog magnitudes and parallel individuation in the construction of the counting principles: An initial investigation. Manuscript submitted for publication.

LeCorre M, Li P and Jia G (2003). *On the role of singular/plural in number word learning.* Paper presented at the biennial meeting of the Society for Research in Child Development, Tampa, FL.

Lemer C, Dahaene S, Spelke ES and Cohen L (2003). Approximate quantities and exact number words: Dissociable systems. *Neuropsychologia,* 41, 1942–1958.

Leslie AM (1994). ToMM, ToBy and Agency: Core architecture and domain specificity. In: LA Hirschfeld and SA Gelman, eds. *Mapping the mind: Domain specificity in cognition and culture,* pp. 119–148. New York: Cambridge University Press.

Li P, LeCorre M, Shui R, Jia G and Carey S (2003). *Effects of plural syntax on number word learning: A cross-linguistic study.* Paper presented at the 28th Boston University Conference on Language Development, Boston, MA.

Link G (1983). The logical analysis of plurals and mass terms: A latttice theoretical approach. In: R Bauerle, C Schwartze, and AV Stechow, eds. *Meaning, use and interpretation of language.* New York: W. de Gruyter.

Lipton JS and Spelke ES (2003). Origins of number sense: Large number discrimination in human infants. *Psychological Science,* 14, 396–401.

Miller KF, Smith CM, Zhu JJ and Zhang HC (1995). Preschool origins of cross-national differences in mathematical competence: The role of number-naming systems. *Psychological Science,* 6, 56–60.

Nersessian NJ (1992). How do scientists think? Capturing the dynamics of conceptual change in science. In: RN Giere, ed. *Cognitive models of science,* pp. 3–45. Minneapolis, MN: University of Minnesota Press.

Piatelli-Palmarini M (1980). *Language learning: The debate between Jean Piaget and Noam Chomsky.* Cambridge, MA: Harvard University Press.

Pica P, Lerner C, Izard V and Dehaene S (2004). Exact and approximate arithemetic in an Amzonian indigene group. *Science,* 306, 499–503.

Pylyshyn Z (1994). Some primitive mechanisms of spatial attention. *Cognition,* 50, 363–384.

Pylyshyn ZW and Storm RW (1998). Tracking multiple independent targets: Evidence for a parallel tracking mechanism. *Spatial Vision,* 3, 179–197.

Quine WVO (1960). *Word and object.* Cambridge, MA: MIT Press.

Sarnecka BW and Gelman SA (2004). Six does not just mean a lot: Preschoolers see number words as specific. *Cognition*, 92, 329–352.

Sarnecka BW, Kamenskaya VG, Ogura T, Yamana Y and Yudovina YB (submitted). How children learn "one," "two," and "three" in English, Russian, and Japanese. Manuscript submitted for publication.

Schaeffer B, Eggleston VH and Scott JL (1974). Number development in young children. *Cognitive Psychology*, 6, 357–379.

Scholl BJ (2001). Objects and attention: The state of the art. *Cognition*, 80, 1–46.

Siegler RS and Robinson M (1982). The development of numerical understanding. *Advances in Child Development and Behavior*, 16, 214–312.

Smith C, Snir J and Grosslight L (1992). Using conceptual models to facilitate conceptual change: The case of weight-density differentiation. *Cognition and Instruction*, 9, 221–283.

Spelke ES and Tsivkin S (2001). Language and number: A bilingual training study. *Cognition*, 78, 45–88.

Treisman AM (1998). Feature binding, attention and object perception. *Philosophical Transactions of the Royal Society, London*, 353, 1295–1306.

Wood J, Koudier S and Carey S (submitted). Acquisition of English singular/plural marking: Evidence from a manual search paradigm. Manuscript submitted for publication.

Wood J and Spelke ES (in press). Infants' enumeration of actions: Numerical discrimination and its signature limits. *Developmental Science*.

Woodward AL (1998). Infants selectively encode the goal object of an actor's reach. *Cognition*, 69, 1–34.

Woodward AL, Sommerville JA and Guajardo JJ (2001). How infants make sense of intentional action. In: BF Malle, LJ Moses and DA Baldwin, eds. *Intentions and intentionality: Foundations of social cognition*, pp. 149–171. Cambridge, MA: MIT Press.

Wynn K (1990). Children's understanding of counting. *Cognition*, 36, 155–193.

Wynn K (1992). Children's acquisition of number words and the counting system. *Cognitive Psychology*, 24, 220–251.

Xu F and Spelke ES (2000). Large number discrimination in 6-month-old infants. *Cognition*, 74, B1–B11.

Part 5

What have we learned (or can we learn) from cognitive neuroscience about developmental change?

Chapter 21

Species comparisons in development: The case of the geometric 'module'

Lynn Nadel and Almut Hupbach

Abstract

Evidence from studies of reorientation in both animals and developing children has been taken to suggest the presence of an encapsulated 'geometric' module, which cannot interact with landmark information until language becomes available as a bridge between these two domains (Hermer and Spelke 1996). We review more recent work in animals and several studies in children that challenge this view. When larger experimental spaces are used, even toddlers can integrate geometric and landmark information in reacting to disorientation. Rather than supporting the notion of strictly separated modules, these data suggest that prelinguistic children, or non-linguistic animals, can integrate multiple information sources under most conditions.

21.1 Introduction

It is said by the Greeks that Paralos, the son of Pericles, *discovered* navigation. If so, he must have been a timid soul, since caution was the defining feature of Greek navigation. Ships stayed within sight of coastlines, sailed only by day, and navigated by strategies we now call 'piloting'.

Matters changed with the Phoenicians' use of the sun and the pole star for purposes of orientation. It is believed the Phoenicians exited the Mediterranean and circumnavigated Africa, sailing around the Cape of Good Horn well before Magellan. Given the prominence of star myths in Phoenician culture, sailors could well have learned to use the night sky to navigate the way South Sea Islanders have done for centuries (Gladwin 1970).

The suggestion that humans had to 'discover' navigation is intriguing. It seems safe to say that humans did not have to 'discover' feeding, or drinking, or sex – these things everyone just knew, as did other animals. But, many other animals also know how to navigate, often over long distances. They presumably didn't have to 'discover' navigation. Why did humans?

In this chapter we briefly discuss navigation, and even more briefly review what is known about its cognitive and neural organization, before focusing on 'reorientation' – the specific task of regaining one's bearings after disorientation. This behavior has received a great deal of attention in recent years, particularly in the domain of cognitive development. Recent studies of reorientation in young children, combined with work in a variety of animal species, have implications for a central debate in this domain. To fully appreciate these implications, we must start by considering some fundamental aspects of navigation.

21.2 Forms of navigation

Animals use a number of navigational 'strategies' to plan and execute outbound and return journeys; in what follows we briefly describe these strategies.

21.2.1 Dead reckoning

Desert ants (*Cataglyphis bicolor*) can find their way back to the nest across long stretches of featureless terrain (e.g. Wehner *et al.* 2004). They maintain a sense of where they are with respect to a known starting point as they move away from it. This ability, called path integration or dead reckoning, is observed in many species, humans included. It involves either: (1) forming and storing a record of every twist and turn taken; or (2) continuously updating a vector that points to the starting place. But, it is a strategy prone to considerable error, and this error accumulates over time and distance. On it's own, dead reckoning could easily fail.

21.2.2 Piloting/guidance

As already noted, the early Greeks navigated by keeping well-known landmarks within sight at all times. Given the density of the islands in the Aegean this was all they needed. A succession of landmarks got them to the goal, and back home again later. This navigational strategy is often called 'piloting', and its central feature is that things in the world, such as islands, mountains, rivers, buildings, etc., can be used to guide an organism, helping it decide which direction to move in, how far to go, and when the goal has been reached (if it's not otherwise obvious). Piloting can be as simple as following an odor plume or as complex as using a constellation of stars, but the basic principles remain the same.

21.2.3 Response learning

Often travels become habitual, so that getting to and from a goal reduces to a stereotyped set of actions – go 10 paces, turn left at the large tree, etc. Note that this 'response'-based navigation often interacts with piloting. The landmarks used while piloting can play a role in setting the conditions for making a particular response – for example turn left at the large tree.

21.2.4 Mapping

Enough experience with an environment, and its relatively fixed features, seems to lead to the formation of what Tolman (1948) referred to as a 'cognitive map', a mental model of the various landmarks and features of the world, and the spatial relations among them. Animals use this spatial representation to calculate routes between any pair of places in the world, and it plays a central role in the acquisition and maintenance of successful navigation in familiar environments. The interested reader is directed to O'Keefe and Nadel (1978) for further development of this idea.

21.3 Neural bases of navigation

Given this range of navigational strategies, it is no surprise that numerous brain systems are involved. Many of the brain systems concerned with space encode egocentric information – for example where parts of the body are with respect to each other, and where the body and all its parts are with respect to features of the external world. Adaptive action, at the moment, is completely dependent on the accuracy of these spatial frameworks. Some, but not all, forms of navigation make use of this egocentric spatial information.

In addition to these various encodings of egocentric space, a brain system coding space allocentrically appears to be centered on the hippocampal formation (O'Keefe and Nadel 1978). The navigational strategy of *mapping* depends on the integrity of this system. The original observation leading to the idea of a cognitive map in the hippocampus, the discovery of 'place' cells in the hippocampus (O'Keefe and Dostrovsky 1971), remains its most compelling support. Active only when the animal is in a specific place in the environment (the 'place field'), these cells are controlled jointly by various features of the environment (O'Keefe and Conway 1978; O'Keefe and Burgess 1996) and the animal's movements within the environment (McNaughton et al.1991).

In addition to the location information provided by these place cells, a cognitive map also requires information about distance and direction. The likely source of direction information was uncovered by Taube, Muller and Ranck (1990), in their report of cells in the rat postsubiculum whose responses were controlled by the rat's heading. These 'head direction' cells have also been reported in the anterodorsal thalamus (Zugaro et al. 2001). There is a strong relation between the head direction cell system and the place cell system. Studies in which rats are disoriented or in which various changes are made to the rat's environment show that these two systems often respond in strikingly similar ways. For example Cressant et al. (1997) have shown that place cells are preferentially controlled by the background cues in the test environment. Objects that were in the foreground did not have the ability to influence place cell firing. The same result has now been reported for the head direction cells (Zugaro *et al.* 2001). The overall impression is that these two systems are 'in register', together contributing to various aspects of navigation, in particular mapping.

Distance information appears to be coded in terms of the firing rates of hippocampal place cells, which vary as a function of the speed of movement of the animal through the 'place field' (Huxter *et al.* 2003).

Taken together, place cells (for location), head direction cells (for heading), and the rate code reflecting speed of movement (for distance) comprise all the neural elements needed to construct an internal cognitive map.

21.3.1 Connecting neural systems and navigation

As this brief review indicates, we have considerable knowledge about the neural mechanisms underlying such things as head direction sense and perhaps cognitive maps. We also have reasonable knowledge about the behavioral manifestations of navigation. Attempts have been made to link these levels with computational models (e.g. Redish and Touretzky 1996; Sharp *et al.*1996; Burgess and O'Keefe 1996; Samsonovich and McNaughton 1997).

Basic questions remain to be answered, however. For example, if multiple navigational strategies are available, how do they interact, and how do their interactions unfold during development? Recent attempts to address this question have focused considerable attention on one particular navigational function: reorientation. This research will be the focus of the remainder of this paper.

21.4 Reorientation

A special problem arises when an animal becomes disoriented. First of all, this is an uncomfortable state. Neither animals, nor humans, enjoy losing their 'bearings'. The organism must find something in the world that permits reorientation. This could be the sun, or a mountain, or river, or some other large land-feature. It apparently can also be the 'shape' of the landscape.

21.4.1 The Cheng (1986) study

In a clever study looking at the information disoriented rats use to reorient themselves, Cheng (1986) reported a surprising result. In the seminal study, rats were shown the location of food in an enclosed rectangular box, which for some rats contained a prominent landmark in one of the corners. Afterward, the rats were taken out of the box and disoriented by being put in a carrying-box and turned around several times. When the rats were put back in a replica of the training box one could judge, by their choices, what information they used to reorient.

Given a rectangular box, the absence of a landmark, and no access to stimuli outside the box, diagonally opposite corners of the box are geometrically indistinguishable.

As expected, rats tested in a box without landmarks split their choices between the two geometrically equivalent 'correct' locations. The surprise in this study was that rats trained in a box *with* landmarks failed to use them to distinguish the two geometrically equivalent locations. Something prevented integration between geometric information and landmarks. Cheng concluded that rats have a 'geometric module' that is used in reorientation situations, and that this module does not interact with landmark information in the solution of the task.

21.4.2 Hermer and Spelke (1996)

Hermer and Spelke replicated this result in young children, and went on in a series of empirical and theoretical papers to assert the existence of an encapsulated 'geometric' module that cannot benefit from landmarks because they are represented in other modules. In their view, young children become capable of overcoming this segregation only with the advent of language.

Hermer and Spelke (1996) went beyond these assertions about geometry. They argued that their 'findings support broader proposals concerning the domain specificity of humans' core cognitive abilities, the conservation of cognitive abilities across related species and over the course of human development, and the developmental processes by which core abilities are extended to permit more flexible, uniquely human kinds of problem solving' (p. 195). These are quite strong and intuitively appealing claims, and they can be tested, it would seem, by making resort to the use of animals. If the ability to integrate geometric and landmark information depends upon language then avians, mammals, and primates ought not to be able to do it at all.

Table 21.1 displays the studies that have been carried out in various animals since the initial report by Cheng. As the Table makes clear, there is little support for the notion of a rigidly encapsulated geometric module. Generally speaking, animals can readily integrate landmark information with information from geometry.

Consider the recent study in fish by Sovrano *et al.* (2002). Fish were tested in a rectangular environment that either did or did not have landmark information. Fish without landmarks preferred the two geometrically equivalent corners, but fish with landmark information were able to restrict their choices largely to the corner that was correct both geometrically and with respect to the landmark.

In the Gouteux *et al.* (2001) study, rhesus monkeys were also tested in a rectangular environment with or without landmarks. Monkeys tested without landmarks showed

Table 21.1 Studies of landmark and geometry information integration in animals

Authors	Species	Result
Vallortigara, Zanforlin and Pasti (1990)	Chicks	Can use landmarks or geometry
Kelly, Spetch and Heth (1998)	Pigeons	Integrate landmarks and geometry
Gouteux, Thinus-Blanc and Vauclair (2001)	Rhesus monkeys	Integrate landmarks and geometry
Deipolyi, Santos and Hauser (2001)	Cotton-top tamarins	Integrate landmarks and geometry
Sovrano, Bisazza and Vallortigara (2002)	Fish	Integrate landmarks and geometry

the typical geometrical solution – making most of their choices in the two diagonally opposite corners. Monkeys tested with a large landmark, either on the wall near the goal or on the opposite wall, combined geometric and landmark information adaptively. In several follow-on studies they demonstrated some kind of relation between the size of the landmark and its utility as a cue to reorientation, a point we return to later.

Perhaps the most thorough exploration of this question is the ongoing work by Hauser and his colleagues investigating various aspects of cognition and cognitive development in cotton-top tamarins. Recently they asked if cotton-tops integrate spatial information across domains (Deipolyi *et al.* 2001; Hauser 2000). The short answer is that they did, at least in some cases, in ways that would not be predicted by Hermer and Spelke.

The work in non-human animals shows quite clearly that language is not a necessary element in integrating geometric and landmark information in the service of reorientation. But, the puzzle of why young toddlers ignored landmarks in Hermer and Spelke's (1994) initial study only deepens as we realize this is not generally the case in animals. Is there something odd about the way humans approach this problem?

21.4.3 **Human reorientation**

A study reported by Stedron *et al.* (2000) hinted at some possible limits on the initial Hermer and Spelke result. The children Stedron *et al.* tested showed clear signs of using landmarks on the very first test trial, although over a series of trials this tendency washed out.

More recently, Learmonth and her colleagues have published a set of studies that impose limits on what one can conclude from the original Hermer and Spelke finding. Learmonth *et al.* (2001) sought to replicate the original result, but in a larger room than that used by Hermer and Spelke (12 × 8 instead of 6 × 4). In this (4 ×) larger space, disoriented toddlers (17–24 months of age) readily integrated information from geometric and landmark features in reorienting themselves. Learmonth *et al.* (2003) repeated this result in a within-subject design. Children were tested on reorientation in both a small room (4 × 6) and a large room (8 ×12), controlling of course for the order of testing in the two environments across subjects. The results are shown in Fig. 21.1. Basically, both results were replicated – young toddlers ignore landmarks in the small room but use them along with geometry in the big room.

More recently, Hupbach and Nadel (in press) have extended this result to a different form of geometry. Their room consisted of four equal length walls, but arranged in the shape of a rhombus. This environment provided direction rather than distance information. Would this kind of geometric information interact with landmarks? The answer appears to be a clear yes. The data for both the landmark and no landmark condition are shown in Fig. 21.2. As soon as children start to use one form of

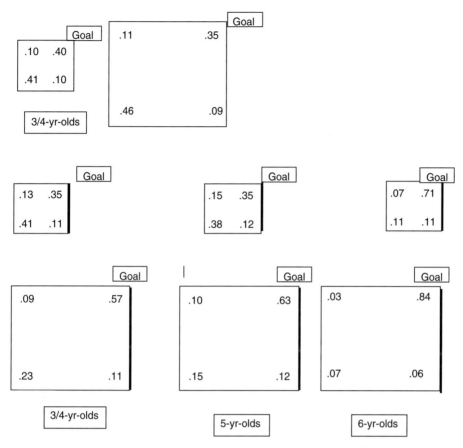

Fig. 21.1 Results of Learmonth *et al.* (2003). Children were shown a toy's hiding place within the experimental room, were then disoriented, and finally, asked to retrieve the hidden toy. (A) Proportion of choices to each corner in two different-sized rectangular rooms by 3/4 year-olds. Note the confusion between the goal corner (X) and its geometrical equivalent in both rooms. (B) Proportion of choices to each corner in a room with a landmark (blue covering – shown by the heavy black line in the figure) on one wall. Note the impact of the landmark in the large room – children of all ages tested used this landmark to choose between the goal corner and its geometrical equivalent. The ability to combine these sources of information improved with age. In the small room only the oldest children (6-year-olds) were able to combine landmarks and geometry in this way.

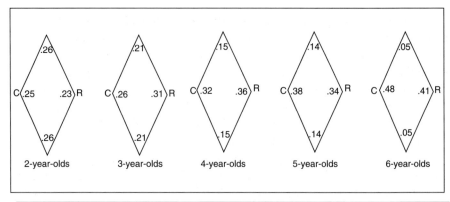

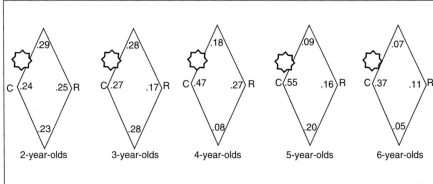

Fig. 21.2 Results of Hupbach and Nadel (in press). Children were shown a toy's hiding place within the experimental room (designated by the 'C' in the figure), were then disoriented, and, finally, asked to retrieve the hidden toy. (A) Proportion of choices to each corner in the rhombic environment, with no landmark. Note the late emergence of the use of angle information – only in the 4-year-olds and beyond. (B) Proportion of choices to each corner in the rhombic environment, with a landmark (blue wall – designated by the symbol) present. As soon as angle information is usable (4-year-olds) it is combined with landmark information.

information, either geometry or landmarks, they simultaneously use the other. There is no stage at which they only use geometry or only use landmarks.

21.5 **Discussion**

Relevant data from studies with various animals, combined with recent studies of children tested in larger rooms, fail to support strong claims about encapsulated geometric modules acting alone in reorientation. But, they also leave us with some explaining to do. Room size seems to matter, especially for the younger children. Why?

An answer to this question requires further discussion of the fundamentals of reorientation. Basically, reorientation involves realigning the (disoriented) direction system with a global framework. What kind of information can be used to accomplish this realignment process? First of all, the framework itself must be specified. In the Cheng study (and the work it inspired), a critical feature of the test environment is that it was cut off from the global environment. When rats could see the outer world, they used this information to specify both the framework and direction, and geometric confusions did not occur (Margules and Gallistel 1988). When this possibility does not exist, rats (and children) must depend upon their own internally-generated global framework, in combination with whatever local information is available to them. In the studies described, this information includes geometry (shape, distance, angle), and what are intended to be usable 'landmarks'.

One factor worth exploring is the status of these putative 'landmarks'? Specifically, do our experimental subjects (rats or humans) consider something like a blue wall a landmark? More generally, what features of objects in the world influence their use as landmarks? Although this is not the most thoroughly researched question, what has been done suggests that two features are critical: stability and distance. Animals strongly prefer to use stable cues to define places and directions, and they also strongly prefer to use distal rather than proximal cues.

21.5.1 Stability

Biegler and Morris (1993) investigated the role of landmark stability in orientation. Rats were trained to find food in a large directionally polarized test arena. The food was located with respect to two prominent landmarks, which for some rats stayed in the same location but for other rats moved around in the bigger space. Even though the relation between the landmarks and food remained constant in both groups, learning was only observed in the rats whose landmarks remained stable with respect to the global framework of the experimental room. When the landmarks moved around, the rats could not use them to locate food, even though to do so would have been rewarded.

There were indications in the Learmonth *et al.* (2001) study that stability might be crucial. Permanent landmarks (e.g. doors or built-in bookshelves) were more likely to be used than landmarks the children had the opportunity to see moving from place to place.

A related finding has recently been reported for hippocampal place cells. Chakraborty *et al.* (2004) tested their rats in a large symmetrical cylinder with high walls, and a single distal cue – a large card on the wall. In this commonly used apparatus the place fields of hippocampal place cells are known to be dependent on this cue card. Chakraborty *et al.* showed that if this distal cue is made unreliable by frequently moving it in full view of the rat, it's ability to define place fields disappears. Thus, only objects that are stable with respect to a global framework can serve as 'landmarks' for the purposes of navigational tasks, including, we imagine, reorientation.

21.5.2 Proximity

In their recent study of head-direction cells Zugaro *et al.* (2004) tested rats in a circular environment containing both a foreground cue near the center of the test apparatus, and a background cue on the wall. Rats were familiarized with this environment, and then were disoriented. The apparatus was also changed – the foreground and background cues rotated 90 degrees in opposite directions. This enabled the investigators to determine whether the foreground or background cues would exert preferential control over reorientation. Finally, rats were tested under two different lighting conditions – either full light or strobe light. In the latter condition the animal was deprived of motion parallax or optic flow information. The results showed that rats with full light used background cues to reorient, but rats tested in the strobe light condition did not. The clear implication of this finding is that it is the distance and direction information conveyed by background cues (via motion parallax and optic flow) that makes them predominant in controlling reorientation. When that information is stripped away in the strobe light condition, background cues no longer exert control.

21.5.3 An hypothesis

These considerations, and the room size effect, suggest a possible explanation, which is not entirely original. Hebb (1938) noticed some time ago that rats prefer to use distal rather than proximal cues for orientation, a point repeated by O'Keefe and Nadel (1978).

The findings just described (Zugaro *et al.* 2004) suggest a neurobiological mechanism through which information about distal stimuli could exert disproportionate influence on direction-finding. If organisms use distal stimuli to orient by, how far away does a stimulus have to be to qualify?

The question of what counts as a 'distal' cue, and what does not, is clearly an empirical one, and presumably reflects the context within which an organism finds itself. It is reasonable to assume the size of the organism makes a difference. We would suggest that for developing children, the answer lies somewhere between 6 and 12 feet. In the small room, a blue wall that cannot be more than 6 feet away (and is usually a lot less), is not treated as a landmark. In the large room, the same blue wall, which can now be up to 12 feet away, is treated as a landmark. Once so treated, it can combine with geometric information to jointly influence the choice.

It is clearly not the case that landmarks and geometry cannot combine to influence reorientation. What comes first is that an environmental feature has to have certain properties to be treated as a landmark at all. Once this step has been negotiated there is no further barrier to combination with geometric information – or so the data seem to suggest. We conclude that the initial Cheng result, and the ensuing Hermer and Spelke results, have a rather more modest explanation than offered by these authors.

Much of the debate surrounding notions of modules such as a geometric module has been posed in extreme form: either encapsulated modules or an all-purpose learning system of initially undifferentiated elements. We prefer to think in terms of systems whose wiring reflects the universe in which we evolved. If there is such a thing as a 'reorientation' system, its various parts are connected by neural pathways whose very presence attests to the importance of the information they convey. Evolution has, we assume, set it up so that information about distal stimuli has priority in the direction system. Exactly how this is accomplished at the neurobiological level is not entirely clear yet, but that it is accomplished seems proven beyond doubt. Does it make sense to talk about this kind of 'hard-wiring' as creating a 'module'? We think not, at least not in this case.

What broader conclusions can we reach? We can think of two. First, studying animals can, under some circumstances, greatly illuminate issues of central concern to human cognitive development. Second, the developing nervous system likely encodes aspects of the world in non-obvious and perhaps even non-intuitive ways. Each case is going to have to be looked at in its own right. The lesson of the spatial story we told here is that the neural organization that matters is one that channels distal information to the direction system. This has consequences for what kinds of environmental objects organisms are willing to treat as landmarks, and this in turn has consequences for how those same organisms attempt to solve reorientation problems.

We cannot conclude without returning to where we started – why did humans, unlike other species, have to 'discover' navigation? The Phoenicians made the critical discovery when they figured out how to use the (quite distant) sun and pole star as orienting cues to navigate by. But why didn't we just know that, the way many species of birds just know it, and use it, to orient, navigate, and migrate considerable distances in the air.

Our colleague Mary Peterson suggested that what makes the situation of the Phoenicians different is that they were seeking to act in spaces *much larger* than the space in which humans evolved. Savanna and its neighbors offer ample scope for complex spatial skills, and there is little reason to doubt that humans could navigate efficiently. Among the sources of information early humans were likely to rely on is optic flow – highly accurate information about distance is available in this channel, especially in an environment replete with varied features.

To effectively use bigger spaces, such as open sea, or desert, humans would have had to cope with the reality that optic flow information in these settings is almost non-existent. Other information in the environment that could be used to navigate in these spaces had to be identified. It is in this context that humans discovered how to use the sun and the pole star in navigation. Combining this knowledge with the neural machinery to build internal 'cognitive maps' of the external world can be said to have opened up the age of exploration. It is not an accident that the system building these cognitive maps, and underpinning navigation, is also central to the behavior of exploration itself (O'Keefe and Nadel 1978).

Acknowledgements

We thank Oliver Hardt and Mary Peterson for their suggestions, which measurably contributed to our thinking. We also thank the Flinn Foundation, the J.S. McDonnell Foundation, NINDS (LN), and Deutsche Forschungsgemeinschaft (AH) for their support of the research described herein.

References

Biegler R and Morris RGM (1993). Landmark stability is a prerequisite for spatial but not discrimination learning. *Nature*, **361**, 631–633.

Burgess N and O'Keefe J (1996). Neuronal computations underlying the firing of place cells and their role in navigation. *Hippocampus*, **7**, 749–762.

Chakraborty S, Anderson MI, Chaudry AM, Mumford JC and Jeffery KJ (2004). Context-independent directional cue learning by hippocampal place cells. *European Journal of Neuroscience*, **20**, 281–292.

Cheng K (1986). A purely geometric module in the rat's spatial representation. *Cognition*, **23**, 149–178.

Cressant A, Muller RU and Poucet B (1997). Failure of centrally placed objects to control the firing fields of hippocampal place cells. *Journal of Neuroscience*, **17**, 2531–2542.

Deipolyi A, Santos L and Hauser MD (2001). The role of landmarks in cotton-top tamarin spatial foraging: evidence for geometric and non-geometric features. *Animal Cognition*, **4**, 99–108.

Gladwin T (1970). *East is a big bird*. Cambridge, MA: Harvard University Press.

Gouteux S, Thinus-Blanc C and Vauclair J (2001). Rhesus monkeys use geometric and nongeometric information during a reorientation task. *Journal of Experimental Psychology: General*, **130**, 505–519.

Hauser MD (2000). *Wild minds: What animals really think*. New York: Henry Holt.

Hebb DO (1938). Studies of the organization of behaviour. I. Behaviour of the rat in a field orientation. *Journal of Comparative Psychology*, **25**, 333–352.

Hermer L and Spelke ES (1994). A geometric process for spatial reorientation in young children. *Nature*, **370**, 57–59.

Hermer L and Spelke ES (1996). Modularity and development: the case of spatial reorientation. *Cognition*, **61**, 195–232.

Hupbach and Nadel L (in press). Reorientation in a rhombic-shaped environment: No evidence for an encapsulated geometric module. *Cognitive Development*, in press.

Huxter J, Burgess N and O'Keefe J (2003). Independent rate and temporal coding in hippocampal pyramidal cells. *Nature*, **425**, 828–832.

Kelly DM, Spetch ML and Heth CD (1998). Pigeons' (*Columba livia*) encoding of geometric and featural properties of a spatial environment. *Journal of Comparative Psychology*, **112**, 259–269.

Learmonth AE, Nadel L and Newcombe NS (2002). Children's use of landmarks: Implications for modularity theory. *Psychological Science*, **13**, 337–341.

Learmonth AE, Newcombe NS and Huttenlocher J (2001). Toddlers' use of metric information and landmarks to reorient. *Journal of Experimental Child Psychology*, 80, 225–244.

Margules J and Gallistel CR (1988). Heading in the rat: determination by environmental shape. *Animal Learning and Behavior*, 16, 404–410.

McNaughton BL, Chen LL and Markus EJ (1991). 'Dead reckoning', landmark learning, and the sense of direction: A neurophysiological and computational hypothesis. *Journal of Cognitive Neuroscience*, 3, 190–202.

O'Keefe J and Burgess N (1996). Geometric determinants of the place fields of hippocampal neurons. *Nature*, 381, 425–428.

O'Keefe J and Conway DH (1978). Hippocampal place units in the freely moving rat: Why they fire where they fire. *Experimental Brain Research*, 31, 573–590.

O'Keefe J and Dostrovsky J (1971). The hippocampus as a spatial map. Preliminary evidence from unit activity in the freely moving rat. *Brain Research*, 34, 171–175.

O'Keefe J and Nadel L (1978). *The hippocampus as a cognitive map*. Oxford: Clarendon Press. Available at http://www.cognitivemap.net

Redish AD and Touretzky DS (1996). Modeling interactions of the rat's place and head direction systems. In: DS Touretzky, MC Mozer and ME Hasselmo, eds. *Advances in neural information processing systems*, vol. 8, pp. 61–71. Cambridge, MA: MIT Press.

Samsonovich AV and McNaughton BL (1997). Path integration and cognitive mapping in a continuous attractor neural network model. *Journal of Neuroscience*, 17, 5900–5920.

Sharp PE, Blair HT and Brown M (1996). Neural network modeling of the hippocampal formation spatial signals and their possible role in navigation: A modular approach. *Hippocampus*, 6, 735–748.

Sovrano VA, Bisazza A and Vallortigara G (2002). Modularity and spatial reorientation in a simple mind: encoding of geometric and nongeometric properties of a spatial environment by fish. *Cognition*, 85, B51–59.

Stedron JM, Munakata Y and O'Reilly RC (2000). Spatial reorientation in young children: A case of modularity? Poster presented at *International Conference on Infant Studies, Brighton, England*.

Taube JS, Muller RU and Ranck Jr JB (1990). Head-direction cells recorded from the postsubiculum in freely moving rats. I. Description and quantitative analysis. *Journal of Neuroscience*, 10, 420–435.

Tolman EC (1948). Cognitive maps in rats and men. *Psychological Review*, 55, 189–208.

Vallortigara G, Zanforlin M and Pasti G (1990). Geometric modules in animals' spatial representations: A test with chicks (*Gallus gallus domesticus*). *Journal of Comparative Psychology*, 104, 248–254.

Wehner R, Meier C and Zollikofer C (2004). The ontogeny of foraging behaviour in desert ants, *Cataglyphis bicolor*. *Ecological Entomology*, 29, 240–250.

Zugaro MB, Arleo A, Dejean C, Burguiere E, Khamassi M and Wiener SI (2004). Rat anterodorsal thalamic head direction neurons depend upon dynamic visual signals to select anchoring landmark cues. *European Journal of Neuroscience*, 20, 530–536.

Zugaro MB, Berthoz A and Wiener SI (2001). Background, but not foreground, spatial cues are taken as references for head direction responses by rat anterodorsal thalamus neurons. *Journal of Neuroscience*, 21, RC154, 1–5.

Chapter 22

Learning about learning and development with modern imaging technology

B. J. Casey, Dima Amso, and Matthew C. Davidson

Abstract

Predictive learning is a cornerstone of cognitive development. Knowing what events to expect when, and in which contexts, is critical for the individual in planning and maintaining appropriate thoughts and actions in different contexts over time. Adjusting behavior when these predictions are violated is an essential element of cognitive control. In this chapter we describe three different neural systems involved in predictive learning and cognitive control: a frontostriatal system that learns about the frequency of events, a frontocerebellar system that learns about their timing, and a hippocampal system that learns about the contexts in which they occur. We provide evidence from neuroimaging studies that track cognitive and neural changes over learning and development. These results suggest an important role for protracted development of prefrontal structures and increasing connectivity within each of these circuits in the development of learning and cognitive control.

22.1 Introduction

With advances in non-invasive imaging technology researchers have begun to track cognitive and neural processes underlying learning and development. A premise of this paper is that learning to predict and anticipate events in our environment is a cornerstone of cognitive development. Knowing when, what, and in which contexts to expect an event is critical for the individual in planning and maintaining appropriate thoughts and actions in different contexts over time. There is evidence to suggest that aspects of this type of learning are present early in life (Saffran *et al.* 1996, 1999; Kirkham *et al.* 2002), and we will argue that adjusting behavior when these expectations are violated is an essential element of the development of cognitive control.

In this chapter, we highlight advances in imaging technology that enable us to track biological changes that underlie behavioral changes in humans. These techniques provide indirect measures of brain maturation that are both progressive (e.g. synaptogenesis, myelination, dendritic arborization) and regressive (e.g. synaptic pruning, cell death) in nature, and can be used to track changes over both short and long periods of time (hours to years). We have used these techniques with children, adolescents, and adults to show the importance of early maturing subcortical systems (e.g. striatum and hippocampus) in learning and later maturing prefrontal connectivity in development of higher cognitive functions such as cognitive control (Casey, in press).

22.1.1 Imaging methodologies

Magnetic resonance imaging (MRI) became especially important to cognitive and developmental psychologists when the functional capabilities were discovered and developed. Whereas MRI is used to produce structural images of individuals brains, useful for anatomical and morphometric studies (Fig. 22.1, Panel A), the functional component allows an *in vivo* measure of brain activity. Functional MRI (fMRI) is sensitive to changes in oxygen levels of the blood in the brain (Kwong *et al.* 1992; Ogawa *et al.* 1992). These changes have been associated with changes in neural activity

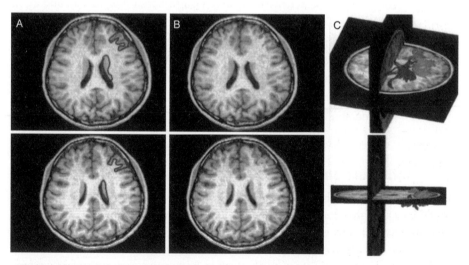

Fig. 22.1 Illustration of most common MR methods used in study of development and learning. MRI-based brain morphometry (Panel A), fMRI-based patterns of brain activity (Panel B) and DTI-based fiber tracking (Panel C) of frontostriatal connections shown in two representative axial slices. See Plate 4 in the centre of this book for a full colour version.

that are accompanied by changes in blood flow and blood oxygenation levels (Logothetis 2001; Raichle 2001).

The fMRI method capitalizes on magnetic differences between oxygenated and deoxygenated blood. In short, hemoglobin in the blood becomes strongly paramagnetic in its deoxygenated state. Deoxygenated hemoglobin can therefore be used as a naturally occurring contrast agent, with highly oxygenated brain regions producing a larger magnetic resonance (MR) signal than less oxygenated regions. Thus, during brain activation, localized increases in blood flow increase blood oxygenation (and consequently reduce deoxygenated hemoglobin), causing the MR signal to increase (Fig. 22.1, Panel B). This method, blood oxygenation level dependent (BOLD) imaging, eliminates the need for exogenous contrast agents, including radioactive isotopes (Kwong *et al.* 1992; Ogawa *et al.* 1992).

Diffusion tensor imaging (DTI) is another relatively new technique that has been applied to questions surrounding learning and development. This method can detect changes in white matter microstructure based on properties of diffusion (Fig. 22.1, Panel C). Diffusion of water in areas of white matter is restricted by myelin and the regularity of fibers. Water diffuses more readily in parallel with a tract, than perpendicular to it, a property termed anisotropic diffusion (e.g. Watts *et al.* 2004). Magnetic resonance imaging can be sensitized to water diffusion to quantify myelination and white matter microstructure *in vivo* and has been used to study prefrontal development in children (Klingberg *et al.* 1999). Taken together these techniques can provide both structural and functional information about the brain that can be used, in combination with carefully designed behavioral assays, to help constrain theories of learning and development.

22.1.2 Regressive and progressive changes with development

It is important to consider all possible constraints to avoid claims of causality between coincidental changes in brain and behavioral development. Such claims are seldom empirically grounded and present a significant trap if we simply assume linear changes across systems and direct associations between these changes. For example, maturation involves both progressive (e.g. proliferation of neurons and glia, cell migration, synaptogenesis, myelination, etc.) and regressive (e.g. cell death and pruning of synapses) changes (Thompson and Nelson 2001; de Haan and Johnson 2003; Brown *et al.* in press; Fig. 22.2). These processes are interactive and, as such, one would be hard pressed to suggest that any single process alone could account for the total increase in neural conduction across development.

Thus, during early development there is an overproduction of synapses followed by a subsequent decline in the number of synapses. Presumably, experience selects which of these synapses survive. However, if we expose the developing organism to experiences earlier than expected, by bringing the animal into the world prematurely, or prevent experiences by blocking sensory input (suturing the eyes and blocking visual

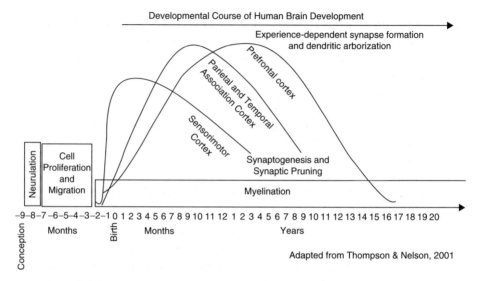

Fig. 22.2 A diagram of regressive and progressive processes in human brain development over the life-span (adapted from Thompson and Nelson 2001).

input to the primary visual cortex), there is still an overproduction of synapses and a subsequent decline that does not change the onset of this overproduction or the number of synapses that survive (Bourgeois *et al.* 1994). Thus, the developmental trajectory in number of synapses appears to be genetically programmed, providing a scaffold upon which further experiences can build, but experiences themselves do not appear to affect the developmental trajectory of synaptogenesis, in the case of number. That is not to say that individual experiences don't have an impact on the efficiency of synapses formed.

The previous example illustrated both progressive (synaptogenesis) and regressive processes (subsequent pruning of synapses) during development. An example of progressive changes with development is that of myelination. Myelin growth increases efficiency in neuronal conduction and increases over childhood and adolescence. Thus, a plausible explanation for the steady increase in cognitive processing speed across development would be increased myelination across development. Yet, the rate and thickness of myelin cannot be measured precisely *in vivo* and related directly to behavioral change in humans. Further, other maturational processes, that may underlie the observed cognitive changes (e.g. synaptic pruning, vasculature changes, dendritic branching, etc.), occur in parallel with changes in myelin. Thus associations between co-occurring neural and cognitive events should be qualified as being only correlative, rather than causal.

In order to better understand biological changes underlying behavioral changes, we need to assess these changes simultaneously. Functional magnetic resonance imaging provides us with an opportunity to explore these changes at a systems level of analysis. Additional animal studies will be needed to specify, definitively, the exact nature or bases of the neural and molecular changes that underlie different aspects of learning and development. For our part, three sets of experiments will be presented that provide clues as to what neural regions may be involved in learning and development of cognitive control. These experiments examine differential patterns of brain activation and connectivity across age groups. We present findings consistent with qualitative shifts in the diffuse recruitment of cortical systems to more focal recruitment of specific cortical regions, with development.

22.1.3 Learning and development: the role of prediction

A routine debate in the developmental literature revolves around how learning and development may be differentiated. As learning occurs within a developmental context, the two could be considered inseparable. The main premise of this paper is that learning to predict temporal and contextual information in guiding our actions is a key component of both learning and cognitive development, that matures relatively early in the human infant. With development, these systems are fine-tuned and modulated by top-down cortical projections from prefrontal cortex that help the organism learn to alter behavior when these learned predictions are violated. The protracted development of prefrontal cortex and projections to and from this region, as opposed to development of learning-related brain centers, are suggested to distinguish learning and development. This review will focus exclusively on development from childhood through adulthood, given the lack of any extensive literature using the previously described methods in infants and toddlers to date.

22.2 Three neural subsystems implicated in learning and development

Three different neural subsystems will be described that support different aspects of learning that include striatal, cerebellar, and hippocampal brain regions. In general, the detection of unpredicted, salient, or novel events has been linked to striatal functioning (Berns *et al.* 1997; Redgrave *et al.* 1999; Shultz *et al.* 1997) whereas monitoring and detecting violations in the timing of events has been linked to cerebellar function (Ivry 1989, 1993). These regions differ from the hippocampus, which has been implicated in learning about contexts that require forming new associations (Gabrieli *et al.* 1994; Squire 1992) as in contextual learning (Davachi *et al.* 2003; Matus-Amat *et al.* 2004), memory for event sequences (e.g. Fortin *et al.* 2002), and novelty related processing (Strange and Dolan 2001; Habib *et al.* 2003). We propose that these neural systems (striatum, cerebellum, and hippocampus) may have independent roles in learning that involve the detection and prediction of events, their timing, and their association with other events, respectively. Although these systems will be described as three unique learning systems, clearly they work together in monitoring the environment and altering behavior in the appropriate context. We propose that these brain regions are able to alter behavior via afferent and efferent connections with prefrontal cortex that are fine-tuned with experience during development (Johnson 2002).

22.2.1 Frequency-based learning of the frontostriatal system

Simple manipulations in the frequency of target events can bias our behavior such that we are faster to respond to frequently occurring ones and slower to respond to less frequent ones. A stimulus becomes familiar or learned through repeated presentations, as in the classic habituation paradigm used with infants (Bornstein 1998; Fantz 1964) or the oddball paradigm used in electrophysiological studies (e.g. Knight 1984). Basically, decisions are biased in favor of frequent or familiar events as evidenced by quicker responses or shorter looking times toward them, and longer responses to rare or novel ones.

22.2.1.1 Animal model of frequency-based learning

Neural circuitry that has been implicated in biasing behavior toward familiar or predictable events includes the midbrain dopamine nuclei and forebrain regions that receive heavy dopaminergic innervation (e.g. Schultz 1997; Robbins and Everitt 1996; Horvitz *et al.* 1997; Berridge and Robinson 1998). Through an extensive series of studies Schultz and colleagues have shown dopamine cells in the midbrain nuclei of alert monkeys to have fairly consistent electrophysiological responses to rewards and stimuli that predict rewards (see Schultz 2002 for review). Rather than indicating the presence or absence of rewards or events *per se*, these neurons are argued to encode a prediction error, signaling the difference between actual and predicted occurrences of an event (Montague *et al.* 1996; Schultz 1997). If an expected event does not occur then there is a depression in the cell's activity (below baseline levels) at the time the event should have occurred. If an unexpected event occurs, the cells firing increases, indicating a bi-directional sensitivity to prediction and violation of expected events.

22.2.1.2 Functional imaging of studies

In our lab, we have examined the neural basis of simple frequency-based learning (i.e. prediction and violation of expected events) using functional magnetic resonance imaging with children and adults (Casey *et al.* 1997c; Durston *et al.* 2002a, b). The primary manipulations have been in the percentage of targets the subject responds to across the task. To establish a learned expectation, the target stimuli are presented more than 50 per cent of the time (typically 70 to 75 per cent) in a go/nogo type task. To examine the bias in performance, we measure the speed of response to the targets and their bias in responding to a stimulus, even when it is a non-target (Fig. 22.3). In

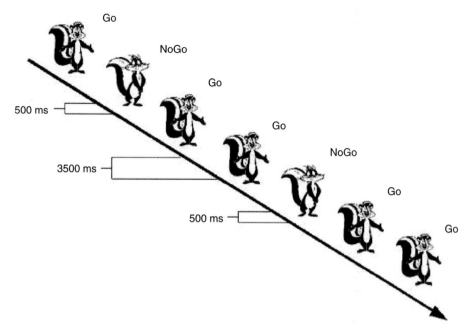

Fig. 22.3 Representative example of the Go/NoGo task with stimulus parameters.

our early studies using a go/nogo task, we examined changes in prefrontal regions as a function of target frequency (Casey *et al.* 1995, 1997c, 2001), but more recently we have examined both cortical and subcortical involvement (Casey *et al.* 2002; Durston *et al.* 2002a, b). Our initial findings from 18 children (7 to 11 years) and young adults, showed poorer performance by children in withholding a response, and a more diffuse pattern of prefrontal activity in children relative to adults. Although ventral, rather than dorsolateral, prefrontal activity was correlated with how well the subject performed, children recruited dorsolateral portions of the prefrontal cortex more. This diffuse recruitment of prefrontal cortex appeared to represent less efficient recruitment of relevant brain regions, or less fine-tuning of this region in performance of the task. This age-related decrease in overall activity may parallel regressive maturational processes such as loss of irrelevant synapses in addition to progressive changes such as strengthening of relevant connections to ventral prefrontal regions. Functional imaging does not provide the opportunity to directly assess such morphometric changes and so such conclusions are speculative at this point. Further, children and adults differed in how well they could perform the task. Thus, controlling for differences in behavioral performance is important when interpreting developmental imaging results.

To address performance differences across age groups and more precisely measure the effects of frequency on learning and behavior with development, we developed another version of the go/nogo paradigm (Durston *et al.* 2002a, b) that varied the number of targets (gos) preceding a non-target (nogo) trial (Casey *et al.* 2001; Durston *et al.* 2002a, b). This version of the task allows for comparisons of perform-ance across groups with different levels of difficulty to control for behavioral differ-ences between groups. The behavioral results showed that as the number of target trials preceding a non-target trial increased, accuracy decreased. Analysis of the imaging data showed that successful inhibition of a response to the less frequent non-target was associated with increased activity in ventral prefrontal cortex and the striatum. Ventral frontostriatal activity correlated with behavioral performance across age with children making more errors overall and maximally recruiting prefrontal regions even when a single target trial preceded a non-target trial. These findings suggest that immature cognition is more susceptible to interference from competing sources and that this pattern of brain activity is paralleled by maturational differences in underlying frontostriatal circuitry, especially at the level of the prefrontal cortex. In our theoretical model of cognitive control (Casey *et al.* 2001), we suggest that the striatum is essential in learning to predict event frequency, whereas the prefrontal cortex adjusts behavior when these predictions are violated and provide a mechanism for how responses to non-targets are overridden.

In sum, we suggest that detection of regularities and irregularities in the environ-ment develops early, even in infancy (Saffran *et al.* 1996, 1999; Kirkham *et al.* 2002), but the ability to adequately adjust behavior when these predictions are violated develops more slowly. We suggest that the maturation of ventral frontostriatal cir-cuitry may underlie the development of this ability, with the striatum having the capacity to detect and predict the occurrence of events early in development, and the prefrontal cortex having a more protracted development in helping to alter behavior when these predictions are violated.

22.2.1.3 Longitudinal imaging studies of frequency-based learning

The previous studies were cross sectional studies of cognitive and brain development. Given the individual differences in brain morphometry (Caviness *et al.* 1996) and behavior, we used functional MRI to assess changes with learning and development, longitudinally (Durston *et al.*, in press). We imaged children at two different time points. The initial scan was acquired at approximately 9 years of age and the second scan was acquired 2 years later, at approximately 11 years. A second group of subjects were scanned once at approximately 11 years (21 scans in total). Overall, the subjects scanned longitudinally got faster in detecting frequently occurring targets, but accur-acy did not change significantly in how well they withheld a response to non-target trials. When we compared the cross-sectional comparison group to the longitudinal group there were no significant changes in behavioral performance.

The longitudinal imaging results showed that most cortical regions showed either no change across time (e.g. primary motor cortex in responding to targets) or else an attenuation in activation (e.g. dorsolateral prefrontal regions in withholding a response) (Fig. 22.4). The only region where activation increased with age within subjects was in the right inferior frontal gyrus, a region shown previously, and in this study, to correlate with behavioral performance (Durston *et al.* 2002a, b, in press). These results suggest that behavioral improvement in target detection is paralleled by an increase in recruitment of ventral prefrontal regions, consistent with less diffuse and more focal patterns of cortical activity with age. For the cross-sectional comparison, a less consistent pattern was observed, where a number of regions that showed a reduction in activation in the longitudinal analysis now showed no clear change. These results suggest that studies tracking development in individuals are more sensitive to subtle changes than cross-sectional comparisons.

22.2.1.4 Adult imaging studies of learning

How do our developmental findings within children compare to changes observed with adults during learning? Karni and others (Karni *et al.* 1995) have shown rapid learning effects in primary motor areas in adults during motor sequence learning within a single session that increased over weeks of training. The activity in motor cortex became less diffuse and increased over time. The example of initial diffuse cortical activity early in learning, followed by an increase in focal activity, in part parallels results just described from developmental cross sectional and longitudinal fMRI studies. These studies show diffuse activity in children relative to adolescents and adults, with adolescents showing the greatest focal activity during performance of behavioral tasks, even when performance is equated (Casey *et al.* 1997c, 2002; Hertz-Pannier *et al.* 1997; Klingberg *et al.* 2001; Schlagger *et al.* 2002). These findings

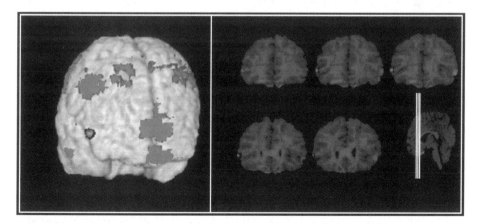

Fig. 22.4 Illustration of fMRI-based changes in MR signal observed with development longitudinally. Blue areas indicate decreases in activity in these regions with age and red areas are those that show increase in activation with age. See Plate 5 in the centre of this book for a full colour version. (Adapted from Durston *et al.* in press.)

highlight a possible approach for addressing the learning versus development question by examining learning within children and tracking whether the pattern of brain activity observed with development is enhanced with intensive exposure to the task.

The cross-sectional and longitudinal imaging data on frequency manipulations are suggestive of regressive maturation processes, but both regressive and progressive brain changes are occurring, especially in the prefrontal cortex. So how can we constrain our functional imaging findings with regard to these maturational changes? One way is to apply a converging methods approach (Casey and Munakata 2002) and use complimentary methods to examine progressive processes such as myelin and connectivity within prefrontal circuitry, and examine the extent to which these change with behavioral changes.

22.2.1.5 Diffusion studies of frequency-based learning

As described earlier, DTI is a relatively new technique that measures the extent of diffusion of water molecules and is sensitive to myelin and regularity of fiber tracts. As water can diffuse more easily between fibers than across them, especially fatty myelinated fibers, we get a measure of directionality and an index of regularity and myelin of these fibers (i.e. connectivity). As such, greater diffusion would be expected in less mature or irregular connections. We (Liston *et al.* in press) used this method to examine whether maturation in prefrontal connectivity may be associated with the ability to predict the frequency of events and to alter behavior when these predictions were violated. Fifteen subjects between the ages of 7 and 31 years were tested on our go/nogo task and scanned using the DTI pulse sequence. As our previous functional imaging studies have shown that performance of this task activates ventral frontostriatal regions, we examined connectivity between these regions (striatum and ventral prefrontal cortex).

The average absolute diffusivity in prefrontal white matter tracts was significantly lower in adults than in children, with a relatively larger decrease in diffusion perpendicular to axons than parallel to them. This decrease suggests that on-going myelination in the maturing prefrontal cortex is contributing to restricted diffusion. This shift was paralleled by developmental changes in performance on the go/nogo task. Although accuracies were not significantly different, children's reaction times were slower than adults, suggesting that inhibitory control demanded greater effort from the younger subjects. Less diffusion (greater connectivity) was associated with faster reaction times ($r = 0.856$, $p < 0.001$), suggesting that connectivity in frontostriatal fiber tracts may contribute to enhanced behavioral inhibition (Fig. 22.5). This result was not attributable to the potentially confounding effects of age or accuracy, since the correlation remained significant even with these variables partialed out ($r = 0.756$, $p < 0.004$). Further, this correlation appeared specific to the frontostriatal fibers and not merely a proxy for general brain maturation as we controlled for this possibility by examining a posterior tract that did not correlate with behavioral inhibition.

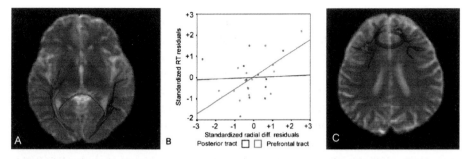

Fig. 22.5 DTI-based anterior (A) and posterior (C) fiber tracts and the correlation with performance of the go/nogo task with prefrontal tracts, but not posterior tracts (B). See Plate 6 in the centre of this book for a full colour version.

Collectively, these results indicate that maturation of frontostriatal connectivity and function contributes to a developing capacity for cognitive control (i.e. adjusting behavior when predictions about the occurrence of events are violated). The fMRI data showed fine-tuning of prefrontal activity with development as the pattern of activity shifted from a diffuse to more focal pattern. Our DTI results suggest that enhanced connectivity between these structures may contribute to this effect.

22.2.2 Detecting regularities and irregularities in timing: role of the cerebellum

The previous studies showed how simple frequency based manipulations could bias behavior and how using different imaging methodologies may constrain our interpretation of what is changing with learning and development. Our findings showed the importance of the development of frontostriatal circuitry in altering behavior when predictions about an event were violated. The predictions formed were based on what event would occur, but when an event will occur is just as important in guiding behavior. We have developed imaging studies in an attempt to dissociate neural systems involved in these different aspects of prediction and learning of what and when events in the environment will occur.

The two circuits of primary interest in the current studies are the frontostriatal and frontocerebellar circuits. These circuits are similar in projections to and from the prefrontal cortex. It is known that the prefrontal cortex projects directly to the basal ganglia and cerebellum and both project back to the prefrontal cortex via the thalamus (Middleton and Strick 1994, 2002). The basal ganglia and cerebellum have been implicated in monitoring the frequency and/or timing of events, respectively (Davidson *et al.* 2004; Hayes *et al.* 1998; Keele *et al.* 2003; McClure *et al.* 2003; Spencer *et al.* 2003; Van Mier and Petersen 2002). Planning and maintaining appropriate thoughts and actions, in different contexts over time, is an important element of cognitive control. Thus, frontostriatal and frontocerebellar circuits may provide neural mechanisms for the maintenance of representations of events over time. Simple detection of violations that presumably allows the system to attend to and learn new information, may be linked to intrinsic inhibitory functions of the basal ganglia and cerebellum, in the absence of prefrontally-driven planned thoughts and actions, early in development.

In an effort to show the importance of predicting what events would occur when, and detecting violations in these predictions, we performed two experiments (Davidson *et al.* 2004). In the first experiment, we modified the previously described parametric go/nogo task such that an expected stimulus occurred (go), or an unexpected stimulus occurred (nogo), or the expected stimulus failed to occur at the expected time. In the second, we attempted to dissociate cognitive and neural processes associated with detection of violations in simple frequency-based learning from those related to temporal-based learning (Fig. 22.6).

Based on data from 12 adults, we showed that the striatum was especially sensitive to frequency manipulations as discussed in the previous section. Specifically, there was a slight increase in striatal activity with the presentation of an unexpected stimulus (Davidson *et al.* 2004) consistent with previous reports (Durston *et al.* 2002a, b, 2003). The insight the findings from this experiment offered was in what

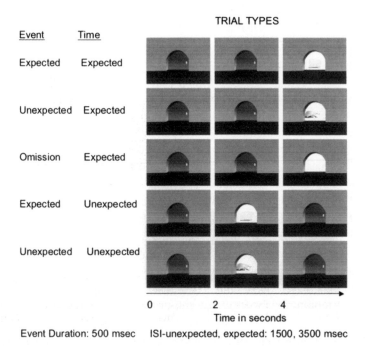

Fig. 22.6 Illustration of the five different trial types for the *what versus when* task. On most trials, the expected target event (cheese) occurred at the expected time (4 seconds).

happens within this region when an expected stimulus fails to occur. The results showed a significant decrease in activity following the omission of an expected stimulus. Thus the striatum is sensitive to whether an expected event occurs or not, as well as whether an unexpected event occurs.

In the previous experiment, the decreased striatal activity when an expected event did not occur may have been due to a violation in timing of the event (i.e. detection of event at an expected time), given it occurred repeatedly at a regular interval. In a second study, we followed up on these findings and explicitly manipulated the temporal presentation of events. The five conditions are presented in Fig. 22.6 that reflect an expected or unexpected stimulus at an expected or unexpected time (Fig. 22.6). We show a dissociation in the sensitivity of the cerebellum and caudate, respectively, in the timing and type of event presented (Fig. 22.7). The cerebellum was recruited when a stimulus was presented at an unexpected time, suggesting sensitivity of this region to the unpredictability of the timing of events. Both the striatum and the

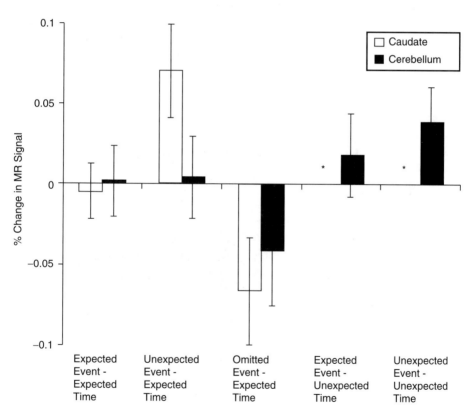

Fig. 22.7 Percent change in MR signal intensity for the rare even trials for the striatum and cerebellum illustrating a differential response in the caudate nucleus and cerebellum regarding what and when an event occurred (* indicates no activity for this region).

cerebellum showed suppressed activity when an expected stimulus did not occur at the expected time (target omission) that reflects both violations in what and when the stimulus occurred. Finally, as shown in the previous experiment, the striatum was recruited when an unexpected stimulus occurred at an expected time, but there was no activation of the striatum when stimuli were presented at an unexpected time. These results suggest that the cerebellum and striatum may help engage control systems by detecting violations in the timing and occurrence of events, respectively (Davidson *et al.* 2004).

22.2.3 Associative learning in the hippocampal system

The previous studies have provided examples of learning about what and when events occur, but we also learn associations among events in their occurrence and timing. In a third study, we attempted to dissociate cognitive and neural processes underlying simple frequency-based versus association-based learning. We manipulated the frequency of the occurrence of cue and target stimuli and their association with one another (Amso *et al.* 2005). The frequency manipulation was designed so that frequent and novel target event stimuli were preceded by and equally associated with the same cue, effectively eliminating the effects of context in the comparison. The association manipulation was such that the target event was identical in the novel and frequent association condition. Here the manipulation rests solely on the probability of an association with the preceding stimulus, thereby controlling for frequency weights in associative learning. Using fMRI, we examined the independent contributions of the striatum and the hippocampus in simple frequency- and association-based learning in young adults.

This *what versus when* task consisted of two cues that predicted each of three targets with varying probabilities (Fig. 22.8). One cue predicted a target 75per cent of the time and predicted the other two targets approximately 12 per cent of the time. A second cue predicted the occurrence of two targets 25 per cent of the time, while predicting a third target 50 per cent of the time. Simultaneously, we varied the frequency with which each target was presented throughout the task, independent of cue-target associations. Frequencies for each of three targets were 50 per cent, 20 per cent, and 30 per cent across the entire experiment (Fig. 22.8). Participants pressed one of three buttons that corresponded to target identity using their index, middle, and pointer finger of their right hand.

The behavioral data showed longer response latencies to novel target stimuli, that is those with a lower frequency of occurrence across the experiment, as well as learning-related behavioral changes (shorter response latencies) for both frequently occurring and frequently associated stimuli. The imaging results showed increased striatal activity for novel (less frequent) targets only and increased left hippocampal activity

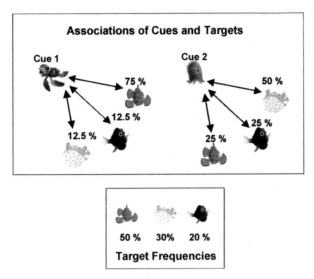

Fig. 22.8 Task learning parameters: frequency of target occurrences, and frequency of associations between cues and targets (Adapted from Amso *et al.* 2005).

to novel (less frequent) associations (Fig. 22.9). This work suggests different neural mechanisms for learning based on simple frequencies and associations simultaneously within a single paradigm. As the frequently presented targets and associations were learned, those stimuli that were more novel (i.e. less frequent occurrence and/or less frequently associated with another stimulus) showed longer response latencies. Thus, the response to novelty or less familiar stimuli served as an index of learning, similar to effects observed in longer looking times to novel stimuli after habituation to a familiar one. Our behavioral data suggests that simple frequency learning takes place earlier than does learning associations with associations posing more difficulty for the learner (Amso *et al.*, submitted).

These behavioral and imaging findings are interesting in light of the developmental work using novelty preferences and looking time measures to show learning in infants. Studies in language learning (Saffran *et al.* 1996; Gomez, Chapter 4, this volume), auditory sequence learning (Saffran *et al.* 1999), and visual sequence learning (Kirkham *et al.* 2002), all suggest that infants can learn simple statistics and probabilities from environmental inputs. The current work has the potential to inform the developmental learning literature by highlighting neural mechanisms that may be supporting such learning early in life.

22.2.4 Summary of imaging studies on learning and development

A premise of this paper is that predictive learning is a cornerstone of cognitive development. Behavioral and neuroimaging evidence was provided that delineated

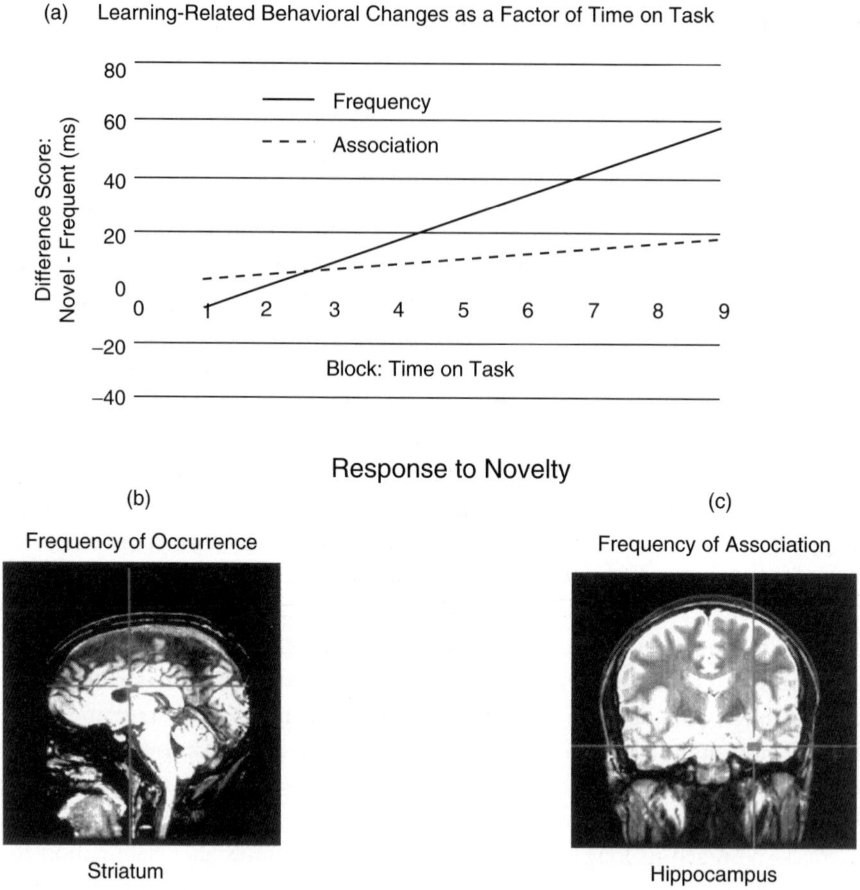

(a) Learning-Related Behavioral Changes as a Factor of Time on Task

Response to Novelty

(b)

Frequency of Occurrence

Striatum

(c)

Frequency of Association

Hippocampus

Fig. 22.9 Behavioral performance (a), striatal activity (b), and hippocampal activity (c) to infrequently presented target stimuli and stimuli associations. See Plate 7 in the centre of this book for a full colour version.

at least three different neural systems underlying predictive learning: a frontostriatal system that learns about the frequency of events; a frontocerebellar system that learns about their timing; and a hippocampal system that learns about associations among events. Within these three systems, we suggest that the striatum, cerebellum, and hippocampus mature as early as infancy and are recruited in learning to predict what events to expect, when to expect them, and in which contexts, respectively. Each system detects both regularities and irregularities in events, passing that information along to the prefrontal cortex that provides top–down control in altering behavior when these expectations are violated. The three sets of imaging studies show that the development of these systems is accompanied by both structural and functional changes in these systems, with more refined recruitment and strengthened connectivity within prefrontal circuitry.

22.3 **Discussion**

How have developments in non-invasive imaging tools helped to inform or constrain our understanding of learning and development? This paper is an attempt to help make a basic distinction on how learning and development may be differentiated by the underlying cognitive and neural processes. Both early and later in life, learning occurs through the recruitment of striatal, cerebellar, and hippocampal regions sensitive to the frequency, timing, and association of events. Only with development of the prefrontal cortex, do we see adjustments in this learning that allows us to flexibly guide and alter behavior when our predictions are violated. We suggest that with development, fine-tuning and modulation by top–down prefrontal projections that mature more slowly than subcortical learning systems (striatum, hippocampus, and cerebellum) which explain differences between early learning and later development. We illustrated how simple learning and prediction of events could be assessed with fMRI showing different neural mechanisms for learning, that were delineated across tasks, depending on the type of information learned. While subcortical systems involved in predicting events in the environment are fairly intact early in development, neural systems involved in altering behavior when these predictions are violated develop more gradually as evidenced by gradual change in recruitment of cortical regions from diffuse to focal, and the simultaneous changes in indices of connectivity, and improvements in cognitive control.

Acknowledgment

This work was supported in part by R21 DA15882 and R01 MH63255 to BJC and Cornell Sackler Biomedical Fellowship to DA.

References

Amso D, Davidson MC, Johnson SP and Casey BJ (2005). Contributions of the hippocampus and the striatum to simple frequency and association-based learning. *Neuroimage*, 27(2): 291–298.

Berns GS, Cohen JD and Mintun M (1997). Brain regions responsive to novelty in the absence of awareness. *Science*, 276, 1272–1275.

Berridge KC and Robinson TE (1998). What is the role of dopamine in reward: hedonic impact, reward learning, or incentive salience? *Brain Research Reviews*, 28, 309–369.

Bornstein MH (1998). Stability in mental development from early life: Methods, measures, models, meanings and myths. In: F Simon and GE Butterworth, eds. *The development of sensory, motor and cognitive capacities in early infancy: From sensation to cognition*, pp. 299–331. Hove, England: Psychological Press.

Bourgeois JP, Goldman-Rakic PS and Rakic P (1994). Synaptogenesis in the prefrontal cortex of rhesus monkeys. *Cerebral Cortex*, 4, 78–96.

Brown, TT *et al.* (in press). Developmental changes in human cerebral functional organization for word generation. *Cereb Cortex.*

Casey, BJ (2000) Development and Disruption of Inhibitory Mechanisms of Attention. In R. S. Siegler & J. L. McClelland (Eds.) Mechanisms of Cognitive Development: The Carnegie Symposium on Cognition, 2000 Vol. 28(pp. 155–168). Hillsdale, NJ: Erlbaum.

Casey BJ (in press). Frontostriatal and frontocerebellar circuitry underlying cognitive control. In: U Mayr, E Awh and SW Keele, eds. *Developing individuality in the brain: a tribute to Michael Posner.* Washington, DC: American Psychological Association.

Casey BJ, Cohen, JD, Jezzard P, *et al.* (1995). Activation of prefrontal cortex in children during a nonspatial working memory task with functional MRI. *Neuroimage,* 2, 221–229.

Casey BJ, Durston S and Fossella JA (2001). Evidence for a mechanistic model of cognitive control. *Clinical Neuroscience Research,* 1, 267–282.

Casey, B. J. and Munakata, Y. Special Issue on Converging Methods Approach in Developmental Science, Invited Editor, Developmental Psychobiology, 2002; 40.

Casey BJ, Thomas KM, Davidson MC, *et al.* (2002). Dissociating striatal and hippocampal function developmentally with a stimulus-response compatibility task. *Journal of Neuroscience,* 22, 8647–8652.

Casey BJ, Trainor RJ, Orendi JL, *et al.* (1997c). A developmental functional MRI study of prefrontal activation during performance of a go-no-go task. *Journal of Cognitive Neuroscience,* 9, 835–847.

Caviness VS Jr, Kennedy DN, Richelme C, Rademacher J, Filipek PA (1996). The human brain age 7–11 years: a volumetric analysis based on magnetic resonance images. *Cerebral Cortex,* 6, 726–736.

Davachi L, Mitchell JP and Wagner AD (2003). Multiple routes to memory: Distinct medial temporal lobe processes build item and source memories. *Proceedings of the National Academy of Sciences,* 100, 2157–2162.

Davidson MC, Horvitz JC, Tottenham N, *et al.* (2004). Dissociation of cingulate and caudate response to unexpected non-rewarding stimuli. *NeuroImage.* 23: 1039–1045.

Davidson MC, Horvitz JC, Tottenham N, Durston S, Fossella JA and Casey BJ (2003). FMRI investigation of circuitry modulated by violations in stimuli and temporal expectations. *Proceedings of the Society for Neuroscience* (abstract).

De Haan M and Johnson M (2003). Mechanisms and theories of brain development. In: M de Hann and M Johnson, eds. *The cognitive neuroscience of development,* pp. 1–18. New York, NY: Psychology Press.

Diamond A (1990). Developmental time course in human infants and infant monkeys and the neural bases of inhibitory control in reaching. In: A Diamond, ed. *The development and neural bases of higher cognitive functions,* pp. 637–676. New York: New York Academy of Sciences Press.

Durston S, Fossella JA, Casey BJ, *et al.* (2005): Differential effects of DRD4 and DAT genotype on fronto-striatal gray matter volumes in boys with ADHD, their unaffected siblings and controls. *Molecular Psychiatry,* 10(7): 478–85.

Durston S, Hulshoff Pol HE, Schnack HG, *et al.* (in press). Magnetic resonance imaging of boys with attention deficit hyperactivity disorder and their unaffected siblings. *JAACAP.*

Durston S, Thomas KM, Worden MS, Yang Y and Casey BJ (2002a). An fMRI study of the effect of preceding context on inhibition. *NeuroImage,* 16, 449–453.

Durston S, Thomas KM, Yang Y, Ulug AM, Zimmerman R and Casey BJ (2002b). A neural basis for development of inhibitory control. *Developmental Science,* 5, 9–16.

Durston S, Tottenham N, Thomas KM, *et al.* (2003). Differential patterns of striatal activation in young children with and without ADHD. *Biological Psychiatry,* 53: 871–878.

Fantz RL (1964). Visual experience in infants: Decreased attention to familiar patterns relative to novel ones. *Science,* 146, 668–670.

Fortin NJ, Agster KL and Eichenbaum HB (2002). Critical role of the hippocampus in memory for sequences of events. *Nature Neuroscience,* 5, 458–462.

Gabrieli JD, Keane MM, Stanger BZ, Kjelgaard MM, Corkin S and Growdon JH (1994). Dissociations among structural-perceptual, lexical-semantic and event-fact memory systems in Alzheimers, amnesic and normal subjects. *Cortex,* 30, 75–103.

Habib R, McIntosh AR, Wheeler MA and Tulving E (2003). Memory encoding and hippocampally-based novelty/familiarity discrimination networks. *Neuropsychologia,* 41, 271–279.

Hayes AE, Davidson MC, Keele SW and Rafal RD (1998). Toward a functional analysis of the basal ganglia. *Journal of Cognitive Neuroscience,* 10, 178–198.

Hertz-Pannier L, Gaillard W D, Mott SH, *et al.* (1997). *Noninvasive assessment* of language dominance in children and adolescents with functional MRI: a preliminary study. *Neurology,* 48, 1003–1012.

Horvitz JC, Stewart T and Jacobs BL (1997). Burst activity of ventral tegmental dopamine neurons is elicited by sensory stimuli in the awake cat. *Brain Research,* 759, 251–258.

Iversen S D and Mishkin M (1970). Perseverative interference in monkeys following selective lesions of the inferior prefrontal convexity. *Experimental Brain Research,* 11, 376–386.

Ivry RB (1993). Cerebellar involvement in the explicit representation of temporal information. In: P Tallal, AM Galaburda, RR Llinas and C vonEuler, eds. *Temporal information processing in the nervous system: Special reference to dyslexia and dysphasia,* pp. 214–230. New York: New York Academy of Sciences.

Ivry RB and Keele SW (1989). Timing functions of the cerebellum. *Journal of Cognitive Neuroscience,* 1, 136–152.

Johnson MH (2002). Neural mechanisms of cognitive development in infancy. In: J McClelland and Thompson, eds. *International encyclopedia of the social and behavioral sciences,* pp. 2103–2108. Elsevier Science. London.

Karni A, Meyer G, Jezzard P, Adams MM, Turner R and Ungerleider LG (1995). Functional MRI evidence for adult motor cortex plasticity during motor skill learning. *Nature,* 377, 155–158.

Keele SW, Ivry R, Mayr U, Hazeltine E and Heuer H (2003). The cognitive and neural architecture of sequence representation. *Psychological Review.* 110 (2), 316–339.

Kirkham NZ, Slemmer JA and Johnson SP (2002). Visual statistical learning in infancy: Evidence for a domain general learning mechanism. *Cognition,* 83, B35–42.

Klingberg T, Forssberg H and Westerberg H (2001). Increased brain activity in frontal and parietal cortex underlies the development of visuospatial working memory capacity during childhood. *Journal of Cognitive Neuroscience,* 14, 1–10.

Klingberg T, Vaidya CJ, Gabrieli JD, Moseley ME and Hedehus M (1999). Myelination and organization of the frontal white matter in children: A diffusion tensor MRI study. *Neuroreport,* 10, 2817–2821.

Knight RT (1984). Decreased response to novel stimuli after prefrontal lesions in man. *Electroencephalography and Clinical Neurophysiology,* 59, 9–20.

Kwong KK, Belliveau JW, Chesler DA, Goldberg IE, Weiskoff RM, Poncelet BP, *et al.* (1992). Dynamic magnetic resonance imaging of human brain activity during primary sensory stimulation. *Proceedings of the National Academy of Sciences, USA,* 89, 5675–5679.

Liston, C, Watts, R, Tottenham, N, Davidson, M, Niogi, M, Ulug, A, *et al.* (in press). Frontostriatal microstructure predicts individual differences in cognitive control. *Cerebral Cortex.*

Logothetis N, Pauls J, Augath M, Trinath T and Oeltermann A (2001). Neurophysiological investigation of the basis of the fMRI signal. *Nature,* 412, 150–157.

Matus-Amat P, Higgins EA, Barrientos RM and Rudy JW (2004). The role of the dorsal hippocampus in the acquisition and retrieval of context memory representations. *Journal of Neuroscience,* 24, 2431–2439.

McClure SM, Berns GS and Montague PR (2003). Temporal prediction errors in a passive learning task activate human striatum. *Neuron,* 38, 1–20.

Middleton FA and Strick PL (1994). Anatomical evidence for cerebellar and basal ganglia involvement in higher cognitive function. *Science,* 226, 458–461.

Middleton FA and Strick PL (2002). Basal-ganglia projections to the prefrontal cortex of the primate. *Cerebral Cortex,* 12, 926–935.

Miller EK and Cohen JD (2001). An integrative theory of prefrontal cortex function. *Annual Review of Neuroscience,* 24, 167–202.

Montague PR, Dayan P and Sejnowski TJ (1996). A framework for mesencephalic dopamine systems based on predictive Hebbian learning. *Journal of Neuroscience,* 16, 1936–1947.

Ogawa S, Tank DW, Menon R, Ellermann JM, Kim SG, Merkle H, *et al.* (1992). Intrinsic signal changes accompanying sensory stimulation: functional brain mapping with magnetic resonance imaging. *Proc. Natl. Acad. Sci.* USA, 89(July), 5951–5955.

Raichle M (2001). Cognitive neuroscience: Bold insights. *Nature,* 12, 128–130.

Redgrave P, Prescott TJ and Gurney K (1999). Is the short-latency dopamine response too short to signal reward error? *Trends in Neuroscience,* 22, 146–151.

Robbins TW and Everitt BJ (1996). Neurobehavioural mechanisms of reward and motivation. *Current Opinion in Neurobiology,* 6, 228–236.

Saffran JR, Aslin RN and Newport EL (1996). Statistical learning by 8-month-old infants. *Science,* 274, 1926–1928.

Saffran JR, Johnson EK, Aslin, RN and Newport EL (1999). Statistical learning of tone sequences by human infants and adults. *Cognition,* 70, 27–52.

Schlaggar BL, Brown TT, Lugar HM, Visscher KM, Miezin FM and Peterson SE (2002). Functional neuroanatomical differences between adults and school-age children in the processing of single words. *Science,* 296, 1476–1479.

Schultz W (1997). Dopamine neurons and their role in reward mechanisms. *Current Opinion in Neurobiology,* 7, 191–197.

Schultz W (2002). Getting formal with dopamine and reward. *Neuron,* 36, 241–263.

Schultz W, Apicella P, Scarnati E and Ljungberg T (1992). Neuronal activity in monkey ventral striatum related to the expectation of reward. *Journal of Neuroscience,* 12, 4595–4610.

Shultz W, Dayan P and Montague RR (1997). A neural substrate of prediction and reward. *Science,* 275, 1593–1599.

Spencer RM, Zelaznik HN, Diedrichsen J and Ivry RB (2003). Disrupted timing of discontinuous but not continuous movements by cerebellar lesions. *Science,* 300, 1437–1439.

Squire LR (1992). Memory and the hippocampus: A synthesis from findings with rats, monkeys and humans. *Psychological Review,* 99, 119–124.

Strange BA and Dolan RJ (2001). Adaptive Anterior hippocampal responses to oddball stimuli. *Hippocampus,* 11, 690–698.

Thompson RA and Nelson CA (2001). Developmental science and the media: Early brain development. *American Psychologist,* **56,** 5–15.

Van Mier HI and Petersen SE (2002). *Role of the cerebellum in motor cognition. Annals of the New York Academy of Science,* **978,** 334–353.

Watts R, Liston C, Niogi S and Ulug AM (2004). Fiber tracking using magnetic resonance diffusion tensor imaging and its application to human brain development. *Mental Retardation and Developmental Disability Research Reviews,* **9,** 168–177.

Chapter 23

Spatial cognitive development following early focal brain injury: Evidence for adaptive change in brain and cognition

Joan Stiles, Brianna Paul, and John R. Hesselink

Abstract

The field of developmental cognitive neuroscience has grown exponentially over the last two decades. The body of findings from both animal and human studies that has emerged has fundamentally changed the way we think about development. The age-old question of nature versus nurture is rapidly losing relevance as study after study demonstrates the essential role of the interaction between biology and experience in development. Development is principled, but dynamic, relying on the careful balance between progressive commitment to stable basic functional systems, while retaining the capacity for adaptation when the demands on the organism change. Further, human development is a protracted process extending at least into adolescence. Indeed, there is substantial evidence that the mammalian brain retains considerable capacity for adaptive reorganization throughout the lifespan.

The study of children with early-occurring focal brain injury provides a model for articulating and specifying this dynamic, adaptive, and protracted view of development. The children in the studies described here suffered focal brain insult in the pre- or perinatal period, long before the acquisition of higher cognitive functions. In many cases, the injuries affect substantial portions of one cerebral hemisphere, resulting in patterns of neural damage that would compromise cognitive ability in adults. However, longitudinal behavioral studies of this population of children have revealed only mild cognitive deficits, and preliminary data from functional brain imaging studies suggest that alternative patterns of functional organization emerge in the wake of early injury. It is argued that the capacity for adaptation is not the *result* of early insult. Rather, it reflects normal developmental processes operating against a backdrop of serious perturbation of the neural substrate. Three examples illustrating profiles of spatial cognitive development and related profiles of functional neural activation provide evidence for adaptive change.

23.1 Introduction

The central debate in the field of developmental psychology has for decades centered on the very old, but perhaps ill-posed, dichotomy of nature versus nurture. While proponents of both positions in this debate acknowledge the role of both nature and nurture in development, from each side the concession to the other view is more often perfunctory than substantive. Proponents of strongly nativist views see no alternative to the positing of innate conceptual constraints on cognitive development, while proponents of a more nurture-based view see no evidence for the plausibility of such constraints. Constructivist views, which dominate the nurture side of the modern psychological debate, argue for adaptive interaction. However, within the field of developmental psychology, there are little actual data documenting the nature of the interaction between experience and biological development. For decades, the central arguments that underlie the various elaborations of the nature–nurture debate have proceeded in the absence of substantive information about the nature and process of brain development. Yet, the debate revolves around claims that must be reconciled with precisely this class of data. Specifically, claims about innateness or interaction must present a biologically feasible mechanism through which development can proceed.

Over the past several decades, significant advances have been made in our understanding of the basic stages and mechanisms of mammalian brain development. While very little of this work has been, or even *could* have been carried out with humans, it has greatly informed our understanding of human brain development (Stiles 2000). Studies elucidating the neurobiology of brain development span the levels of neural organization from the molecular, to the cellular, to the macroanatomic. This large body of work provides a picture of brain development as the product of a complex series of dynamic and adaptive processes operating within a genetically organized but constantly changing context (Waddington 1939; Morange 2001). The view of brain development that has emerged from the developmental neurobiology literature presents both challenges and opportunities to psychologists seeking to understand the fundamental processes that underlie social and cognitive development, and the neural systems that mediate them.

This chapter is intended to provide a brief introduction to the neuropsychological approach to studying basic questions about cognitive development. It begins with a summary of key questions and issues in the study of neurocognitive development in human children, emphasizing the important role of special populations of children with neurodevelopmental disorders in understanding the emergence of basic brain–behavior relations. The chapter then turns to findings from a longitudinal study of spatial cognitive development in children with pre- and perinatal focal brain injury to illustrate how a neuropsychological approach can inform and constrain our understanding of the processes that underlie the development of this basic cognitive function.

23.2 Contributions from neurobiology and neuropsychology

While studies of psychological development have made little progress toward specifying the nature of the relations between brain and cognitive development, more compelling data have begun to emerge from work in developmental neurobiology. From the very first stages of embryonic brain development through the experience-mediated organizational changes in the adolescent brain, the evidence of interaction and the capacity for adaptive change abounds. Development is a process defined by the progressive and interdependent commitment of neural and cognitive resources to specific functions and processes. This view of brain and cognitive development as dynamic and interactive is critical to addressing the very important questions posed by those who seek to understand the origins of human thought and social interaction. This view argues strongly for the need for psychologists to fundamentally rethink the constructs of interaction and adaptation, and their essential role in human development.

23.2.1 The development of higher cognitive functions

While data from animal models have established basic principles of brain and behavioral development, they can provide only limited insight into the development of higher cognitive functions. There is, however, a small but growing body of data from human studies. One important class of studies involves functional neuroimaging, including electrophysiology, magnetoencephalography, near-infrared optical tomography, and functional magnetic resonance imaging (fMRI). To date, the most widely used of these methods with pediatric populations has been electrophysiology, but the other methods are rapidly becoming more prevalent. The application of functional neuroimaging to child populations offers great promise for exploring directly the dynamic nature of developmental change in brain–behavior relations.

By far the largest body of the work with human children involves studies of clinical populations in which specific perturbations of normal development are used to map the range of possible developmental trajectories and outcomes. The accumulating work documenting profiles of developmental change in children with a wide range of neurodevelopmental disorders strongly supports the notion that there is no single developmental pathway. Rather, development reflects the interaction of highly specified (and sometimes pathological) biological factors and the experience of the individual (see Maurer and Mondloch and Karmiloff-Smith, Chapters 19 and 24, this volume). The remainder of this chapter will focus on one such clinical population, children with pre- or perinatal focal brain injury.

23.3 Children with pre- or perinatal focal brain lesions

One clinical population that has proven particularly helpful in elucidating the dynamic and adaptive nature of brain and cognitive development has been children with pre- or perinatal focal brain lesions (PL). Within the adult neuropsychological literature, patients with localized brain injury have been widely used as a model for understanding mature patterns of brain organization. The logic of this very large body of work is typically one of subtraction and dissociation in which the goal is to identify the functional *loss* that is uniquely associated with injury to a particular brain region. However, in the study of child populations, the question of functional localization is clearly subordinate to the issue of delineating the mechanisms that underlie the dynamic features of cognitive and neural development that are so prominent in the data. Indeed, simple models of functional deficit or sparing typically fail to capture profiles of either developmental change or outcome in populations of children with neurological disorders. The study of cognitive development following early neural insult does not typically focus on defining a single, uniform profile of functional organization. Rather, the central questions concern the multiple, *alternative* patterns of brain organization that can arise following early injury to the developing brain (Moses and Stiles 2002).

Our population of children with PL suffered a single, unilateral neurological insult (most commonly a stroke) very early in development. The cause of the insult is typically unknown. Patients with medical complications that might result in more global neural involvement such as infection or maternal drug or alcohol use were explicitly excluded from the sample. The strokes are frequently large. Approximately half of the children in our sample have injury involving distribution of the middle cerebral artery, thus affecting temporal and parietal, and sometimes the margin of occipital and frontal, brain regions. However, many children have smaller injuries confined to a single cerebral lobe or to a more limited subcortical region. The children in the population are typically born full term, with normal or corrected-to-normal sensory functions, and IQs in the normal range. Over a period of more than 20 years, our research group has followed, prospectively, a large sample of children with PL with a goal of addressing four key questions:

1. Are specific behavioral deficits evident early in development?
2. Are associations between pattern of behavioral deficit and site of brain injury among children comparable to the patterns of association observed among adults?

3. Do we find evidence of persistent behavioral deficit over time, or is there significant compensation, adaptation, and development?

4. Do patterns of behavioral deficit change over time, and if so what is the nature of the change and how does this change occur?

Our principle focus has been on the development of language, spatial cognitive functioning, and affect. Our studies are prospective in that we identify children as early as possible, and study their development over time. This approach allows us to examine development in detail during periods when children are acquiring or elaborating cognitive skills and abilities. All of this work is done in conjunction with large cross-sectional, and in some cases longitudinal, studies of typically developing children. These studies are designed to provide profiles of typical developmental change for targeted measures against which the developmental profiles for the PL group can be compared. One important finding, common to all of our domains of cognitive inquiry, is that the patterns of deficit observed among children with PL are milder than those observed among adults with comparable injury and with development children manifest considerable capacity for behavioral, and possibly neural, compensation. Equally interesting, each domain of inquiry has yielded a somewhat different set of answers to the four questions that guide our work (Stiles *et al.* 2002). Space does not permit a full discussion of each of these areas of study. Rather, this paper will focus on spatial cognitive development, and more specifically on the development of visual pattern processing.

23.4 Spatial cognitive development in children with prenatal focal brain lesions

One major focus of inquiry in our study of spatial cognitive processing in children with PL has been visual pattern processing. Processing of any visuospatial pattern requires specification of both the parts and the overall configuration. It thus involves both the ability to segment a pattern into a set of constituent parts, and the ability to integrate those parts into a coherent whole. Further, there is evidence that the two cerebral hemispheres play complementary roles in processing visual pattern information. Studies of adult stroke patients have shown that injury to left posterior brain regions results in disorders involving difficulty in defining the parts of a spatial array, while patients with right posterior lesions have difficulty with the configural aspects of spatial pattern analysis (e.g. McFie and Zangwill 1960; Piercy *et al.* 1960; Warrington *et al.* 1966; Delis *et al.* 1986; Robertson and Delis 1986; Swindell *et al.* 1988; Robertson and Lamb 1991). Data from a study by Delis, Robertson, and Efron (1986), provides a particularly graphic example of this dissociation (Fig. 23.1). Adult stroke patients were asked to study a model hierarchical stimuli (i.e. a stimulus in which small, local elements are arranged to form a larger, global configuration) and after a brief delay, to reproduce the pattern from memory. As illustrated in the figure, memory for global level information was compromised in the patients with right-hemisphere (RH) injury;

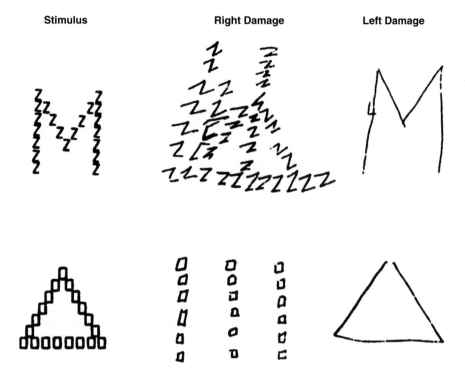

Fig. 23.1 Examples of memory reproductions of hierarchical form stimuli by adult stroke patients with either right or left hemisphere injury. Adapted with permission from Delis *et al*. (1986).

while memory for local level information was affected in patients with left-hemisphere (LH) injury.

Given these findings with adult patients, the question for our investigation was whether, or to what extent, children with PL would manifest similar profiles of deficit. The three studies summarized here were conducted as part of the larger longitudinal study of development in children with PL. Most of the data presented here have been published in more complete reports elsewhere. The three studies were selected to provide an overview of our major developmental findings for this domain of inquiry. However, before turning to a discussion of these studies, it is important to provide an overview of the principle neural systems involved in visual pattern processing, as well as summaries of major findings from behavioral studies of visual pattern processing for adults and children.

23.4.1 Two visual streams

In the early 1980s, Ungerleider and Mishkin (1982) proposed that the cortical visual system can be functionally and anatomically subdivided into two principal processing streams, a dorsal pathway that mediates attention to movement and location, and a ventral stream involved in processing information about patterns and objects. It is this ventral 'object' processing stream that is the primary focus of our studies of visual pattern processing. The ventral visual pathway begins at the retina and projects via the lateral geniculate nucleus of the thalamus to primary visual cortex, area V1. The pathway proceeds to areas V2 and V4, and then projects ventrally to the posterior and anterior regions of the inferior temporal lobe.

23.4.2 Visuospatial processing in adults

Studies of typical adults provide evidence that brain systems mediating configural and featural processing are lateralized to the RH and LH, respectively. It has been suggested that the hemispheres differ in terms of higher-order perceptual processes. The RH is preferentially involved in processing lower spatial frequencies, which are important for detecting global form, while the LH processes higher spatial frequencies which are important for processing fine detail (Sergent 1982). Consistent with these findings, event-related potentials (ERPs) recorded to visual presentation of sinusoidal gratings with either high or low spatial frequency content have documented laterality differences (e.g. Martinez *et al.* 1997a). Brain responses to low spatial frequencies have larger amplitude over the RH whereas responses to high spatial frequency showed greater amplitude over lateral LH scalp sites. Functional imaging studies have provided greater functional and anatomical specification of these findings, showing functional localization to inferior occipital temporal (IOT) regions of the RH and LH for configural and featural processing, respectively (Martinez *et al.* 1997b; Fink *et al.* 1999). For example, Fink's (1996, 1997, 1999) positron emission tomography (PET) studies of hierarchical stimulus processing showed increases in functional activity in the RH-IOT area during processing of the overall configuration (global processing) and in the LH-IOT area during feature processing (local processing). They controlled specifically for spatial frequency in the target stimuli, and thus the activation observed was associated with configural or featural processing *per se*. Martinez (1997b) used a similar global–local task design with fMRI and reported laterality findings consistent with those of Fink. In addition, she compared the activation findings with data from a reaction time (RT) task in which hierarchical stimuli were presented to either the left visual field (LVF/RH) or right visual field (RVF/LH). She reported that the patterns of functional activation closely mirrored subjects' RT performance.

Faces, a particularly important (and some have argued special) category of visual pattern, seem to exploit this configural processing capacity of the RH. Behavioral phenomena such as the face inversion effect (the disproportionately large decrement in recognition caused by inversion of faces compared with other objects) (Yin 1969) are thought to reflect processing of holistic or configural aspects of face stimuli (disrupted when faces are inverted) (Young *et al.* 1987; Tanaka and Farah 1993; Freire *et al.* 2000). Neuroimaging studies with adults find a RH bias for face activation in ventral occipito-temporal cortices (McCarthy *et al.* 1997), with the highly active 'fusiform face area' (FFA), residing in the fusiform gyrus of the right temporal lobe (Kanwisher *et al.* 1997). Increasing levels of expertise with faces, and other categories of objects, results in enhanced activation of the FFA (Gauthier *et al.* 1999, 2000) and, for faces, may reflect an increased reliance on configural processing strategies (Diamond and Carey 1986; Rhodes *et al.* 1989).

23.4.3 The development of visuospatial processing

Studies of typically developing children have shown that even young infants are capable of analyzing spatial patterns. Early competence has been demonstrated at least for rudimentary global and local pattern information (Cohen and Younger 1984). Further, systematic increases with development in the complexity of information that infants can process have been reported. Deruelle and de Schonen (1991, 1995) have shown lateralized differences in global and local processing among infants as young as 4 months that are similar to those described earlier in the adult fMRI study reported by Martinez *et al.* (1997b). Thus, it is clear that basic spatial analytic abilities emerge early in development. However, there is also evidence for substantial change in visual pattern processing as children develop. Change in the complexity and sophistication of spatial analytic processing has been documented across the preschool and school-age period (Akshoomoff and Stiles 1995a, b; Dukette and Stiles 1996, 2001; Feeney and Stiles 1996; Tada and Stiles 1996; Stiles and Stern 2001). Prather and Bacon (1986), for example, showed that children can attend to either the parts or whole of a spatial pattern, but that performance can be influenced by specific task and stimulus manipulations. Data from a large series of studies from our laboratory using different measures and testing children ranging in age from 3 to 12 years, have shown that pattern complexity affects how children approach the problem of spatial analysis. In studies of toddlers using block modeling (Stiles and Stern 2001) and of school-age children using both the Rey-Osterrieth Complex Form and simplified variants, we demonstrated that simplification of a pattern can induce more advanced reproduction strategies (Akshoomoff and Stiles 1995a, b).

Face processing also appears to be an early available ability that undergoes substantial change with development. A large body of data has shown that infants can process faces and may even show adult-like processing biases (de Schonen and Mathivet 1990; Cohen and Cashon 2001; Nelson 2001; Simion *et al.* 2001; Thompson *et al.* 2001), leading to claims that even newborns have elaborate representations of faces (Slater *et al.* 2000; Slater and Quinn 2001). Early characterizations of developmental gains during the school-age period suggested that featural strategies may initially predominate face processing in children (Carey and Diamond 1977). However, later work has shown that even preschool children, like adults, rely on holistic and configural information (e.g. Baenninger 1994; Tanaka *et al.* 1998; but see Schwarzer 2002;

Pellicano and Rhodes 2003). A recent fMRI study of face processing in 10-year-olds reported that children activate very similar areas within the IOT system as adults, but activation may be less well focused in children than adults (Passarotti *et al.* 2003).

23.5 Three studies of spatial cognitive processing in children with PL

The three studies presented here provide an overview of our major findings on visual pattern processing in children with PL. Each of the studies examined a different developmental period: preschool, school-age, and adolescence. Each used a task developed to be challenging, and thus diagnostic, of abilities for the targeted age group: copying models of blocks; reproduction of simple patterns from memory; RT measures of face matching from memory, for the three ages, respectively. Importantly, each, in different ways, used a multimeasure approach to assess performance, that takes account of both the product of the child's efforts, but also the processes by which the child solves the spatial task presented. In all three cases, product was assessed by some measure of accuracy; while process was assessed via examination of strategy, speed of response, or pattern of neural mediation. The product/process distinction has proven to be critical for understanding development in this population of children. On virtually every spatial processing task we have used, children with PL eventually achieve ceiling levels of performance as assessed by the product measures, that is, by the measures of accuracy. However, accurate performance is not always achieved via the same processing strategy used by typically developing children. These performance profiles have important implications for our understanding of how brain–behavior systems develop, and suggest that there are multiple, alternative developmental pathways. Even when there is substantial damage (injury that would leave an adult permanently impaired), development is adaptive and dynamic. It is the product of progressive biological specification interacting in concert with the specific experience of the child.

23.5.1 Study 1: block construction

The block construction task was used to test the ability of 4- to 6-year-old children with PL to evaluate and reproduce a series of spatial configurations (Fig. 23.2A). The task requires children to both identify the relevant parts or features of each construction and to combine those parts to form an accurate and integrated whole. In this task, children were presented with a series of six model block constructions, and given exactly the number of blocks needed to reproduce each model. Models were produced by the experimenter behind a screen, and presented one at a time to the child. The child was given unlimited time to complete the construction. The testing session was videotaped for later transcription and scoring. Children with either LH or RH PL were tested at age 4, and at age 5 to 6 (Fig. 23.2). Their performance was contrasted with a

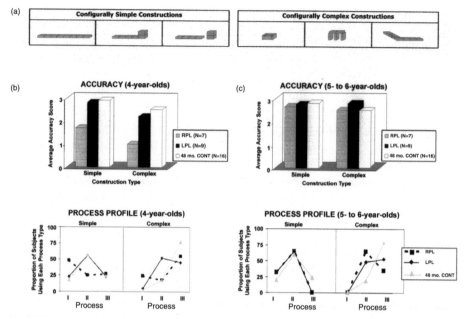

Fig. 23.2 (A) Model constructions used in the block construction task. Based on two earlier studies of typically developing 24- to 60-month-old children, two sets were identified. One set included three configurally simple and the other three configurally complex models. (B) Accuracy and process type results for 4-year-old children with RH injury (gray), LH injury (black), and typically developing controls (white). (C) Accuracy and process type results for 5- to 6-year-old children. Adapted with permission from Stiles *et al.* (1996).

sample of typically developing 4-year-olds, that is, with children who had basically mastered all of the target constructions.

The selection of constructions and development of scoring protocols was based upon two large studies of typically developing children, age 2 to 5 years (Stiles-Davis 1988; Stiles and Stern 2001). The six constructions used in the study of children with PL included both 'simple' and 'complex' constructions (Fig. 23.2A). Simple constructions were accurately produced by typical children under 36 months, while complex constructions were not mastered until approximately 48 months. Developmental differences reflected both the complexity of the target construction and processing difficulty (see Stiles and Stern 2001). Accuracy was measured on a three point scale: 1 = no resemblance to the model, 2 = partial reproduction, 3 = accurate reproduction of construction parts and configuration. The process measure defined three levels of performance that were found to be characteristic of typically developing children at different ages in the early preschool period. Process I was defined as the use of a single reiterative relation in a single direction. It is the optimal procedure for making a stack, but can also be used to construct a line if each new block is placed next to the last block placed in the line. Process II was defined as the use of different relations in sequence, for example producing a line and then a stack, or producing a line by placing half the blocks to right of the initial block, and then the remaining blocks to the left. Process III was defined by the flexible use of multiple relations, where a participant shifted back and forth between parts of his or her construction. A process score was assigned to each construction without regard to accuracy.

The results of this study document early, subtle spatial processing deficits for both groups of children with PL, but they also provide considerable evidence of the children's capacity for compensation and adaptation. The performance profiles of the LH and RH groups differed at age 4 (Fig. 23.2B). Children with LH injury produced accurate constructions, but the procedures they used in copying the forms were greatly simplified, particularly on the complex constructions. While typically developing children overwhelmingly used the most efficient Process III strategy when reproducing complex constructions, the dominant strategy among children with LH injury was the cognitively simpler Process II. This dissociation between product and process, which is not observed among typically developing children, persisted among the children with LH injury through at least age 6 (Fig. 23.2C).

The evidence of early deficit and development were even more pronounced among children with RH injury. At age 4, they produced disordered, poorly configured constructions, even when copying the simple constructions (Fig. 23.2A). During this period, the procedures the children used to generate their ill-formed constructions were mixed. For simple constructions, they used the simplest procedure, Process 1. However, for the complex constructions they, like their age-matched controls, used the most complex construction procedure, Process III. However, by the time these children were 6 years of age their performance profiles changed. At age 6, they accurately copied all of the target constructions, but now, like their LH-injured peers, they used simpler procedures to generate those constructions.

The results of this study suggest that there is impairment in spatial processing following early injury, but there is also compensation with development. On this task, the deficits among children with RH injury were more pronounced than those of children with LH injury, but the performance of both groups was affected relative to controls. Subtle forms of the deficits appear to persist into the early school-age period. However, there is also clear evidence for development of alternative spatial processing strategies that allow the children to compensate for their deficits. This compensation is reflected in the very high accuracy scores for the product measures at age 6, coupled with the unusual predominance of Process II construction strategies.

23.5.2 Study 2: global–local processing of hierarchical forms

Hierarchical stimuli have been used extensively to assess two different aspects of visual pattern processing: processing of the 'global' configuration and processing of the 'local' elements. As discussed earlier, they have been a valuable tool for examining lateralized spatial processing differences in both typical adults and in patient populations. Two studies of global–local processing are presented. The first is a large behavioral study in which 5- to 12-year-old children (both children with PL and typical controls) were asked to reproduce from memory a series of hierarchical forms. Both cross-sectional and longitudinal data samples were obtained over the course of this study. The second is a case report study examining patterns of functional brain activation in two children with PL scanned while performing a hierarchical form detection task.

23.5.2.1 Study 2A: reproducing hierarchical forms from memory

The behavioral study was adapted for use with children from the task used by Delis and colleagues (1986) with adult stroke patients (Fig. 23.1). The original adaptation of the task involved a large cross-sectional study of typically developing 4- to 8-year-old children (Dukette and Stiles 2001). The stimuli incorporated global and local elements that were balanced for perceptual features, familiarity, and complexity appropriate to children (Fig. 23.3A). On each of the four memory trials, children were shown one hierarchical stimulus for 10 s and told they would be asked to reproduce the form from memory. A 30-s story-card distractor task was then administered, after which the child was given a blank 14 × 21.6 cm sheet of white paper and a felt tip pen and asked to reproduce the form from memory. The memory reproductions were scored on two separate, but developmentally calibrated, 6-point (0–5) accuracy scales: one assessed accuracy of the global configuration and the other accuracy of the local forms. The scoring system was developed and validated as a part of the larger study of typically developing children discussed earlier (Dukette and Stiles 2001). The cross-sectional study included 31 children age 5 to 7 years (RH = 9, LH = 10, Controls = 12) and 31 children age 8 to 12 years (RH = 10, LH = 9, Controls = 12). All groups were matched for age and IQ. The longitudinal sample consisted of a total of 20 children from the cross-sectional sample who had completed the two data points (RH = 6, LH = 7, Controls = 7).

The results of this study mirror the profile of results found in the study of block construction with younger children in that there is evidence of both subtle deficit and substantial improvement in performance with development (Stiles *et al.* submitted). In addition, the design of this study provides more precise evidence of lesion specific deficits than did the block construction task, in that the three groups show distinctive performance profiles for global and local processing. Children with RH injury showed a strong dissociation in the accuracy of reproductions at the global and local levels. Their accuracy scores for the local level were comparable to those of age and IQ matched control children, and significantly higher than that of children in the LH group (Fig. 23.3B). However, they were significantly less accurate than controls in the accuracy of their global level reproduction. Although the older group of children with RH injury was significantly more accurate overall than the younger group, the pattern of differential performance on global and local levels was observed at both

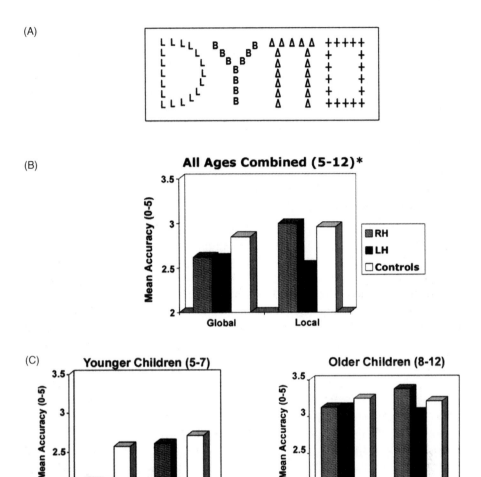

Fig. 23.3 (A) Stimuli used in the hierarchical forms memory reproduction task. (B) Results from the longitudinal sample of children with RH injury (gray), LH injury (black), and age and IQ matched controls (white). The interaction of group by stimulus level (global vs. local) was significant at p <0.01. Children with RH injury had difficulty reproducing the global but not the local level of pattern structure, while children with LH injury had difficulty reproducing both levels of the pattern. (C) The interaction with age was not significant, but is presented to illustrate the consistency of the pattern of data over ages. Adapted from Stiles *et al.*, submitted.

ages (Fig. 23.3C). By contrast, children with LH injury were significantly less accurate than controls in reproducing both levels of the pattern, although their performance on global was marginally better than their performance on local. Control children's accuracy was comparable on global and local levels of pattern structure. Further, when the frequency of specific error types is examined, children in the RH group were significantly more likely to make errors of omission or form substitution at the global level, while children with LH injury made errors of omission or substitution at the local level. Very similar patterns of results were observed in the cross-sectional and longitudinal samples. The major findings are illustrated in Fig. 23.3B with the data from the longitudinal sample.

The current study provided clearer profiles of specific deficit than did the block construction study. Marked deficits in global level processing accompanied by preserved local level processing were found for children with RH injury, while both global and local level processing was affected in the LH group. The apparent deficits in global processing for the LH group on this task needs to be viewed with some caution, however. This is not a profile we have observed on other tasks, and it does not appear to be the product of the most common type of global processing error found among the children with RH injury, specifically, errors of global omission or substitution. It is possible that, for this particular task, pronounced deficits in local level processing compromise the child's ability to accurately produce a configured global form. Thus the apparent global level deficit may be an artifact of the difficulty with local level processing.

It is notable that the profiles of deficit for each group mirror the findings from studies of adults with similar injuries, suggesting basic early functional specification of the IOT system. However, it is also important to consider the degree of improvement in performance observed in both groups of children. Note that although there was no significant interaction of age and group in any of the analyses in this study, the performance data for the two age groups have been presented separately in Fig. 23.3C. This has been done to emphasize that *overall* performance improves across the two age points, and yet the *pattern* of performance does not change. These findings suggest persistent, subtle deficit within the context of considerable functional and behavioral compensation. A critical outstanding question concerns the nature of this compensation. Functional neuroimaging studies can provide important complementary data to these behavioral findings. Identification of alternative profiles of neural activation in children with early brain injury will allow us to begin to address directly the question of neural mediation and to begin to define the nature and organization of compensatory functional pathways. Data in the form of two case reports of brain activation profiles during a hierarchical stimulus processing task offers a preliminary look at this issue.

23.5.2.2 Study 2B: fMRI case reports of hierarchical form processing

Data from the two case reports were compared to findings from two earlier fMRI studies of hierarchical form processing, one with adults and one with a sample of 20 12- to 14-year-olds. These two studies provide both information on the mature pattern of activation associated with the task and data on developmental change in profiles of neural activation. Both are important for interpreting the data from the two children with PL.

The fMRI task used a block design in which a global or local form detection task alternated with a control task. On separate imaging runs children were asked to attend to either the global or local level of the stimulus patterns. Functional images were acquired on a GE 1.5T SIGNA magnet using a single-shot EPI sequence (TE = 40 ms, TR= 5000 ms, flip angle = 90°, FOV = 240 mm, 64 × 64 matrix, 74 repetitions, 20 5-mm coronal slices). The EPI images were superimposed on a set of whole-brain anatomical images (MP-RAGE: TE = 5.2 ms, TR = 10.7 ms, flip angle = 10°, FOV = 240 mm, 256 × 256 matrix, 1.5 mm thickness).

Our study with adults (Martinez *et al.* 1997b), yielded a pattern of results consistent with other fMRI studies of global–local processing. Specifically, greater activation was observed in IOT regions of the RH when adults attended to the global pattern level, and greater LH IOT activation was observed when they attended to the local level. Two distinct profiles of activation were observed among the children, one mirroring the adult pattern, and one reflecting a more immature pattern of activation (Moses *et al.* 2002). Children with an immature RT profile showed bilateral activation for both tasks, with a tendency toward greater RH activation overall. For both groups of children, as well as the adults, patterns of brain activation were consistent with RT performance on a visual hemifield task using hierarchical stimuli. The close link between RT performance and brain activation suggests that a changing pattern of neural activation accompanies the developmental shift toward greater proficiency and increased lateralization of local processing.

The case reports include two teenage boys with comparatively small lesions to the RH or LH. The two children (M-RH and K-LH) were selected because they are representative of our larger population with regard to both their neuropathology and their longitudinal profiles of behavioral development. For this first study, cases of children with small lesions were selected to allow us to examine the possibility of alternative *intra*hemispheric organization; very large lesions would not permit such profiles. Table 23.1 provides an overview of basic neuropsychological testing data as well as a summary of the neuroradiological findings for each child.

Both of the children in these case reports presented with distinctive and complementary profiles of neural activation on the global–local processing task. In contrast to either adults or typically developing children, each child activates predominantly in one hemisphere and it is activated during both global and local processing tasks. In both cases, ventral temporal regions of the *contra*lesional hemisphere are activated (Fig. 23.4). Specifically, K-LH shows extensive activation on the right and little or no activation on the left on both the global and local processing tasks, while M-RH showed extensive activation of the LH and very little activation of the RH.

Table 23.1 Summary of neuropsychological and neuroradiological findings for M-RH and K-LH

	M-RH	K-LH	Radiological findings: M-RH	Radiological findings: K-LH
WISC-R:			White matter lesion of right parietal lobe and to a lesser degree the frontal lobe. Periventricular lesion affects white matter of the postcentral, superior parietal, angular and supramarginal gyri in the parietal region. Lesion extends superior and lateral to the anterior horn of lateral ventricle into frontal lobe where it involves white matter of the precental and inferior frontal gyri. Lesion marginally affects superior and middle temporal gyri. Thalamus and optic radiations in injured hemisphere are smaller than in intact hemisphere. Measurement of gray and white matter volumes of intact occipital lobe shows increase in gray-to-white matter ratio.	Damage to the left post central gyrus with the exception of the most superior aspect of the gyrus. Lesion impinges upon adjacent gray matter of the supramarginal gyrus posteriorly and marginally involves the precentral gyrus anteriorly. Lesion involves white matter underlying the supramarginal and superior temporal gyri. Left thalamus shows atrophy; atrium of the left lateral ventricle is dilated. Within the cerebral lobes, the intact ipsilesional occipital and frontal lobes show significant reduction in white matter volume.
Age at test	15,06	11,08		
Verbal	106	120		
Performance	93	102		
Full Scale	100	113		
VMI:				
Age at least	13,01	11,00		
Raw	19	15		
Standard	84	69		
%-ile	14	2		
Age Equivalent	8,09	6,06		

The two children in this study have a documented history of subtle, but specific, spatial deficit consistent with the side of their injury. The brain activation data provide insight into the relation between brain and behavioral development following early injury. In each case, processing of both global and local level pattern information is strongly lateralized to the contralesional hemisphere. These findings document the capacity of the developing brain to establish alternative patterns of neural mediation for this basic cognitive function.

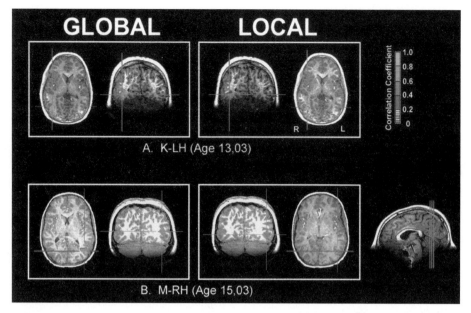

Fig. 23.4 fMRI activation data from two teenagers with prenatal focal brain injury on a hierarchical form processing task. Each child participated in separate imaging runs where they were asked to attend to either the global or local level of the stimulus pattern. Unlike typical controls who show different patterns of lateralization for global and local processing, the two children with lesions showed activation largely confined to the uninjured hemisphere. (A) Activation for the child with LH injury. (B) Activation for the child with RH injury. Adapted with permission from Stiles *et al.* (2003). See Plate 8 in the centre of this book for a full colour version.

23.5.3 Study 3: face processing

Faces are an important class of visual pattern stimuli that play a key role in early social and cognitive development. Face processing typically activates occipito-temporal regions, including the fusiform gyrus bilaterally (Haxby *et al.* 1994). Consistent with the notion that face discrimination may rely more on the holistic and configural processing capacity of the RH than on the featural processing system of the LH (Hillger and Koenig 1991; Rhodes 1993; Rossion *et al.* 2000), many studies report a RH bias for this activation (Kanwisher *et al.* 1997; McCarthy *et al.* 1997). Face processing may, thus, be differentially affected by early, unilateral brain injury. Like Study 2, Study 3 consists of two experiments, both using the same face-matching task. The first looks at the behavioral performance of a large group of participants with PL ages 9 to 23 years, while the second takes a case study approach, examining patterns of functional brain activation in two adolescents with PL.

23.5.3.1 Study 3A: face-matching, reaction-time

The data on face processing reported here were collected as part of a larger, ongoing study of face and location processing with both typically developing children and children with a variety of neurological disorders (e.g. Paul *et al.* 2002; Passarotti *et al.* 2003). Accordingly, the data for the current study (Paul *et al.* in preparation) represent only part of the data collected during the RT and imaging sessions for each participant. For the current study we focus only on the face-matching task (Fig. 23.5A), in which children are presented with a series of face-matching trials involving presentation of three black-and-white face photographs. The first two faces constitute the memory set, the third is the memory probe. The task is to indicate whether the probe face matches one of the faces in the memory set. Data from a total of 42 participants between 9 and 23 years of age were included in this preliminary study (RH = 11, L = 15, Controls = 16). Groups were matched for age and IQ.

Developmental studies report at least some degree of early proficiency with face processing, and imaging studies suggest RH dominance. Consistent with these data, the children with RH injury were significantly less accurate and slower than controls on the

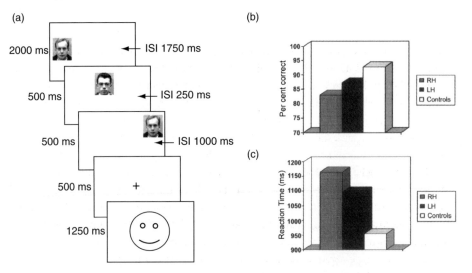

Fig 23.5 (A) An example of one trial in the face-matching task. (B) Accuracy results for the face-matching task for children with RH injury (gray), LH injury (black), and age and IQ matched controls (white). The effect of group was significant at p < .005. Children with RH injury were significantly less accurate then controls (p < .005), while children with LH injury were marginally less accurate (p = .08). The two lesion groups were not significantly different in accuracy. (C) RT results for the face-matching task for children with RH injury (gray), LH injury (black), and age and IQ matched controls (white). The effect of group was significant at p < .05. Children with RH injury were slower then controls (p = .038), while children with LH did not differ from either the RH group or the controls.

Table 23.2 Summary of neuropsychological and neuroradiological findings for A-RH and L-LH

	A-RH	L-LH	Radiological findings: A-RH	Radiological findings: L-LH
WISC-3:			Focal lesion in the posterior right perisylvian region. The lesion affects the posterior lateral inferior frontal gyrus. It encompasses the most inferior aspects of the pre and postcentral gyri, as well as the supramarginal gyrus.	Lesion involves an area of porencephaly in the left cerebral hemisphere. It involves the deep white matter of the middle and posterior portions of the superior and inferior frontal gyri, up to and including the precentral gyrus. It also involves the corticospinal and corticobulbar tracts of the coronal radiate, as well as the corpus callosum in the same region. There is sparing of the subcortical U-fibers and cortical association fibers.
Age at test	12,00	14,03		
Verbal	122	126		
Performance	135	111		
Full Scale	130	121		
VMI:				
Age at least	11,10	11,00		
Raw	25	24		
Standard	113	113		
%-ile	81	81		
Age Equivalent	14,00	14,00		

face-matching task. Accuracy of children with LH injury was marginally worse than controls (Tukey HSD = .079), and did not differ from the RH group. Their RTs were intermediate and did not differ significantly from either the RH group or controls. These somewhat different performance profiles suggest a marked deficit in face processing among the RH group and a measurable, but less pronounced, deficit in the LH group. The face-matching task should place different demands on featural and configural aspects of processing and account for the pattern of results. A configural processing deficit among children in the RH group should affect encoding of any face stimulus, affecting both the memory set stimuli and the probe in our task. This may account for the substantial difficulty reflected in both the accuracy and RT performance of this group. On the other hand, a featural processing deficit may have only a limited effect on processing of the memory set stimuli, but the task of matching faces from memory may place greater demands on featural processing (e.g. remembering salient or important features such as eyes, Taylor *et al.* 2001). This may account for the accuracy decrement in the LH group. Like the study of memory for hierarchical forms, these findings suggest that the ventral temporal system may begin to adopt its functional roles early in development. However, it is also a developing system and thus capable of considerable adaptation and compensation. Thus, while performance is affected, it is not compromised. As before, the neural correlates of this change, specifically the possibility of alternative patterns of functional organization, can be examined with functional imaging of the PL population as we have performed with our face processing task in Study 3B.

23.5.3.2 Study 3B: fMRI case reports of face processing

As with Study 2B, for this study we have selected two cases of children with smaller lesions. A-RH was 12,01 at the time of imaging; L-LH was 14,02 (see Table 23.2 for an overview of neuropsychological and radiological findings). Their activation data are compared with a group of ten 12- to 14-year-old controls (five females). The fMRI face-matching task was adapted from the one used in the behavioral study. It employed a block design in which blocks of face-matching trials were alternated with control trials, over two imaging runs. Functional and anatomical images were acquired on a 1.5T Siemens Vision scanner (EPI: TE = 40 ms, TR = 2500 ms, flip angle = 90°, FOV = 220 mm, 64 × 64 matrix, 122 repetitions, 27 5-mm slices; MP-RAGE: TE = 5.2 ms, TR = 10.7 ms, flip angle = 10°, FOV = 256 mm, 180 sagittal slices, resolution = 1 mm^3).

Given our uncertainty about the topography of face processing activation in children with early brain injury, we defined our region of inquiry broadly, exploring activation in the temporal fusiform gyrus and immediately adjacent areas. Beginning with more inferior aspects of this region (Fig. 23.6, left) we notice that both children with PL (A-RH, Fig. 23.6B; L-LH, Fig. 23.6C) show a pattern similar to that found in typically-developing controls (Fig. 23.6A). Controls show bilateral activation with the typical RH > LH bias. A-RH, the child with RH injury, also shows a RH > LH profile in these more inferior areas (though his activation here is less reliable than in other regions). L-LH, the child with LH injury, like controls, shows bilateral activation. All ten typical children reliably recruited a small region in the fusiform gyrus that likely corresponds to the classically-defined FFA (Fig. 23.6A, arrow). Both children with PL also activate this region (Fig. 23.6B and C, arrows). Thus, activation in both children with PL resembles controls in these more ventral face regions, suggesting that the basic neural organization for face processing can emerge, even after an early insult to the system has occurred. This is surprising given the results from the global–local task, and suggests that activation related to face processing, an ability essential to healthy social and cognitive development, may take precedence early on.

However, examination of more superior aspects of the face-responsive regions (Fig. 23.6, right) suggests there is more to the story. In these regions, both children with PL show enhanced activation within the LH in contrast to controls who show little or no activation in this region. It has recently been suggested (Gerlach et al. 1999; Joseph and Gathers 2003) that enhanced activity in this region may be associated with visual discrimination tasks that are particularly difficult. For example Joseph and Gathers (2003) presented pairs of stimuli from the same category (animals or geo-

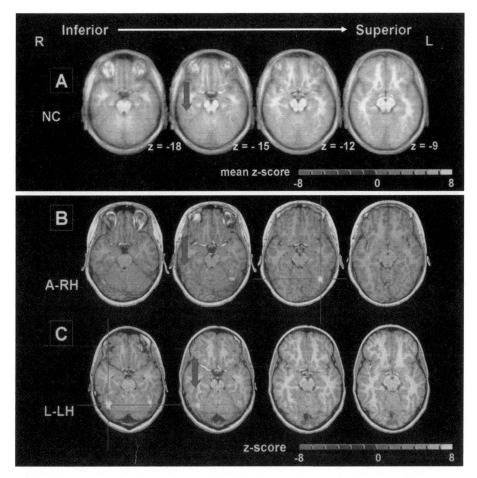

Fig. 23.6 Brain activation data for the face processing task from: (A) controls (N = 10, active voxels with group t-score > 6.6, p <0.05, Bonferroni corrected); (B) A-RH (z-score > 4.4, p <0.00001 per voxel uncorrected); and (C) L-LH (z-score > 4.4, p <0.00001 per voxel uncorrected). Cross-hairs indicate the single most active region for each of the two children with PL. A region-of-interest (ROI) was employed which included the temporal lobe fusiform gyrus, presumably including the FFA. The distribution of activation in the inferior regions of the ROI was very similar for all participants (arrows), suggesting that basic neural organization for face processing can emerge, even after an early insult to the system has occurred. However, activation in more superior regions of the ROI, particularly within the LH, may index residual deficit. This more superior LH fusiform region represents the most active focus for case A-RH. None of the children in the control group displayed this pattern. Those regions have been shown to selectively activate during difficult visual discrimination tasks. See Plate 9 in the centre of this book for a full colour version.

metric shapes) that systematically varied in perceptual similarity, and thus presumably in visual processing demands. They found enhanced activation for perceptually similar stimulus pairs within a region of fusiform that corresponds closely to the activation observed in our children; further, they found greater LH than RH activation. Thus in our children, this region of activation may reflect enhanced task demands associated with their subtle, but persistent spatial processing deficits. Most striking is the case of A-RH, for whom this more superior LH focus is, in fact, his most significant area of activation (Fig. 23.6B, region marked by crosshairs). This was not the case for any of the control children. Study 3A provided evidence that RH lesions are particularly associated with behavioral deficits in face processing. Thus, while A-RH can process faces, and appears to engage very similar regions of the inferior fusiform as typically developing children, his persistent subtle deficit may be indexed by the enhanced activation in the more superior fusiform regions in the LH. These imaging data, thus, provide a very different index of residual visuospatial deficits than did the global–local processing task.

23.6 Discussion: adaptation and development – the case of children with early focal brain injury

A constant refrain from our work with children from the PL population has been the dual theme of subtle specific deficit, and the capacity for adaptation and development. On the one hand, our work leaves no question about the fact that brain damage is a bad thing. In answer to the first of our central questions: Yes, there is evidence of subtle persistent deficit following early focal brain injury. In answer to our second question: Yes, for visuospatial functioning[1], the associations between site of lesion and type of deficit are similar in adult and child populations. Both of these answers confirm the presence of deficit following early brain injury, and thus document the limitations on the capacity of the developing system to compensate for early neuropathology. But the answers to our third and fourth questions are more hopeful. To our third question, the answer is: Yes, subtle deficits persist, but there is also significant

---

[1] It is critical to note that our study of language acquisition in children with PL presents a very different answer to this question. Virtually all of the children with PL that we have studied are delayed in language acquisition, regardless of side or site of lesion. However, the lesion-specific profiles of deficit observed in this population would not be predicted from the classic adult model of aphasia. For example comprehension deficits are typically associated with RH injury, while language production deficits are associated with left posterior temporal injury. Further, by the early school years, children in our population 'catch-up'. Regardless of early deficit profile, by age 7 they test within the normal range on standardized tests of language ability, and after this age there are no significant differences in language ability based on site of lesion (Stiles *et al.* 2002).

evidence for adaptation and compensation. Our approach to the study of developmental change in both typical and atypical populations involves an emphasis on both product and process. Evaluation of product provides a measure of quantitative developmental change; that is, do children at a given age or representing a particular group succeed in solving the spatial problem presented to them? In contrast, evaluation of process entails the examination of *how* the child solves a problem. It thus provides a measure of how success is achieved. As such, process measures provide a richer and more specific window on developmental change. They are, thus, a metric for evaluating both developmental progression and, in the case of our patient population, developmental divergence. Measures of process have, thus, been critical to addressing the issues of compensation and development raised in question 3.

Question 4 evokes a larger and very different sense of the word process. It refers to the problem of understanding developmental change at a much more detailed and fundamental level. Question 4 asks: What is the nature of developmental change and how does it occur? This is the really difficult question, the one that is at the heart of the nature vs. nurture debate. We have argued that the developmental neuroscience perspective suggests that, at this level, process entails the interaction of biological systems and the experience of the organism in an ongoing, interleaved fashion. While we are far from providing a complete or definitive demonstration of development defined at this level of description, we have noted that animal models have begun to provide substantial support for this position. Further, there is corroborating evidence from human studies, even within our own limited data set. One source of evidence comes from the explicit correspondence of behavioral profiles and profiles of brain activation in the data from both our typically developing children and our children with focal brain injury. One example from our own work will illustrate the importance of these kinds of data to the issue of process, in the larger sense. For brevity, we will use the data from the global–local processing study, but data from the face processing study would make a different, but equally interesting case.

The activation data from the case reports of children with PL demonstrated that different profiles of brain organization *can* emerge following early perturbation of the neural system. However, consideration of these data within the context of the data from the sample of typically developing children may also provide insight as to *how* such alternative profiles of brain organization might arise. In our studies of typically developing 12- to 14-year-olds, the RT performance differences were used to define two groups: one showed a lateralized, functionally specialized processing profile and the other showed a comparatively undifferentiated (non-lateralized) profile. The RT profiles were mirrored in their patterns of brain activation. One interpretation of the group differences in the performance/activation data is that the more efficient, mature strategies *selectively* engage specialized visuospatial processing systems; while the less efficient, immature strategies require the marshalling of *all available* spatial processing resources. For typically developing children, 'marshalling all available visuospatial processing resources' would result in bilateral activation of the ventral temporal system. For the typical child, then, the development of more efficient processing strategies should allow for more selective engagement of neural processing subsystems, which would be reflected in the increasing patterns of lateralization in the activation data. This is, in fact, what is observed in our data. By contrast, for the children with focal brain injury, 'marshalling all available resources' would result in activation of the more limited pool of resources compared to typically developing children. Further, those resources would also be distributed disproportionately to the contralesional hemisphere, thus concentrating both global and local processing within the non-injured hemisphere throughout development. The reduction of processing resources should reduce the capacity for specialization, resulting in a functional, but less efficient, spatial processing system. The behavioral and brain activation data from both of the children with PL in the current study confirm this pattern, and, in combination with the data from the typically developing children, provide much clearer definition of how behavioral and neurological compensation may develop.

In the case of early, localized brain injury, a normal developmental process – that is the progressive functional specialization as observed in the data from typically developing children – becomes adapted to the circumstance of a specific neural pathology with an outcome that minimizes, but cannot eliminate, deficit for the child. While brain damage is never a good thing, when it occurs in a child, it is, by definition, a part of a developmental profile and thus part of a larger developmental process. Because developing systems are progressively adaptive, the final functional organization of the brain in a child with PL reflects an alternative developmental pathway, a variant of the typical pathway, which is itself developmentally constructed. The developmental pathway of the child with PL incorporates both the neuropathology, and the cognitive and neural consequences of that pathology, into an ongoing developmental process that is unique to that individual, giving rise to the patterns of deficit, adaptation, and compensation that are the hallmark of development in this population.

References

Akshoomoff NA and Stiles J (1995a). Developmental trends in visuospatial analysis and planning: I. Copying a complex figure. *Neuropsychology*, **9**, 364–377.

Akshoomoff NA and Stiles J (1995b). Developmental trends in visuospatial analysis and planning: II. Memory for a complex figure. *Neuropsychology*, **9**, 378–389.

Baenninger M (1994). The development of face recognition: Featural or configurational processing? *Journal of Experimental Child Psychology*, **57**, 377–396.

Carey S and Diamond R (1977). From piecemeal to configurational representation of faces. *Science*, **195**, 312–314.

Cohen LB and Cashon CH (2001). Do 7-month-old infants process independent features or facial configurations? *Infant and Child Development*, **10**, 83–92.

Cohen LB and Younger BA (1984). Infant perception of angular relations. *Infant Behavior and Development*, **7**, 37–47.

Delis DC, Robertson LC and Efron R (1986). Hemispheric specialization of memory for visual hierarchical stimuli. *Neuropsychologia*, 24, 205–214.

Deruelle C and de Schonen S (1991). Hemispheric asymmetries in visual pattern processing in infancy. *Brain and Cognition*, 16, 151–179.

Deruelle C and de Schonen S (1995). Pattern processing in infancy: Hemispheric differences in the processing of shape and location of visual components. *Infant Behavior and Development*, 18, 123–132.

de Schonen S and Mathivet E (1990). Hemispheric asymmetry in a face discrimination task in infants. *Child Development*, 61, 1192–1205.

Diamond R and Carey S (1986). Why faces are and are not special: an effect of expertise. *Journal of Experimental Psychology: General*, 115, 107–117.

Dukette D and Stiles J (1996). Children's analysis of hierarchical patterns: Evidence from a similarity judgment task. *Journal of Experimental Child Psychology*, 63, 103–140.

Dukette D and Stiles J (2001). The effects of stimulus density on children's analysis of hierarchical patterns. *Developmental Science*, 4, 233–251.

Feeney SM and Stiles J (1996). Spatial analysis: An examination of preschoolers' perception and construction of geometric patterns. *Developmental Psychology*, 32, 933–941.

Fink GR, Halligan PW, Marshall JC, Frith CD, Frackowiak RSJ and Dolan RJ (1996). Where in the brain does visual attention select the forest and the trees? *Nature*, 382, 626–628.

Fink GR, Halligan PW, Marshall JC, Frith CD, Frackowiak RSJ and Dolan RJ (1997). Neural mechanisms involved in the processing of global and local aspects of hierarchically organized visual stimuli. *Brain*, 120, 1779–1791.

Fink GR, Marshall JC, Halligan PW and Dolan RJ (1999). Hemispheric asymmetries in global/local processing are modulated by perceptual salience. *Neuropsychologia*, 37, 31–40.

Freire A, Lee K and Symons LA (2000). The face-inversion effect as a deficit in the encoding of configural information: direct evidence. *Perception*, 29, 159–170.

Gauthier I, Skudlarski P, Gore JC and Anderson AW (2000). Expertise for cars and birds recruits brain areas involved in face recognition. *Nature Neuroscience*, 3, 191–197.

Gauthier I, Tarr MJ, Anderson AW, Skudlarski P and Gore JC (1999). Activation of the middle fusiform 'face area' increases with expertise in recognizing novel objects. *Nature Neuroscience*, 2, 568–573.

Gerlach C, Law I, Gade A and Paulson OB (1999). Perceptual differentiation and category effects in normal object recognition: a PET study. *Brain*, 122, 2159–2170.

Haxby JV, Horwitz B, Ungerleider LG and Maisog JM (1994). The functional organization of human extrastriate cortex: A PET-rCBF study of selective attention to faces and locations. *Journal of Neuroscience*, 14, 6336–6353.

Hillger LA and Koenig O (1991). Separable mechanisms in face processing: Evidence from hemispheric specialization. *Journal of Cognitive Neuroscience. Special Issue: Face perception*, 3, 42–58.

Joseph JE and Gathers AD (2003). Effects of structural similarity on neural substrates for object recognition. *Cognitive Affective and Behavioral Neuroscience*, 3, 1–16.

Kanwisher N, McDermott J and Chun MM (1997). The fusiform face area: a module in human extrastriate cortex specialized for face perception. *Journal of Neuroscience*, 17, 4302–4311.

Martinez A, Anllo-Vento L and Hillyard SA (1997a). Brain electrical activity during selective attention to spatial frequency. *Society for Neuroscience Abstracts*.

Martinez A, Moses P, Frank L, Buxton R, Wong E and Stiles J (1997b). Hemispheric asymmetries in global and local processing: evidence from fMRI. *Neuroreport*, 8, 1685–1689.

McCarthy G, Puce A, Gore JC and Allison T (1997). Face-specific processing in the human fusiform gyrus. *Journal of Cognitive Neuroscience*, 9, 605–610.

McFie J and Zangwill OL (1960). Visual-constructive disabilities associated with lesions of the left cerebral hemisphere. *Brain*, 83, 243–259.

Morange M (2001). *The misunderstood gene.* Cambridge, MA: Harvard University Press.

Moses P, Roe K, Buxton RB, Wong EC, Frank LR and Stiles J (2002). Functional MRI of global and local processing in children. *Neuroimage*, 16, 415–424.

Moses P and Stiles J (2002). The lesion methodology: contrasting views from adult and child studies. *Developmental Psychobiology*, 40, 266–277.

Nelson CA (2001). The development and neural bases of face recognition. *Infant and Child Development*, 10, 3–18.

Passarotti AM, Paul BM, Bussiere JR, Buxton RB, Wong EC and Stiles J (2003). The development of face and location processing: An fMRI study. *Developmental Science*, 6, 100–117.

Paul B, Carapetian S, Hesselink J, Nass R, Trauner D and Stiles J (in preparation). Face and location processing in children with early unilateral brain injury.

Paul BM, Stiles J, Passarotti A, Bavar N and Bellugi U (2002). Face and place processing in Williams syndrome: evidence for a dorsal-ventral dissociation. *Neuroreport*, 13, 1115–1119.

Pellicano E and Rhodes G (2003). Holistic processing of faces in preschool children and adults. *Psychological Science*, 14, 618–622.

Piercy M, Hecaen H and De Ajuriaguerra J (1960). Constructional apraxia associated with unilateral cerebral lesions: left and right sided cases compared. *Brain*, 83, 225–242.

Prather PA and Bacon J (1986). Developmental differences in part/whole identification. *Child Development*, 57, 549–558.

Rhodes G (1993). Configural coding, expertise, and the right hemisphere advantage for face recognition. *Brain and Cognition*, 22, 19–41.

Rhodes G, Tan S, Brake S and Taylor K (1989). Expertise and configural coding in face recognition: Erratum. *British Journal of Psychology*, 80, 526.

Robertson LC and Delis DC (1986). 'Part-whole' processing in unilateral brain-damaged patients: Dysfunction of hierarchical organization. *Neuropsychologia*, 24, 363–370.

Robertson LC and Lamb MR (1991). Neuropsychological contributions to theories of part/whole organization. *Cognitive Psychology*, 23, 299–330.

Rossion B, Dricot L, Devolder A, *et al.* (2000). Hemispheric asymmetries for whole-based and part-based face processing in the human fusiform gyrus. *Journal of Cognitive Neuroscience*, 12, 793–802.

Schwarzer G (2002). Processing of facial and non-facial visual stimuli in 2–5-year-old children. *Infant and Child Development*, 11, 253–270.

Sergent J (1982). The cerebral balance of power: Confrontation or cooperation? *Journal of Experimental Psychology: Human Perception and Performance*, 8, 253–272.

Simion F, Cassia VM, Turati C and Valenza E (2001). The origins of face perception: Specific versus non-specific mechanisms. *Infant and Child Development*, 10, 59–65.

Slater A and Quinn PC (2001). Face recognition in the newborn infant. *Infant and Child Development*, 10, 21–24.

Slater A, Quinn PC, Hayes R and Brown E (2000). The role of facial orientation in newborn infants' preference for attractive faces. *Developmental Science*, 3, 181–185.

Stiles J (2000). Neural plasticity and cognitive development. *Developmental Neuropsychology*, 18, 237–272.

Stiles J, Bates EA, Thal D, Trauner DA and Reilly J (2002). Linguistic and spatial cognitive development in children with pre- and perinatal focal brain injury: a ten-year overview from the san diego longitudinal project. In: MH Johnson, Y Munakata and RO Gilmore, eds. *Brain development and cognition: a reader*, pp. 272–291. Malden, MA: Blackwell.

Stiles J, Moses P, Roe K, *et al.* (2003). Alternative brain organization after prenatal cerebral injury: convergent fMRI and cognitive data. *Journal of the International Neuropsychological Society*, 9, 604–622.

Stiles J and Stern C (2001). Developmental change in spatial cognitive processing: Complexity effects and block construction performance in preschool children. *Journal of Cognition and Development*, 2, 157–187.

Stiles J, Stern C, Trauner D and Nass R (1996). Developmental change in spatial grouping activity among children with early focal brain injury: Evidence from a modeling task. *Brain and Cognition*, 31, 46–62.

Stiles J, Stern C, Appelbaum M, Nass R, Trauner D and Hesselink J (submitted). Effects of early focal brain injury on memory for visuospatial patterns: Selective deficits of global-local processing.

Stiles-Davis J (1988). Developmental change in young children's spatial grouping activity. *Developmental Psychology*, 24, 522–531.

Swindell CS, Holland AL, Fromm D and Greenhouse JB (1988). Characteristics of recovery of drawing ability in left and right brain-damaged patients. *Brain and Cognition*, 7, 16–30.

Tada WL and Stiles J (1996). Developmental change in children's analysis of spatial patterns. *Developmental Psychology*, 32, 951.

Tanaka JW and Farah MJ (1993). Parts and wholes in face recognition. *Quarterly Journal of Experimental Psychology: Human Experimental Psychology*, 46A, 225–245.

Tanaka JW, Kay JB, Grinnell E, Stansfield B and Szechter L (1998). Face recognition in young children: When the whole is greater than the sum of its parts. *Visual Cognition*, 5, 479–496.

Taylor MJ, Edmonds GE, McCarthy G and Allison T (2001). Eyes first! Eye processing develops before face processing in children. *Neuroreport*, 12, 1671–1676.

Thompson LA, Madrid V, Westbrook S and Johnston V (2001). Infants attend to second-order relational properties of faces. *Psychonomic Bulletin and Review*, 8, 769–777.

Ungerleider LG and Mishkin M (1982). Two cortical visual systems. In: DJ Ingle, MA Goodale and RJW Mansfield, eds. *Analysis of visual behavior*, pp. 549–586. Cambridge, MA: MIT Press.

Waddington CH (1939). *An introduction to modern genetics*. New York: Macmillan.

Warrington EK, James M and Kinsbourne M (1966). Drawing disability in relation to laterality of cerebral lesion. *Brain*, 89, 53–82.

Yin RK (1969). Looking at upside-down faces. *Journal of Experimental Psychology*, 81, 141–145.

Young AW, Hellawell D and Hay DC (1987). Configurational information in face perception. *Perception*, 16, 747–759.

Chapter 24

Modules, genes, and evolution: What have we learned from atypical development?

Annette Karmiloff-Smith

Abstract

If the atypical brain presented with a neat juxtaposition of parts intact and parts impaired, then atypical development might be a direct window on normal developmental change, with clear-cut single and double dissociations. Such a view emanates from the model of adult neuropsychological patients whose brains were fully and normally developed until their brain insult. The *developing* brain is very different. It is neither localized nor specialized at birth, and many months and years are required for the progressive modularization of the adult brain to occur. Because development plays such a crucial role in normal and atypical development and, early on, brain regions are highly interconnected, a tiny impairment in the initial state of the brain of a child with a genetic disorder may affect several brain regions and have cascading effects over time on the phenotypic outcome. This chapter considers what we have learned from atypical development about modules, genes, and evolution. Each section first looks at the Nativist claims found in the literature, and then re-evaluates them within a neuroconstructivist perspective. The final section considers what remains to be learned from developmental disorders.

24.1 Introduction

As it becomes increasingly clear that biology and the environment both play vital roles in human development, most scholars of human cognition reject the Nature *or* Nurture controversy in favor of theories in which Nature and Nurture interact. Even the staunchest Chomskyan Nativist and the most domain-general Empiricist concur that development involves contributions from both genes and environment. However, first because we still lack a testable theory of the precise processes by which genes and environment interact, and second because of entrenched philosophical views about what it is to be human, the debate remains as to whether it is Nature or Nurture that plays the greater role in constraining the developing brain. For some, consistent regularities in the physical and social environments to which children are exposed play a critical role, whereas for others the environment is merely a trigger for the onset of the functioning of our biological endowment. For the latter position, data from adult neuropsychological patients and from studies of developmental disorders of genetic origin are often used to motivate strong claims about the evolution of the neonate brain in terms of innate cognitive modules, the contents of which are argued to be specified in our genes (Barkow *et al.* 1992; Duchaine *et al.* 2001; Pinker 1997). By contrast, behavioral genetics addresses the Nature–Nurture issue as it applies to individual variation within a species, apportioning the variance into genetic, shared environmental, and non-shared environmental influences (Plomin 2004). The present paper is focused on the former issues about species-general development and the extent to which genetic mutations that disrupt development can inform the nature and origins of our species-general cognitive architecture.

The paper is divided into three sections on modularity, genes, and evolution. Each section starts by exploring some major Nativist claims to be found in the literature, and subsequently evaluates them within the context of a neuroconstructivist approach to human development. The final section considers what remains to be learned from atypical development, that is what should be given priority in future studies of genetic disorders. Before we proceed, it is crucial to be clear about how I will be using the terms 'innate' and 'module'. The term 'innate' has been employed in many different ways. A useful division can be made between architectural constraints, chronotopic (temporal) constraints, and representational constraints (Elman *et al.* 1996). No-one denies that there are architectural and chronotopic constraints governing human cognition. The question is whether representational innateness exists. In other words, does the neonate brain come equipped with innate knowledge (representations with content) of, say, the abstract structure of human language, prior to any experience? For example Pinker (1994) claimed that children are born expecting language to contain nouns and verbs. This must constitute representational innateness. My criticism of innate knowledge in this paper is with respect to representational constraints that would seem to require a prespecified pattern of synaptic connectivity within the cortical microcircuitry of a specific neural system (Karmiloff-Smith *et al.* 1998).

My criticism here of modularity concerns the concept 'module' in the Fodorian sense (Fodor 1983). Fodor specified a number of criteria that must hold for something to be a module: modules are hard-wired (not assembled from more primitive processes), of fixed neural architecture, domain-specific, fast, autonomous, mandatory (higher-level cognitive processes cannot curtail their operation), stimulus driven, give rise to shallow outputs, are insensitive to central cognitive goals, process only proprietary inputs, and, most importantly, are informationally encapsulated. It is the *co-occurrence* of all these properties that constitute, for Fodor, a module (see critical discussion in Karmiloff-Smith 1992). In my view, once one weakens these co-occurring criteria, as many authors have done, then the notion of a module loses its theoretical power. In other words, one cannot have one's modular cake and eat it!

24.2 Modularity

24.2.1 The claimed modularity of mind

Insults to particular brain regions from accidents or stroke are claimed to have provided some of the most convincing evidence that the brain has modular structure (Rapp 2002). Agrammatic patients, for example, are claimed to present with severe impairments in the grammatical structures of their language, but otherwise normal vocabulary and cognition (Grodzinsky 2000). Other patients with different brain lesions seem to present with normal grammar but have serious word-finding difficulties (Miozzo 2003). Yet others may retain completely normal language but have extreme difficulties in recognizing faces, that is prosopagnosia (Farah *et al.* 1995). Data from other adult patients display interesting dissociations between, say, semantic aspects of number and the semantics of other cognitive domains (Cappelletti *et al.* 2001). Cases of this kind have been used to bolster claims about the existence of independently functioning cognitive modules in the brain.

One particularly impressive case of the seeming dissociation between language and the rest of cognition is that of a savant linguist (Smith 1999; Smith and Tsimpli 1995). Christopher, who is in his 30s, has learned some 20 languages, yet cannot tie his shoelaces. His non-linguistic Performance IQ is low, and this dissociation has led to the claim that his language skills must have developed independently of the rest of his intelligence (Smith and Tsimpli 1995). Other theorists have argued for smaller modular specializations between, say, Arabic numerals and other forms of numerical representation (Cipolotti *et al.*1995), or between nouns and verbs (Rapp and Caramazza 2002). The most crucial data for this type of argument lie in the existence of double dissociations in which patient A can process, say, faces but not objects and patient B can process objects but not faces, or patient C has impaired semantics but intact syntax and patient D impaired syntax but intact semantics. These and other such claims using the double dissociation logic have abounded in the literature from studies in adult neuropsychology (see discussion in Karmiloff-Smith *et al.* 2003b).

Espousing similar theoretical aims, many studies of children with genetic disorders have used the same logic as adult neuropsychology, seeking modular impairments and dissociations alongside normal scores in other domains claimed to be 'intact/-preserved/spared' (Baron-Cohen 1998; Leslie 1992; Smith and Tsimpli 1995;

Tager-Flusberg *et al.* 1998; Temple 1997; see discussion in Karmiloff-Smith *et al.* 2003b). Researchers have focused on a number of genetically-based disorders to assert the existence of a juxtaposition of deficits and preservations. For example language and face processing have been claimed to be preserved in Williams syndrome (WS) (Bellugi *et al.* 1988; Bellugi *et al.* 1994; Clahsen and Almazan 1998; Pinker 1994, 1999; Rossen *et al.* 1996; Tager-Flusberg *et al.* 1998, 2003), a neurodevelopmental disorder caused by the deletion of some 25 contiguous genes on one copy of chromosome 7 (Donnai and Karmiloff-Smith 2000). The impressive behavioral proficiency with language and face processing in WS was found to coexist with a mean IQ of 58 (Mervis *et al.* 2004) and seriously impaired spatial and numerical cognition (Bellugi *et al.*1994). Impaired dorsal versus intact ventral pathways in the brain have been argued to explain some of the visuospatial problems encountered in WS (Atkinson *et al.* 2001).

Modularity claims have also been made with respect to Specific Language Impairment (SLI) (Gopnik and Crago 1991; Rice 2002; van der Lely 1997) and developmental prosopagnosia (Kress and Daum 2003), that is one aspect of the cognitive system is seriously impaired (grammar in the former case, face processing in the latter), with remaining cognitive functions operating normally. Arguments for double dissociations in developmental disorders have also been marshaled, as the following claim from Pinker (1999) bears witness: '...overall, the genetic double dissociation is striking ... ...The genes of one group of children [SLI] impair their grammar while sparing their intelligence; the genes of another group of children [WS] impair their intelligence while sparing their grammar.'

These various developmental data and interpretations thereof, using the logic of adult neuropsychology, seem to suggest that the brain is strictly modular, with genetic disorders helping the scientist to discover that the content of modules is likely to be innately specified in our genetic make-up.

24.2.2 The modularity of mind: a neuroconstructivist critique

Let us now re-examine the data presented in Section 24.2.1 that have been used to bolster claims about the innate specification of language and other cognitive modules. We will first reconsider the case of Christopher, the so-called linguistic savant (Smith and Tsimpli 1995). Is Christopher really the language machine that he is claimed to be? It is true that this young man has, over the years, taught himself a large number of languages to a surprising degree of proficiency. This has astonished researchers, given Christopher's low IQ (Smith and Tsimpli 1995). However, using an IQ measure rather than Mental Age can be misleading (see discussion in Karmiloff-Smith 1998). This 30-year-old's non-verbal IQ is indeed low, but in terms of Mental Age, Christopher reaches a non-verbal level of a 9-year-old. Moreover, unlike most normal individuals, he spends a very large percentage of his waking hours studying languages. Another critical factor is that, in the main, Christopher learns his languages through written media. In other words, Christopher is not an oral 'linguistic savant'; he is capable of *reading*, and he has learned to do so in several different scripts. As impressive and interesting the feats of what we might call 'this language spotter', the fact that Christopher has a non-verbal Mental Age of 9 and can read fluently challenges the notion of an isolated oral language capacity that has developed independently of general intelligence. In my view, many 9-year olds who were to spend so much of their time devoted almost exclusively to learning languages would reach comparable or even greater achievements. In other words, the innate specification of a language module developing independently of intelligence is not demonstrated by this (albeit fascinating) case.

As mentioned earlier, several developmental disorders have been highlighted as presenting examples of a single deficit alongside a pattern of normality throughout the rest of the cognitive system. Such disorders have been used to sustain arguments for the innate modularity of the mind/brain. However, the arguments that pure cases of single deficits exist in children, as they may perhaps in adult neuropsychological patients (although this remains debatable), turn out to be difficult to sustain. For example a metareview by Nunn, Postma, and Pearson (2001) of so-called developmental prosopagnosia concluded that the face-processing deficit in young children *never* occurred in the absence of object processing deficits. This suggests that the relative independence of object/face processing found in adults *emerges* gradually as a function of ontogenetic development, but starts in young children with some *common* processing.

Similar arguments are now being marshaled with respect to Specific Language Impairment (SLI). This is, by definition, considered to involve a single impairment in language, with the rest of the cognitive system operating normally. However, in recent years disorders such as SLI have been shown to stem from lower-level deficits and to be accompanied by numerous other subtle impairments in the hitherto presumed 'intact' non-linguistic domains (Benasich and Spitz 1999; Bishop 1997, 2002; Botting 2005; Chiat 2001; Norbury *et al.* in press). Moreover, even when performance IQ falls within the normal range, the IQ of the SLI individual is often significantly lower than that of his siblings (Botting 2005), pointing to a general impairment despite so-called 'normal' scores. Furthermore, longitudinal studies have shown that the pattern of deficits and normal scores in developmental disorders change quite considerably over developmental time, with drops in non-verbal scores of some 10 to 20 points (Conti-Ramsden and Botting 1999; Krassowski and Plante 1997; Mawhood *et al.* 2000a, b). All of these data highlight the fact that, contrary to the views discussed in Section 24.2.1, developmental disorders rarely display a neat juxtaposition of intact and impaired modules.

Are there processes of general developmental change that might be evaluated by patterns of deficit in developmental disorders? In earlier work on normal development, I hypothesized that two parallel developmental processes occur over developmental time: progressive modularization and progressive explicitation (Karmiloff-Smith

1992). The former involves a process by which, over developmental time, domains become increasingly segregated, fast, and automatic. Thus, instead of modules being preformed, they were argued to be the product of the dynamics of development, with representations remaining implicit within the system. The fact that some adult neuro-psychological patient data seem to suggest a modular brain is actually orthogonal to the issue of whether modules are innately specified because, as I hypothesized, modules could be the product of development, not its starting point. Hence, to address these questions, a developmental perspective is essential, as we shall see below. The second process, progessive explicitation, runs in parallel with progressive modularization and involves domains becoming increasingly associated and available to consciousness. In the explicitation process, representations are considered to be explicit redescriptions of the implicit knowledge that remains embedded in developing modules (for details, see Karmiloff-Smith 1992). Are childhood disorders informative about these hypothesized processes of developmental change?

In our studies of Williams syndrome (WS) and Down's syndrome (DS), we assessed these two hypothesized developmental processes. With respect to progressive mod-ularization, we examined face processing since this is a domain for which many authors have claimed intactness of the functioning of a face-processing module in WS, analogous to that found in typical development (e.g. Bellugi *et al.* 1994; Rossen *et al.* 1995; Tager-Flusberg *et al.* 2003). We challenged this conclusion on several fronts (Karmiloff-Smith *et al.* 2004). First, although people with WS display proficient behavior which falls in the normal range on some standardized face processing tasks like the Benton (Rossen *et al.* 1995) or the Rivermead (Udwin and Yule 1991), the means by which they achieve this success turn out to be different from controls. Whereas controls in our studies used configural processing, the WS group used featural or holistic processing of faces, just as they do for non-face spatial stimuli (Karmiloff-Smith *et al.* 2004; see also, Deruelle *et al.* 1999; Karmiloff-Smith 1998). Moreover, our brain imaging studies of WS face processing and spatial stimuli, using high-density event related potentials (HD-ERP), point to similar conclusions (Grice *et al.* 2001, 2003). When comparing brain processing to human faces, monkey faces, and cars, it was found that typical controls displayed a strong N170 (the electro-physiological marker of face processing) for human and monkey faces, with no such increase in amplitude for the brain processing of cars. By contrast, the adolescents and adults with WS showed a very reduced N170, which was similar for all three stimuli. In other words, for the WS group, faces were processed in the same way as cars. Thus, the behavioral scores on some standardized tasks where people with WS fall 'in the normal range' seem to be sustained by different cognitive and brain processes from controls. It is not the case, then, that individuals with WS have an impaired spatial module and an intact facial module; both domains are impaired in similar ways. Rather, people with Williams syndrome fail to modularize their face processing over developmental time. So, a lack of modularization in developmental disorders may reveal *common initial processes* across domains, before each domain would normally have become increasingly segregated and modularized over time.

What about earlier claims regarding an intact language module in WS (Bellugi *et al.* 1994; Pinker 1994, 1999; Smith 1999)? First, an abundance of empirical studies from numerous laboratories across the world now challenge these claims in respect of all aspects of WS language (e.g. the lexicon: Jarrold *et al.* 2000; Temple *et al.* 2002; morpho-syntax: Grant *et al.* 2002; Karmiloff-Smith *et al.* 1997; Thomas *et al.* 2001; Volterra *et al.* 2001; phonology: Grant *et al.* 1997; pragmatics: Laws and Bishop 2004). Brain imaging of language processing again points to atypical processing in WS (Neville *et al.* 1994). Moreover, despite the superficially fluent language peppered with erudite-sounding words of adolescents and adults with WS, language onset in this clinical population is very late, often not until the fifth or sixth year (Singer Harris *et al.* 1997). Why is WS language so delayed? Is this due to a late-maturing module? Or is there a *developmental* explanation? In my view, the roots of the delay reside in deficits in multiple earlier processes. For example infants and toddlers with WS are extremely delayed in hand movements and babbling (Masataka 2001), as well as in segmenting the speech stream (Nazzi *et al.* 2003), a capacity seen as early as 8 months in typically developing infants. Second, unlike typical controls, toddlers and young children with WS rely more on perceptual cues than linguistic labels when identifying new objects (Nazzi *et al.*, in press). Furthermore, early categorization abilities in WS are impaired (Nazzi and Karmiloff-Smith 2002), and exhaustive sorting follows word onset rather than preceding it as is the normal case (Mervis and Bertrand 1997). Pointing is also atypical in WS toddlers. Whereas in typical development, referential pointing precedes the onset of language, in WS this order is unusually reversed (Mervis and Bertrand 1997). Moreover, our recent studies revealed that WS toddlers do not use or follow eye gaze for referential communication and do not understand the referential function of pointing (Laing *et al.* 2002). Finally, in the normal case, young children's comprehension outstrips their levels of production. This clear-cut asymmetry does not hold for Williams syndrome (Paterson *et al.* 1999). In sum, many different aspects of communication show an early, unusual pattern in WS, jointly contributing in very complex ways to the explanation of the late onset of their language.

However, an even earlier deficit outside the domain of language may offer a compelling explanation of some of these early deficits: atypical eye movement planning. In a study of saccadic planning in infants and toddlers with WS, DS compared to Mental Age and chronological age controls, we found that although children with DS resembled controls, although slower, the infants and toddlers with WS displayed a range of impairments (Brown *et al.* 2003). Some stayed fixated on one stimulus without moving their eyes at all, whereas others made a single eye movement but failed to make the two saccades made by the controls and infants with DS. For the infants with WS who did make a double saccadic movement, two errors appeared:

either they failed to update their retinal imagine after the first eye movement and ended in the wrong location after their second saccade (the retinocentric error). Or they summated the two saccades before moving, thus making the vector summation error typical of normal 2-months-olds. In other words, making eye movements to explore the environment, as well as to follow another's eye gaze and pointing gestures, is atypical in infants and toddlers with WS. Thus, early visuospatial deficits in the WS developmental trajectory *outside the domain of language* can have cascading developmental effects over time on several *emerging* higher-level linguistic and cognitive domains. The fact that domains are highly interrelated early in brain development (Huttenlocher 2002; Neville, Chapter 13, this volume) turns out to play a critical role in the formation of more general, albeit sometimes subtle, deficits in later development.

Finally, what about the hypothesized process of increasing explicitation (Karmiloff-Smith 1992)? Can developmental disorders inform us about this aspect of developmental change? Little work has hitherto been carried out to explore this possibility. Our unpublished longitudinal case study of a 9- to 11-year-old child with Down's syndrome is suggestive, however. Using a technique developed for normal development (Karmiloff-Smith and Inhelder 1975), we assessed longitudinally, over a period of 19 months, one DS child's progress in balancing blocks on a narrow support. Some blocks balanced at their geometric center, but others either had a cube stuck visibly to one end or had lead drilled invisibly inside one end. These two types of block balanced off-centre towards their heavier end. In a cross-sectional study of typically developing children (Karmiloff-Smith and Inhelder 1975), it was found that 5-year-olds managed to balance all the blocks during an experimental session by feeling proprioceptively the direction of fall and progressively adjusting until balance was achieved. Seven-year olds, by contrast, resolutely placed each of the blocks, irrespective of their weight distribution, at their geometric centre on the support. Even if the Experimenter placed a weighted block in balance and asked the child to copy this with another identical block, the 7-year old would place his own block at its geometric centre. We termed this powerful constraint the 'geometric center theory-in-action' because most children were unable to explain their behavior verbally. Finally, by 9 years, children were again successful with all blocks but, unlike the 5-year-olds, they assessed the weight distribution before attempting to balance, used previous successes on other blocks to guide attempts on similar new blocks, and placed blocks close to their center of gravity (Karmiloff-Smith and Inhelder 1975). We also ascertained that if 7-year-lds had a lot of practice over time, they gradually also moved towards taking counterexamples into account.

What about our 9- to 11-year-old with DS? To his own delight and that of his parents, he managed after two sessions to balance all the blocks, using the proprioceptive strategy of 5-year-olds. But he continued to repeat the success in exactly the same way on all our subsequent visits. Never did he try to use the balance from one weighted block to copy it for another similar item. He treated each block as an isolated problem and, using proprioceptive feedback, managed to bring each one into balance. At no time did we witness any signs of the 'geometric center theory-in-action'. Of course, case studies can only be suggestive, but this example does imply that people with developmental disorders may not change their level of processing a problem space to a more explicit one. The block-balancing task is interesting because progressive explicitation in this case does not require *verbal* metacognition. So the child with DS is not constrained by any verbal problems in this respect. A change in the level of representation to a more explicit one merely entails demonstrating in one's actions that a new theory-in-action dominates one's behavior. This failed to emerge over developmental time in this boy with Down's syndrome.

Even when atypically developing children have very fluent language, the lack of progressive explicitation or reorganization of knowledge also seems to hold. In a study of adolescents and adults with WS, a syndrome with proficient language, it was shown that although the participants had accumulated a large amount of factual knowledge about the biological concept under study (that of 'alive'), they had never reorganized that knowledge nor made it more explicit (Johnson and Carey 1998). By contrast, typically developing children as young as 9 to 10 years of age demonstrate such conceptual reorganization and progressive explicitation across a wide variety of domains (Carey 1985).

In sum, despite accumulating large amounts of piecemeal knowledge across several domains, it seems that individuals with developmental disorders often fail to demonstrate the two parallel processes of developmental change hypothesized to operate in typically developing children: progressive modularization and explicitation/reorganization of knowledge.

24.3 **Genetics**

24.3.1 **The claimed genetic underpinnings to cognitive-level modules**

Because of our differences from other species, human language has been the domain most consistently claimed to be specified in our genes. Leading linguists and psycholinguists, such as Wexler and Pinker, have consistently asserted that language is an innately specified endowment of our biology, as the following quotations bear witness *(italics added)*: 'It is uncontroversial that the development [of Universal Grammar] is essentially guided by a biological, *genetically-determined program*' (Wexler 1996); 'The mind is likely to contain *blueprints for grammatical rules*[. . .] and a *special set of genes* that help wire it in place' (Pinker 1994).

Much excitement for such claims was recently reinforced with the revelation of a specific genetic mutation in a family pedigree with speech and language deficits. The now well-known KE family was genotyped across several generations. It was found that affected family members had a point mutation on one copy of the FOXP2 gene on chromosome 7 that encodes a protein of 715 amino acids belonging to the forkhead class of transcription factors. The point mutation was not found in family members with normal language (Fisher *et al.* 1998; Lai *et al.* 2001). Although the geneticists remained cautious about the conclusions to be drawn from these cases, some linguists were quick to claim that a gene directly implicated in speech and language had been identified (Gopnik and Crago 1991), a seemingly exciting discovery which Pinker claimed to mark the 'dawn of cognitive genetics' (Pinker 2001). One implication from such a claim is that we may soon be able to map more or less directly from genes and their protein products to the cognitive level.

Other work on variable gene mapping and animal models also seemed to hold the promise of direct mapping between genes and cognitive-level outcomes. For example WS has been used to support claims of direct gene-behavior mappings. Identifying patients with a small deletion within the WS critical region (WSCR), researchers have attempted to delineate the functions of certain genes. Families were discovered, some of whose members had a small deletion of two genes within the WSCR (Elastin and Limkinase1), with other family members having no such deletion. Elastin is a gene implicated in the building of connective tissue throughout the body, particularly the arterial walls, and likely to be linked to the supravalvular aortic stenoses suffered by people with WS and by these small-deletion patients (Curran *et al.* 1993; Frangiskakis *et al.* 1996). Limkinase1(LIMK1) is a protein kinase gene, expressed in the developing brain (Proschel *et al.* 1995; Tassabehji *et al.* 1996). Interestingly, it turned out that family members with the LIMK1 deletion displayed spatial deficits similar to people with WS, whereas family members without the deletion had no spatial problems (Frangiskakis *et al.* 1966). From these data, the Frangiskakis group concluded that the half dosage of LIMK1 plays a vital role in contributing to the visuospatial constructive cognition deficits that occur in WS.

The fact that a mouse knockout model came to similar conclusions about the function of LIMK1 seems to make such claims even more plausible. Chromosome 5G on the mouse genome conserves all of the WS-relevant genes on chromosome 7 and their order (albeit reversed). So the mouse is a potentially excellent model of the WS human case. Meng and collaborators (2002) created a single knockout of LIMK1 and demonstrated serious spatial learning problems in the mouse's behavior in the Morris water maze. Thus, both the mouse model and the small-deletion patient data seem to point to the same conclusion: deletion of the LIMK1 gene is directly linked to the impaired visuospatial module in WS. This again implies that it is possible to map more or less directly from genes and their protein products to the cognitive level.

24.3.2 Genetic underpinnings to cognitive-level modules: a neuroconstructivist critique

Let us now return to the KE pedigree in whom family members with the allelic mutation on FOXP2 display speech and language deficits. It turns out that their problems are not specific to speech and language (Alcock *et al.* 2000a, b; Vargha-Khadem *et al.* 1998). Family members with the mutation display impairments in multiple domains such as: fine motor control, gait, oro-facial movement, perception and production of rhythm, all of which may subsequently impact on speech and language from infancy onwards. The KE family's problems may be more overtly obvious in speech and language, but this does not mean that they were originally rooted only in speech and language modules. The origins may have been at a much lower level, that is in the learning of skilled co-ordination of rapid movement sequences and their timing, as is the case for FOXP2 expression in avian learners (to be discussed in Section 24.4 below).

Not only is the genetic origin of the language deficit in the KE family far more indirect than implied in the original claims (Gopnic and Crago 1991; Pinker 2001), but this gene is likely to be a very tiny and even non-necessary contributor to impaired linguistic outcome. Indeed, different laboratories have genotyped (for the FOXP2 allelic mutation) hundreds of children selected for their low language scores (Meaburn *et al.* 2002; Newbury *et al.* 2002). Not a single individual was found to have the FOXP2 mutation, despite all having serious language deficits. This again points to the premature nature of claims about the discovery of genes thought to be implicated in a deficit in the cognitive outcome of development. If FOXP2 is implicated in language, its contribution is likely to be minute and extremely indirect, in interaction with multiple other genes.

What about animal models of the genetics of human disorders? Do they not suggest fairly direct gene–outcome mappings? We discussed in Section 24.3.1 Meng and colleagues' mouse knockout model of LIMK1, one of the genes situated in the WS critical region (Meng *et al.* 2002). The spatial deficit found in the mouse's behavior in the Morris water maze seemed to replicate the spatial deficit found in individuals with WS who also all have a deletion of LIMK1. However, there are several problems with this model. First, it is a single gene knockout whereas WS involves the deletion of some 25 contiguous genes that may interact with one another. Second, LIMK1 does not target a specific brain region responsible for spatial cognition, but is expressed widely across the brain early in embryonic development. Its protein products are thought to contribute to something far more general developmentally: dendritic spine growth and synaptic regulation across the brain. Moreover, although the mouse–human comparison stressed the spatial deficits found in both species, other impairments were found in the knockout mouse which do not occur in WS and *vice versa*. Moreover, even if the function of LIMK1 were the same in human development as in the mouse, then it is highly unlikely to target a spatial module in parietal cortex, but to have subtle widespread effects. Indeed, it probably has a broad general influence on embryonic and postnatal development. So, the generalization from animal models to the human case must always been treated with extreme prudence.

Other animal models require similar caution. This was made particularly clear in a recent chimpanzee model of Down's syndrome (The International Chimpanzee

Chromosome 22 Consortium 2004). A group of researchers modeled the human trisomy on chromosome 21 on the chimpanzee orthologue, chromosome 22. They found that in some cases over-expression of a gene had no measurable effect, whereas for other genes, particularly transcription factors, the effects were cascading. But above all, despite the similarity of the human and chimpanzee genomes, the scientists concluded that: 'the biological consequences due to the genetic differences are much more complicated than previously speculated.' Thus, even when two species are more similar than mouse and man, multiple differences remain, and simple generalizations from animal to human are to be avoided.

Another seemingly clear example of direct links between genes and cognitive-level outcomes discussed in Section 24.3.1 came from the variable deletion mapping of patients with small deletions in the WS critical region (Frangiskakis *et al.* 1996). Family members with Elastin and Limkinase1 deletions turned out to have spatial problems, attributed to LIMK1 because it is expressed in the brain, whereas family members without the deletion displayed no spatial problems. However, other patients with similar or even larger deletions in the WS critical region, including LIMK1, failed to corroborate these conclusions (Karmiloff-Smith *et al.* 2003; Tassabehji *et al.* 1999). Our study with Tassabehji and collaborators included four patients with centromeric deletions including LIMK1, and yet none showed an imbalance between their language and spatial scores. Two of these patients had normal intelligence, one well above normal intelligence, and one was in the lower end of the normal range. Yet none displayed a spatial deficit. An in-depth follow-up study of two of the patients, using over 40 neuropsychological tests of spatial and navigational cognition (Gray *et al.* in press; Smith *et al.* 2004), found no deficits whatsoever in these patients despite their half dosage of LIMK1. Further comparisons of a case study of a high-functioning woman with WS and a girl with a relatively large deletion within the WSCR, matched on their verbal scores, revealed in the former case an uneven cognitive profile including the spatial deficits typical of WS and in the latter case a completely even profile (Karmiloff-Smith *et al.* 2003). Yet again, it turns out that the claims of a direct link between spatial cognition and a specific gene, LIMK1 (Frangiskakis *et al.* 1996), were premature and based, in my view, on a false assumption, that is specific genes will turn out to be linkable to specific cognitive-level outcomes. If LIMK1 plays a role, then it is probably in low-level processes, interacting with other genes at the telemetric end of the typical WS deletion, ultimately to *result* over developmental time in the spatial cognition deficit.

24.4 Evolutuion

24.4.1 The claimed evolutionary underpinnings of cognitive-level modules

With the discovery of the FOXP2 mutation in some humans and its potential relationship to speech and language, researchers moved to genotyping our closest cousin, the ape. The FOXP2 proteins of the chimpanzee, gorilla, and rhesus macaque are identical to one another. FOXP2 is an extremely conserved gene across mammalian species, and has shown no changes in the chimp lineage since it separated from the human lineage some 4 to 6 million years ago. By contrast, it acquired two amino acid changes on the human lineage, one of which is likely to be functional, dated to some 200 000 years ago (Enard *et al.* 2002). Not surprisingly, this was an exciting discovery, since the timing of the protein changes on the human lineage coincide with estimates of when language started to emerge in our species (Hurford *et al.* 1998; Botha 2004; Newmeyer 2004). Put together with the data from the KE family, it is a small step to then claim that the change in a single base pair in FOXP2 altering protein synthesis must be a direct contributor to the evolution of human language. Likewise, outside the field of language, a number of authors have made sweeping claims about the evolutionary underpinnings of cognitive-level modules (e.g. Barkow *et al.* 1992; Duchaine *et al.* 2001; Pinker 1997).

24.4.2 Evolutionary underpinnings of cognitive-level modules: a neuro-constructivist critique

First, it should be recalled that FOXP2 is a transcription factor – its expression affects many other genes. Second, while the evidence from primate comparisons of FOXP2 is at first blush very exciting, more recent research on FOXP2 expression in birds, which is very similar to FOXP2 in humans, tends to make the original claims about the relation of FOXP2 to language seem premature. Researchers compared songbirds that learn their vocalization (e.g. zebra finches, canaries, etc.) with songbirds that produce their vocalization without learning (Haesler *et al.* 2004). The findings were revealing. In the avian learners, FOXP2 had greater expression in the equivalent of basal ganglia during phases of song *learning* than during song production. The scientists concluded that FOXP2 expression is associated with the learning of skilled co-ordination of rapid movement sequences and their timing, that is FOXP2 expression was an important contributor to *vocal plasticity* (Haesler *et al.* 2004). Such findings tend to challenge the notion that evolution has created increasingly complex genes that specify the content of cognitive-level modules. Rather, evolution may well have opted for genetic changes that contribute to increased plasticity for learning. Of course, the claim that FOXP2 is found in birds and contributes to vocal plasticity does not automatically contradict the finding of rapid recent evolution of FOXP2 in primates or the claim that the allelic mutation may be a contributor to human language. What it does challenge is any notion that the FOXP2 mutation gave rise to a 'grammar gene'(Gopnik and Crago 1991). Moreover, as I have repeatedly argued, one cannot simply take for granted homology of function or identical timing of genetic expression of the same gene across different species (Karmiloff-Smith *et al.* 2002). It has to be demonstrated empirically. None the less, the fact that FOXP2 in birds is not a gene that encodes a specific bird song, but rather facilitates the ability to learn, highlights the need for extreme caution in assuming that FOXP2 is a gene contributing directly to language in humans.

24.5 What remains to be learned from atypical development?

I have stressed throughout this paper the need for a truly developmental, neuroconstructivist perspective on the study of developmental disorders (see, also, Karmiloff-Smith 1992, 1998). But when does development begin? We now know from numerous, carefully controlled, experimental studies that the fetus is not passively waiting to be born. At least during the final trimester of intrauterine life, the fetus is actively learning, particularly in the auditory domain given that by this stage of gestation the hearing system is well formed. By measuring changes in fetal heart beat and/or leg kicking, studies have now shown that the fetus learns about its mother's voice, the language family to which its mother tongue belongs, as well as the sound patterns of songs or stories heard repeatedly, and can remember all of these at birth (Hepper 1989, 1991; see review in Karmiloff-Smith 1995). Yet we know little if anything about the learning and memory capacities of the atypically developing fetus, despite the fact that we now have completely non-invasive research techniques to do so. If deficits in simple discriminations are already apparent in fetal learning prior to birth in developmental disorders, it is crucial to identify these in the hope of finding very early intervention strategies. So, future research should focus on fetal learning in those developmental disorders that are identified prior to birth.

Another vital issue for future consideration is the fact that we now know from studies of normal development that the microcircuitry of the brain develops massively during the postnatal months, followed by a period of pruning when non-used connections are weakened and used connection weights are strengthened. Yet we know very little about atypical development in this respect. What is this process like in infants with developmental disorders? Does pruning fail to occur, due to the lack of progressive modularization? Do brain areas in atypical development remain more interconnected over time, failing to progressively modularize, than is the case for typical development? Is this the same across different disorders, or does each syndrome display its own particular brain signature? In sum, there is an urgent need for longitudinal cross-syndrome, cross-domain studies of infant behavior and of progressive brain development in a variety of developmental disorders.

How can we achieve a coherent, non-modular developmental explanation of the contrasting profiles found in different developmental disorders? Should we focus more on associations between disorders than on the search for dissociations? How do genetic mutations alter the way in which brains develop over time? Finally, it is also vital for scientists to understand how having a developmental disorder changes the social and physical environment in which a child is raised (Ciccetti 2002; Karmiloff-Smith and Thomas 2004). Parental expectations alter with the knowledge of a child's condition and, however subtle these changes may be, they impact on the learning situation and the interaction between parent and child over time.

24.6 Concluding comments

In conclusion, we have seen that simple, direct mappings between genes and cognitive-level outcomes are not sustainable. In fact, genes are more likely to contribute to much more general outcomes such as developmental timing, neuronal migration, neuronal type/size/ density/orientation, myelination, lamination, ratio of gray matter to white matter, firing thresholds, neurotransmitter differences, and so forth (Elman *et al.* 1996), any or all of which may be atypical in developmental disorders. Any of these factors may turn out to be domain-relevant, that is more appropriate for one domain of processing than others. Over time, in normal development such domain relevance can, with repeated processing, become domain specific and modularized (Karmiloff-Smith 1992). But if deficient early on, domain specificity of processing may not emerge developmentally. I have repeatedly argued that the neonate brain does not start out with domain-specific higher-level modular processing, but that this emerges gradually. In my view, the study of developmental disorders has helped us to come to this conclusion.

In sum, genetic developmental disorders can inform theories of developmental change, as long as they are considered against the backdrop of the plastic, activity-driven nature of normal cortical specialization, rather than as illustrations of a juxtaposition of 'intact' versus 'impaired' static modules. Developmental disorders point to altered constrains on neural plasticity in a *developing* organism, often affecting plasticity itself (Karmiloff-Smith 1998; Karmiloff-Smith and Thomas 2004). Although plasticity is seen by some as a response solely to injury (Wexler 1996), for others plasticity is the rule for development, normal or atypical, and not the exception (Bates and Roe 2001; Cicchetti and Tucker 1994; Elman *et al.* 1996; Huttenlocher 2002; Johnson 2001; Karmiloff-Smith and Thomas 2004). But plasticity is not, of course, unconstrained, and developmental disorders may turn out to be very informative about the constraints on plasticity. In sum, once one thinks from a truly *developmental* perspective, it is easy to imagine how even a tiny asynchrony or impairment early on in development can have a huge, cascading impact on the subsequent outcome.

Acknowledgements

This paper was written with the support of grants from Fogarty/NIH, USA, (Grant No. R21TW06761–01) and from Procter and Gamble, Geneva.

References

Alcock KJ, Passingham RE, Watkins K and Vargha-Khadem F (2000a). Pitch and timing abilities in inherited speech and language impairment. *Brain and Language,* 75, 34–46.

Alcock KJ, Passingham RE, Watkins KE and Vargha-Khadem F (2000b). Oral dyspraxia in inherited speech and language impairment and acquired dysphasia. *Brain and Language,* 75, 17–33.

Atkinson J, Anker S, Braddick O, Nokes L, Mason A and Braddick F (2001). Visual and visuospatial development in young children with Williams syndrome. *Developmental Medicine and Child Neurology,* 43, 330–337.

Barkow JH, Cosmides L and Tooby J, eds (1992). *The adapted mind: evolutionary psychology and the generation of culture.* New York, NY: Oxford University Press.

Baron-Cohen S (1998). Modularity in developmental cognitive neuropsychology: Evidence from autism and Gilles de la Tourette syndrome. In: JA Burack, RM Hodapp and E Zigler, eds. *Handbook of mental retardation and development,* pp. 334–348. Cambridge, UK: Cambridge University Press.

Bates E and Roe K (2001). Language development in children with unilateral brain injury. In: CA Nelson and M Luciana, eds. *Handbook of developmental cognitive neuroscience,* pp. 281–307. Cambridge, MA: MIT Press.

Bellugi U, Marks S, Bihrle A and Sabo H (1988). Dissociation between language and cognitive functions in Williams syndrome. In: D Bishop and K Mogford, eds. *Language development in exceptional circumstances,* pp.177–189. London: Churchill Livingstone.

Bellugi U, Wang P and Jernigan TL (1994). Williams syndrome: an unusual neuropsychological profile. In: S Broman and J Grafman, eds. *Atypical cognitive deficits in developmental disorders: Implications for brain function,* pp. 23–56. Hillsdale, NJ: Erlbaum.

Benasich AA and Spitz RV (1999). Insights from infants: temporal processing abilities and genetics contribute to language impairment. In: K Whitmore, H Hart and G Willems, eds. *A neurodevelopmental approach to specific learning disorders.* London: MacKeith Press.

Bishop DVM (1997). *Uncommon understanding: development and disorders of language comprehension in children.* Hove: Psychology Press.

Bishop DVM (2002). Motor immaturity and specific speech and language impairment: evidence for a common genetic basis. *American Journal of Medical Genetics: Neuropsychiatric Genetics,* 114, 56–63.

Botha R (2004). Windows with a view on language evolution. *European Review,* 12, 235–243.

Botting N (2005). Non-verbal cognitive development and language impairment. *Journal of Child Psychology and Psychiatry,* 46, 317–326.

Brown J, Johnson MH, Paterson S, Gilmore RO, Gsödl M, Longhi E, *et al.* (2003). Spatial representation and attention in toddlers with Williams syndrome and Down syndrome. *Neuropsychologia,* 41, 1037–1046.

Cappelletti M, Butterworth B and Kopelman M (2001). Spared numerical abilities in a case of semantic dementia. *Neuropsychologia,* 39, 1224–1239.

Carey S (1985). *Conceptual change in childhood.* Cambridge, MA: MIT Press.

Chiat S (2001). Mapping theories of developmental language impairment: Premises, predictions and evidence. *Language and Cognitive Processes,* 16, 113–142.

Cicchetti D (2002). The impact of social experience on neurobiological systems: illustration from a constructivist view of child maltreatment. *Cognitive Development,* 17, 1407–1428.

Cicchetti D and Tucker D (1994). Development and self-regulatory structures of the mind. *Development and Psychopathology*, 6, 533–549.

Cipolotti L, Butterworth B and Warrington E (1995). Selective impairment of the manipulation of arabic numerals. *Cortex*, 31, 73–86.

Clahsen H and Almazan M (1998). Syntax and morphology in Williams syndrome. *Cognition*, 68, 167–198.

Conti-Ramsden G and Botting N (1999). Classification of children with specific language impairment: Longitudinal considerations. *Journal of Speech, Language, and Hearing Research*, 42, 1195–1204.

Curran ME, Atkinson DL, Ewart AK, Morris CA, Leppert MF and Keating MT (1993). The elastin gene is disrupted by a translocation associated with supravalvular aortic stenosis. *Cell*, 73, 159–168.

Deruelle C, Mancini J, Livet MO, Cassé-Perrot C and de Schonen S (1999). Configural and local face processing in children with Williams syndrome. *Brain and Cognition*, 41, 276–298.

Donnai D and Karmiloff-Smith A (2000). Williams syndrome: From genotype through to the cognitive phenotype. *American Journal of Medical Genetics: Seminars in Medical Genetics*, 97, 164–171.

Duchaine B, Cosmides L and Tooby J (2001). Evolutionary psychology and the brain. *Current Opinion in Neurobiology*, 11, 225–230.

Elman JL, Bates EA, Johnson MH, Karmiloff-Smith A, Parisi D and Plunkett K (1996). *Rethinking innateness: A connectionist perspective on development*. Cambridge, MA: MIT Press.

Enard W, Przeworski M, Fisher S, Lai CSL, Wiebe V, Kitano T, *et al.* (2002). Molecular evolution of *FOXP2*, a gene involved in speech and language. *Nature*, 418, 869–872.

Farah MJ, Levinson KL and Klein KL (1995). Face perception and within-category discrimination in prosopagnosia. *Neuropsychologia*, 33, 661–674.

Fisher SE, Vargha-Khadem F, Watkins KE, Monaco AP and Pembrey ME (1998). Localisation of a gene implicated in a severe speech and language disorder. *Nature Genetics*, 18, 168–170.

Fodor J (1983). *The modularity of mind*. Cambridge, MA: MIT Press.

Frangiskakis JM, Ewart AK, Morris AC, Mervis CB, Bertrand J, Robinson BF, *et al.* (1996). LIM-kinase1 hemizygosity implicated in impaired visuospatial constructive cognition. *Cell*, 86, 59–69.

Gopnik M and Crago MB (1991). Familial aggregation of a developmental language disorder. *Cognition*, 39, 1–30.

Grant J, Karmiloff-Smith A, Gathercole SA, Paterson S, Howlin P, Davies M, *et al.* (1997). Phonological short-term memory and its relationship to language in Williams syndrome. *Cognitive Neuropsychiatry*, 2, 81–99.

Grant J, Valian V and Karmiloff-Smith A (2002). A study of relative clauses in Williams syndrome. *Journal of Child Language*, 29, 403–416.

Gray, V., Karmiloff-Smith, A., Funnell, E. & Tassabehji, M. (in press) In-depth Analysis of Spatial Cognition in Williams Syndrome: A Critical Assessment of the Role of the *LIMK1* gene. *Neuropsychologia*.

Grice S, Spratling MW, Karmiloff-Smith A, Halit H, Csibra G, de Haan M, *et al.* (2001). Disordered visual processing and oscillatory brain activity in autism and Williams Syndrome. *Neuroreport*, 12, 2697–2700.

Grice SJ, de Haan M, Halit H, Johnson MH, Csibra G, Grant J, *et al.* (2003). ERP abnormalities of visual perception in Williams syndrome. *NeuroReport*, 14, 1773–1777.

Grodzinsky Y (2000). The neurology of syntax: language use without Broca's area. *Behavioral and Brain Sciences*, 23, 1–71.

Haesler S, Wada K, Nshdejan A, Morrisey EE, Lints T, Jarvis ED, *et al.* (2004). FoxP2 expression in avian vocal learners and non-learners. *Journal of Neuroscience*, 24, 3164–3175.

Hepper PG (1989). Foetal learning: Implications for psychiatry? *British Journal of Psychiatry*, 155, 289–293.

Hepper PG (1991). An examination of fetal learning before and after birth. *Irish Journal of Psychology*, 12, 95–107.

Hurford JR, Studdert-Kennedy M and Knight C, eds (1998). *Approaches to the evolution of language*. Cambridge, UK: Cambridge University Press.

Huttenlocher PR (2002). *Neural plasticity: the effects of environment on the development of the cerebral cortex*. Cambridge, MA: Harvard University Press.

Jarrold C, Hartley SJ, Phillips C and Baddeley AD (2000). Word fluency in Williams syndrome: Evidence for unusual semantic organisation? *Cognitive Neuropsychiatry*, 5, 293–319.

Johnson MH (2001). Functional brain development in humans. *Nature Reviews Neuroscience*, 2, 475–483.

Johnson SC and Carey S (1998). Knowledge enrichment and conceptual change in folkbiology: Evidence from Williams syndrome. *Cognitive Psychology*, 37, 156–200.

Karmiloff-Smith A (1992). *Beyond modularity: A developmental perspective on cognitive science*. Cambridge, MA: MIT Press/Bradford Books.

Karmiloff-Smith A (1995). Annotation: The extraordinary cognitive journey from foetus through infancy. *Journal of Child Psychology and Child Psychiatry*, 36, 1293–1313.

Karmiloff-Smith A (1998). Development itself is the key to understanding developmental disorders. *Trends in Cognitive Sciences*, 2, 389–398.

Karmiloff-Smith A, Grant J, Berthoud I, Davies M, Howlin P and Udwin O (1997). Language and Williams syndrome: how intact is 'intact'? *Child Development*, 68, 246–262.

Karmiloff-Smith A, Grant J, Ewing S, Carette MJ, Metcalfe K, Donnai D, *et al.* (2003a). Using case study comparisons to explore genotype/phenotype correlations. *Journal of American Medical Genetics*, 40, 136–140.

Karmiloff-Smith A and Inhelder B (1975). If you want to get ahead, get a theory. *Cognition*, 3, 195–212.

Karmiloff-Smith A, Plunkett K, Johnson M, Elman JL and Bates E (1998). What does it mean to claim that something is 'innate'. *Mind and Language*, 13, 588–597.

Karmiloff-Smith A, Scerif G and Ansari D (2003). Double dissociations in developmental disorders? Theoretically misconceived, empirically dubious. *Cortex*, 39, 161–163.

Karmiloff-Smith A, Scerif G and Thomas MSC (2002). Different approaches to relating genotype to phenotype in developmental disorders. *Developmental Psychobiology*, 40, 311–322.

Karmiloff-Smith A and Thomas M (in press). Can developmental disorders be used to bolster claims from evolutionary psychology? A neuroconstructivist approach. In: J Langer, S Taylor Parker and C Milbrath, eds. *Biology and knowledge revisited: from neurogenesis to psychogenesis*, Erlbaum, New Jersey.

Karmiloff-Smith A, Thomas M, Annaz D, Humphreys K, Ewing S, Brace N, *et al.* (2004). Exploring the Williams syndrome face processing debate: the importance of building developmental trajectories. *Journal of Child Psychology and Psychiatry*, 45, 1258–1274.

Krassowski E and Plante E (1997). IQ variability in children with SLI: Implications for use of cognitive referencing in determining SLI. *Journal of Communication Disorders*, **30**, 1–9.

Kress T and Daum I (2003). Developmental prosopagnosia: a review. *Behavioral Neurology*, **14**, 109–121.

Lai CSL, Fisher SE, Hurst JA, Vargha-Khadem F and Monaco A (2001). A forkhead-domain gene is mutated in a severe speech and language disorder. *Nature*, **413**, 519–523.

Laing E, Butterworth G, Ansari D, Gsödl M, Longhi E, Panagiotaki G, et al. (2002). Atypical development of language and social communication in toddlers with Williams syndrome. *Developmental Science*, **5**, 233–246.

Laws G and Bishop DVM (2004). Pragmatic language impairment and social deficits in Williams syndrome: a comparison with Down's syndrome and specific language impairment. *International Journal of Language Communication Disorders*, **39**, 45–64.

Leslie AM (1992). Pretence, autism, and the theory-of-mind-module. *Current Directions in Psychological Science*, **1**, 18–21.

Masataka N (2001). Why early linguistic milestones are delayed in children with Williams syndrome: late onset of hand banging as a possible rate-limiting constraint on the emergence of canonical babbling. *Developmental Science*, **4**, 158–164.

Mawhood L, Howlin P and Rutter M (2000a). Autism and developmental receptive language disorder: A comparitive follow-up in early adult life. I: Cognitive and language outcomes. *Journal of Child Psychology and Psychiatry*, **41**, 547–559.

Mawhood L, Howlin P and Rutter M (2000b). Autism and developmental receptive language disorder: A comparitive follow-up in early adult life. I: Social, behavioural, and psychiatric outcomes. *Journal of Child Psychology and Psychiatry*, **41**, 561–578.

Meaburn E, Dale PS and Craig IW (2002). Language-impaired children: No sign of the FOXP2 mutation. *Neuroreport*, **12**, 1075–1077.

Meng Y, Zhang Y, Tregoubov V, Janus C, Cruz L, Jackson M, et al. (2002). Abnormal spine morphology and enhanced LTP in LIMK-1 knockout mice. *Neuron*, **35**, 121–133.

Mervis C and Bertrand J (1997). Developmental relations between cognition and language: Evidence from Williams syndrome. In: LB Adamson and MA Romski, eds. *Research on communication and language disorders: Contributions to theories of language development*, pp. 75–106. New York: Brookes.

Mervis CB, Robinson BF, Rowe ML, Becerra AM and Klein-Tasman BP (2004). Relations between language and cognition in Williams syndrome. In: S Bartke and J Siegmüller, eds. *Williams syndrome across languages*, pp. 63–92. Philadelphia, PA : John Benjamins.

Miozzo M (2003). On the processing of regular and irregular forms of verbs and nouns: evidence from neuropsychology. *Cognition*, **87**, 101–127.

Nazzi T, Gopnik A and Karmiloff-Smith A (in press). Asynchrony in the cognitive and lexical development of young children with Williams syndrome. *Journal of Child Language*.

Nazzi T and Karmiloff-Smith A (2002). Early categorization abilities in young children with Williams syndrome. *NeuroReport*, **13**, 1259–1262.

Nazzi T, Paterson S and Karmiloff-Smith A (2003). Early word segmentation by infants and toddlers with Williams syndrome. *Infancy*, **4**, 251–271.

Neville HJ, Mills DL and Bellugi U (1994). Effects of altered auditory sensitivity and age of language acquisition on the development of language-relevant neural systems: preliminary studies of Williams syndrome. In: S Broman and J Grafman, eds. *Atypical cognitive deficits in developmental disorders: Implications for brain function*, pp. 67–83. Hillsdale, NJ: Erlbaum.

Newbury DF, Bonora E, Lamb JA, Fisher SE, Lai CSL, Baird G, *et al.* and International Molecular Genetic Study of Autism Consortium (2002). FOXP2 is not a major susceptibility gene for autism or specific language impairment (SLI). *American Journal of Human Genetics*, 70, 1318–1327.

Newmeyer FJ (2004). Cognitive and functional factors in the evolution of grammar. *European Review*, 12, 245–264.

Norbury CF, Bishop DVM and Biscoe J (in press). Does impaired grammatical comprehension provide evidence for an innate grammar module? *Applied Psycholinguistics.*

Nunn JA, Postma P and Pearson R (2001). Developmental prosopagnosia: Should it be taken at face value? *Neurocase*, 7, 15–27.

Paterson SJ, Brown JH, Gsödl MK, Johnson MH and Karmiloff-Smith A (1999). Cognitive modularity and genetic disorders. *Science*, 286, 2355–2358.

Pinker S (1994). *The language instinct.* London: Penguin.

Pinker S (1997). *How the mind works.* New York: Norton.

Pinker S (1999). *Words and rules.* London: Weidenfeld and Nicolson.

Pinker S (2001). Talk of genetics and vice-versa. *Nature*, 413, 465–466.

Plomin R (2004). Genes and developmental psychology. *Merrill-Palmer Quarterly*, 50, 341–352.

Proschel C, Blouin MJ, Gutowski NJ, Ludwig R and Noble M (1995). L1MK1 is predominantly expressed in neural tissue and phosphorylates serine, threonine and tyrosine residues in vitro. *Oncogene*, 11, 1271–1281.

Rapp B, ed. (2002). *The handbook of cognitive neuropsychology: what deficits reveal about the human mind.* Philadelphia: Psychology Press.

Rapp A and Caramazza A (2002). Selective difficulties with spoken nouns and written verbs: A single case study. *Journal of Neurolinguistics*, 15, 373–402.

Rice ML (2002). A unified model of specific and general language delay: Grammatical tense as a clinical marker of unexpected variation. In: Y Levy and J Schaeffer, eds. *Language competence across populations: Toward a definition of Specific Language Impairment*, pp. 63–95. Mahwah, New Jersey: Lawrence Erlbaum.

Rossen ML, Jones W, Wang PP and Klima ES (1995). Face processing: Remarkable sparing in Williams syndrome. *Genetic Counseling, Special Issue*, 6, 138–140.

Rossen M, Klima ES, Bellugi U, Bihrle A and Jones W (1996). Interaction between language and cognition: Evidence from Williams syndrome. In: JH Beitchman, N Cohen, M Konstantareas and R Tannock, eds. *Language learning and behavior*, pp. 367–392. New York, NY: Cambridge University Press.

Singer Harris NG, Bellugi U, Bates E, Jones W and Rossen M (1997). Contrasting profiles of language development in children with Williams and Down syndromes. *Developmental Neuropsychology*, 13, 345–370.

Smith A, Hood B and Karmiloff-Smith A (2004). Manuscript in preparation on navigations skills in Williams syndrome.

Smith N (1999). *Chomsky: Ideas and ideals.* Cambridge: Cambridge University Press.

Smith N and Tsimpli I-M (1995). *The mind of a savant: language, learning and modularity.* Oxford: Blackwell.

Tager-Flusberg H, Boshart J and Baron-Cohen S (1998). Reading the windows to the soul: Evidence of domain-specific sparing in Williams syndrome. *Journal of Cognitive Neuroscience*, 10, 631–639.

Tager-Flusberg H, Plesa-Skwerer D, Faja S and Joseph RM (2003). People with Williams syndrome process faces holistically. *Cognition*, 89, 11–24.

Tassabehji M, Metcalfe K, Fergusson WD, Carette MJ, Dore JK, Donnai D, *et al.* (1996). LIM-kinase deleted in Williams syndrome. *Nature Genetics*, **13**, 272–273.

Tassabehji M, Metcalfe K, Karmiloff-Smith A, Carette MJ, Grant J, Dennis N, *et al.* (1999). Williams syndrome: use of chromosomal microdeletions as a tool to dissect cognitive and physical phenotypes. *American Journal of Human Genetics*, **63**, 118–125.

Temple C (1997). *Developmental cognitive neuropsychology.* London: Psychology Press.

Temple C, Almazan M and Sherwood S (2002). Lexical skills in Williams syndrome: a cognitive neuropsychological analysis. *Journal of Neurolinguistics*, **15**, 463–495.

The International Chimpanzee Chromosome 22 Consortium (2004). DNA sequences and comparative analysis of chimpanzee chromosome 22. *Nature*, **429**, 382–388.

Thomas MSC, Grant J, Gsödl M, Laing E, Barham Z, Lakusta L, *et al.* (2001). Past tense formation in Williams syndrome. *Language and Cognitive Processes*, **16**, 143–176.

Udwin O and Yule W (1991). A cognitive and behavioural phenotype in Williams syndrome. *Journal of Clinical and Experimental Neuropsychology*, **13**, 232–244.

van der Lely HKJ (1997). Language and cognitive development in a grammatical SLI boy: Modularity and innateness. *Journal of Neurolinguistics*, **10**, 75–107.

Vargha-Khadem F, Watkins KE, Price CJ, Ashburner J, Alcock K, Gadian DG, *et al.* (1998). Neural basis of an inherit speech and language disorder. *Proceedings of the National Academy of Sciences, USA*, **95**, 12695–12700.

Volterra V, Capirci O and Caselli MC (2001). What atypical populations can reveal about language development: The contrast between deafness and Williams syndrome. *Language and Cognitive Processes*, **16**, 219–239.

Wexler K (1996). The development of inflection in a biologically based theory of language acquisition. In: ML Rice, ed. *Toward a genetics of language.* Mahwah, NJ: Lawrence Erlbaum Associates.

Chapter 25

Connectionist models in developmental cognitive neuroscience: Critical periods and the paradox of success

Mark S. Seidenberg and Jason D. Zevin

Abstract

Connectionist models have made significant contributions to understanding developmental phenomena, mainly by providing novel computational accounts of behavioral emergence and change. What is the fate of such models given the increasing interest in, and information about, the biological bases of development? We consider this issue with respect to the classical idea of a critical period for acquiring language. The standard view is that neurobiological developments on a strict maturational timetable create limits on language learning capacity. Computational analysis suggests the opposite: that learning itself creates neurobiological conditions underlying the 'closing' of the critical period. The critical period example suggests how connectionist models can continue to provide a necessary level of analysis intermediate between behavior and brain.

25.1 Introduction

Our task in being invited to contribute to this volume was to critically assess the contributions of computational models to the study of the developmental issues that were the focus of the conference. This task seemed unmanageable, given the variety of computational architectures in the marketplace and the range of issues in brain and cognitive development to which they have been applied. We therefore set a more modest goal: to consider the role of such models in light of the rapidly increasing body of knowledge about the brain bases of behavior and its development. To further simplify our task, we will focus on connectionist models of the parallel distributed processing (PDP) variety (Rumelhart *et al.* 1986), for several reasons:

- because they are intrinsically developmental: they simulate the course of acquiring a skill or type of knowledge. Many other computational models are not;

- because they are explicitly intended to bridge overt behavior and its brain basis, providing insight about both;

- because they have been applied to a broader range of phenomena in cognition and development than other frameworks, and so there is a significant body of work to consider, including other work described in this volume;

- because many of the issues that arise concerning connectionist models are not specific to this type of model but rather concern the role of computational models more generally;

- because we happened to have worked extensively with such models.

25.2 What have we learned from PDP models about development?

It is nearly 20 years since the publication of the PDP 'bible,' the two volumes edited by Rumelhart and McClelland that introduced the basic concepts and initial applications of their approach. As one of us said at the time, 'The authors have laid out an approach that will be discussed and developed for years to come.' (Seidenberg 1986) and so it has. There have been many applications of this approach to developmental phenomena, which is unsurprising given its emphasis on learning. Any summary of the advances achieved within this framework relevant to development would have to include the following (see also Munakata and McClelland 2003). This list is not exhaustive, and not every model instantiates every point.

A. *Unifying acquisition and skilled performance within a single theoretical framework.* Connectionist models are intrinsically developmental. The models learn to perform tasks, such as predicting the location of a hidden object (Munakata *et al.* 1997), determining the meaning of a written word (Plaut and Shallice 1993; Harm and Seidenberg 2004), or generating the past tense of a verb (e.g. Rumelhart and McClelland 1986; Joanisse and Seidenberg 1999). Each model instantiates a developmental trajectory in the course of learning the task. Overt performance changes over time; however, the same principles govern acquisition and skilled performance which are merely different points on a developmental continuum (Seidenberg and MacDonald 1999).

The importance of linking acquisition and skilled performance should not be underestimated; in many areas, such as language, acquisition and skilled performance are studied largely separately with different principles used to explain phenomena in the two areas (see Seidenberg and McDonald 1999, for discussion). This dissociation occurs in many domains, including perception (e.g.

object recognition), motor performance (e.g. walking, reaching), and cognition (e.g. numerical knowledge).

B. *Identifying mechanisms of developmental change.* Connectionist models have provided mechanisms that explain why developmental changes occur, a significant step beyond the often acute descriptions of behavioral change in the developmental literature. Changes in overt behavior are closely tied to – and emerge from – specific computational properties of these models, which affect knowledge representations and their use in performing different tasks.

The classic illustration of this point is the reconceptualization of stage-like behavior in development, initiated by McClelland (1989) whose modeling demonstrated how developmental stages in performance of the balance-beam problem (Siegler 1976) could arise from non-linear transitions in network behavior. In standard PDP networks, knowledge acquisition is gradual and continuous. However, the overt behavior of the system may change more abruptly, reflecting the aggregate effects of many small weight changes. A second example is provided by research on stages in learning to read. Beginning readers have been described as proceeding through a series of stages (Ehri 1995): logographic, alphabetic, orthographic; prealphabetic, partial alphabetic, full alphabetic, consolidated alphabetic; and so on, depending on how finely the stages are stratified. These observations capture some broad facts about reading acquisition, at a level that engages many educators. These developments are usually ascribed to changes in the child's reading 'strategy,' based on developing metalinguistic awareness of how writing relates to speech. However, children's behavior is not strictly stage-like insofar as at any one point in time they read different words by different strategies (as Ehri has noted). The 'strategy' idea suggests a level of conscious intent that may not be present. Moreover, it is not clear what kinds of processes each strategy entails, or the extent to which they differ. Finally, the description leaves open the crucial question as to the forces that cause the child to change strategy. These behavioral changes arise in a different manner in connectionist models of reading (Seidenberg and McClelland 1989; Harm and Seidenberg 1999). The phenomena reflect the child's growing sensitivity to the internal structure of the written and spoken forms of words. This occurs in a connectionist model as a byproduct of the learning process. Our reading models initially learn on a word by word basis. As the model is exposed to a broader sample of words, it begins to pick up on statistical regularities over various levels of structure that the orthographic and phonological representations potentially afford. Thus the model progressively differentiates the orthographic and phonological structures of words and the mappings between them, ending up with knowledge that spans multiple levels (letters, digraphs, onset, rime, and other subword structures, words). The network is then a representation of the statistical structure of the lexicon, which varies across writing systems. This is a form of implicit learning. There is no homunculus guiding the model's choice of 'strategy;' rather the characteristics that the strategy description are intended to capture fall out of basic computational properties of the model. The point here is not to deny that children ever engage in explicit learning or problem solving strategies; rather it is that as applied to this aspect of early reading the strategy notion is, at best, a broad characterization of developmental processes that have a particular computational basis, which is relevant to understanding the fine detail of the behavior, why it occurs, and how it could be facilitated or remediated.

C. *Determining the extent to which behavior reflects general vs. domain-specific types of learning or processing mechanisms, or types of knowledge representation.* One of the main ideas in the PDP approach is that behavior (and its brain bases) can be explained in terms of a relatively small number of principles concerning knowledge representation, learning, processing, and so on. This aspect of the approach is clearly related to Piaget's attempt to describe general cognitive principles underlying learning and developmental change. As in Piaget's day (Piatelli-Palmarini 1980), controversy explodes when this type of approach is applied to language (cf. the Rumelhart and McClelland 1986, verb learning model). Such models have challenged a core tenet of modern linguistic theory, that language involves highly abstract, domain-specific forms of knowledge, and thus cannot be derived from general capacities to think and learn (Seidenberg 1997). There continue to be strongly divergent views on this matter. The main complaint about the application of Piaget's concepts to language was that they could not account for any interesting aspect of grammar (see discussion in Piatelli-Palmarini 1980).[1] However, there now are several plausible applications of PDP principles to specific grammatical phenomena, including ones that have been difficult to explain within grammatical theory. For example Haskell *et al.* (2003) provide an account of how children acquire a subtle grammatical distinction, the dispreference for plural modifiers in compounds (e.g. *rats-eater), which had been repeatedly argued (Pinker 1999, and elsewhere) to provide evidence for a type of innate grammatical knowledge (that word formation rules operate at ordered levels or strata in the mental lexicon: Kiparsky 1982; Gordon 1985). Inadequacies of the level-ordering theory had been noted almost since its creation (Spencer 1991), and the phenomena had resisted systematic explanation. Haskell *et al.* showed that the phenomena relate to phonological and semantic properties of the modifier, from which different degrees of modifier acceptability follow. The Haskell *et al.* work suggests a

---

[1] One could say the same about current theories of language evolution, which are more focused on explaining the fact of language evolution rather than the existence of particular aspects of grammar. Such theories do not explain any of the aspects of language that are said to be highly abstract and unmarked in the overt structure of utterances.

plausible account of the *rats-eater* data and promising directions for future research. (See articles in Christiansen, Chater, and Seidenberg (1999) and citations therein for other applications of connectionist concepts to linguistic phenomena.)

This research is part of a broader reconceptualization of the language acquisition problem (e.g. Bates 1994; Saffran *et al.* 1996; Seidenberg 1997), largely motivated by the PDP approach. In the standard linguistic characterization of the 'logical problem of language acquisition,' the child's goal is to converge on the grammar of a language and the main problem is the poverty and variability of the input (Pinker 1989). Within this framework there is indeed a puzzle about how a child could ever acquire a particular language. However, many of the considerations that make language learning difficult and seem to implicate innate grammatical knowledge (e.g. the lack of explicit negative evidence, the lack of consistent feedback about grammaticality) are moot if the acquisition task is reformulated as acquiring the neural networks that support comprehension and production (Seidenberg 1997, 2003; Lewis and Elman 2002).

D. *Unifying phenomena previously thought to be unrelated.* One result of applying a common set of theoretical principles to a broad range of phenomena has been the discovery of unexpected commonalities among them. Consider, for example, the inflectional and spelling systems of English. Inflection is a component of natural language, which has evolved over eons in one species, humans. Spelling is a technology, a method for representing speech invented only a few thousand years ago. Hence one might expect the two systems to have little in common. Parallel programs of research within the connectionist framework suggest otherwise, however. In brief, there are close commonalities between the two types of knowledge. Both are quasiregular (Seidenberg and McClelland 1989): they are dominated by rule-like regularities but admit forms that deviate from these central tendencies in differing degrees; the 'exceptions' partially overlap with the rule-governed forms and so are rarely arbitrary; the deviant forms tend to cluster among the higher frequency words in the language, and so on. These properties are handled by connectionist networks that learn probabilistic mappings between codes (spelling, sound, meaning). The correspondences between these types of knowledge extend beyond mere similarity: they are both parts of a lexical system that encodes relations among sound, spelling, and meaning (Harm and Seidenberg 2004). It follows from this view that these types of knowledge should be similarly affected by neuropathology, which recent research has confirmed. Patterson *et al.* (in press) show that semantic impairments in a group of patients with a progressive neurodegenerative disorder exhibit similar deficits on six tasks. For example patients who regularize past tenses (e.g. *leaved*) also regularize the pronunciations of words such as *listen*. The explanation for both is the greater role of semantics in determining the correct forms of atypical lower frequency words (Plaut *et al.* 1996; Joanisse and Seidenberg 1999).

Two other major components of this approach that play significant roles in explaining developmental phenomena should be mentioned. One is the *non-linear combination of probabilistic constraints*. It is a fundamental insight that bits of information that are not very informative in isolation can become highly constraining when taken together. For example the infant learning to identify the boundaries between spoken words relies on several types of information, no one of which is highly reliable. The connectionist framework provides a mechanism whereby such probabilistic constraints could be learned and combined efficiently. This is a significant insight about a basic characteristic of learning and skilled performance. In the language acquisition literature, it is often observed that various structures (or cues) occur too infrequently to provide a basis for learning a linguistic generalization, leading to the inference that innate knowledge is required. There is a further intuition that the existence of multiple, unreliable cues merely worsens the learning problem. However, such intuitions do not take into account the possibility of non-linear combinations of constraints, which connectionist models illustrate.

The other major concept *is division of labor* (Seidenberg 1992; Plaut *et al.* 1996; Harm and Seidenberg 2004). The idea is that learning to perform a complex task involves finding an efficient partitioning of the problem among interacting subsystems. The load that one subsystem carries depends on what is happening in other systems that are also contributing to performance. Division of labor (DOL) is the opposite of modularity, the idea of independent, isolable subsystems whose functions are determined in advance (e.g. by evolution). The DOL idea has been worked out in greatest detail with respect to reading, but represents a more general ideal about how the brain solves complex problems (see Gordon and Dell 2003, for another application of the concept).

What is clear from this partial survey is that connectionist models have mainly contributed to understanding developmental phenomena by explaining how they arise from what Rumelhart and McClelland called the microstructure of cognition. That is, the models (and the broader theoretical framework they instantiate) explain how prominent aspects of behavior emerge from a particular type of computational system. Although this type of computation was said to be 'neurally inspired' and broadly consistent with basic characteristics of brain function, the models that most directly bear on cognitive and linguistic development have been only weakly constrained by facts about neurobiology. Of course, many people are actively exploring how the same computational principles can be used to understand neurobiology (e.g. brain bases of learning and memory), but our focus is on models that account for behavior and its development. Looking at the literature one is struck by an apparent tradeoff between biological fidelity and level of phenomenon: the further the phenomena from higher level cognition, the more biologically realistic the model.

Thus a questions arises: what is the fate of connectionist models in light of advances in, and a growing emphasis on, understanding the brain bases of behavior, at levels ranging from the neural circuits revealed by neuroimaging to cellular neurobiology? One possibility is that current models of language and cognition are an intermediate step: the limiting factor is our lack of knowledge about aspects of neurobiology that are relevant to cognition and its development. When such information becomes available, models will be developed that are based on it. Current-generation cognitive models will be replaced by neurobiological ones. Some enthusiastic neuroimagers go further, asserting that knowledge about brain circuitry will obviate computational theories of behavior entirely.

An alternative view is that the natural progression is one in which computational models are not just an interim stage but necessary for achieving the goal of linking brain and behavior. The main constraint is not lack of knowledge of the brain bases of cognition (although what is known is indeed limited). Rather, in many areas of cognition we have not achieved the understanding of basic *computational* mechanisms that are a prerequisite for understanding their brain bases. On this view, computation modeling complements other methodologies: behavioral experiments can tell us what the effects of stimulus and task manipulations are on overt responses. Imaging can tell us what brain regions and circuits are involved in processing. There is a further need for computational models that explain how brain mechanisms give rise to behavior. Otherwise the behavioral work is isolated from the brain and the neuroimaging has an atheoretical, descriptive character.

One can also argue, as we will here, that computational models serve a further function: they have explanatory value insofar as they provide an appropriate level for understanding basic characteristics of complex cognitive and developmental phenomena. This function does not merely reflect lack of knowledge about brain mechanisms, but rather reflects a deeper issue about the levels of analysis that are relevant to explaining behavior.

This last claim may seem a throwback to an earlier era in which much less was known about the brain. It may merely be the case that we still know too little about the brain bases of cognition to build biologically realistic models that account for detailed aspects of cognitive functions and how they develop. Or perhaps modelers merely need to work harder on their neurobiology. Surely neuroimaging techniques are on an upward trajectory toward identifying neural circuits underlying many aspects of cognition. Even neural development is within our grasp: we can image the brains of 3-month-olds (Dehaene-Lambertz *et al.* 2002). Perhaps we will all be neurobiologists in the end.

These issues matter insofar as they reflect different views about where cognitive neuroscience should be heading. But really, who knows what will happen and who's to say what should? Fields make these decisions, not individuals. Still, we might remove this discussion from the realm of pure speculation and gain some insight by pursuing the following strategy: let us consider some aspect of cognition for which a considerable amount is already known about its neurobiological and computational bases, and then examine how they each contribute to understanding the phenomena. With that in mind, we turn to critical periods.

25.3 Critical periods in language acquisition and other domains

The term *critical period* has been used with reference to several types of developmental phenomena, including neurobiological (e.g. critical periods for gene expression), sensory-motor (e.g. development of the visual system), and cognitive (e.g. language). Our focus is on the sense of critical period (dating from Lenneberg 1967) referring to a time window during which species-typical communicative behaviors (e.g. song in zebra finches, language in humans) are learned (Doupe and Kuhl 2000). This rapid and efficient early learning contrasts with subsequent restrictions on learning capacity (often termed a loss of plasticity). Evidence for a critical period in language acquisition (CPLA) derives from studies of diverse aspects of normal and atypical language acquisition, including observations such as:

1. Languages are learned on a consistent maturational timetable despite input that is impoverished (relative to what is learned) and highly variable (across languages, individuals, and cultures). This consistency extends across modalities, insofar as signed and spoken languages are learned on much the same timetable (Petitto 1999).

2. Learning a second language later in life is difficult even with extended experience (Johnson and Newport 1989; Flege *et al.* 1999; Birdsong and Molis 2002), in contrast to learning two languages from birth.

3. Late learning of a first language (e.g. by deaf individuals whose exposure to sign language is delayed) results in incomplete mastery (Newport 1990; Neville and Bavelier 2000; Mayberry *et al.* 2002).

4. The timing rather than amount of exposure to a language apparently determines the level of mastery (Johnson and Newport 1989).

5. The high degree of plasticity during the critical period affords reorganization in the presence of atypical input (e.g. recruitment of 'auditory' language areas given signed input; Neville *et al.* 1998) and following early brain injury or neuropathology (Dennis 2000; Vargha-Khadem and Polkey 1992). Thus these conditions do not preclude acquiring normal language. In contrast, recovery of linguistic functions following brain injury in adulthood is typically limited (Holland 1989), paralleling the limits on ability to learn a first or second language post critical period.

The standard view is that these facts can be explained in terms of a 'language faculty' that evolved in humans (Chomsky 1986). The realization of the language capacity in an individual requires exposure to a native language coinciding with the maturation or expression of this faculty under genetic control. This theory is thought to simultaneously explain many other facts as well, such as the universal properties of language; the creation of language without a model (Senghas 2003); creolization and other cases where the child's language is more systematic the parents' (Singleton and Newport 2004); and the species-specificity of language. The fact that language is learned during a critical period can be taken as independent evidence for the biological basis of the language faculty.

Within this standard approach, the brain bases of language and the critical period are often ignored because they are thought to shed little light on the nature of language *qua* language. When they are discussed, it is usually by analogy to the development of the visual system, often ocular dominance columns in cat. For example, as noted by Stromswold (1995), 'Although the ability to learn language appears to be innate, exposure to language during childhood is necessary for normal language development, just as the ability to see is innate yet visual stimulation is necessary for normal visual development (Hubel and Wiesel 1970). The hypothesis that exposure to language must occur by a certain age in order for language to be acquired normally is called the critical period hypothesis.' The factors that close the critical period for language are not known but are discussed by reference to aspects of neurobiological maturation such as synaptic pruning, the development of inhibitory synaptic connections, and other events that have been identified with the loss of plasticity in other species (Hensch 2003).

Three broad issues arise in connection with this account.

1. There are controversies about each of the types of behavioral evidence seen as evidence for a CPLA. For example the limits on language learning following the close of the putative critical period are not absolute; there are well-attested cases of late acquisition of native-like competence (e.g. Birdsong and Molis 2002). The idea of a CPLA seems somewhat Anglocentric, of less concern perhaps in cultures where it is common to achieve high competence in a second or third language at different points in life. Data concerning the effects of age vs. amount of exposure to L2 (Johnson and Newport 1989) have been strongly contested (e.g. Bialystok and Hakuta 1994). Second language learning outcomes are greatly affected by the conditions under which learning occurs (Flege *et al.* 1999). Studies of late learners of a first language raise questions about what their communicative experience was like prior to exposure to a natural language and how it affected subsequent learning. Non-linguistic aspects of these individuals' experiences may also have differed greatly from those that prevail in the usual L1 learning situation. Evidence that language can be acquired despite severe injury to (indeed, complete removal of) left hemisphere tissue that normally supports language raises questions as to the locus and role of the putative language organ. Languages

created without a model do not appear to exhibit the deep, abstract properties said to be characteristic of grammar, and the studies leave open whether development reflects strictly grammatical or more general cognitive processes. Thus, the standard account relies heavily on data that are at best open to other interpretations.

For linguists such as Jackendoff (2003), the definitive evidence concerning the innateness of grammar comes from recent studies of the emergence of sign language without a formal model in Nicaragua (Senghas 2003). These findings are fascinating but the view that they are the pure expression of innate universal grammar is questionable. The extent to which the emerging communicative system will come to exhibit various properties of grammar, including the abstract ones thought to differentiate language from other types of cognition, is not yet clear. Utterances in the early stages of the development of the system were closely tied to actions and individuals in the immediate environment. The language is changing over time, but this may be due to general perceptual and memory forces rather than language-specific ones. In short, this research may be yielding elegant evidence for how language emerges from communicative needs and general cognitive factors.

2. The analogy to critical periods in visual development does not advance the issues very far. Analogies are not facts, no matter how forcefully asserted and repeated. Many interesting issues arise in comparing language and vision that are not captured by statements such as 'the child's language 'grows in the mind' as the visual system develops the capacity for binocular vision.' (Chomsky 1993, p. 29). Language involves multiple types of sensory information (audition, vision), motoric output systems, a cognitive system that thinks and reasons, and so on. These components do not all develop exclusively in the service of language and thus have their own developmental trajectories. Language also consists of multiple subsystems, which represent different types of information, have different properties and exploit different capacities in different ways. Phonology, for example, which is tied to hearing and speaking, is different from word learning, which involves conceptual knowledge. There is a grain mismatch in comparing the development of this system of interlocking skills and parts with the development of a component of early vision. Even at the level of perceptual processing, the ability to interpret rapidly varying acoustic signals in speech is clearly different in kind and complexity from the segregation of inputs from different sensory organs at the periphery.[2]

[2] Chomsky has compared the innateness of language to many aspects of vision, including perception of three-dimensional space, color perception, object perception, visual attention, and binocular vision, going so far as to claim there is an innate 'grammar of vision' (Werry 2002). These analogies are not a substitute for actual visual science. For example the common comparison between language and the development of ocular dominance columns echoed in the Stromswold quote is vexed given recent evidence that the latter is even more hard-wired than previously thought. Using modern visualization methods, Crair et al. (2001)

3. The standard story assumes that language is essentially unlearned (and unlearnable) except for minor language-specific elements (Pinker 1994). Given this view it is plausible to equate language with other capacities that are fully realized within a limited window in early development. However, other recent theories of language and how it is acquired view the language acquisition problem very differently. One such alternative account emphasizes the role of statistical learning and the structure of the input to the child in converging on knowledge that supports the use of language (Saffran *et al.* 1996; Seidenberg 1997; Gomez, Chapter 4, this volume). This approach provides a different way of thinking about critical period phenomena, which we explore below.[3]

In summary, the standard evidence and arguments for critical periods attempt to establish the plausibility of the idea but leave open basic questions of fact. Still, acquiring language early in life seems patently easier than learning it later. We do not want to conclude from uncertainties about particular findings that the emperor has no clothes; perhaps merely a wardrobe malfunction. Moreover, learning language appears both easier than learning many other things and more age-dependent. Apparently, there is something to be explained here but the characterization of what is to be explained may need modification, which will in turn affect how it is explained.

25.4 Biological bases of critical/sensitive periods

Plausibility arguments and analogies aside, is there direct biological evidence for a critical period in acquiring language? The loose coupling of the critical period concept to neurobiology is reflected in the fact that even the date at which it is said to close varies greatly, from 5 to 6 years (Pinker 1994) to puberty (Lenneberg 1967) and points beyond (Hakuta and Bialystock 1994). There is, however, an extensive literature on the biological bases of critical/sensitive periods as studied in other species. In brief, there are many candidates for intrinsic changes to neural networks that may limit plasticity, including synaptic pruning, changes in the number and distribution of neurotransmitter receptors, and the maturation of inhibition. These developments can be experience-independent. For example the development of inhibitory circuitry can be controlled by genetic (Hensch *et al.* 1998; Huang *et al.* 1998; Fagiolini *et al.* 2004) and pharmacological (Fagiolini and Hensch 2000) factors that can be de-coupled from activity-dependent changes in plasticity evident during the critical

---

demonstrated that the earliest inputs from thalamus to primary visual cortex in cat are already segregated by eye. In ferrets, which are highly altricial, complete removal of visual experience does not interfere with the development of ODCs (Issa *et al.* 1999; Crowley and Katz 1999). This is quite unlike language which definitely requires substantial experiential input.

[3] Insofar as statistical learning plays a central role in both language and vision (compare, e.g. Saffran *et al.* 1996, and Kirkham *et al.* 2002), the two may indeed turn out to be similar but not for the reasons Chomsky suggested.

period. For example whatever the environment in which the animal is raised, interventions that induce the maturation of inhibitory circuitry also induce the onset and closure of a critical period for plasticity.

However, there is also strong evidence that learning itself also plays a role in limiting plasticity (Hensch 2003; McClelland *et al.* 1999; Zevin and Seidenberg 2002). Song learning in zebra finches provides an example that turns out to be relevant to language learning (more so than ocular dominance columns). Zebra finches typically learn song during a sensitive period that closes in early adulthood, after which new song elements are not added, and existing elements are not lost or rearranged. There is variability across bouts of song (e.g. with respect to number of repetitions of a song element) but it is highly constrained. In isolation, this fact could be taken as evidence for a classical biologically-determined critical period, the closing of which shuts down the organism's capacity to learn. However, this view is contradicted by a wealth of recent data implicating learning and environment in the critical period and its aftermath.

Although song is learned within a typical time frame, zebra finches exhibit plasticity well beyond the closing of this period. For example the critical period can be extended by altering the bird's experience: adult birds raised in isolation can learn new song material from a tutor (Jones *et al.* 1996). Songs learned under these conditions are slightly abnormal, either because of the experience-independent developments summarized above or because of learning from the bird's own song that occurs in isolation and interferes with subsequent learning. Plasticity can also be reinstated in adults via methods that disrupt motor output (Williams and Mehta 1999) or auditory feedback (Brainerd and Doupe 2000; Leonardo and Konishi 1999). These findings sparked interest in the hypothesis that some form of maintenance learning continues to occur throughout adulthood. When normal feedback is available, the bird's output matches his target and reinforces the existing song representation. Disruptions of feedback lead to maladaptive adjustments of song via this same mechanism. Indeed, lesions of brain regions known to be critical for initial song acquisition prevent changes of song in deafened birds (Brainerd and Doupe 2000), providing strong support for this view.

Zevin, Bottjer and Seidenberg (2004) explored this further using white noise to prevent adult birds from being able to hear their own songs without damaging their hearing. Under these conditions the birds' songs degrade to varying degrees. This suggests that continued exposure to the bird's own song is necessary for maintenance, that is, keeping the song network tuned. When noise was removed, the subjects showed no evidence of learning from exposure to a tutor, suggesting a limit on adult plasticity and learning capacity. However, song did change over time with new access to auditory feedback, suggesting a continued capacity to learn.

Finally, results from a large-scale, cross-sectional study suggest that plasticity continues to decline gradually late into adult life (Lombardino and Nottebohm 2000). Variability in adult song, as characterized by the frequency and consistency with which particular song elements are produced, declines throughout adulthood, suggesting a progressive entrenchment of the representations that underlie song production. Critically, the response to deafening was also shown to differ as a function of age, such that the effects of deafening were progressively slower and less severe with age.

What conclusions follow from this research? First, there is evidence for reductions in plasticity after the sensitive period, possibly related to non-experience-dependent neurobiological developments that extend into adulthood. Second, song birds nonetheless retain plasticity beyond the critical period; continued exposure to song is required for maintenance, and song degrades when it is not available. Finally, learning itself plays a role in limiting plasticity. Degradation of feedback induces song change in a manner that depends on the integrity of nuclei involved in initial song acquisition. Susceptibility to disruption of auditory feedback declines steadily with age throughout the life span, in a manner that is highly correlated with behavioral stereotypy. These observations suggest that the acquisition and gradual entrenchment of representations that support stereotyped song become increasingly resistant to change as a result of the process of learning itself.

Of course birds are not people and songs are not language. Nonetheless the zebra finch research suggests a picture that may plausibly extend to language learning, with a combination of independent neurobiological events and learning contributing to rapid initial learning followed by a gradual decline in plasticity. Close causal connections between developmental neurobiological events and language learning have not been established, however, and it is unclear whether they are the proximal causes of the major phenomena seen as evidence for a critical period in language acquisition. Of particular interest is the extent to which the landmark phenomena are attributable to learning itself. To investigate this question, we need a computational model.

25.5 A computational view of critical periods

What we seek is a computational-level theory of the basic CPLA phenomena, including the early rapid learning of L1, the gradual decrease in plasticity/language learning ability, and other facts such as differences in plasticity associated with different components of language and the effects of both the timing of exposure to a second language and structural relations between first and second languages. What follows are some steps toward such an account. PDP networks have not, as yet, incorporated facts about neurobiological development; the network's architecture, processing dynamics, and capacity to learn are typically fixed (leaving aside the cascade correlation approach; Shultz, Chapter 3, this volume). Changes in network behavior are therefore due to how learning occurs given these initial constraints. Thus such networks can be used as a tool to gain evidence as to whether learning itself determines critical period phenomena. In effect, the networks can be used to decouple the confounds between experience and brain development that complicate the interpretation of many other types of data. Because the networks are pitched at this computational rather than neurodevelopmental level, we know in advance that there are some boundary phenomena that they will not capture correctly. For example, there are neurobiological developments associated with normal aging that affect plasticity, which this type of account ignores. The idea, however, is that an account pitched at a computational level intermediate between brain and behavior can provide important insight about – indeed a different view of – critical periods. Such a theory, taken with other facts about neurodevelopment that influence plasticity, should account for the range of observed behavioral outcomes.

25.5.1 PDP networks and the paradox of success

Learning in PDP networks involves changes to weights on connections between units that are intended to capture the behavior of large ensembles of neurons (see O'Reilly and Munakata 2000, for further detail). Models are typically initialized with small random weights, consistent with the idea that although early neurobiological development establishes preconditions for learning, humans are not born with highly structured knowledge. We know that early language learning is rapid, given appropriate experiential input. In PDP networks this occurs for specifiable technical reasons related to several aspects of the architecture (see also Munakata and McClelland 2003). Early exposure to target patterns results in large weight changes. The system is highly plastic at this point because unit outputs tend to fall toward the middle of the sigmoidal activation function, that is on the steep linear portion; as a result, the behavior of the system can change significantly as the weights change, supporting rapid learning. Early learning is mainly sensitive to pattern frequency. As the model learns from patterns sampled from a structured domain such as language, units begin to approach extremal values (e.g. 1 or −1) and several important effects are observed. First, some weights fall to small values, contribute little to accurate performance or additional learning, and are effectively pruned (as seen in neurobiological development). Second, the model becomes less sensitive to pattern frequency; once a pattern is learned, the error signal it produces is very small. Additional exposures have little effect, creating a discrepancy between the statistics of the input (i.e. actual frequency) and network performance. Thus learning in such systems involves transforming rather than merely matching the input statistics (see Singleton and Newport 2004). Third, the model becomes more sensitive to similarities across patterns; new learning is easiest for patterns that overlap with previously-trained ones. This property also supports generalization: correct performance on novel stimuli in virtue of their similarity to trained patterns.

Learning to perform a task correctly, then, means that the weights have assumed values that push activations close to desired values. Exposure to additional patterns from the same target set (e.g. language) produces small error signals. Except perhaps under extreme conditions in which the input to the network is radically changed

(McClelland *et al.* 1999), the weights are difficult to adjust further because of their contributions to successful performance. The net result is that the model becomes less plastic in the sense of no longer allowing large weight changes with few exposures. This effect has been termed 'entrenchment' (Ellis and Lambon Ralph 2000; Zevin and Seidenberg 2002; Elman *et al.* 1996).

These network properties establish a basis for early rapid learning followed by a decline in plasticity, the classic 'critical period' pattern. The 'closing' of the critical period, then, is the loss of plasticity associated with success in learning a task, that is entrenchment. A problem arises because weights that are highly favorable for skilled performance of one task (e.g. using a first language) are unfavorable for other tasks (e.g. learning a second language). We call this the *paradox of success*: learning to perform a task with a high degree of proficiency may create conditions that interfere with further learning.

In the case of language, this loss of plasticity is not a wholly negative thing. The knowledge that is acquired is systematic and represented in a way that supports generalization, a defining characteristic of language. The network is trained on examples but generalizes to novel patterns via similarity and recombination of existing elements. In effect, the network assimilates new utterances to the existing structure. However, the network's capacity to generalize also gives it a strong tendency to assimilate L2 utterances as well. Running French utterances through a highly trained English network is not an efficient way to learn French. The obvious extreme cases are ones in which novel phonological contrasts in L2 are not perceived because they are assimilated to existing categories in L1 (e.g. Best *et al.* 2001). Interference due to increasing entrenchment of L1 provides a basis for the decline in plasticity associated with the 'closing' of the critical period.

The situation described above contrasts with the learning of unsystematic facts, such as names for things and individuals, which afford little generalization but do not show critical period effects or a decline in plasticity over time (modulo independent developments such as effects of aging on hippocampal function). In fact the learning of arbitrary facts exhibits tiny entrenchment ('age of acquisition') effects. In brief, there is empirical and computational modeling evidence that arbitrary associations learned earlier in life show a long-lasting advantage over associations learned later (Ellis and Lambon Ralph 1999; Zevin and Seidenberg 2002). In practice it takes less time to name an object or person if it was learned early in life, other factors aside. Note, however, that AoA effects differ from critical periods in two important respects. First, AoA effects concern particular items rather than systematic aspects of knowledge. Second, conditions that give rise to AoA effects do not typically result in a failure to acquire novel items. Rather, performance is merely poorer. In contrast, sensitive period effects result in the inability to acquire generalizable, systematic knowledge, for example the ability to categorize novel speech sounds.

Thus, the loss of plasticity associated with the CPLA seems to be specifically related to the capacity to generalize. If this is correct it suggests that there is no critical period-like loss of plasticity in cognitive domains that do not afford generalization. This would be a step toward explaining why only some types of knowledge show the critical period type of developmental profile.

25.6 Applications to 'late' language learning

The above analysis emphasizes computational factors thought to underlie the rapid learning followed by decline in plasticity characteristic of first language learning. With minor extensions we can apply this account to phenomena concerning 'late' language learning, two types of which have been studied:

1. Learning a second language, which can occur at varying time lags relative to a first language.
2. Late learning of a first language. This condition has mainly been studied with regard to deaf children of hearing parents who are not exposed to a signed natural language (e.g. American Sign Language, ASL) until relatively late (e.g. the onset of formal schooling; Mayberry *et al.* 2002; Newport 1990; Singleton and Newport 2004). Late exposure to ASL is typically preceded by the development of home sign communicative systems that exhibit some important properties of natural language (Goldin-Meadow and Mylander 1990).

In both cases, the phenomena concern language learning by individuals who have already had experience with another communicative system (L1 in the case of L2 learners, home sign in the case of late ASL learners). For brevity we will refer to both cases as L1 followed by L2, although ASL is referred to as L1 in the late acquisition cases, in part because home sign, though rich, may not exhibit the full range of properties of natural languages. The main point is that experience with one communication system precedes experience with another. We can now identify several computational and experiential factors that interact to determine L2 learning outcomes.

One factor is the structure of the learner's experience. There has been considerable research about how the conditions that govern language learning vary. For example a child learns a first language under different conditions than an adult learning a second language (e.g. as an immigrant; in a classroom). The late L2 learner already knows a language, the L1 learner does not. Motivational and environmental factors, including the range of conditions under which L2 is used, account for considerable variance in L2 learning outcomes (Flege *et al.* 1999), much more so than in L1 learning. Similarly, home sign is learned (created, really) under conditions that differ from those in standard L1 learning. These differences among the conditions under which language is learned are important and contribute to observed outcomes. However, here our concern is with other major aspects of the learning environment, suggested by the computational framework, which relate to the timing and consequences of learning.

L1 learning in the monolingual context is *blocked*: the child has extensive exposure to a single language. Language is learned rapidly and, as noted above, there is an increase in the capacity to generalize accompanied by a decrease in plasticity. It is then difficult (though not impossible of course) to assimilate L2 to this functioning language system. Other social and motivational factors aside, an important characteristic of late exposure to a second language is L1 and L2 experiences are *interleaved*: the individual continues to use L1 but is also exposed to L2. This condition is Blocked Early–Interleaved Late. The complement of this situation is a bilingual environment from birth, in which the child is exposed to both L1 and L2 (Interleaved Early). These conditions (summarized in Table 25.1) represent extreme points on a continuum determined by how well-learned L1 is at the time of exposure to L2. Similar considerations apply to the home sign vs. L1 situation, keeping in mind the likelihood that home sign differs in some respects from natural languages.

Two computational factors are operating here. One is the degree to which one system has been learned prior to exposure to the second system. L1 monolingual learning is easy: there is no prior entrenched knowledge to interfere with learning, and plasticity is high. Learning both L1 and L2 in the Interleaved Early condition is also relatively easy: no entrenchment here either, and plasticity is again high; the task is harder than learning a single language but ultimately learnable. L2 learning in the Interleaved Late condition is hard: L1 is entrenched and plasticity is low; thus knowledge of L1 interferes with learning L2. Note that this analysis does not make reference to any changes over time in the substrates that support learning or the capacity to learn except those that are a consequence of learning itself.

A second factor is whether the experiences with the two systems are interleaved or not. In the Early (bilingual) case, interleaving is good: neither language is entrenched and they both can be learned. This contrasts with the Blocked Early–Interleaved Late situation typical of late L2 learning. Experience with L2 is interleaved with L1. It is the continued experience with L1 that keeps the language network entrenched, interfering with the attempt to accommodate L2. Thus interleaved language experience has radically different effects at different points in time.

Table 25.1 Language learning conditions

	TIMING	
LEARNING CONDITION	**Early**	**Late (L2 exposure)**
Blocked	Monolingual	L2 interferes with L1 (CI)
Interleaved	Bilingual	L1 interferes with L2

'Early' refers to the child's language experience from birth. 'Late' refers to exposure to L2 following initial acquisition of L1. CI = Catastrophic interference; LP = 'loss of Plasticity'.

25.6.1 **Catastrophic interference, L1 loss and L2 interference**

The interfering effect of L1 on L2 turns on the maintenance of L1 weights. As we have noted, zebra finches actively maintain song through continued feedback from the bird's own song. Disrupting this feedback causes the song to drift. (This drift is similar to that which occurs in the speech of individuals with adult hearing loss.) The role of continued experience with L1 in interfering with L2 learning can be understood with reference to the phenomenon of catastrophic interference in PDP networks. McCloskey and Cohen (1989) trained a simple feedforward network on a set of arithmetic problems (e.g. the 'ones' problems: 1+0, 1+1, ... 1+9). Once the model learned these problems, training switched to the twos problems (2+0, 2+1, etc.). McCloskey and Cohen observed that learning the twos problems resulted in loss of knowledge about the ones. They termed this retroactive interference effect in feedforward networks 'catastrophic interference'. It was thought to be a problem for such networks because learning new information typically does not cause unlearning of old information. However, the effect is not very general. It depends on strict blocking of the problem sets (Hetherington and Seidenberg 1989); thus the ones are maintained if there are even a few additional exposures to them during training on the twos. The conditions that give rise to catastrophic interference rarely occur in human learning, outside the context of a verbal learning experiment. In real life, experiences of different things are interleaved, thankfully.

The relevance of these effects to the language learning case should be clear. Learning a second language does not result in unlearning of a first language because experience with L1 does not cease. Catastrophic interference is not a problem for human learners because experience is rarely blocked to the extent the effect demands. However, the down side is that maintenance of L1 interferes with learning L2; L1 remains entrenched for reasons discussed above. When it comes to language learning, then, proactive interference from L1 is more a problem than retroactive interference from L2.

It is interesting to note that catastrophic interference – unlearning of L1 via learning of L2 – does occur on rare occasions. Pallier *et al.* (2003) studied adults who were born in Korea but adopted by French families in childhood (between the ages of 3 and 8 years old). These individuals had been exposed to Korean during the 'critical period' but then became French speakers. fMRI data suggested that knowledge of Korean had not been preserved into adulthood; the activation patterns elicited by Korean stimuli were similar for these subjects and speakers who had not been exposed to Korean. Pallier *et al.*'s interpretation is that L2 (French) replaced L1 (Korean), a naturalistic example of catastrophic interference. Experience with the two languages was strictly blocked; without any additional L1 'trials,' knowledge of the language was lost.

This analysis is supported by the results of two other studies that used designs similar to Pallier *et al.*'s but yielded somewhat different results. Tees and Werker

(1984) found that English-speaking adults who had been exposed to Hindi during infancy could discriminate Hindi speech sounds better than subjects without prior Hindi experience. Oh *et al.* (2003) found similar results for adults who had been exposed to Korean 'prior to age 5 and very little afterward' (p. 54). They observed residual effects of early exposure among college students enrolled in Korean courses. Perhaps the crucial difference between the conditions in these studies compared to Pallier *et al.*'s is whether there was continued exposure to L1 or not. In the Pallier case, there was essentially no additional exposure to L1 following adoption and relocation. In the Tees and Werker case, the subjects stopped using Hindi as their main language, but they were raised in a Hindi-Canadian community and would have continued to hear Hindi. Subjects in the Oh *et al.* study also experienced more exposure to the abandoned L1 than in Pallier *et al.*'s experiment (the subjects were either born in Korea and immigrated to the US with their Korean families, or were US born offspring of Korean speakers). This set of results is consistent with the strict blocking interpretation of catastrophic interference: L1 is unlearned when experience with the two languages is strictly blocked; however, even intermittent re-exposure to L1 is sufficient to keep it maintained at level that facilitated adults' phonological perception.

This analysis makes a further prediction. Hetherington and Seidenberg (1989) showed that even in the highly artificial blocked condition that produced 'catastrophic' interference, the model that had 'unlearned' the ones problems could rapidly relearn them with additional training. This savings in relearning indicated that although the model produced incorrect responses, the early learning had not been completely erased. This finding suggests that it would be valuable to look at relearning among individuals such as those studied by Pallier *et al.* Although residual knowledge of Korean was not detectable at the resolution provided by fMRI, it might be observed in relearning, indicating that the original language was not completely replaced.

25.6.2 Interleaving effects in L2 learning

The more common circumstance is the one in which continued experience with L1 interferes with learning of L2. These effects are predicted to depend on the degree of entrenchment of the first language. The clearest cases are ones in which a high degree of L1 entrenchment interferes with aspects of late L2 learning. This phenomenon is likely to be relevant to the well-studied problem of teaching adult Japanese speakers the r-l discrimination in English (Bradlow *et al.* 1997; McClelland *et al.* 2002). The English phonemic categories /r/ and /l/ are mapped onto a single category in Japanese (an alveolar tap closer to English /l/ than /r/). Adult Japanese speakers have difficulty discriminating and producing /r/ and /l/, even with extensive exposure to English. Several methods have been used to train this discrimination in adult Japanese speakers, with varying degrees of success (see references above). Whatever the upper limits on how well the discrimination can be learned and maintained, it is clear that the problem is a difficult one. This difficulty could be due in part to continued use of Japanese during training. That is, regardless of how intensive or extended the training regime, or how it is structured, the Japanese subject continues to use Japanese, including the phoneme category to which English /r/ and /l/ are typically assimilated. No language training regime can enforce cessation of L1 usage (although minimizing L1 usage is an apparent goal of 'immersion' programs). Because the Japanese category is so well learned, even a small number of additional trials with it are sufficient to maintain the category and interfere with learning the remapping required for /r/–/l/ discrimination in English.

McClelland *et al.* (2002; Chapter 2, this volume) have explored the hypothesis that the difficulty that Japanese speakers have in learning the r/l distinction is an unwanted byproduct of a Hebbian learning mechanism. In brief, with Hebbian learning the speaker's own incorrect perception of /r/ and /l/ as alveolar flaps will tend to strengthen the existing phonemic structure rather than promote learning the English phonemic categories. This account is similar to ours in that it is the speaker's continued experience with, and maintenance of, L1 phonology that interferes with additional learning. McClelland *et al.* place this effect in the learning algorithm itself; we place it in the interleaving of English and Japanese experiences. The two positions might be different faces of the same coin if the brain utilizes a learning mechanism that has both Hebbian and supervised aspects, as some believe (see O'Reilly and Munakata 2000, for discussion).

Above we discussed cases in which L2 overwrote L1 in differing degrees. The Pallier *et al*, Oh *et al*, and Tees and Werker studies all emphasized the extent to which L1 knowledge had been lost as function of L2. It would be interesting to know whether the converse also occurred: initial exposure to L1 interfering with mastery of L2, which became the primary language. This would be consistent with evidence that late learners do not fully master subtle aspects of L2 grammar. These effects would be modulated by how much L1 learning occurred prior to exposure to L2 and the degree to which L1 continued to be experienced. Greater experience with the 'abandoned' L1 would be expected to create greater interference with L2. This type of investigation would shed light on how much L1 entrenchment has to occur to create interference with L2.

25.6.3 Late learners of ASL

The situation in which a sign language such as ASL is learned late is a particularly interesting one. The literature emphasizes the fact that late learners do not achieve full command of the language's grammar, despite many years of experience with it (e.g. Newport 1990). This data seems to parallel similar limitations on L2 mastery (Johnson and Newport 1989): in both cases the age at which the individual is exposed to the language has an impact on outcome; this seems a more powerful factor than the amount of experience with the language (a factor that Johnson and Newport attempted to control). We have already suggested that in assessing outcomes associated with L2 learning, it is necessary to consider the degree of language learning that preceded onset of L2 experience. And Flege (1999; Flege *et al.* 1999) has perhaps been the most effective in identifying environmental and experiential factors that differ in L1 vs. L2 learning. Both of these considerations come into play in interpreting late ASL learning outcomes.

The late ASL learner will typically have used a home sign communicative system. Such children are not communicatively bereft; they are merely receiving highly degraded natural language input. The important finding from studies of such invented communicative systems (e.g. Goldin-Meadow and Feldman 1975; Goldin-Meadow and Mylander 1990) is that they exhibit some properties of natural languages. Thus the relationship of this experience to late ASL learning is similar to the role of L1 in learning L2. There are some potential differences in these situations that are difficult to assess (Mayberry 1993); home sign may not exhibit all the properties of natural languages, and it may not be as entrenched as a typical L1, because of the more limited conditions under which it is used. Still, the late ASL learner is not *tabula rasa* with respect to communicative ability, and the impact of this knowledge on later ASL acquisition needs to be considered. Note also that the late learner of ASL will typically continue to interleave home sign with ASL. Thus the situation has many of the characteristics of Late-Interleaved learning. Finally, the conditions that exist when the late learner is finally exposed to ASL differ from those in L1 learning. The child may be learning from peers or teachers whose own early language experiences (e.g. home sign, ASL, signed English) and level of ASL mastery are highly variable. These factors cannot be overlooked in considering why late learners fail to asymptote at the same level of grammatical competence as a child who learned ASL as a first language from deaf signing parents. Thus, although many aspects of the late ASL learner's experience differ from the other language learning conditions we have discussed, the same principles and factors may govern outcomes in all these cases.

25.6.4 Similarity effects

Finally, we must mention another major factor that contributes to L2 learning outcomes: the degree of similarity or overlap between the two languages. We have emphasized the negative impact of L1 learning on L2 acquisition. This emphasis was due to the fact that such data are typically seen as providing evidence for a critical period in language acquisition. However, the effects of L1 on L2 are not uniformly negative. Effects of L1 on L2 are governed by a complex equation whose variables are not fully understood. There is typological variation in phonology, morphology, syntax, organization of the lexicon, and other components of language. Similarity between L1 and L2 could facilitate learning: the fact that one language has inflectional morphology might make it easier to learn a second inflectional language. Similarity could interfere with learning, as in the r/l case, where sounds that are contrastive in English get absorbed into an existing attractor (perceptual category) for the Japanese. Dissimilarity could be helpful: the distinctiveness of Zulu clicks might make them easy for an English speaker to learn. Dissimilarity could also create difficulty: Chinese lacks determiners but that apparently does not make them easy to learn in L2 English.

It is clear that similarity relations between languages affect L2 outcomes (Bialystock and Hakuta 1994), possibly by modulating effects of language entrenchment, the timing of exposure to a second language, and the interleaving of language experiences. Although progress has been made in understanding these effects, particularly in phonological learning (e.g. Best *et al.* 2001), models of language learning are not advanced enough to make strong, detailed predictions about relative ease of learning across components of different languages. Here we can only reiterate the important point that language is not homogeneous; it consists of multiple components involving different types of knowledge, which exhibit different information structures. These differences among types of linguistic knowledge will affect L2 learning. For example lexical learning has a high degree of arbitrariness (i.e. in the mapping between form and meaning), which makes it susceptible to modest entrenchment (AoA) effects but creates little interference with later learning. In contrast, other domains of language (e.g. speech perception) require a high degree of generalization, which can give rise to effects of pernicious overassimilation.

25.7 Critical periods: complementary roles of biological and computational accounts

We have presented a summary of some of the biological factors that affect plasticity in non-human species, but noted that their connection to the loss of plasticity associated with the classic CPLA hypothesis was conjectural at best. We then sketched a computational learning theory of some of the major phenomena related to L1 and L2 acquisition ascribed to the CPLA.

Although a great deal remains to be learned about early neurobiological development, the findings and observations we have summarized suggest the tentative conclusion that there is no classical CPLA; at best the term describes what normally happens (language is learned rapidly with a gradual loss of capacity to learn other languages). However, there is little evidence for further claim that it is tied to biological developments on a maturational timetable. To the contrary, the major phenomena can be explained in terms of a theory of learning that specifies what is learned, how well it is learned, when it is learned, and how learning one system (e.g. L1) affects subsequent learning (e.g. L2). The crucial explanatory concept is entrenchment, which emerged from considering the phenomena computationally rather than biologically. This factor interacts with the systematic, generative aspect of language to create interference with later language learning. In our account, learning *creates* neurobiological changes that reduce plasticity; this is the opposite of the standard theory, in which intrinsic neuromaturational changes limit learning. In short, it is a viable working hypothesis that there simply *is no* critical period for language acquisition in any theoretically interesting sense, merely learning phenomena that create the Paradox of Success (see Bever 1981, who also proposed that critical period effects are a byproduct of normal acquisition; however, his 'psychogrammar' hypothesis involved wholly different ideas about what is learned and how).

Returning to the broader question about the role of connectionist-computational models in the era of the brain with which we began this chapter, the investigation of critical period phenomena suggests that the models continue to play an important role in clarifying phenomena and why they occur. Surprisingly, some relatively simple principles about learning in PDP networks can explain many of the major critical period phenomena, including ones often thought to implicate biological rather than experiential factors. The account presented above is only schematic; much of the simulation research that is needed to assess this analysis has not been completed (although see Zevin and Seidenberg 2002; Ellis and Lambon Ralph 2000). However, we have built this account on a much more extensive body of PDP modeling and it turns on some rather generic properties of such networks rather than specialized machinery.

What about the neurobiological evidence concerning the brain bases of changes in plasticity? We see this evidence as complementing the computational analysis in several ways. First, neurobiology establishes the preconditions and substrate for the learning phenomena we have described. There is no learning without the relevant neurobiological substrate and the learning effects we have modeled obviously have a neurobiological basis. The critical distinction is between neurobiological events that change the substrate of learning (e.g. proliferation and pruning) and changes in what has been learned within this substrate (e.g. a song or language). Second, some of the neurobiological facts lend corroborative support to the computational analysis. For example the modeling predicts that if the relevant experience were withheld (without introducing other pathologies as in the case of Genie), language could still be learned outside the notional critical period. These conditions cannot be created with human subjects, but the predicted effect is seen in zebra finches. As we have discussed, other details about song learning in this species are consistent with a learning-based view of the critical period for language.[4] Third, neurobiology is relevant to accounting for detailed facts about observed outcomes. There are changes in neurobiology over the lifespan that affect the capacity to learn. They are not the kinds of changes that create the decline in plasticity characteristic of language learning, which is better explained by the computational learning theory. However, they play a role in explaining other facts, such as age-related changes in language, memory, and learning, and indeed set the boundary conditions on language learning outcomes. Thus at least for the behavioral phenomena we have discussed, the theoretical equation that provides the

---

[4] Of course, comparisons between the species break down at some point, given the vast differences in perceptual, cognitive, and learning capacities. For example the loss of plasticity in zebra finches is not related to generalization, contrary to our conjecture about humans. One song may simply exhaust the finch's capacity to learn, whereas learning one language does not exhaust ours. An issue such as why humans exhibit a severe loss of plasticity in acquiring one type of knowledge (language) but not many other types does not arise with respect to other species, to our knowledge.

most explanatory leverage is one in which a computational theory of learning + neurodevelopmental boundary conditions yield a range of observed behavioral outcomes.

In summary, examining one phenomenon in detail has led to the conclusion that computational and biological accounts play complementary roles in understanding at least some major cognitive phenomena. It seems likely that what is true of critical periods in language acquisition will carry over to many other phenomena for which our current level of understanding is similarly limited. In many areas of cognition, the limiting factor on understanding their brain bases is not a lack of neurobiological knowledge (although what we know is indeed limited). Rather it a lack of understanding of the phenomena at the computational level represented by neural networks. The computational level theory provides insight about many phenomena, and suggests directions for additional behavioral and neurobiological research. This seems to be a vivid realization of the vision of the originators of the PDP approach (Rumelhart and McClelland 1986).

Acknowledgements

Research supported by NIMH grant P50-MH64445, a Research Scientist Development Award from NIMH to MSS, and an NIH NRSA postdoctoral fellowship to JDZ. We benefited from feedback at the conference, particularly from Annette Karmiloff-Smith and Lynn Nadel.

References

Bates E (1994). Modularity, domain specificity and the development of language. *Discussions in Neuroscience*, 10, 136–149.

Best CT, McRoberts GW and Goodell E (2001). Discrimination of non-native consonant contrasts varying in perceptual assimilation to the listener's native phonological system. *Journal of the Acoustical Society of America*, 109, 775–794.

Bever TG (1981). Normal acquisition processes explain the critical period for language learning. In: KC Diller, ed. *Individual differences and universals in language learning aptitude*. Rowley, MA: Newbury House Publishers .

Bialystok E and Hakuta K (1994). *In other words: The science and psychology of second language acquisition*. New York: Basic Books.

Bialystok E and Hakuta K (1999). Confounded age: Linguistic and cognitive factors in age differences for second language acquisition. In D. Birdsong ed *Second language acquisition and the Critical Period Hypothesis* pp. 161–181. Mahwah, NJ: Erlbaum.

Birdsong D and Molis M (2002). On the evidence for maturational constraints in second-language acquisition. *Journal of Memory and Language*, 44, 215–249.

Bradlow AR, Pisoni DB, Yamada RA and Tohkura Y (1997). Training Japanese listeners to identify English /r/ and /l/ IV: Some effects of perceptual learning on speech production. *Journal of the Acoustical Society of America*, 101, 2299–2310.

Brainard M and Doupe A (2000). Interruption of a basal ganglia-forebrain circuit prevents plasticity of learned vocalizations. *Nature, 404,* 762–766.

Chomsky N (1986). *Knowledge of language: Its nature, origin and use.* New York: Praeger.

Chomsky N (1993). *Language and thought.* Wakefield, RI: Moyer Bell.

Christiansen MH, Chater N and Seidenberg MS, eds. (1999). Connectionist models of human language processing: Progress and prospects. *Cognitive Science,* Special issue, **23,** 415–634.

Crair MC, Horton JC, Antonini A and Stryker MP (2001). Emergence of ocular dominance columns in cat visual cortex by 2 weeks of age. *Journal of Cognitive Neurology,* **430,** 235–249.

Crowley JC and Katz LC (1999). Development of ocular dominance columns in the absence of retinal input. *Nature Neuroscience,* **2,** 1125–1130.

Curtiss, S. (1977). Genie: a psycholinguistic sutdy of a modern–day "wild child." New York: Academic Press.

Dehaene-Lambertz G, Dehaene S and Hertz-Pannier L (2002). Functional neurogimaging of speech perception in infants. *Science,* **298,** 2013–2015.

Dennis M (2000). Developmental plasticity in children: The role of biological risk, development, time and reserve. *Journal of Communication Disorders,* **33,** 321–332.

Doupe AJ and Kuhl PK (1999). Birdsong and human speech: Common themes and mechanisms. *Annual Review of Neuroscience,* **22,** 567–631.

Ehri L (1995). Phases of development in learning to read words by sight. *Journal of Research in Reading,* **18,** 116–125.

Ellis AW and Lambon Ralph MA (2000). Age of acquisition effects in adult lexical processing reflect loss of plasticity in maturing systems: Insights from connectionist networks. *Journal of Experimental Psychology: Learning, Memory and Cognition,* **26,** 1103–1123.

Elman J, Bates E, *et al.* (1996). *Rethinking innateness.* Cambridge, MA: MIT Press.

Fagiolini M and Hensch TK (2000). Inhibitory threshold for critical period activation in primary visual cortex. *Nature,* **404,** 183–186.

Fagiolini M, Fritschy J-M, Löw K, Möhler H, Rudolph U, et al. (2004). Specific $GABA_A$ circuits for visual cortical plasticity. *Science* 303: 1681–1683.

Flege JE (1999). Age of learning and second-language speech. In: DP Birdsong, ed. *New perspectives on the critical period hypothesis for second language acquisition,* pp. 101–132. Hillsdale, NJ: Lawrence Erlbaum.

Flege JE, Yeni-Komshian G and Liu S (1999) Age constraints on second language acquisition. *Journal of Memory and Language,* **41,** 78–104.

Goldin-Meadow S and Feldman H (1975). The creation of a communication system: A study of deaf children of hearing parents. *Sign Language Studies,* **8,** 226–236.

Goldin-Meadow S and Mylander C (1990). Beyond the input given: The child's role in the acquisition of language. *Language,* **66,** 323–355.

Gordon J and Dell G (2003). Learning to divide the labor: An account of deficits in light and heavy verb production. *Cognitive Science,* **27,** 1–40.

Gordon P (1985). Level-ordering in lexical development. *Cognition,* **21,** 73–93.

Harm MW and Seidenberg MS (1999). Phonology, reading and dyslexia: Insights from connectionist models. *Psychological Review,* **163,** 491–528.

Harm MW and Seidenberg MS (2004). Computing the meanings of words in reading: Cooperative division of labor between visual and phonological processes. *Psychological Review,* **111,** 662–720.

Haskell TR, MacDonald MC and Seidenberg MS (2003). Language learning and innateness: Some implications of *compounds research. Cognitive Psychology*, **47**, 119–163.

Hensch TK (2003). Controlling the critical period. *Neuroscience Research*, **47**, 17–22.

Hensch T, Fagiolini M, Mataga N, Stryker M, Baekkeskov S and Kash SF (1998). Local GABA circuit control of experience-dependent plasticity in developing visual cortex. *Science*, **282**, 1504–1508.

Hetherington P and Seidenberg MS (1989). Is there "catastrophic interference" in connectionist networks? In *Proceedings of the 11th annual conference of the cognitive science society* (p. 26–33). Hillsdale, NJ: Erlbaum.

Holland A (1989). Recovery in aphasia. In: F Boller and J Grafman, eds. *Handbook of neuropsychology*, vol. 2, pp. 83–90. North Holland: Elsevier.

Huang Z, Kirkwood A, Pizzorusso T, Porciatti V, Morales B, Bear M, *et al*. (1999). BDNF regulates the maturation of inhibition and the critical period of plasticity in mouse visual cortex. *Cell*, **98**, 739–755.

Hubel DH and Wiesel TN (1970). The period of susceptibility to the physiological effects of unilateral eye closure in kittens. *Journal of Physiology*, **206**, 419–436.

Issa N, Trachtenberg J, Chapman B, Zahs K and Stryker M (1999). The critical period for ocular dominance plasticity in the ferret's visual cortex. *Journal of Neuroscience*, **19**, 6965–6978.

Jackendoff R (2003). Precis of *Foundations of Langauge*: brain, meaning, grammar, evolution. *Behavioral and Brain Sciences*, **26**, 651–665.

Joanisse MF and Seidenberg MS (1999). Impairments in verb morphology following brain injury: A connectionist model. *Proceedings of the National Academy of Sciences*, **96**, 7592–7597.

Johnson JS and Newport EL (1989). Critical period effects in second language learning: The influence of maturational state on the acquisition of English as a second language. *Cognitive Psychology*, **21**, 60–99.

Jones AE, ten Cate C and Slater PJB (1996). Early experience and plasticity of song in adult male zebra finches (*Taeniopygia guttata*). *Journal of Comparative Psychology*, **110**, 154–169.

Kiparsky P (1982). From cyclic phonology to lexical phonology. In: H van der Hulst and N Smith, eds. *The structure of phonological representations*. Dordrecht, The Netherlands: Foris.

Kirkham NZ, Slemmer JA and Johnson SP (2002). Visual statistical learning in infancy: evidence of a domain general learning mechanism. *Cognition*, **83**, B35–B42.

Lenneberg EH (1967). *Biological foundations of language*. New York: Wiley.

Leonardo A and Konishi M (1999). Decrystallization of adult birdsong by perturbation of auditory feedback. *Nature*, **399**, 466–470.

Lewis JD and Elman JL (2001). Learnability and the statistical structure of language: Poverty of stimulus arguments revisted. In: B Skarabela, S Fish, and AH-J Do, eds. *Proceedings of the 26th Annual Boston University Conference on Language Development*, pp. 359–370. Somerville. MA: Cascadilla Press.

Lombardino AJ and Nottebohm F (2000). Age at deafening affects the stability of learned song in adult male zebra finches. *Journal of Neuroscience*, **404**, 5054–5064.

Mayberry RI (1993). First-language acquisition after childhood differs from second-language acquisition: The case of American Sign Language. *Journal of Speech and Hearing Research*, **36**, 1258–1270.

Mayberry RI, Lock E and Kazmi H (2002). Linguistic ability and early language exposure. *Nature*, **417**, 38.

McClelland JL (1989). Parallel distributed processing: Implications for cognition and development. In: RGM Morris, ed. *Parallel distributed processing: Implications for psychology and neurobiology*, pp. 8–45. Oxford: Oxford University Press.

McClelland JL, Thomas A, McCandliss BD and Fiez JA (1999). Understanding failures of learning: Hebbian learning, competition for representational space, and some preliminary experimental data. In J. A. Reggia, E. Ruppin & D. Glanzman (Eds.), *Progress in Brain Research, 121*, 75–80.

McCloskey, M and Cohen, NJ, (1989). Catastrophic interference in connectionist networks: The sequential learning problem. In GH Bower ed. *The psychology of learning and motivation* (Vol 23) pp. 109–164. New York, NY: Academic Press.

Munakata Y, McClelland JL, Johnson MH, and Siegler RS. (1997). Rethinking infant knowledge: Toward an adaptive process account of successes and failures in object permanence task. *Psychological Review, 104*, 686–713.

Munakata Y and McClelland JL (2003). Connectionist models of development. *Developmental Science, 6*, 413–429.

Neville HJ and Bavelier D (2000). Specificity and plasticity in neurocognitive development in humans. In: MS Gazzaniga, ed. *The new cognitive neurosciences*, pp. 83–98. Cambridge, MA: MIT Press.

Neville HJ, Bavelier D, Corina D, Rauschecker J, Karni AL, Lalwani A, *et al.* (1998). Cerebral organization for language in deaf and hearing subjects: Biological constraints and effects of experience. *Proceedings of the National Academy of Sciences, 95*, 922–929.

Newport EL (1990). Maturational constraints on language learning. *Cognitive Science, 14*, 11–28.

Oh JS, Jun S, Knightly L and Au TK-F (2003). Holding on to childhood language memory. *Cognition, 86*, 53–64.

Pallier C, Dehaene S, Poline J-B, LeBihan D, Argenti A-M, Dupoux E, *et al.* (2003) Brain imaging of language plasticity in adopted adults: can a second language replace the first? *Cerebral Cortex, 13*, 155–161.

Patterson K, Lambon Ralph MA, Jefferies E, Jones R, Hodges JR and Rogers TT (in press). 'Pre-semantic' cognition in semantic dementia: Six deficits in search of an explanation. Journal of Cognitive neuroscience.

Petitto LA (1999). The acquisition of natural signed languages. In: C Chamberlain, J Morford and R Mayberry, eds. *Language acquisition by eye*, pp. 41–50. Mahwah NJ: Erlbaum.

Piatelli-Palmarini M (1980). *Language and learning: The debate between Jean Piaget and Noam Chomsky*. Harvard University Press.

Pinker S (1989). *Learnability and cognition: The acquisition of argument structure*. Cambridge, MA: MIT Press.

Pinker S (1994). The language instinct. New York: William Morrow.

Pinker S (1999). *Words and rules*. New York: Basic Books.

Plaut DC, McClelland JL, Seidenberg MS and Patterson KE (1996). Understanding normal and impaired word reading: Computational principles in quasiregular domains. *Psychological Review, 103*, 56–115.

Plaut DC and Shallice T (1993). Deep dyslexia: A case study of connectionist neuropsychology. *Cognitive Neuropsychology, 10*, 377–500.

Rumelhart DE, McClelland JL and the PDP Research Group (1986). *Parallel distributed processing*, Vol. 1. Cambridge, MA: MIT Press.

Saffran JR, Aslin RN and Newport EL (1996). Statistical learning by 8-month-old infants. *Science, 274*, 5294.

Seidenberg MS (1986). [Jacket, hard cover editions]. In: DE Rumelhart and JL McClelland, eds. *Parallel distributed processing*, vols 1 and 2. Cambridge, MA: MIT Press.

Seidenberg MS (1992). Beyond orthographic depth: Equitable division of labor. In: R Frost and L Katz, eds. *Orthography, phonology, morphology and meaning*. North Holland: Amsterdam.

Seidenberg MS (1997). Language acquisition and use: Learning and applying probabilistic constraints. *Science*, 275, 1599–1603.

Seidenberg MS and McClelland JL (1989). A distributed, developmental model of visual world recognition and naming. *Psychological Review.* 96, 523–568.

Seidenberg MS and MacDonald MC (1999). A probabilistic constraints approach to language acquisition and processing. *Cognitive Science*, 23, 569–588.

Senghas A (2003). Intergenerational influence and ontogenetic development in the emergence of spatial grammar in Nicaraguan Sign Language. *Cognitive Development,* 18, 511–531.

Siegler R (1976). Three aspects of cognitive development. *Cognitive Psychology,* 8, 481–520.

Singleton JL and Newport EL (2004). When learners surpass their models: The acquisition of American Sign Language from inconsistent input. *Cognitive Psychology,* 49, 370–407.

Spencer A (1991). *Morphological theory: An introduction to word structure in generative grammar.* Cambridge, MA: Blackwell.

Stromswold K (1995). The cognitive and neural bases of language acquisition. In: M Gazzaniga, ed. *The cognitive neurosciences*, pp. 855–870. Cambridge, MA: MIT Press.

Tees RC and Werker JF (1984). Perceptual flexibility: maintenance or recovery of the ability to discriminate non-native speech sounds. *Canadian Journal of Psychology,* 38, 579–590.

Vargha-Khadem F and Polkey CE (1992). A review of cognitive outcome after hemidecortication in humans. In: FD Rose and DA Johnson, eds. *Recovery from brain damage: reflections and directions, pp.* 137–151. New York: Plenum Press.

Werry C (2002). *Rhetoric and reflexivity in Chomskyan and cognitive linguistics.* Unpublished doctoral dissertation, Carnegie Mellon University.

Williams H and Mehta H (1999). Changes in adult zebra finch song require a forebrain nucleus that is not necessary for song production. *Journal of Neurobiology,* 39, 14–28.

Zevin JD and Seidenberg MS (2002). Age of acquisition effects in reading and other tasks. *Journal of Memory and Language,* 47, 1–29.

Zevin JD, Seidenberg MS and Bottjer SW (2004). Limits on reacquisition of song in adult zebra finches exposed to white noise. *Journal of Neuroscience,* 24, 5849–5862.

Chapter 26

Processes of change in brain and cognitive development: The final word

Richard N. Aslin

Abstract

In this discussion, many of the key issues that emerged during the conference are critically evaluated. These include the correlational vs. causal nature of behavioral and neural data, the utility of animal models of development, the homogeneity assumption in models of brain activity, the value of computational models, of lesion studies, and of atypical populations, the mechanisms of brain plasticity, reorganization, and recovery, what is meant by the terms representation and generalization, the mechanisms of learning, and the ways in which these learning mechanisms are constrained.

26.1 Introduction

The task facing a discussant whose charge is to 'wrap up' a 5-day conference encompassing 26 presentations entails two types of risks. The first is the risk of reiterating the obvious. The second is the risk of going well beyond the data and proposing the outrageous. My charge, which I welcome, is to purposely take both of these risks. Often, researchers embedded in their own 'little' world need to hear the simple caveats that are taken for granted but which are often glossed over in an attempt to push a subfield forward. I will, therefore, reiterate the obvious in an attempt to provide cautionary notes to researchers who may tend to go beyond their data. Speculation is not a bad thing, of course, because it can lead to potentially fruitful new hypotheses, provided those hypotheses are testable. Yet speculations are usually limited to the next step in the logic of an argument rather than to whole-scale questioning of where that argument may ultimately lead. In my concluding remarks, I hope to question these core principles by asking what *could* be learned about the processes of change in brain and cognitive development if we had access to a complete description of the states of the brain and of the cognitive competencies of the developing child.

26.2 **The obvious restated**

Developing organisms undergo profound changes in their behavior and, in the case of humans, in their ability to operate using mechanisms that are not shared with other species (e.g. the morphology and syntax of language or the cardinal numbers greater than three). Descriptive behavior alone, without recourse to a model or an underlying neural mechanism, does not provide a sufficient explanation of developmental change. For example infants get progressively longer (taller) from birth to postadolescence, but that descriptive fact says nothing about why growth occurs. In the absence of data about the brain (or other underlying physiology), it is often (though not always) impossible to determine what factor(s) cause a change in human behavioral development. For example it is surely the case that infants must be exposed to a natural language (spoken or signed) to acquire that language, but beyond this minimal requirement of exposure it is unclear what mechanisms internal to the human infant (compared to a dog or a chimp; see Hauser *et al.* 2002) enable that language to be acquired. In many other cases, however, behavior alone is sufficient to draw conclusions about underlying developmental mechanisms, provided that there is a good animal model of that behavior. For example in the domain of visual development the rhesus macaque is an excellent animal model of the human visual system, and invasive studies (even those limited to the behavioral level, such as visual deprivation) can reveal much about the underlying mechanisms of developmental change (Kiorpes and Movshon 1990).

Neural data, of course, are relevant to providing a more detailed account of the mechanisms of developmental change. But neural data themselves, in the absence of a model about how they influence behavior, are no more useful than descriptive data at the behavioral level. For example knowing that the number of neurons rises and falls at particular points in development may say nothing about correlated changes in behavior unless we know the mechanism by which neural number influences behavior. In the songbird, this mechanism is known and can be experimentally manipulated (Bottjer and Arnold 1997), but in humans (and most other mammals) it is not known, except in rare cases. One such case is the neural mechanism that subserves color vision.

It has long been known that color vision in humans is mediated by three classes of photoreceptor (cone) pigments corresponding to short (blue), medium (green), and long (red) wavelengths. These three cone types are not distributed in equal proportion across the retina (e.g, there are no blue cones in the fovea), and the ratio of red:green cones was thought to be approximately 1:1 based on psychophysical data. Although these facts were obtained from psychophysical studies of humans and anatomical studies of retinal tissue, it was not until recently that a technique called adaptive optics (AO) was used to image the photoreceptor mosaic of the living human eye to determine the precise layout of the array of cone types. These data revealed that among adults with normal color vision the ratio of red:green cones in the central retina ranges from about 1:1 to 4:1 (Roorda and Williams 1999). Additional data from a larger sample revealed that this ratio ranges from 0.5:1 to 10:1 (Neitz *et al.* 2002). This is a truly astounding fact because it suggests that postretinal mechanisms compensate for huge variations in the chromatic signals coming from the retina.

The foregoing example, while illustrating the utility of a new technique (AO) and the linkage of neural data to behavior, raises a number of developmental questions. For example is this same variability in cone distributions present in the newborn retina? Obviously, we cannot know the answer without developmental data. AO raises the possibility of obtaining such data from human infants. As a first step such data could be obtained from an animal model, but it would still be necessary to gather data from human infants to be certain that the same underlying ratios were present in both species. Thus, the dilemma facing researchers who wish to account for developmental change in humans is that an animal model is not enough (thereby demanding new non-invasive techniques), and in many cases there is no good animal model (e.g. for language).

Because non-invasive studies of the brain cannot be conducted in humans (for obvious ethical reasons), a set of less invasive techniques have been used to study the human brain, including electroencephalography (EEG), event-related potentials (ERP), positron emission tomography (PET), magnetic resonance imaging (MRI), functional magnetic resonance imaging (fMRI), magnetoencephalography (MEG), and a variety of other less direct physiological measures (e.g. heart rate). There are two ways in which these measures can be used: (1) as just another dependent measure (like reaction time); or (2) as a more 'direct' indicator of the neural generators that cause behaviors to be triggered. The first use is rather conservative and, in the case of heart rate, is completely justified. No one thinks that a slight decline in heart rate *causes* heightened attention. However, the second use is commonly accepted in much of the literature, although in my judgment such acceptance is controversial and potentially illusory.

Consider any measure of brain state as if it were a number (or set of numbers). For example the number(s) could indicate the level of summed neural activity from one or more electrode sites on the scalp or the amount of hemodynamic (BOLD) signal from one or more voxels. The typical strategy for studying brain–behavior relations is to obtain these measures separately, hoping that what happens in one set of subjects at time-1 when behavioral data are collected is sufficiently stable that it can be related to time-2 when brain states are measured. Although it would be preferable, these brain and behavioral data are rarely gathered at the same time in the same subjects. But even under such optimal conditions, these data are merely correlational. There are no experimental manipulations of brain states to determine how they alter behavioral performance. Thus, it is seductive but risky to draw any conclusions about causal relations between brain states and behavior, and it is doubly risky to do so in infants and young children because extraneous task variables are often less well controlled.

These issues of cross-age comparisons raise daunting concerns when interpreting any dependent measure of brain states. For example the ERP technique assumes that the underlying neural generators are homogenous in their summation; that is, when pools of parietal neurons are compared to pools of temporal neurons, the metric by which these summed activations are compared uses the same 'ruler'. Similarly, for fMRI it is assumed that the BOLD signal obtained from two different brain regions is based on a homogenous linkage between neural firing and the underlying vasculature (thereby rendering the subtraction algorithm sensible). In both cases, this homogeneity assumption is surely wrong in detail, although it may be correct to a first approximation. But if, as discussed earlier, effects in the brain are highly non-linear, then a little bit of violation of an underlying assumption can go a long way toward misinterpretation of brain state data, particularly when that assumption is extended across age.

Similar limitations resulting from reliance on correlational data are also true for computational models. The beauty of such models is that they are explicit (or should be), they provide quantitative outputs, they enable the rapid testing of hypotheses (particularly for data that would be difficult or impossible to obtain from real subjects), and they can generate interesting outcomes that lead to empirical studies. But like brain states, computational models are seductive when they 'work', not only because many models are so powerful that they cannot fail in any real sense, but also because different models can 'work' for different reasons. If the goal is to find the model that accounts for human behavior (which is often not the goal of computer scientists), then models whose performance is identical must be examined in more detail to determine which one best captures the computational algorithms and architectures used by the human brain.

Where both brain states and computational models play a critical role is in revealing hidden mechanisms. By hidden mechanisms I mean the situation in which behavior alone is insufficient to tease apart a phenomenon. For example take the case of a highly practiced skill that is extremely robust to perturbations and which cannot be decomposed to test competing theories of potential underlying mechanisms. Brain states and computational models may provide a window on whether a single underlying mechanism is sufficient to characterize this behavior or whether two (or more) mechanisms are consistent with the behavior. If two mechanisms are possible, then arguments for parsimony are typically raised and single mechanisms are preferred. But parsimony is an argument, not a proof, and so direct empirical tests of possible underlying mechanisms must be conducted.

Like computational models, similar power comes from lesion studies and studies of atypical populations. In both of these cases, the hope is that removal or alteration of one component of a complex (brain) system will have isolated effects. For example it would be less interesting for models of brain organization if a lesion anywhere in the brain or a deviation from normality among atypical subjects had uniformly negative effects on a wide range of behaviors. On the contrary, lesions and atypical subjects often show highly differentiated effects in their brain and in their behavior. However, the presence of non-uniform effects does not imply that the resultant mechanism(s) remaining postlesion or in the presence of a genetic- or environmental-induced anomaly are the same as those that are functional in the intact organism. Brain plasticity, particularly early in development, may enable recovery of the same tissue, reorganization of pathways to rely on undamaged tissue, and/or recruitment of tissue from other areas that leads to recovery, but at the cost of reduced function in those recruited areas (i.e. compensation). Moreover, small quantitative differences in an underlying mechanism may result in large qualitative differences in behavior. This is, of course, also true for normal development and emphasizes that in a large, inter-connected system like the brain it is unrealistic to expect that effects will be linear. The flip side of this 'quantitative change leads to qualitative effects' is the fact that, while genes operate as discrete units, their effects are often graded because few genes operate as single mechanisms (i.e. behaviors are assembled from the action of many genes except in the case of single genes whose absence is lethal).

The foregoing discussion highlights the fact that context matters: both the context provided by evolutionary history (i.e. which genes are activated and when during development) and the context provided by the local developmental environment (i.e. how opportunities for learning are influenced by passive and active stimulation). Context matters not only for how we think about underlying mechanisms, but also for how those mechanisms operate. Consider the question of developmental continuity. Since Piaget (1952) coined the term décalage, researchers have worried about the fact that behaviors which should, in principle, be present at the same age regardless of context, often are not. This led to both shallow and deep discussions of the distinction between competence and performance. The shallow discussions state the obvious: behavior is not equivalent to the 'potential' for behavior (i.e. wait long enough or put the organism in a new situation and new behaviors will be exhibited). The deep discussions quickly lead to the Fodorian conundrum: in the limit any new behavior must have emerged from an already existing competence (i.e. Plato was right).

Can we get out of this dilemma without reverting to behaviorism? The key seems to lie with two concepts: representational fidelity and generalization (or transfer). With regard to representational fidelity, no one would deny that organisms store information. We cannot observe that information directly (i.e. there is no window on the skull that reveals a set of memory registers and their contents). Some refer to stored information as a 'representation', and admittedly many researchers use that term too loosely. But the hypothesis that organisms store information for future access to guide their behavior seems uncontroversial. At issue is how this information gets acquired, in what format it is encoded, and how it is utilized to guide future behavior. Imagine an adult who is, by all accepted definitions, perfectly normal and a native speaker of a language. No one would be surprised if that adult, under less than ideal circumstances, showed decrements in language processing (e.g. misinterpreting words in noise or failing to follow directions while intently watching a football game on TV). Does this mean that the underlying representation for language is changing from moment to moment or as a function of context, or does it simply mean that a variety of other factors are influencing the underlying principles of access to that representation? Similarly, when an infant shows by a looking time measure that something about an occlusion event is different under one set of circumstances than under another, whereas that same infant a year later fails on a task that appears to tap the same underlying representation, should we conclude that the underlying representation has changed? Different tasks place different demands on the representational system (if we can call it that), even though, to an adult, these demands appear to be very similar for the infant or child being tested.

The second factor, generalization (or transfer), bears on the question of how representations change. Piaget (1952) proposed a rich, but largely untestable, set of principles by which representations (mental structures) change during development. When infants encounter environmental inputs that do not 'fit' current representations, modified representations are induced (or the inputs are not processed veridically). According to this view, representations are the causal agents of behavior. But in some domains, representations are modified because new behaviors alter the form or frequency of occurrence of inputs that, in turn, cause representational change. For example when infants are able to stand and walk unaided, their perspective on the visual world and the rate at which visual information is available for encoding changes dramatically (Campos *et al.* 2000). Even if infants have the same representational mechanisms before and after this developmental transition, the content of their representations is likely to be quite different, and these differences may lead to qualitative shifts in behavior.

What happens, then, when such a qualitative shift in behavior occurs? Adolph (2000) suggests that after such transitions in locomotion infants must reacquire the knowledge that they apparently had prior to the transition. That is, they show little or no evidence of generalization to the new locomotor context. But this lack of generalization does not appear to characterize all domains of development. For example infants and young children are not provided with all possible grammatical sentences, yet they acquire the ability to make grammaticality judgments for novel sentences. Here is a contrast across domains where data on brain states could potentially clarify the underlying representational mechanisms. In the case of the transition from crawling to walking, visual, vestibular, and motor systems undergo some form of development. But does the perception of depth change during this transition? Adolph's work suggests that it does because naïve walkers make gross errors in gap judgment that were not made weeks earlier by the same infants who were well-practiced crawlers. Would activation of extrastriate visual areas mediating depth perception remain invariant during this transition? If so, then the lack of generalization would not be attributable to depth perception mechanisms, but rather to the locomotor system itself that relies on depth to guide infants across gaps in a surface.

A similar logic could be applied to questions of domain-general vs. domain-specific cognitive abilities. When there is behavioral evidence of a specialized ability (e.g. recognition of faces), it is seductive to conclude that the representational mechanism itself is specialized. But there may be a homogenous representational system whose inputs are biased, either because the environment contains a skewed distribution of stimuli or because access to those stimuli is biased by other non-representational constraints (e.g. attention to vertical asymmetry). Alternatively, the domain-specificity may reside not in the content of the representation, but rather in how the learning mechanism is applied to that content.[1] Brain states may provide a window on this distinction that would otherwise be invisible to behavioral measures of domain-specificity. Unfortunately, at present we have very little idea as to how learning mechanisms and representational mechanisms are segregated in the brain (if in fact they are). Until we do, brain states may offer little clarification of the debate about 'modules' in the brain and the usefulness of concepts like 'core knowledge'.

What are the mechanisms of learning and how are they sufficiently constrained to enable infants to learn just what they need to learn with limited resources? Several points are critical. First, without biological constraints, some of which are likely to be species-specific, a uniform learning mechanism could not limit the number of potential stimulus inputs to avoid the combinatorial explosion problem. That is, there are so many possible stimulus correlations in even the simplest of environments that a limited capacity learning mechanism would be overwhelmed. One type of constraint is to add feedback from the environment to serve as a 'teacher' and thereby limit the information that is learned. However, only in a very few domains (e.g. motor systems) does feedback appear to be a viable constraint. Associative (Hebbian) learning, including statistical learning of the distributional properties of the input (Fiser and Aslin 2002; Saffran *et al.* 1996), suffers from the combinatorial explosion problem, even though associative learning has been demonstrated in human infants and in non-human primates in the absence of feedback.

One way to constrain associative learning is to have built-in biases on what elements serve as inputs to the learning mechanism. This is clearly operative in the visual domain because of the poor spatial resolution (acuity and contrast sensitivity) of young infants, which reduces the number of potential stimulus inputs. Infants also appear to have very poor working memory (Káldy and Leslie in press; Ross-Sheehy *et al.* 2003), thereby reducing the number of elements stored in memory for access by a distributional learning mechanism. Both of these constraints on learning have been

---

[1] Nancy Kanwisher made this point in the discussion led by Isabel Gauthier, and Susan Carey elaborated on the same point in her presentation.

discussed from the behavioral (Newport 1990) and computational (Elman 1993) perspectives on language acquisition.

Another way to constrain the learning mechanism is to build-in or learn, by a separate mechanism, a set of prior probabilities. According to the first of these Bayesian approaches, evolutionary constraints are essential, as proposed by researchers who match the statistics of natural images to elementary feature detectors in early levels of the visual system (Simoncelli and Olshausen 2001). Alternatively, Bayesian priors may be extracted from the environment by a statistical learning mechanism with a high threshold that limits encoding to a small number of elements. Brain states may provide a useful window on these two alternatives. If priors are present at birth, then they should serve as a 'filter' on environmental inputs. If priors are acquired by experience, then they should change depending on the input.

Another set of constraints appears to involve the timing of inputs and how effectively they are incorporated into the underlying representational system. Unless priors completely determine the content of this representational system, the effects of learning should change during development. In some cases, as capacity improves, learning should also improve. But in other cases, where the elements that are learned initially form the units for subsequent encoding, learning should become more constrained with development. The latter is an example of a critical or sensitive period. According to one view (see Seidenberg and Zevin, Chapter 25, this volume), there is nothing special about a sensitive period: it merely reflects the bias to use prior inputs as the units for encoding future inputs. Thus, the more these encoding units are firmly established, the harder it is to introduce new encoding units (because the priors are so strong). As a result, representations compete and the dominant one (first is usually best) wins (see Knudsen 1998 for a counter example in the domain of auditory–visual adaptation by the barn owl). An alternative view is that underlying neural mechanisms of encoding and/or learning undergo changes with development. Although these changes may be regulated intrinsically by some physiological process (e.g. the presence of hormones), they also may be regulated by capacity limitations on the encoding system itself. Regardless, the notion of a sensitive period is incomplete without a consideration of the manner in which experience affects development. Gottlieb (1976) provided such a detailed taxonomy of the roles of experience (see also Aslin 1981), and they provide a useful guideline for thinking about underlying mechanisms of development at both the behavior and brain state levels.

26.3 Rampant speculation about a thought problem

Thirty years ago, in a graduate course at the University of Minnesota on philosophy of mind taught by Keith Gunderson, he posed the following question. What if we had access to *all* brain states? What would that information tell us about cognition? Let's assume that we could develop sophisticated tools for data analysis to deal with the massive amount of neural information and the details of overt behavioral responses provided by human subjects. Given the implicit assumptions of modern neuroscience, these new and complete data from the brain would not only be welcome but they would clarify how the brain works. In contrast to that view, I believe such data would be useless without a theory of neural coding and brain organization. To take an example from another domain, what would knowing the time series of the states of all the molecules in a thunderstorm provide to the weather forecaster? The information provided by knowing molecular states, or brain states, is often at the wrong level to be useful in predicting behavior. This is because we do not yet have sufficiently detailed models of the dynamics of the complex system by which neurons themselves behave, much less how these neurons affect behavior.

This is not to say that having access to brain states is a bad thing. It is simply another source of information that requires an explicit linking hypothesis to make behavioral predictions. But brain states offer much more promise than they currently have delivered in our explanations of behavior. Hopefully, in the proper hands and with the development of new measures that complement those already in use, the precise mechanisms of cognitive development will be revealed.

References

Adolph KE (2000). Specificity of learning: Why infants fall over a veritable cliff. *Psychological Science,* 11, 290–295.

Aslin RN (1981). Experiential influences and sensitive periods in perceptual development: A unified model. In: RN Aslin, JR Alberts and MR Petersen, eds. *Development of perception: Psychobiological perspectives,* vol 2, pp. 45–93. New York: Academic Press.

Bottjer SW and Arnold AP (1997). Developmental plasticity in neural circuits for a learned behavior. *Annual Review of Neuroscience,* 20, 459–481.

Campos JJ, Anderson DI, Barbu-Roth MA, Hubbard EM, Hertenstein MJ and Witherington D (2000). Travel broadens the mind. *Infancy,* 1, 149–219.

Elman JL (1993). Learning and development in neural networks: The importance of starting small. *Cognition,* 48, 71–99.

Fiser J and Aslin RN (2002). Statistical learning of new visual feature combinations by infants. *Proceedings of the National Academy of Sciences,* 99, 15822–15826.

Gottlieb G (1976). The roles of experience in the development of behavior and the nervous system. In: G Gottlieb, ed. *Neural and behavioral specificity,* pp. 25–54. New York: Academic Press.

Hauser MD, Chomsky N and Fitch WT (2002). The faculty of language: What is it, who has it, and how did it evolve? *Science,* 298, 1569–1579.

Káldy Z and Leslie AM (in press). A memory span of one? Object identification in 6.5-month-old infants. *Cognition.*

Kiorpes L and Movshon JA (1990). Behavioral analysis of visual development. In: JR Coleman, ed. *Development of sensory systems in mammals,* pp. 125–154. New York: Wiley.

Knudsen EI (1998). Capacity for plasticity in the adult owl auditory system expanded by juvenile experience. *Science,* 279, 1531–1533.

Neitz J, Carroll J, Yamauchi Y, Neitz M and Williams DR (2002). Color perception is mediated by a plastic neural mechanism that is adjustable in adults. *Neuron,* 35, 783–792.

Newport EL (1990). Maturational constraints on language learning. *Cognitive Science,* 14, 11–28.

Piaget J (1952). *The origins of intelligence in children.* New York: W. W. Norton.

Roorda A and Williams DR (1999). The arrangement of the three cone classes in the living human eye. *Nature,* 397, 520–522.

Ross-Sheehy S, Oakes LM and Luck SJ (2003). The development of visual short-term memory capacity in infants. *Child Development,* 74, 1807–1822.

Saffran JR, Aslin RN and Newport EL (1996). Statistical learning by 8-month-old infants. *Science,* 274, 1926–1928.

Simoncelli EP and Olshausen B (2001). Natural image statistics and neural representation. *Annual Review of Neuroscience,* 24, 1193–1216.

Author Index

Subject Index

WITHDRAWN